W9-CFP-182

This Book Comes With a Website

Nolo's award-winning website has a page dedicated just to this book, where you can:

KEEP UP TO DATE – When there are important changes to the information in this book, we'll post updates

READ BLOGS – Get the latest info from Nolo authors' blogs

LISTEN TO PODCASTS – Listen to authors discuss timely issues on topics that interest you

WATCH VIDEOS – Get a quick introduction to a legal topic with our short videos

You'll find the link in the introduction.

And that's not all. Nolo.com contains thousands of articles on everyday legal and business issues, plus a plain-English law dictionary, all written by Nolo experts and available for free. You'll also find more useful **books, software, online services,** and **downloadable forms.**

Get updates and more at
www.nolo.com

NOLO **The Trusted Name**
(but don't take our word for it)

"In Nolo you can trust."
THE NEW YORK TIMES

"Nolo is always there in a jam as the nation's premier publisher of do-it-yourself legal books."
NEWSWEEK

"Nolo publications…guide people simply through the how, when, where and why of the law."
THE WASHINGTON POST

"[Nolo's]…material is developed by experienced attorneys who have a knack for making complicated material accessible."
LIBRARY JOURNAL

"When it comes to self-help legal stuff, nobody does a better job than Nolo…"
USA TODAY

"The most prominent U.S. publisher of self-help legal aids."
TIME MAGAZINE

"Nolo is a pioneer in both consumer and business self-help books and software."
LOS ANGELES TIMES

12th Edition

Patent, Copyright & Trademark

Attorney Richard Stim

TWELFTH EDITION	MARCH 2012
Cover Design	SUSAN PUTNEY
Book Design	TERRI HEARSH
Proofreading	ROBERT WELLS
Index	JULIE SHAWVAN
Printing	BANG PRINTING

Stim, Richard.
Patent, copyright & trademark / by Richard Stim. — 12th ed.
    p. cm.
Includes index.
Summary: "Gives an encyclopedic overview of intellectual property (IP) law, plus includes definitions of common IP terms."—Provided by publisher.
ISBN 978-1-4133-1680-3 (pbk.) — ISBN 978-1-4133-1693-3 (epub ebook)
1. Intellectual property—United States—Popular works. I. Title. II. Title: Patent, copyright and trademark.
KF2980.E44 2012
346.7304'8—dc23

                    2011032244

Please note

We believe accurate, plain-English legal information should help you solve many of your own legal problems. But this text is not a substitute for personalized advice from a knowledgeable lawyer. If you want the help of a trained professional—and we'll always point out situations in which we think that's a good idea—consult an attorney licensed to practice in your state.

Dedication

This book is dedicated to Steve Elias who passed away in 2012. Steve wrote and edited the first three editions at a time when intellectual property was just beginning to surface in mainstream media. His contributions to the legal self-help movement were immense and the world is a different place for his efforts.

About the Author

Richard Stim is an attorney specializing in intellectual property and is an editor at Nolo. He is the author of seven other intellectual property books, including *Getting Permission: How to License & Clear Copyrighted Materials Online & Off* (Nolo); *Music Law: How to Run Your Band's Business* (Nolo); and *Profit From Your Idea: How to Make Smart Licensing Deals* (Nolo). He enjoys watching movies but not if they're longer than two hours.

Table of Contents

Your Legal Companion 1

Introduction 3

How Intellectual Property Law Works 5

Determining What Rights Apply to Your Work 8

Intellectual Property Laws Chart 9

Self-Help Intellectual Property Resources From Nolo 9

Part 1: Patent Law 15

Patent Law: Overview 17

Patent Law: Definitions 31

Patent Law: Forms 173

Patent Application Basics 173

Preparing a Design Patent Application 191

Part 2: Copyright Law 195

Copyright Law: Overview 197

Copyright Law: Definitions 209

Copyright Law: Forms 349

Preparing a Copyright Application 349

Preparing a Form CO Copyright Application 350

Preparing an Electronic (eCO) Copyright Application 363

Preparing a Traditional Print Copyright Application 366

Part 3: Trademark Law 377

Trademark Law: Overview 379

Trademark Law: Definitions 391

Trademark Law: Forms 503

Preparing a Federal Trademark Application 503

The Trademark Application: the TEAS System 504

Example of a TEAS Plus Application 509

Part 4: Trade Secret Law 517

Trade Secret Law: Overview 519

Trade Secret Law: Definitions 523

Trade Secret Law: Forms 569

Preparing a Nondisclosure Agreement 569

Index 581

Your Legal Companion

A photographer is wondering why an advertising agency can copy her photographs without permission. An inventor is wondering why he cannot stop a foreign manufacturer from making his patented invention. A man named McDonald is wondering why he cannot open a restaurant called McDonald's. And a woman who spends $600 on a software program is wondering why it's illegal to share copies with her friends.

Welcome to the *wonder*ful world of intellectual property.

Writers, inventors, and artists transform ideas into tangible property. When this property qualifies under law for protection it's known as intellectual property (or IP)—for example, patents, copyrights, trademarks, and trade secrets. Creators of IP are granted certain rights. For example, the author of a book can prevent others from copying it; and the owner of a patented invention can prevent others from making, using, or selling the device.

After a time, these exclusive rights may be lost or taken from the owner and given to the public. For example, copyright protection has ended for Mark Twain and anyone is free to copy his books *Huckleberry Finn* and *The Adventures of Tom Sawyer*. The patent on the original roller blade invention has expired and companies are now free to copy the device.

But not all products of the mind can achieve protection under intellectual property law. Determining what can be protected and why used to be the exclusive domain of patent, copyright, and trademark lawyers. Unfortunately, few businesses, nonprofits, or educational institutions can afford to call an attorney with every question. And lately, there are a lot more questions. Globalization, digital data, and the Internet have all contributed to a greater need for information about IP.

The truth is that intellectual property is not an inscrutable discipline. Anybody can understand the basics. This book is proof that IP law is not a mystery. For over a decade, engineers, scientists, businesspeople, academics, *and* attorneys have used this book as a reference for understanding basic patent, copyright, trademark, and trade secret principles.

This helpful desk reference has—over 12 editions—evolved to include hundreds of definitions, statutes, forms, and bits of how-to information about protecting and preserving intellectual property.

So before you pick up the phone to call an attorney, check out this book. It may save you time and money … and it will hopefully make your job easier, your employer more secure, and your business more prosperous.

Get Updates and More Online

When there are important changes to the information in this book, we'll post updates online, on a page dedicated to this book: **www.nolo.com/back-of-book/PCTM12.html**. You'll find other useful information there, too, including author blogs, podcasts, and videos.

Introduction

How Intellectual Property Law Works..5

    Types of Intellectual Property Laws 5

    Intellectual Property Overlap..6

    International Laws 7

Determining What Rights Apply to Your Work...8

Intellectual Property Laws Chart...9

Self-Help Intellectual Property Resources From Nolo 9

ntellectual property refers to products of the human intellect that have commercial value and that receive legal protection. Typically, intellectual property encompasses creative works, products, processes, imagery, inventions, and services and is protected by patent, copyright, trademark, or trade secret law.

The commercial value of intellectual property comes from the ability of its owner to control and exploit its use. If the owner could not legally require payment in exchange for use, ownership of the intellectual property would have little if any commercial value.

> **EXAMPLE 1:** At the end of the 1930s Walt Disney took a big gamble. Nobody had ever made a full-length animated feature. Many people felt the idea was foolish, including Mr. Disney's business partner and brother, Roy. But Walt Disney believed that the public was ready for full-length animated features, and in 1937 he borrowed heavily from Bank of America to make the film *Snow White and the Seven Dwarfs*. The success of that film led to other classic animated features including *Fantasia, Lady and the Tramp,* and *101 Dalmations.* These films are now among the most valuable copyright properties in the world and have been rereleased numerous times and in different formats. The Disney Company has earned billions of dollars from the monopoly created by its copyrights on full-length animated films. The company has successfully used copyright law to prevent others from copying and selling the films without authorization.

> **EXAMPLE 2:** In the 1990s, Lonnie Johnson, an ex-NASA engineer, improved upon a staple of every child's toy weapons arsenal when he created one of the most popular toys of the 1990s, a squirt gun with phenomenal spraying power. Mr. Johnson acquired a U.S. patent for his invention (U.S. Pat. 4591071) and was able to license the rights to several companies who paid millions of dollars in royalties to Mr. Johnson. The product was sold under the trademarked name "Super Soaker," and the exclusive right to use this name further enhanced the value and goodwill of the product. Under patent law, Mr. Johnson was able to stop others, during the term of his patent, from the unauthorized making, using, and selling of his invention.

How Intellectual Property Law Works

Intellectual property laws, along with court decisions and regulations, establish rules for the following activities:
- selling or licensing of intellectual property
- resolving disputes between companies making or selling similar intellectual property products and services, and
- the registration and administration of intellectual property.

Intellectual property laws don't prevent someone from stepping on the owner's rights. But the laws do give an owner the ammunition to take a trespasser to court. This is the most well-known benefit of owning intellectual property: The owner acquires exclusive rights and can file a lawsuit to stop others who use the property without authorization. If the intellectual property owner does not confront the person or company who has acted without permission, then the illegal activity will likely continue.

Types of Intellectual Property Laws

Intellectual property law consists of several separate and overlapping legal disciplines, each with its own characteristics and terminology.
- **Patent law.** There are three types of patents: utility, design, and plant. Utility patents (the most common type) are granted to the inventor of a new, nonobvious invention. The utility patent owner has the exclusive right to make, use, and sell the invention for a limited term—usually 17 to 18 years. A design patent (for a new but nonfunctional design) lasts 14 years after the date the patent issues. A plant patent expires 20 years from the date the patent was filed.
- **Copyright law.** Copyrights are granted for original creative expressions produced by authors, composers, artists, designers, programmers, and similar creative individuals. Copyright law does not protect ideas and facts, only the manner in which those ideas and facts are expressed. Copyright protection lasts a long time, often more than 100 years.
- **Trademark law.** Trademark law protects the rights of businesses that use distinctive names, designs, logos, slogans, or other signifiers to identify and distinguish their products and services. This protection can last as long as the company uses the trademark in commerce—for example, many

trademarks, such as Coca-Cola and General Mills, have been protected for over a century.

- **Trade secret law.** A trade secret is any confidential information that gives a business a competitive advantage. Under trade secret law, the owner of this confidential information can prevent others from using the information if it was obtained illegally. Trade secret protection lasts for as long as the business maintains the secret.

Legal Basis of Intellectual Property Laws

The sources of intellectual property laws vary according to the subject matter. Copyright and patent laws are derived from powers originating in the U.S. Constitution and are specifically and exclusively implemented by federal statutes. In all of these areas, court decisions provide important principles governing the application of intellectual property laws. Trademark and trade secret laws originate primarily in both federal and state statutes but also are derived from court decisions that apply principles developed by earlier courts as part of the common law.

Intellectual Property Overlap

Sometimes, trade secret, copyright, patent, and trademark laws intersect with each other with respect to a particular product or service. Some common examples of this are as follows:

- **Trade secret and patent.** It is possible to pursue a patent application while simultaneously maintaining the invention as a trade secret, at least for the first 18 months of the U.S. patent application process. The U.S. Patent and Trademark Office (USPTO) treats applications as confidential until they are published. Unless the applicant files a Nonpublication Request (NPR) at the time of filing, and doesn't file for a patent outside the United States, the PTO will publish the application within 18 months of the filing date.
- **Copyright and trademark.** It's not uncommon for an item to be protected under both trademark and copyright law. For example, the expressive artwork in a package design may be protected by copyright, while

the overall look and feel of the package may be protected as a form of trademark. Likewise, an advertisement may include some material covered by copyright (for example, a jingle) and other material covered by trademark (the product or company name). The difference here is that copyright protects the literal expression, while trademark protects whatever is used to designate the source of a product or service being offered in the marketplace.

- **Patent, copyright, and trademark.** Patent law can intersect with copyright and trademark law in the case of certain products. For example, the designer of a toy or of jewelry may protect the device's name or appearance (as a trademark), the design of the item (design patent), the appearance of any artwork or graphics (copyright), and the novel, nonobvious functionality of the device (utility patent).

Intellectual Property and the Internet

Intellectual property laws came under intense scrutiny with the popularization of the Internet at the end of the 20th century. The ability to transform documents, movies, music, and other expressions into digital copies suddenly made near-perfect copying possible for everyone, not just bootleggers and pirates. The Internet enabled the widespread distribution of these unauthorized copies as well as a plethora of other issues relating to trademarks and domain names, the publication of trade secrets, the linking of websites, and the invention of patentable business processes (business method patents). Along with these changes came disputes and new laws. Throughout this book, we have included Internet-related definitions and issues.

International Laws

Most countries in the world have entered into intellectual property treaties that afford members mutual rights. This does not mean that anything protected in the United States will be protected abroad. However, intellectual property that is protected in America may achieve protection abroad under the standardized rules established by the various treaties. For example, the Madrid Protocol has standardized the process for obtaining trademark protection among member countries. Similarly, the Berne Convention establishes international copyright principles, and the Paris Convention and the Patent Cooperation Treaty offer harmonization for owners of patents. Trade secrets may receive international protection under GATT (General Agreement on Tariffs and Trade).

Determining What Rights Apply to Your Work

If you are concerned with a creation of your own, you'll first need to know what form (or forms) of intellectual property applies to it. On the next few pages, we've provided a detailed chart that classifies how creative works are protected.

These basic rules can help you get started.

- **Utility patents** are awarded for new processes, machines, manufactures, or compositions of matter, or new uses of any of the above
- **Design patents** are awarded to nonfunctional, ornamental, or aesthetic design elements of an invention or product.
- **Plant patents** a granted for asexually or sexually reproducible plants (such as flowers).
- **Copyright law** protects expressions of creative ideas such as songs, artwork, writing, films, software, architecture, and video games.
- **Trademark law** protects marketing signifiers such as the name of a product or service or the symbols, logos, shapes, designs, sounds, or smells used to identify it.
- **Trade secret law** commonly protects confidential designs, devices, processes, compositions, techniques, formulas, information, or recipes.

Is It Primarily Functional or Aesthetic?

Intellectual property rights are often divided between functional elements (protected by utility patents and trade secrets) and nonfunctional elements (protected by trademarks, copyrights, and design patents). Sometimes you can start your analysis of intellectual property protection by asking the question: "Does this creation accomplish a task or goal or is it done primarily to appeal to the senses or provide information or entertainment?"

Intellectual Property Laws Chart

Below, we've provided a detailed chart to further help you identify the applicable law. The chart lists categories of creations, followed by indications of what sorts of intellectual property laws generally apply.

Self-Help Intellectual Property Resources From Nolo

If you're interested in intellectual property, Nolo, the publisher of this book, offers a number of excellent self-help resources. You can find more information at the back of this book or at the Nolo website, www.nolo.com.

Books

- *All I Need Is Money: How to Finance Your Invention*, by Jack Lander, is packed with advice and strategies to help the reader find sources of funding for new inventions.
- *Getting Permission: How to License & Clear Copyrighted Materials Online & Off*, by Richard Stim, spells out how to obtain permission to use art, music, writing, or other copyrighted works.
- *What Every Inventor Needs to Know About Business & Taxes*, by Stephen Fishman, provides the information you will need if you want to make a profit from your invention, or if you have to understand legal protections, business rules, and tax deductions.
- *Profit From Your Idea: How to Make Smart Licensing Deals*, by Richard Stim, guides the reader through the important process of giving others permission to use, develop, and market an invention.
- *Nolo's Patents for Beginners*, by David Pressman and Richard Stim, is a quick and easy guide to patent law that sets out the basics for protecting, searching, documenting, and registering patentable inventions.
- *Patent It Yourself*, by David Pressman, a patent attorney and former patent examiner, takes inventors through the entire process—from conducting a patent search to filing a successful application.
- *Patent Pending in 24 Hours*, by Richard Stim and David Pressman, shows you how to prepare, assemble, and file a provisional patent application— an abbreviated patent application that preserves your priority of invention for 12 months.

Guide to Use of Intellectual Property Protections

CREATIVE WORK	Trade Secret	Copyright	Patent	Trademark	Unfair Competition	No Rights
advertisement (billboard, card, flyer, sign)		■		■		
advertising copy		■				
architectural drawings, renderings		■				
arrangement of facts		■				
artwork (see specific entries)		■		■		
biography		■				
biological inventions	■		■			
blueprints		■				
book design				■		■
book titles						■
carpet design			■	■		
cartoons		■		■		
characters—animated		■		■		
characters—books						■
characters—comic strips		■		■		
characters—TV or movies						■
charts		■				
chemical inventions	■		■			
choreographed works		■				
clothing accessories and designs (belts, hats, scarves, suspenders)			■			
comic strips		■		■		
commercial names				■	■	
computers	■		■			
containers			■	■		
cosmetics	■		■			
databases		■				
decorative hardware			■	■		
design (see specific entries)		■	■	■		
drawings		■				
electrical inventions	■		■			
electronic inventions	■		■			

The header row **APPLICABLE LEGAL RIGHTS** spans the columns: Trade Secret, Copyright, Patent, Trademark, Unfair Competition, No Rights.

Guide to Use of Intellectual Property Protections (continued)

CREATIVE WORK	Trade Secret	Copyright	Patent	Trademark	Unfair Competition	No Rights
		APPLICABLE LEGAL RIGHTS				
engineering plans		■				
etchings		■				
fabric	■		■			
fabric design		■	■	■		
facts						■
flow charts	■	■				
food inventions	■		■			
forms		■				
formulas—chemical	■		■			
formulas—cosmetic	■		■			
formulas—food	■		■			
furniture design			■	■		
games—board, box, and instructions		■	■	■		
hardware			■	■		
housewares			■	■		
ideas by themselves	■					
interior design		■		■		
Internet domain names				■		
jewelry		■	■	■		
labels				■		
landscape designs		■	■			
laser light show	■	■				
law of nature						■
lectures		■				
lithographs		■				
logos				■	■	
machines	■		■			
machines—internal parts	■		■			
magazines		■		■		
magic tricks or techniques	■		■			
manufacturing process			■			
maps		■				

Guide to Use of Intellectual Property Protections (continued)

CREATIVE WORK	Trade Secret	Copyright	Patent	Trademark	Unfair Competition	No Rights
			APPLICABLE LEGAL RIGHTS			
mathematical algorithms	■					
mechanical inventions	■		■			
medical accessories, devices (splints, braces, supports)		■	■			
method of doing business	■		■			
movie—film or video		■				
movie—plot (not written)	■					
movie—script	■	■				
movie—treatment	■	■				
murals		■				
musical composition		■				
musical instrument		■	■			
names—business				■	■	
names—entertainer/celebrity				■	■	
names—famous animals				■		
names—product or service				■	■	
odors—new use/process	■		■			
odors—used in marketing				■		
packaging			■	■		
paintings		■				
pamphlets		■				
periodicals		■		■		
photographic processes	■		■			
photographs		■				
plants and plant inventions	■		■			
plays—written or performances		■				
pottery		■		■		
prints		■				
project designs	■	■				
radio programs		■		■		
record books		■				
recreational gear			■	■		
reproductions		■				

Guide to Use of Intellectual Property Protections (continued)

CREATIVE WORK	APPLICABLE LEGAL RIGHTS					
	Trade Secret	Copyright	Patent	Trademark	Unfair Competition	No Rights
schedules		■				
scientific treatises		■	■			
sculpture		■				
shapes			■	■		
shoes			■	■		
signs		■		■	■	
slogans				■	■	
software	■	■	■			
software titles				■		
songs—jingles for marketing		■		■	■	
songs—not written or recorded	■					
songs—recorded or written		■				
sounds—new ways to make	■		■			
sounds—original sequence		■				
sounds—used in marketing				■	■	
sporting goods—designs		■	■	■		
sporting goods—equipment			■			
stained glass		■				
structural plans		■				
symbols				■	■	
titles—books, plays					■	
titles—magazines				■	■	
titles—movies, songs, TV shows					■	
toys		■	■	■		
translations		■				
videotape		■				
wallpaper design		■				
weavings		■		■		
Web pages		■		■	■	
words by themselves						■
writing—articles, essays, poems, novels, short stories, nonfiction books		■				

- *Patent Savvy for Managers: Spot & Protect Valuable Innovations in Your Company*, by patent attorney Kirk Teska, provides all the information you need to identify and evaluate company patents, organize patent committees, work with patent attorneys, and read and understand patents.
- *The Copyright Handbook: What Every Writer Needs to Know*, by Stephen Fishman, takes the reader through the process of protecting all kinds of written expression under copyright law.
- *The Inventor's Notebook: A Patent It Yourself Companion*, by Fred Grissom and David Pressman, is an annotated book that can be used to document the creation of an invention.
- *How to Make Patent Drawings: A Patent It Yourself Companion*, by Jack Lo and David Pressman, teaches how to use pen and ink, computerized drawing programs, and photography to prepare patent drawings.
- *The Public Domain: How to Find Copyright-Free Writings, Music, Art & More*, by Stephen Fishman, is an essential road map for determining whether music, writing, artwork, and movies are free to use.
- *Trademark: Legal Care for Your Business & Product Name*, by Stephen Elias and Richard Stim, shows how to choose a distinctive name, conduct a trademark search, and register a mark with the U.S. Patent and Trademark Office.
- *Legal Guide to Web & Software Development*, by Stephen Fishman, covers website development, software development, intellectual property laws, and the legalities of working with independent contractors and employees.

Online Resources

- *Dear Rich: Nolo's Patent, Copyright & Trademark Blog* (www.patentcopyrighttrademarkblog.com) provides answers to many common intellectual property questions.
- *Nolo Podcasts* (www.nolocast.com) offer a series of audio podcasts on legal subjects including several episodes discussing intellectual property.
- *Nolo's Online Trademark Application* (www.nolo.com) assists applicants filing for federal registration.
- *Nolo's Online Provisional Patent Application* (www.nolo.com) assists applicants filing a provisional patent application with the U.S. Patent and Trademark Office.

Part 1: Patent Law

Patent Law: Overview..17

What is a patent?...17

How do inventors benefit by holding a patent?...17

What kinds of patents may be issued?...17

What types of inventions qualify for a utility patent?..18

What is the procedure for applying for a utility patent and
   a provisional patent application?...19

What happens if there are multiple applications for the same invention?............19

Under what circumstances is a utility patent application approved?.....................20

How are patent rights enforced?..20

When does a patent expire or otherwise come to an end?..................................21

What about international protection for U.S. patents?..21

What's new in patent law since the last edition?..22

The America Invents Act..22

Changes that took place immediately (upon enactment)....................................22

Other changes to patent law..25

Patent resources...29

Patent Law: Definitions..31

Patent Law: Forms.. 173

Patent Application Basics.. 173

Preparing a Utility Patent Application 173

Who Files the Utility Application?... 175

Preparing a Design Patent Application... 191

Patent Law: Overview

There are three types of patents: utility patents, design patents, and plant patents. Commonly, when people refer to a patent, they are referring to a utility patent, which allows the creator of a useful, novel, nonobvious invention to stop others from making, using, or selling that invention for a period of approximately 17 to 18 years.

What is a patent?

A patent is a grant by the U.S. Patent and Trademark Office (USPTO) that allows the patent owner to maintain a monopoly for a limited period of time on the use and development of an invention.

How do inventors benefit by holding a patent?

Most patent owners make arrangements with an existing company to commercialize an invention. Typically, the arrangement takes the form of a license agreement under which a company (the licensee) is authorized to commercially exploit the invention in exchange for paying the patent owner royalties for each invention sold.

A license may be exclusive (only one company is licensed to exploit the invention) or nonexclusive (a number of companies are licensed to make and sell it). The license may be for the duration of the patent or for a shorter period of time. Sometimes the patent is sold outright (an assignment) to the company for a lump sum payment.

On occasion, a licensee may sublicense other companies to market or distribute the invention. The right to do this and the extent to which the patent owner will benefit from these sublicenses depends on the terms of the agreement between the patent owner and the licensee.

Licenses are often limited by geography (for instance, different licenses for different countries or for different parts of one country) and by use. In many cases, one company will trade licenses with other companies—called cross-licensing—so that companies involved in the trade will benefit from each other's technology.

What kinds of patents may be issued?

The U.S. Patent and Trademark Office issues three types of patents:

- **Utility patents.** New, nonobvious, useful inventions that fall into one of five categories—a process, a machine, a manufacture, a composition of matter, or an improvement of an existing idea—may qualify for a utility patent. Often, an invention will fall into more than one of the categories. For instance, computer software can usually be described both as a process (the steps that it takes to make the computer do something) and as a machine (a device that takes information from an input device and moves it to an output device). Regardless of the number of categories in which an invention falls, only one utility patent may be issued on it.
- **Design patents.** New and original designs that ornament a manufactured article can qualify for a design patent. For example, a new shape for a car fender, bottle, or flashlight that doesn't improve its functionality would qualify.
- **Plant patents.** The least-frequently issued type of patent are plant patents—granted for any asexually or sexually reproducible plants (such as flowers) that are both novel and nonobvious.

What types of inventions qualify for a utility patent?

Most types of inventions (the term we'll use for innovative ideas) qualify for a utility patent if they offer something new (are novel) and are particularly clever (that is, nonobvious). However, some types of inventions do not qualify for a patent, no matter how nonobvious they are. For instance, mathematical formulas, newly discovered laws of nature, and newly discovered substances that occur naturally in the world traditionally have been considered to be unpatentable.

When deciding whether an invention qualifies for a patent, the USPTO first must determine whether the invention is novel in some way—that is, a new development in at least one or more of its constituent elements—as of the date of invention (usually the date the inventor conceived it or when the patent application was filed).

If the USPTO determines that the invention is novel, it then must make another decision: Is the invention nonobvious? To make this determination, the USPTO asks this question: Would someone who was skilled in the particular field as of the invention date consider the invention to be an unexpected or surprising development?

If the invention is found to be both novel and nonobvious, and it fits within one or more of the five statutory categories discussed above, it may qualify to receive a patent. (Note: with the passage of the America Invents Act in September 2011, the date of invention becomes less relevant and the date of filing becomes the new standard by which novelty and nonobviousness are measured. This change will occur in March 2013. See "What's new in patent law since the last edition?" below.)

Among the many types of creative works that might qualify for a utility patent are biological inventions; new chemical formulas, processes, or procedures; computer hardware and peripherals; computer software; cosmetics; electrical inventions; electronic circuits; food inventions; housewares; machines; magic tricks or techniques; mechanical inventions; medical accessories and devices; medicines; musical instruments; odors; and sporting goods (designs and equipment).

What is the procedure for applying for a utility patent and a provisional patent application?

To apply for a U.S. patent, the inventor files an application with the USPTO, a branch of the U.S. Department of Commerce.

For the purpose of obtaining an early filing date, the inventor may file what is known as a Provisional Patent Application (PPA). The only requirement for a PPA is that it must adequately describe how to make and use the invention. However, to obtain a patent, the inventor must file a formal patent application (within one year of the PPA date if one is filed) that follows technical conventions and contains words and drawings to clearly:

- demonstrate how to make and use the invention
- explain why the invention is different from all previous and similar developments (known as the prior art), and
- precisely describe what aspects of the invention deserve the patent (the patent claims).

This patent application will be the subject of much discussion between the applicant and the USPTO patent examiner.

What happens if there are multiple applications for the same invention?

If the patent examiner discovers that another pending application involves the same invention, and that both inventions appear to qualify for a patent, the patent examiner will declare that a conflict (called an interference) exists between the two applications. In that event, a hearing is held to determine who is entitled to the patent. Affidavits or declarations are submitted, and often live testimony is taken.

Who may be awarded the patent depends on such variables as who first conceived of the invention and worked on it diligently, who first actually built and tested the invention, and who filed the first provisional or regular patent application. (Note: With the enactment of the America Invents Act in September 2011, the rules about conflicting applications will change to reflect the new "first to file" rules. This change to a first-to-file system will occur in March 2013. See "What's new in patent law since the last edition?" below.)

Under what circumstances is a utility patent application approved?

Once a patent application is received by the USPTO, a patent examiner is assigned to the application. The examiner is responsible for deciding whether the application meets all technical requirements, whether the invention qualifies for a patent, and, assuming it does, what the scope of the patent should be.

Usually, communications occur between the applicant and the examiner regarding these issues. Typically, this takes between one and three years and involves significant amendments by the applicant. The most serious and difficult issue to fix is whether the invention qualifies for a patent in light of previous developments—that is, whether the invention is novel and nonobvious in light of the prior art.

If the examiner's objections are overcome by the applicant, the invention is approved for a patent. Then, the applicant pays a patent issue fee and receives an official copy of the patent.

To keep a patent in effect, three additional fees must be paid over the life of the patent. The total patent fee for a small inventor ("small entity"), from application to issue to expiration, is approximately $5,000 to $6,000. For large corporations, it is twice this amount.

How are patent rights enforced?

Once a patent is granted, the owner may enforce it by bringing a patent infringement action (lawsuit) against anyone who makes, uses, or sells the invention without the patent owner's permission. Normally, when a patent infringement action is filed, the alleged infringer counters by attacking the validity of the patent. Patents may be held invalid on a number of grounds. The most common are if an alleged infringer can show that the invention really wasn't novel or nonobvious or that the patent examiner simply made a mistake in issuing the patent.

If the defendant is unsuccessful and the patent is not invalidated, the court will take one of two approaches. It may issue a court order (injunction) preventing the infringer from any further use or sale of the infringing device and award damages to the patent owner. Alternatively, the court may work with the parties to hammer out an agreement under which the infringing party will pay the patent owner royalties in exchange for permission to use the infringing device.

When does a patent expire or otherwise come to an end?

The most common reason for a patent to come to an end is that the statutory period during which it is in force expires. For utility and plant patents, the statutory period is 20 years after the application date. For design patents, the statutory period is 14 years from date of issuance.

Another common reason why patents expire is that the patent owner fails to pay required maintenance fees. Usually this occurs because attempts to commercially exploit the underlying invention have failed and the patent owner chooses not to throw good money after bad.

A patent may also be declared invalid (and no longer in force) if it is later shown that the patent application was insufficient, that the applicant committed fraud on the USPTO (usually by lying about or failing to disclose the applicant's knowledge about prior art that would legally preclude issuance of the patent), or that the inventor engaged in illegal conduct when using the patent—such as conspiring with a patent licensee to exclude other companies from competing with them.

Once a patent has terminated for any reason, the invention described by the patent falls into the public domain: It can be used by anyone without permission, and the patent owner has no more rights to the invention than any member of the public. The basic technologies underlying television and personal computers are good examples of valuable inventions that are no longer covered by in-force patents.

The fact that an invention is in the public domain does not mean that subsequent developments based on the original invention are also in the public domain. Rather, new inventions that improve public domain technology are constantly being conceived and patented. For instance, televisions and personal computers that roll off today's assembly lines employ many recent inventions that are covered by in-force patents.

What about international protection for U.S. patents?

The right to control, or monopolize, an invention that a patent owner enjoys in the United States originates in the U.S. Constitution and is implemented exclusively by federal laws passed by Congress. These laws define the kinds of inventions that

Patent Law: Overview

are patentable and the procedures that must be utilized to apply for, receive, and maintain the patent in full force for its entire period.

All other industrialized countries also offer inventors protection in the form of a patent. While the standards of what is patentable and the period that patents last differ from country to country, several international treaties (including the Patent Cooperation Treaty and the Paris Convention) allow U.S. inventors to obtain patent protection in certain other countries if they take certain required steps, such as filing a patent application in the countries on a timely basis and paying required patent fees.

What's new in patent law since the last edition?

Below are the major events in patent law since the last edition of this book was published.

The America Invents Act

The America Invents Act (also referred to as the "Patent Reform Act of 2011") was enacted in September, 2011, and is the most sweeping change to patent law in the past 50 years. Although the Act is intended to go into effect 12 months after enactment, many provisions went into effect immediately and the most important change—switching to a first-to-file system—will not go into effect until 18 months from enactment. To help you understand the timing of when various provisions of the Act take place, we've reviewed the 37 proposed changes to patent law and created a listing by date, below. (Note: we haven't included many of the technical or relatively unimportant changes—for example, renaming the Detroit Patent Library—but you can read the full list of changes online at http://thomas.loc.gov.) After each bullet point, we have included a cross-reference to the relevant sections from the Act.

Changes that took place immediately (upon enactment)

- **Higher fees**. Patent filers will pay a 15% surcharge on all patent fees. (Sec. 11.)
- **Tougher to obtain an inter partes reexam**. It will be harder to obtain patent reexamination. (The Director can only authorize a reexam if "there is a reasonable likelihood that the petitioner would prevail with respect to at least 1 of the claims challenged in the petition.") And there will be no more federal court review of USPTO reexaminations. (Sec. 6.)

- **Easier for prior users to defend.** If you're sued for infringement but you were commercially using the patented technology more than one year before the filing date of the claimed invention, you have a defense against a claim that you infringed (although that defense doesn't invalidate the patent). The Act includes a definition of "commercial use." (Sec. 5.)
- **Goodbye to tax strategy patents.** The USPTO will stop granting patents for strategies for reducing, avoiding, or deferring tax liability.
- **Goodbye best mode defense**. Accused patent infringers often use the "best mode defense" in which they argue that the patent holder failed to disclose the best mode of carrying out the invention. The best mode defense will no longer be available. (Sec. 15.)
- **Hello virtual website marking.** Virtual marking—the process of using a publicly accessible website to provide a link between a patented invention and its patent number—shall be considered as sufficiently providing public notice for that patent. This change will apply to all cases filed including cases pending at the time of enactment. (Sec. 16.)
- **Harder to go after false markers.** It has become common practice for parties to bring a lawsuit claiming (or making a counterclaim) that an invention is falsely marked, especially if the mark exists on copies of the invention after the patent has expired. The Act provides that privately filed false marking claims (those claims not brought by the government) will require proof of competitive injury. Marking with the number of a patent that covered that product but has expired will no longer be considered false marking. This provision will apply to all cases filed including cases pending at the time of enactment. (Sec. 16(b).)
- **New rules when joining defendants.** Joinder of unrelated accused infringers will be limited in actions commenced on and after enactment (Sec. 19(d), and
- **No patenting humans**. Issuance of patent claims directed to or encompassing a human organism will be barred as of enactment. (Sec. 33.)

10 days after enactment

- **Paying for being prioritized.** There's a new $4,800 fee for filing a prioritized application (effective after ten days). Small entities pay only $2,400. (Sec. 11(h).)

60 days after enactment

- **The Luddite penalty.** A new $400 fee ($200 for small entities) must be paid by those applicants who do not file utility patent applications electronically. (Sec. 10(b).)

12 months after enactment

- **The Inventor's Oath/Assignment.** The Act modifies certain requirements regarding the oath or declaration required of an inventor. If an inventor has assigned (or is obligated to assign) an invention, the assignee can file the application for the patent. (Sec. 4.)

- **Narrows postgrant reviews.** The Act provides that inter partes hearings after a patent has been issued are now limited to challenges for novelty and nonobviousness—that is, to issues relating to Section 102 and 103 of the patent law. Such claims can only be based on prior art consisting of patents and printed publications and must be filed nine months after the patent issued. This provision also establishes many additional technical and procedural rules for postgrant reviews, generally making it more difficult to bring postgrant reviews. For example, it prohibits a postgrant review and inter partes review if the party filing has filed a related civil action before filing the petition. (Sec. 6.)

- **Changes to Patent Trial and Appeal Board.** The Act sets forth new rules about the Board and provides for appeals to the Court of Appeals for the Federal Circuit (CAFC) from certain Board decisions. (Sec. 7.)

- **Submitting "gotcha" documentation.** Prior to the USPTO's granting of a patent, the Act allows a third party to submit relevant publications for the patent examiner to consider (commonly referred to as preissuance submissions). (Sec. 8.)

- **Patent owner's right to supplemental exam.** The Act establishes a system of supplemental examinations for a patent owner "to consider, reconsider, and correct information believed to be relevant to the patent." (Sec. 12.)

- **A new look at business patents**. The Act requires the Director to establish a transitional postgrant review proceeding to consider the validity of business-method patents. (Sec. 18.)

18 months after enactment

- **First to file; not first to invent.** Patents filed 18 months after enactment will be subject to new first-to-file and prior art rules, effectively ending centuries of first-to-invent rules. The current one-year on sale bar—that permits sale or disclosure of the claimed invention less than one year before filing—is terminated, although the Act establishes a limited one-year grace if the inventor (or anyone who obtained the subject matter from the inventor) made certain disclosures of the claimed invention. The novelty and nonobviousness sections of the patent law (Sections 102 and 103) are amended and existing provisions relating to inventions made abroad and statutory invention registration are terminated. (Sec. 3.)

- **New rules for fighting earlier effective patent filing.** The Act permits a patent owner to bring a "derivation hearing" at the USPTO (replacing interference proceedings) against another patent owner claiming to have the same invention and who has an earlier effective filing date. The derivation hearing must be filed within a one-year period beginning on the date of the first publication of a claim in the earlier filed application. Alternatively, the owner of a patent may sue the owner of another patent that claims the same invention and has an earlier effective filing date. These lawsuits can only be brought if the invention claiming priority was derived directly from the person seeking relief. (Sec. 3.)

Other changes to patent law

- **The willful blindness standard: inducing infringement does not require actual knowledge of infringement.** A company, SEB, patented a "cool touch" deep-fryer whose exterior was cool to the touch. GlobalTech Appliances, operating outside the U.S. copied everything but the cosmetic aspects of the SEB deep-fryer. GlobalTech then branded these deep-fryers for sale by Sunbeam, Montgomery Ward, and others. SEB sued GlobalTech for inducing others to infringe its cool-touch patent. GlobalTech defended itself by arguing that it couldn't induce others to infringe because it had no actual knowledge it was infringing SEB's patent. (GlobalTech had vetted its device with a patent attorney but had failed to disclose to the attorney that their device was copied directly from the SEB deep-fryer.) The Supreme Court ruled for the patent owner, SEB. The court said that inducing infringement required knowledge of the existing patent, but that knowledge could be inferred using a legal standard referred to as "willful blindness." As the Court stated: "Many criminal statutes require proof that a defendant acted knowingly or willfully, and courts applying the doctrine of willful blindness hold that defendants cannot escape the reach of these statutes by deliberately shielding themselves from clear evidence of critical facts that are strongly suggested by the circumstances." The Court went on to distinguish willful blindness from a lower court's standard known as "deliberate indifference." As for the differences, the bottom line is that when asking an attorney to render a legal opinion ("Does my deep-fryer infringe?"), don't hide information (like, "I copied this from another deep-fryer"). (*GlobalTech Appliances v. SEB*, __ U.S. __ (2011).)

- **Proving invalidity requires clear and convincing evidence.** The Supreme Court refused to alter the standard for invalidating a patent in a battle between tech companies. Microsoft was sued for patent infringement by i4i, a Canadian company, over an XML feature of Microsoft's *Word* software. At trial, Microsoft argued that i4i failed to disclose a prior invention that might have invalidated the application (a principle known as the "one-year rule"). The jury was instructed that the patent could only be invalidated if there was "clear and convincing" evidence of invalidity. Microsoft and many other tech companies wanted the court to use the lower standard of "preponderance of the evidence" which would make it easier to invalidate many of the iffy patents used by nonpracticing entities (also known as patent trolls). The justices refused to change the standard, although the Court threw one small bone to troll victims: they could tell juries about any evidence that hadn't been considered by the patent office, like the facts Microsoft had advanced about i4i's patent. Bottom line: Tech companies will need to petition Congress for a change (unlikely) and big Pharma is happy with the decision. (*Microsoft Corp. v. i4i Limited Partnership*, __ U.S. __ (2011).)

- **Clear language in conflicting assignments determinative of ownership (not Bayh-Dole Act).** In a case involving Stanford University and the Roche pharmaceutical company, the Supreme Court was faced with two agreements signed by a university scientist: one in which he promised to assign rights to the university; and another in which he actually assigned rights to a company that was later purchased by Roche. The Supreme Court ruled that the agreement in which rights were actually assigned took precedence over the agreement in which rights were promised. Stanford's position was that the inventor's rights automatically vested in the university under the Bayh-Dole Act. The Bayh-Dole Act, enacted in 1980, permits universities to claim patent rights in inventions created with federal funding at a university. The university may then license these discoveries to private industry—a practice some critics have likened to corporate welfare. Curiously, one of the prerequisites for the university to claim these rights is that the university must have written agreements with its faculty and technical staff requiring disclosure and assignment of inventions. The ruling won't invalidate past assignments. But problems may occur in cases like this one, where two assignments appear to conflict. In addition, you can expect that universities will stop using language in which inventors promise to assign and instead automatically assign inventions. (*Stanford v. Roche,* 563 U. S. __ (2011).)

- **Human genes are unpatentable as "products of nature."** A federal district court determined that certain patent claims for BRCA1 and BRCA2 human genes were invalid. The genes are found in the cells of breast and other tissue, where they help repair damaged DNA. The genes are a factor in breast cancer diagnosis. The court held that the subject matter was unpatentable because genes are the physical embodiment of [genetic] information. (*Association for Molecular Pathology v. USPTO,* 702 F. Supp. 2d 181 (S.D. N.Y. 2010).)

- **Filing date of provisional patent application establishes prior art references.** An inventor, Giacomini, filed a patent application claiming a method of selectively storing sets of electronic data. Another inventor, Tran, filed a patent application after Giacomini for a similar invention. However, Tran's application was based on a provisional patent application that accurately described the invention and was filed before Giacomini's application. In that case, the Federal Circuit held that Tran as "first inventor," could claim patent rights and use his patent application as prior art against Giacomini. (*In re Giacomini*, 612 F.3d 1380 (Fed. Cir. 2010).)

- **Registered copyright and deposit copy are not necessarily publicly accessible prior disclosures.** Printed publications function as prior art if they are publicly accessible, no matter how burdensome it is to obtain the publication. In this case, an inventor, Lister, filed a copyright registration and furnished a deposit to the Copyright Office. However, the Copyright Office's database had such limited search capabilities that the Federal Circuit determined that the evidence was insufficient and remanded the case. (*In re Lister,* 583 F.3d 1307 (Fed. Cir. 2009).)

- **Nonobviousness determination can be based on common sense**. In this case, a court invalidated a patent for email distribution. The patent claimed a method for managing bulk email distribution to groups of consumers including selecting recipients, sending emails to that group, and tabulating the number of emails successfully transmitted. If the number did not exceed a certain minimum, the last step called for repeating the previous steps. The district court summarized the last step as obvious since it was based on the commonsense principle, "If at first you don't succeed, try again." (*Perfect Web Technologies, Inc. v. InfoUSA, Inc,* 587 F.3d 1324 (Fed. Cir. 2009).)

- **Patent misuse standard narrowed.** The Federal Circuit narrowed the scope of patent misuse in a case involving compact disc patents. Under the Federal Circuit's new standard, there must be evidence of anticompetitive effects associated in addition to restrictions on use. Alleging wrongful conduct is not enough. (*Princo Corp. v. International Trade Commission,* 616 F.3d 1318 (Fed. Cir. 2010).)

- **Employment agreement is not conclusive as to invention assignment.** A scientist signed an employee invention agreement that required that inventions created during employment would belong to his employer unless:

  1. the invention was developed entirely on his own time;
  2. equipment, supplies, facility, or trade secret of the Company was not used in its development, and
  3. (i) it does not relate to the business or actual or demonstrably antici-pated research, or development of the Company, or (ii) it does not result from any work performed by [him] for the Company.

  The scientist invented a method of sequencing DNA on his own time using his home computer and without the assistance of any company trade secrets. The Federal Circuit determined that under California law, the scientist need only meet either of the two requirements established in the third criteria. The court determined the invention did not result from work performed for the company and on that basis, there was no assignment. (*Applera Corp. Applied Biosystems Group v. Illumina, Inc.,* 2009-1260, 2010 WL 1169936 (Fed. Cir. Mar. 25, 2010).)

- **A coinventor does not have to make a complete conception of invention.** A dispute arose as to whether Vanderbilt professors could be added as coinventors on a patent for an inhibitor, useful for treating erectile dysfunction. A district court held that coinventorship required that each coinventor have a full conception of the inhibitor. The Federal Circuit determined this was an error because each coinventor must only engage with the others in some significant way toward that end. (The error was considered harmless because Vanderbilt failed to prove its methodology was used in the patent.) (*Vanderbilt University v. ICOS Corp.,* 601 F.3d 1297 (Fed. Cir. 2010).)

Patent resources

If you're interested in hands-on, step-by-step instructions on applying for a patent or simply want more information on patent law, consult one of these Nolo resources:

- *Patent It Yourself,* by David Pressman
- *Patent Pending in 24 Hours,* by Richard Stim and David Pressman
- *How to Make Patent Drawings: A Patent It Yourself Companion,* by Jack Lo and David Pressman
- *What Every Inventor Needs to Know About Business & Taxes,* by Stephen Fishman
- *The Inventor's Notebook: A Patent It Yourself Companion,* by Fred Grissom and David Pressman
- *Profit From Your Idea: How to Make Smart Licensing Deals,* by Richard Stim
- *All I Need Is Money: How to Finance Your Invention,* by Jack Lander, and
- *Nolo's Patents for Beginners,* by David Pressman and Richard Stim.

You may also find valuable information related to patents at the following sites:

- **Patents and Business (www.patentsandbusiness.com).** Nolo offers information about patent law, patent news, and running an invention business at this site.
- **The USPTO (www.uspto.gov).** This is the place to go for recent policy and statutory changes and transcripts of hearings on various patent law issues. You may also use this site to conduct a search of patents issued since 1971.
- **Dear Rich: Nolo's Patent, Copyright & Trademark Blog (www.dearrichblog.com).** Nolo's intellectual property blog operates as a companion to this book. Answers are provided to common intellectual property questions.

Patent Law: Overview

Patent Law: Definitions

B elow are definitions of the words and phrases commonly used in patent-related activities.

abandonment of patent application

The U.S. Patent and Trademark Office (USPTO) considers a patent application abandoned if the applicant fails to respond in a timely manner to actions or requests initiated by the USPTO.

The USPTO's response to most patent applications is to send the applicant a notice (called an office action) rejecting one or more aspects of the application. The applicant must then amend the application—usually the claims, which are precise descriptions of the invention—or provide some other suitable response within three months to keep the application alive.

In the event an application is treated by the USPTO as abandoned, the applicant may:

- petition the Director of the USPTO to set aside the abandonment decision
- file a substitute application—which means paying additional fees and being given a later filing date (harmful if another applicant files an application for a similar invention between the first and second filing dates), or
- forget about the patent and utilize another available method of protection, such as trade secrecy (assuming the invention has not been published or publicly disclosed) or trademark (for example, you can use a clever name for the invention to capture market share, such as "The Club").

Related terms: claims; prosecution of a patent application; substitute patent application.

abstract

This paragraph in the patent application (also known as the "Abstract of the Disclosure") concisely summarizes the general nature, structure, and purpose of the invention.

Related terms: *Official Gazette* (OG); patent application.

accused device

An accused device is an invention that is alleged to have been used or sold in a manner that infringes a patented invention.

actual reduction to practice

See reduction to practice.

admissions by inventor

Statements by an inventor about his or her invention may be used by the U.S. Patent and Trademark Office (USPTO) to reject a patent application or cause a court to rule against the invention's validity. An inventor should avoid writing anything in a patent application or in correspondence with the USPTO that derogates the invention, since the statement will constitute an admission that can later be introduced by the USPTO or by a competitor to fight the patent.

Related terms: certificate of correction; duty of candor and good faith; file wrapper estoppel.

AEP (Accelerated Examination Program)

Under the Accelerated Examination Program (AEP), the USPTO will advance an application out of turn for examination if the applicant files a Petition to Make Special under the AEP program, and the petition is granted. The AEP program supersedes (although it does not replace) the process whereby applicants file petitions to make special (PTMS). The USPTO has revised the procedures for petitions to make special, except those based on applicant's health or age. Other petitions to make special (i.e., based on: manufacture, infringement, environmental quality, energy, recombinant DNA, superconductivity materials, HIV/AIDS and cancer, countering terrorism, and biotechnology applications filed by small entities; see MPEP § 708.02) will be processed using the revised AEP procedure. The AEP requires that an applicant file electronically using EFS-Web and Form SB28 at the same time. For more information see the USPTO explanation at www.uspto.gov/web/patents/accelerated.

AIPLA

The AIPLA (American Intellectual Property Law Association) is the largest organization of intellectual property lawyers in the United States (www.aipla.org).

algorithms

An algorithm is a mathematical procedure that can be used to solve a problem or class of problems. Common examples of algorithms are mathematical formulas, geometry axioms, and algebraic equations. Algorithms as such are not patentable, because the patent would create a huge and fundamental monopoly over laws of nature.

> EXAMPLE: The Heisenberg uncertainty principle, a well-known law of nature, states that you cannot design an apparatus to simultaneously determine the location and the momentum of a subatomic particle. This principle is relevant to many scientific and electrical engineering applications; thus a patent on it would give exclusive control of the development of these applications to the owner of the patent. Effectively, a patent on the Heisenberg uncertainty principle would either halt progress in any field where the principle applies or force all would-be developers to pay license fees to the patent holder.

The rule against patenting algorithms was at one time applied to computer software, because software largely consists of procedural instructions in mathematical form that make a computer accomplish a certain and definite result. Now, however, the U.S. Patent and Trademark Office will allow patents on that aspect of software that accomplishes a useful, concrete, and tangible result, and provided that the software process is tied to a particular machine or transforms an article into a different state.

Related terms: laws of nature exception to patents; software patents.
See also Part 2 (Copyright Law): computer software.

allowance

The decision by the U.S. Patent and Trademark Office (USPTO) to award a patent to an applicant is referred to as an allowance (the application is "allowed"). The applicant is sent a notice of allowance by the USPTO; this usually occurs after the initial claims were amended at least once during the prosecution of the patent application.

Related terms: certificate of correction; prosecution of a patent application.

amendment of patent application

A patent application may be amended (changed) in response to an initial rejection by the U.S. Patent and Trademark Office. Patent examiners often reject the initial application as filed, most commonly because the scope of the patent being applied for is too broad in light of previous developments in that field (the prior art). Other common reasons for rejection are noncompliance with certain rules governing how the invention must be described in words or portrayed in drawings.

This initial rejection includes an explanation and copies of any patents that seem very similar (called prior art references) and have contributed to the rejection. Upon receiving a rejection, an applicant usually files an amendment, in one part changing the application in accordance with the examiner's requirements, and in the other part contesting such requirements. Alternatively, an applicant may contest the examiner's decisions completely or file an amendment that completely conforms the application to the examiner's requirements.

Related terms: office action; prosecution of a patent application.

America Invents Act

Modifications to the patent law were enacted in September 2011, with the passage of the America Invents Act (also known as the Leahy-Smith America Invents Act). Although referred to as "patent reform," commentators have noted that the Act does little to "reform" the problems associated with the patent system—notably, an underfunded PTO, inadequate examination procedures, and burdensome litigation. In the end, the Act turned out to be an example of special interest policy-making that favors large companies over independent inventors. The major change of the Act is that the U.S. switches to a first-to-file system in March 2013, 18 months after enactment. Below is a timeline for the changes in the Act.

Changes that took place in September 2011 (upon enactment)

- **Higher fees.** Patent filers will pay a 15% surcharge on all patent fees
- **Tougher to obtain an inter partes reexam.** It will be harder to obtain patent reexamination. (The Director can only authorize a reexam if "there is a reasonable likelihood that the petitioner would prevail with respect to at least 1 of the claims challenged in the petition.") And there will be no more federal court review of USPTO reexaminations.
- **Easier for prior users to defend.** If you're sued for infringement but you were commercially using the patented technology more than one year before the filing date of the claimed invention, you have a defense against a claim that you infringed (although that defense doesn't invalidate the patent). The Act includes a definition of "commercial use."

- **Goodbye to tax strategy patents.** The USPTO will stop granting patents for strategies for reducing, avoiding, or deferring tax liability.
- **Goodbye best mode defense.** Accused patent infringers often use the "best mode defense" in which they argue that the patent holder failed to disclose the best mode of carrying out the invention. The best mode defense will no longer be available.
- **Hello virtual website marking.** Virtual marking—the process of using a publicly accessible website to provide a link between a patented invention and its patent number—shall be considered as sufficiently providing public notice for that patent. This change will apply to all cases filed including cases pending at the time of enactment.
- **Harder to go after false markers.** It has become common practice for parties to bring a lawsuit claiming (or making a counterclaim) that an invention is falsely marked, especially if the mark exists on copies of the invention after the patent has expired. The Act provides that privately filed false marking claims (those claims not brought by the government) will require proof of competitive injury. Marking with the number of a patent that covered that product but has expired will no longer be considered false marking. This provision will apply to all cases filed including cases pending at the time of enactment.
- **New rules when joining defendants.** Joinder of unrelated accused infringers will be limited in actions commenced on and after enactment.
- **No patenting humans.** Issuance of patent claims directed to or encompassing a human organism will be barred as of enactment.
- **Paying for being prioritized.** There's a new $4,800 fee for filing a prioritized application (effective after ten days). Small entities pay only $2,400.

Changes that took place in November 2011

- **The Luddite penalty.** A new $400 fee ($200 for small entities) must be paid by those applicants who do not file utility patent applications electronically.

Changes that take place in September 2012

- **The Inventor's Oath/Assignment.** The Act modifies certain requirements regarding the oath or declaration required of an inventor. If an inventor has assigned (or is obligated to assign) an invention, the assignee can file the application for the patent.

- **Narrows postgrant reviews.** The Act provides that inter partes hearings after a patent has been issued are now limited to challenges for novelty and nonobviousness—that is, to issues relating to Section 102 and 103 of the patent law. Such claims can only be based on prior art consisting of patents and printed publications and must be filed nine months after the patent issued. This provision also establishes many additional technical and procedural rules for postgrant reviews, generally making it more difficult to bring postgrant reviews. For example, it prohibits a postgrant review and inter partes review if the party filing has filed a related civil action before filing the petition.

- **Changes to Patent Trial and Appeal Board.** The Act sets forth new rules about the Board and provides for appeals to the Court of Appeals for the Federal Circuit (CAFC) from certain Board decisions.

- **Submitting "gotcha" documentation.** Prior to the USPTO's granting of a patent, the Act allows a third party to submit relevant publications for the patent examiner to consider (commonly referred to as preissuance submissions).

- **Patent owner's right to supplemental exam.** The Act establishes a system of supplemental examinations for a patent owner "to consider, reconsider, and correct information believed to be relevant to the patent."

- **A new look at business patents.** The Act requires the Director to establish a transitional postgrant review proceeding to consider the validity of business-method patents.

Changes that take place in March 2013

- **First to file; not first to invent.** Patents filed 18 months after enactment will be subject to new first-to-file and prior art rules, effectively ending centuries of first-to-invent rules. The current one-year on sale bar—that permits sale or disclosure of the claimed invention less than one year before filing—is terminated, although the Act establishes a limited one-year grace if the inventor (or anyone who obtained the subject matter from the inventor) made certain disclosures of the claimed invention. The novelty and nonobviousness sections of the patent law (Sections 102 and 103) are amended and existing provisions relating to inventions made abroad and statutory invention registration are terminated.

- **New rules for fighting earlier effective patent filing.** The Act permits a patent owner to bring a "derivation hearing" at the USPTO (replacing interference proceedings) against another patent owner claiming to have the same invention and who has an earlier effective filing date. The derivation hearing must be filed within a one-year period beginning on the date of the first publication of a claim in the earlier filed application. Alternatively, the owner of a patent may sue the owner of another patent that claims the same invention and has an earlier effective filing date. These lawsuits can only be brought if the invention claiming priority was derived directly from the person seeking relief.

Anticipation

Note: The rules regarding anticipation, below, will change dramatically in March 2013 when the U.S. switches to a first-to-file system (as a result of passage of the America Invents Act). The current one-year on sale bar—that permits sale or disclosure of the claimed invention less than one year before filing—is terminated, although the Act establishes a limited one-year grace if the inventor (or anyone who obtained the subject matter from the inventor) made certain disclosures of the claimed invention. The novelty and nonobviousness sections of the patent law (Sections 102 and 103) are amended and existing provisions relating to inventions made abroad and statutory invention registration are terminated. Until March 2013, you can rely on the standards provided below.

An invention is said to be anticipated when it is too similar to an earlier invention to be considered novel. Because novelty is a requirement for patentability, anticipated inventions are not patentable.

An invention may be anticipated in any of the following ways:

- Prior publication in such writings as a news article, trade journal article, academic thesis, or prior patent. For example, Fred invents a low-cost kit that permits a car's driver to monitor ten different engine functions while driving. If all of the primary characteristics (elements) of this kit had been described by someone else in a publication or patent before Fred invented his kit, the invention would be considered anticipated by the published reference and would be barred from receiving a patent.

- By existence of a prior invention, if all significant elements of the later invention are found in an earlier one prior to the date of invention or the application's filing date. Suppose Sam "invents" an electric generator that is driven by the kinetic energy of a car's moving wheels. If all basic elements used by Sam in his "invention" can be found in a prior invention (whether patented or not) by Jake, who used his invention openly—without suppressing or concealing it—Sam's generator has been anticipated.

- By placing the invention on sale more than one year prior to an application's being filed. "On sale" means not only an actual sale, but any offer of sale. For example, if Sam offers to sell his invention to a major car manufacturer more than one year previous to his filing a patent application on it, the offer will anticipate the invention even if the sale never takes place.
- By public use or display of the invention more than a year prior to filing the patent application. For example, if Fred publicly demonstrated his kit a year or more prior to filing for a patent, the invention would be considered "anticipated" because the earlier public display would render the invention no longer "novel" at the time of filing the application. However, if the public demonstrations were predominately for experimental purposes, the one-year period might not apply. In fact, anticipation through public use or display rarely occurs.

Anticipation by a prior invention or printed publication—that is, a prior art reference—can occur only if all of the later invention's basic elements are contained in a single invention or a single publication. For example, if a news article describes some elements of an invention, and a prior invention shows the rest, no anticipation has occurred, because no single reference contained all the elements.

In a case involving a new use for a composition, the Court of Appeals for the Federal Circuit (CAFC) held that claims were anticipated when (1) the prior references disclosed each and every element of the claimed invention, and (2) the prior references enabled a person of ordinary skill in the art to practice the invention without undue experimentation (*In re Marin Gleave and Maxim Signaevsky*, 560 F.3d 1331 (Fed. Cir. 2009).) In another case, the CAFC held that prior art—in order to anticipate an invention—must not only disclose all elements of a claim, but also must disclose those elements as arranged in the claim. The CAFC analogized to a recipe in which the ingredients must be combined in a certain order. (*Net MoneyIn, Inc. v. Verisign*, 545 F.3d 1359 (Fed. Cir. 2008).)

Related terms: novelty; printed publication as statutory bar; prior art reference; public use.

antishelving clause

This provision in a licensing agreement makes permission to use a patented invention contingent on the willingness of the party receiving the license to use the patent commercially within a designated period of time (rather than acquiring the patent in order to put the invention out of commission—that is, "putting it on the shelf".)

antitrust law (federal) and patents

Federal antitrust laws generally prohibit businesses from engaging in monopolistic activities—that is, to engage in practices purposely designed to give the business dominant control over a particular market segment. However, by definition, a patent is a legal monopoly over the production, use, and distribution of an invention. In an attempt to reconcile these conflicting legal goals, the United States (and most countries) restricts the ways companies holding patents may use them in the marketplace.

In addition to preventing monopolistic activities, antitrust laws prohibit business practices that restrain the free flow of commerce (called restraint of trade). Among the more common types of patent-related activity that may potentially cause antitrust violations are:

- price fixing—for example, a patent owner requiring licensees of a patent to charge certain prices for goods manufactured under the patent
- exclusive dealing agreements—for example, a patent owner encouraging patent licensees not to deal with certain customers
- tying agreements—that is, requiring a customer who wishes to purchase the patented invention to also purchase other goods or services as a condition of the purchase; for instance, putting a provision in a license agreement that requires the licensee of a mainframe computer to use the licensor to service the computer would tie the purchase of the computer to the purchase of the service
- requirements contracts, whether mandatory or encouraged by price reductions—for example, prohibiting a purchaser of goods covered by a patent from purchasing comparable items from another source
- patent thickets—a collection of patents owned by various companies that prevent a newcomer from entering a field of technology or invention
- territorial restrictions—for example, restricting licensees to certain geographical areas in their marketing of goods covered by the patent, and
- concerted refusal to deal—for example, excluding some potential customers from use of the device or process covered by the patent while including others.

Practically speaking, antitrust laws should not be a concern for most patent owners, as few patents have a large enough impact on the related market or

Patent Law: Definitions

industry to raise the antitrust warning flag. If, however, a patent is so broad in its coverage that the actual ebb and flow of commerce might be affected by it, there is no substitute for good knowledge of antitrust law. This is especially true when important inventions are involved in patent infringement lawsuits, because defendants often charge that the plaintiff committed an antitrust violation and therefore cannot enforce the patent.

Related terms: defenses to a patent infringement claim; patent misuse; patent thickets; price fixing.

appeals

See Board of Patent Appeals and Interferences (BPAI).

application filing fees

Fees to file a patent application typically include a filing fee (which is reduced if you file electronically), a search fee, and an examination fee. The fees are twice as much for large entities as for small entities. Generally, independent inventors, nonprofit corporations, and businesses with fewer than 500 employees qualify for small entity status. However, if an assignment has or will be made by a small entity to a large entity, large entity fees must be paid. For information on current patent application fees, check the USPTO website.

Related terms: issue fee.

application issue fees

See issue fee.

assignment of a patent

Because a patent is a type of property, it can be sold (assigned) to others. An assignment is a document that transfers a patent owner's rights in exchange for money payable in a lump sum or royalties on future sales of the invention.

Many inventors assign their invention, either to the company they work for under an employment agreement or, in the case of independent inventors, to outside development or manufacturing companies. These assignments typically transfer ownership of any patent that issues on the invention and may (although usually not in the case of employed inventors) provide for compensation for the inventor, although employed inventors often receive little or no additional compensation, because they are getting paid to invent.

As of September 2012 (as result of passage of the America Invents Act), assignees of invention rights rather than the inventor may apply for the patent.

Sec. 118. Filing by other than inventor [Effective September 2012]

A person to whom the inventor has assigned or is under an obligation to assign the invention may make an application for patent. A person who otherwise shows sufficient proprietary interest in the matter may make an application for patent on behalf of and as agent for the inventor on proof of the pertinent facts and a showing that such action is appropriate to preserve the rights of the parties. If the Director grants a patent on an application filed under this section by a person other than the inventor, the patent shall be granted to the real party in interest and upon such notice to the inventor as the Director considers to be sufficient.

Related terms: licensing of an invention; patent owner.

attorney fees, infringement action

See infringement action.

Attorneys and Agents Registered to Practice Before the U.S. Patent and Trademark Office

See patent attorneys.

Bayh-Dole Act

The Bayh-Dole Act, enacted in 1980, permits universities to claim patent rights in inventions created at the university with federal funding. The university may license these discoveries to private industry—a practice some critics have likened to corporate welfare.

As a result of Bayh-Dole, university patent acquisition and licensing has expanded dramatically. Before 1980, U.S. universities acquired fewer than 150 patents per year. However, 20 years later, the University of California alone obtained 324 patents (and earned $261 million in licensing revenue). Regulations for the Bayh-Dole law (35 United States Code, Sections 200-212) can be found at 37 C.F.R. Part 401.

The key regulations are as follows:

- The university must have written agreements with its faculty and technical staff requiring disclosure and assignment of inventions.
- The university has an obligation to disclose each new invention to the federal funding agency within two months after the inventor discloses it in writing to the university.

- The decision whether or not to retain title to the invention must be made within two years after disclosing the invention to the agency.
- The university must file a patent application within one year, or prior to the end of any statutory period in which valid patent protection can be obtained in the United States.
- Any company holding an exclusive license to a patent that involves sales of a product in the United States must substantially manufacture the product in the U.S.
- In their marketing of an invention, universities must give preference to small business firms (fewer than 500 employees), provided such firms have the resources and capability for bringing the invention to practical application. However, if a large company has also provided research support that led to the invention, that company may be awarded the license.
- Universities may not assign their ownership of inventions to third parties, except to patent-management organizations.
- Universities must share with the inventor(s) a portion of any revenue received from licensing the invention. Any remaining revenue, after expenses, must be used to support scientific research or education.
- Under certain circumstances, the government can require the university to grant a license to a third party, or the government may take title and grant licenses itself (these are called "march-in rights").

In 2004, in a demonstration of federal government's power under Bayh-Dole, the Court of Appeals for the Federal Circuit invalidated a patent because the patent owner, a recipient of federal funds, failed to make adequate disclosures regarding its invention as required under the Act. (*Campbell Plastics v. Brownlee* 389 F.3d 1243 (Fed. Cir. Nov. ten, 2004).)

In a 2011 case involving Stanford University and the Roche pharmaceutical company, the Supreme Court was faced with two agreements signed by a university scientist: one in which he promised to assign rights to the university; and another in which he actually assigned rights to a company that was later purchased by Roche. The Supreme Court ruled that the agreement in which rights were actually assigned took precedence over the agreement in which rights were promised. Stanford's position was that the inventor's rights automatically vested in the university under the Bayh-Dole Act. The Bayh-Dole Act, enacted in 1980, permits universities to claim patent rights in inventions created with federal funding at a university. The university may then license these discoveries to private industry—a practice some critics have likened to corporate welfare.

Curiously, one of the prerequisites for the university to claim these rights is that the university must have written agreements with its faculty and technical staff requiring disclosure and assignment of inventions. The ruling won't invalidate past assignments. But problems may occur in cases like this one, where two assignments appear to conflict. In addition, you can expect that universities will stop using language in which inventors promise to assign and instead automatically assign inventions. *Stanford v. Roche*, 563 U. S. ___ (2011)

Related terms: march-in rights.

best mode disclosure requirement

See disclosure requirement for patents.

biotechnology and patents

See genetic engineering and patents.

blocking patent

When patents have claims that overlap each other in a manner that the invention claimed in one patent cannot be used or sold ("practiced" in patent lingo) without infringing the claims of the other patent and vice versa, each patent is referred to as a "blocking patent" since it blocks the use of the other.

Related terms: patent pools.

Board of Patent Appeals and Interferences (BPAI)

A tribunal of administrative judges of the U.S. Patent and Trademark Office that handles appeals of rejected applications and decides who is entitled to a patent when an interference occurs (when two or more inventors lay claim to the same invention). This administrative body combines the former functions of the Board of Appeals and the Board of Patent Interferences.

Related terms: Court of Appeals for the Federal Circuit (CAFC); final office action; interference; prosecution of a patent application.

breaking (or busting) a patent

To break a patent means to establish that an existing patent is invalid or unenforceable because of either of the following:

- It was improperly issued by the U.S. Patent and Trademark Office in the first place.
- It was legally misused by the patent owner.

Patents are normally broken in the course of defending against a patent infringement charge brought by the patent owner.

Related terms: antitrust law (federal) and patents; defenses to a patent infringement claim; infringement action; patent misuse.

building and testing an invention

After conceiving of an invention, an inventor's next step is usually to build and test a working model (called "actually reducing an invention to practice"). Although not necessary to get a patent, building and testing an invention before applying for a patent on it is strongly advised, because a working model will:

- more definitively establish the exact nature of the invention
- make it much easier to describe the invention in the patent application
- help to sell the invention to a company, and
- prove a crucial date in case of an interference or a prior use reference having a date up to one year before the applicant's filing date.

Related terms: experimental use of an unpatented invention; interference; reduction to practice.

business methods as statutory subject matter

For many years it was assumed that methods of doing business were not patentable subject matter. However, in the case of *State Street Bank and Trust v. Signature,* 149 F.3d 1368 (Fed. Cir. 1998), the Court of Appeals for the Federal Circuit ruled that there is no logical basis for the business methods exception, and that a business method constitutes statutory subject matter if it produces a useful, concrete, and tangible result. The business method approved of in the *State Street* case was part of a computer program that facilitates mutual fund investing. The principle established in the *State Street* case—that business methods are suitable patent subject matter—was affirmed in *AT&T Corp. v. Excel Communications, Inc.,* 179 F.3d 1352 (Fed. Cir. 1999).

The term "business method patent" has also been used to describe a group of utility patents whose inventions combine software programs and methods of doing business, most of which relate to Internet uses. These are also sometimes referred to as "Internet patents," and one of the most well-known is Amazon.com's "One-Click" system, a method that allows a repeat customer to bypass address and credit card data entry forms when placing an online order. (U.S. Pat. No. 5,960,411.)

Although the terms "business method patent" and "Internet patent" have been used interchangeably in the media, these patents may deal with mutually exclusive concepts. For example, a patented method of doing business does not have to pertain to an online application. Likewise, a patent for a process used on the Internet may be more accurately described as a software patent than as a business method.

Regardless of their categorization, all of these patents seem to have one thing in common: They expand ways of doing business in new technologies. Since the *State Street* case, the number of applications filed in the principal class for business methods (Class 705) has exploded.

In 2008, the existence of business method patents was threatened by a ruling (*In re Bilski*) by the Court of Appeals for the Federal Circuit (CAFC). The CAFC that stated that any new process must either (1) be tied to a particular machine or apparatus, or (2) transform an article into a different state or thing. In 2010, the Supreme Court held that this "machine or transformation" test was "a useful and important clue, an investigative tool" but that it should not be used as the sole test to determine patentability. The Supreme Court refused to categorically deny patentability to any class or category of otherwise patentable subject matter. In doing so, the Supreme Court basically preserved the status quo and kept alive the concept of software, business method, and other process patents. (*Kappos v. Bilski*, 561 U.S. ___ (2010).)

Sometimes a business may have been using a particular business method prior to another company acquiring a patent on that method. For example, if Business A files for a business method patent, but Business B can show that it implemented and commercially used the method publicly more than a year prior to the filing, Business B has a good defense against the patent. This defense was created under a 1999 amendment to the patent law. (35 United States Code, Section 273(b).)

Note: The America Invents Act, enacted in September 2011, requires that in September 2012, the Director must establish a transitional postgrant review proceeding to consider the validity of business-method patents. In other words, it will likely become harder to obtain a business method patent.

Related terms: software patents; statutory subject matter.

Patent Law: Definitions

CCPA (Court of Customs and Patent Appeals)

Formerly, this court handled appeals from determinations by the U.S. Patent and Trademark Office. Appeals are now heard by the Court of Appeals for the Federal Circuit (CAFC).

Related terms: Court of Appeals for the Federal Circuit (CAFC).

certificate of correction

The USPTO issues a certificate of correction form when an inventor wishes to make minor technical or clerical corrections in an application after the USPTO has decided to issue the patent. These corrections may not, however, consist of new matter that changes the invention covered by the patent.

Related terms: new matter; prosecution of a patent application.

chemicals as patentable subject matter

See composition of matter.

CIP

See continuation-in-part application (CIP).

claims

Claims are statements included in a patent application that describe (or "recite") the structure of an invention in precise and exact terms, using a long-established formal style and precise terminology. Claims serve as a way:

- for the U.S. Patent and Trademark office (USPTO) to determine whether an invention is patentable, and
- for a court to determine whether a patent has been infringed (someone has made, used, or sold a patented device without the patent owner's permission).

Most patent applications contain more than one claim, each of which describes the invention from a slightly different viewpoint. Claims may be "independent" (standing on their own) or "dependent" (referring to other claims on which they depend for some or all of their elements). Examples of independent and dependent claims are below.

Each claim must "particularly point out and distinctly claim" the invention for which the patent is being sought. To this end, the USPTO requires that each claim be:

- stated in one unit (a sentence fragment which can and almost always does have numerous clauses and subclauses)

Example of Independent and Dependent Claims	
	I claim:
Independent Claim	1. A target comprising substrate means and target pattern means formed on one side of said substrate means in a layer substantially covering said one side of said substrate means, said substrate means and said target pattern means being mutually contrasting visually, said substrate means and said target pattern means being arranged such that when struck by a high-speed projectile, a substantially larger-than-projectile-size portion of said target pattern means at the projectile's point of impact will be physically separated and remove from the rest of said target pattern means, and a hole, of a size smaller than said removed portion of said target pattern means, will be made in said substrate means, whereby a portion of said substrate means around said hole will be exposed by the impact of said projectile.
Dependent Claims	2. The target of claim **1** wherein said substrate means is contrastingly colored to said target pattern means by means of a fluorescent dye.
	3. The target of claim **1** wherein said substrate means comprises a transparent film backed by a layer of material having a contrasting color to said target pattern means.
	4. The target of claim **1** wherein said substrate means comprises an ionomer resin and said target pattern means comprises an ink layer.
	5. The target of claim **4** wherein said ionomer resin is transparent and is backed by layer of material having a contrasting color to said target pattern means.
	6. The target of claim **4** wherein said ionomer resin has a contrasting color to said target pattern means.
	7. The target of claim **1** wherein said substrate means has a target pattern congruent with the target pattern on said target pattern means.
	8. The target of claim **7** wherein said substrate means comprises a transparent film backed by a layer of material having contrasting color to said target pattern means, said congruent target pattern being formed on said layer of material.
	9. The target of claim **8** wherein said layer of material is paper which is dyed with a brightly colored fluorescent ink.
	10. The target of claim **1** wherein said target pattern means comprises at least one substantially larger-than-bullet-size flat member adhesively secured to said substrate means.
	11. The target of claim **1** wherein said target pattern means comprises a mosaic of substantially larger-than-bullet-size flat members adhesively secured to and covering said substrate means and carries a target pattern thereon.

Patent Law: Definitions

- very specific
- clear
- distinct from other claims, and
- consistent with the narrative description of the patent contained in the patent application.

Claims may be broad or narrow in terms of the scope of the invention they address. The greater the scope of the invention defined in the claims (that is, the broader the claims), the wider the reach of the patent. Similarly, the narrower the scope of a patent claim, the more restricted the reach of the patent—and the easier it is for another inventor to come up with a somewhat similar invention that does not infringe the claim.

EXAMPLE 1: A claim to a new type of writing implement states that the invention is "a hand-held device containing means by which marks may be made on a surface." Because the language of this claim literally reaches every writing implement that ever has been or ever could be manufactured, it would be considered extremely broad. If a patent were issued (extremely unlikely, as discussed below), any subsequent invention that was held by hand and made marks on a surface would infringe the claim and therefore the patent.

EXAMPLE 2: Suppose the inventor of a type of writing implement claims the invention as follows: "A 3-inch by ½-inch plastic tube containing liquid and for making an indelible $1/32$-inch line on a flat paper surface." If another company makes a 4-inch by ¼-inch metal tube containing a charcoal substance capable of making variable width lines on any flat surface, the claim is not infringed, because it recited very specific elements that are different from the elements of the later invention.

Although broad claims promise to give the inventor more protection, there is a rub: They may preclude the issuance of a patent. To qualify for a patent, an invention must be both novel (different in some way from previous inventions) and nonobvious (produce an unexpected or surprising result). The broader the claims, the more likely that they overlap with previous developments, and the greater the risk that the invention described in the claims won't be considered novel and nonobvious. (The writing implement discussed above is a good example.) Conversely, narrower claims for an invention provide a greater chance that the invention will be considered novel and nonobvious, because the claims are less likely to overlap with previous developments.

EXAMPLE: The first writing implement claim, described earlier, was so broad that it clearly read on (described) prior inventions (such as pencil, chalk, pen, quill, crayon). This fact should preclude the issuance of a patent and would make invalid any patent that did issue on the invention described in that claim. The narrower version of the second writing implement claim, however, tended to exclude many prior inventions. For instance, by limiting the claim to a liquid means, the claim excluded pencils and chalk. The narrower claim would therefore have a better chance of being considered novel and nonobvious.

Because claims must be narrow enough to distinguish the invention from previous developments, but broad enough to provide meaningful protection, the primary goal of all patent claim drafters is to draft claims as broadly as possible, given the constraints of the state of prior knowledge or art (inventions and developments).

Related terms: dependent claim; independent claim; infringement, patent; limiting reference; means plus function clause; multiple claims; patent application; prior art; specification.

Class Definitions manual

See classification of patents.

classification of patents

The U.S. Patent and Trademark Office (USPTO) assigns numbered classes and subclasses to inventions for the purpose of classifying patents issued on them and facilitating retrieval of these patents in the course of a patent search. To conduct a search for prior patents relevant to an invention, one must first determine its proper classification.

There are roughly 300 main classes, and an average of more than 200 subclasses under each main class. An invention will fall within at least one of the 66,000 separate classifications, and sometimes several.

Fortunately, the USPTO provides resources, available at the USPTO website (www.uspto.gov), to help a patent searcher find the correct classification(s):

- *Index of U.S. Patent Classification.* All 66,000 categories (classes and subclasses) used to classify patented U.S. inventions are listed alphabetically. To conduct a patent search for prior patents relevant to an invention, it is useful to first determine the class and subclass within which the invention falls.
- *Manual of Classification.* This manual lists by number the 66,000 classes and subclasses used by the USPTO to categorize inventions.

- *Class Definitions.* This manual contains brief definitions of each classification and subclassification used to categorize patents. The manual helps a patent searcher determine the appropriate categories to search in.

Related terms: patent search.

coinventors

In situations where an invention is attributable to the creative effort of more than one person, everyone who makes a creative contribution to the invention (as described in at least one claim in the patent application) is considered a coinventor.

> EXAMPLE: Tom and Bonnie jointly conceive of and design a miniature EEG machine (a machine that measures brain waves), which allows its wearer to monitor his or her own brain waves via a wristwatch-like device. To make sure the concept is viable, Tom and Bonnie get their engineer friend, Clark, to build a test model according to their specifications. Bonnie and Tom would be listed as "coinventors" of the invention because they were the sole creative contributors to the invention's structure. Clark would not be considered a coinventor, assuming his model was made according to set specifications and did not encompass creative additions to the invention. If, on the other hand, Clark had significantly altered the invention's basic specifications and design while building the test model, he also might qualify as a coinventor.

In a case involving an invention that provided lumbar supports for car seats, the Court of Appeals for the Federal Circuit (CAFC) ruled that "one who simply provides the inventor with well-known principles or explains the state of the art without ever having a firm and definite idea of the claimed combination as whole does not qualify as a joint inventor." (*Nartron Corp. v. Schukra U.S.A., Inc.*, 558 F.3d 1352 (Fed Cir. 2009).) In another case, the CAFC held that project members new to a research effort were not inventors because their peers had already formed a definite and permanent idea of the invention even though their knowledge was not scientifically certain. The latecomers to the research effort simply helped the inventors formulate the scientific certainty. As the CAFC indicated, "'knowledge' does not mean proof to a scientific certainty … the belief that an invention will work is enough to establish a conception." (*Univ. of Pittsburgh of the Commonwealth Sys. of Higher Educ. v. Hedrick*, 573 F.3d 1290 (Fed. Cir. 2009).)

When filing a patent application, it is extremely important to accurately identify the inventor or coinventors. Leaving an inventor out or listing someone who doesn't qualify may later cause an issued patent to be declared invalid and unenforceable (if an action is brought in court to enforce the patent), because an accurate description of the true inventors in the patent application is one of the basic requirements for a valid patent.

In 2010, the Third Circuit ruled that a coinventor does not have to make a complete conception of an invention. In that case, a dispute arose as to whether Vanderbilt professors could be added as coinventors on a patent for an inhibitor, useful for treating erectile dysfunction. A district court had ruled that the law required that each coinventor have a full conception of the inhibitor. The Federal Circuit determined this was an error because each coinventor must only engage with the others in some significant way toward that end. (The error was considered harmless because Vanderbilt failed to prove its methodology was used in the patent.) (*Vanderbilt University v. ICOS Corp.*, 601 F.3d 1297 (Fed. Cir. 2010).)

Related terms: inventor, defined; patent application.

combination patent

This is a colloquial phrase for patents on inventions that are combinations of prior existing inventions or technology. Suppose an inventor combines a public domain bicycle frame with a public domain movable tread design previously utilized on a snowmobile and creates a new type of device that travels efficiently on sand. Because the invention combines two public domain inventions, a patent issued on it will commonly be referred to as a "combination patent."

Earlier court decisions in patent cases suggested that a combination invention had to demonstrate a new or surprising result, called "synergism," before it could qualify for a patent. However, the Court of Appeals for the Federal Circuit has ruled that the phrase "combination patent" has no operational meaning under the patent laws, and that virtually all inventions can be said to be combinations of prior existing technology. In short, under the reasoning of this decision, an invention need only meet the basic requirements for a patent (statutory subject matter, novelty, nonobviousness, and utility). The fact that it is a combination of prior developments has no legal effect, and no showing of synergism is required.

Commissioner for Patents

The Commissioner for Patents is the title of the person who manages the patent division of the U.S. Patent and Trademark Office. The previous title for this position was "The Assistant Commissioner for Patents."

Related terms: Director of the U.S. Patent and Trademark Office; U.S. Patent and Trademark Office (USPTO).

community patent

See European Patent Convention.

composition of matter

A composition of matter is one of the five categories of things (collectively, statutory subject matter) that qualify for a patent. Generally, compositions of matter consist of chemical compositions, conglomerates, aggregates, or other chemically significant substances that are usually supplied in bulk, in liquid, gas, or solid form. They include most new chemicals, new forms of life created by gene-splicing techniques (the genetic mixing constitutes the composition), drugs, road-building compositions, gasoline, fuels, glues, and paper.

Related terms: nonstatutory subject matter; statutory subject matter.

compulsory licensing of a patent

In some countries, a patent owner is legally required to allow others to utilize his or her invention in exchange for reasonable compensation. Compulsory licensing of a patent doesn't happen in the United States, because a U.S. patent owner has the right to not produce, manufacture, create, or implement his or her invention. This, of course, means that the public may never benefit from the invention—at least until the patent has expired.

Under the General Agreement on Tariffs and Trade (GATT), compulsory patent licenses are disfavored and will probably disappear from the countries that used to provide for them.

Related terms: GATT (General Agreement on Tariffs and Trade); licensing of an invention; working a patent.

computer programs and patents

See software patents.

computerized patent search

See patent search, computerized.

conception

There are two foundations of patent rights: conception and reduction to practice. Conception is the mental part of inventing, including how an invention is formulated or how a problem is solved. Reduction to practice means that the inventor can demonstrate that the invention works for its intended purpose. These two events and the dates upon which they occur can affect determinations of prior art and the date of invention.

Inventors can document conception by maintaining a notebook. It is a common myth that an inventor can document conception by mailing a description of the invention to him- or herself by certified or registered mail and keeping the sealed envelope. The USPTO has ruled that such "Post Office Patents" have little legal value.

In 2010, the Third Circuit ruled that a coinventor does not have to make a complete conception of an invention. (*See* coinventors.) (*Vanderbilt University v. ICOS Corp.*, 601 F.3d 1297 (Fed. Cir. 2010).)

Related terms: date of invention; Disclosure Document Program (DDP); reduction to practice.

concerted refusal to deal

If two or more businesses jointly boycott (discriminate against, refuse to buy from, or refuse to sell to) one or more other businesses, such activity can be an antitrust violation if commerce has been significantly affected. If a concerted refusal to deal stems from the selective use of one or more patents, these patents may be declared invalid if the antitrust laws have been violated.

> EXAMPLE: The three largest genetic engineering laboratories agree to share their patents through a patent pool arrangement. Competitors are not allowed to use the patents. This exclusion of competitors may constitute a concerted refusal to deal, resulting in the patents being unenforceable.

Related terms: antitrust law (federal) and patents; breaking (or busting) a patent.

confidentiality of patent application

The U.S. Patent and Trademark Office (USPTO) treats patent applications as confidential, making it possible to apply for a patent and still maintain the underlying information as a trade secret, at least for the first 18 months of the application period. Unless the applicant files a Nonpublication Request (NPR) at the time of filing and doesn't file for a patent outside the United States, the USPTO will publish the application within 18 months of the filing date. Because an application is published by the USPTO, all of the secret information becomes public and the trade secret status of the application is lost.

However, if an applicant files an NPR at the time of filing the application, the information in the patent application will become publicly available only if and when a patent is granted. If the applicant is not filing abroad and the patent is rejected, confidentiality is preserved because the USPTO does not publish rejected applications. If the USPTO approves the patent application, it will be published in the *Official Gazette*. Inventors are willing to accept this trade-off—loss of trade secrecy for patent rights—because the patent can be used to prevent anyone else from exploiting the underlying information.

If an applicant files an NPR and then later files abroad, the applicant must notify the USPTO within 45 days of the foreign filing. The USPTO will then publish the application 18 months after the U.S. filing date (or as soon as possible after the 18-month period), and the applicant must pay a publication fee. If the USPTO is not notified within 45 days, the application will be abandoned unless the applicant can demonstrate that the delay was unintentional and a stiff fee is paid.

Related terms: patent search; submarine patent.
See also Part 4 (Trade Secret Law): patent application, effect on trade secrets.

constructive reduction to practice

An invention may legally be considered to have been reduced to practice even though no actual building and testing has occurred.

An invention is considered reduced to practice when any one of the following three events occurs:

- The inventor actually builds and tests the invention (actual reduction to practice).
- The inventor files a patent application on the invention (constructive reduction to practice).
- The inventor files a Provisional Patent Application (PPA) on the invention (also a constructive reduction to practice).

The timing of when an invention was reduced to practice is important because, in the event of a conflict between inventions, it is necessary to identify the first inventor, who is entitled to the patent. This determination depends on a number of important factors, including:

- who first conceived the invention
- after conception, who was most diligent in developing the invention, and
- who first reduced the invention to practice.

Note: The rules regarding reduction to practice will diminish in importance after March 2013 when the U.S. switches to a first-to-file system. Patents filed after March 2013 will be subject to new first-to-file and prior art rules, effectively ending centuries of first-to-invent rules. In short, it will become less important to prove when an invention was created.

Related terms: building and testing an invention; diligence in reducing to practice; interference; reduction to practice.

continuation application

This type of patent application may keep an original patent application alive after the patent examiner has issued a final office action rejecting one or more of the claims. A "continuation application" must be filed within three months after a patent application is rejected, unless an extension is obtained by filing an extension application and paying the appropriate fee.

A continuation application requires a new fee and new claims and will receive a new serial number and filing date. However, in the event an interference (a conflict between two pending applications) occurs, and for purposes of determining the existence of prior art, the inventor will be entitled to the benefit of the original filing date. In other words, if someone else comes up with the same invention between an applicant's original filing date and the continuation application filing date, the original filing date will control and the corresponding invention will be given priority.

The term "continuation application" is often used interchangeably with a "file wrapper continuing application (FWC)."

Related terms: continuation-in-part application (CIP); prosecution of a patent application; Request for Continued Examination.

continuation-in-part application (CIP)

A continuation-in-part application (CIP) is an application filed subsequent to an original application which includes new material not covered in the original application. A CIP provides a way for an inventor to supplement an earlier patent application with new matter to cover improvements made since the first application was filed. The CIP receives the same filing date for matter that it and the original (or parent) application have in common. However, any claim in the CIP that covers the new subject matter is treated as being filed as of the date of the CIP.

Note: Continuation-in-part application should be distinguished from a continuation application, where the applicant reformulates his or her claims after a rejection by the U.S. Patent and Trademark Office.

Related terms: continuation application; final office action; prosecution of a patent application; Request for Continued Examination.

contributory infringement of patent

The sale of an item that has been especially designed to work as a material part of a patented invention may be considered an infringement of the patent, called a contributory infringement, if the item itself lacks independent noninfringing use. Contributory infringement can occur even when the item being sold is itself not patentable. In essence, the contributory infringement doctrine recognizes that items especially modified for a patented invention will not generally be sold unless they are being used for an infringing purpose.

> EXAMPLE: Bionics, Inc., a manufacturer of artificial human organs, patents and manufactures an artificial kidney containing several unique (but non-patentable) valves. If Empire Hospital Equipment Ltd. starts selling the modified valve separately, they may be held to be a contributory infringer of the kidney patent, unless they can show that the valves have an independent use that does not infringe the kidney invention.

The act of actively inducing another to infringe a patent is also considered an act of infringement.

Related terms: inducing infringement; infringement action; infringement, patent.

Convention application

A patent application may be filed in accordance with the Convention for the Protection of Industrial Property, sometimes known as the Paris Convention. Under this treaty, a patent application must be filed in every country where patent protection is desired, within one year of the date that an application is first filed in any other member country. So, if a U.S. patent application has a filing date of February 5, 2010, all additional Convention filings in other countries or jurisdictions, including the Patent Cooperation Treaty and the European Patent Office, must be made by February 5, 2011.

Each Convention filing must be made in the language of the country where it takes place, and separate filing and search fees must be paid. Generally speaking,

Convention applications in individual countries utilize a different and more costly procedure than do Convention applications under the Patent Cooperation Treaty.

Related terms: international patent protection for U.S. inventions; Patent Cooperation Treaty (PCT).

Convention for the Protection of Industrial Property

See Convention application.

Court of Appeals for the Federal Circuit (CAFC)

Often referred to as "Kafka," this special federal court of appeals is responsible for hearing and deciding all appeals from patent infringement actions decided in the U.S. District Courts, as well as all appeals from decisions by the Board of Patent Appeals and Interferences (a branch of the U.S. Patent and Trademark Office). The CAFC convenes in Washington, DC, and also hears cases in other parts of the United States.

cross-licensing

In a cross-licensing arrangement, two or more owners of separate patents cooperate so that each may use the other's inventions. Because technologies such as automobile manufacturing, genetic engineering, and semiconductor chip fabrication depend heavily on many inventions owned by a number of different companies, these companies commonly share their patents through cross-licensing agreements. By doing this, they can benefit from the state-of-the-art improvements in the particular field without having to pay royalties to all the relevant patent owners.

Related terms: improvement inventions; patent pools; patent thickets.

damages, patent infringement

In the event a court determines that a patent has been infringed, the judge or jury may award the patent owner damages for loss of income or for profits resulting from the infringement from the time the invention was properly marked (when the word "patent" and the patent number were affixed to the invention) or from when the infringer was first put on actual notice of the infringement, whichever occurred first. In the event the infringement was willful or flagrant (it continued without a reasonable defense after notification by the patent owner, or infringement occurred through a direct copying without any ground to believe the plaintiff's patent was invalid), the court may award the plaintiff three times the actual damages established in court plus reasonable attorney fees.

When determining lost profits as damages in a patent infringement case, two questions are asked: (1) How many of the infringer's historical sales would not have been made absent the infringing feature or invention? and (2) How many of those sales would have been made by the patent owner if the infringer had not been competing in the marketplace? The Court of Appeals for the Federal Circuit established that as for the first question, when a patent owner seeks damages for more than one patent, the patent owner must distinguish the effects of each patent on marketability. For example, what is the effect if one of several infringing patents were invalid? As for the second question, the court determined that an effective analysis of the marketplace competition requires going beyond broad categories of products and providing evidence of actual competitive patterns as to the accused products. (*Ferguson Beauregard/Logic Controls v. Mega Sys.*, 350 F.3d 1327 (Fed. Cir. 2003); *Utah Medical Products v. Graphic Controls Corp.*, 350 F.3d 1376 (Fed. Cir. 2003).)

§ 284. Damages

Upon finding for the claimant the court shall award the claimant damages adequate to compensate for the infringement, but in no event less than a reasonable royalty for the use made of the invention by the infringer, together with interest and costs as fixed by the court.

When the damages are not found by a jury, the court shall assess them. In either event the court may increase the damages up to three times the amount found or assessed. Increased damages under this paragraph shall not apply to provisional rights under section 154 (d) of this title.

The court may receive expert testimony as an aid to the determination of damages or of what royalty would be reasonable under the circumstances.

Related terms: improvement inventions; infringement action.

date of invention

Note: The rules regarding prior art and date of invention will diminish in importance after March 2013 when the U.S. switches to a first-to-file system. Patents filed after this date will be subject to new first-to-file and prior art rules, effectively ending centuries of first-to-invent rules. In short, it will become less important to prove the date when an invention was created. For more information, check the entry for the America Invents Act.

In order to decide what prior art is with respect to any given invention, it's first necessary to determine the date of invention. Most inventors think this is the date on which one files a patent application. However, the date of invention is the earliest of the following dates:

- The date an inventor filed the patent application (provisional or regular).
- The date an inventor can prove that the invention was built and tested (known as "reduction to practice") in the United States or a country that is a member of North American Free Trade Association (NAFTA) or the World Trade Organization (WTO). (35 United States Code, Section 104.)
- The date an inventor can prove that the invention was conceived in a NAFTA or WTO country, provided the inventor can also prove diligence in building and testing it or filing a patent application on it. Most industrial countries are members of the WTO, and a listing of WTO signatories is provided at the U.S. Patent and Trademark Office website (www.uspto.gov).

An inventor who maintains proper records and is diligent afterward in the invention process will be able to use the date of conception, which is usually several months before the filing date. Once the date of invention is determined, the relevant prior art comprises everything available before that date or anything available about the invention more than one year prior to filing the application.

Related terms: reduction to practice.

declaratory judgment of noninfringement, invalidity and unenforceability of patent

This is a court ruling that allows a business to proceed making or using a device without fear that it might later be held to infringe a particular patent. This type of ruling is commonly sought when a business desires to commercially utilize a device or process arguably described in a patent owned by someone else but is unable to reach a satisfactory licensing agreement with that party. The business files an action in court, requesting a judge to declare (issue a declaratory judgment) that the patent is either invalid or unenforceable, or that it doesn't apply to the device or process in question. If the business wins, it can go ahead to develop the invention unless the patent owner appeals the case. If the business loses, it can appeal but most likely will end up having to license the invention from the patent owner.

Related terms: infringement, patent; licensing of an invention.

defenses to a patent infringement claim

When a patent owner takes legal action to enforce a patent by alleging that it has been infringed (that is, the invention described in the patent has been made, used, or sold without the patent owner's permission), there are a number of common defenses.

In addition to the most common defense—that the allegedly infringing invention does not infringe on the claims of the patented invention and the two inventions are not substantially similar—the following defenses are also often raised.

Patent Invalidity. A lawsuit for patent infringement almost always becomes two separate battles—one in which the plaintiff claims damage from infringement, and the other in which the defendant attempts to terminate the patent rights by proving the patent is invalid. For example, the Polaroid company sued Kodak for infringement of ten instant photography patents. The court determined that Kodak infringed seven Polaroid patents but that the other three Polaroid patents were invalid.

To prove that a patent is invalid, the defendant must attack the patent on the basis of lack of novelty or nonobviousness—that is, show prior art that anticipates or renders the patent's claims obvious or prove that sales or disclosure of the patented invention occurred more than one year prior to filing the patent application.

Note: The one-year rules regarding prior art discussed below will terminate in March 2013 when the U.S. switches to a first-to-file system. After that date, patents will be subject to new first-to-file and prior art rules, effectively ending centuries of first-to-invent rules. Prior art will generally refer to anything that existed prior to filing (not materials published or sold more than one year preceding the filing). For more information, check the entry for the America Invents Act.

> EXAMPLE: A company was sued for infringement of a patented device for displaying computer text on a television monitor. The company defended itself by proving that more than one year prior to filing its patent application the company filing the suit had submitted a proposal for sale of the invention. On that basis, the patent was invalidated and there was no infringement. (*RCA Corporation v. Data General Corporation,* 887 F.2d 1056 (Fed. Cir. 1989).)

In 2011, the Supreme Court refused to alter the standard for invalidating a patent in a battle between tech companies. Microsoft was sued for patent infringement by i4i, a Canadian company, over an XML feature of Microsoft's *Word* software. At trial, Microsoft argued that i4i failed to disclose a prior invention that might have invalidated the application (a principle known as the "one-year rule"). The jury was instructed that the patent could only be invalidated if there was "clear and convincing" evidence of invalidity. (*Microsoft Corp. v. i4i Limited Partnership,* ___ U.S. ___ (2011).)

Inequitable Conduct. If the defendant can prove that a patent owner intentionally misled a patent examiner or should have known that withheld information was material (important) to the examination process, the issued patent will be declared invalid.

Exhaustion (First-Sale Doctrine). Once a patented item is sold, rights to that item are exhausted and it is not an infringement to resell it. The defense in this situation is known as either the "first-sale exemption" or the "exhaustion doctrine." This defense does not apply if the defendant purchased an infringing invention, one that was initially sold without authorization from the patent owner. For example, this defense is not available if someone purchases infringing spark plugs and resells them at retail outlets.

Repair Doctrine. It is not an infringement to repair a patented device and replace worn out unpatented components. It is also not contributory infringement to sell materials used to repair or replace a patented invention. This defense does not apply if the defendant completely rebuilt an invention or repaired an infringing invention.

> EXAMPLE: A company owned a patent for a convertible-top apparatus used in automobiles. The fabric used in the top was not patented. Under the repair doctrine, the sale of fabric to legitimate purchasers of the patented convertible top was not an infringement or contributory infringement. However, a second company was making an infringing version of the convertible-top apparatus. Any repair on these devices was an infringement. The sale of fabric for these infringing devices was a contributory infringement. (*Aro Mfg. Co. v. Convertible Top Replacement Co.,* 365 U.S. 336 (1961).)

File Wrapper Estoppel. The official file in which a patent is contained at the U.S. Patent and Trademark Office is known as a "file wrapper." All statements, admissions, correspondence, or documentation relating to the invention are placed in the file wrapper. If, during the patent application process, the inventor admits limitations to the invention or disclaims certain rights, those admissions or disclaimers will become part of the file wrapper and the patent owner cannot later sue for infringement over any rights that were disclaimed in the file wrapper. This defense is known as file wrapper estoppel (or prosecution history estoppel). Estoppel means that a party is prevented from contradicting a former statement or action.

> EXAMPLE: A medical company owned a patent for an inflatable thermal blanket. The patent claimed a design that caused the inflated blanket to "self-erect" into a Quonset-hut-like shape, preventing contact of the blanket with

the patient. The prosecution history of the patent showed that the applicant relinquished rights to any forced-air blanket other than a "self-erecting" convective thermal blanket. On that basis there could not be infringement of an allegedly equivalent blanket that rested on a patient and did not inflate itself into a self-supporting structure. (*Augustine Medical Inc. v. Gaymar Industries Inc.*, 181 F.3d 1291 (Fed. Cir. 1999).)

Outside U.S. Borders. If a defendant manufactures and sells an invention in a foreign country, a U.S. patent owner cannot stop the manufacture, use, or sale of inventions in that country unless the owner has patented the invention in that country. However, it is an infringement of a U.S. patent:

- to import an infringing device into the United States, or
- to create all of the parts of a patented invention in the United States and ship those parts to a foreign company with instructions for assembly.

Patent Misuse. A patent owner who has misused a patent cannot sue you for infringement. Common examples of misuse are violations of the antitrust laws, or unethical business practices. For example, if a patent owner conspired to fix the price of the patented item, this would violate antitrust laws. If the patent owner later sued for infringement, the defendant could argue that the owner is prohibited from suing because he or she has misused the patent rights. Tying is a form of patent misuse in which, as a condition of a transaction, the buyer of a patented device must also purchase an additional product.

EXAMPLE: A company had a patent on a machine that deposited salt tablets in canned food. Purchasers of the machine were also required to buy salt tablets from the patent owner. The Supreme Court determined that the seller of the machine misused its patent rights and, on that basis, was prevented from suing for infringement. (*Morton Salt Co. v. G.S. Suppiger Co.*, 314 U.S. 488 (1942).)

In 1988, Congress enacted the Patent Misuse Amendments, which require courts to apply a "rule of reason" standard—meaning that the court must view all the relevant factors to determine if the tying arrangement is in any way justified.

In a 2010 case, the Federal Circuit narrowed the scope of patent misuse. Under the Federal Circuit's new standard, there must be evidence of anticompetitive effects associated in addition to restrictions on use. Alleging wrongful conduct is not enough. (*Princo Corp. v. International Trade Commission*, 616 F.3d 1318 (Fed. Cir. 2010).)

Waiting Too Long to File the Lawsuit. There is no time limit (or statute of limitations) for filing a patent infringement lawsuit, but monetary damages can be recovered only for infringements committed during the six years prior to the filing of the lawsuit. Despite the fact that there is no law setting a time limit, courts will not permit a patent owner to sue you for infringement if the owner has waited an unreasonable amount of time to file the lawsuit (a principle known as "laches"). Generally, courts consider anything over a six-year period an unreasonable delay in filing the suit, unless the patent owner can provide some excuse for the delay.

> EXAMPLE: A company owned a patent for concrete highway barriers. The company threatened litigation against a competitor but did not file the infringement lawsuit until eight years later. Since the company could not provide a reasonable basis for the delay, the case was dismissed because the company had waited too long to file the lawsuit. (*A.C. Aukerman Co. v. R.L. Chaides Construction Co.,* 960 F.2d 1020 (Fed. Cir. 1992).)

New Prior User Defense. The America Invents Act, passed in September 2011, provides for a defense for prior commercial users of the invention. If you're sued for infringement but you were commercially using the patented technology more than one year before the filing date of the claimed invention, you have a defense against a claim that you infringed (although that defense doesn't invalidate the patent). The Act includes a definition of "commercial use." (See below.)

Because of the variety of potential defenses to an infringement action, many observers feel that a patent is not worth a great deal if there's significant economic motivation to infringe it. According to this view, the more valuable a patent, the more likely it is that large economic interests will mount a fierce and expensive court challenge to the patent's validity. And the more difficult it is to enforce a patent, the less it is worth to its rightful owner. (Sound like a paradox? Welcome to patent law.)

On the other hand, billions of dollars are awarded to patent owners every year as a result of successful infringement actions, and numerous inventors (both small and institutional) make good money from licensing others to use the inventions covered by their patents.

[New Section Effective September 2012, as a result of passage of the America Invents Act] § 273. Defense to infringement based on prior commercial use
(a) In General. A person shall be entitled to a defense under section 282(b) with respect to subject matter consisting of a process, or consisting of a machine, manufacture, or

Patent Law: Definitions

composition of matter used in a manufacturing or other commercial process, that would otherwise infringe a claimed invention being asserted against the person if—

(1) such person, acting in good faith, commercially used the subject matter in the United States, either in connection with an internal commercial use or an actual arm's length sale or other arm's length commercial transfer of a useful end result of such commercial use; and

(2) such commercial use occurred at least 1 year before the earlier of either—

   (A) the effective filing date of the claimed invention; or

   (B) the date on which the claimed invention was disclosed to the public in a manner that qualified for the exception from prior art under section 102(b).

(b) Burden of Proof. A person asserting a defense under this section shall have the burden of establishing the defense by clear and convincing evidence.

(c) Additional Commercial Uses.

   (1) PREMARKETING REGULATORY REVIEW. Subject matter for which commercial marketing or use is subject to a premarketing regulatory review period during which the safety or efficacy of the subject matter is established, including any period specified in section 156(g), shall be deemed to be commercially used for purposes of subsection (a)(1) during such regulatory review period.

   (2) NONPROFIT LABORATORY USE. A use of subject matter by a nonprofit research laboratory or other nonprofit entity, such as a university or hospital, for which the public is the intended beneficiary, shall be deemed to be a commercial use for purposes of subsection (a)(1), except that a defense under this section may be asserted pursuant to this paragraph only for continued and noncommercial use by and in the laboratory or other nonprofit entity.

(d) Exhaustion of Rights. Notwithstanding subsection (e)(1), the sale or other disposition of a useful end result by a person entitled to assert a defense under this section in connection with a patent with respect to that useful end result shall exhaust the patent owner's rights under the patent to the extent that such rights would have been exhausted had such sale or other disposition been made by the patent owner.

(e) Limitations and Exceptions.

   (1) PERSONAL DEFENSE.

      (A) IN GENERAL. A defense under this section may be asserted only by the person who performed or directed the performance of the commercial use described in subsection (a), or by an entity that controls, is controlled by, or is under common control with such person.

      (B) TRANSFER OF RIGHT. Except for any transfer to the patent owner, the right to assert a defense under this section shall not be licensed or assigned or transferred to another person except as an ancillary and subordinate part of a good-faith assignment or transfer for other reasons of the entire enterprise or line of business to which the defense relates.

(C) RESTRICTION ON SITES. A defense under this section, when acquired by a person as part of an assignment or transfer described in subparagraph (B), may only be asserted for uses at sites where the subject matter that would otherwise infringe a claimed invention is in use before the later of the effective filing date of the claimed invention or the date of the assignment or transfer of such enterprise or line of business.

(2) DERIVATION. A person may not assert a defense under this section if the subject matter on which the defense is based was derived from the patentee or persons in privity with the patentee.

(3) NOT A GENERAL LICENSE. The defense asserted by a person under this section is not a general license under all claims of the patent at issue, but extends only to the specific subject matter for which it has been established that a commercial use that qualifies under this section occurred, except that the defense shall also extend to variations in the quantity or volume of use of the claimed subject matter, and to improvements in the claimed subject matter that do not infringe additional specifically claimed subject matter of the patent.

(4) ABANDONMENT OF USE. A person who has abandoned commercial use (that qualifies under this section) of subject matter may not rely on activities performed before the date of such abandonment in establishing a defense under this section with respect to actions taken on or after the date of such abandonment.

(5) UNIVERSITY EXCEPTION.

(A) IN GENERAL. A person commercially using subject matter to which subsection (a) applies may not assert a defense under this section if the claimed invention with respect to which the defense is asserted was, at the time the invention was made, owned or subject to an obligation of assignment to either an institution of higher education (as defined in section 101(a) of the Higher Education Act of 1965 (20 U.S.C. 1001(a)), or a technology transfer organization whose primary purpose is to facilitate the commercialization of technologies developed by one or more such institutions of higher education.

(B) EXCEPTION. Subparagraph (A) shall not apply if any of the activities required to reduce to practice the subject matter of the claimed invention could not have been undertaken using funds provided by the Federal Government.

(f) Unreasonable Assertion of Defense. If the defense under this section is pleaded by a person who is found to infringe the patent and who subsequently fails to demonstrate a reasonable basis for asserting the defense, the court shall find the case exceptional for the purpose of awarding attorney fees under section 285.

(g) Invalidity. A patent shall not be deemed to be invalid under section 102 or 103 solely because a defense is raised or established under this section ....

Related terms: infringement action; infringement, patent; intervening right; statute of limitations, infringement action; unenforceable patent.

defensive disclosure

Publishing the details of an invention legally transforms the invention into prior art, which in turn precludes others from obtaining a patent on it. A defensive disclosure consists of publishing a description of an invention in the *Official Gazette* or another publication that is likely to be noticed by the U.S. Patent and Trademark Office, prior to a patent being issued.

A defensive disclosure is often used after an inventor files a patent application and decides not to pursue it further but also doesn't want a subsequent filer of an application on the same or similar invention to have monopoly rights. Defensive disclosures are also used by companies that don't think a particular area of technology (such as software) should be subject to the patent laws and therefore disclose their technology to prevent others from patenting it and extracting royalties.

There are two basic approaches to making a defensive disclosure: a Statutory Invention Registration procedure offered by the USPTO and a preemptive private publication. The USPTO procedure is much more expensive than the private approach.

To publish defensively under the Statutory Invention Registration program, an inventor can file a document with the USPTO that:

- requests that the USPTO publish the patent application's abstract in the *Official Gazette*
- formally abandons the patent application, and
- authorizes the USPTO to open the patent application to public inspection.

EXAMPLE: Lou Swift invents a new form of portable energy source that allows most residential users of electricity to disconnect from the common electrical grid. After Lou applies for a patent, she comes to believe that the cause of peace and freedom would best be served by the invention being placed in the public domain, therefore becoming unpatentable. She utilizes the procedures described above to turn her application into a prior art reference that precludes anybody else from obtaining a patent on her invention. (This example is based on a theme developed in *Ecotopia Emerging,* by Ernest Callenbach.)

The private and less-expensive approach to making a defensive disclosure is to publish the invention in journals published just for this purpose, such as *International Technical Disclosure* and *Research Disclosure.* Also, the Software

Patent Institute (www.spi.org) provides a defensive disclosure program for software-based inventions.

Related terms: confidentiality of patent application; *Official Gazette* (OG); prior art reference; Software Patent Institute; Statutory Invention Registration (SIR).

dependent claim

The scope of a patent is determined by the way the underlying invention is described in the patent claims (precise, single-sentence statements that articulate the exact nature of the invention). There are two basic types of patent claims: independent and dependent. Independent claims are statements that stand by themselves. Dependent claims are statements that rely on another claim for part of their description. In other words, each dependent claim must be read (interpreted) by incorporating the wording of each claim to which it refers, which may be an independent claim or another dependent claim.

The typical patent application contains several independent claims, each of which is referred to by several additional dependent claims. (Samples of dependent and independent claims are provided in "claims, defined.")

Related terms: claims; independent claim.

derivation hearings

Derivation hearings are one of the many changes implemented by the America Invents Act. As of March 2013, the USPTO will permit a patent owner to bring a derivation hearing at the USPTO (replacing interference proceedings) against another patent owner claiming to have the same invention and who has an earlier effective filing date. The derivation hearing request must be filed within a one-year period beginning on the date of the first publication of a claim in the earlier filed application. Alternatively, the owner of a patent may sue the owner of another patent that claims the same invention and has an earlier effective filing date. These lawsuits can only be brought if the invention claiming priority was derived directly from the person seeking relief.

Sec. 135. Derivation proceedings (Effective March 2013)

(a) Institution of Proceeding. An applicant for patent may file a petition to institute a derivation proceeding in the Office. The petition shall set forth with particularity the basis for finding that an inventor named in an earlier application derived the claimed invention from an inventor named in the petitioner's application and, without authorization, the earlier application claiming such invention was filed. Any such petition may be filed only within the 1-year period beginning on the date of the first publication of a claim to an invention that is the same or substantially the same as the earlier application's claim to the invention, shall be made under oath, and shall be supported by substantial evidence. Whenever the Director determines that a petition filed under this subsection demonstrates that the standards for instituting a derivation proceeding are met, the Director may institute a derivation proceeding. The determination by the Director whether to institute a derivation proceeding shall be final and nonappealable.

(b) Determination by Patent Trial and Appeal Board. In a derivation proceeding instituted under subsection (a), the Patent Trial and Appeal Board shall determine whether an inventor named in the earlier application derived the claimed invention from an inventor named in the petitioner's application and, without authorization, the earlier application claiming such invention was filed. In appropriate circumstances, the Patent Trial and Appeal Board may correct the naming of the inventor in any application or patent at issue. The Director shall prescribe regulations setting forth standards for the conduct of derivation proceedings, including requiring parties to provide sufficient evidence to prove and rebut a claim of derivation.

(c) Deferral of Decision. The Patent Trial and Appeal Board may defer action on a petition for a derivation proceeding until the expiration of the 3-month period beginning on the date on which the Director issues a patent that includes the claimed invention that is the subject of the petition. The Patent Trial and Appeal Board also may defer action on a petition for a derivation proceeding, or stay the proceeding after it has been instituted, until the termination of a proceeding under chapter 30, 31, or 32 involving the patent of the earlier applicant.

(d) Effect of Final Decision. The final decision of the Patent Trial and Appeal Board, if adverse to claims in an application for patent, shall constitute the final refusal by the Office on those claims. The final decision of the Patent Trial and Appeal Board, if adverse to claims in a patent, shall, if no appeal or other review of the decision has been or can be taken or had, constitute cancellation of those claims, and notice of such cancellation shall be endorsed on copies of the patent distributed after such cancellation.

(e) Settlement. Parties to a proceeding instituted under subsection (a) may terminate the proceeding by filing a written statement reflecting the agreement of the parties as to the correct inventors of the claimed invention in dispute. Unless the Patent Trial and Appeal Board finds the agreement to be inconsistent with the evidence of record, if any, it shall take action consistent with the agreement. Any written settlement or understanding of the parties shall be filed with the Director. At the request of a party to the proceeding, the agreement or understanding shall be treated as business confidential information, shall be kept separate from the file of the involved patents or applications, and shall be made available only to Government agencies on written request, or to any person on a showing of good cause.

(f) Arbitration. Parties to a proceeding instituted under subsection (a) may, within such time as may be specified by the Director by regulation, determine such contest or any aspect thereof by arbitration. Such arbitration shall be governed by the provisions of title 9, to the extent such title is not inconsistent with this section. The parties shall give notice of any arbitration award to the Director, and such award shall, as between the parties to the arbitration, be dispositive of the issues to which it relates. The arbitration award shall be unenforceable until such notice is given. Nothing in this subsection shall preclude the Director from determining the patentability of the claimed inventions involved in the proceeding.

design around

To design or build a device or process that is similar to but doesn't infringe on an invention protected by a patent is referred to as "designing around" the patent. The scope of protection acquired under a patent is determined by the wording of the patent's claims. Thus, any device, process, or substance containing the same elements described in a patent's claims can be said to infringe the patent. Conversely, a device or process that contains fewer or different elements does not infringe the patent (technically, the patent's claims do not "read on," or literally describe, the infringing device). Therefore, by studying the claims associated with a specific patent, it is often possible to build or design a device or process very similar to that described in the patent without legally infringing the patent's claims.

> EXAMPLE: Fred invents and patents a small radiator-type device that uses hot water to dry and warm towels. One of the claims for his invention describes it as consisting of plastic. Bonanza Bathroom Products (BBP) creates a similar device but uses a metal alloy that doubles the ability of the device to retain heat. BBP probably has not infringed Fred's patent, because it designed around the invention by using a different element that produces a different result.

To try to prevent such "designing around" activity, Fred's patent claim should have been broader to start with. Instead of limiting his invention to plastic, Fred's claim might have described "an inflexible means through which hot water can be channeled at normal domestic water pressures, the heat retained over a period of time, and towels folded over for the purpose of drying."

There is one important legal restriction on the ability to design around a patent claim. A court can decide that the differences in the basic elements of the two inventions—in the previous example, the type of substance used and the extra heat retention—are immaterial (unimportant) to the overall invention. In that event, infringement will have occurred under the doctrine of equivalents, which allows infringement to be found when two inventions work in the same way to produce substantially the same result.

Related terms: claims; doctrine of equivalents.

design patents

A design patent will be issued by the U.S. Patent and Trademark Office for any "new, original, and ornamental design for an article of manufacture." (35 United States Code, Section 171.) This includes three types of designs:

- surface ornamentation—that is, a design applied to or embodied in an article of manufacture
- a product shape or configuration, and
- a combination of the first two categories.

Courts have limited design patents to one sense, vision—that is, the appearance presented by the article. A design patent will not be granted for sounds, smells, or tastes that ornament products. In addition, the design must be capable of reproduction and not merely the chance result of a method. A water fountain display—the combined appearance of the water and the underlying sculpture—is suitable subject matter for a design patent because it is definite (even though not permanent) and can be reproduced.

The protected design must be ornamental, not functional.

EXAMPLE: A personal computer designed to resemble a classical robot might qualify for a design patent as long as the robot characteristics were purely ornamental. But if the robot characteristics were functional in some way—for instance, they provided the computer with mobility—a design patent on these characteristics would be precluded.

Often, two patents will be submitted for the same device: a utility patent covering the device's functional characteristics, and a design patent protecting the device's ornamental characteristics. In our robot computer example, it might be possible to obtain both types of patents if they cover different aspects of the device.

Although design patents are relatively easy to obtain, the fact that the design by definition lacks utility normally makes it easy to create another design that will also be novel and interesting without violating the design patent.

Prior to 2008, the Court of Appeals for the Federal Circuit (CAFC) used two standards to demonstrate design patent infringement: (1) The Ordinary Observer Test, in which the court compares the allegedly infringing device with design patent drawings to determine whether the allegedly infringing design is substantially similar; and (2) The Point of Novelty Test, in which the court compares the patented design with the prior art to determine "the point of novelty" of the patented design and whether the allegedly infringing design appropriates the novelty.

The CAFC terminated the "point of novelty" test in a 2008 case involving a claim of infringement of a nail buffer design, *Egyptian Goddess v. Swisa, Inc.,* 543 F.3d 665, 88 USPQ2d 1658 (Fed. Cir. 2008) (en banc). Instead, the court held that only an "ordinary observer" test was required. The CAFC also discouraged the "over-verbalization" of design patent claims, preferring more reliance on design patent drawings. In a post-*Goddess* case, a district court applied the new standard to a design patent for a "curvilinear zipper." The district court applied the ordinary observer test, first comparing the differences between the patented design and the infringing design, and then considering the differences in relation to the prior art. The conclusion: no infringement. (*Arc'Teryx Equipment, Inc. v. Westcomb Outerwear, Inc.,* 2008 WL 4838141 (D. Utah, November 3, 2008).) The CAFC also extended the ordinary observer test for design patents when determining if a design patent is anticipated by prior art. (*International Seaway Trading Corp. v. Walgreens Corp.,* 589 F.3d 1233, 93 U.S.P.Q.2d 1001 (Fed. Cir. 2009).)

Related terms: design around.

diligence in reducing to practice

An inventor's diligence in reducing an invention to practice consists of steady progress toward the goal of either:

- actual reduction to practice—building and testing a working model of the invention, or
- constructive reduction to practice—filing a provisional or regular patent application on it.

If two inventors come up with the same invention about the same time, the first inventor who can also show diligence in reducing the invention to practice, usually through documentation of building and testing activity or activity related to the preparation of a patent application, is most likely to get the patent.

Patent Law: Definitions

EXAMPLE 1: In March 2008, Joe conceives of an invention that produces heat from a car heater the instant the car is started. Joe steadily applies himself during the next six months to building a working model of the insta-heater and in October 2008 applies for a patent on it. Sal independently conceives of the same invention in June 2008, but rather than building and testing a working model, Sal files a patent application on the invention in July 2008. Under these facts, Joe should get the patent, because he was first to conceive of the invention and was diligent in reducing the invention to practice, even though his patent application was later than Sal's. Although Sal was also diligent in reducing the invention to practice (called constructive reduction to practice in this case), by filing the patent application a month after he conceived of the invention, he wasn't the first to invent, so he would lose out to Joe.

EXAMPLE 2: Using the same insta-heater invention, assume now that Joe didn't get around to building and testing his working model until September 2008. He then filed a patent application in December 2008. Under these facts, the patent would probably go to Sal, because Joe was not diligent in reducing the invention to practice, while Sal was.

Related terms: constructive reduction to practice; interference; reduction to practice.

direct infringement of patent

See infringement, patent.

Director of the U.S. Patent and Trademark Office

This is the title of the person who runs the USPTO, a branch of the U.S. Department of Commerce. The full title is actually Undersecretary of Commerce for Intellectual Property and Director of the U.S. Patent and Trademark Office. Prior to 2000 the title for this position was the Commissioner of Patents and Trademarks.

Related terms: Commissioner for Patents; U.S. Patent and Trademark Office (USPTO).

Disclosure Document Program (DDP)

This USPTO program, eliminated in February 2007, previously allowed inventors, for a nominal fee, to file a signed document called a "disclosure" that preliminarily described their invention. Later, when the inventor applied for a patent on the invention, the disclosure could be used to prove the date of conception of the invention, should this become necessary because of an interference with another patent application.

There are other ways to document inventive efforts, such as keeping a notebook or producing disclosures that are signed and witnessed.

Related terms: disclosure requirement for patents; interference; notebook, inventor's; Provisional Patent Application (PPA).

disclosure requirement for patents

A patent application must disclose enough about the invention to enable a person with ordinary skill in the art (technology used in the invention) to build or develop it. In addition, a patent application is required to disclose the best means ("best mode") known to the applicant of practicing the invention as of the date of filing the application. The reason for the disclosure requirement is simple. A disclosure that is detailed enough to enable the invention to be built enhances the public's knowledge of the technology and ideas involved in the invention. In exchange for this public benefit, an inventor earns the right to a statutory monopoly over the right to make, use, and sell the invention.

Prior to passage of the America Invents Act in September 2011, if the information necessary to build the invention was not sufficiently disclosed in the application (also known as "best mode"), a patent that was issued on the invention might be declared invalid and therefore not enforceable. This was a common defense in infringement actions. The America Invents Act eliminated this defense.

Related terms: patent application.

divisional application

If a patent examiner rejects a patent application because it claims two or more inventions (a patenting no-no), the common inventor response is to restrict the application to one invention of the inventor's choosing. But if the inventor doesn't wish to abandon the other "nonelected" invention, he or she can file a separate divisional application to cover it. The divisional application will be entitled to the filing date of the original application (which is referred to as the parent application, once a divisional application is filed).

What happens if the patent examiner was wrong, and a court later finds that there was, in fact, only one invention, even though the U.S. Patent and Trademark Office (USPTO) issued two (or more) patents on it? Although this

Patent Law: Definitions

violates another patenting rule (the statutory rule against double patenting), both patents will be upheld because the restriction of the original patent application was imposed by the USPTO.

§ 121. Divisional applications

If two or more independent and distinct inventions are claimed in one application, the Director may require the application to be restricted to one of the inventions. If the other invention is made the subject of a divisional application which complies with the requirements of section 120 of this title it shall be entitled to the benefit of the filing date of the original application. A patent issuing on an application with respect to which a requirement for restriction under this section has been made, or on an application filed as a result of such a requirement, shall not be used as a reference either in the Patent and Trademark Office or in the courts against a divisional application or against the original application or any patent issued on either of them, if the divisional application is filed before the issuance of the patent on the other application. If a divisional application is directed solely to subject matter described and claimed in the original application as filed, the Director may dispense with signing and execution by the inventor. The validity of a patent shall not be questioned for failure of the Director to require the application to be restricted to one invention.

Related terms: abandonment of patent application; double patenting; nonelected claims; prosecution of a patent application.

doctrine of equivalents

A secondary method for deciding whether a patent is being infringed, the doctrine of equivalents considers whether a later device or process does the same work in substantially the same way to accomplish the same result as a patented invention. If it does, then patent infringement will be found to exist.

The primary method used by the courts to assess possible patent infringement is to compare the literal language of each element of the patent's claims with each element of the device or process claimed to be infringing. (In patent jargon, do the patent claims "read on" the infringing device or process?) However, even if a patent's claims don't literally "read on" an allegedly infringing device or process, infringement may be found under the doctrine of equivalents so long as the element of the device is the "equivalent" of the claimed element. A device element is equivalent if it performs the same function in the same way to achieve the same result as the claim element, or the role of the device element is substantially the same as that of the claim element.

The doctrine of equivalents is intended to prevent designing around a patent on hypertechnical grounds. Unfortunately, there is no logical dividing line between (1) noninfringement based on legitimate designing around an invention, and (2) infringement based on the doctrine of equivalents. It is up to the courts to decide, on a case-by-case basis, if inventions are substantially equivalent.

In 2000, a federal appeals court barred the use of the doctrine of equivalents for any amended patent claims. In 2002, the U.S. Supreme Court struck down this absolute bar to the doctrine of equivalents and replaced it with a less-arbitrary standard. Under the Supreme Court's standard, all amended claims are presumed to be narrowed so as to bar the doctrine of equivalents. But this presumption can be rebutted if a patent owner can demonstrate that the amendment involved a feature that was "unforeseeable at the time of the application" or "for some other reason" could not be included in the original claim. In that case, the patent owner can use the doctrine of equivalents. (*Festo Corp. v. Shoketsu Kinzoku Kabushiki Co. Ltd.,* 535 U.S. 722 (2002).)

Related terms: design around; *Festo v. Shoketsu;* infringement, patent; negative doctrine of equivalents.

double patenting

If two patents are obtained on (or claim) a single invention, it's referred to as double patenting. Double patenting is not allowed under the patent laws, and both patents can later be invalidated. However, if double patenting results from a divisional application required by the U.S. Patent and Trademark Office (USPTO) because of the USPTO's misperception that two inventions were being described in the original patent application, under a special statute (35 United States Code, Section 121) this rule does not apply and the patents will be considered valid.

Related terms: divisional application.

drawings, patent application

Visual representations of an invention must be included in the patent application. These drawings should show all the features recited (described) in the claims.

If an invention is a thing (including machines or articles of manufacture), the drawings must show features of the invention that are different from those known in the prior art. A drawing for a process should consist of a flow chart showing its sequence of steps.

Drawings are generally not required for inventions consisting of compositions of matter unless either of the following is true:

- The inventions consist of structures that can be shown in a cross-sectional representation.
- A flow chart showing the process of manufacture is relevant.

Related terms: disclosure requirements for patents; patent application.

duration of patents

Utility patents—the most common kind—expire 20 years after the filing date of the regular formal patent application. This means that the period of time the patent is actually in force will depend on how long it takes the patent to be examined. For instance, if the regular patent application is filed on December 1, 2008, and the patent issues on December 1, 2011, the patent will be in force for 18 years.

Effective June 2000, every patent is guaranteed an in-force period of at least 17 years. The patent term will be extended for as long as necessary to compensate for any of the following:

- any delay caused by the U.S. Patent and Trademark Office (USPTO) failing to examine a new application within 14 months of filing
- any delay caused by the USPTO failing to take any one of the following actions within four months:
  - reply to an amendment or to an appeal brief
  - issue an allowance or office action after a decision on appeal, or
  - issue a patent after the issue fee is paid and any required drawings are filed
- any delay caused by the USPTO failing to issue a patent within three years from filing, unless the delay was due to the applicant filing a continuation application or buying a delay to reply to an Office Action, or
- any delay due to secrecy orders, appeals, or interferences.

Because the law creating the 20-year patent term became effective June 8, 1995, patents issued prior to that date—or that were pending on that date—will expire 20 years from their filing date or 17 years from their issue date, whichever period is longer. (35 United States Code, Section 154(c)(1).)

Design patents last for 14 years from the date the patent issues, and plant and utility patents last for 20 years from the date of filing.

Related terms: filing date; in-force patent; patent term extension.

duty of candor and good faith

This duty is owed to the U.S. Patent and Trademark Office (USPTO) by every patent applicant in connection with the information and disclosures contained in the patent application. Under rules issued by the USPTO, the applicant must disclose:

- all known instances of anticipation (events or references that might cause the USPTO to determine that the invention isn't novel)
- pertinent prior art that might bear on the question of nonobviousness
- the preferred embodiment (best mode) of the invention, and
- any other information known to the applicant that bears on the patentability of the invention and the proper scope of the patent claims.

Failure to comply fully with the duty of candor and good faith can result in rejection of the patent application by the USPTO or a later finding in an infringement action that the applicant committed fraud on the USPTO (if the noncompliance was willful or negligent). In the latter case, the patent may be declared invalid even if the undisclosed information would not have invalidated the patent as such.

EXAMPLE: In 2006, Patricia invented a device and a process that allowed wind velocities to be differentially measured according to very small portions of space. The results of the measurements could then be fed into a computer, and the best placement for windmills could be determined. Patricia made the invention for her own home in the country and decided not to patent it, due to the plentiful supply of centralized electrical energy at that time. Patricia let some of her neighbors use the invention on an as-needed basis, which may have constituted prior public use of the invention, which in turn could be considered prior art.

Three years later, oil prices soar and Patricia applies for and receives a patent. In her patent application, she neglects to mention the use of the device by her neighbors, a fact she should have disclosed under the applicant's duty to disclose known relevant prior art. In 2011, a leading power company begins to market Patricia's device across the country without a license from Patricia. If Patricia sues the company for infringement or her patent, she may find that her patent cannot be enforced. Why? Because she failed to disclose relevant prior art to the USPTO, even though the information in question, if disclosed at the time, might not have barred issuance of the patent. If this information

Patent Law: Definitions

comes out at trial, the judge may find that she violated her duty of candor and good faith.

Related terms: anticipation; defenses to a patent infringement claim; disclosure requirement for patents; fraud on the U.S. Patent and Trademark Office.

electronic filing of patent applications

The USPTO has implemented an Electronic Filing System (EFS-Web) that enables patent applications, amendments, and other documents to be filed over the Internet. It replaces the former EFS, which was difficult to learn and use. The EFS-Web is a considerable improvement. However, it still requires some time to master, as well as time for conversion of documents to the Portable Data Format (PDF). The EFS-Web does have some practical advantages. Using it, you can (1) file an application anytime and from anywhere that has Internet access, (2) obtain instant confirmation of receipt of documents by the PTO, (3) send an application to the PTO without having to go to the post office to get an Express Mail receipt or having to wait for a postcard receipt, and (4) file an application without having to prepare an application transmittal, a fee transmittal, receipt postcard, or check or Credit Card Payment Form (CCPF).

elements of invention

See claims.

employed to invent

It is possible that even without a written employment agreement, an employer may own rights to an employee's patent or trade secret under the "employed to invent" doctrine. How might this rule apply? If a person were employed—even without a written employment agreement—for inventing or designing skills, or was hired or directed to create an invention, the employer would own all rights to any resulting inventions. This doctrine is derived from a Supreme Court ruling that stated, "One employed to make an invention, who succeeds, during his term of service, in accomplishing that task, is bound to assign to his employer any patent obtained." Generally, most companies prefer to use a written agreement, which is more reliable and easier to enforce than this implied agreement. However, the issue of "employed to invent" still arises.

EXAMPLE: An engineer had no written employment agreement with his employer. He was assigned as the chief engineer on a project to devise a method of welding a "leading edge" for turbine engines. The engineer spent at least 70% of his time on the project. He developed a hot forming process (HFP) for welding a leading edge and built the invention on his employer's time and using his employer's employees, tools, and materials. The engineer claimed that he was the sole owner of patent rights. A court held that the company owned the patent rights because the engineer was hired for the express purpose of creating the HFP process. That fact, combined with the use of the employer's supplies, payment for the work, and payment by the employer for the patent registration, demonstrated that there was an implied contract to assign the patent rights to the employer. Therefore, even without a written employment agreement, the employer acquired ownership.

enabling disclosure

The description of an invention included ("disclosed") in a patent application must be in sufficient detail as to "enable" a person with ordinary skill in the art to build or develop it ("work it") without having to apply any inventiveness of his or her own.

Related terms: disclosure requirement for patents.

equivalents, doctrine of

See doctrine of equivalents.

European Patent Convention

This treaty covers patent law relationships, primarily among the members of the European Union (EU), plus a few other countries.

Under the European Patent Convention (EPC), an inventor need make only one filing and undergo one examination procedure to obtain patent protection in all member countries. Filings and examinations are conducted by the European Patent Office in Munich, Germany, and The Hague, Netherlands. A patent issued under the EPC lasts for 20 years from the date of application but must be registered in each country.

Related terms: Convention application; Patent Cooperation Treaty (PCT).

European Patent Office

See European Patent Convention.

Patent Law: Definitions

examiners, patent

See patent examiners.

exclusive patent license

A binding agreement in which a patent owner (the licensor) grants another party (the licensee) the sole (exclusive) right to make, use, and/or sell an invention covered by the patent is known as an exclusive patent license.

Sometimes the grant of rights is for all purposes, but often it is limited to a specific context. For example, sales may be restricted to the United States, to a particular period of time, or for a particular purpose. However, the particular right is granted exclusively to the person or business receiving it. For example, a patent owner could grant one company the exclusive right to make and sell the invention in the United States and another company the exclusive right to make and sell it in the European community.

Related terms: geographic patent license; nonexclusive patent license.

exhaustion

Patent exhaustion is a legal doctrine that prohibits a patent owner from seeking further patent payments for that particular product when it has been sold. For example, the buyer of a patented lawn mower cannot be sued by the patent owner if the buyer later resells the mower (or uses the mower in his gardening business). The principle is also known as the "first-sale doctrine," a term that also applies in copyright law for a similar principle. This principle was reinforced in 2008 by the Supreme Court's ruling in *Quanta v. LG Electronics*, 553 U.S. 617 (2008). In that case, a company (LG) that sold licensed chipsets entered into licenses with direct purchasers. When another company (Quanta) purchased these chipsets from one of LG's customers, LG claimed infringement. The Supreme Court ruled that a patent owner cannot later sue a customer who purchased an authorized copy of a patented product. In other words, the patent owner's rights are exhausted after the sale.

exhibiting an unpatented invention

Using or exhibiting an unpatented invention in public in an unrestricted (nonconfidential) context prior to filing a provisional or regular patent application can constitute a public use, which would qualify as prior art and later bar a patent from being issued under the anticipation doctrine.

Related terms: anticipation; experimental use of an unpatented invention; public use.

experimental use of an unpatented invention

An unpatented invention may be used or exhibited in public for experimental purposes—that is, to test or improve the invention. Experimental use is not considered a public use or a disclosure and therefore won't bar a patent under the anticipation rule.

Many inventions need to be tested in public one or more times before the inventor is ready to file a patent application. However, if the public use is not truly experimental in nature, such use may bar a patent unless an application for the patent is filed within one year of the use.

A clinical trial application that results in a publicly accessible record is not an experimental use. (*In re Natures Remedies,* 315 Fed. App'x 300 (Fed. Cir. 2009).) Eleven installations of a claimed method—primarily made for regulators within the industry—were not experimental when the invention had been reduced to practice before the installations. (*Clock Spring, L.P. v. Wrapmaster, Inc.,* 560 F.3d 1317 (Fed Cir. 2009).)

Note: The one-year rules cited above will (with some exceptions), terminate in March 2013 when the U.S. switches to a first-to-file system. After that date, anything published or sold prior to filing of the application will be considered prior art unless it qualifies under a very limited one-year grace period for certain disclosures. For more information, check the entry for the America Invents Act.

Related terms: anticipation; exhibiting an unpatented invention; public use.

expert witness

A witness who has special knowledge of a subject so that the court may rely on the expert's opinion. In patent litigation, expert witnesses are commonly used to explain complex scientific or mechanical innovations. In 2005, the Court of Appeals for the Federal Circuit indicated that a patent owner of a complex technology will have a difficult time proving infringement unless expert witness testimony is provided. (*Centricut LLC v. Esab Group, Inc.,* 390 F.3d 1361 (Fed. Cir. 2004).)

expiration of patent

See duration of patents.

Patent Law: Definitions

false marking of invention

See marking of an invention.

Federal Circuit Court of Appeals

See Court of Appeals for the Federal Circuit (CAFC).

Federal Trade Commission proceeding

Under this administrative process, a patent owner can get an order barring devices that infringe the patent from being imported into the United States.

Related terms: international patent protection for U.S. inventions.

Festo v. Shoketsu

In 2000, in a case involving a patent on parts used in robotic arms, a federal appeals court ruled that a patent owner could not assert the doctrine of equivalents if the patent claim at issue had been amended during the application process. The doctrine of equivalents allows a patent owner to stop an infringer who, by using equivalent parts or elements, manages to create an invention that performs the same function in the same manner as a patented invention—for example, if an infringer uses aluminum wire when the original patent claimed the use of copper wire.

In 2002, the U.S. Supreme Court struck down this absolute bar to the doctrine of equivalents and replaced it with a less arbitrary standard. Under the Supreme Court's standard, all amended claims are presumed to be narrowed so as to bar the doctrine of equivalents. But this presumption can be rebutted if a patent owner can demonstrate that the amendment involved a feature that was "unforeseeable at the time of the application" or "for some other reason" could not be included in the original claim. In that case, the patent owner can use the doctrine of equivalents. For example, the patentee could show that, at the time of the amendment, one skilled in the art could not reasonably be expected to have drafted a claim that would have literally encompassed the alleged equivalent. (*Festo Corp. v. Shoketsu Kinzoku Kabushiki Co. Ltd.*, 535 U.S .722 (2002).)

field of invention

The "field" of an invention is colloquial for the classification or subclassification into which an invention falls. For instance, an invention involving gene splicing might be said to be in the "genetic engineering field," while an invention involving computers would fall within the "electronics field."

These terms have no legal significance. The similar phrase "field of search" is related to how patents are categorized for search purposes.

Related terms: classification of patents; patent search.

file wrapper

The file the U.S. Patent and Trademark Office (USPTO) maintains for each patent application is known as a file wrapper. This file contains the application itself, as well as copies and notes of all correspondence between the USPTO and the applicant regarding amendment and issuance of the patent. For example, if a letter is sent to the USPTO regarding a pending patent application, it will be added to the applicant's file wrapper.

Related terms: continuation application; file wrapper estoppel; patent application.

file wrapper continuing application (FWC)

See continuation application.

file wrapper estoppel

This is a rule of court under which patent applicants are bound by the statements they make in their patent application and subsequent correspondence and documents filed with the U.S. Patent and Trademark Office (USPTO) in the course of prosecuting the application. The term "file wrapper" is jargon for the file the USPTO maintains on an invention, and the term "estoppel" is a legal principle that holds people to their words even if they later want to weasel out of them.

The file wrapper estoppel rule becomes pertinent if the patent owner should ever seek enforcement of his or her patent in court. In that event, the inventor would be prevented from describing the scope of the invention differently from how it was described in earlier documents in the USPTO patent file (again, colloquially referred to as the file wrapper). In short, an inventor is stuck with what's already been told to the USPTO—and cannot later try to broaden a patent's coverage that has been surrendered by original claim language, or in an amendment or a written argument during the earlier prosecution stage.

Because of the file wrapper estoppel rule, it is good practice to follow these two rules:

- Do not say anything negative about an invention in a patent application (your words may come back to haunt you).
- Draft patent claims as broadly as possible in light of the pertinent prior art.

EXAMPLE: Otto invents a medical tool that uses a fiber optic strand, laser light, specially cloned antibodies, and certain chemicals to detect the presence of various substances in human tissue. In his patent application, Otto drafts his claims very broadly, without a limiting reference to his use of fiber optics. After the USPTO rejects the initial claims, Otto amends his application so that the claims now specify fiber optics as the method of transmitting the laser light. In his cover letter transmitting the amendment to the USPTO, Otto admits that his original claim was wildly overbroad and thanks the examiner for helping him pare his claim down to the appropriate scope. The patent is then granted. Ten years later, Lewis, a famous heart surgeon, makes and uses a similar diagnostic tool, using a magnetic rather than fiber optic means for transmitting the laser light waves. If Otto brings an infringement action against Lewis, alleging that his patent is sufficiently broad in scope to preclude Lewis's device, the court will hold Otto to his admission about the overly broad scope of his original claim, as found in the file wrapper, which clearly limits his patent to a fiber optic means.

Related terms: claims; prosecution of a patent application.

filing date

Assigned to every application by the U.S. Patent and Trademark Office (USPTO), the filing date is indicated on a "filing receipt" that the USPTO sends to the applicant. The date is usually the date that application is received by electronic filing, or one to four days after the patent application was mailed, or the date it's mailed if sent by U.S. Postal Service Express Mail.

Note: The filing date will have more importance after the U.S. switches to a first-to-file system in March 2013. (Until that, time, the rules below are still applicable.) After March 2013, issues regarding date of invention and reduction to practice will become, for the most part, irrelevant, unless there is a battle between two competing applications. The same is true for the one-year bar—it effectively disappears. In summary, the filing date will become the crucial date that establishes an inventor's claim to patent ownership. For more information, check the entry for the America Invents Act.

Until March 2013, the filing date is crucial for a number of reasons, including the following:

- The filing date starts the period within which a patent application must be filed in other countries to receive patent protection. If a Convention application in Germany, for instance, is not filed within one year after the

U.S. filing date, German patent protection will be precluded. If, however, the applicant files under the Patent Cooperation Treaty within one year of the U.S. filing date, the applicant is allowed a longer time period to file in Germany.

- The filing date closes the one-year period during which an inventor can publicly use, work, describe, or place the invention on sale in the United States without the anticipation rule being applied to bar a patent on it.
- The filing date shuts the door on all subsequent developments by other inventors from being considered as prior art. That is, any developments that occur after the filing date will not be considered as prior art that would preclude a patent (which must be novel or nonobvious).
- The filing date is when the law considers an invention to be first reduced to practice (called constructive reduction to practice), absent evidence that it was actually reduced to practice at an earlier time by building and testing it. In the event of an interference (pending applications by different inventors covering the same invention), the inventor who filed first will receive the patent unless another inventor can show that he or she conceived of the invention first and then diligently set about to reduce it to practice or actually reduced it to practice first by building and testing it.

A Provisional Patent Application (PPA) may be filed up to one year prior to filing a regular patent application. The PPA filing date will count as a constructive reduction to practice and serve as the date for deciding whether the invention has been anticipated by prior art. However, the regular patent application filing date—not the PPA filing date—will count as the beginning of the patent term, which expires 20 years from date of filing, and will also begin the year period in which a patent application must be filed in many foreign jurisdictions—if patent protection is sought in them. The same rules should apply in March 2013, after the U.S. adopts the first-to-file system.

To take advantage of the earlier filing date, the regular patent application must specifically claim that date, and the PPA must meet the rigorous standard for disclosure of the invention required of regular patent applications.

Related terms: anticipation; interference; international patent protection for U.S. inventions; prosecution of a patent application; Provisional Patent Application (PPA).

filing fees

See application filing fees; issue fee.

final office action

The patent examiner's decision as to whether or not to issue a patent is known as a final office action. Despite the name, final office actions are not necessarily final. A patent examiner can be petitioned to reconsider the application. And, even if the examiner refuses to budge, the applicant can:

- file a continuation application
- agree to amend the application to exclude a claim altogether (if the argument is about a particular claim), or
- appeal the decision to the Board of Patent Appeals and Interferences.

Normally, the final office action occurs after the patent applicant has been afforded at least one opportunity to amend the application (in response to a first office action which raised problems with the application). Most commonly, the applicant will be expected to revise one or more of the claims in the amendment, thereby avoiding an overlap with prior art that otherwise would preclude a patent from issuing. Also, technical mistakes in how the application describes the invention, how the claims are constructed, and how the drawings depict the invention are typical subjects of an amendment.

Related terms: Board of Patent Appeals and Interferences (BPAI); continuation application; prosecution of a patent application.

first office action

This term refers to the patent examiner's first response to a patent application. Often, the first office action involves the rejection of all or most of the claims in an application (in the trade, humorously termed a "shotgun rejection") on the ground that one or more prior art references render the invention obvious. The applicant can file a response within three months (extendable for up to six months) that either amends the claims or satisfactorily explains to the patent examiner why the prior art references found troublesome by the examiner are not pertinent.

Related terms: prosecution of a patent application; swearing behind a prior art reference.

first sale (patent)

See exhaustion.

first-to-file countries

The U.S. switches to a first-to-file system in March 2013, 18 months after enactment of the America Invents Act. After the switch, the filing date will become the crucial date that establishes an inventor's claim to patent ownership. Under a first-to-file system, an inventor who is the first to file an application for a patent on an invention is given absolute priority over other inventors. Until passage of the America Invents Act, all countries except the United States use the first-to-file system.

The laws providing for this absolute priority are sometimes termed "race statutes," because they award a patent to the inventor who wins the race to the patent office.

Related terms: first-to-invent countries; international patent protection for U.S. inventions.

first-to-invent countries

Until March 2013, the United States will award a patent to the first party to actually come up with an invention (first to invent), as opposed to the first party to file a patent application (first to file). After March 2013, the U.S. will use a first-to-file system.

Related terms: first-to-file countries; international patent protection for U.S. inventions.

fraud on the U.S. Patent and Trademark Office

Any behavior by an applicant for a patent that attempts to mislead the U.S. Patent and Trademark Office (USPTO) in regard to whether the invention deserves a patent is considered fraud. The most common type of fraud is failure to inform the USPTO about one or more relevant prior art references known to the applicant. This issue is usually raised by an alleged infringer as a defense to court litigation seeking enforcement of a patent. Once found to exist by a court, fraud on the USPTO usually results in the patent being judged unenforceable or invalid.

Related terms: defenses to a patent infringement claim; duty of candor and good faith; infringement action; unenforceable patent.

fully met by a prior art reference

When any single previous development or publication (prior art reference) contains all of the specific elements and limitations set out in a patent claim, the claim is said to be fully met by the prior art. If a claim is fully met, the invention is considered anticipated and is therefore not entitled to a patent.

EXAMPLE: Unaware of prior developments, Gary invents a mechanical match. When he tries to patent it, however, the U.S. Patent and Trademark Office points out a patent that shows (teaches) all of the elements in the claim describing Gary's device. Because Gary's claims are fully met, his device has been "anticipated" and is not entitled to a patent.

Related terms: claims; novelty; prior art reference.

GATT (General Agreement on Tariffs and Trade)

The General Agreement on Tariffs and Trade (GATT) is among the most important international trade treaties in our history. And it has had a large effect on U.S. patent law.

Under GATT, for patents filed after June 7, 1995, the U.S. patent monopoly ends 20 years from the application's filing date, regardless of when the patent issues. However, effective June 2000, every patent is guaranteed an in-force period of at least 17 years. Previously, the patent monopoly lasted for 17 years from the date of issue, regardless of when the application was filed. (Patent applications that were pending—and patents which were in force—as of June 8, 1995, expire 20 years from filing or 17 years from issue, whichever period is longer.)

Another GATT-related change involves the Provisional Patent Application or PPA. Filing a PPA will legally "reduce an invention to practice," provided that the inventor files an actual patent application within a year or filing the PPA. The reduction to practice date is crucial if an inventor is faced with a competing patent application or a prior art reference with a close date. Formerly, an invention could be reduced to practice only by building and testing it or by filing a regular patent application.

Another GATT-related change involves foreign inventors. Under current U.S. law, an inventor may establish a date of invention earlier than the filing date of the inventor's patent application in order to:

- obtain the patent in the face of a competing application ("win an interference"), or
- show that the invention predates a particular prior art reference ("swear behind cited prior art").

But to do this, the inventor must show conception of the invention and either:

- actual reduction to practice (building and testing), or
- diligent efforts to reduce the invention to practice or file a patent application.

Before GATT, inventors could rely on activities only in the United States, Mexico, or Canada. For applications filed on or after January 1, 1996, inventors are also able to rely on activities in any GATT country.

The final GATT-related change enhances protection against patent infringement. Prior to GATT, a patent only gave its owner the right to exclude others from making, using, or selling the patented invention. GATT expanded this right to include the situation when anyone else offers for sale or imports a patented invention, or, in the case of a process patent, imports products made abroad by the patented process.

genetic engineering and patents

Ordinarily, patents will not be issued on "inventions" consisting of items or substances that are found to exist in a natural state. The reason for this is obvious. Something occurring in nature without human intervention cannot have been the product of inventive activity.

There are several categories of patentable inventions that do, however, involve "natural" materials. One category is novel and nonobvious plants created through asexual breeding. Plant patents for new plants involving human inventiveness (breeding skill) are specifically authorized by statute (the patent laws and the Plant Variety Protection Act) in the United States.

Genetic engineering is another field where "natural" materials (that is, bacteria, DNA, RNA) have been manipulated by humans through gene splicing and cloning techniques (such as Polymerase Chain Reaction, or PCR) to produce new organic materials and life forms. These new substances and forms, and the processes used to create them, are also considered to be patentable under authority of the U.S. Supreme Court's decision in the case of *Diamond v. Chakrabarty,* 447 U.S. 303 (1980), as long as they meet the basic patent requirements of novelty, nonobviousness, and utility.

Because Congress wants basic research in biotechnology to develop as quickly as possible, federal law permits a company to utilize biotechnical inventions patented by another company if the purpose of the use is strictly for research. This is an exception to the general rule that a patent prohibits the manufacture or use of an invention covered by an in-force patent. If, however, the company doing the research desires to commercially exploit the substance or process being utilized, it must obtain permission from the patent owner (usually accomplished by paying a license fee).

Patent Law: Definitions

In 2010 a federal district court determined that certain patent claims for BRCA1 and BRCA2 human genes were invalid. The genes are found in the cells of breast and other tissue, where they help repair damaged DNA. The genes are a factor in breast cancer diagnosis. The court held that the subject matter was unpatentable because genes are the physical embodiment of [genetic] information. (*Association for Molecular Pathology v. USPTO*, 702 F. Supp. 2d 181 (S.D. N.Y. 2010).)

In September 2011, the U.S. enacted the America Invents Act that bars the issuance of patent claims directed to or encompassing a human organism.

Related terms: laws of nature exception to patents; nonstatutory subject matter.

geographic patent license

This type of exclusive license grants its holder (the licensee) the right to make, use, or sell a patented invention within a specified geographic region only. For example, one license might allow its holder to exploit the invention commercially in the United States, while another license might provide similar rights to another company, to be exercised solely in the European Community countries.

Related terms: exclusive patent license.

Graham v. John Deere

This 1966 Supreme Court case created the guidelines for determining when an invention is nonobvious—a statutory requirement for an invention to be patentable. (The text of this case can be located in 383 U.S. 1.)

According to the *Deere* case, the following steps help to determine if an invention is nonobvious:

- Determine the scope and content of the prior art.
- Determine the novelty of the invention.
- Determine the skill level of artisans in the pertinent technology (art).
- Against this background, determine the obviousness or nonobviousness of the inventive subject matter.
- Consider relevant secondary factors, such as the commercial success experienced with the invention, whether there was a long-felt but unsolved need for the invention, and whether others tried but failed to produce the invention.

In practice, these guidelines boil down to whether, taking all relevant factors into account, a person reasonably skilled in the art involved in the invention would find the invention to be a surprising or unexpected development at the time it was made.

Related terms: nonobviousness; obviousness.

grant of patent

A patent is granted when the U.S. Patent and Trademark Office issues a patent on an invention.

group art unit

The group art unit is an internal division of the U.S. Patent and Trademark Office to which a filed patent application is assigned for examination.

Related terms: prosecution of a patent application; U.S. Patent and Trademark Office (USPTO).

improvement inventions

Technically, almost all inventions are "improvement inventions"—that is, inventions that improve upon other, prior inventions.

Patent protection for small improvements on existing inventions in well-developed fields (many of them technological developments) is relatively easy to obtain. Conversely, in relatively new fields such as genetic engineering, small improvements may be considered too trivial or obvious to be granted a patent. This is true primarily because new fields of invention are much more supportive of new developments than are established fields, where the areas of potential improvement in existing techniques are more obvious.

A patent on an improvement invention covers only the improvement itself and is thus subject to the rights of any holders of in-force patents on the other technology involved. This means that to commercially exploit the improvement invention, its owner must license the right to use the underlying invention. Often this is accomplished by cross-licensing the two patents ("You can use mine if I can use yours"). Cross-licensing is extremely common throughout the industrial world.

EXAMPLE: A computer manufacturer makes an unexpected and novel improvement on an existing patented data bus (a device included in most microcomputers to move data from one part of the computer to another in an orderly way). The value of this improvement patent will depend heavily upon the degree to which appropriate arrangements can be made with the owner of the patent on the original data bus. This may not be difficult, because the original patent owner will likely want the right to commercially exploit the improvement patent. If so, the parties can enter into a cross-license agreement permitting them to use each other's inventions for agreed-upon compensation.

If there were two in-force patents covering the original data bus, the improvement patent owner would have to come to terms with both patent owners to exploit the invention.

Related terms: cross-licensing; patent pools.

independent claim

An independent claim by itself describes an aspect of the invention without reference to any other claim. By contrast, a dependent claim refers to another independent or dependent claim. (Samples of dependent and independent claims are provided in "claims.")

Related terms: claims; dependent claim.

Index of U.S. Patent Classification

See classification of patents.

inducing infringement

35 USC § 271(b) provides that an act of actively inducing another to infringe a patent shall itself be treated as an act of infringement. To prove inducement to infringe, the patent owner must demonstrate some positive act of inducement by the person being sued. That may include instructing, directing, or advising the third party as to how to carry out a infringement.

What is the standard for inducing infringement? The Supreme Court looked at the issue in 2011. A company, SEB, patented a "cool-touch" deep-fryer whose exterior was cool to the touch. GlobalTech Appliances, operating outside the U.S., copied everything but the cosmetic aspects of the SEB deep-fryer. GlobalTech then branded these deep-fryers for sale by Sunbeam, Montgomery Ward, and others. SEB sued GlobalTech for inducing others to infringe its cool-touch patent. GlobalTech defended itself by arguing that it couldn't induce others to infringe because it had no actual knowledge it was infringing SEB's patent. (GlobalTech had vetted its device with a patent attorney but had failed to disclose to the attorney that their device was copied directly from the SEB deep-fryer.) The Supreme Court ruled for the patent owner, SEB. The court said that inducing infringement required knowledge of the existing patent, but that knowledge could be inferred using a legal standard referred to as "willful blindness." As the Court stated: "Many criminal statutes require proof that a defendant acted knowingly or willfully, and courts applying the doctrine of willful blindness hold that defendants cannot escape the reach of these statutes by deliberately shielding themselves from clear evidence of critical facts that are strongly suggested by the circumstances." The Court went on to distinguish willful blindness from a lower court's standard known as "deliberate indifference." As for the differences, the bottom line is that when asking an attorney to render a legal opinion ("Does my deep-fryer infringe?"), don't hide information (like, "I copied this from another deep-fryer"). (*GlobalTech Appliances v. SEB*, ___ U.S. ___ (2011).)

A patent is said to be in force (in effect) if all of the following are true:

- The patent's statutory term has not yet expired.
- Appropriate maintenance fees have been paid when due.
- The patent has not been ruled invalid by the U.S. Patent and Trademark Office or a court.

Even when a patent is no longer in force, it still is considered prior art when determining if a later invention qualifies for a patent.

Related terms: patent term extension; reexamination of patent.

Information Disclosure Statement

A statement must be filed with a regular patent application (or within the following three months) that describes all relevant prior art references known to the applicant and also provides actual copies of such references when they have appeared in print. Known as an Information Disclosure Statement, an IDS, or USPTO Form 1449, this statement provides the U.S. Patent and Trademark Office (USPTO) with a head start in determining whether the invention deserves a patent. An IDS need not be filed with a Provisional Patent Application.

An applicant's knowing failure to disclose any known and relevant prior art reference is considered fraud on the USPTO. If a patent was granted in this circumstance, it may be held unenforceable in court, although the deliberately omitted prior art reference might not have resulted in any claim being disallowed.

When examining a patent application, the USPTO conducts its own patent search in addition to what it learns from an applicant's IDS and often picks up omitted prior art references. These references may then be used to reject the application on novelty or nonobviousness grounds, but the USPTO seldom presumes that the omission was intentional. If, however, the USPTO fails to find the omitted prior art reference and proceeds in its ignorance to issue a patent, the reference will usually only be brought to light if an infringement lawsuit is filed. This is because the infringer, as part of its defense, can be counted on to do an exhaustive prior art search (called a validity search) to prove that the patent was improperly issued and therefore invalid. If the prior art reference is found in the course of this search, the infringer can then be expected to argue that the omission was deliberate. If the court agrees, it will invalidate the patent because of fraud on the USPTO, without regard to how the reference affects the invention's novelty and nonobviousness.

Related terms: defenses to a patent infringement claim; patent search; Provisional Patent Application (PPA); validity search.

infringement, patent

Infringement of a utility patent occurs when someone makes, uses, or sells an item covered by the claims of an in-force patent without the patent owner's permission. If a court finds that infringement occurred, every patent infringer can be ordered by a court to stop all infringing activity. Any of the infringers who profited from the infringement may also be found liable for money damages. Only an infringer who had reason to know that a patent was being infringed can be held liable for treble damages as a willful infringer.

> **EXAMPLE:** Owens Organic Products invents and patents a simple computerized sprinkler system that turns on and off according to the moisture level of the soil. Although Phil Prendergast has been independently working on the same invention, he failed to beat Owens to the Patent and Trademark Office and is unable to prove that he was the first to invent. However, figuring that Owens will probably never find out, Phil licenses Garden Development Corp. to construct and market his invention in exchange for royalties. Garden Development manufactures and distributes the system on a wholesale basis to a chain of retail garden-supply stores, which then sell the sprinklers to consumers, who use them in their gardens. Phil, Garden Development, the retail stores, and the consumers are all guilty of patent infringement— even though none except Phil knew about Owens's patent. Phil, Garden Development, and the retail stores may be ordered to stop infringing and to pay money damages. However, only Phil would be liable for treble damages, unless Garden Development and the retail stores knew, or should have known, that their activity infringed Owens's patent.

Infringement of a design patent occurs when two distinct standards are met: (1) The Ordinary Observer Test: The court first compares the allegedly infringing device with design patent drawings under the ordinary observer test to determine whether the allegedly infringing design is substantially the same as the patented design; and (2) The Point of Novelty Test: The court compares the patented design with the prior art to determine the novelty of the patented design. Then, the court determines whether the allegedly infringing design appropriates the novelty. (*Lawman Armor Corp. v. Winner Intl.*, CAFC 2006.)

Related terms: contributory infringement of patent; infringement action.

infringement action

An infringement action is a lawsuit alleging that one or more parties (defendants) have, without permission, made, used, or sold an invention protected under a patent owned by the party bringing the lawsuit (plaintiff). Patent infringement actions must be filed in the U.S. District Court within a maximum of six years after the date the infringement occurred—or sooner, if a delay in filing would obviously cause undue hardship to the defendant.

Although it is possible to have a jury trial in a patent infringement case, the judge alone is responsible for interpreting the patent claims. (*Markman v. Westview Instruments, Inc.*, 517 U.S. 370 (1996).) The judge or jury then examines the plaintiff's patent and compares the elements recited in its claims with those of the accused infringer's device or process. On this basis, the judge or jury decides whether the plaintiff's claims, as interpreted by the judge, cover the defendant's device or process—that is, fully describe the elements contained in the device or process. If the plaintiff's claims cover ("read on") the device or process, infringement is found. If the claims do not cover the defendant's device or process, then no infringement has occurred.

Even if the claims don't literally read on the infringing device, the judge or jury could find infringement by applying the doctrine of equivalents: The two devices are sufficiently equivalent in what they do and how they do it to warrant a finding of infringement. Also possible, but extremely rare, is the converse: finding no infringement because the two devices are sufficiently dissimilar in what they accomplish or how they work, even though the claims are the same (in patent speak, the negative doctrine of equivalents).

If infringement is found to exist, the judge may:
- issue an injunction (court order) preventing further infringement
- award the patent owner damages for loss of income or for profits resulting from the infringement from the time the invention was properly marked (when the word "patent" and the patent number were affixed to the invention) or from when the infringer was first put on actual notice of the infringement, whichever occurred first, and

- in the event the infringement was willful or flagrant (it continued without a reasonable defense after notification by the patent owner, or infringement occurred through a direct copying without any ground to believe the plaintiff's patent was invalid), the court may award the plaintiff three times the actual damages established in court plus reasonable attorney fees.

The Supreme Court has determined that a court should not automatically issue an injunction based on a finding of patent infringement. (Alternatively, an injunction should not be denied simply on the basis that the plaintiff does not make, sell, or use the patented invention.) Instead, a federal court must still weigh the four factors traditionally used to determine if an injunction should be granted. (*eBay Inc. v. MercExchange, L.L.C.*, 126 S.Ct. 1837 (2006).)

Patent infringement lawsuits are risky for the patent owner, because the defendant will almost always attack the underlying validity of the patent on such grounds as:

- The invention was obvious or lacked novelty when the patent issued. The defendant proves this by introducing relevant prior art references not picked up by the U.S. Patent and Trademark Office (USPTO) in the course of examining the patent application.
- The patent application failed to fully disclose the best mode of the invention, as is required by the patent laws.
- The patent applicant failed to disclose relevant prior art known to the applicant (fraud on the USPTO).

Until the late 1980s, courts ruled against the validity of the patent in over half of all patent infringement cases. Lately, however, under the leadership of the U.S. Court of Appeals for the Federal Circuit, the courts are upholding significantly more patents than they strike down.

Related terms: breaking (or busting) a patent; contributory infringement of patent; defenses to a patent infringement claim; infringement, patent.

infringement defenses

See defenses to a patent infringement claim.

infringement search

An infringement search is conducted for the purpose of discovering whether an invention infringes any in-force patent. This type of search is typically conducted by an invention developer as a preliminary step to deciding whether to develop a particular invention. It is much narrower in scope than a patentability search, which is concerned with all prior art—including expired patents and relevant unpatented technology. It also differs from a validity search, which typically is conducted by a defendant in a patent infringement lawsuit for the purpose of discovering information that would invalidate the patent.

Related terms: patent search.

injunctions and injunctive relief

See infringement action.

inter partes proceeding

If someone—for example, another patent owner, a potential infringer, or the U.S. Patent and Trademark Office (USPTO)—seeks to reexamine an existing patent to determine its validity, an *inter partes* proceeding can be brought at the USPTO. This type of administrative hearing is less expensive, less formal, and faster than challenging a patent owner in court. In addition, *inter partes* decisions are rendered by technical specialists, not juries.

After September 2011 (following enactment of the America Invents Act), it became more challenging to obtain an *inter partes* reexam. The Director can only authorize a reexam if "there is a reasonable likelihood that the petitioner would prevail with respect to at least one of the claims challenged in the petition." In September 2012, the provisions of the America Invents Act will make it even more difficult for anyone to obtain an *inter partes* hearing after a patent has been issued. Such proceedings will be limited to challenges for novelty and nonobviousness— that is to issues relating to Section 102 and 103 of the patent law. These claims can only be based on prior art consisting of patents and printed publications and must be filed nine months after the patent issued. This provision also establishes many additional technical and procedural rules for postgrant reviews, generally making it more difficult to bring postgrant reviews.

[Effective September 2012 as a result of passage of the America Invents Act]

§ 311. Inter partes review

(a) In General. Subject to the provisions of this chapter, a person who is not the owner of a patent may file with the Office a petition to institute an inter partes review of the patent. The Director shall establish, by regulation, fees to be paid by the person requesting the review, in such amounts as the Director determines to be reasonable, considering the aggregate costs of the review.

(b) Scope. A petitioner in an inter partes review may request to cancel as unpatentable 1 or more claims of a patent only on a ground that could be raised under section 102 or 103 and only on the basis of prior art consisting of patents or printed publications.

(c) Filing Deadline. A petition for inter partes review shall be filed after the later of either—

   (1) the date that is 9 months after the grant of a patent or issuance of a reissue of a patent; or

   (2) if a postgrant review is instituted under chapter 32, the date of the termination of such postgrant review.

Sec. 312. Petitions

(a) Requirements of Petition. A petition filed under section 311 may be considered only if—

   (1) the petition is accompanied by payment of the fee established by the Director under section 311;

   (2) the petition identifies all real parties in interest;

   (3) the petition identifies, in writing and with particularity, each claim challenged, the grounds on which the challenge to each claim is based, and the evidence that supports the grounds for the challenge to each claim, including—

      (A) copies of patents and printed publications that the petitioner relies upon in support of the petition; and

      (B) affidavits or declarations of supporting evidence and opinions, if the petitioner relies on expert opinions;

   (4) the petition provides such other information as the Director may require by regulation; and

   (5) the petitioner provides copies of any of the documents required under paragraphs (2), (3), and (4) to the patent owner or, if applicable, the designated representative of the patent owner.

(b) Public Availability. As soon as practicable after the receipt of a petition under section 311, the Director shall make the petition available to the public.

Sec. 313. Preliminary response to petition

If an inter partes review petition is filed under section 311, the patent owner shall have the right to file a preliminary response to the petition, within a time period set by the Director, that sets forth reasons why no inter partes review should be instituted based upon the failure of the petition to meet any requirement of this chapter.

Sec. 314. Institution of inter partes review

(a) Threshold. The Director may not authorize an inter partes review to be instituted unless the Director determines that the information presented in the petition filed under section 311 and any response filed under section 313 shows that there is a reasonable likelihood that the petitioner would prevail with respect to at least 1 of the claims challenged in the petition.

(b) Timing. The Director shall determine whether to institute an inter partes review under this chapter pursuant to a petition filed under section 311 within 3 months after—

    (1) receiving a preliminary response to the petition under section 313; or

    (2) if no such preliminary response is filed, the last date on which such response may be filed.

(c) Notice. The Director shall notify the petitioner and patent owner, in writing, of the Director's determination under subsection (a), and shall make such notice available to the public as soon as is practicable. Such notice shall include the date on which the review shall commence.

(d) No Appeal. The determination by the Director whether to institute an inter partes review under this section shall be final and nonappealable.

Related terms: reexamination of patent.

interference

An "interference" is patent jargon for an administrative proceeding scheduled by the U.S. Patent and Trademark Office (USPTO) to determine who gets the patent in situations where two pending applications (or a pending application and a patent issued within one year of the pending application's filing date) both claim the same invention.

Note: Among the changes implemented by the America Invents Act, enacted in September 2011, is that commencing in March 2013, the USPTO will terminate interference process and instead permit a patent owner to bring a "derivation hearing" at the USPTO against another patent owner claiming to have the same invention and who has an earlier effective filing date. Alternatively, the owner of a patent may sue the owner of another patent that claims the same invention and has an earlier effective filing date.

The Board of Patent Appeals and Interferences determines the priority of inventorship according to the following analytical steps.

Step 1: The Board decides which inventor was the first to reduce the invention to practice. This will be the first inventor to either:

- constructively reduce the invention to practice by filing a provisional or regular patent application (the senior party), or
- actually reduce the invention to practice by building and testing a working model of the invention.

Step 2: Based on evidence introduced in the interference proceeding, the Board decides whether the inventor who was second to reduce to practice can prove both that (1) he or she was first to conceive of the invention, and (2) he or she was also diligently attempting to reduce the invention to practice at the time the other inventor conceived the invention.

The inventor who can prove both prior conception and diligence in reduction to practice will be awarded the patent; otherwise, the inventor who was first to reduce the invention to practice (either actually or constructively) gets the patent.

The reasoning behind these priorities is relatively simple. The patent laws attempt to balance three goals:

- get the inventor to file as quickly as possible so the invention can become known to the public
- get the inventor to come up with the best possible version of the invention, and
- reward the inventor who is first to conceive of the invention.

By initially presuming that the first inventor to reduce the invention to practice should get the patent, the patent laws serve the first two goals. But all three goals can be served by giving the patent to the first to conceive the invention if that inventor also worked diligently to reduce the invention to practice.

Because an inventor may later be called on to prove when an invention was first conceived and what steps were taken to reduce it to practice, most inventors maintain detailed records of their inventive activities in notebooks that are signed and witnessed.

EXAMPLE: Bellingham Medical Supplies and Boca Raton Pharmaceuticals both have pending applications for a patent on a painkilling device designed to allow patients to self-medicate small doses of certain opiates without running the risk of an overdose or addictive reaction. An interference is declared and a hearing scheduled. At the hearing, the research scientists at Bellingham Medical produce their notebooks showing that they were the first to conceive of the invention. Boca Raton, on the other hand, establishes that it filed its patent application first and was thus the first to constructively reduce the invention to practice.

If Bellingham can establish that it was the first to actually reduce the invention to practice by building a working model before Boca Raton filed its application, or that it was diligently working to reduce the invention to practice at the time Boca Raton first conceived of the invention, Bellingham will be awarded the patent. If neither of these showings is made, however, Boca Raton will be awarded the patent (even though it was the second to conceive the invention), because it was the first to reduce the invention to practice by filing the patent application, and Bellingham failed to show the necessary diligence toward reduction to practice after its initial conception of the invention.

Related terms: Disclosure Document Program (DDP); filing date; interference; notebook, inventor's; Provisional Patent Application (PPA); reduction to practice.

International Bureau of the World Intellectual Property Organization

This administrative arm of the World Intellectual Property Organization (WIPO) in Geneva, Switzerland, is designated by the Patent Cooperation Treaty of 1970 as the clearinghouse for international patent applications.

Related terms: Patent Cooperation Treaty (PCT).
See also Part 4 (Trade Secret Law): World Intellectual Property Organization (WIPO).

international patent protection for U.S. inventions

U.S. inventors can gain patent protection in countries outside the United States in two ways:

- by filing separately in each country where protection is desired under certain rules established by the Paris Convention, or
- by filing an "international application" with the International Bureau of the World Intellectual Property Organization, an office established under the Patent Cooperation Treaty (PCT). This single filing establishes a filing date good in all member countries, although the patent owner must file separate "national" applications in each member country where the owner wants coverage. The European Patent Office is considered a single entity for the purpose of the PCT.

Although other treaties exist between the United States and certain countries pertaining to reciprocal patent protection, the two mentioned above provide the primary international protection for U.S. inventors.

Related terms: Convention application; European Patent Convention; Federal Trade Commission proceeding; Patent Cooperation Treaty (PCT).

Internet, patent searching

See patent search, computerized.

Internet patent

The term "Internet patent" has, for the most part, been supplanted by the term "business method patent," though technically an Internet patent is a subset of

Patent Law: Definitions

business method patents. In general, the term is used to describe a group of utility patents issued for software programs and for methods of doing business, most of which relate to Internet uses. The most well-known example of an Internet patent is Amazon.com's "One-Click" system, a method that allows a repeat customer to bypass address and credit card data entry forms when placing an online order. (U.S. Pat. No. 5,960,411.)

What was considered different about Internet patents was their subject matter—a method of doing online business. For most of the 20th century, the courts and the USPTO believed that business methods could not be patented. But in 1998 a federal court ruled that patent laws were intended to protect any method, whether or not it required the aid of a computer, so long as it produced a "useful, concrete, and tangible result." (*State Street Bank & Trust Co. v. Signature Financial Group, Inc.*, 149 F.3d 1368 (Fed. Cir. 1998).) Thus, with one stroke, the court legitimized both software patents and methods of doing business, opening the way for these so-called Internet patents. Regardless of their categorization, business method, software, or Internet patents have one thing in common: They were all affected by the Supreme Court's 2010 ruling in *Kappos v. Bilski*. The Supreme Court rejected the view held by the Court of Appeals for the Federal Circuit (CAFC) that the so-called "machine or transformation" test should be the sole standard for patentability. The Supreme Court refused to categorically deny patentability to any class or category of otherwise patentable subject matter, preserved the status quo, and kept alive the concept of Internet, software, business method, and other process patents. (*Kappos v. Bilski*, 561 U.S. ___ (2010).)

Note: In September 2012 (one year after enactment of the America Invents Act), the Director must establish a transitional postgrant review proceeding to consider the validity of business-method patents. In other words, in coming years it may become more difficult to obtain a so-called Internet patent.

Related terms: business methods as statutory subject matter; software patents.

intervening right

When an in-force patent is reissued on the basis of broadened claims, there exists the possibility that someone relying on the wording of the claims in the original patent developed or used a device that would not have infringed the original patent, but that does infringe the reissue patent. When this occurs, the infringing business is said to have "intervening" rights, which preclude an infringement suit under the new broadened claims. However, these intervening rights are considered personal to the business in question and cannot be transferred to another business or owner.

Related terms: defenses to a patent infringement claim; reissue patent.

invalid patent

See defenses to a patent infringement claim; unenforceable patent.

invention

As defined by patent attorney David Pressman in his book *Patent It Yourself* (Nolo), an invention is any thing, process, or idea that:
- is not generally and currently known
- without too much skill or ingenuity can exist or be reduced to tangible form or used in a tangible thing
- has some value or use to society, and
- was thought up or discovered by someone.

In addition to this description, an invention is said to happen when at or about the time the thing, process, or idea is first conceived, efforts are then continually made to build a working model of the invention or file a patent application on it—that is, reduce it to practice.

Related terms: inventor; patent.

inventor

An inventor is a person who contributes significant creative input into an invention. Until September 2012, an application for a patent on an invention must be made in the name of the inventor (or names of all inventors if more than one), even if a commercial or nonprofit organization actually owns the invention. Failing to accurately name the true inventor or inventors in a patent application can result in an issued patent later being declared invalid.

As result of passage of the America Invents Act, in September 2012 assignees of invention rights may apply for the patent, rather than the inventor.

Sec. 118. Filing by other than inventor [Effective September 2012]

A person to whom the inventor has assigned or is under an obligation to assign the invention may make an application for patent. A person who otherwise shows sufficient proprietary interest in the matter may make an application for patent on behalf of and as agent for the inventor on proof of the pertinent facts and a showing that such action is appropriate to preserve the rights of the parties. If the Director grants a patent on an application filed under this section by a person other than the inventor, the patent shall be granted to the real party in interest and upon such notice to the inventor as the Director considers to be sufficient.

Related terms: coinventors; patent applicant; patent owner; prosecution of a patent application; shop rights.

issue fee

In addition to the fees required for filing a patent application, additional fees also must be paid for the patent to issue after allowance by the U.S. Patent and Trademark Office. The fees are twice as much for large entities as for small entities. Generally, independent inventors, nonprofit corporations, and businesses with fewer than 500 employees qualify for small entity status. However, if an assignment has been or will be made by a small entity to a large entity, large entity fees must be paid. For the current fees, check the USPTO website (www.uspto.gov).

Related terms: application filing fees; prosecution of a patent application.

joint inventors

See coinventors.

junior party in interference proceedings

When an interference is scheduled by the U.S. Patent and Trademark Office, the inventor who was last to file a patent application is known as the junior party.

Related terms: interference proceeding; senior party in interference proceedings.

jury, role of in patent infringement cases

See infringement action.

Kappos v. Bilski

Coinventors Bernard Bilski and Rand Warsaw sought to patent a three-step process to limit risks in hedge fund investments. The examiner rejected the applications because the claims merely "manipulated an abstract idea" and solved a "purely mathematical problem." On appeal, the Court of Appeals for the Federal Circuit (CAFC) affirmed the rejection. The CAFC held that in order for a process claim to be patentable it must either (1) be tied to a particular machine or apparatus, or (2) transform an article into a different state or thing. (*In re Bilski*, 545 F.3d 943 (Fed. Cir. 2008).) The ruling threatened the validity of many business method and software patents. In 2010, the Supreme Court agreed with the CAFC that the Bilski process was unpatentable because it was an abstract idea. However, the Supreme Court rejected the CAFC's view that the so-called "machine or transformation" test should be the sole standard for patentability. ("There are reasons to doubt whether the test should be the sole criterion for determining the patentability of inventions in the Information Age," the Court stated.) The Supreme Court refused to categorically deny patentability to any class or category of otherwise patentable subject matter and in doing so, the Court preserved the status quo and kept alive the concept of software, business method, and other process patents. (*Kappos v. Bilski* 561 U.S. ___ (2010).)

KSR v. Teleflex

Teleflex owned a patent that combined two well-known components—a gas pedal that can be adjusted relative to the driver's seating position and an electronic (as opposed to a mechanical) sensor that senses and transmits to the vehicle's throttle computer the position of the pedal. Teleflex sued its competitor, KSR International, of Canada, for supplying General Motors with adjustable gas pedals with their own sensors for use with electronic throttle controls.

The Supreme Court decided that when elements, techniques, items, or devices are combined, united, or arranged, and when, in combination, each item performs the function it was designed to perform, the resulting combination—something the court called "ordinary innovation"—is not patentable. Therefore, ordinary engineering that engineers perform in the course of their usual day-to-day activities may not be patentable. (*KSR v. Teleflex*, 550 U.S. 398 (2007).)

laboratory notebook

See notebook, inventor's.

large entity

A for-profit company that has over 500 employees is considered a large entity by the U.S. Patent and Trademark Office (USPTO). When a large entity owns the patent rights to an invention, or is entitled to have ownership of these rights transferred to it, the fees payable to the USPTO for various aspects of the patent application and prosecution process are double those for small entities.

Related terms: issue fee; maintenance fees; small entity.

laws of nature exception to patents

This rule states that general scientific and mathematical principles are not patentable, even if they meet the other required statutory requirements for patentability (such as utility, novelty, and nonobviousness). Laws of nature are

Patent Law: Definitions

considered to be part of the public domain rather than products of human inventiveness.

Related terms: algorithms; genetic engineering and patents; naturally occurring substances as nonpatentable; nonstatutory subject matter; statutory subject matter.

lay judge

This term is used by patent law practitioners to refer to any judge sitting in a patent case who is not a patent attorney or especially experienced in patent law.

lay patent searchers

See patent searcher.

letters patent

See patent deed.

licensing of an invention

The process by which an owner gives permission to another party to make, use, or sell his or her patented invention is most often given in the form of a written document called a license. A license of patent rights can be either an exclusive license (only the licensee is entitled to exercise the rights set out in the license) or a nonexclusive license (the licensee may exercise the rights set out in the license but cannot prevent others from exercising the same right under a different license).

Related terms: assignment of a patent; exclusive patent license; nonexclusive patent license.

limiting reference

A limiting reference consists of any element in a patent claim that operates to both define the invention and, by defining it, limit its scope.

Related terms: claims.

machines as patentable subject matter

Generally defined as any devices with moving parts, machines are one of the five categories of inventions (called statutory subject matter) that can be patented. Electronic circuits are also considered machines, even though their parts, strictly speaking, don't move.

Related terms: statutory subject matter.

maintenance fees

Fees must be paid to the U.S. Patent and Trademark Office (USPTO) (or the patent office of another country where a patent has been obtained) to keep an issued patent in effect. For the current maintenance fees, check the USPTO website (www.uspto.gov).

Effective with applications filed after June 7, 1995, the patent term changed from 17 years from the date of issue to 20 years from the date of filing. This means that the final maintenance fee may extend beyond the 17th year until the patent term actually expires. The USPTO will accept credit card payments online for maintenance fees at its website (www.uspto.gov).

A number of other industrialized countries require inventors to pay even larger maintenance fees, reaching into the thousands of dollars per renewal period, in order to maintain the validity of their patent.

Related terms: large entity; small entity.

Manual of Classification

See classification of patents.

Manual of Patent Examining Procedure (MPEP)

The MPEP is a manual of internal procedures followed by U.S. Patent and Trademark Office (USPTO) examiners in processing patent applications (often termed "The Examiner's Bible"). The MPEP is available online at the USPTO website (www.uspto.gov) and may be obtained from the USPTO, for a fee, on CD-ROM.

Related terms: classification of patents; patent application.

manufactures as patentable subject matter

Relatively simple objects that don't have working or moving parts, "manufactures," sometimes also called "articles of manufacture," is one of the five categories of inventions (statutory subject matter) that can be patented. There can be some overlap between the "machines" and "manufactures" categories—especially in the case of inventions involving electronic circuits, which lack moving parts but which are frequently classified as machines because of how they operate.

Examples of more typical manufactures include erasers, desks, houses, wire, tires, books, cloth, chairs, containers, and transistors.

Related terms: statutory subject matter.

march-in rights

The U.S government retains the right (though rarely uses it) to use an invention that has been developed as a result of a government contract if the actual inventor fails to develop and exploit the invention sufficiently.

Related terms: Bayh-Dole Act; patent owner; shop rights.

marking of an invention

Affixing the marks "Patent Pending" or "Pat. Pend." to an invention after a patent application or provisional patent application has been filed, or affixing the patent number after a patent has issued, is known as marking the invention.

The marks "Patent Pending" or "Pat. Pend." have no immediate legal significance, but they do place potential infringers on notice that, should a patent ultimately issue, they will not be allowed to make, use, or sell the invention without the patent owner's permission. During the patent pending period, an inventor cannot stop an infringer or collect damages. However, under the new 18-month publication statute (see "confidentiality of patent application"), an inventor whose application is published prior to issuance may obtain royalties from an infringer from the date the application is published. There are two requirements: (1) the application later issues as a patent; and (2) the infringer had actual notice of the published application. (35 United States Code, Sections 122, 154.) An infringer will have actual notice of a publication if he or she sees the published application. This can be accomplished by sending a copy to the infringer by registered mail. Otherwise, the inventor has no rights whatsoever against infringers during the pendency period—only the hope of a future monopoly, which doesn't commence until a patent issues.

Marking an invention with a patent number (for example, "patent #5,040,387" or "pat. #5,040,387") after a patent is issued puts infringers on notice that any use of the invention may result in an injunction and damages. If an infringement action is later filed, the patent owner will be able to collect damages from the date he or she began properly marking the invention. By contrast, if the invention is not marked, damages may be collected only from the time the infringer received actual notice (usually a demand letter from the patent owner) or the date the patent infringement suit was first filed, whichever occurred earlier.

Many inventors prefer not to place the patent number on their invention. Why? Because marking the invention makes it easier for a competitor to obtain a copy of the patent and design around it. A competitor may have a much more difficult time locating the patent on an unmarked invention. In an attempt to avoid this problem, some patent holders just use the mark "patent," without an accompanying number. This doesn't have any legal clout, however, since this type of notice is not legally sufficient to start the period running for which damages may be recovered. As with an unmarked invention, damages on an inadequately marked invention are recoverable only for the period after the infringer received actual notice, or after the suit was filed.

The America Invents Act initiated two changes regarding patent marking:

- **Virtual marking**. Virtual marking is the process of using a publicly accessible website to provide a link between a patented invention and its patent number. After September 2011, this is considered as sufficiently providing public notice for that patent.

- **Harder to claim false marking defense**. It has become common practice for parties to bring a lawsuit claiming (or making a counterclaim) that an invention is falsely marked, especially if the mark exists on copies of the invention after the patent has expired. The America Invents Act provides that privately filed false marking claims (those claims not brought by the government) will require proof of competitive injury. Marking with the number of a patent that covered that product but has expired will no longer be considered false marking.

Related terms: confidentiality of patent application; infringement action; patent pending.

Markman v. Westview Instruments

This U.S. Supreme Court case (517 U.S. 370 (1976)) ruled that the judge rather than the jury is responsible for interpreting patent claims in a patent infringement case. Since the scope of the claims can often determine the outcome of an infringement case, the power of the jury in such cases has been sharply diminished.

mathematical formulas

See algorithms.

means plus function clause

This jargon refers to a way of defining an invention in a patent claim that describes an element of the invention in terms of its function (as the means by which a specific function is performed), rather than in terms of its specific structure.

The use of a means plus function clause broadens the claim and makes the claim harder to design around, since a patent on the "means" will then support all possible structures that can perform the specified function. A means plus function clause must include the term "means" followed by the specific function of the element.

> **EXAMPLE:** One of the claims in a patent application filed on fundamental multimedia search technology begins by stating: "A computer search system for retrieving information, comprising: ... *means for storing* interrelated textual information and graphical information."

In this claim element, the words "means for storing ... information" theoretically are broad enough to include a CD-ROM, a computer hard disk, or any other information storage method that exists now or may exist in the future. However, the scope of this or any other claim using a means plus clause is not as unlimited as the words may suggest. When determining the scope of a claim containing a means plus function clause, the U.S. Patent and Trademark Office (USPTO) and courts look to other references to the invention contained in the patent or patent application and limit the reach of the claim to those references. Also, because historically there has been some dispute as to how broadly means plus function claims can read (that is, how many devices/processes they can cover), it is often wise to draft one set of claims using means plus function clauses and a duplicate set of claims citing specific devices and processes so that the patent will be both as broad and as specific as the USPTO will allow.

A 2007 court decision emphasized that every means and even every nonmeans component in the patent claims portion of a patent application must also be clearly described and identified in the specification. (*Biomedino, LLC v. Waters Technologies Corp.*, 490 F.3d 946, 950 (Fed. Cir. 2007).)

Related terms: claims; prosecution of a patent application.

MedImmune v. Genentech

In 2007, the Supreme Court ruled that a licensee in good standing can challenge the validity of the patents it has licensed without having to break the license agreement before doing so. In other words, without a contractual clause limiting such behavior, the licensee has an unfettered right to prove that the underlying patent is void. The Supreme Court did not limit this holding to patents—indicating that perhaps trademark and copyright licensees can also challenge the validity of the title. (*MedImmune v. Genentech*, 549 U.S. 118 (2007).)

methods as patentable subject matter

See processes (or methods) as patentable subject matter.

misuse

See patent misuse.

multiple claims

A single patent application may contain two or more claims describing a single invention. A patent application typically contains more than one claim, because there is often more than one way a single invention can be novel and/or useful.

> EXAMPLE: A robotics invention that keeps a running account of a kitchen's ingredients can be viewed as a device for maintaining general inventory, a specific process of managing a kitchen's stock of food, and a new physical manifestation of certain robotics principles. At least three different independent claims might be used to describe the invention in these different ways.

Related terms: claims; dependent claim; independent claim.

narrowing a claim

A claim in a patent application that was initially rejected by a patent examiner as being too broad (over the prior art) may be redrafted (narrowed) so that the claim no longer overlaps with the prior art and, therefore, describes a novel and non-obvious invention. Narrowing can be done by adding more elements to the claim or by reciting the existing elements more specifically.

Related terms: claims; first office action.

naturally occurring substances as nonpatentable

Items or substances that are found to exist in a natural state are not eligible for patent protection (they are nonstatutory subject matter). In other words, the discovery of natural substances and processes does not by itself qualify as an invention. However, if natural substances are manipulated and repackaged to meet specific human needs—as is true with many drugs—they may qualify as patentable inventions.

The rule prohibiting the patenting of naturally occurring substances previously was used to bar patents on most living matter. However, the late 20th century saw the development of technologies that allow the genetic alteration of living plants

Patent Law: Definitions

and animals into something different from a "naturally occurring substance." Accordingly, patents have issued on such items as genetically manipulated DNA molecules, enzymes, proteins, bacteria, viruses, plants, and even a mouse, as well as on the processes of manipulation themselves.

Related terms: genetic engineering and patents; nonstatutory subject matter; plant patents.

negative doctrine of equivalents

Under this doctrine, a later device or process may be held to not infringe the patent on an earlier invention, even though the patent's claims fully cover (read on) the later device or process, if the structure, function, or result of the two inventions is substantially different.

This is the rarely used converse of the doctrine of equivalents, which requires a finding of infringement when an invention and a later item are basically the same, even though the patent's claims do not, strictly speaking, cover the later item.

Related terms: doctrine of equivalents; infringement action.

new combinations of old inventions

See combination patent.

new matter

Technical information about an invention that was not included in the original patent application is referred to as new matter. Once an application has been filed, the U.S. Patent and Trademark Office (USPTO) does not allow an applicant to add new matter that would change the scope and nature of the invention. This is because the filing date often determines the date of the invention, and if new matter could continually be added to an application, the filing date would no longer serve this purpose.

However, an applicant for a patent who wants to bring new matter before the USPTO may do so by filing a special supplementary application called a continuation-in-part application.

Related terms: continuation-in-part application (CIP); filing date; patent application.

new-use invention

A new-use invention consists of a new way to use an old device or process, such that the new use is nonobvious—generally remote or surprising to one skilled in the art.

EXAMPLE: Utilizing a known physical property of color dyes that causes them to expand at a different rate when applied to cloth, Tony invents a new process for transferring color patterns into textiles. Assuming that the process is considered nonobvious, it will be entitled to a patent as a "new use" of an old principle.

Related terms: nonobviousness; statutory subject matter.

nondisclosure of patent applications by U.S. Patent and Trademark Office

See confidentiality of patent application.

nonelected claims

A patent may only claim one invention. An applicant may voluntarily choose (elect) not to prosecute a claim or claims in a pending patent application in response to a patent examiner's decision that the application impermissibly claims two inventions. However, an applicant can file a "divisional application" on the nonelected claims, so that they are not abandoned.

Related terms: abandonment of patent application; divisional application; double patenting.

nonexclusive patent license

A nonexclusive patent license is an agreement by which a patent owner (the "licensor") authorizes (licenses) another (the "licensee") to make, use, and/or sell the patented invention but retains the right to license it to others as well. For example, the inventor of a new, more efficient fuel injection system would most likely grant nonexclusive licenses to all the major car companies able to utilize the system, rather than just license it to one company on an exclusive basis.

Related terms: antishelving clause; exclusive patent license; infringement action.

nonobviousness

The quality of nonobviousness refers to the ability of the invention to produce unexpected or surprising new results—results that were not anticipated by the prior art. (The statute that sets forth the nonobviousness requirements is found in 35 United States Code, Section 103.)

To be patentable, an invention must be nonobvious to a person with ordinary skill in the art. Thus, an invention involving video technology would need to be considered nonobvious to a video engineer thoroughly familiar with prior art in the video field.

Analyzing an invention for nonobviousness is difficult primarily because it is a subjective exercise. In addition, whether or not an invention is nonobvious is supposed to be determined as of the date of invention—which in most cases is considered to be the date a provisional or regular patent application is filed.

This means that the U.S. Patent and Trademark Office (USPTO) usually must decide whether an invention is nonobvious well after the date of the invention, because of delays inherent in the patent prosecution process. If the issue of nonobviousness is raised as a defense in a patent infringement lawsuit, the court must look back over an even longer period of time to decide whether the invention was nonobvious as of the date of invention.

Note: After March 2013, the date for determining nonobviousness shall be the filing date, not the date of invention.

The initial determination of whether an invention is (was) nonobvious is made by the patent examiner in the course of deciding whether a patent should issue. The patent examiner generally approaches this task by examining all pertinent prior art references that existed as of the date of invention. Because the patent examiner is usually knowledgeable in the area of the patent being examined, his or her expertise may also be brought to bear as a person with ordinary skill in the art.

However, once a patent issues, the patent may be attacked (usually in court) on the ground that the patent examiner made a mistake on the question of non-obviousness. In this situation, both sides will typically produce experts who provide opposing opinions ("Yes, it was nonobvious"; "No, it absolutely wasn't"). The inventor will also attempt to establish that the invention enjoyed commercial success or solved an unperceived need and should therefore be considered to be nonobvious on the basis of actual developments in the marketplace, regardless of what the experts say. In addition to this evidence, the court will evaluate from scratch the prior art existing at the time of the invention.

One danger of relying on this type of retrospective analysis is that the experts and judge will be unconsciously affected by the intervening technical improvements, and the invention might later be considered obvious even though it wasn't at the time of invention.

In 2007, the U.S. Supreme Court attempted to clarify the issue of nonobviousness regarding combination inventions. The Supreme Court recognized that most, if not all, patentable inventions rely on known building blocks and combinations that, in some sense, are already known. The Court held that when elements, techniques, items, or devices are combined, and when, in combination, each item performs the function it was designed to perform—something the court called "ordinary innovation"—the result may not be patentable. (*KSR v. Teleflex*, 550 U.S. 398 (2007).)

The Court of Appeals for the Federal Circuit (CAFC) applied the *KSR* standard in a case involving a glass sexual aid, concluding that a person of ordinary skill would have known that the results of certain glass experimentation were predictable. (*Ritchie v. Vast Resources, Inc.*, 563 F.3d 1334 (Fed. Cir. 2009).) The CAFC also applied the *KSR* standard in *Aerosol and Specialty Container, Inc. v. Limited Brands, Inc.* 555 F.3d 984 (Fed. Cir. 2009). In that case, the court reviewed a candle tin whose cover could also serve as the candle's base. The court held that prior art references, when combined, made the candle claims obvious.

In 2009, the Federal Circuit provided some hopeful news: nonobviousness determinations can be based on common sense. The court invalidated a patent for email distribution. The patent claimed a method for managing bulk email distribution to groups of consumers including selecting recipients, sending emails to that group, and tabulating the number of emails successfully transmitted. If the number did not exceed a certain minimum, the last step called for repeating the previous steps. The district court summarized the last step as obvious since it was based on the commonsense principle, "If at first you don't succeed, try again." (*Perfect Web Technologies, Inc. v. InfoUSA, Inc.*, 587 F.3d 1324 (Fed. Cir. 2009).)

§ 103. Conditions for patentability; nonobvious subject matter (effective until March 2013)

(a) A patent may not be obtained though the invention is not identically disclosed or described as set forth in section 102 of this title, if the differences between the subject matter sought to be patented and the prior art are such that the subject matter as a whole would have been obvious at the time the invention was made to a person having ordinary skill in the art to which said subject matter pertains. Patentability shall not be negatived by the manner in which the invention was made.

(b) (1) Notwithstanding subsection (a), and upon timely election by the applicant for patent to proceed under this subsection, a biotechnological process using or resulting in a composition of matter that is novel under section 102 and nonobvious under subsection (a) of this section shall be considered nonobvious if

   (A) claims to the process and the composition of matter are contained in either the same application for patent or in separate applications having the same effective filing date and

   (B) the composition of matter, and the process at the time it was invented, were owned by the same person or subject to an obligation of assignment to the same person.

(2) A patent issued on a process under paragraph (1)

    (A) shall also contain the claims to the composition of matter used in or made by that process, or

    (B) shall, if such composition of matter is claimed in another patent, be set to expire on the same date as such other patent, notwithstanding section 154.

(3) For purposes of paragraph (1), the term "biotechnological process" means

    (A) a process of genetically altering or otherwise inducing a single- or multi-celled organism to

        (i) express an exogenous nucleotide sequence,

        (ii) inhibit, eliminate, augment, or alter expression of an endogenous nucleotide sequence, or

        (iii) express a specific physiological characteristic not naturally associated with said organism.

    (B) cell fusion procedures yielding a cell line that expresses a specific protein, such as a monoclonal antibody and

    (C) a method of using a product produced by a process defined by subparagraph (A) or (B), or a combination of subparagraphs (A) and (B).

(c) Subject matter developed by another person, which qualifies as prior art only under one or more of subsections (e), (f), and (g) of section 102 of this title, shall not preclude patentability under this section where the subject matter and the claimed invention were, at the time the invention was made, owned by the same person or subject to an obligation of assignment to the same person.

EFFECTIVE MARCH 2013: § 103 as amended by America Invents Act

Sec. 103. Conditions for patentability; nonobvious subject matter

A patent for a claimed invention may not be obtained, notwithstanding that the claimed invention is not identically disclosed as set forth in section 102, if the differences between the claimed invention and the prior art are such that the claimed invention as a whole would have been obvious before the effective filing date of the claimed invention to a person having ordinary skill in the art to which the claimed invention pertains. Patentability shall not be negated by the manner in which the invention was made.

Related terms: *Graham v. John Deere*; obviousness; person with ordinary skill in the art; statutory subject matter.

Nonpublication Request (NPR)

The U.S. Patent and Trademark Office (USPTO) treats patent applications as confidential, so it is possible to apply for a patent and still maintain the underlying information as a trade secret, at least for the first 18 months of the application period. The USPTO will publish a patent application 18 months after the earliest claimed filing date, but they will not publish it if, at the time of filing, the inventor files a Nonpublication Request (NPR) stating that that it will not be foreign-filed. (The 18-month publication statute was enacted in order to make U.S. patent laws more like those of foreign countries.) If an inventor does not file the NPR, the application will be published after 18 months and the trade secret status of the application will be lost. If the inventor files an NPR and decides later to foreign-file the application, the NPR must be rescinded within 45 days.

If the inventor files an NPR, the information in the patent application becomes publicly available only if and when a patent issues. If the patent is refused so that the application is not published, the competition will not know about the invention and any competitive advantage inherent in that fact can be maintained.

nonstatutory subject matter

To qualify for a patent, an invention must fit into one or more categories established by the federal patent laws (statutes). The categories are compositions of matter, processes, machines, manufactures, and new uses of inventions falling within any of the first four categories. Inventions that don't fall within any of these classes are said to be "nonstatutory subject matter" and are not patentable. Examples of nonstatutory subject matter are:

- processes done entirely by human motor coordination, such as choreographed dance routines
- printed matter that has no unique physical shape or structure associated with it
- naturally occurring matter, even though its external characteristics may be modified, and
- abstract scientific principles, mathematical formulas, and natural laws (algorithms) or ideas that don't produce a useful, concrete, or tangible result.

The term "nonstatutory subject matter" has a second, less obvious meaning: Any invention that doesn't qualify for a patent for any reason is also termed nonstatutory subject matter. So even if an invention fits within one of the five statutory categories above, it would still be considered nonstatutory subject matter if it failed to meet the additional basic patent qualifications of novelty, non-obviousness, and utility.

Related terms: algorithms; genetic engineering and patents; laws of nature exception to patents; naturally occurring substances as nonpatentable; statutory subject matter.

Patent Law: Definitions

not invented here (NIH) syndrome

A handicap to inventors trying to market their inventions is the refusal by many companies to buy, develop, or distribute inventions owned by outside inventors—inventions that are "not invented here."

This all-too-common policy is often attributable to corporate ego: If it wasn't invented here, it can't be any good. But, in addition, it can be the understandable result of the sincere desire to avoid potential and expensive disputes over who owns the patents held or applied for by the company. By never looking at outsiders' inventions, a business can at least partially protect itself from such claims.

Related terms: infringement action; patent owner.

notebook, inventor's

Many inventors maintain a journal in which they record when and how they conceived of an invention and specify all procedures, dates, actions, failures, successes, contacts, and other events that occur in the course of building and testing the invention. Every inventor is advised to maintain such a journal, diary, or notebook, and to have the notebook entries signed, dated, and witnessed as they are made.

A statutory alternative to the patent notebook method of documenting an invention is the Provisional Patent Application (PPA), a program effective June 8, 1995, under which an inventor may submit a full disclosure of his or her invention to the USPTO up to a year prior to filing the actual patent application. A properly filed PPA operates as a (constructive) reduction to practice in case of an interference or conflicting prior art.

Related terms: interference proceeding; Provisional Patent Application (PPA).

notice of allowance

A notice of allowance is sent to an applicant when a patent examiner decides that a patent should issue on an invention (technically, the claims are allowed).

Related terms: office action; prosecution of a patent application.

notice of references cited

This form is sent by the U.S. Patent and Trademark Office (USPTO) to a patent applicant citing the various prior art references used by the USPTO as a basis for rejecting the application's claims. Copies of the references are also enclosed, so the applicant can respond to the rejection by either explaining why they don't apply or by amending the rejected claims.

Related terms: office action; prior art reference; prosecution of a patent application.

novelty

An invention must have novelty to qualify for a patent. In this context, "novelty" means that the invention is different from the prior art (that is, all previous products, devices, methods, and documents describing these things). An invention is considered different from the prior art—and therefore novel—when no single prior art item describes all of the invention's elements. The statute setting out the novelty requirement is 35 United States Code, Section 102.

Even if an invention is novel in that it is different from the prior art, it can still flunk the novelty test if it has been described in a published document or put to public use more than one year prior to a patent application being filed on it (known as the one-year rule).

Note: The one-year rules cited above will, for the most part, terminate in March 2013 when the U.S. switches to a first-to-file system. Patents filed after that date will be subject to new first-to-file and prior art rules, effectively ending centuries of first-to-invent rules. In short, as a general rule for purposes of determining novelty, anything published or sold prior to filing of the application will be considered prior art unless it qualifies under a very limited one-year grace period for certain disclosures. For more information, check the entry for the America Invents Act.

Although an invention may meet the novelty test, it still may be denied a patent if the patent examiner finds that the invention is obvious—that is, it isn't innovative enough to deserve a patent.

§ 102. Conditions for patentability; novelty and loss of right to patent (effective until March 2013)

A person shall be entitled to a patent unless

(a) the invention was known or used by others in this country, or patented or described in a printed publication in this or a foreign country, before the invention thereof by the applicant for patent, or

(b) the invention was patented or described in a printed publication in this or a foreign country or in public use or on sale in this country, more than one year prior to the date of the application for patent in the United States, or

(c) he has abandoned the invention, or

(d) the invention was first patented or caused to be patented, or was the subject of an inventor's certificate, by the applicant or his legal representatives or assigns in a foreign country prior to the date of the application for patent in this country on an application for patent or inventor's certificate filed more than twelve months before the filing of the application in the United States, or

(e) the invention was described in

(1) an application for patent, published under section 122 (b), by another filed in the United States before the invention by the applicant for patent, or

(2) a patent granted on an application for patent by another filed in the United States before the invention by the applicant for patent, except that an international application filed under the treaty defined in section 351 (a) shall have the effects for the purposes of this subsection of an application filed in the United States only if the international application designated the United States and was published under Article 21(2) of such treaty in the English language; or

(f) he did not himself invent the subject matter sought to be patented, or

(g) (1) during the course of an interference conducted under section 135 or section 291, another inventor involved therein establishes, to the extent permitted in section 104, that before such person's invention thereof the invention was made by such other inventor and not abandoned, suppressed, or concealed, or

(2) before such person's invention thereof, the invention was made in this country by another inventor who had not abandoned, suppressed, or concealed it. In determining priority of invention under this subsection, there shall be considered not only the respective dates of conception and reduction to practice of the invention, but also the reasonable diligence of one who was first to conceive and last to reduce to practice, from a time prior to conception by the other.

EFFECTIVE MARCH 2013: § 102 as amended by America Invents Act

Sec. 102. Conditions for patentability; novelty

(a) Novelty; Prior Art- A person shall be entitled to a patent unless—

(1) the claimed invention was patented, described in a printed publication, or in public use, on sale, or otherwise available to the public before the effective filing date of the claimed invention; or

(2) the claimed invention was described in a patent issued under section 151, or in an application for patent published or deemed published under section 122(b), in which the patent or application, as the case may be, names another inventor and was effectively filed before the effective filing date of the claimed invention.

(b) Exceptions—

(1) DISCLOSURES MADE 1 YEAR OR LESS BEFORE THE EFFECTIVE FILING DATE OF THE CLAIMED INVENTION- A disclosure made 1 year or less before the effective filing date of a claimed invention shall not be prior art to the claimed invention under subsection (a)(1) if—

(A) the disclosure was made by the inventor or joint inventor or by another who obtained the subject matter disclosed directly or indirectly from the inventor or a joint inventor; or

(B) the subject matter disclosed had, before such disclosure, been publicly disclosed by the inventor or a joint inventor or another who obtained the subject matter disclosed directly or indirectly from the inventor or a joint inventor.

(2) DISCLOSURES APPEARING IN APPLICATIONS AND PATENTS- A disclosure shall not be prior art to a claimed invention under subsection (a)(2) if—

(A) the subject matter disclosed was obtained directly or indirectly from the inventor or a joint inventor;

(B) the subject matter disclosed had, before such subject matter was effectively filed under subsection (a)(2), been publicly disclosed by the inventor or a joint inventor or another who obtained the subject matter disclosed directly or indirectly from the inventor or a joint inventor; or

(C) the subject matter disclosed and the claimed invention, not later than the effective filing date of the claimed invention, were owned by the same person or subject to an obligation of assignment to the same person.

(c) Common Ownership Under Joint Research Agreements- Subject matter disclosed and a claimed invention shall be deemed to have been owned by the same person or subject to an obligation of assignment to the same person in applying the provisions of subsection (b)(2)(C) if—

(1) the subject matter disclosed was developed and the claimed invention was made by, or on behalf of, 1 or more parties to a joint research agreement that was in effect on or before the effective filing date of the claimed invention;

(2) the claimed invention was made as a result of activities undertaken within the scope of the joint research agreement; and

(3) the application for patent for the claimed invention discloses or is amended to disclose the names of the parties to the joint research agreement.

(d) Patents and Published Applications Effective as Prior Art- For purposes of determining whether a patent or application for patent is prior art to a claimed invention under subsection (a)(2), such patent or application shall be considered to have been effectively filed, with respect to any subject matter described in the patent or application—

(1) if paragraph (2) does not apply, as of the actual filing date of the patent or the application for patent; or

(2) if the patent or application for patent is entitled to claim a right of priority under section 119, 365(a), or 365(b), or to claim the benefit of an earlier filing date under section 120, 121, or 365(c), based upon 1 or more prior filed applications for patent, as of the filing date of the earliest such application that describes the subject matter.

Related terms: anticipation; nonobviousness; one-year rule; prior art.

Patent Law: Definitions

obviousness

The quality of an obvious invention is such that a person with ordinary skill in the art could reasonably believe that, at the time of its conception, the invention was to be expected. An obvious invention (that is, one that lacks the quality of nonobviousness) doesn't qualify for a patent.

> **EXAMPLE:** A new metal that is significantly lighter and stronger than current alloys hits the market. It is "obvious" that someone will build a bicycle containing the material, since lightness is a desirable aspect of high-quality bicycles. Thus, while the inventor of the metal may be entitled to a patent, the developer of the new bicycle made from that metal will not.

Related terms: nonobviousness; person with ordinary skill in the art; prior art.

office action

A letter sent by a patent examiner to an applicant regarding the pending application is called an office action. Generally, one or two office actions are sent per patent application. The first office action typically describes what's wrong with the application and why it can't be allowed. Most often, the first office action rejects the application because of:

- lack of novelty (35 United States Code, Section 102)
- obviousness (35 United States Code, Section 103), or
- claim indefiniteness (35 United States Code, Section 112).

The applicant is permitted to amend the application to overcome the rejection as long as no new subject matter is added. If the application is acceptable as amended, a notice of allowance will be sent (that is, a patent is granted). If the application is still not acceptable, the patent examiner will send a final office action that partially or completely rejects the application.

Related terms: final office action; first office action; prosecution of a patent application.

Official Gazette (OG)

The *Official Gazette* consists of two weekly online publications produced by the U.S. Patent and Trademark Office (USPTO). There is one for trademarks and another for patents. Each is colloquially known as the OG.

The patent edition contains official announcements concerning USPTO policy and patent rules and information on patents issued that week. For each patent, the *Official Gazette* contains:

- its patent number

- all inventors' names and addresses
- the assignee (usually a company to which the inventor has transferred ownership of the patent), if any
- the filing date
- the application's serial number
- the international classification number
- the U.S. classification number
- the main figure or drawing
- the number of claims, and
- a sample claim or abstract.

The *Official Gazette* contains the essence of the invention, not the entire patent. The full text of the patent contains far more technical information.

Anyone wishing to keep up with the patents being issued in a specific field should regularly read the *Official Gazette*. It is now also possible to track issued patents by subscribing to an online new-patent service available through the USPTO's Internet site (www.uspto.gov).

Related terms: abstract; Patent and Trademark Depository Libraries; patent search.

on-sale statutory bar

Part of the one-year rule, the on-sale statutory bar holds that any invention that is placed on sale more than one year before a patent application is filed on it is not eligible for a patent. In this case, the patent is barred by statute from issuing. (35 United States Code, Section 102.)

"On sale" means not only the actual selling, but also any sales effort or solicitation. Such actions are considered public use in violation of the novelty requirement.

Note: The one-year on-sale rule cited above will terminate in March 2013 when the U.S. switches to a first-to-file system. After that date, anything sold prior to filing of the application will be considered prior art. For more information, check the entry for the America Invents Act.

Related terms: anticipation; novelty; one-year rule; statutory bar; public use.

one-year rule

The one-year rule (35 United States Code, Section 102) requires a patent application on an invention to be filed within one year of:

- any public use of the invention by the inventor
- an actual sale of the invention
- an offer to sell the invention, or
- any description of the invention by the inventor in a published document.

Failure to file a patent application within this one-year period results in the invention passing into the public domain. An invention in the public domain is not considered novel and is therefore not eligible for a patent.

The filing of a Provisional Patent Application (PPA) does not trigger the one-year rule for purposes of determining the invention's novelty in the United States but does trigger the one-year period for filing patent applications in other countries. Also, if a regular patent application is not filed within one year of the PPA's filing date, the PPA's date cannot be claimed as the filing date for purposes of deciding whether the invention has been anticipated by prior art or reduced to practice (in case of an interference).

Note: The one-year rule cited above will, with some minor exceptions, terminate in March 2013 when the U.S. switches to a first-to-file system. Patents filed after that date will be subject to new first-to-file and prior art rules, effectively ending centuries of first-to-invent rules. For more information, check the entry for the America Invents Act.

Related terms: anticipation; filing date; novelty; on-sale statutory bar; patent application; Provisional Patent Application (PPA); public use.

online patent searching

See patent search, computerized.

operability

An invention must (theoretically at least) work in order to qualify for a utility patent. Although this does not mean the device must actually be built and working, it does mean that the patent application must disclose sufficient information to demonstrate the theoretical operability of the invention.

A patent examiner who believes an invention will not work (is nonoperable) can require proof of its operability (such as a demonstration) before the patent application will be allowed. However, the fact that a patent has been issued on an invention is not a guarantee that the invention will work—only that it appears on paper to work.

Related terms: disclosure requirement for patents; utility patents.

opposing a patent (international rules)

In most countries, a party may register its opposition to a pending patent application after it has been officially published. If the opposing party can establish that relevant prior art exists, an opposition proceeding is held to determine whether a patent should be issued. This process opens up the initial patent determination to all interested parties.

Related terms: defenses to a patent infringement claim; infringement action; reexamination of patent.

ordinary skill in the art

See person with ordinary skill in the art.

ownership of patent

See patent owner.

PAD

See Patent Application Declaration (PAD).

parent application

During the prosecution of a patent, an applicant may need to file additional applications such as a divisional application, a substitute application, a continuation application, a continuation-in-part application, or an application for a reissue patent. If one of these subsequent applications is filed, the original application will be referred to as the parent application.

> **EXAMPLE:** Rory applies for a patent for a tennis racket with an electronic device embedded in the handle that keeps track of the score. The patent examiner rejects the application because it claims two inventions—the racket/device combination and the device by itself. Rory then restricts his application by withdrawing or canceling the claims to the device itself and files a divisional application on it. In this scenario, the application that now only claims the combination will be considered the parent application.

Related terms: continuation application; divisional application; double patenting; prosecution of a patent application; reissue patent; substitute patent application.

Paris Convention

See Convention application; European Patent Convention.

patent

A patent is a right provided by a government that allows an inventor to prevent others from manufacturing, selling, or using the patent owner's invention. This right covers the invention as specifically described in the patent application's claims allowed by the U.S. Patent and Trademark Office (USPTO) or other patent-examining agencies in other countries.

Physically, a U.S. patent consists of the following:

- a cover sheet bearing the patent number; the name of the invention as provided by the inventor; the name of all inventors; the name of the assignee (the person or company to whom the patent has been assigned), if any; the application filing date; a list of the prior art references found by the patent examiner to be pertinent to the invention; and the patent abstract (a concise summary of the invention)
- one or more pages containing drawings of the invention submitted by the patent applicant
- the patent specification as submitted in the patent application (a detailed narrative description of the invention's structure and function), and
- the patent claims as finally approved by the patent examiner.

The original physical patent issued by the USPTO is termed a "patent deed" or "letters patent" and has a blue ribbon and gold seal for adornment. The physical patent retained by the USPTO and others interested in the patent is often termed a "patent copy" or a "soft copy" and lacks the adornment found on the patent deed. As with a college diploma or deed, the patent in any of its forms has no intrinsic value. The patent derives its value from the offensive rights it provides in the event of an infringement.

Related terms: claims; infringement action; prosecution of a patent application.

patent agents

Patent agents are nonattorneys with technical training who are legally permitted— under a license issued by the U.S. Patent and Trademark Office (USPTO)—to draft, file, and prosecute patent applications on behalf of inventors. If necessary, a patent agent also can represent applicants before the Board of Patent Appeals and Interferences. However, if a patent becomes the subject of litigation in court, only a patent attorney may appear on behalf of the inventor.

Related terms: patent attorneys; patent searcher.

Patent and Trademark Depository Libraries

Over 80 libraries around the United States have been designated as Patent and Trademark Depository Libraries (PTDLs). These public or special libraries contain copies of patents and the reference tools necessary to carry out a reasonably informative U.S. patentability search. A list of PTDLs can be found at the U.S. Patent and Trademark Office (USPTO) website.

Related terms: patent search; patent search, computerized.

Patent and Trademark Office

See U.S. Patent and Trademark Office (USPTO).

patent applicant

The inventor or organization who files the patent application (and, often, who will own the patent if the application is granted) is termed the patent applicant. Patent applicants typically are independent inventors who choose to build and distribute their own inventions, companies to which independent inventors have sold (assigned) their invention, or large R&D companies that employ the actual inventor. Even if an entity other than the inventor will own the patent, the application must be filed in the name of the inventor.

Related terms: coinventors; inventor; patent application; patent owner.

patent application

An inventor must transmit a voluminous packet of documents to the USPTO, either electronically or by mail, to obtain a patent. Usually included in a patent application (and depending on whether it is filed electronically or via mail) are:
- a self-addressed receipt postcard
- a transmittal letter
- a check for the filing fee
- a fee transmittal form
- drawings
- a specification (a sample is provided in the Forms section at the end of this part of the book)
- one or more patent claims
- an abstract
- a Patent Application Declaration (PAD), and
- an Information Disclosure Statement (IDS).

Patent Law: Definitions

A regular patent application can also include a Petition to Make Special (to speed the processing), an assignment and assignment cover sheet (if the invention was sold by its owner), a Disclosure Document Reference Letter (if a disclosure document was previously filed with the USPTO), and a transmittal letter claiming the Provisional Patent Application filing date, if a PPA was filed.

One to two weeks after the application is mailed, the applicant will receive the receipt post card back from the USPTO with the filing date and number stamped on it. The filing date applies to this application and will provide the starting date for determining the patent term (20 years from date of filing). However, if a Provisional Patent Application was filed, its filing date will provide the basis for determining the invention's novelty and deciding any interference that is declared by the USPTO.

The receipt of the post card means that the USPTO has established a separate file (called a file wrapper) in which the application and all future correspondence between the applicant and the USPTO are kept.

An inventor can also file a patent application electronically with the USPTO's Electronic Filing System (EFS-Web). Using it you can (1) file an application anytime and from anywhere that has Internet access, (2) obtain instant confirmation of receipt of documents by the PTO, (3) send an application to the PTO without having to go to the post office to get an Express Mail receipt or having to wait for a postcard receipt, and (4) file an application without having to prepare an application transmittal, a fee transmittal, receipt postcard, or check or Credit Card Payment Form (CCPF).

Once a regular patent application is on file, the applicant is said to be in the patent prosecution stage, which averages 18 months but which can take much longer in specific cases.

Related terms: electronic filing of patent applications; prosecution of a patent application; Provisional Patent Application (PPA).

Patent Application Declaration (PAD)

A Patent Application Declaration (PAD) is a written statement, made under penalty of perjury, that must accompany a patent application. In the statement, the patent applicant states (avers) that:

- The applicant is the first and true inventor.
- The applicant has reviewed and understands the specification and claims.
- The applicant has disclosed all information material to the examination of the application.

Related terms: duty of candor and good faith; fraud on the U.S. Patent and Trademark Office; patent application; prosecution of a patent application.

patent attorneys

Patent attorneys must be licensed to practice law and also be licensed by the U.S. Patent and Trademark Office (USPTO) to practice before it. Patent attorneys prepare and prosecute patent applications, represent clients in interference proceedings, and bring and defend patent-related lawsuits in federal court.

Patent attorneys are required to have a technical higher education degree as well as a legal background and must pass a USPTO examination in order to obtain their license. A complete listing of all licensed patent attorneys can be obtained in the USPTO publication "Attorneys and Agents Registered to Practice Before the U.S. Patent and Trademark Office."

Related terms: infringement action; interference; patent agents.

patent claim

See claims.

Patent Cooperation Treaty (PCT)

This international agreement establishes streamlined procedures for obtaining uniform patent protection in its member countries. The PCT is administered by the World Intellectual Property Organization (WIPO) in Geneva, Switzerland. U.S. inventors applying for PCT patent protection can file with the U.S. Patent and Trademark Office, which has been designated a receiving office of the International Bureau.

In addition to filing the one PCT application, an inventor must still file a national patent application in every country in which patent protection is desired. However, the primary advantages of using PCT's procedures are as follows:

- By filing one PCT application, the applicant obtains a filing date that is good in every member country in which he or she ultimately seeks patent protection.
- An initial international patent search is conducted on the PCT application, and the member countries will rely heavily on this search. Thus, the applicant is saved the great expense and delay that can result from having to conduct separate searches in each country and convince each country's patent examining agency that an invention is novel and nonobvious over the prior art.

Patent Law: Definitions

- The PCT applicant need not decide whether to prosecute the international application in the individual countries until 18 months after the initial patent application filing date in his or her original country.

For more specific information on filing under the Patent Cooperation Treaty, a booklet called the "PCT Applicant's Guide" can be obtained from the World Intellectual Property Organization (www.wipo.org).

Related terms: International Bureau of the World Intellectual Property Organization; international patent protection for U.S. inventions.
See also Part 4 (Trade Secret Law): World Intellectual Property Organization (WIPO).

patent deed

This official document, sometimes termed "letters patent," is sent to applicants by the U.S. Patent and Trademark Office when their patent issues.

Related terms: final office action; notice of allowance; patent.

patent examination process

See prosecution of a patent application.

patent examiners

U.S. Patent and Trademark Office examiners are employees who examine patent and trademark applications. On the patent side, the examiners correspond with applicants and decide whether inventions deserve patents. All patent examiners must have a technical degree in some field, such as electrical engineering, chemistry, or physics. Many are also attorneys.

Related terms: U.S. Patent and Trademark Office (USPTO).

patent infringement action

See infringement action.

patent issue fees

See issue fee.

patent license agreements

See exclusive patent license; nonexclusive patent license.

patent misuse

Use of a patent in a manner that violates federal patent or antitrust laws may result in the patent being declared invalid or unenforceable by a court. Most often, the issue of patent misuse is raised as a defense to a patent infringement action. If the court in such an action finds that the patent was misused, it will not enforce the patent unless the owner can show that the misuse was involuntary and completely cured ("purged"). If the misuse was an antitrust violation, however, no such cure is possible and the patent will simply be declared invalid.

In 2010, the Federal Circuit narrowed the scope of patent misuse in a case involving compact disc patents. Under the Federal Circuit's new standard, there must be evidence of anticompetitive effects associated in addition to restrictions on use. Alleging wrongful conduct is not enough. (*Princo Corp. v. International Trade Commission*, 616 F.3d 1318 (Fed. Cir. 2010).)

Related terms: antitrust law (federal) and patents; breaking (or busting) a patent; defenses to a patent infringement claim; infringement, patent.

patent number

The number assigned to each patent by the U.S. Patent and Trademark Office is known as the patent number.

Related terms: marking of an invention.

patent number marking

See marking of an invention.

patent owner

The inventor is usually the patent owner unless the invention and patent rights were assigned (ownership rights were transferred to another person or entity—for instance, because the invention arose in the course of an employment relationship).

Many inventors assign ownership of their invention to development or manufacturing companies in exchange for compensation in the form of a lump sum or royalties on sales realized from the invention. These assignments typically also include ownership of the patent, whether already issued or to be issued in the future.

Large companies, and often universities and laboratories, usually require employees to assign their future inventions to the institution as a condition of employment. Under these assignments, the institution will be considered the patent owner. In some states, such requirements are prohibited for inventions that:
- were made on the employee's own time
- did not involve the use of the employer's equipment, supplies, facilities, or trade secret information, and

- do not relate to the business of the employer and do not result from any work prepared by the employee for the employer or relate to the employer's actual or demonstrably anticipated research or development.

Even if an inventor retains the right to the invention and is therefore considered the patent owner, employers retain the right (called "shop rights") to make and use an invention created in the course of the employment relationship and with the employer's tools and facilities.

Related terms: assignment of a patent; coinventors; shop rights.

patent pending

Once a patent application (regular or provisional) has been filed in the U.S. Patent and Trademark Office, the invention has patent pending status. The inventor can then mark the device "patent pending" to deter potential competitors from copying it by informing them that it may soon receive a patent. However, unless and until a patent is actually issued, an inventor has no right to prevent others from making, using, and selling the invention. In other words, simply applying for a patent does not earn the applicant the right to behave like a patent owner.

However, under the new 18-month publication statute (see "confidentiality of patent applications"), an inventor whose application is published prior to issuance may obtain royalties from an infringer from the date the application is published. There are two requirements: (1) the application later issues as a patent, and (2) the infringer had actual notice of the published application. (35 United States Code, Sections 122, 154.) An infringer will have actual notice of a publication if he or she sees the published application. This can be accomplished by sending a copy to the infringer by registered mail. Otherwise, the inventor has no rights whatsoever against infringers during the pendency period.

The patent pending label can also provide a way for an inventor to show the invention to a potential developer without fear that the developer will rip it off and later claim to be the true inventor. This is especially useful when a developer refuses to sign a nondisclosure agreement for fear of a later lawsuit by the inventor.

Before June 8, 1995, obtaining patent pending status involved the considerable expense of preparing and filing a full patent application. Under the Provisional Patent Application program, however, patent pending status costs considerably less ($100 for small entities, current as of April 2007).

Related terms: marking of an invention; not invented here (NIH) syndrome; office action; opposing a patent (international rules); Provisional Patent Application (PPA).

patent pools

Under a patent pool arrangement between two or more companies, the companies assign (sell) their patents to a third party which, in turn, licenses any or all of the patents back to participating companies. This allows the participating companies to share their patents by providing them with access to each other's patents on a reciprocal basis.

Patent pools run a substantial risk of violating the antitrust laws in the event they are not open to all competitors in a particular industry.

Related terms: antitrust law (federal) and patents; concerted refusal to deal; cross-licensing; patent thickets.

patent prosecution

See prosecution of patent application.

patent search

The term "patent search" generally means a search for documents that will help one decide whether a particular invention was novel and nonobvious when it was invented. While a patent search usually starts with the patent database (all previously issued patents), it also covers other types of documents that may describe the invention being searched, such as journal articles and scientific papers.

There are normally three discrete types of patent searches:

- **Patentability searches.** This kind of search is normally conducted by, or on behalf of, an inventor to familiarize the inventor with previous developments in the field of invention and to help the inventor determine whether it is worthwhile to develop the invention and/or apply for a patent in the first place. Also, once a patent application is filed, the U.S. Patent and Trademark Office will conduct its own patentability search in the course of examining the application.
- **Infringement searches.** An infringement search is usually much narrower in scope than a patentability search and is conducted for the purpose of deciding whether a particular invention will infringe an in-force patent.
- **Validity searches.** This search is usually conducted by the defendant in a patent infringement case for the purpose of discovering documents that will adversely bear on the validity of the patent as issued.

Related terms: infringement search; nonobviousness; novelty; Patent and Trademark Depository Library (PTDL); patent search, computerized; patent searcher; patentability search; prior art; validity search.

patent search, computerized

All patents issued by the U.S. Patent and Trademark office (USPTO) since 1972 now are available online through a number of different public and private services. The USPTO website (www.uspto.gov) is a free online full-text searchable database of patents and drawings that covers the period from January 1976 to the most recent weekly issue date.

In addition, you can search the USPTO database with a speedier search engine using **Google Patent Search** (www.google.com/patents). Google has entered the free patent searching business by converting the entire image database of U.S. patents (from 1790 to the present) in a format that's easy to search. At the time this book went to press, it did not include patent applications, international patents, or U.S. patents issued over the last few months, but the company plans to expand coverage in the future.

Below are several fee-based patent search engines:

- **Delphion (www.delphion.com).** The Delphion website has evolved from the former IBM patent website. The site offers U.S. patents searchable from 1971 to the present (and it is expected to add pre-1971 patents), as well as full-text patents from the European Patent Office, the World Intellectual Property Organization PCT collection, and abstracts from Derwent World Patent Index (which includes 40 international patent-issuing authorities).
- **Micropatent (www.micropatent.com).** Micropatent offers U.S. and Japanese patents searchable from 1976 to the present, international PCT patents from 1983, European patents from 1988, and the *Official Gazette* for patents.
- **LexPat (www.lexis-nexis.com).** This site provides U.S. patents searchable from 1971 to the present. In addition, the LEXPAT library offers extensive prior-art searching capability of technical journals and magazines.
- **Pantros IP (www.patentcafe.com).** The Decision Support System offers various levels of patent research and reports.
- **PatBase (www.patbase.com).** PatBase is a relatively new database that can search back to the 1800s through many nations' patents, and permits batch downloading.

The services described above are all accessible from a personal computer connected to the Internet. USPTO computer databases can also be accessed through the terminals at the USPTO and through the APS Search terminals at 32 of the Patent Trademark Deposit Libraries (PTDLs) listed at the USPTO website.

All prior art is relevant to a patent application—even patents that were issued decades ago and that have long since expired. For this reason, it may be necessary

Patent Law: Definitions

to search for pre-1972 patents as well as the patents in the computer database—all of which were issued after that date. This would especially be true for gadget-type inventions that might resemble something invented hundreds of years ago. For instance, the finger grooves in certain types of old swords were considered relevant prior art for the finger indentations found in many modern automobile steering wheels.

Pre-1972 patents are not normally relevant to patent searches involving inventions based on modern technologies such as computers and software, integrated circuits, superconductivity, nanotechnology, artificial intelligence, robotics, and bioengineering. For these types of inventions, an online computer search should do the entire job.

Two other Internet sources of information are:

- **Software Patent Institute (www.spi.org)**, which maintains, catalogs, and has the best software prior art database in the world. The SPI also likes to receive prior art on software inventions, such as old instruction books and manuals.

- **Source Translation and Optimization Patent Website (www.bustpatents.com)**, which is directed by Gregory Aharonian, one of the USPTO's most vocal critics. The site provides a free email newsletter, critiques, legal reviews, file wrappers, and information about infringement lawsuits relating to software patents.

Computerized patent searches are usually carried out by typing certain key words at a computer terminal and instructing the computer to produce a list of all patents that contain those words in the order that you specify. For example, if your search involves a bicycle chain, you might ask for a listing of all patents that contain the words "bicycle" and "chain," where "bicycle" comes before "chain." When the list appears on your terminal, you can then view the full text of any entry on the list or any selected portion (such as the abstract of patent, drawing, claims, or specification).

If you find that no patent contains the words "bicycle" and "chain" in that order, then you will need to reformulate your request (try "bipedal vehicle" and "wheel pulling device"). Often it takes a number of attempts to cover all possible words used in all relevant patents. Unless you come up with all the correct words, you may miss patents and thus perform an incomplete search.

A copy of a patent can be acquired by:

- contacting the USPTO by phone or fax, ordering from the USPTO website, or writing a letter listing the number of the patent to Commissioner for

Patent Law: Definitions

Patents, Washington, DC 20231, along with a payment for the price per patent (see the Fee Schedule at the USPTO website) times the total number of patents being ordered

- downloading a text copy or image copy of the patent, if available, from the Delphion, Google, or USPTO search sites, or
- ordering a copy from a private supply company such as PatentFetcher (www.patentfetcher.com), or Micropatent (www.micropatent.com).

Related terms: classification of patents; patent search; Patent and Trademark Depository Libraries.

patent searcher

A number of individuals and firms specialize in conducting patent searches. In the United States, patent searchers tend to be concentrated in Washington, DC, and Virginia, because the U.S. Patent and Trademark Office (USPTO) library is located nearby and it is therefore the best place to conduct a patent search.

There are three options for getting a patent search done by someone else:

- patent attorneys
- patent agents, and
- lay searchers.

Patent attorneys usually have their favorite searchers and can help you assess the results of the search. However, this is the most expensive option.

A less costly option is a patent agent. Patent agents are licensed by the USPTO and have demonstrated their competence by passing a USPTO-administered test.

The least expensive option is a lay searcher. However, lay searchers are not licensed, and you should be careful when selecting one to do your search.

The yellow pages are a good place to locate a patent searcher. Look under "patent searcher" for lay searchers and under "attorney," "legal," or "lawyer" for patent attorneys and patent agents.

Related terms: patent agents; patent attorneys; patent search.

patent term extension

Under 35 United States Code, Sections 155 and 156, the statutory period during which a patent is in force can be extended if the inventor's ability to realize gain from the invention will be adversely affected by a regulatory process. For instance, a new drug or food may be withheld from the market for a number of years because of a requirement that the Food and Drug Administration must approve such items as safe and effective.

Related terms: duration of patents; in-force patent.

patent thickets

A patent thicket is a collection of patents—often owned by different companies—that must be licensed in order to commercialize a new technology. The name refers to the fact that new companies in a tech industry must "hack" their way through in order to get in the marketplace. For example, companies performing gene research often encounter a network of overlapping patent rights. A patent thicket has the effect of limiting the players in an industry and, because of that, it raises antitrust concerns.

Related terms: antitrust law (federal) and patents.

patent troll

"Patent troll" is a disparaging term for someone who sues for patent infringement but who does not make or sell any products using the patented technology. In other words, the patent troll is in the business of suing companies, not in the business of making or selling anything. A friendlier term for the practice is "patent assertion company." Patent trolls are sometimes disliked because they seek licensing fees that are disproportionate to the patent's value, often because they are well funded and can afford litigation costs (while their opponents cannot).

In a case that affected the dynamics of patent troll litigation, eBay was sued by a company that owned several auction patents. The patent owner sought a permanent injunction, which was granted by the Court of Appeals for the Federal Circuit (CAFC). Patent trolls typically rely on the fear of permanent injunctions to elicit licensing fees. eBay appealed the case, and the Supreme Court determined that courts should not automatically issue an injunction based on a finding of patent infringement. (Alternatively, an injunction should not be denied simply on the basis that the plaintiff does not make, sell, or use the patented invention.) Instead, a federal court must still weigh the four factors traditionally used to determine if an injunction should be granted. The case is seen as a blow to patent trolls. (*eBay v. MercExchange, L.L.C.*, 126 S.Ct. 1837 (2006).)

patentability

Not all inventions qualify for a patent. To qualify for a utility patent, an invention must:

- fit within one of the five statutory subject matter classes
- have novelty

Patent Law: Definitions

- be nonobvious, and
- have some usefulness.

To qualify for a plant patent, the plant must meet the first three of these tests. To qualify for a design patent, the novel features of a design must meet the first three qualifications and must be purely ornamental (have no practical function other than ornamental).

Related terms: nonstatutory subject matter; statutory subject matter.

patentability search

Once an invention is conceived, the inventor will normally conduct (or have conducted) a search of previous and existing patents and other documents that might describe the invention to discover whether the invention is novel and nonobvious enough over the prior art to qualify for a patent. A search conducted for this purpose is commonly termed a patentability search. The primary reason for a patentability search is to avoid wasting time and money developing an invention that is not patentable.

Related terms: classification of patents; novelty; patent search; patent search, computerized; patent searcher; prior art reference.

patentable subject matter

See statutory subject matter.

patents as prior art

All patents, whether expired or in force, and whether issued in the United States or in other countries, are considered prior art when determining whether an invention qualifies for a patent.

Related terms: anticipation; prior art; prior art reference.

PCT

See Patent Cooperation Treaty (PCT).

person with ordinary skill in the art

This is a hypothetical person whose educational or occupational credentials would make him or her competent in the field of the invention. For example, an electrical engineer would be a person with ordinary skill with respect to integrated circuits, whereas a prosthetics engineer would be a person with ordinary skill in the art of designing knee braces.

How this hypothetical person would view a particular invention is used as a standard to make some important determinations. Among the questions that must be answered in deciding whether a patent should issue, or whether an in-force patent is valid, are:

- whether a person with ordinary skill in the art would find the invention an obvious development in light of the relevant prior art (the technology and knowledge existing at the time the invention was first conceived), and
- whether the patent application sufficiently discloses the nature of the invention to permit a person with ordinary skill in the art to build it in a routine manner.

Related terms: disclosure requirement for patents; *Graham v. John Deere*; nonobviousness.

Petition to Make Special

An applicant can, under certain circumstances, have an application examined sooner than the normal course of USPTO examination (one to three years). Prior to 2008, this was accomplished by filing a "petition to make special" (PTMS), together with a supporting declaration. In 2007, the USPTO introduced a process for filing petitions to make special (PTMS) known as the Accelerated Examination Program (AEP). Under the new procedures, the USPTO will advance an application out of turn for examination if the applicant files a grantable petition to make special under the accelerated examination program (AEP). The USPTO is similarly revising the procedures for other petitions to make special, except those based on the applicant's health or age. Other petitions to make special (i.e., based on manufacture, infringement, environmental quality, energy, recombinant DNA, superconductivity materials, HIV/AIDS and cancer, countering terrorism, and biotechnology applications filed by small entities; see MPEP § 708.02) will be processed using the revised AEP procedure. AEP requires that an applicant file electronically using EFS-Web and Form SB28 at the same time. For more information, see www.uspto.gov/web/patents/accelerated.

Related terms: patent applicant; patent application.

plant patents

Since 1930, the United States has been granting plant patents under the Plant Patent Act to any person who first appreciates the distinctive qualities of a plant and reproduces it asexually. Asexual reproduction means reproducing the plant by a means other than seeds, usually by grafting or cloning the plant tissue. If a plant cannot be duplicated by asexual reproduction, it cannot be the subject of a plant patent. In addition, the patented plant must also be novel and distinctive. Generally, this means that the plant must have at least one significant distinguishing characteristic to establish it as a distinct variety. For example, a rose may be novel and distinctive if it is nearly thornless and has a unique two-tone color scheme. Tuber-propagated plants (such as potatoes) and plants found in an uncultivated state cannot receive a plant patent. (35 United States Code, Sections 161–164.)

There is a limit on the extent of plant patent rights. Generally, a plant patent can only be infringed when a plant has been asexually reproduced from the actual plant protected by the plant patent. In other words, the infringing plant must have more than similar characteristics—it must have the same genetics as the patented plant.

A human-made plant can also be the subject of a utility patent. These plants can be reproduced either sexually (by seeds) or asexually. For example, utility patents have been issued for elements of plants such as proteins, genes, DNA, buds, pollen, fruit, plant-based chemicals, and the processes used in the manufacture of these plant products. To obtain a utility patent, the plant must be made by humans and must fit within the statutory requirements (utility, novelty, and nonobviousness). The patent must describe and claim the specific characteristics of the plant for which protection is sought. Sometimes the best way to meet this requirement is to deposit seeds or plant tissue at a specified public depository. For example, many countries have international depositories for such purposes.

Although a utility patent is harder and more time-consuming to acquire than a plant patent, a utility patent is considered to be a stronger form of protection. For example, a plant protected by a utility patent can be infringed if it is reproduced either sexually or asexually. Since the utility patent owner can prevent others from making and using the invention, does this mean the purchaser of a patented seed cannot sell the resulting plants to the public? No, under patent laws, the purchaser can sell the plants but cannot manufacture the seed line.

Related terms: genetic engineering and patents; nonstatutory subject matter.

Plant Variety Protection Act

This statute authorizes the U.S. Department of Agriculture to grant patent protection for certain types of plants.

Related terms: plant patents.

practicing an invention

See reduction to practice; working a patent.

preinvention assignments

Some employment agreements have a provision requiring the employee to assign any inventions to the employer. Because these employment agreements are signed before the employee creates the invention, they are sometimes referred to as preinvention assignments.

To protect employees, eight states, including California, impose restrictions on the permissible scope of assignments of employee-created inventions. These restrictions apply only to "inventions" an employee creates—that is, items for which a patent is sought. These limitations on employee invention assignments are usually not very generous to employees. The only inventions an employee can't be required to assign to the employer are true independent inventions—those that are developed completely without company resources and that don't relate to the employee's work or the employer's current business or anticipated future business. The following states impose restrictions:

- California (California Labor Code § 2870)
- Delaware (Delaware Code Annotated, Title 19, § 805)
- Illinois (Illinois Revised Statutes, Chapter 140, §§ 301–303)
- Kansas (Kansas Statutes Annotated §§ 44–130)
- Minnesota (Minnesota Statutes Annotated § 181.78)
- North Carolina (North Carolina General Statutes §§ 66-57.1, 66-57.2)
- Utah (Utah Code Annotated §§ 34-39-2, 34-39-3), and
- Washington (Washington Revised Code Annotated §§ 49.44.140, 49.44.150).

In a 2010 case, the Federal Circuit ruled that an employment agreement is not conclusive as to a preinvention assignment. A scientist signed an employee invention agreement that required that inventions created during employment would belong to his employer unless:

(1) the invention was developed entirely on his own time;

(2) equipment, supplies, facility, or trade secret of the Company was not used in its development, and

(3) it does not relate to the business or actual or demonstrably anticipated research or development of the Company, or it does not result from any work performed by [him] for the Company.

The scientist invented a method of sequencing DNA on his own time using his home computer and without the assistance of any company trade secrets. The Federal Circuit determined that under California law, the scientist need only meet either of the two requirements established in the third criterion. The court determined the invention did not result from work performed for the company and on that basis, there was no assignment. (*Applera Corp. Applied Biosystems Group v. Illumina, Inc.*, 2009-1260, 2010 WL 1169936 (Fed. Cir. Mar. 25, 2010).)

preliminary look at prior art

This preliminary investigation by inventors consists of checking stores, catalogs, reference books, product directories, and similar sources to discover whether a proposed invention already exists. Such preliminary looks should be done before investing time and money developing an invention.

If a preliminary look finds no relevant previous development, then work on the invention may be initiated, with a more serious patentability search to follow before significant resources are expended.

Related terms: patent search; patentability search.

presumption of validity

In an infringement suit brought by a patent owner against an alleged infringer, it is legally presumed that the patent owner's patent is valid. Practically, this means the legal responsibility (burden) is on the alleged infringer to prove that the patent is invalid, if he or she wants to raise this defense.

Related terms: defenses to a patent infringement claim; infringement action.

price fixing

If two or more separate businesses enter into an agreement (formal or informal) to maintain their prices at a certain level, it is known as price fixing. Price fixing is considered a restraint of trade, which is a violation of the antitrust laws. A patent owner who uses the patent monopoly for the purpose of fixing prices may also be deemed guilty of misusing the patent and accordingly lose the patent rights.

Related terms: antitrust law (federal) and patents; concerted refusal to deal; patent misuse.

printed publication as statutory bar

Under patent law, published writings are considered prior art references, so a previous publication that discusses or describes the essential ideas, functional means, or structures that underlie an invention can render that invention ineligible for a patent (the patent is barred by statute from issuing). This will happen if the article describing the invention was published:

- by someone other than the inventor any time before the date of the invention, or
- by the inventor (or someone else) more than one year before the patent application for the patent was filed.

Related terms: anticipation; one-year rule; statutory bar; thesis as prior art.

prior art

"Prior art" refers to all previous developments that are used by the U.S. Patent and Trademark Office and the courts (in the event of an infringement action) to decide whether a particular invention is sufficiently novel and nonobvious to qualify for a U.S. patent.

Prior art relevant to a particular invention generally includes:

- any published writing (including any patent) that was publicly available either (1) before the date of invention, or (2) over one year before the patent application filing date
- any U.S. patent that has a filing date earlier than the date of invention
- any relevant invention or development (whether described in writing or not) existing prior to the date the invention was conceived, or
- any public or commercial use, sale, or knowledge of the invention more than one year prior to the application filing date.

Any specific instance of prior art is generally referred to as a prior art reference.

Note: The one-year rules cited above will, for the most part, terminate in March 2013 when the U.S. switches to a first-to-file system. Patents filed after this date will be subject to new first-to-file and prior art rules, effectively ending centuries of first-to-invent rules. Anything published or sold prior to filing of the application will be considered prior art unless it qualifies under a very limited one-year grace period for certain disclosures. For more information, check the entry for the America Invents Act.

§ 102. Conditions for patentability; novelty and loss of right to patent (effective until March 2013)

A person shall be entitled to a patent unless

(a) the invention was known or used by others in this country, or patented or described in a printed publication in this or a foreign country, before the invention thereof by the applicant for patent, or

(b) the invention was patented or described in a printed publication in this or a foreign country or in public use or on sale in this country, more than one year prior to the date of the application for patent in the United States, or

(c) he has abandoned the invention, or

(d) the invention was first patented or caused to be patented, or was the subject of an inventor's certificate, by the applicant or his legal representatives or assigns in a foreign country prior to the date of the application for patent in this country on an application for patent or inventor's certificate filed more than twelve months before the filing of the application in the United States, or

(e) the invention was described in

(1) an application for patent, published under section 122 (b), by another filed in the United States before the invention by the applicant for patent, or

(2) a patent granted on an application for patent by another filed in the United States before the invention by the applicant for patent, except that an international application filed under the treaty defined in section 351 (a) shall have the effects for the purposes of this subsection of an application filed in the United States only if the international application designated the United States and was published under Article 21(2) of such treaty in the English language; or

(f) he did not himself invent the subject matter sought to be patented, or

(g) (1) during the course of an interference conducted under section 135 or section 291, another inventor involved therein establishes, to the extent permitted in section 104, that before such person's invention thereof the invention was made by such other inventor and not abandoned, suppressed, or concealed, or

(2) before such person's invention thereof, the invention was made in this country by another inventor who had not abandoned, suppressed, or concealed it. In determining priority of invention under this subsection, there shall be considered not only the respective dates of conception and reduction to practice of the invention, but also the reasonable diligence of one who was first to conceive and last to reduce to practice, from a time prior to conception by the other.

EFFECTIVE MARCH 2013: § 102 as amended by America Invents Act

Sec. 102. Conditions for patentability; novelty

(a) Novelty; Prior Art- A person shall be entitled to a patent unless—

(1) the claimed invention was patented, described in a printed publication, or in public use, on sale, or otherwise available to the public before the effective filing date of the claimed invention; or

(2) the claimed invention was described in a patent issued under section 151, or in an application for patent published or deemed published under section 122(b), in which the patent or application, as the case may be, names another inventor and was effectively filed before the effective filing date of the claimed invention.

(b) Exceptions—

    (1) DISCLOSURES MADE 1 YEAR OR LESS BEFORE THE EFFECTIVE FILING DATE OF THE CLAIMED INVENTION- A disclosure made 1 year or less before the effective filing date of a claimed invention shall not be prior art to the claimed invention under subsection (a)(1) if—

        (A) the disclosure was made by the inventor or joint inventor or by another who obtained the subject matter disclosed directly or indirectly from the inventor or a joint inventor; or

        (B) the subject matter disclosed had, before such disclosure, been publicly disclosed by the inventor or a joint inventor or another who obtained the subject matter disclosed directly or indirectly from the inventor or a joint inventor.

    (2) DISCLOSURES APPEARING IN APPLICATIONS AND PATENTS- A disclosure shall not be prior art to a claimed invention under subsection (a)(2) if—

        (A) the subject matter disclosed was obtained directly or indirectly from the inventor or a joint inventor;

        (B) the subject matter disclosed had, before such subject matter was effectively filed under subsection (a)(2), been publicly disclosed by the inventor or a joint inventor or another who obtained the subject matter disclosed directly or indirectly from the inventor or a joint inventor; or

        (C) the subject matter disclosed and the claimed invention, not later than the effective filing date of the claimed invention, were owned by the same person or subject to an obligation of assignment to the same person.

(c) Common Ownership Under Joint Research Agreements- Subject matter disclosed and a claimed invention shall be deemed to have been owned by the same person or subject to an obligation of assignment to the same person in applying the provisions of subsection (b)(2)(C) if—

    (1) the subject matter disclosed was developed and the claimed invention was made by, or on behalf of, 1 or more parties to a joint research agreement that was in effect on or before the effective filing date of the claimed invention;

    (2) the claimed invention was made as a result of activities undertaken within the scope of the joint research agreement; and

    (3) the application for patent for the claimed invention discloses or is amended to disclose the names of the parties to the joint research agreement.

(d) Patents and Published Applications Effective as Prior Art- For purposes of determining whether a patent or application for patent is prior art to a claimed invention under subsection (a)(2), such patent or application shall be considered to have been effectively filed, with respect to any subject matter described in the patent or application—

    (1) if paragraph (2) does not apply, as of the actual filing date of the patent or the application for patent; or

(2) if the patent or application for patent is entitled to claim a right of priority under section 119, 365(a), or 365(b), or to claim the benefit of an earlier filing date under section 120, 121, or 365(c), based upon 1 or more prior filed applications for patent, as of the filing date of the earliest such application that describes the subject matter.

Related terms: anticipation; nonobviousness; novelty; patentability; prior art reference.

prior art reference

Any printed publication, prior patent, or other document that contains a discussion or description relevant to an invention for which a patent is currently being sought or enforced is a prior art reference.

When applying for a patent, an applicant who knows of any prior art references is required to submit an Information Disclosure Statement (IDS) in which all such references must be listed, and to which copies of these references must be appended.

In the event a patent examiner rejects one or more claims on the ground they are anticipated by (or are obvious over) the prior art, the U.S. Patent and Trademark Office sends out a Notice of Prior Art References, with copies of the actual references attached, which identifies the prior art references upon which the rejection is based.

Related terms: anticipation; Information Disclosure Statement; prior art.

processes (or methods) as patentable subject matter

Ways of doing or making things (termed processes or methods) are one of the five categories of statutory subject matter—that is, types of inventions that can be patented. Processes always have at least two steps, each of which expresses some activity or occurrence. Examples of processes include heat-treatment processes, chemical reactions, surgical techniques, gene-splicing procedures, applied robotics, and computer software.

To be patentable, a process must produce a useful, concrete, and tangible result.

Related terms: nonstatutory subject matter; software patents; statutory subject matter.

product-by-process claim

A patent claim for a product that is defined in terms of the method (or the manipulative steps) used to manufacture the product. Even though product-by-process claims are limited by, and defined by, the process, their patentability is based on the product itself (because the patentability of a product does not depend on its method of production). If the product in the product-by-process claim is the same as or obvious from a product of the prior art, the claim is unpatentable even though the prior product was made by a different process. (*In re Thorpe,* 777 F.2d 695 (Fed. Cir. 1985).) Previously, the use of a product-by-process claim was limited to situations where the product could not be defined or distinguished from the prior art except by reference to the process of creating the product. The Court of Appeals for the Federal Circuit ruled that in an infringement analysis, a product-by-process claim would be limited by the process in the claim. (*Abbott Labs v. Sandoz,* 566 F.3d 1282 (Fed Cir. 2009).) *See also* MPEP 2113 (Product-by-Process Claims).

prosecution of a patent application

Once a regular patent application has been filed, the full gamut of procedures that must be followed to actually obtain the patent is referred to as the prosecution of a patent application. (The patent prosecution process does not apply to Provisional Patent Applications (PPAs).)

The first step in the patent prosecution process is when a U.S. Patent and Trademark Office (USPTO) patent examiner who has been assigned to the application sends the applicant a written form (called the first office action), which sometimes takes place up to a year after the application is received. This form will typically deny all or most of the application's claims on a variety of grounds.

If the rejection was due to lack of novelty (35 United States Code, Section 102), the office action will identify the reasons. If the rejection was due to obviousness over the relevant prior art (35 United States Code, Section 103), the office action will list the prior art references in a Notice of Prior Art References. In both Sections 102 and 103 rejections, the USPTO will attach copies of the relevant prior art references and designate the claims to which the references pertain.

Note: If a valid PPA was previously filed on the invention, and the PPA filing date is claimed in the regular patent application, the examiner will use that earlier date to assess the prior art and only base a rejection on prior art references that came before it.

Claims also may be rejected under 35 United States Code, Section 112, because they are too broad or are formulated incorrectly. If so, the inventor will be provided the opportunity to make amendments suggested by the examiner. On occasion, the patent examiner will determine that the application impermissibly claims two or more inventions. In this case, the applicant will be informed in the first office action that he or she must "elect" (choose to include) the claims covering one of the inventions in the original (parent) application and optionally file one or more divisional applications for the nonelected claims (the ones that weren't kept in the parent application) that recite the additional inventions.

Sometimes, an inventor will improve his or her invention while the application is pending or will want to broaden or better define the claims. If so, he or she can file a continuation-in-part (CIP) application incorporating the changes.

Whatever the recommendations made by the patent examiner and the reasons given for the claims being rejected, the applicant must either file a response to the first office action within three months or pay a fee and obtain up to a three-month extension. If he or she fails to do either, the application will be deemed abandoned.

Once the applicant has responded, the patent examiner will respond again, usually with a final office action. This will either reject all of the claims with suggested modifications that would make them allowable or reject some of the claims and accept others. If amended claims are rejected on anticipation or obviousness grounds, any pertinent prior art references that were not cited the first time around will be listed (and copies sent). Suggestions may also be made for how to narrow claims that are too broad.

After the final office action, the applicant has five basic choices:

- amend the claims as suggested by the patent examiner
- request that the patent examiner reconsider one or more of the decisions contained in the final office action
- appeal to the Board of Patent Appeals and Interferences
- file a continuation application (essentially a new application with new claims, with the benefit of the original filing date for the purpose of determining the effect of relevant prior art references), or
- file a Request for Continued Examination (RCE), which effectively removes the final action so that the applicant can submit further amendments, for example, new claims, new arguments, a new declaration, or new references.

Whatever the choice, it must be done within three months of the final office action, or up to a three-month extension must be obtained. Otherwise, the application will be deemed legally abandoned. If the application has not been published by the USPTO, it won't serve as a prior art reference after being abandoned—unless a defensive publication is made by the applicant.

Assuming that the final action results in an allowance of one or more claims, either as drafted or as amended in response to the final office action, the applicant will receive a Notice of Allowability. This will be followed or accompanied by a formal Notice of Allowance and a form specifying the issue fee that is due. At this time it is still possible to file minor amendments. Also, if any amendments to claims that have occurred in the course of prosecution are not covered by the formal Patent Application Declaration signed by the applicant, a Supplemental Declaration should also be filed.

If the issue fee is sent to the USPTO within three months of the formal Notice of Allowance, the applicant will receive a patent deed (a decorative document describing the patent with a USPTO seal on the front) and a regular photocopy of the patent. Although the formal patent prosecution process is now over, the inventor may later wish to amend his or her in-force patent in some material way, perhaps because a new ramification is spotted or the inventor now sees that one or more of the claims could have been made broader. If the amendment broadens one or more claims, and the application is filed within two years of the patent issue date, a reissue patent may be obtained. This will carry the same issue date as the original patent but will incorporate the claims as amended.

Related terms: claims; continuation application; continuation-in-part application (CIP); filing date; issue fee; office action; patent application; Provisional Patent Application (PPA); reconsideration request; reissue patent; Request for Continued Examination; supplemental declaration; swearing behind a prior art reference.

Provisional Patent Application (PPA)

An inventor may file an interim patent application (called a provisional patent application or PPA) to constructively reduce his or her invention to practice. If the PPA sufficiently discloses the invention, and a regular patent application is filed within one year of the PPA's filing date, the inventor gets the benefit of the PPA filing date for the purpose of deciding whether prior art is relevant and, in the event an interference exists, who is entitled to the patent. In addition, the inventor gets the full 20-year term from the date the regular application is filed.

The PPA need contain only a portion of the information presently required in a patent application specification—a complete description of the invention (structure and operation) and any drawings that are necessary to understand the description. The PPA need not include claims, formal drawings, a Patent Application Declaration, or an Information Disclosure Statement. In order to

Patent Law: Definitions

claim the benefit of the PPA's filing date, the applicant must file an amendment in the regular patent application referring to the earlier filed PPA.

The PPA currently (as of January 2012) costs $125 to file ($250 for large entities), which means an inventor can now afford to get an invention registered with the U.S. Patent and Trademark Office (USPTO) and have a year to show the invention to potential developers before filing a regular patent application. An inventor who files a PPA may claim patent pending status.

In a 2010 case, the Federal Circuit determined that the filing date of a provisional patent application establishes prior art references. An inventor, Giacomini, filed a patent application claiming a method of selectively storing sets of electronic data. Another inventor, Tran, filed a patent application after Giacomini for a similar invention. However, Tran's application was based on a provisional patent application that accurately described the invention and was filed before Giacomini's application. In that case, the Federal Circuit held that Tran, as "first inventor," could claim patent rights and use his patent application as prior art against Giacomini. (*In re Giacomini*, 612 F.3d 1380 (Fed. Cir. 2010).)

Related terms: filing date; patent application; patent pending; prosecution of a patent application.

PTDL

See Patent and Trademark Depository Libraries.

PTO

See U.S. Patent and Trademark Office (USPTO).

public domain

When an idea, design, or expression does not belong to anyone under the patent (or copyright) laws, it is said to exist in the public domain and may be used by anyone for any purpose without permission from its originator or author.

Any invention that is published, put in public use, sold, or placed on sale more than one year prior to the filing of a patent application is considered to be in the public domain. Also in the public domain are inventions whose patents are no longer in force (that is, the patent period has expired).

Related terms: anticipation; defensive disclosure; on-sale statutory bar; printed publication as statutory bar; prior art; Statutory Invention Registration (SIR).

public use

When an invention is worked (used by the inventor in the presence of one or more members of the public in a nonconfidential context), it is considered to have been publicly used. Public use of an invention constitutes a statutory bar to a patent under the anticipation doctrine, unless the patent application is filed within a one-year period after the public use.

There are exceptions to the public use rule for:

- experimental tests (to develop and improve an invention), and
- uses that are not, in fact, public (for instance, when witnesses to the use sign nondisclosure agreements or are otherwise required to maintain secrecy).

Whether any particular use of an invention is a public use must be determined on a case-by-case basis.

> EXAMPLE: Julian, a motel keeper, invents a counterweighting device that allows a king-size bed to be easily moved on very thick carpets. Julian actually constructs a bed that uses the device and uses it in his motel for a little over a year. If Julian then attempts to obtain a patent, the U.S. Patent and Trademark Office (USPTO) will probably deny it. Why? The use of the bed in the motel probably would be considered a public use, and therefore a statutory bar to the patent, because the patent application was not filed within one year of the "use." Julian is required to disclose this use of the invention in his patent application.
>
> What about the exception for experimental uses? If Julian can show that he was engaged in both monitoring the experiences of cleaning personnel with the bed and actively modifying the bed's basic design according to what he learned, he might escape the statutory one-year bar. What if Julian only allowed one customer to use the bed, and only for two nights, but he still failed to file the patent application within one year? He will be barred from the patent unless he can establish that the two nights' use was really for experimental purposes or he had the user sign a nondisclosure agreement.

Note: The one-year rules cited above will, for the most part, terminate in March 2013 when the U.S. switches to a first-to-file system. Patents filed after that date will be subject to new first-to-file and prior art rules, effectively ending centuries of first-to-invent rules. Anything published or sold prior to filing of the application will be considered prior art. For more information, check the entry for the America Invents Act.

Patent Law: Definitions

Related terms: anticipation; exhibiting an unpatented invention; experimental use of an unpatented invention; statutory bar.

race statutes

See first-to-file countries.

read on

In the patent context, "read on" means to literally describe. A patent is infringed if the patent's claims read on (literally describe) all elements of the infringing device.

Related terms: anticipation; claims; infringement, patent.

recite

When the claims of a prior patent literally describe or "read on" the elements of a later invention, the claims are said to "recite" such elements.

Related terms: read on.

reconsideration request

A patent applicant may request that the patent examiner reconsider an application whose claims were rejected in the final office action. If this reconsideration request is rejected, the applicant may:

- amend the claims in the manner suggested by the patent examiner, if this option was presented to the applicant in the office action
- appeal to the Board of Patent Appeals and Interferences, or
- file a continuation application.

Related terms: continuation application; final office action; prosecution of a patent application.

reduction to practice

After conceiving an invention, the inventor's next step is to reduce the invention to practice. This can be done in several ways:

- build and test the invention (called actual reduction to practice)
- file a Provisional Patent Application (PPA) on the invention (called constructive reduction to practice), or
- file a regular patent application (also a constructive reduction to practice).

While it's not legally required to get a patent, many inventors find that building and testing a working model of an invention is necessary to convince others to finance the invention's development. Also, if the invention consists of something generally thought highly improbable, such as a perpetual motion machine (a machine that will perpetually produce more energy than it uses), the U.S. Patent and Trademark Office (USPTO) may ask that its operability be demonstrated.

Prior to March 2013, the date of when an invention was first reduced to practice will remain extremely important if an interference occurs—that is, two or more pending applications claim the same underlying invention. That's because under the first-to-invent system, the inventor who was first to reduce the invention to practice, whether by building and testing it or by filing a provisional or regular patent application, will normally be entitled to the patent. However, under this system, if the other inventor can prove that he or she was first to conceive the invention and thereafter was diligent in attempting to either build and test the invention or to file a provisional or regular patent application on it, that inventor will be entitled to the patent.

Note: The rules regarding date of invention, conception, and reduction to practice will diminish in importance when the U.S. switches to a first-to-file system in March 2013, and it will become less important to prove the date when an invention was created. For more information, check the entry for the America Invents Act.

Related terms: constructive reduction to practice; interference; Provisional Patent Application (PPA).

reexamination of patent

The U.S. Patent and Trademark Office (USPTO) may hold a formal proceeding in which it reexamines an in-force patent to determine whether newly cited prior art references adversely affect the validity of the patent. A patent may be reexamined any time while it is in force. The patent owner or anyone else may initiate the reexamination. Upon request, the requester's identity will be kept confidential. (The statute establishing the reexamination process is 35 United States Code, Section 302.)

Note: After September 2012 (and enactment of the America Invents Act) it will be more difficult to obtain an inter partes reexamination. The Director can only authorize a reexam if "there is a reasonable likelihood that the petitioner would prevail with respect to at least one of the claims challenged in the petition." And there will be no more federal court review of USPTO reexaminations

The patent reexamination process can be useful to patent owners as well as alleged (or would-be) infringers.

EXAMPLE 1: A patent owner discovers infringement and the infringer counters that the patent is invalid in light of certain prior art. The owner decides to refer the prior art in question to the USPTO and request a reexamination before filing an infringement lawsuit. If the USPTO upholds the claims as drafted, the owner can feel secure about bringing the infringement action, because the results of the reexamination will be admissible in court and the court will almost always honor the USPTO's determination.

EXAMPLE 2: A business wants to use an invention covered by an in-force patent that it believes is invalid because of certain prior art. The reexamination process is a relatively inexpensive way for the business to anonymously "test the water" without actually infringing the patent.

The party requesting the reexamination must pay a reexamination fee. The requester must also describe the way in which prior art references specifically bear on the validity of the claims contained in the patent.

Upon request for a reexamination, the USPTO has three months to decide whether a "substantial new question of patentability has been raised." If not, the requester will be refunded the bulk of the reexamination fee, with the balance retained by the USPTO.

If the requester adequately demonstrates why prior art references are relevant, the patent will be reexamined and the claims possibly rejected or amended based on the prior art. Also, the USPTO may choose to invite the public into the reexamination process by asking it to submit any known instances of prior art relevant to the reexamination.

If a reexamination finds that the patent claims are still valid, the USPTO will issue a Certification of Validity. If it finds that one or more claims are not valid as drafted, the inventor will have an opportunity to redraft the claims to the patent examiner's satisfaction. In the event of such a change, the amended claims will be entitled to the original filing date.

Related terms: in-force patent; nonobviousness; prior art reference.

references

See prior art reference.

regular patent application

See patent application.

reissue patent

To revise the specification or claims of an in-force patent, the patent owner may apply for a reissue patent. If it seeks to broaden the claims, the reissue patent must be applied for within two years of the issue date of the original patent. If issued, the reissue patent takes the place of the original patent and expires when that patent would have.

Reissue patents can be used to correct any significant error in the claims of the original patent or to narrow or broaden its claims. In fact, reissue patents are relatively rare, because the push and pull of the patent prosecution process tends to make the claims both accurate and as broad as the U.S. Patent and Trademark Office will allow.

Related terms: in-force patent; intervening right; patent application.

rejection of patent application

See office action.

repair doctrine

Anyone who is authorized to make, use, or sell a patented device is also permitted to repair and replace unpatented components. This right is asserted as an affirmative defense in a patent infringement lawsuit. The defense does not apply to completely rebuilt inventions, unauthorized inventions, or items that are made or sold without authorization of the patent owner.

Request for Continued Examination

A Request for Continued Examination (RCE) is filed when a patent applicant wishes to continue prosecuting an application that has received a final office action. Filing the RCE with another filing fee effectively removes the final action so that the applicant can submit further amendments, for example, new claims, new arguments, a new declaration, or new references.

An RCE must cover the same invention as the parent or basic application, and the parent or basic application must be abandoned when a continuation is filed. When an RCE continuation is filed, the USPTO uses the same file jacket and papers as the parent or basic filing. After an RCE is filed, prosecution of the same application simply continues as if there were no final action. The RCE is entitled to the benefit of the filing date of the parent or prior application for purposes of overcoming prior art.

It is also possible to file a continuation of an RCE. In fact, it's theoretically possible to file an unlimited sequence of RCEs or continuation applications. However, an RCE is not an end-run around a previous objection by the USPTO. The RCE or continuation will be quickly rejected unless the inventor comes up with a truly different slant on or definition of the invention that was not previously considered by the USPTO. When a patent issues on an RCE, the heading of the patent will not indicate that it's based on the RCE.

An RCE must be mailed before the period for response to the final rejection expires or before any extensions expire. The RCE can be mailed on the last day of the period for response.

reverse engineering

The process of figuring out how a device is built by taking it apart and studying its components.

See also Part 4 (Trade Secret Law): reverse engineering and trade secrets.

search of patentability

See patentability search.

secrecy of patent application

See confidentiality of patent application.

senior party in interference proceedings

The first inventor to file a provisional or regular patent application on an invention is considered the senior party if the USPTO declares an interference (when two or more inventors file separate patent applications on the same invention). Senior party status does not necessarily entitle that party to the patent. This will depend on which inventor was first to conceive of the invention and how diligently that inventor moved to reduce the invention to practice.

Related terms: interference; junior party in interference proceedings; reduction to practice.

sequence listing

For biotech inventions, the USPTO requires an attachment to a patent application that includes a sequence listing of a nucleotide or amino acid sequence. The applicant attaches this information on separate sheets of paper and refers to the sequence listing in the application. (PTO Rule 77.)

shelving of invention

See antishelving clause.

shop rights

Most employers acquire ownership of invention rights created by employees either through written employment agreements (preinvention assignments) or under the "employed to invent" rule. In another situation the employer may not acquire ownership of a patent but may acquire a limited right to use these innovations, known as a shop right. Under a shop right, the employee retains ownership of the patent, but the employer has a right to use the invention without paying for it. A shop right can occur only if the employee uses the employer's resources (materials, supplies, time) to create an invention. Other circumstances may be relevant, but use of employer resources is the most important criterion. Shop right principles are derived from state laws and precedents in court cases. Generally, the shop right claim arises when an inventor sues a former employer for patent infringement. The employer defends itself by claiming a shop right.

Related terms: employed to invent; march-in rights; nonexclusive patent license; patent owner; preinvention assignment.

shotgun rejection of claims

This slang term refers to the U.S. Patent and Trademark Office's (USPTO's) habit of rejecting all claims in its first office action (its first formal response to the application) on the premise that it will deal more seriously with the application if and when the applicant submits amended claims or a more detailed explanation of why the existing claims should be allowed. Although discouraging, a shotgun rejection does not necessarily mean that an applicant should abandon trying to patent the invention. As mentioned, a shotgun rejection has much more to do with general USPTO practices than with the merits of a particular patent application.

Related terms: first office action; prosecution of a patent application.

single application rule

See divisional application.

small entity

A for-profit company with 500 or fewer employees, a nonprofit organization, or an independent inventor is referred to by the U.S. Patent and Trademark Office (USPTO) as a small entity. The USPTO charges small entities half the fees

Patent Law: Definitions

charged large entities for filing a patent application and for issuing and maintaining the patent. A small entity qualifies for these lower fees provided that the company or inventor has not assigned or licensed, or agreed to assign or license, its patent rights to a large entity (a for-profit company with over 500 employees).

Related terms: issue fee; large entity; maintenance fees.

smart money

The colloquial phrase "smart money" is used by patent attorneys to describe the extra damages that can be imposed on defendants found guilty of willful or flagrant infringement. These extra damages—up to three times the actual damages established in court—are awarded to teach the infringers a lesson and make them "smart."

Related terms: infringement action.

software-based inventions

See software patents.

Software Patent Institute

This independent nonprofit corporation (www.spi.org) collects and organizes nonpatented prior art references in the software field.

The purpose of the SPI is to facilitate more complete patent searches. Because most software is not patented, a search of the patent database usually produces a small fraction of the prior art in the software field. By collecting as many samples of nonpatented software as possible, SPI hopes to provide patent searchers with a truer picture of the relevant prior art.

Related terms: patent search, computerized; prior art; prior art reference.

software patents

Patents don't issue on software itself, although they issue on inventions that use innovative software to produce a useful, concrete, and tangible result—that is, "software-based" inventions.

When first faced with applications for patents on software-based inventions in the 1950s, the U.S. Patent and Trademark Office (USPTO) routinely rejected the applications on the grounds that software consists of mathematical algorithms (abstract methods for solving problems not tied to a particular use or tangible structure), which were considered to be unpatentable for the same reason abstract laws of nature are unpatentable.

In the late 1980s, however, the USPTO began granting patents on inventions that rely heavily on innovative software. Now the USPTO issues patents on software if the patent application describes the software in relation to computer hardware and related devices and limits the software to specific uses.

Software-based inventions that have qualified for patents often involve software that connects to and runs hardware components. For example, consider a device that monitors a patient's heart functions, feeds the raw information into a computer where a program analyzes the information according to a set of algorithms, and causes the results of this analysis to be displayed on a monitor in a format that shows whether the person is at risk for a heart attack. While none of the components of this invention would qualify for a patent (the physical items have already been invented and the algorithm itself is unpatentable), the overall invention did qualify for a U.S. patent, even though the software was the key aspect of the invention.

It is also possible to obtain a patent on the process or method used by software as well as on the machine aspect of the invention—that is, the combined software and hardware. For instance, the heart monitor invention described above received a patent on a machine claim (a claim that described the structure which produced the result) as well as a method claim (a claim that described the process by which the structure worked). Other examples of software-based inventions that have received patents are a device that converts sound waves into smooth wave forms for display on an oscilloscope (a rasterizer), and software that moves the cursor on a computer screen.

In 2010, the Supreme Court kept alive software patents when it rejected the view held by the Court of Appeals for the Federal Circuit (CAFC) that the so-called "machine or transformation" test should be the sole standard for patentability. The Supreme Court preserved the status quo and kept alive the concept of software patents (as well as business method, and other process patents). (*Kappos v. Bilski*, 561 U.S. ___ (2010).)

Despite the fact that software-based inventions may qualify for a patent, most do not because they are considered obvious over the prior art and must therefore be protected in another manner—usually under trade secret or copyright laws.

Note: As of September, 2011, the USPTO will stop granting patents for strategies for reducing, avoiding, or deferring tax liability. In September 2012 (one year after enactment of the America Invents Act), the Director must establish a transitional postgrant review proceeding to consider the validity of business-method patents. In other words, in coming years it may become more difficult to obtain a so-called software patent.

Virtually all patents that have been obtained on software-based inventions are utility patents, although design patents have been issued on computer screen icons.

Related terms: algorithms; business methods as statutory subject matter; nonstatutory subject matter; *State Street Bank and Trust v. Signature Financial Group.*

sovereign immunity

Sovereign immunity is a principle that a government is immune from civil suit or criminal prosecution. For purposes of patent law, it refers to the fact that state governments cannot be liable for patent infringement. In 1999, the Supreme Court ruled that was so, even though Congress had previously amended the patent laws to circumvent state sovereign immunity. In one case, the State of Florida was sued by a patent holder for utilizing a patented financing methodology. (*Fla. Prepaid Postsecondary Educ. Expense Bd. v. College Sav. Bank,* 527 U.S. 627 (1999).)

Neither the federal government nor local municipal or county governments enjoy similar sovereign immunity. Moreover, civil patent remedies can be pursued against any government employee (federal, state, or local) who commits infringement in their individual capacity. Finally, a state institution should not assume it has carte blanche to commit patent infringement. State laws vary, and some states may waive or limit sovereign immunity in certain situations.

specification, defined

The narrative portion of a patent application is called a specification. A specification includes descriptions of:
- the type of invention
- the pertinent prior art (previous developments in the technology utilized in the invention) known to the applicant
- the purpose of the invention
- the invention itself (for example, how it's constructed and what it's made of)
- the operation of the invention (how it works), and
- any accompanying drawings.

As defined by the patent laws, the specification also includes the patent claims and an abstract: a one-paragraph summary of the specification. (A sample specification is provided in the Forms section at the end of this part of the book.)

Essentially, the specification must provide enough information about the invention so that a person having ordinary skill in the art (proficient in the particular area of expertise involved in the invention) could build it without having to be "inventive." Because the specification is where the fullest disclosure of the invention is made, it (rather than the claims) is commonly used to determine whether a later invention has been anticipated by the patent.

§ 112. Specification

This statute sets out the detailed requirements for how an invention must be described in a patent application, known as the specification and claims.

The specification shall contain a written description of the invention, and of the manner and process of making and using it, in such full, clear, concise, and exact terms as to enable any person skilled in the art to which it pertains, or with which it is most nearly connected, to make and use the same, and shall set forth the best mode contemplated by the inventor of carrying out his invention.

The specification shall conclude with one or more claims particularly pointing out and distinctly claiming the subject matter which the applicant regards as his invention.

A claim may be written in independent or, if the nature of the case admits, in dependent or multiple dependent form.

Subject to the following paragraph, a claim in dependent form shall contain a reference to a claim previously set forth and then specify a further limitation of the subject matter claimed. A claim in dependent form shall be construed to incorporate by reference all the limitations of the claim to which it refers.

A claim in multiple dependent form shall contain a reference, in the alternative only, to more than one claim previously set forth and then specify a further limitation of the subject matter claimed. A multiple dependent claim shall not serve as a basis for any other multiple dependent claim. A multiple dependent claim shall be construed to incorporate by reference all the limitations of the particular claim in relation to which it is being considered.

An element in a claim for a combination may be expressed as a means or step for performing a specified function without the recital of structure, material, or acts in support thereof, and such claim shall be construed to cover the corresponding structure, material, or acts described in the specification and equivalents thereof.

Related terms: claims; disclosure requirements for patents.

State Street Bank and Trust v. Signature Financial Group

In this 1998 case (149 F.3d 1368 (Fed. Cir. 1998)), the Court of Appeals for the Federal Circuit made it much easier to obtain a patent on computer software and on methods of doing business. The software invention at issue in this case was designed solely to make financial calculations dealing with advantageous mutual fund investing techniques. In the past, such a program would have been considered to be nothing more than a mathematical algorithm, which does not constitute statutory subject matter. However, in *State Street,* the court ruled that the mathematical algorithms are nonpatentable only when they are nothing more than abstract ideas consisting of disembodied concepts that are not useful. In the court's words: "Today we hold that the transformation of data, representing discrete dollar amounts, by a machine through a series of mathematical calculations into a final share price, constitutes a practical application of a mathematical algorithm, formula, or calculation, because it produces a useful, concrete, and tangible result—a final share price momentarily fixed for recording and reporting purposes and even accepted and relied upon by regulatory authorities and in subsequent trades."

The court also shed new light on the long-held belief that methods of doing business do not constitute statutory subject matter. The court pointed out that the patent statutes do not specifically exclude business methods from being patentable and that no authoritative case law supported the concept.

Related terms: business methods as statutory subject matter; *Kappos v. Bilksi*

statement of prior art references

See Information Disclosure Statement.

statute of limitations, infringement action

In patent law there is no time limit (statute of limitations) for filing a patent infringement lawsuit, but monetary damages can only be recovered for infringements committed during the six years prior to filing the lawsuit. For example, if a patent owner sues after ten years of infringement, the owner cannot recover monetary damages for the first four years of infringement. Despite the fact that there is no law setting a time limit, courts will not permit a patent owner to sue for infringement if the owner has waited an unreasonable time to file the lawsuit (this is the doctrine called "laches").

§ 286. Time limitation on damages

Except as otherwise provided by law, no recovery shall be had for any infringement committed more than six years prior to the filing of the complaint or counterclaim for infringement in the action.

In the case of claims against the United States Government for use of a patented invention, the period before bringing suit, up to six years, between the date of receipt of a written claim for compensation by the department or agency of the Government having authority to settle such claim, and the date of mailing by the Government of a notice to the claimant that his claim has been denied, shall not be counted as part of the period referred to in the preceding paragraph.

Related terms: defenses to a patent infringement claim.

statutory bar

A statutory bar is any federal statutory provision that requires the U.S. Patent and Trademark Office or a court to disqualify an invention for a patent. Among the most common types of statutory bars are:

- the rule that prior patents, or other printed publications that describe the invention, may preclude the invention from being considered novel
- the rule that a later invention is precluded from receiving a patent by an earlier invention that contains all of the same elements
- the rule that a patent may not be obtained on an invention if the application has been abandoned by the inventor, or
- the rule that a description in a printed publication, public use, or on-sale status of the invention more than one year prior to the application filing date precludes a patent from issuing.

Note: The one-year rule cited above will, for the most part, terminate in March 2013 when the U.S. switches to a first-to-file system. For more information, check the entry for the America Invents Act.

Related terms: anticipation; on-sale statutory bar; printed publication as statutory bar; prior art reference; public use; swearing behind a prior art reference.

Statutory Invention Registration (SIR)

A patent applicant can abandon an application and prevent anyone else from getting a patent on the underlying invention by in effect putting the invention in the public domain. This is done by converting a patent application to an SIR.

The U.S. Patent and Trademark Office in turn will publish the abstract of the patent included in the original application in the *Official Gazette*, thereby transforming the invention into a prior art reference effective on the original application's filing date. No patent can issue on the invention unless another inventor has already claimed it in a pending application and is entitled to priority because of an earlier date of conception or reduction to practice.

Note: As a result of the passage of the America Invents Act in September 2011, the Statutory Invention Registration procedure will no longer be available after March 2013.

It is also possible to turn an invention into a prior art reference (thereby placing it in the public domain) by publishing an article on it or by listing it with an invention register and the effective date of the reference will be the date of publication.

Related terms: defensive disclosure; interference.

statutory subject matter

The U.S. Patent and Trademark Office issues utility patents, design patents, and plant patents. To qualify for a utility patent, an invention must fit into at least one of five categories defined in 35 United States Code, Section 101. Qualifications for a design or plant patent are not, however, governed by these statutory categories.

The statutory categories for utility patents are:

- compositions of matter
- manufactures (or articles of manufacture)
- machines (or apparatuses)
- processes (or methods), and
- new and useful improvements of any of the above categories.

Any invention that does not fall within at least one of these categories does not qualify for a utility patent, no matter how novel or nonobvious it may otherwise prove to be. On the other hand, it is not necessary to define exactly which category applies to a particular invention as long as the patent examiner concludes that at least one of them does.

> EXAMPLE: A patent application on an automated database invention that answers legal questions can be viewed as claiming a machine (apparatus) or a process (method). Because the invention can fit within one or the other of these categories, it is deemed to be statutory subject matter.

To qualify for a utility patent, an invention must be novel, useful, and non-obvious, in addition to fitting within at least one of the five statutory categories. The phrase "statutory subject matter" is often used to refer not only to inventions that fall within one of the five statutory classes, but to those that satisfy these other patent requirements as well.

Related terms: nonstatutory subject matter; prosecution of a patent application.

submarine patent

A patent may be deliberately held up in the U.S. Patent and Trademark Office by the applicant while the technology covered by the patent is developed by companies that have no knowledge of the pending application. Then, once the patent issues, it is like a submarine, suddenly emerging from the patent office and forcing the users of the invention to pay hefty license fees. Two changes in patent law have substantially eliminated the possibility of submarine patents. In 1995, the patent laws were amended to limit the duration of patents to 20 years from the date of filing. In 1999, the patent laws were amended to require publication of patent applications within 18 months of filing unless the patent applicant will not be filing the patent application in a foreign country.

Related terms: confidentiality of patent application.

substitute patent application

Inventors sometimes file a new patent application after abandoning an earlier application on the same invention. For example, if an applicant who failed to respond to the U.S. Patent and Trademark Office's first office action within three months refiles a duplicate application, the later application is considered a substitute of the abandoned parent application. The substitute application does not get the benefit of the original filing date, so any prior art that has surfaced in the meantime may operate to anticipate the invention and thus bar the patent from issuing.

Related terms: abandonment of patent application; parent application.

supplemental declaration

When claims are broadened or changed in any substantial way in the course of a successful patent prosecution, the applicant must file a supplemental declaration with the U.S. Patent and Trademark Office after receiving a notice of allowance. Under oath, the inventor must:

- specify which claims have been altered in the course of the prosecution, and
- declare that the applicant was the inventor of the subject matter contained in the altered claims and knows of no prior art that would anticipate the claims as altered.

Related terms: prosecution of a patent application.

swearing behind a prior art reference

Swearing behind a prior art reference is a way of eliminating a prior art reference cited by a patent examiner against an application.

To swear behind a cited prior art reference, the applicant must show that the date his or her invention was conceived of or reduced to practice was before the effective date of the prior art reference. The evidence to establish these facts typically consists of the inventor's testimony under oath and appropriate entries from his or her notebook.

If the prior art reference is a publication dated less than one year before the patent application's filing date, a showing that the invention was conceived of prior to the publication and diligent attempts were made to reduce it to practice will eliminate the reference as a statutory bar.

EXAMPLE: An article appearing in the November 2009 issue of a leading popular science magazine details an efficient portable photovoltaic cell able to run various electronic devices. Lou has already conceived of such a cell and has been busy designing it so that a patent application can be filed. Lou may still be able to obtain a patent if she files a patent application within one year of the article's publication date and shows (swears behind) that she conceived her invention prior to such publication date and was diligently engaged in reducing it to practice.

When a prior art reference is a U.S. patent with a filing date preceding the applicant's filing date and an issue date that is less than one year before the applicant's filing date, a showing that the inventor conceived of the invention prior to the patent's filing date, and thereafter exercised diligence to reduce it to practice, will eliminate the patent acting as a statutory bar to the application.

EXAMPLE: Lou invents a photovoltaic cell, but before she files a patent application she discovers that another inventor has patented the same invention (the patent issued on July 1, 2010). The other patent will be eliminated from consideration if Lou (1) files her application within one year of the date the patent issued (that is, by July 1, 2011), (2) is able to prove that she conceived of her invention prior to the date the other patent application was filed, and (3) can show that she was diligently attempting to reduce her invention to practice at the time the other patent application was filed.

Related terms: first office action; interference; notebook, inventor's; prior art reference; reduction to practice; statutory bar.

teach the invention

When a prior publication, invention, or patent discusses the elements of, or technology associated with, an invention for which a patent is being sought, it is said to "teach" the invention.

temporary presence exception

This rule permits foreign ship and aircraft owners with otherwise infringing technology to dock or land here without being sued provided: (1) the ship or aircraft enters the U.S. on a temporary or accidental basis, and (2) the patented technology or device is used exclusively for the needs of the ship or aircraft.

thesis as prior art

A published college or university thesis may count as a prior art reference, even if published in an obscure publication, and thus operate as a statutory bar to a patent if it describes (teaches) the essential characteristics of an invention on which a patent is being sought. This applies to a patent sought by anyone other than the thesis author, and to the thesis author as well if he or she did not file the patent application within one year of the date the thesis was first published.

Because a thesis can count as prior art, a thorough patent search will usually cover listings of theses, as well as prior patents and publications in trade journals.

Related terms: printed publication as statutory bar; prior art reference.

Title 35 of the United States Code

This part of the United States Code (sometimes abbreviated as USC) contains the patent statutes. The entire code can be found in 35 United States Code Annotated (USCA) or 35 United States Code Service, Lawyers Edition (USCS).

transfer of patent or patent application

See assignment of a patent.

transmittal letter for patent application

See patent application.

treaties on international patent protection

See Patent Cooperation Treaty (PCT); Convention application; international patent protection for U.S. inventions.

treble (triple) damages for patent infringement

See infringement action.

tying

In some circumstances, patent owners may violate the antitrust laws by using their patents to unfairly require that companies purchasing the patented technology also purchase unpatented products as well. For example, a clothing manufacturing

Patent Law: Definitions

company patents a new machine for sewing buttons. The clothing company licenses the machine and also insists that manufacturers buy buttons from it as a condition of the license. In general, deciding whether a particular activity violates the antitrust laws involves such variables as the intent of the actors, the degree of harm done to other companies, and the level of commerce that is affected (local, state, national, or international). In a 2005 case the Court of Appeals for the Federal Circuit established that there is a rebuttable presumption that the company requiring the tying of products has sufficient market power to make the action an antitrust violation. (*Independent Ink v. Illinois Tool Works,* 396 F.3d 1342 (Fed. Cir. 2005).)

Related terms: antitrust law (federal) and patents.

unenforceable patent

A patent may be declared unenforceable if the alleged infringer can show that the patent owner has misused the patent. Among the specific types of misuse that can render a patent unenforceable are:

- falsely marking an invention, such as putting a patent number on it that doesn't apply
- illegal or unfair licensing practices
- an extended delay in bringing the infringement lawsuit to the detriment of the defendant (called "laches"), or
- fraud on the U.S. Patent and Trademark Office (USPTO), such as failing to include a pertinent prior art reference in the patent application.

Patents may be declared invalid if a court finds any of the following:

- The USPTO didn't discover or properly analyze relevant prior art references that affect the novelty or nonobviousness of the invention (in short, the invention really didn't qualify for a patent).
- The invention doesn't or won't work.
- The disclosure of the invention in the patent application contains insufficient information to teach an ordinary person skilled in the art to build the invention.
- The patent claims are vague and indefinite.
- The patent was issued to the wrong inventor.
- Antitrust violations occurred.
- Any other facts exist that operate to retroactively invalidate the patent.

Related terms: defenses to a patent infringement claim.

unobviousness

See nonobviousness.

U.S. Patent and Trademark Office (USPTO)

An administrative branch of the U.S. Department of Commerce, the U.S. Patent and Trademark Office (www.uspto.gov), is charged with the responsibility for overseeing and implementing the federal laws on patents and trademarks. Also known as the USPTO or Patent Office, this agency is responsible for examining, issuing, classifying, and maintaining records of all patents issued by the United States. It also serves as a filing agency for Patent Cooperation Treaty (PCT) applications.

The USPTO publishes online the *Official Gazette* (both the patent and trademark versions), a weekly periodical that describes newly issued patents, new regulations, and other information of interest to patent practitioners. The USPTO also maintains a library in which a complete patent search may be conducted by classification.

Related terms: Patent Cooperation Treaty (PCT).

usefulness, required for patents

See utility patents.

utility

See utility patents.

utility model

This provision in Japanese and German law states that inventions that do not qualify for a regular patent may nonetheless receive some protection for a shorter period of time.

utility patents

Patents may issue on inventions that have some type of usefulness (utility) even if the use is humorous, such as a musical condom or a device to hold your big toes together to prevent sunburned inner thighs. However, the invention must work, at least in theory. Thus, a new drug that hasn't been tested or a new chemical for which no use is now known will not receive a patent. Design patents and plant patents, the other two types of patents obtained in the United States, do not require utility.

Related terms: design patents; plant patents; statutory subject matter.

Patent Law: Definitions

validity search

A patent search may be conducted after a patent has issued for the purpose of discovering any fact that might be used to invalidate, and thus break, the patent. Generally conducted by the defendant in a patent infringement action, a validity search is often more thorough than the initial patentability search conducted by the inventor prior to filing a patent application, which was used to determine whether the invention was anticipated.

Related terms: defenses to a patent infringement claim; patent search.

willful infringement

Willful patent infringement occurs when someone deliberately and in "wanton disregard" of the patent owner's rights, copies a patented invention. Willfulness is usually demonstrated when an infringer copies an invention without any grounds for believing that the patent is invalid, or when an infringer continues unauthorized copying after being notified of the infringement. In cases of willful infringement, the court may award the plaintiff three times the actual damages established in court plus reasonable attorney fees. Previously, a court would infer willful infringement occurred if an alleged patent infringer did not produce or obtain an opinion of counsel as to the use of an infringing invention. The Court of Appeals for the Federal Circuit reversed this 20-year precedent when it ruled that the absence of an opinion of counsel is only one of several factors to be considered when determining if patent infringement is willful. (*Knorr-Bremse Systeme fuer Nutzfahrzeuge GmbH v. Dana Corp. et al.*, 383 F.3d 1337 (Fed.Cir. 2004).)

Related terms: damages, patent infringement; infringement, patent

working a patent

Actually developing and commercially exploiting the underlying invention covered by a patent is known as working a patent. In many countries outside the United States, a patent owner's failure to work the patent within a specific period of time may result in the owner's being forced to grant a license (called a compulsory license), at government-set fees, to any party that wants to be licensed.

Related terms: compulsory licensing of a patent.

World Intellectual Property Organization (WIPO)

See International Bureau of the World Intellectual Property Organization; Patent Cooperation Treaty (PCT).

World Trade Organization (WTO)

This organization was created by the General Agreement on Tariffs and Trade (GATT) for the purpose of enforcing the intellectual property and other trade agreements contained in that treaty.

Related terms: GATT (General Agreement on Tariffs and Trade).

World Wide Web and patent searches

See patent search, computerized.

Patent Law: Definitions

Patent Law: Forms

Patent Application Basics

In this section, we explain the basic principles involved in filing a utility patent application and a design patent application. We also provide a completed example of both types of patents. Applicants can also obtain help from the instructions provided at the U.S. Patent and Trademark Office (USPTO) website (www.uspto.gov).

Preparing a Utility Patent Application

If you opened a typical utility patent application package at the USPTO mailroom, it would contain the following:

- **Transmittal Form.** The Transmittal Form serves as a cover letter for the application. It describes what is being filed, the names of the inventors, the number of pages, the fee, and other information used by the USPTO to categorize the filing. All of the inventors must sign the transmittal form. (All of the USPTO forms required for an application are downloadable from the USPTO website, at www.uspto.gov.)
- **Fee Transmittal Form.** This form provides information about your fee, including whether you are claiming Small Entity Status. (Most inventors claim this reduced-fee status unless they have transferred their invention rights to a for-profit business with more than 500 employees.)
- **Credit Card Transmittal Form.** You must complete this additional form if you are paying by credit card.
- **Fee.** You can pay by personal check, money order, or credit card. Check the UPSTO website for current fees. The fee depends on several variables, including the number of independent and dependent claims, whether the applicant qualifies for Small Entity Status, and whether an assignment is being filed (transferring rights from the inventor to another entity). You can review current filing fees at the USPTO website.
- **Patent Application Declaration (PAD).** The PAD certifies the accuracy of the statements in the application—in other words, that you are telling the truth.
- **Drawings.** Patent drawings (also known as "drawing sheets") are visual representations of the invention that must be included with the application,

if necessary to explain the invention. The drawings must show every feature recited in the claims. There are strict standards for patent drawings as to materials, size, form, symbols, and shading. For help in preparing drawings, consult *How to Make Patent Drawings,* by Jack Lo and David Pressman (Nolo). If you'd prefer to have a patent draftsperson prepare the drawings, you can expect to pay between $75 to $150 per drawing sheet.

- **The Specification.** This document will make up the bulk of your application. It describes the invention so that someone knowledgeable in the field of the invention can make and use it without any further experimenting. It also discloses the "best mode" of creating and using the invention. In other words, the specification is a statement that explains the best way to make and use an invention. If the inventor knew of a better way (or "best mode") and failed to disclose it, that failure could result in the loss of patent rights. The specification consists of several sections including:

  - title
  - background of the invention—this usually includes cross-references to any related applications, references to a microfiche appendix, a statement regarding federally sponsored research or development, the field of the invention, and a discussion of prior art
  - summary of the invention—this usually includes the objects (what the invention accomplishes) and advantages (why the invention is superior to the prior art) of the invention
  - description of the drawings
  - detailed description of the invention and how it works
  - abstract—a concise, one-paragraph summary of the structure, nature, and purpose of the invention, and
  - claims. Of all the elements, claims are often the hardest to draft (and hardest to decipher). One reason is that claims follow strict grammatical requirements: They are sentence fragments, always start with an initial capital letter, and contain one period and no quotation marks or parentheses (except in mathematical or chemical formulas). Claims are usually made up of independent and dependent claims. One claim is stated as broadly as possible (the "independent claim") and then followed by successively narrower claims designed to specifically recite possible variations on the invention ("dependent claims"). The independent claim

stands by itself, while a dependent claim always refers back and incorporates the language of another independent or dependent claim.

In addition to these documents, the following documents might also be included in the utility patent application:

- **Information Disclosure Statement.** This should be included if you know of any relevant prior art. You don't have to include it with the application; you can file it within three months after you file the application.
- **Petition to Make Special.** Include this if you want to accelerate the examination process by a few months. You can request it only if you meet one of the requirements in the patent law—for example, your invention relates to HIV/AIDS or cancer research, counters terrorism, or results in significant energy savings, or if the applicant's health is poor.
- **Assignment and Cover Sheet.** Include this if you are transferring ownership of the patent. You don't have to provide it with the application; you can file it any time.
- **Disclosure Document Reference Letter.** Include this if a Disclosure Document was filed previously.
- **Return Receipt Postcard.** This is optional, but it provides proof that the application was received by the USPTO.

Who Files the Utility Application?

A patent application must be filed in the name of the true inventor or inventors. If there is more than one inventor, each becomes an applicant for the patent, and each automatically owns equal shares of the invention and any resulting patents.

Inventorship can be different from legal ownership. Often, all or part of the ownership rights to the invention and the patent application must be transferred to someone else, either an individual or a legal entity. For example, some inventors are hired to invent for companies; they may be required to transfer ownership of any inventions they create as a condition of employment. To make the transfer, the inventor must legally transfer the interest by filing an assignment, either with the patent application or at any time afterward. Some inventors prefer to wait until they have a received a serial number for the application before filing the assignment.

If an assignment has been recorded and the applicant refers to it in the issue fee transmittal form, the USPTO will print the patent with the assignee's interest indicated.

Even if the patent doesn't indicate the assignment, the assignment will still be effective if the USPTO has recorded it.

For more on employer ownership of invention, see *What Every Inventor Needs to Know About Business & Taxes,* by Stephen Fishman (Nolo).

Should You Do Your Own Utility Patent Application or Hire a Professional?

Many inventors have obtained patents on their own, often using the method David Pressman explains in detail in his book, *Patent It Yourself* (Nolo). Doing your own patent requires considerable diligence. If you have sufficient funds but don't have the time or writing skills to do it on your own, you may be better off hiring a professional.

Of course, you can do some of the work yourself and hire a professional to do the rest. You can, for example, draft your application then have an attorney review it, or hire an attorney only if your application runs into problems with a USPTO examiner. Or you can familiarize yourself with the patent drafting rules so that you can save time explaining your invention and preparing your patent.

An example of a completed patent specification is provided below.

Interested in Filing a Provisional Patent Application?

If you are interested in preparing a provisional patent application (PPA), Nolo offers two resources. You can prepare and file the PPA yourself using the book *Patent Pending in 24 Hours,* by Richard Stim and David Pressman, or you can file your PPA directly on the Web using Nolo's interactive online PPA filing procedures (www.nolo.com).

Patent: Law: Forms

Specification of Sample Patent Application

A2-Koppe

Lam.SB

Patent Application of

Lou W. Koppe

for

TITLE: PAPER-LAMINATED PLIABLE CLOSURE FOR FLEXIBLE BAGS

CROSS-REFERENCE TO RELATED APPLICATIONS   Not Applicable

FEDERALLY SPONSORED RESEARCH   Not Applicable

SEQUENCE LISTING OR PROGRAM   Not Applicable

BACKGROUND OF THE INVENTION—FIELD OF INVENTION

This invention relates to plastic tab closures, specifically to such closures which are used for closing the necks of plastic produce bags.

BACKGROUND OF THE INVENTION

Grocery stores and supermarkets commonly supply consumers with polyethylene bags for holding produce. Such bags are also used by suppliers to provide a resealable container for other items, both edible and inedible.

Originally these bags were sealed by the supplier with staples or by heat. However, consumers objected since these were of a rather permanent nature: The bags could be opened only by tearing, thereby damaging them and rendering them impossible to reseal.

Thereafter, inventors created several types of closures to seal plastic bags in such a way as to leave them undamaged after they were opened. U.S. patent 4,292,714 to Walker (1981) discloses a complex clamp which can close the necks of bags without causing damage upon opening; however, these clamps are prohibitively expensive to manufacture. U.S. patent 2,981,990 to Balderree (1961) shows a closure which is of

Patent Application of Lou W. Koppe for "Paper-Laminated
Pliable Closure for Flexible Bags" continued

expensive construction, being made of PTFE, and which is not effective unless the bag has a relatively long "neck."

Thus, if the bag has been filled almost completely and consequently has a short neck, this closure is useless. Also, being relatively narrow and clumsy, Balderree's closure cannot be easily bent by hand along its longitudinal axis. Finally, his closure does not hold well onto the bag, but has a tendency to snap off.

Although twist closures with a wire core are easy to use and inexpensive to manufacture, do not damage the bag upon being removed, and can be used repeatedly, nevertheless they simply do not possess the neat and uniform appearance of a tab closure, they become tattered and unsightly after repeated use, and they do not offer suitable surfaces for the reception of print or labeling. These ties also require much more manipulation to apply and remove.

Several types of thin, flat closures have been proposed—for example, in U.K. patent 883,771 to Britt et al. (1961) and U.S. patents 3,164,250 (1965), 3,417,912 (1968), 3,822,441 (1974), 4,361,935 (1982), and 4,509,231 (1985), all to Paxton. Although inexpensive to manufacture, capable of use with bags having a short neck, and producible in break-off strips, such closures can be used only once if they are made of frangible plastic since they must be bent or twisted when being removed and consequently will fracture upon removal. Thus, to reseal a bag originally sealed with a frangible closure, one must either close its neck with another closure or else close it in makeshift fashion by folding or tying it. My own patent 4,694,542 (1987) describes a closure which is made of flexible plastic and is therefore capable of repeated use without damage to the bag, but nevertheless all the plastic closures heretofore known suffer from a number of disadvantages:

(a) Their manufacture in color requires the use of a compounding facility for the production of the pigmented plastic. Such a facility, which is needed to compound the primary pigments and which generally constitutes a separate production site, requires the presence of very large storage bins for the pigmented raw granules. Also, it presents great difficulties with regard to the elimination of the airborne powder which results from the mixing of the primary granules.

(b) If one uses an extruder in the production of a pigmented plastic—especially if one uses only a single extruder—a change from one color to a second requires purging the extruder of the granules having the first color by introducing those of the second color. This process inevitably produces, in sizeable volume, an intermediate product of an undesired color which must be discarded as scrap, thereby resulting in waste of material and time.

(c) The colors of the closures in present use are rather unsaturated. If greater concentrations of pigment were used in order to make the colors more intense, the plastic would become more brittle and the cost of the final product would increase.

Patent Application of Lou W. Koppe for "Paper-Laminated
Pliable Closure for Flexible Bags" continued

(d) The use of pigmented plastic closures does not lend itself to the production of multicolored designs, and it would be very expensive to produce plastic closures in which the plastic is multicolored—for example, in which the plastic has stripes of several colors, or in which the plastic exhibits multicolored designs.

(e) Closures made solely of plastic generally offer poor surfaces for labeling or printing, and the label or print is often easily smudged.

(f) The printing on a plastic surface is often easily erased, thereby allowing the alteration of prices by dishonest consumers.

(g) The plastic closures in present use are slippery when handled with wet or greasy fingers.

(h) A closure of the type in present use can be very carefully pried off a bag by a dishonest consumer and then attached to another item without giving any evidence of such removal.

BACKGROUND OF INVENTION—Objects and Advantages

Accordingly, besides the objects and advantages of the flexible closures described in my above patent, several objects and advantages of the present invention are:

(a) to provide a closure which can be produced in a variety of colors without requiring the manufacturer to use a compounding facility for the production of pigments;

(b) to provide a closure whose production allows for a convenient and extremely rapid and economical change of color in the closures that are being produced;

(c) to provide a closure which both is flexible and can be brightly colored;

(d) to provide a closure which can be colored in several colors simultaneously;

(e) to provide a closure which will present a superior surface for the reception of labeling or print;

(f) to provide a closure whose labeling cannot be altered;

(g) to provide a closure which will not be slippery when handled with wet or greasy fingers; and

(h) to provide a closure which will show evidence of having been switched from one item to another by a dishonest consumer—in other words, to provide a closure which makes items tamper-proof.

Further objects and advantages are to provide a closure which can be used easily and conveniently to open and reseal a plastic bag without damage to the bag, which is simple to use and inexpensive to manufacture, which can be supplied in separate tabs en masse or in break-off links, which can be used with bags having short necks, which can be used repeatedly, and which obviates the need to tie a knot in the neck of the bag or fold

Patent Application of Lou W. Koppe for "Paper-Laminated
Pliable Closure for Flexible Bags" continued

the neck under the bag or use a twist closure. Still further objects and advantages will become apparent from a consideration of the ensuing description and drawings.

SUMMARY

In accordance with the present invention, a bag closure comprises a flat body having a notch, a gripping aperture adjacent the notch, and a layer of paper laminated on its side.

DRAWINGS—FIGURES

In the drawings, closely related figures have the same number but different alphabetic suffixes.

Figs 1A to 1D show various aspects of a closure supplied with a longitudinal groove and laminated on one side with paper.

Fig 2 shows a closure with no longitudinal groove and with a paper lamination on one side only.

Fig 3 shows a similar closure with one longitudinal groove.

Fig 4 shows a similar closure with a paper lamination on both sides.

Fig 5 shows a similar closure with a paper lamination on one side only, the groove having been formed into the paper as well as into the body of the closure.

Figs 6A to 6K show end views of closures having various combinations of paper laminations, longitudinal grooves, and through-holes.

Figs 7A to 7C show a laminated closure with groove after being bent and after being straightened again.

Figs 8A to 8C show a laminated closure without a groove after being bent and after being straightened again.

DRAWINGS—Reference Numerals

10	base of closure	12	lead-in notch
14	hole	16	gripping points
18	groove	20	paper lamination
22	tear of paper lamination	24	corner
26	longitudinal through-hole	28	neck-down
30	side of base opposite to bend	32	crease

DETAILED DESCRIPTION—FIGS. 1A AND 1B—PREFERRED EMBODIMENT

A preferred embodiment of the closure of the present invention is illustrated in Fig 1A (top view) and Fig 1B (end view). The closure has a thin base 10 of uniform cross

Patent Application of Lou W. Koppe for "Paper-Laminated
Pliable Closure for Flexible Bags" continued

section consisting of a flexible sheet of material which can be repeatedly bent and straightened out without fracturing. A layer of paper 20 (Fig 1B) is laminated on one side of base 10. In the preferred embodiment, the base is a flexible plastic, such as poly-ethylene-tere-phthalate (PET—hyphens here supplied to facilitate pronunciation) available from Eastman Chemical Co. of Kingsport, TN. However, the base can consist of any other material that can be repeatedly bent without fracturing, such as polyethylene, polypropylene, vinyl, nylon, rubber, leather, various impregnated or laminated fibrous materials, various plasticized materials, cardboard, paper, etc.

At one end of the closure is a lead-in notch 12 which terminates in gripping points 16 and leads to a hole 14. Paper layer 20 adheres to base 10 by virtue either of the extrusion of liquid plastic (which will form the body of the closure) directly onto the paper or the application of heat or adhesive upon the entirety of one side of base 10. The paper-laminated closure is then punched out. Thus the lamination will have the same shape as the side of the base 10 to which it adheres.

The base of the closure is typically .8 mm to 1.2 mm in thickness, and has overall dimensions roughly from 20 mm x 20 mm (square shape) to 40 mm x 70 mm (oblong shape). The outer four corners 24 of the closure are typically beveled or rounded to avoid snagging and personal injury. Also, when closure tabs are connected side-to-side in a long roll, these bevels or roundings give the roll a series of notches which act as detents or indices for the positioning and conveying of the tabs in a dispensing machine.

A longitudinal groove 18 is formed on one side of base 10 in Fig 1. In other embodiments, there may be two longitudinal grooves—one each side of the base—or there may be no longitudinal groove at all. Groove 18 may be formed by machining, scoring, rolling, or extruding. In the absence of a groove, there may be a longitudinal through-hole 26 (Fig 6L). This through-hole may be formed by placing, in the extrusion path of the closure, a hollow pin for the outlet of air.

Figs 2-5—Additional Embodiments

Additional embodiments are shown in Figs 2, 3, 4, and 5; in each case the paper lamination is shown partially peeled back. In Fig 2 the closure has only one lamination and no groove; in Fig 3 it has only one lamination and only one groove; in Fig 4 it has two laminations and only one groove; in Fig 5 it has two laminations and one groove, the latter having been rolled into one lamination as well as into the body of the closure.

Figs 6A-6B—Alternative Embodiments

There are various possibilities with regard to the relative disposition of the sides which are grooved and the sides which are laminated, as illustrated in Fig 6, which presents end views along the longitudinal axis. Fig 6A shows a closure with lamination on one side only and with no groove; Fig 6B shows a closure with laminations on both sides and with no

Patent Application of Lou W. Koppe for "Paper-Laminated
Pliable Closure for Flexible Bags" continued

groove; Fig 6C shows a closure with only one lamination and only one groove, both being on the same side; Fig 6D shows a closure with only one lamination and only one groove, both being on the same side and the groove having been rolled into the lamination as well as into the body of the closure; Fig 6E shows a closure with only one lamination and only one groove, the two being on opposite sides; Fig 6F shows a closure with two laminations and only one groove; Fig 6G shows a closure with two laminations and only one groove, the groove having been rolled into one lamination as well as into the body of the closure; Fig 6H shows a closure with only one lamination and with two grooves; Fig 6I shows a closure with only one lamination and with two grooves, one of the grooves having been rolled into the lamination as well as into the body of the closure; Fig 6J shows a closure with two laminations and with two grooves; Fig 6K shows a closure with two laminations and with two grooves, the grooves having been rolled into the laminations as well as into the body of the closure; and Fig 6L shows a closure with two laminations and a longitudinal through-hole.

Operation—Figs 1, 6, 7, 8

The manner of using the paper-laminated closure to seal a plastic bag is identical to that for closures in present use. Namely, one first twists the neck of a bag (not shown here but shown in Fig 12 of my above patent) into a narrow, cylindrical configuration. Next, holding the closure so that the plane of its base is generally perpendicular to the axis of the neck and so that lead-in notch 12 is adjacent to the neck, one inserts the twisted neck into the lead-in notch until it is forced past gripping points 16 at the base of the notch and into hole 14.

To remove the closure, one first bends it along its horizontal axis (Fig 1C—an end view—and Figs 7 and 8) so that the closure is still in contact with the neck of the bag and so that gripping points 16 roughly point in parallel directions. Then one pulls the closure up or down and away from the neck in a direction generally opposite to that in which the gripping points now point, thus freeing the closure from the bag without damaging the latter. The presence of one or two grooves 18 or a longitudinal through-hole 26 (Fig 6L), either of which acts as a hinge, facilitates this process of bending.

The closure can be used to reseal the original bag or to seal another bag many times; one simply bends it flat again prior to reuse.

As shown in Figs 1C, 7B, and 8B (all end views), when the closure is bent along its longitudinal axis, region 30 of the base will stretch somewhat along the direction perpendicular to the longitudinal axis. (Region 30 is the region which is parallel to this axis and is on the side of the base opposite to the bend.) Therefore, when the closure is flattened again, the base will have elongated in the direction perpendicular to the longitudinal axis. This will cause a necking down 28 (Figs 1D, 7C, and 8C) of the base, as well as either a tell-tale tear 22, or at least a crease 32 (Figs 7A and 8A) along the axis of

Patent Application of Lou W. Koppe for "Paper-Laminated
Pliable Closure for Flexible Bags" continued

bending. Therefore, if the closure is attached to a sales item and has print upon its paper lamination, the fact that the closure has been transferred by a dishonest consumer from the first item to another will be made evident by the tear or crease.

Figs 7A and 8A show bent closures with and without grooves, respectively. Figs 7C and 8C show the same closures, respectively, after being flattened out, along their longitudinal axes, paper tear 22 being visible.

Advantages

From the description above, a number of advantages of my paper-laminated closures become evident:

(a) A few rolls of colored paper will contain thousands of square yards of a variety of colors, will obviate the need for liquid pigments or a pigment-compounding plant, and will permit the manufacturer to produce colored closures with transparent, off-color, or leftover plastic, all of which are cheaper than first-quality pigmented plastic.

(b) With the use of rolls of colored paper to laminate the closures, one can change colors by simply changing rolls, thus avoiding the need to purge the extruder used to produce the closures.

(c) The use of paper laminate upon an unpigmented, flexible plastic base can provide a bright color without requiring the introduction of pigment into the base and the consequent sacrifice of pliability.

(d) The presence of a paper lamination will permit the display of multicolored designs.

(e) The paper lamination will provide a superior surface for labeling or printing, either by hand or by machine.

(f) Any erasure or alteration of prices by dishonest consumers on the paper-laminated closure will leave a highly visible and permanent mark.

(g) Although closures made solely of plastic are slippery when handled with wet or greasy fingers, the paper laminate on my closures will provide a nonslip surface.

Figs 7A and 8A show bent closures with and without grooves, respectively. Figs 7C and 8C show the same closures, respectively, after being flattened out, along their longitudinal axes, paper tear 22 being visible.

Conclusion, Ramifications, and Scope

Accordingly, the reader will see that the paper-laminated closure of this invention can be used to seal a plastic bag easily and conveniently, can be removed just as easily and without damage to the bag, and can be used to reseal the bag without requiring a new closure. In addition, when a closure has been used to seal a bag and is later bent and removed from the bag so as not to damage the latter, the paper lamination will tear or crease and thus give visible evidence of tampering, without impairing the ability of the closure to reseal the original bag or any other bag. Furthermore, the paper lamination has the additional advantages in that:

• it permits the production of closures in a variety of colors without requiring the manufacturer to use a separate facility for the compounding of the powdered or liquid pigments needed in the production of colored closures;

• it permits an immediate change in the color of the closure being produced without the need for purging the extruder of old resin;

• it allows the closure to be brightly colored without the need to pigment the base itself and consequently sacrifice the flexibility of the closure;

• it allows the closure to be multicolored since the paper lamination offers a perfect surface upon which can be printed multicolored designs;

• it provides a closure with a superior surface upon which one can label or print;

• it provides a closure whose labeling cannot be altered or erased without resulting in telltale damage to the paper lamination; and

• it provides a closure which will not be slippery when handled with wet or greasy fingers, the paper itself providing a nonslip surface.

Although the description above contains many specificities, these should not be construed as limiting the scope of the invention but as merely providing illustrations of some of the presently preferred embodiments of this invention. For example, the closure can have other shapes, such as circular, oval, trapezoidal, triangular, etc.; the lead-in notch can have other shapes; the groove can be replaced by a hinge which connects two otherwise unconnected halves; etc.

Thus the scope of the invention should be determined by the appended claims and their legal equivalents, rather than by the examples given.

CLAIMS: I claim:

1. In a bag closure of the type comprising a flat body of material having a lead-in notch on one edge thereof and a gripping aperture adjacent to and communicating with said notch, the improvement wherein said closure has a layer of paper laminated on one of its sides.

    2. The closure of claim 1 wherein said body of material is composed of polyethyleneterephthalate.

    3. The closure of claim 1 wherein said body is elongated and has a longitudinal groove which is on said one side of said body and extends the full length of said one side, from said gripping aperture to the opposite edge.

Patent Application of Lou W. Koppe for "Paper-Laminated
Pliable Closure for Flexible Bags" continued

4. The closure of claim 3 wherein said groove is formed into and along the full length of said lamination.

5. The closure of claim 1 wherein said body is elongated and has a longitudinal groove which is on the side of said body opposite to said one side thereof and extends the full length of said one side, from said gripping aperture to the opposite edge.

6. The closure of claim 1 wherein said body is elongated and has two longitudinal grooves which are on opposite sides of said body and extend the full lengths of said sides, from said gripping aperture to the opposite edge.

7. The closure of claim 6 wherein the groove on said one side of said body is formed into and along the full length of said lamination.

8. The closure of claim 1 wherein said body has a paper lamination on both of said sides.

9. The closure of claim 8 wherein a groove is on one side of said body and extends the full length of said one side, from said gripping aperture to the opposite edge.

10. The closure of claim 8 wherein two grooves, on opposite sides of said body, extend the full lengths of said sides, from said gripping aperture to the opposite edge.

11. The closure of claim 10 wherein said grooves are rolled into and along the full lengths of said laminations, respectively.

12. The closure of claim 1 wherein said paper lamination is colored.

13. The closure of claim 1 wherein said body is elongated and has a longitudinal through-hole.

14. A bag closure of the type comprising a flat body of material having a lead-in notch on one edge thereof, a gripping aperture adjacent to and communicating with said notch, characterized in that one of its sides has a layer of paper laminated thereon.

15. The closure of claim 14 wherein said body of material is composed of polyethyleneterephthalate.

16. The closure of claim 14 wherein said body is elongated and has a longitudinal groove on said one side of said body and which extends the full length of said one side, from said gripping aperture to the opposite edge.

17. The closure of claim 14 wherein said body is elongated and has a longitudinal groove which is on the side of said body opposite to said one side thereof and extends the full length of said one side, from said gripping aperture to the opposite edge.

Patent Application of Lou W. Koppe for "Paper-Laminated
Pliable Closure for Flexible Bags" continued

18. The closure of claim 14 wherein said body is elongated and has two longitudinal grooves which are on opposite sides of said body and extend the full lengths of said sides, from said gripping aperture to the opposite edge.

19. The closure of claim 14 wherein said body has a paper lamination on both of said sides.

20. The closure of claim 19 wherein a groove is on one side of said body and extends the full length of said one side, from said gripping aperture to the opposite edge.

21. The closure of claim 19 wherein two grooves, on opposite sides of said body, extend the full lengths of said sides, from said gripping aperture to the opposite edge.

22. The closure of claim 14 wherein said paper lamination is colored.

23. The closure of claim 14 wherein said body is elongated and has a longitudinal through-hole.

24. A method of closing a plastic bag, comprising:

(a) providing a bag closure of the type comprising a flat body of material having a lead-in notch on one edge thereof, a gripping aperture adjacent to and communicating with said notch, and a layer of paper laminated on one of its sides,

(b) providing a plastic bag and inserting contents into said plastic bag,

(c) twisting said plastic bag so that it forms a neck portion to hold said contents from falling out of said plastic bag,

(d) inserting said bag closure onto said neck portion of said plastic bag so that said neck portion of said plastic bag passes said lead-in notch and into said gripping aperture,

whereby said bag closure can be easily marked to identify and/or price said contents in said plastic bag.

25. The method of claim 24 wherein said flat body of material is composed of polyethyleneterephthalate.

26. The method of claim 24 wherein said layer of paper is colored.

Abstract: A thin, flat closure for plastic bags and of the type having at one edge a V-shaped notch (12) which communicates at its base with a gripping aperture (14). The base (10) of the closure is made of a flexible material so that it can be repeatedly bent, without fracturing, along an axis aligned with said notch and aperture. In addition, a layer of paper (20) is laminated on one or both sides of the closure. The axis of the base may contain one or two grooves (18) or a through-hole (26), either of which acts as a hinge to facilitate bending.

Patent: Law: Forms

1/4

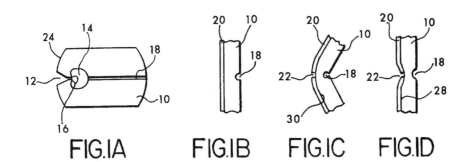

FIG.IA FIG.IB FIG.IC FIG.ID

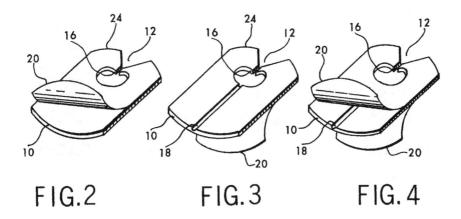

FIG.2 FIG.3 FIG. 4

2/4

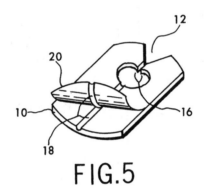

FIG.5

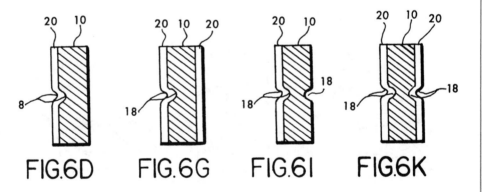

FIG.6D   FIG.6G   FIG.6I   FIG.6K

3/4

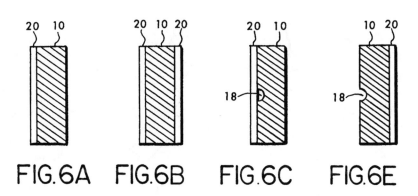

FIG.6A   FIG.6B   FIG.6C   FIG.6E

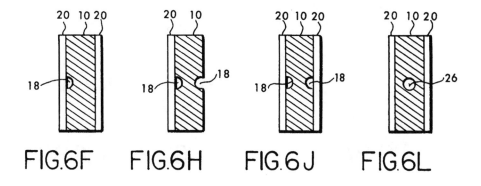

FIG.6F   FIG.6H   FIG.6J   FIG.6L

Patent Law: Forms

4/4

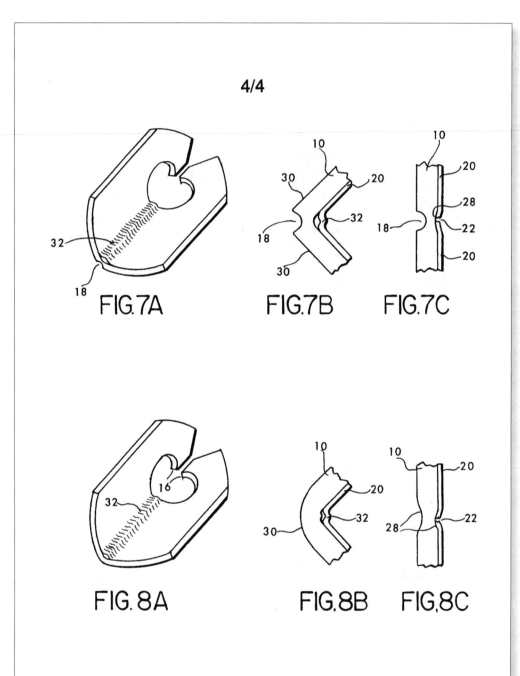

FIG.7A

FIG.7B

FIG.7C

FIG. 8A

FIG.8B

FIG.8C

Preparing a Design Patent Application

Preparing and filing a design patent is fairly simple—especially when compared to preparing and filing a utility patent. If you're a self-starter with a do-it-yourself mindset, you can, with a bit of work, prepare your own design patent application and save anywhere from $500 to $1,000. Below, we present basic instructions for preparing a design patent application. If you would like more information, read *Patent It Yourself,* by David Pressman (Nolo), or read and download the design patent information provided at the USPTO website, at www.uspto.gov. Even if you prepare the rest of the application yourself, however, you may need to hire a patent draftsperson to create professional drawings.

If you're not the do-it-yourself type, you can always hire an attorney or patent agent to review and analyze your design and advise you on whether pursuing a design patent is worthwhile. The attorney or agent can prepare the application. If there is a problem at the USPTO—for example, an examiner challenges your application—the attorney or agent can respond and keep the application on track.

If you don't want to do it all yourself, you'll have to pay between $750 and $1,500 for:

- an attorney to draft the application
- a patent draftsperson to create the drawings, and
- the filing fee ($110, plus $50 for search fee and $70 for examination fee).

Unless you pay for expedited processing of your application, you will have to wait one to two years for your design patent, and you cannot use it to stop others from copying your design until the patent has been granted. (The USPTO has indicated that it will place design patents on a faster track than utility patents, which can take two to three years.) Design patents automatically expire 14 years after they're issued, and you cannot renew them.

As the inventor, only you have the right to apply for the patent. (For historical reasons, the USPTO often refers to the designer as the inventor and to the design as the invention.) Even if you signed away your rights to someone else or you were employed to create the design, you must still be listed as the inventor and sign the application. However, the issued patent application will indicate that your rights have been assigned. If someone else contributes to a new, nonobvious element of your design, that person is a coinventor, and the two of you should reach an agreement as to ownership of the patent.

Patent Law: Forms

If you're employed to create designs, your employer may own rights in any resulting design patents. Who owns the design depends on the contents of your employment agreement, your employer's policies, whether you used your employer's time and resources to create the design, and state laws regarding employee ownership rights.

The design patent application consists of:

- the "specification"—a short written document describing your design. The specification is quite simple to prepare. We've provided a sample one for a table design, created by a furniture designer. The elements of the specification are fairly straightforward. Here's a quick breakdown:
  - Preamble—one or two boilerplate sentences announcing that you're seeking a design patent.
  - Specification—the place to introduce your design by name. A basic title such as "glass bowl," "puppet," or "steel table" will work best.
  - Cross References to Related Applications—here, you indicate whether you have filed a previous design patent application to which this one is related.
  - Statement Regarding Federally Sponsored R & D—indicate here whether the design was prepared under a government grant or as part of government research.
  - Description of the Figure(s) of the Drawings—describe the view presented in each of the drawing sheets.
  - Feature Description—provide a short description of your design; for example, "My candle is characterized by a pinwheel effect that gradually slopes outward."
- drawing(s) showing the appearance of your design. Design patent drawings are technical and stylized. Each element—for example, stippling (use of dots), linear shading (use of lines), and distinctive patterns (for indicating colors)—has a special meaning. You are allowed to provide informal drawings, such as rough sketches or photographs, with your design patent application, but no one will examine your application until you provide formal drawings similar to those shown in this chapter. To avoid delay, we recommend that you provide formal drawings in the first place. (The only time you should furnish informal drawings is when you are in a hurry to obtain an early filing date but haven't had a chance to draft the drawings.) With a little drawing skill or computer graphics knowledge, you can prepare formal drawings for your design patent application. In their book *How to Make Patent Drawings* (Nolo),

Jack Lo and David Pressman explain how to prepare these drawings using computer software or pen and ink. One chapter is devoted solely to design patent drawing rules. If you prefer to have a professional draft your drawings, you can accomplish this relatively inexpensively (about $80 per drawing sheet; each sheet may contain one or two figures). Designs are commonly depicted in different views—for example, top views, side views, or disassembled views. You should present as many views as are necessary to demonstrate your design. Each view provides another way of "seeing" the design. Each view is given a discrete figure number (abbreviated as "Fig" in patent law). Keep in mind that the design patent only protects what is disclosed in the drawings. If you later change the design substantially, you can't protect it unless you apply for a new design patent.

- the Design Patent Application Transmittal—a cover sheet that accompanies your application. You must submit a cover sheet with your design patent application. The USPTO has prepared one that we recommend you use. To obtain this form, go to the USPTO home page at www.uspto.gov and click "Patents" on the left side of the screen. Click "Forms," then follow the instructions to download Form SB0018.

- the Declaration—an oath provided by the designer. The declaration, Form SB/01, is a two-page form that you can download from the USPTO website. Check the box "Declaration Submitted With Initial Filing" and provide the title of your design. On page 2, list the designers and their addresses. Sign the declaration where it is marked "Inventor's Signature."

- the Fee Application Transmittal Form. The Fee Transmittal, Form SB/17, is a one-page form that you can download from the USPTO website. Indicate your method of payment.

- A fee (check current fees).

Design Patent Application—Preamble, Specification, and Claim

Mail Stop Designs—United States Patent and Trademark Office
Commissioner for Patents
P.O. Box 1450
Alexandria, VA 22313-1450

PREAMBLE:

The petitioner whose signature appears on the declaration attached respectfully requests that Letters Patent be granted to such petitioner for the new and original design set forth in the specification.

SPECIFICATION:

Petitioner has invented a new, original, and ornamental design for a table entitled "I Cannot Tell a Lie Table," of which the following is a specification. Reference is made to the accompanying drawings which form a part hereof, the figures of which are described below.

CROSS-REFERENCE TO RELATED APPLICATIONS: None

STATEMENT REGARDING FEDERALLY SPONSORED RESEARCH: None

DRAWING FIGURES:

Fig. 1 is a perspective view of my new table design

Fig. 2 is a right side view of my new table design

Fig. 3 is a top view of my new table design

Fig. 4 is a left end view of my new table design

FEATURE DESCRIPTION: My table design is characterized by wooden hatchets, hanging wooden cherries, and the written expression "I cannot tell a lie."

CLAIM: I (We) Claim:

The ornamental design for a table as shown and described.

Express Mail Label # EU121293846US

Date of Deposit: 2004 _____

Part 2: Copyright Law

Copyright Law: Overview 197

    What is a copyright? 197

    How is a copyright created? 198

    Who owns a copyright? 198

    Can copyrights be divided or transferred? 199

    How long does copyright protection last? 200

    What happens if a copyright is infringed? 200

    When can a copyrighted work be used without an owner's permission? 201

    What laws cover copyright protection in the United States
       and other countries? 202

    What's new in copyright law since the last edition? 202

    Copyright resources 207

Copyright Law: Definitions 209

Copyright Law: Forms 349

    Preparing a Copyright Application 349

    Preparing a Form CO Copyright Application 350

    Preparing an Electronic (eCO) Copyright Application 363

    Preparing a Traditional Print Copyright Application 366

Copyright Law: Overview

Copyright law protects a variety of original expressions, including art, sculpture, literature, music, songs, choreography, crafts, poetry, software, photography, movies, video games, videos, websites, architecture, and graphics. Protection occurs automatically—that is, you acquire copyright once you fix the work in a medium—but this automatic protection can be enhanced by registering the work with the U.S. Copyright Office.

Copyright lasts for the life of the work's creator (its author) plus 70 years. In cases where the creator is a business, the copyright lasts between 95 and 120 years. Most nations of the world offer copyright protection to works by U.S. citizens and nationals, and the United States offers its copyright protection to the citizens and nationals of these same nations.

What is a copyright?

A copyright gives the owner of a creative work the right to keep others from unauthorized use of the work. Under copyright law, a creative work (often referred to as a "work of authorship") must meet all of these three criteria to be protected:

- It must be original—that is, the author must have created rather than copied it.
- It must be fixed in a tangible (concrete) medium of expression—for example, it should be recorded or expressed on paper, audio or videotape, computer disk, clay, or canvas.
- It must have at least some creativity—that is, it must be produced by an exercise of human intellect. There is no hard and fast rule as to how much creativity is enough. To give an example, it must go beyond the creativity found in the telephone white pages, which involve a nondiscretionary alphabetic listing of telephone numbers rather than a creative selection of listings.

Copyright does not protect ideas or facts; it protects only the unique way in which ideas or facts are expressed. For instance, copyright may protect an author's science fiction novel about a romance between an earthling and a space alien, but the author cannot stop others from using the underlying idea of an intergalactic love affair.

How is a copyright created?

A creative work is protected by copyright the moment the work assumes a tangible form—which in copyright circles is referred to as "fixed in a tangible medium of expression." Contrary to popular belief, providing a copyright notice or registering the work with the U.S. Copyright Office is not necessary to obtain basic copyright protection. But there are some steps that can be taken to enhance the creator's ability to sue or stop others from copying:

- Place a copyright notice on a published work. The copyright notice, or "copyright bug" as it is sometimes called, commonly appears in this form: "© (year of publication) (author or other basic copyright owner)." Placing this notice on a published work (distributed to the public without restriction) prevents others from claiming that they did not know that the work was covered by copyright. This can be important if the author is forced to file a lawsuit to enforce the copyright, since it is much easier to recover significant money damages from a deliberate (as opposed to innocent) copyright infringer.
- Register works with the U.S. Copyright Office. Timely registration of the copyright with the U.S. Copyright Office—that is, registration within three months of the work's publication date, or before the infringement actually begins—makes it much easier to sue and recover from an infringer. Registration creates a legal presumption that the copyright is valid and, if accomplished prior to someone copying the work, allows the copyright owner to recover up to $150,000 (and possibly attorney fees) without proving any actual monetary harm. Registration is accomplished by filing a simple form and depositing one or two samples of the work (depending on what it is) with the U.S. Copyright Office. The U.S. Copyright Office registration currently costs $65 for each paper registration, $50 for each Form CO application (a hybrid paper/electronic form), and $35 for each online registration.

Who owns a copyright?

With three important exceptions, a copyright is owned by the person who created the work. In copyright lingo, these people are all called "authors."

The exceptions are:

- If a work is created by an employee in the course of employment, the work is called a "work made for hire" and the copyright is owned by the employer (and the employer is considered the "author" for copyright purposes).
- If the work is commissioned (created by an author working as an independent contractor) and the parties sign a written work-made-for-hire agreement, the copyright will be owned by the commissioning party as long as the work falls within one of the statutory categories of commissioned works that can qualify as works made for hire.
- If the author sells ("assigns") the copyright to someone else, the purchasing person or business owns the copyright.

Can copyrights be divided or transferred?

A copyright actually encompasses a bundle of separate exclusive rights, including the exclusive right to:
- reproduce the work
- display or perform the work
- distribute the work, and
- prepare adaptations of the work (derivative works).

When a copyright owner wishes to commercially exploit the work, the owner typically transfers one or more of these rights to the publisher or other entity who will be responsible for getting the work to market. It is also common for the copyright owner to place some limitations on the exclusive rights being transferred. For example, the owner may limit the transfer to a specific period of time, allow the right to be exercised only in a specific part of the country or world, or require that the right be exercised only on certain computer platforms (those with Linux operating systems, for example).

When all copyright rights are transferred unconditionally, it is generally termed an "assignment." When only some of the rights associated with the copyright are transferred, it is known as a "license." An exclusive license exists when the right being licensed can only be exercised by the licensee, and no one else. If the license allows others to exercise the same rights being transferred in the license, the license is said to be nonexclusive.

The U.S. Copyright Office allows buyers of exclusive and nonexclusive copyright rights to record the transfers in the U.S. Copyright Office. This helps to protect the buyers in case the original copyright owner later decides to transfer the same rights to another party.

How long does copyright protection last?

As a result of the Copyright Term Extension Act of 1998, most copyrights for works published after January 1, 1978, last for the life of the author plus 70 years. However, in the following circumstances, the copyright lasts between 95 and 120 years, depending on the date the work is published:

- The work belongs to the author's employer under work-made-for-hire principles.
- The work was commissioned under a work-made-for-hire agreement (and fits within one of the categories of works that qualify for work-made-for-hire treatment).
- The author publishes and registers the work anonymously or under a pseudonym.

After a copyright expires, the work goes into the public domain, meaning it becomes available for anyone's use.

For works created before 1978, the duration times are different:

- If the work was published before 1923, it is in the public domain (available for use without permission).
- If the work was published between 1923 and 1963 and not renewed, it is in the public domain.
- If the work was published between 1923 and 1963 and it was renewed, the copyright lasts 95 years from the date of first publication.
- If the work was published between 1964 and 1977, the copyright lasts for 95 years from the date of publication.
- If the work was created before 1978 and published before December 31, 2002, the copyright lasts at least until December 31, 2047; if created before 1978 and *not* published before December 31, 2002, the copyright has expired and the work is in the public domain in the United States.

What happens if a copyright is infringed?

In the event someone infringes (violates) the exclusive rights of a copyright owner, the owner is entitled to sue in federal court and ask the court to:

- issue orders (restraining orders and injunctions) to prevent further violations
- award money damages if appropriate, and
- in some circumstances, award attorney fees.

Whether the lawsuit will be effective and whether damages will be awarded depends on whether the alleged infringer can raise one or more legal defenses to the charge. Common legal defenses to copyright infringement are:

- Too much time has elapsed between the infringing act and the lawsuit (the statute of limitations defense).
- The infringement is allowed under the fair use defense.
- The infringement was innocent (the infringer had no reason to know the work was protected by copyright).
- The infringing work was independently created (that is, it wasn't copied from the original).
- The copyright owner authorized the use in a license.

When can a copyrighted work be used without an owner's permission?

Some uses of a copyrighted work are considered fair use—that is, the use may infringe, but the infringement is excused because the work is being used for a transformative purpose such as research, scholarship, criticism, or journalism. When determining whether an infringement should be excused on the basis of fair use, a court will use several factors including the purpose and character of the use, amount and substantiality of the portion borrowed, and effect of the use on the market for the copyrighted material.

It's important to understand that fair use is a defense rather than an affirmative right. This means that a particular use only gets established as a fair use if the copyright owner decides to file a lawsuit and the court upholds the fair use defense. There is, therefore, no way to find out in advance whether something will or won't be considered a fair use. Of course, if the copyright owner is willing to grant permission for the use, then the uncertainty surrounding the use goes away. For this reason, most people who propose to use a copyrighted work do what they can to obtain permission and only rely on the fair use defense if permission is not granted or the copyright owner can't be located.

A person who infringes a copyright but has good reason to genuinely believe that the use is a fair use is known as an innocent infringer. Innocent infringers usually don't have to pay any damages to the copyright owner but do have to cease the infringing activity or pay the owner for the reasonable commercial value of that use.

What laws cover copyright protection in the United States and other countries?

In the United States, copyright protection derives from the U.S. Constitution, which requires that original works of authorship be protected by copyright. The current (and exclusive) source of this protection is the federal Copyright Act of 1976, as amended. There are no state copyright laws.

Copyright protection rules are fairly similar worldwide, due to several international copyright treaties, the most important of which is the Berne Convention. Under this treaty, all member countries (in excess of 100 countries, including virtually all industrialized countries) must afford copyright protection to authors who are nationals of any member country. This protection must last for at least the life of the author plus 50 years and must be automatic, without the need for the author to take any legal steps to preserve the copyright.

In addition to the Berne Convention, the GATT (General Agreement on Tariffs and Trade) treaty contains a number of provisions that affect copyright protection in signatory countries. Together, the Berne Copyright Convention and the GATT treaty allow U.S. authors to enforce their copyrights in most industrialized nations and allow the nationals of those nations to enforce their copyrights in the United States.

What's new in copyright law since the last edition?

Below are the major changes in copyright law since the last edition was published.

- **Copyright Cleanup, Clarification, and Corrections Act of 2010.** (December 2010.) This Act, as its name suggests provides various corrections and clarifications to copyright law, most of which are of little interest to the general public. For example, the law provides for repeal of 17 USC Sec. 601 that prohibited the importation of certain types of works manufactured outside the U.S. It also permits sublicensing of copyrighted works in the absence of a written agreement, and changes the regulations for recording documents with the Copyright Office.
- **Ringtones are not a public performance.** ASCAP, a society that collects money for songwriters, claimed that Verizon's sale of ringtones amounted to violation of the public performance right and required payment of licensing fees. A court held that the ringtones—which were stored on users' phones—were exempt from public performance licensing under 17 USC Sec. 110(4). (*In re Application of Cellco Partnership*, 663 F. Supp. 2d 363 (S.D. N.Y. 2009).)

- **Blank emergency room forms not copyrightable.** The Eleventh Circuit determined that blank forms used for emergency room purposes were not copyrightable because the forms did not convey information. (*Utopia Provider Systems, Inc. v. Pro-Med Clinical Systems, LLC*, 596 F.3d 1313 (11th Cir. 2010).)

- **Unfinished artwork is protected by VARA.** A Swiss artist, unhappy with the manner in which his art was being installed in a museum, sued under the Visual Artists Rights Act (VARA). The First Circuit determined that VARA was intended to protect the integrity of works of art, even uncompleted artwork. (*Massachusetts Museum of Contemporary Art Foundation, Inc. v. Buchel*, 593 F.3d 38 (1st Cir. 2010).)

- **DRM-breaking not excused by availability of DRM-cracking tools.** Apple sued a company that had circumvented its Digital Rights Management (DRM) system. The company argued in defense that tools for cracking the DRM were widely available and that therefore, the DRM itself was so ineffective as to be meaningless. The court disagreed and held that if the DRM could not be circumvented without outside information or tools, it would be considered as effective DRM. (*Apple Inc. v. Psystar Corp.,* 673 F. Supp. 2d 931 (N.D. Cal. 2009).)

- **Usefulness not a bar to protecting toys and furniture.** The original design of a toy or an item of furniture can qualify for copyright protection if it is created for expressive rather than functional purposes. In cases, where this issue arises, a court must attempt to separate form from function. This issue arose in two 2010 cases. In *Universal Furniture International, Inc. v. Collezione Europa USA, Inc.,* 618 F. 3d 417 (4th Circuit 2010), the Fourth Circuit ruled that highly ornate furniture design can be separable and copyrightable despite its utilitarian function. In *Lanard Toys Ltd. v. Novelty Inc.*, 2010 U.S. App. LEXIS 7585 (9th Cir. 2010), the Ninth Circuit held that there was sufficient evidence to demonstrate that a launcher and flying toy were copyrightable despite their function.

- **Complications for registrants of photo compilations and databases.** Two cases highlighted the confusion regarding registration of databases and compilations. In one case, a photographer licensed 150 works to Corbis. Corbis included the photos in a group registration of approximately 12,000–16,000 photographs. A district court ruled that the photographer could not rely on the group registration because it identified Corbis as the author of the works, not the photographer. Because each author must be identified, the compilation registration did not register copyrights in the individual works. (*Bean v. Houghton Mifflin Publishing, Co.,* 95 USPQ 2d 1489 (D. Ariz. 2010).) A related result occurred in *Muench Photography, Inc. v. Houghton Mifflin Harcourt Publishing,* 712 F. Supp. 2d 84 (S.D. N.Y. 2010). In that case, a New York district court ruled that copyright registration in an automated database of photographs must contain the names of each of the photographers in order for an individual photographer to sue for infringement.

- **Jailbreaking exempt from DMCA rules.** The Library of Congress issued rules in 2010 stating that wireless phone owners could break access controls on their phones in order to switch wireless carriers (known as "jailbreaking"). Other rules issued: computer users could bypass security dongles if the dongle no longer works and can't be replaced; users of eBook readers could break digital locks to use read-aloud software, and educators and filmmakers could circumvent DVD protection for noncommercial purposes.

- **First-sale doctrine does not apply to gray market goods.** Costco imported "gray market" Omega watches that featured a copyrighted image of a globe. Omega sued for copyright infringement and Costco argued that the sale was permitted under the first-sale doctrine. In a per curiam decision (a brief statement unaccompanied by an explanation), the Supreme Court affirmed the Ninth Circuit decision that the "first-sale" doctrine applies only to copyrighted items that are made and distributed in the United States. (*Costco Wholesale Corporation v. Omega, S.A.* 131 S.Ct. 565 (2010).)

- **Determining statutory damages for music infringement.** A Tennessee District Court ruled that separate sound recordings embodying a single song constituted one work when determining statutory damages. (*MCS Music America v. Yahoo! Inc.,* ___ F. Supp. 2d ___ (M.D. Tenn. 2010).) In a related issue, the Second Circuit determined that copying and selling an album of music constituted one infringement for purposes of statutory damages rather than computing damages based on the number of tracks. (*Bryant v. Media Right Productions,* 603 F.3d 135 (2010).)

- **More than "likelihood of infringement" required for preliminary injunction.** A preliminary injunction used to be relatively easy to obtain once substantial evidence was presented to the court showing a probability that an infringement occurred. The Second Circuit held that this simple test no longer applied in light of the Supreme Court's ruling in *eBay v. MercExchange, L.L.C.* In the *eBay* case (a patent case), the Supreme Court ruled that showing a likelihood of infringement was not enough; the party seeking the preliminary injunction must apply a more traditional four-factor test for injunctions. (*Salinger v. Colting,* 607 F.3d 68 (2d Cir. 2010).)

- **Before requesting takedown under DMCA, copyright owners must consider fair use defense.** Universal Music issued a takedown notice for a video of a child dancing to the song, "Let's Go Crazy," by Prince. The owner of the video claimed that since Universal didn't consider the issue of fair use, Universal could have not had a "good faith belief" they were entitled to a takedown. Faced with this novel issue a district court agreed that the failure to consider fair use when sending a DMCA notice could give rise to a claim of failing to act in good faith. (*Lenz v. Universal Music Corp.,* 572 F. Supp 2d 1150 (N.D. Cal. 2008).) (One curious element of the case: During the resulting lawsuit, a series of emails was discovered. In one, a friend was amused that the woman had "injured [Universal] substantially and irreparably" to which the woman replied. "I have ;–)." Universal claimed that this demonstrated bad faith in regard to the DMCA counter notice. The court disagreed and threw out the bad faith claim.)

- **Filing for copyright registration does not create a presumption of validity.** A company filed for, but had not received, a copyright registration prior to seeking a preliminary injunction against an alleged infringer. The court refused to grant an injunction absent evidence of the registration. The district court held that someone who has acquired a registration is entitled to the presumption of copyright validity, but that is not true for someone who has simply applied for registration. (*CHM Industries Inc. v. Structural and Steel Products, Inc.,* 2008 WL 4693385 (N.D. Tex. 2008).)

- **Compilation of health care provider ratings is protectable.** A district court held that a compilation prepared by a fee-based website that specialized in grading health care professionals and other providers, was protected under copyright. The compilation achieved copyright protection because it involved selection, evaluation, and arrangement of facts. (*Health Grades Inc. v. Robert Wood Johnson University Hospital,* 634 F. Supp. 2d 1226 (D. Colo., 2009).)

- **Use of monster magazine covers in book about artist is a fair use.** A district court held that the reproduction of movie monster magazine covers, in a book about the cover artist, was a fair use. In that case, a publisher of monster magazines from the 1950s, 60s, and 70s sued the creator and publisher of a book, *Famous Monster Movie Art of Basil Gogos.* (Gogos created covers for the magazines.) The book publisher had obtained licenses from the artist directly but not from the magazine publisher who claimed copyright under work-made-for-hire principles. The district court did not address the ownership issues but focused only on fair use and determined that the use was transformative—it was a biography/retrospective of the artist, not simply a series of covers for magazines devoted to movie monsters. In addition, the magazines were no longer in print, and the covers amounted to only one page of the magazine, not the "heart" of the magazine. (*Warren Publishing Co. v. Spurlock d/b/a Vanguard Productions*, 645 F. Supp. 2d 402, (E.D. Pa., 2009).)

- **A 2-D representation of a sculpture on a stamp is not a fair use.** The U.S. Postal Service (USPS) licensed the use of a photograph of the Korean War veterans' memorial sculpture for a postage stamp but failed to obtain permission from the sculptor who held copyright in the three-dimensional work. The U.S. Court of Appeals for the Federal Circuit held that the stamp was not a fair use because the 2-D replication was not sufficiently transformative (even though the lower court held that it had new and different character and was enhanced by additional "surrealistic elements"). (*Gaylord v. United States*, 595 F.3d 1364 (2010).)

- **Illegal acts don't preclude an award of damages.** The Ninth Circuit ruled that actual damages should be awarded despite the fact that the plaintiff (the person bringing the case) had violated the law. In this case, the owner of copyright in an electronic video bingo game sued a competitor for infringement and was awarded $25,000 in statutory damages. The trial court refused to award actual damages for lost profits because the plaintiff had offered its game in Utah and Wyoming, two states in which the game has been ruled to be illegal. The Ninth Circuit held that illegal operation of a copyrightable work doesn't preclude copyright remedies. (*Dream Games of Arizona Inc. v. PC Onsite*, 561 F.3d 983 (9th Cir. 2009).)

- **Resale of foreign published textbooks not permitted under first-sale doctrine.** A New York district court ruled that an importer of less expensive foreign-published textbooks was prohibited from claiming the first-sale doctrine as a defense to copyright infringement for distributing those books in the U.S. (an issue also currently in front of the U.S. Supreme Court at the time this book went to print). (*John Wiley & Sons Inc. v. Kirtsaeng*, 2009 WL 3364037 (S.D. N.Y, 10/19/09).)

- **Chronology of facts about Pope's death is unprotectable.** In a case involving a play and a book—both examining the death of Pope John Paul I—a New York district court ruled that historical facts, theories interpreting those facts and plots based on the chronology of historical events are unprotectible. (*Crane v. Poetic Products, Ltd.*, 593 F. Supp. 2d 585 (S.D. NY 2009).)

- **Tree frogs do not require "absolute identicality."** In a case comparing two plush toys, both based on a Puerto Rican brown tree frog (*coquí común*), the defendant argued that the only similarities were elements based on the actual appearance of the frog. In other words, there is only one way to present the *coquí común* and so all copies would have to be substantially similar (a principle known as "the merger doctrine"). Alternatively, the defendant argued that it had distinguished its frog. The First Circuit disagreed stating that there were numerous ways to depict *coquí común*, and that when it comes to tree frogs, "absolute identicality" is not required for a finding of substantial similarity. (*Coquico Inc. v. Rodríguez-Miranda*, 562 F.3d 62, (1st Cir. 2009).)

- **Federal prisoner cannot sue government over distribution of calendar art.** 28 USC Sec. 1498(b) prohibits copyright infringement suits against the U.S. when the copyrighted work at issue was prepared by someone in the "employment or service" of the federal government. Walton was a federal prisoner instructed to prepare desk blotter calendars later sold to private companies and individuals. The Court of Appeals for the Federal Circuit determined that Walton was in the "service" of the federal government when he created the calendars and therefore barred from claiming copyright and suing the federal government over its distribution of the calendars. (*Walton v. U.S.*, 551 F.3d 1367 (Fed. Cir. 2009).)

Copyright resources

You can find valuable information about copyright by using any of the following Web resources:

- **Nolo (www.nolo.com).** Nolo offers self-help information about a wide variety of legal topics, including copyright law. (See the intellectual property topic in the Legal Encyclopedia, which incidentally includes selected entries from this part of the book.)

- **Copyright Office (www.copyright.gov).** The U.S. Copyright Office's website offers forms, circulars, and a wide range of helpful copyright information.

- **Copyright and Fair Use (http://fairuse.stanford.edu).** Operated by the Stanford University Libraries, this site provides a through overview of copyright and fair use.

- **Dear Rich: Nolo's Patent, Copyright & Trademark Blog.** (www.dearrichblog. com). Have a question about copyright law? Nolo's intellectual property blog operates as a companion to this book.

Copyright Law: Definitions

n this section, we provide concise definitions of the words and phrases commonly used when dealing with copyrights.

abridgment

See derivative work.

access

In order to prove that a work was copied, sold, or performed without authorization, the copyright owner must demonstrate that the person accused of infringement had a reasonable opportunity to view or hear the copyrighted work and that the two works—the infringer's and the copyright owner's—are substantially similar. The first requirement—the occasion to view or hear the copyrighted work— is referred to as access. If the infringement involves identical copies, such as photographs copied from a magazine, access may be presumed and does not need to be proved. That's because in cases of verbatim copying, it is virtually impossible that two works could have been independently created.

> EXAMPLE: The makers of Beanie Babies successfully sued a company market-ing a pig bean bag known as "Preston the Pig" that was identical to the Beanie Baby known as "Squealer." The similarity between the two was so close as to create a reasonable presumption of access. (*Ty Inc. v. GMA Accessories Inc.,* 132 F.3d 1167 (7th Cir. 1997).)

When the copies are not identical, access can be proven in various ways.

> EXAMPLE 1: The owners of copyright in popular children's characters proved access because the representatives of a fast-food chain had visited their head-quarters and discussed use of the characters in commercials. (*Sid & Marty Krofft Television Prods., Inc. v. McDonald's Corp.,* 562 F.2d 1157 (9th Cir. 1977).)

> EXAMPLE 2: The owners of the song "He's So Fine" sued George Harrison, alleging that Harrison's song "My Sweet Lord" infringed their copyright. It

was determined that Harrison had access to "He's So Fine" because the song was on the British pop charts in 1963 during the same period when a song by the Beatles was also on the British charts. (*Abkco Music, Inc. v. Harrisongs Music, Ltd.*, 722 F.2d 988 (2d Cir. 1983).)

As a general rule, the more popular a work, the easier it is to prove access. Conversely, if a work was not published, the copyright owner has a harder time proving access.

Proving access generally requires direct evidence. For example, a T-shirt company alleged access by its claim that a representative of the company that made Bratz dolls attended the Los Angeles County Fair where the T-shirt company had a display. The Ninth Circuit Court of Appeals dismissed this as a mere "bare possibility" because there was no direct evidence of the representative seeing the design or of the design being widely disseminated. (*Art Attacks Ink LLC v. MGA Entertainment Inc.*, 581 F.3d 1138 (9th Cir. 2009).)

Of course, in order to prove access, the party alleging infringement should be able to demonstrate a chronology that makes sense.

EXAMPLE: Two men alleged that they had sent their version of a song to a talent scout representing Britney Spears and claimed it was later infringed by the Spears song "What U See Is What U Get." However, the undisputed evidence at trial showed that Spears had recorded her version several months before the two men had even submitted their composition. (*Cottrill v. Spears*, 2003 U.S. Dist. LEXIS 8823 (E.D. Pa. 2003).)

In some federal circuits, noticeably the Ninth Circuit, the higher the degree of access to a work, the less the degree of similarity required, a principle known as the "inverse ratio" rule.

Related terms: copyright infringement; infringement action.

actual damages for copyright infringement

A copyright owner is entitled to recover the actual damages suffered as a result of an infringement, as well as any profits of the infringer that are attributable to the infringement and are not taken into account in computing the actual damages. In establishing the infringer's profits, the copyright owner is required to present proof only of the infringer's gross revenue, and the infringer is required to prove his or her deductible expenses and the elements of profit attributable to factors other than the copyrighted work. In some cases, a copyright owner may elect to recover statutory damages instead of actual damages. (*See* damages for copyright infringement.)

Related terms: copyright infringement; damages for copyright infringement.

adaptations or alterations

See derivative work.

advertising injury

This is the title of a provision in insurance contracts (usually found in comprehensive general liability policies used by most businesses) that often triggers coverage for the defense of copyright or trademark claims. Typically, the provision is worded to provide coverage when "infringing upon another's copyright, trade dress or slogan in your advertisement" (quoting from the 2003/2007 ISO Comprehensive General Liability Form). Although initially written (and interpreted broadly), such provisions now commonly include strict exclusions relating to intellectual property infringement. They key for triggering insurance coverage is for the policyholder to demonstrate a causal connection between the business's advertising and the infringement—for example, an artist alleges that the policyholder's unauthorized distribution and marketing of a promotional T-shirt infringes one of the artist's work.

affirmative rights

Many people use the term "protections" to refer to the benefits that go along with ownership of copyrights and other intellectual property such as trade secrets, patents, and trademarks. For example, one might say, "My poem is protected by copyright." However, a number of commentators prefer to describe these legal protections as "affirmative rights," because works are not protected unless the owners affirmatively exercise their rights if their copyright is infringed.

Affirmative rights include the owner's right to file a lawsuit, the right to recover damages, and the right to obtain an injunction (a court order preventing the infringer from taking certain actions, such as using or selling the infringing material). Although observing this linguistic difference may lead to a better understanding of how intellectual property laws work, this book generally uses the more accepted and commonly used term "protection."

all rights reserved

This phrase was required as part of a copyright notice by the Buenos Aires Convention international treaty. Until recently, the term appeared in many

Copyright Law: Definitions

copyright notices in an attempt to secure complete protection under that treaty. However, all signatory countries to the Buenos Aires Convention are now also members of other international agreements that don't require the "all rights reserved" phrase, so it is no longer required.

Related terms: international copyright protection; international rules on notice of copyright.

Altai case

See Computer Associates Int'l v. Altai.

anonymous

An author's contribution to a work is anonymous if the author (a natural person) is not identified on the copies or phonorecords (audio recordings) of the work. Copyright protection for anonymous and pseudonymous works is 95 years from the date of publication or 120 years from creation, whichever is shorter. However, if the name of the author is disclosed in the records of the Copyright Office, the work will be protected for the author's life plus 70 years.

> **EXAMPLE:** The 1995 best seller *Primary Colors* was published anonymously. The media eventually determined that the book's author was Joe Klein, a writer for *Newsweek* magazine. If Mr. Klein died in 2030 without disclosing his name to the Copyright Office, the term of copyright for *Primary Colors* would end in 2090 (95 years from publication). If Mr. Klein disclosed his name, protection would extend until 2100 (70 years from his death.)

Copyright Act: § 101. Definitions
An "anonymous work" is a work on the copies or phonorecords of which no natural person is identified as author.

Related terms: author as owner of copyright; duration of copyrights; pseudonym.

anthologies, copyrightability of

See compilations.

Apple Computer, Inc. v. Franklin

In this influential 1983 court decision, a federal Court of Appeals for the first time extended copyright protection to computer operating systems consisting of object code embedded in read-only memory chips, or ROMs. (*Apple Computer, Inc. v. Franklin Computer Corporation,* 714 F.2d 1240 (3d Cir. 1983), *affirmed* 35 F.3d 1435 (1994).)

Related terms: computer software, copyright of.

Apple Computer, Inc. v. Microsoft Corp.

This seminal case established that the metaphor—your computer screen is a desktop in which you can click on icons to accomplish tasks—employed by the Macintosh user interface was an unprotectable idea. Further, most of the individual elements that made up this desktop metaphor were not protected by copyright, either because they were functional rather than original expression or because they were unprotectable ideas. (*Apple Computer, Inc. v. Microsoft Corp.,* 717 F. Supp. 1428 (N.D. Cal. 1989), 779 F. Supp. 133 (N.D. Cal. 1992), *affirmed,* 35 F.3d 1435 9th Cir. 1994).)

Related terms: computer software, copyright of.

architectural work

The appearance, architectural plans, drawings, or photographs of an architectural work (a building) created after 1990 cannot be reproduced without the consent of the owner of copyright in the architectural work—usually the architect or developer. There are some exceptions. For example, if the building is located in a place that is ordinarily visible to the public, photos or pictures of the building can be taken, distributed, or publicly displayed. Standard features such as common bathroom or kitchen design elements are not protected. Even if the building contains sculptural elements like vampire figures, you can still photograph those elements and in one case, it was permissible to use such architectural elements as part of the backdrop in a Batman movie. (*Leicester v. Warner Bros.,* 232 F.3d 1212 (9th Cir. 2000).) As with all copyright infringement, the copyright owner must demonstrate that the alleged infringer had access to the plans or design. For example, in one case, the Tenth Circuit Court of Appeals found no evidence that the defendant architect had access to the plaintiff's plans and concluded that any similarities in the designs of two homes were because both architects took direction and ideas from the same person. (*La Resolana Architects P.A. v. Reno, Inc.,* 555 F.3d 1171 (10th Cir. 2009).)

Copyright Act: § 101. Definitions

An "architectural work" is the design of a building as embodied in any tangible medium of expression, including a building, architectural plans, or drawings. The work includes the overall form as well as the arrangement and composition of spaces and elements in the design, but does not include individual standard features.

Copyright Law: Definitions

Copyright Act: § 120. Scope of exclusive rights in architectural works

This statute governs when architectural works may be reproduced, altered, or destroyed.

(a) Pictorial Representations Permitted.—The copyright in an architectural work that has been constructed does not include the right to prevent the making, distributing, or public display of pictures, paintings, photographs, or other pictorial representations of the work, if the building in which the work is embodied is located in or ordinarily visible from a public place.

(b) Alterations to and Destruction of Buildings.—Notwithstanding the provisions of section 106 (2), the owners of a building embodying an architectural work may, without the consent of the author or copyright owner of the architectural work, make or authorize the making of alterations to such building, and destroy or authorize the destruction of such building.

archival copies

The Computer Software Protection Act of 1980 defines archival copies as copies of software made by a software owner strictly for backup purposes—that is, to use if something happens to the original copy. The Act permits a computer program owner to make archival copies of the program as long as the owner retains the original copy of the program. But if the purchaser sells or gives away the original software to a new owner, all archival copies must either be included in the transfer or destroyed. The intention is to prevent two or more people from legally possessing copies of a program that has only been purchased from the copyright owner once.

arrangements, musical

See musical works and sound recordings distinguished.

assignment of copyright

The transfer of all or a portion of a copyright to a new owner is referred to as an assignment. Usually, an assignment involves the permanent transfer of the entire copyright, as when a freelance writer assigns all copyright interests in a particular article to a magazine. But an assignment may also transfer less than the whole copyright. For example, an author might assign the right to promote, display, and distribute a novel to a publisher while reserving the right to create derivative works (such as a screenplay) from that novel.

As a general rule, assignments are unconditional transfers of the rights in question, without limitations on how long the transfer lasts or the conditions under which the rights may be used. By contrast, licenses give permission for a party to use a copyright expression under certain specified conditions for a defined period of time. For works published after January 1, 1978, any assignment by the author may be terminated by the author, the author's surviving spouse, or the author's children or grandchildren 35 years after publication or 40 years after the transfer, whichever comes first.

Related terms: licensing of copyrights; transfers of copyright ownership; termination of transfer.

attorney fees in infringement actions

See infringement action.

attribution

Many people mistakenly believe that they can use copyrighted material as long as they credit the author. This is not true. For example, providing the author's name for a quotation will not, by itself, excuse someone from a charge of infringement (or qualify the use as a fair use). That said, judges and juries may take attribution into consideration. For example, an author who provides attribution may be considered more favorably when a judge or jury makes a fair use determination or awards damages.

There is no requirement for attribution when reproducing public domain works. In a 2003 case, a film company had created film footage that had fallen into the public domain. When the footage was reproduced in another documentary, the film company argued that it should be credited. Why? Because the failure to do so would violate trademark laws, because it would confuse consumers as to the source of the footage. The United States Supreme Court disagreed and ruled that people who use public domain materials don't violate trademark laws by failing to provide credit to the creator of the materials. In other words, if you use public domain works, you don't need to provide attribution. (*Dastar Corp. v. Twentieth Century Fox Film Corp.,* 539 U.S. 23 (2003).)

Audio Home Recording Act

The Audio Home Recording Act of 1992 (AHRA) requires the manufacturers of certain digital devices to register with the Copyright Office and pay a statutory royalty on each device and piece of media sold. The Act is, for the most part, outdated because it covers only devices that are designed or marketed for the primary purpose of making digital musical recordings, such as DAT players and minidisc players—technologies that no longer account for much of the marketplace. Had personal computers or CD burners been included in the AHRA, much of the battle about musical downloading might have been

Copyright Law: Definitions

circumvented by a system that accounted for copying of musical compositions. Under the AHRA manufacturers also are obligated to use a copyright management system that permits a copy to be made from an original only (or first-generation copy). By following these rules, manufacturers are immune from lawsuits claiming copyright infringement. Consumers are also immune from claims of infringement when using devices covered by the AHRA so long as the copying is done for noncommercial use.

Related terms: Internet, copyright regulation of; MP3.

audiovisual works

The Copyright Act defines audiovisual works as ones consisting of "a series of related images intended to be shown on machines such as projectors, viewers, or electronic equipment, with accompanying sounds, if any, whether the works are recorded on film, tape, or other material." (17 USC § 101.) The Copyright Act specifically protects movies, videotapes, videodiscs, CD-ROM multimedia packages, training films, and computer games as audiovisual works.

Related terms: Copyright Act of 1976; Form PA.

author

The "author" of a work of expression subject to copyright protection is one of the following:

- the person who creates the work
- the person or business that pays another to create the work in the employment context, or
- the person or business that commissions the work under a valid work-made-for-hire contract.

For example, a songwriter may author a song, a movie producer may author a movie, a computer programmer may author a program, and a toy designer may author a toy (unique toys with designs unrelated to their functions are protectable by copyright). In all these situations, however, if the creator does not work independently but creates the work in an employment relationship or under a valid work-made-for-hire contract, the employer or person paying for the work is the author for copyright purposes. The author is the initial owner of the work and remains the owner unless the ownership rights are transferred, typically by an assignment.

Related terms: assignment of copyright; transfers of copyright ownership; work made for hire.

authorized use as defense

A person accused of infringing another's copyright may seek to prove as a defense that the owner granted permission for the use—in other words that it was authorized, usually through a license or other transfer. Even in the absence of a written agreement, a defendant may make the argument that the use was authorized orally or was implied by the actions of the copyright owner. Were such a case to go to court, the judge would seek to determine the conditions under which the license or transfer was granted, what was transferred, and to whom.

Related terms: copyright infringement; infringement action; transfers of copyright ownership.

automated databases

See computer databases.

based on an earlier work

See derivative work.

Berne Convention

Originally drafted in 1886, the Berne Convention is an international treaty that standardizes basic copyright protection among all of the countries signing it (currently over 100 member countries). For copyright purposes, a member country will afford the same treatment to an author from another country as it does to authors in its own country. In addition, each member country has agreed to protect what are called the author's "moral rights" in the work (generally, the right to proclaim or disclaim authorship and the right to protect the reputation of the work) and to extend copyright protection for at least the life of the author plus 50 years. No notice of copyright or other formality is required for basic copyright protection under the Berne Convention.

Under the General Agreement on Tariffs and Trade (GATT) treaty, enacted into U.S. law in December 1994, all signatories to GATT must also adhere to the Berne Convention if they don't already do so.

Related terms: GATT (General Agreement on Tariffs and Trade); international rules on notice of copyright; Universal Copyright Convention (U.C.C.).

best edition of a work

To register a work with the U.S. Copyright Office, the author must deposit the best edition of the work with the application. The "best edition of a work" is usually the best-quality version of the work available at the time of registration or

Copyright Law: Definitions

deposit. The U.S. Copyright Office has published a circular explaining the best version of a work for different types of deposits. Download Circular 7b from the U.S. Copyright Office's website (www.copyright.gov).

Copyright Act: § 101. Definitions
The "best edition" of a work is the edition, published in the United States at any time before the date of deposit, that the Library of Congress determines to be most suitable for its purposes.

Related terms: deposit with U.S. Copyright Office; U.S. Copyright Office.

BitTorrent

BitTorrent is an Internet software protocol that is especially efficient when transfer-ring large files such as music, movies, or videogames. Unauthorized BitTorrent transfers are sometimes difficult for copyright owners to stop because the complete file is rarely stored in one piece; instead, the file is broken into identically sized pieces that are stored on different computers. The file is reassembled as the user makes a download. On the other hand, users of BitTorrent sites are usually not anonymous, and IP addresses (the unique numerical address for each computer) can be tracked by copyright owners with access to tracking logs. It is estimated that as of 2011, there are over 100 million users.

In 2010, a district court determined that BitTorrent protocols—when used to facilitate infringement—violated copyright law in the same manner as other peer-to-peer infringements despite the lack of a central server containing infringing copies of the material. (*Columbia Pictures Industries, Inc. v. Fung*, 447 F. Supp. 2d 306 (C.D. Cal. 2009).)

blank forms

Since the U.S. Supreme Court's decision in *Baker v. Selden*, (101 U.S. 99 (1879)), courts have considered blank forms to be unprotectable. The principle has been adopted in 37 C.F.R. 202.1(b) which states that registration will not be entertained for "blank forms, such as time cards, graph paper, account books, diaries, bank checks, scorecards, address books, report forms, order forms and the like, which are designed for recording information and do not in themselves convey information." This rule is based on the idea that these documents are either functional works, ideas, or works that can only be expressed in a limited number of ways. For example, the Eleventh Circuit determined that blank forms used for emergency room purposes were not copyrightable because the forms did not convey information. (*Utopia Provider Systems, Inc. v. Pro-Med Clinical Systems, LLC,* 596 F.3d 1313 (11th Cir. 2010).)

blog

A blog (an abbreviation of "Web log") is a website (or portion of a website) where users post chronological journal entries. Blogs range from personalized vanity sites (for example, a teenager's diary, and so on) to corporate communication tools (for example, a business bulletin board). Each blog post usually contains one or more hyperlinks to other sites or references. In terms of copyright law, the same legal principles that apply to websites apply to blogs—that is, reproduction of unauthorized materials requires permission unless excused by fair use principles, and the use of links that encourage infringement can give rise to copyright infringement claims.

bootlegging of live performance

In 1994, as part of the implementation of the GATT Agreement, the United States passed legislation that allows a performer or record company to prevent the unauthorized recording of a live performance, even if the performer or record company does not own a copyright in any of the songs being performed. (17 USC § 1101.) Under this law, performers or record companies did not have to register with the Copyright Office in order to receive protection, and there was no time limit for how long the protection lasts. In 2007, the Second Circuit upheld the law despite the fact that some critics contended the law provided "seemingly perpetual protection for unfixed musical performances." (*United States v. Martignon,* 492 F.3d 140 (2d Cir. 2007).)

Buenos Aires Convention

The Buenos Aires Convention establishes copyright reciprocity between the United States and most Latin American nations. However, because all of these member nations are now also members of larger international treaties that supersede the Buenos Aires Convention, this treaty has little, if any, remaining significance.

When the Buenos Aires Convention had more importance, it guaranteed copyright protection in its member countries if the statement "all rights reserved" was placed on all expressions for which copyright protection was being claimed. This is why the "all rights reserved" phrase appears as a part of so many copyright notices on published works, even if there is no longer any legal reason for it.

Related terms: international copyright protection; international rules on notice of copyright.

Copyright Law: Definitions

caching

A "cache" refers to a storage area (usually temporary) where digital data is stored, enabling rapid access. It's commonly used to store an archival copy of an image of part or all of a website. With cached technology it is possible to search Web pages that the website owner has permanently removed from display. In one case an attorney/author sued Google when the company's cached search results provided end users with copies of copyrighted works. The court held that Google did not infringe. Google was considered passive in the activity—users chose whether to view the cached link. Also, Google had an implied license to cache Web pages because owners of websites have the ability to turn on or turn off the caching of their sites using tags and code. In this case, the attorney/author knew of this ability and failed to turn off caching, making his claim against Google more tenuous. (*Field v. Google Inc.*, 412 F. Supp. 2d 1106 (D. Nev. 2006).)

Related terms: website

cease and desist letter

The opening salvo in any copyright dispute is usually a cease and desist letter from the copyright owner's attorney. This letter typically informs the alleged infringer of the validity and ownership of the copyrighted work, the nature of the infringement, and the remedies that are available to the copyright holder unless the infringement is halted.

Related terms: copyright infringement; damages for copyright infringement; infringement action.

certificate of registration

When the U.S. Copyright Office approves a copyright application for registration, it mails the author (or other owner) a certificate of registration. This certificate consists of the information in the copyright application, a copyright registration number, a registration date, the U.S. Copyright Office seal, and the signature of the Register of Copyrights.

If the copyright owner sues another party for infringement, the certificate can be used as evidence that the copyright is valid. There is also a legal presumption that the certificate contains true statements—for example, the year the work was created, the fact of authorship, and whether other works are incorporated in the work being copyrighted. Copyright owners must register their work prior to suing for infringement under the provisions of 17 USC § 411(a). However, the Fifth, Seventh, and Ninth Circuits have interpreted this to mean that a lawsuit can proceed if an application has been filed, provided that a registration eventually issues. The Tenth and Eleventh Circuits have held to a stricter requirement and require a Certificate of Registration.

Related terms: copyright infringement; infringement action; supplemental registration.

characters, fictional

Fictional characters can be protected separately from their underlying works as derivative copyrights, provided that they are sufficiently unique and distinctive—for example, James Bond, Fred Flintstone, Hannibal Lecter, and Snoopy. Judge Learned Hand established the standard for character protection in *Nichols v. Universal Pictures Corp.*, 45 F.2d 119 (2d Cir. 1930), when he stated that, "… the less developed the characters, the less they can be copyrighted; that is the penalty an author must bear for marking them too indistinctly."

For example, alien characters stranded on earth is a popular and recurring theme as portrayed in *My Favorite Martian, Starman, Alien Nation, Transformers, District 9, Predators*, and *The Man Who Fell to Earth*. The idea of a stranded alien character, without embellishment, is not protectable.

> **EXAMPLE:** A relatively unknown play (*Lokey From Maldemar*) featured an alien with powers of levitation and telepathy, stranded on earth and pursued by authoritarian characters. The playwright sued the owners of the movie *E.T.: The Extra-Terrestrial*, claiming that her character was infringed by the E.T. character. A federal court disagreed, ruling that that the character from Lokey was too indistinct to merit protection. (*Litchfield v. Spielberg*, 736 F.2d 1352 (9th Cir. 1984).)

However, once the stranded alien acquires more distinctive characteristics—for example, a big-headed, long-necked alien with a glowing finger who murmurs "Phone home"—it is distinct enough to merit protection and its owners can prevent others from using his image and expression. (*Universal Studios, Inc. v. J.A.R. Sales, Inc.*, 216 U.S.P.Q. 679 (C.D. Cal. 1982); *Universal Studios, Inc. v. Kamar Indus. Inc.*, 217 U.S.P.Q. 1165 (S.D. Tex. 1982).)

Exploitation of fictional characters is a crucial source of revenue for entertainment and merchandising companies. Characters such as Superman and Mickey Mouse are the foundations of massive entertainment franchises and are commonly protected under both copyright and trademark law.

The protection afforded to fictional characters sometimes clashes with the fair use right to comment upon or criticize those characters. This is particularly common in parody cases. For example, one court refused to permit an X-rated parody, *Scarlett Fever,* that used characters from *Gone With the Wind.* (*Metro-Goldwyn-Mayer, Inc. v. Showcase Atlanta Cooperative Productions, Inc.,* 479 F. Supp. 351 (N.D. Ga. 1979).) Another court permitted publication of a novel using characters from *Gone With the Wind* but written from a slave's perspective. (*Suntrust Bank v. Houghton Mifflin Co.,* 268 F.2d 1257 (11th Cir. 2001).) The disparity in the two opinions—both based on *Gone With the Wind*—may be due to the fact that in one work the characters were lampooned in a broad sexual farce, while in the other the characters were used to provoke discussion about racial stereotypes.

Related terms: derivative work; parody and fair use.
See also Part 4 (Trademark Law): characters as trademarks.

charts, copyrightability of

See flow charts, registration of.

choreography and pantomime

Choreography is the composition and arrangement of dance movement and patterns, often accompanied by music. A registrable choreographic work should be capable of being performed and usually includes direction for movement. Popular dance steps such as the cha-cha and other simple routines are not copyrightable.

Pantomime or "mime" is considered a mute performance with expressive communication. Because it is a form of acting that consists mostly of gestures, there is an overlap in the categorization of pantomime and dramatic works. Traditionally, pantomime and choreographic works are fixed in a system of written notation, but the copyright act provides that they also may be fixed in any tangible medium including film, video, or photographs.

Like all copyrightable works, choreographic and pantomimic productions can qualify for copyright protection when fixed in a tangible medium of expression such as film, video, written score, or recording. To register these types of works with the U.S. Copyright Office, the owner must use Form PA.

Although choreography and pantomime cases are rare under copyright law, they arise occasionally.

EXAMPLE: The works of dancer Martha Graham came under scrutiny in 2002 when a federal court ruled that the bulk of her dance compositions (45 out of

61) belonged to the Martha Graham Center for Contemporary Dance because she had composed them while she worked as an employee for the Center. In addition, ten of her dance compositions were found to be in the public domain. (*Martha Graham School and Dance Foundation, Inc., v. Martha Graham Center for Contemporary Dance, Inc.,* 224 F. Supp. 2d 567 (2002).)

Related terms: Form PA; parody and fair use; registration.

clearinghouses, copyright

Copyright clearinghouses organize and license works by their members. A person who wants to use one of these works contacts the clearinghouse and—depending on how the organization is structured—pays a fee and acquires a limited right to use the work for a specific purpose. Clearinghouses speed up the permissions process by providing a central source for a class or type of work. For example, Copyright Clearinghouse (www.copyright.com) provides permission for written materials. BMI (www.bmi.com) and ASCAP (www.ascap.com) provide permission for musical performances. Harry Fox Agency (www.harryfox.com) provides permission to reproduce songs. Corbis (www.corbis.com) and Time, Inc. (www.thepicturecollection.com) are among several clearinghouses that grant permission to use photographs. Art Resource (www.artres.com) and the Visual Artists and Galleries Association (www.vaga.co.uk) grant permission for famous artwork. The Cartoonbank (www.cartoonbank.com) is one of several clearinghouses that licenses cartoons.

Related terms: permission.

clickwrap agreement

See end-user license (aka EULA, shrinkwrap or clickwrap agreement).

coauthors

Two or more people who have contributed significant creative input to a work of expression are legally considered coauthors. Coauthorship can take several forms and the most common is a joint work, where the authors intend that their separate contributions be merged into a unified whole. Coauthors of a joint work share in the copyright of the whole work equally, unless they have signed a joint ownership agreement that provides differently. Absent an agreement to the contrary, any coauthor may use the expression covered by the copyright without permission of other coauthors but must account to the other coauthors and equally share with them any profits realized from the use.

Other forms of coauthorship appear in collective works and derivative works with more than one author, where each author owns only the copyright of the material he or she created:

- **Collective works.** Coauthors intend to keep their contributions separate—for instance, where one coauthor is separately credited for chapters 1 through 10 and the other coauthor is credited for chapters 11 through 20.
- **Coauthored derivative works.** Two or more authors create separate works and only later decide to combine them in one work.

Related terms: collaboration agreement; collective work; derivative work; joint work.

collaboration agreement (coauthor agreement)

When coauthors want to specify their rights, obligations, and percentage of copyright ownership and revenues, they enter into a collaboration (or coauthor) agreement. Without a collaboration agreement or other evidence to the contrary, a court will presume that the coauthors share equally.

Related terms: coauthors; collective work; joint work.

collective work

A work such as a periodical, anthology, wiki, or encyclopedia, in which a number of separate and independent works are assembled into one work, is referred to as a collective work. (17 USC § 101.) A collective work is a type of compilation, but, unlike other compilations such as a directory or book of quotes, the underlying elements assembled into a collective work can be separately protected; for example, a collection of short stories by John Updike or a collection of "greatest disco hits" recordings from the 1970s. Other examples of collective works would include a newspaper, a group of film clips, or a poetry anthology. To create a collective work, either public domain materials must be used or the owners of the copyrights in the constituent parts must give their permissions. Assuming that these rules are followed, the creativity involved in organizing and selecting the constituent materials is itself subject to independent copyright protection.

EXAMPLE: Phil prepares an anthology of what he considers to be the best American poems published in the years 1900 and 2000, calling this collective work *American Poetry—A Century of Difference.* Each poem from 2000 is a separate and independent work protected by its own copyright. To use these poems, Phil must get the permission of each copyright owner. But because copyright protection has run out on the 1900 poems, they are now in the public domain and Phil can use them without obtaining anyone's permission. Once all needed permissions are assembled, Phil has created a new protectable collective work and owns a copyright in the choice and organization of the poems, but not in any specific poem.

Many collective works have been preserved in digital format. However, when a collective work (or compilation) is provided in conjunction with a software program—for example, a program that organizes or creates clip art versions of images on a disk—two separate copyrights are at work. One copyright is in the collective work, for example, the collection of images, and the other copyright is in the underlying program. In order to assert rights in both, each must be separately registered. (*Xoom, Inc. v. Imageline, Inc.*, 323 F.3d 279 (4th Cir. 2003).)

Copyright Act: § 101. Definitions
A "collective work" is a work, such as a periodical issue, anthology, or encyclopedia, in which a number of contributions, constituting separate and independent works in themselves, are assembled into a collective whole.

Related terms: compilations; original work of authorship.

commissioned work
See work made for hire.

common law copyright laws
Prior to 1978, copyright law protected only published works. Unpublished works were protected under rules known as common law copyright (also sometimes referred to as "state copyright"). The 1976 Copyright Act (effective 1978) extended protection to unpublished works and replaced common law copyright rules). Issues of common law copyright rarely arise except in cases of sound recordings created prior to February 15, 1972 (when the Copyright law was amended to include sound recordings).

Related terms: Copyright Act of 1909; Copyright Act of 1976.

compilations
A compilation is a work formed by selecting, collecting, and assembling pre-existing materials or data in a novel way that forms an original work of authorship. Examples of compilations are databases (collections of information arranged

in a way to facilitate updating and retrieval), anthologies, and collective works. (17 USC § 101.)

The creative aspects of a compilation—such as the way it is organized and the selection of the materials to be included—are entitled to copyright protection whether or not the individual parts are in the public domain or are subject to another owner's copyright.

> **EXAMPLE:** Harry assembles sheet music of national anthems (public domain) for a music book. If Harry simply published the anthems in alphabetical order without enhancing or organizing them in a special way or combining them with other materials, the collection would not be protected, because it is not considered to be creative. If, on the other hand, Harry compiled a selection of his anthems for countries that have been at war with each other ("Battling Anthems"), the compilation (but not the music) is more likely to qualify for copyright protection, because the act of selecting the anthems involved some creative work on Harry's part. If it did qualify, Harry could stop others who copied his work from creating a similar compilation.

Copyright Act: § 101. Definitions

A "compilation" is a work formed by the collection and assembling of preexisting materials or of data that are selected, coordinated, or arranged in such a way that the resulting work as a whole constitutes an original work of authorship. The term "compilation" includes collective works.

Copyright Act: § 103. Subject matter of copyright: Compilations and derivative works

(a) The subject matter of copyright as specified by section 102 includes compilations and derivative works, but protection for a work employing preexisting material in which copyright subsists does not extend to any part of the work in which such material has been used unlawfully.

(b) The copyright in a compilation or derivative work extends only to the material contributed by the author of such work, as distinguished from the preexisting material employed in the work, and does not imply any exclusive right in the preexisting material. The copyright in such work is independent of, and does not affect or enlarge the scope, duration, ownership, or subsistence of, any copyright protection in the preexisting material.

Related terms: *Feist Publications Inc. v. Rural Telephone Service Co.*; original work of authorship.

compulsory license

Normally, in order for someone to reproduce, perform, or distribute a copyrighted work, permission must be obtained from the copyright owner. However, in a few circumstances—known as compulsory licenses—a copyright owner's permission is not required provided that the user follows certain rules and pays fees set by law. Such compulsory licenses are commonly used by satellite TV providers, cable providers, webcasters, and music companies.

One of the most common uses of a compulsory license is in the music industry. Once a song has been recorded and distributed to the public on recordings, any person or group is entitled to record and distribute the song without obtaining the copyright owner's consent, provided they pay a fee and meet copyright law requirements.

In order to take advantage of this compulsory license, a notice must be sent to the copyright owner along with a fee set by the Copyright Office known as the statutory fee or statutory rate. The fee for recordings is currently 9.1 cents per song (or 1.75 cents per minute of playing time). To verify the current rate, check the Copyright Office website (www.copyright.gov/carp) and click "Mechanical Royalty Rate." If a song is three minutes long and an artist makes 10,000 compact discs containing the song, the fee paid to the song's owner would be $910. A recording artist does not have to use the compulsory license, and many recording artists seek permission directly from the song owner and negotiate for a lower rate.

> EXAMPLE: Lou writes and releases the song "Up the Stairs." Later, Barry decides he wants to record "Up the Stairs." If Barry is willing to pay the statutory fee, he does not need to ask Lou for permission—but if he wants to pay less per copy, he must obtain permission from Lou.

Keep in mind that the compulsory license for recording music (the mechanical license) only authorizes the use of the song for nondramatic musical compositions and you could not, under the compulsory license, use the song for dramatic purposes such as in an opera or an overture to a musical. The compulsory license only applies to phonorecords distributed to the public. Therefore, it cannot be used to record a song for use on a television show's soundtrack. In that case, permission must be obtained from the copyright owner.

Under the terms of a compulsory license, the licensee is permitted to make a new arrangement of the composition as long as the basic melody or fundamental character of the work is not altered.

Copyright Law: Definitions

EXAMPLE: Sammy composes and records a country ballad. Later, Pauline, a punk rap star, acquires a compulsory license and records Sammy's song but changes the words and eliminates the melody. Sammy can have Pauline's compulsory license revoked and prevent the recording from being distributed further or played.

In a different context, and without regard to the type of work involved, the concept of a compulsory license can arise in a copyright infringement action. A court has the power to order a copyright owner to grant a license to an innocent infringer instead of ordering the infringement stopped.

Finally, in countries that subscribe to the Universal Copyright Convention (U.C.C.), including the United States, an author may be required to grant a compulsory license to a subscribing government to translate his or her work into that country's primary language if no translation has been published within seven years of the work's original date of publication. This rule precludes copyright owners in most countries from preventing the translation of works covered by their copyrights into different languages.

Related terms: derivative work; innocent infringement of copyright; mechanical rights; musical works and sound recordings distinguished.

Computer Associates Int'l v. Altai
See filtration.

computer databases

A computer database, sometimes known as an automated database, is a collection of information or resources placed in a computer and organized to allow for rapid updating and retrieval. Examples of computer databases are:
- a mailing list organized so that mailings can be made according to certain criteria such as the residential area, average personal income, or interests of the recipient
- a compilation of articles published on a particular subject (for example, female Parkinson's disease sufferers over 80) organized so that people can quickly retrieve and read the article dealing with their particular point of interest, and
- a listing of all items in a store's inventory arranged to permit an analysis by such variables as supplier, kind of product, price, and length of time in stock.

Computer databases commonly consist both of materials protected by copyright and materials that are said to be in the public domain, either because their copyright has run out or because they consist of ideas and facts that themselves do not receive copyright protection.

Despite the fact that the database owner may not own any copyright interest in any of the material in the database, the structure and organization of the database itself can qualify as an original work of authorship and thus be subject to copyright protection as a compilation.

Although the original expression implicit in the structure and organization of a computer database is entitled to copyright protection, the labor and cost associated with building a database is not protected by copyright. For instance, the labor and cost associated with compiling an alphabetical telephone directory does not protect the information in the directory from being copied by others, because there was no creativity exercised in building the database.

Similarly, copyright owners of a software program that gathers public domain information cannot seek to extend database protection over the information that the users gather with the software.

> EXAMPLE: A company owned by the Multiple Listing Service (MLS) sought public data about real estate from county and municipal assessors. Several municipalities refused to furnish it, claiming that to do so would violate the copyright of a rival company that had already solicited and categorized the information in a database using customized software. The Seventh Circuit Court of Appeals ruled that the process of furnishing (or extracting) the raw data did not violate copyright law and did not create a derivative work (*Assessment Technologies of WI LLC v. WIREData Inc.,* 350 F.3d 640 (7th Cir 2003).)

Computer databases can be registered with the U.S. Copyright Office. For more information on preparing the registration, see Copyright Office Circulars 65 and 66.

Related terms: compilations; *Feist Publications Inc. v. Rural Telephone Service Co.*; Form TX.

computer software

Under a 1980 amendment to the copyright law, computer software is protected in the same manner as other original works of authorship. Any computer program, defined as "a set of statements or instructions to be used directly or indirectly in a computer to bring about a certain result," can be protected by copyright if it constitutes an original work of authorship. The 1980 amendment also specifies the situations in which computer programs may be copied and altered without permission of the copyright owner.

The early years of software protection consisted of battles of protection for code in object code form, for example as mechanically reproduced in a silicon chip as part of an integrated circuit (ROM chips), and in templates (mask works) used in making ROM chips. Most disputes were resolved in favor of copyright protection for software regardless of its form (that is, whether it is source code or object code), and regardless of whether it is embedded in a chip or exists as an independent work on a computer disk. The leading case in this area is *Apple Computer, Inc. v. Franklin Computer Corporation,* 714 F.2d 1240 (3d Cir. 1983). (Under a different line of cases, software can also be protected by patent law, too.)

In the late 1980s and early 1990s, new questions arose about what aspects of software could receive copyright protection. Some of the issues have been:

- Should copyright protection be limited to the literal code as written, or is the structure, sequence, and organization of software code also entitled to copyright protection? In *Whelan v. Jastrow,* 797 F.2d 1222 (3d Cir. 1986), a federal circuit court of appeals held that protection for software code goes beyond the code's literal expression and extends to its structure, sequence, and organization. Other courts have found this approach unworkable and have adopted the filtration approach taken in *Computer Associates Int'l. v. Altai,* 982 F.2d 693 (2d Cir. 1992). That approach separates the code's ideas and other public domain elements from its expression and then extends protection only to the expression.

- What aspects of computer screen displays and graphical user interfaces (GUIs) are entitled to copyright protection? The filtration approach taken in the *Altai* case has been used by a number of courts to decide which aspects of a program interface are protected by copyright. The most prominent of these cases involved a suit by Apple against Microsoft, which claimed that the Microsoft Windows operating system violated a copyright owned by Apple in the Macintosh interface. (*Apple Computer, Inc. v. Microsoft Corp.,* 717 F. Supp. 1428 (N.D. Cal. 1989), 779 F. Supp. 133 (N.D. Cal. 1992).) Using the filtration approach, the court eliminated from copyright protection most individual elements of the Macintosh interface and refused to provide protection for the interface as a whole. In short, Microsoft won and Apple lost. The overall result of applying the filtration approach to computer user interfaces has been to afford computer user interfaces very little copyright protection.

- How much originality must a factual database have to qualify for copyright protection? In *Feist Publications Inc. v. Rural Telephone Service Co.,* 111 S.Ct. 1282 (1991), the U.S. Supreme Court ruled that an alphabetically arranged telephone directory involved insufficient creativity to qualify for copyright. As a result, the Copyright Act could not be used to compensate Feist Publications Inc. for the labor and expense involved in originally compiling the directory. The question remains, however, as to how much creativity is required to qualify a factual database for copyright. By its very nature, this issue can only be decided on a case-by-case basis.

Related terms: *Apple Computer, Inc. v. Franklin*; *Apple Computer, Inc. v. Microsoft Corp.*; copyright; copyright infringement; infringement action.

Computer Software Protection Act of 1980

See archival copies; computer software.

Computer Software Rental Amendments Act of 1990

See first-sale doctrine.

contributory infringement

Contributory infringement occurs when someone knows of (or should have known of) infringing activity and induces or substantially contributes to it. Technology developments brought the issue of contributory infringement more to the forefront. In the 1980s the issue arose as to whether the sale of videocassette recorders amounted to contributory infringement because the manufacturer knew that some buyers of the device used it for infringing purposes. The Supreme Court held that manufacturers of devices that are capable of substantial noninfringing uses should not be held liable as contributory infringers. (*Sony Corp. of America v. Universal City Studios, Inc.,* 464 U.S. 417 (1984).) Thirty years later, the Supreme Court held that a company that distributes software that enables file sharing on peer-to-peer networks, could be considered a contributory infringer. (*Metro-Goldwyn-Mayer Studios, Inc. v. Grokster, Ltd.,* 545 U.S. 913, 936-37 (2005).) Another line of contributory infringement cases deals with the liability of entities that rent space to infringers. For example, a department store owner that rented space with the knowledge that some of is tenants were selling bootleg merchandise was a contributory infringer. (*Shapiro, Bernstein and Co. v. H.L. Green Co.,* 316

F.2d 304 (2d Cir. 1963).) Similarly, a flea market operator that leased stalls with knowledge that some vendors were selling infringing merchandise was liable as a contributory infringer. (*Fonovisa, Inc. v. Cherry Auction, Inc.,* 76 F.3d 259 (9th Cir. 1996).)

copies

For purposes of the copyright law, a copy is the physical form in which an expression is retained over time, no matter how brief. This includes such things as photocopies, tape recordings, photographs, manuscripts, printings, molds (for example, for plastic toy designs), computer disks and diskettes, videotapes, videodiscs, CDs, DVDs, hard drives, thumb drives, and ROMs. The placing of a program in dynamic computer memory (RAM) for a brief period of time has also been treated as copying, which may constitute an infringement under the copyright act. (*Mai v. Peak,* 991 F.2d 511 (9th Cir. 1993).)

The Copyright Act defines copies as "material objects, other than phonorecords, in which a work is fixed by any method now known or later developed, and from which the work can be perceived, reproduced, or otherwise communicated, either directly or with the aid of a machine or device." (17 USC § 101.)

The right to prepare copies of an original work of authorship—that is, put the work into some fixed form—is one of the primary rights protected by the overall copyright.

Copyright Act: § 101. Definitions

"Copies" are material objects, other than phonorecords, in which a work is fixed by any method now known or later developed, and from which the work can be perceived, reproduced, or otherwise communicated, either directly or with the aid of a machine or device. The term "copies" includes the material object, other than a phonorecord, in which the work is first fixed.

Related terms: copyright; copyright infringement; photocopies and copyright law.

Copyleft

Copyleft refers to a grassroots movement formed in protest to perceived abuses of copyright—for example, cases brought under the Digital Millennium Copyright Act or the extension of copyright per the Copyright Term Extension Act. Comprising librarians, legal scholars, historians, artists, musicians, archivists, website creators, and many others, the Copyleft seeks through public awareness and litigation to rebalance the rights of authors and the public under copyright law. Leaders of the Copyleft such as professors Larry Lessig and Jonathan Zittrain believe that copyright has become a permission-based enterprise and that it should be returned to its Jeffersonian roots—that is, to encourage rather than stifle creativity. The Copyleft movement was a strong supporter of Eric Eldred and his unsuccessful effort to terminate the 1998 copyright extension. (*Eldred v. Ashcroft,* 537 U.S. 186 (2003).)

Related terms: *Eldred v. Ashcroft*; Creative Commons.

copyright

A copyright consists of a bundle of rights held by the author or developer of an original work of authorship. The term "copyright" applies both to the entire bundle of rights and to any individual right or part of an individual right:

- the exclusive right to make copies
- the exclusive right to authorize others to make copies
- the exclusive right to make derivative works (that is, similar works based on the original, such as translations or updated versions)
- the exclusive right to sell (market) the work
- the exclusive right to display the work
- the exclusive right to perform the work (such as plays and musical compositions), and
- the exclusive right to obtain court relief in the event others infringe (violate) these rights.

Each of these exclusive rights can be sold separately through transfers of copyright ownership. For example, a transfer may give a party the exclusive right to make derivative works from an original work. In addition, each right may be divided, giving different parties exclusive rights during different periods of time or in different geographical areas.

Under the laws of most countries, any original work of authorship is considered the property of its owner; others are prevented from using this property without the owner's consent. The owner is usually the originator of the work—the actual author or somebody who paid for the work under an employment agreement or work-made-for-hire contract. Sometimes, however, full ownership is transferred to somebody else before the work is finished. For instance, it is common for free-lance software programmers to assign all of their copyright rights in a program to the publisher before programming begins, in exchange for advance royalties or payments to be received in phases as the project progresses. Usually termed a "grant of rights," this type of transfer shifts ownership of the copyright from the author to the publisher.

Among the categories of expressive works that are protected by copyright throughout the world are:

- literary works
- audiovisual works
- computer software
- graphic works
- musical arrangements, and
- sound recordings.

In short, practically any type of expression that can be fixed in a tangible medium of expression is eligible for copyright protection, assuming it is original and has at least some creativity. It is important to understand, however, that copyright law protects only the expression itself—not the underlying facts, ideas, or concepts. This means it is often possible to legitimately produce an expression very similar to one that is already protected by copyright, as long as the original expression itself is not copied or used as a basis for the later work. The more factual in nature the original work, the more similar the second work can be without infringement occurring. Conversely, works of fiction are more susceptible to infringement claims, because they tend to involve far more original expression than do nonfiction works.

Although a copyright owner's permission must be obtained to make copies for commercial purposes, it is sometimes possible to copy without permission in situations collectively labeled as "fair use." These tend to be for educational and nonprofit purposes—situations where there is little or no commercial motive for using the material and the use of the material won't interfere with the natural market for the work being used.

Under the Copyright Act of 1976, an original work of authorship gains copyright protection the instant it becomes fixed in a tangible form. This means that such protection is available for both published and unpublished works. The protection lasts for:

- the life of the author plus 70 years, or
- 95 years from the date of publication or 120 years from the date of creation, whichever is shorter, if the author is an employer or commissioner of a work made for hire, or if the author uses a pseudonym or remains anonymous.

In addition to the automatic protection extended a copyright owner by the law, it is possible to gain crucially important protective benefits in the United States by placing a proper copyright notice on the work and registering it with the U.S.

Copyright Office. If the registration occurs in a timely manner (either within three months of publication or before the infringing activity begins), it is easier for the copyright owner to obtain effective relief against infringers.

Related terms: copyright infringement; copyright owner; duration of copyrights; fair use; timely registration; transfers of copyright ownership.

Copyright Act of 1909

This federal statute governed copyrights in the United States between 1910 and 1978. Works first published prior to January 1, 1978, are still covered by the 1909 Act, unless the copyright has expired. The main practical differences between the 1909 Copyright Act and the 1976 Copyright Act (which replaced the 1909 Act) are:

- The 1909 Act granted protection only to published works. The 1976 Act extends its protection to both published and unpublished works.
- Protection under the 1909 Act could be permanently lost if even a single copy was distributed without the proper notice of copyright. The 1976 Act provided that the absence of a proper notice could be cured under certain circumstances. Moreover, as of March 1989, there is no longer any requirement for a notice.

Note: The GATT (General Agreement on Tariffs and Trade) has restored copyright protection for works of foreign authors that fell into the public domain in the United States prior to March 1989 because of faulty notice. These restored copyrights have the same duration as they would have had if they not been considered to be in the public domain.

Related terms: common law copyright laws; copyright; Copyright Act of 1976; notice of copyright; restored copyright under GATT.

Copyright Act of 1976

This comprehensive federal statute governs copyright protection for original works of authorship created after January 1, 1978. Found in Title 17, United States Code, Sections 100 and following, the 1976 Copyright Act (as amended from time to time) is the exclusive source of copyright law in the United States for works published after January 1, 1978. It preempts (replaces) all state laws that affect rights covered by this Act.

Related terms: audiovisual works; copyright; Copyright Act of 1909; infringement action; original work of authorship.

copyright and patent compared

As a general matter, the copyright and patent laws cover entirely different kinds of items and offer different protections. Copyright law protects all forms of expression fixed in a tangible medium, but not the underlying ideas. Patents protect ideas that take the form of useful, novel, and nonobvious inventions—for instance, production methods, devices, substances, and mechanical processes.

Copyright and patent do intersect, however, in two important areas:

- **Product design.** Both copyright and design patent law may be used to protect a product's design, as long as the design does not affect how the product functions. A design patent is more time-consuming and expensive to obtain than a copyright, but it offers a broader scope of protection. That's because under design patent law you can stop anyone who uses the same design, but under copyright law you can stop only those who copy your design; you cannot stop someone who independently created the same design. On the other hand, copyright protection lasts for the life of the author, whereas design patent protection lasts for only 14 years from the date the patent issues. As mentioned, these two approaches to protecting original designs are not exclusive of each other. For instance, a truly innovative but functionless design for a computer might qualify for both copyright protection (as a pictorial, graphic, or sculptural work) and for a design patent (as a purely ornamental design of an article of manufacture).

- **Computer software.** Both copyright and patent may be used to protect computer software. A copyright may protect the program's literal expression and perhaps its structure, sequence, and organization. A patent may issue on the program's innovative approach to solving a particular problem or producing a particular result in a computer or other type of machine, such as a robot or remote vehicle. As with designs, patent protection is broader than that afforded by copyright because the patent creates a monopoly over the ideas covered by the patent, whereas the copyright only protects the expression itself. In addition, a copyright owner can only stop someone who has copied the software. A patent owner can stop anyone who is making, selling, or using the software, regardless of whether it has been copied or developed independently.

Related terms: computer software; pictorial, graphic, and sculptural works.
See also Part 1 (Patent Law): design patents; software patents.

copyright claimant

A copyright claimant is the party considered to be the basic owner of the copyright in a work being registered with the U.S. Copyright Office. The copyright claimant may be any of the following:

- the actual author of the work
- an employer (also considered the actual author) whose employee created the work in the scope of employment
- a party who commissioned a work made for hire, as defined in the Copyright Act (also considered the actual author)
- a party to whom all rights in a work have been assigned, or
- a party who has come to own all of the exclusive rights that make up the copyright.

The name of the copyright claimant must be put in the copyright registration form filed with the U.S. Copyright Office as part of the registration process.

Related terms: registration.

copyright infringement

Any unauthorized use of a copyrighted work that violates the copyright owner's exclusive rights in the work constitutes an infringement. Common examples of infringement are copying computer software, songs, photos, or eBooks, or adapting a photo or text for your own purposes.

Once a copyright owner suspects infringement, the owner may file a lawsuit against the infringer for damages in a federal court. Copyright owners must register their work prior to suing for infringement under the provisions of 17 USC § 411(a). However, the Fifth, Seventh, and Ninth Circuits have interpreted this to mean that a lawsuit can proceed if an application has been filed, provided that a registration eventually issues. The Tenth and Eleventh Circuits have held to a stricter requirement and require a Certificate of Registration before filing.

If the infringement began before the registration occurred the owner usually has less leverage in regard to the remedies available in court.

Whether or not a work will be found to have infringed an earlier copyrighted work largely depends on three factors:

- Was the first work the subject of a proper copyright? This factor is satisfied if the first work was independently created, has enough creativity, and is fixed in a tangible medium.
- Did the infringer copy the work? In the absence of an admission that copying occurred, this factor depends on whether the author of the second

work had access to the earlier work and whether there is a substantial similarity between the two works. The stronger the similarity, the greater the chance that a court will find that infringement occurred. Generally, a greater similarity is required for factual or nonfiction works to be considered infringing than is required for works of fiction.

- Did the infringer improperly use the copied material? The third factor addresses whether the infringer copied by paraphrasing or by repeating the expression verbatim, and how much was copied. Again, the key determination is how substantially similar the two works are. An infringement might be found based on several paraphrased passages of a few hundred words each, or on just 20 words copied verbatim.

Some courts use a three-step approach to decide whether the substantial similarity element (in the second factor) has been shown. First, they identify the aspects of the two works that are subject to copyright protection. Then they make an objective comparison of these aspects to see how alike they are. If they are similar enough to warrant a suspicion of infringement, the courts then make a subjective determination as to whether the works are substantially similar enough to justify a finding of infringement.

Below are two examples showing the basic principles involved in copyright infringement.

EXAMPLE 1: The photographer Art Rogers created the photograph entitled "Puppies" that features a man and a woman sitting on a bench and holding eight puppies. The artist Jeff Koons purchased two postcards of the image and, without obtaining Mr. Rogers's authorization, created a wood sculpture based on the image. Because the sculpture was substantially similar and was prepared without the authorization of Mr. Rogers, a court determined it was an infringement of Mr. Rogers's right to adapt the work. In other words, even though Koons had demonstrated sufficient originality in his statues, he could not sell his works, because he failed to obtain permission from the photographer of the underlying copyrighted work. (*Rogers v. Koons,* 960 F.2d 301 (2d Cir. 1992).)

EXAMPLE 2: In 1983, the owners of *Star Wars* sued the owners of the television show *Battlestar Galactica* for copyright infringement. There was no duplication of *Star Wars* dialogue in the television show but there were many nonliteral similarities. In their brief to the court, the owners of *Star Wars* listed 34 such nonliteral similarities; for example: the central conflict of each story is a war between the galaxy's democratic and totalitarian forces; a friendly robot who aids the democratic forces is severely injured (*Star Wars*) or destroyed (*Battlestar*) by the totalitarian forces; there is a romance between the hero's friend (the cynical fighter pilot) and the daughter of one of the leaders of the democratic forces; and there is a scene in a cantina (*Star Wars*) or casino (*Battlestar*) in which musical entertainment is offered by bizarre, nonhuman creatures. On the basis of the 34 nonliteral similarities, the owners of *Star Wars* were able to prove infringement. (*Twentieth Century-Fox Film Corp. v. MCA Inc.*, 715 F.2d 1327 (9th Cir. 1983).)

Related terms: derivative work; fair use; infringement action; registration.

copyright management information

Copyright management information (CMI) is information conveyed with a copyrighted work that identifies the owner and nature of that copyright. The Digital Millennium Copyright Act of 1998 prohibits the removal or falsification of CMI as well as the distribution of such altered works. The Act specifically defines copyright management information as:

- The title and other information identifying the work, including the information set forth on a notice of copyright.
- The name of, and other identifying information about, the author of a work.
- The name of, and other identifying information about, the copyright owner of the work, including the information set forth in a notice of copyright.
- With the exception of public performances of works by radio and television broadcast stations, the name of, and other identifying information about, a performer whose performance is fixed in a work other than an audiovisual work.
- With the exception of public performances of works by radio and television broadcast stations, in the case of an audiovisual work, the name of, and other identifying information about, a writer, performer, or director who is credited in the audiovisual work.

In 2011, the Third Circuit determined that the CMI rules also applied to non-digital works.

> EXAMPLE: A photographer's copyrighted picture of two nude radio "shock jocks" was published in the *New Jersey Monthly*. The radio station that employed the men scanned and posted the photo online (after removing the photo credit that ran alongside the photo known in the trade as a "gutter

credit"). The station then encouraged listeners to download the photo, modify it, and resubmit the photos to the station for posting. The Third Circuit ruled that the "gutter credit" qualified as CMI and cutting it off the photo violated the DMCA. (*Murphy v. Millennium Radio Group*, ___ F.3d ___ (3d Cir. 2011).)

Related terms: Digital Millennium Copyright Act of 1998; digital rights management (DRM).

copyright notice

See notice of copyright.

copyright office

See U.S. Copyright Office.

copyright owner

Under the Copyright Act of 1976, the term "copyright owner" has two distinct meanings. First, it refers to the person or entity listed as the owner in the U.S. Copyright Office and on any notice attached to the copyrighted work. This is either the original author or a person or entity to whom all rights under the copyright have been transferred.

Second, "copyright owner" also refers to a person or entity who owns one or more of the five exclusive rights that make up the whole copyright, and who therefore has a right to sue infringers of that right. These constituent rights, which may be separately owned and assigned (sold), consist of the following:

- the right to reproduce (copy) the work
- the right to prepare derivative works
- the right to distribute copies of the work
- the right to perform the work, and
- the right to display the work.

EXAMPLE: June writes a novel and owns the copyright on the expression contained in it. June grants an exclusive worldwide license (permission) to Henry to publish and distribute her novel. She also gives Ernest the exclusive right to prepare a screenplay (a derivative work) based on the novel. Because these rights are exclusive, both Henry and Ernest are legally considered copyright owners.

In addition to separately licensing basic copyright rights, a copyright owner can separately license subparts of each right.

EXAMPLE: Vixen Publications purchases the entire copyright in Andrew's book before it is written, in exchange for a royalties advance. Vixen is now the copyright owner and has the right to transfer parts of its copyright ownership to others. Vixen licenses exclusive German language book rights to a German publisher, exclusive French language book rights to a French publisher, and exclusive Russian language book rights to a Russian publisher. Each of the entities receiving exclusive rights under these licenses would also be considered a copyright owner.

Although different people or entities can own different rights based on a copyright and be considered copyright owners, there is only one actual "copyright." Unless the original owner (the author, employer, commissioner of a work made for hire, or assignee of all rights) transfers all of the five exclusive rights set out above to one or more parties, that original owner is still considered by the U.S. Copyright Office to be the copyright owner.

Copyright Act: § 201. Ownership of copyright

(a) Initial Ownership.—Copyright in a work protected under this title vests initially in the author or authors of the work. The authors of a joint work are coowners of copyright in the work.

(b) Works Made for Hire.—In the case of a work made for hire, the employer or other person for whom the work was prepared is considered the author for purposes of this title, and, unless the parties have expressly agreed otherwise in a written instrument signed by them, owns all of the rights comprised in the copyright.

(c) Contributions to Collective Works.—Copyright in each separate contribution to a collective work is distinct from copyright in the collective work as a whole, and vests initially in the author of the contribution. In the absence of an express transfer of the copyright or of any rights under it, the owner of copyright in the collective work is presumed to have acquired only the privilege of reproducing and distributing the contribution as part of that particular collective work, any revision of that collective work, and any later collective work in the same series.

Related terms: author as owner of copyright; copyright claimant; transfers of copyright ownership.

copyright protection

See affirmative rights.

copyright registration

See registration.

copyright registration forms

The Copyright Office provides applicants for registration with three methods of copyright registration. Applicants may (1) file using the online eCO system (currently $35 per application); (2) file Form CO, an all-purpose form that uses an innovative bar code technology (currently $50 per application); or (3) file using traditional paper forms (currently $65 per application) such as Form TX for nondramatic literary works, including computer programs, Form PA for audiovisual works, Form VA for graphic art and sculptural works, Form SR for sound recordings, and Form SE for serials and periodicals. Copyright forms can be downloaded from the copyright office website (www.copyright.gov).

Related terms: registration of copyright.

creation of work, when protected by copyright

Under the Copyright Act, the following three rules determine when a work is first entitled to copyright protection—that is, when it is first "created":

Rule 1: Creation of a work occurs when it first becomes "fixed" in some form.

Rule 2: Drafts and other intermediate forms in the development of a work receive copyright protection just like the underlying work does.

Rule 3: Each new version of an original work is a separate creation.

EXAMPLE: Todd creates complex charts showing the relationships among scientific concepts in different fields. Todd often carries an idea for a particular chart around in his head for weeks before he jots it down in physical (tangible) form. Once his idea becomes fixed in a tangible form, whether on paper, programmed on a computer, or constructed out of plastic or other materials, Todd has created a work of authorship. Todd typically changes and improves the physical representation of his original idea. Each new version of Todd's chart becomes an original work as of the moment it becomes fixed in a tangible form. As long as Todd is working on a given chart, he has created only one work, despite a number of incremental changes. If, however, Todd produces his chart both in a print version and in a specially tailored computerized slide show, he would have two different versions of the same work and could obtain separate copyright protection for each. Separate copyrights may also be available for two different charts based on the same idea, regardless of the medium used.

Copyright Act: § 101. Definitions

A work is "created" when it is fixed in a copy or phonorecord for the first time; where a work is prepared over a period of time, the portion of it that has been fixed at any particular time constitutes the work as of that time, and where the work has been prepared in different versions, each version constitutes a separate work.

Related terms: derivative work; fixed in a tangible medium of expression.

Creative Commons

The Creative Commons is a nonprofit enterprise that encourages copyright owners to share their works with the public in various innovative ways including dedications to the public domain or through a series of licenses. For example, under one system, copyright owners can elect to use what the Commons calls "Founders' Copyright"—the original copyright term adopted by the first copyright law in 1790. This consists of an initial term of 14 years after publication, and an additional 14 years if the copyright owner wants it. The copyright owner fills out an online application and sells the copyright to the Creative Commons for $1, and then the organization gives the owner an exclusive license to the work for 14 or 28 years. If desired, users of the dedicated works can be required to provide attribution to the original author. Works so dedicated to the public domain are listed in the Creative Commons website so people can find them easily. For detailed information, see the Creative Commons website (www.creativecommmons.org).

Related terms: Copyleft.

credit line

A written acknowledgment of authorship is referred to as a credit line. When authors give permission for somebody else to use a portion or an entire work, they commonly condition the permission on including a line crediting the original author in the new work. Credit lines may become part of a work's copyright management information (CMI) and removal of this information may violate the Digital Millennium Copyright Act.

Related terms: attribution; copyright management information

criminal copyright infringement

Infringement of a copyright can be treated as a federal crime under the Copyright Act (17 USC § 506) if it is done intentionally and with full knowledge that an infringement is occurring. As a practical matter, the U.S. Department of Justice only brings criminal charges against copyright infringers when a substantial amount of money is at stake and the purpose of the infringement is commercial gain.

An infringer who commits one or more infringements during a 180-day period for "purposes of commercial advantage or private financial gain" can be fined and imprisoned for one to five years depending upon the value of the infringements. Repeat violations can result in fines and imprisonment for up to ten years.

Regardless of whether there is financial gain, an infringer may be liable for fines and up to three years in jail if the infringement is ten or more copies of one or more copyrighted works that have a total retail value of $2,500. Repeat offenders may be liable for jail time of up to six years.

The government will also prosecute anyone who knowingly and willfully aids in a criminal infringement. The government will not prosecute innocent infringers, that is, persons who had a good-faith reason to believe that copying was permitted, although those persons can still be subject to a civil law suit.

Willful violators (and those who do it for purposes of financial gain) of the Digital Millennium Copyright Act may be subject to fines of not more than $500,000 or imprisonment for not more than five years, or both, for the first offense, and fines of not more than $1,000,000 or imprisonment for not more than ten years, or both, for any subsequent offense.

Finally, the Family Entertainment and Copyright Act of 2005 made it a crime to videotape or transmit video signals from inside a movie theater, and to knowingly place a copyrighted computer program, musical work, motion picture, or other audiovisual work or sound recording on a computer network accessible to the public for purposes of copying.

Copyright Act: § 506. Criminal offenses

This statute authorizes criminal penalties for certain types of copyright infringement and establishes fines for certain dishonest copyright-related activities.

(a) **Criminal Infringement.** Any person who infringes a copyright willfully either—

 (1) for purposes of commercial advantage or private financial gain, or

 (2) by the reproduction or distribution, including by electronic means, during any 180-day period, of 1 or more copies or phonorecords of 1 or more copyrighted works, which have a total retail value of more than $1,000, shall be punished as provided under section 2319 of title 18, United States Code. For purposes of this subsection, evidence of reproduction or distribution of a copyrighted work, by itself, shall not be sufficient to establish willful infringement.

(b) **Forfeiture and Destruction.** When any person is convicted of any violation of subsection (a), the court in its judgment of conviction shall, in addition to the penalty therein prescribed, order the forfeiture and destruction or other disposition of all infringing copies or phonorecords and all implements, devices, or equipment used in the manufacture of such infringing copies or phonorecords.

(c) **Fraudulent Copyright Notice.** Any person who, with fraudulent intent, places on any article a notice of copyright or words of the same purport that such person knows to be false, or who, with fraudulent intent, publicly distributes or imports for public distribution any article bearing such notice or words that such person knows to be false, shall be fined not more than $2,500.

(d) **Fraudulent Removal of Copyright Notice.** Any person who, with fraudulent intent, removes or alters any notice of copyright appearing on a copy of a copyrighted work shall be fined not more than $2,500.

(e) **False Representation.** Any person who knowingly makes a false representation of a material fact in the application for copyright registration provided for by section 409, or in any written statement filed in connection with the application, shall be fined not more than $2,500.

(f) **Rights of Attribution and Integrity.** Nothing in this section applies to infringement of the rights conferred by section 106A (a).

customs, preventing importing of infringing works

See importing of infringing works.

cyberspace

See Internet, copyright regulation of.

damages for copyright infringement

Money damages in copyright infringement actions are commonly awarded under three legal theories, actual damages, profits, and statutory damages:

- **Actual damages.** Also called compensatory damages, this consists of the dollar amount of any demonstrable loss the owner suffered as a result of the infringing activity. This loss may be from lost sales, lost licensing revenue, or any other provable financial loss directly attributable to the infringement.

- **Profits.** This consists of any money made by the infringer as a result of the infringement. These damages are only awarded if they exceed the amount of profits lost by the copyright owner (actual damages) as a result of the infringement.

  EXAMPLE: A book on self-defense, authored by Susan, contains a practical chapter on how to purchase and care for a handgun. Rachel also writes a book on self-defense and substantially borrows from Susan's chapter on handguns without first obtaining her permission. Rachel has infringed Susan's copyright. A court could award Susan actual damages if Susan proves that she lost sales of her book because people bought Rachel's book instead, at least in part because of the handgun chapter. Alternatively, if Susan has licensed chapters of her books to other authors, the amount she typically receives for such licensing could be her actual damages. In addition, the court could award Susan any profits that Rachel realized from the infringement to the extent such profits exceeded the amount of Susan's lost profits.

- **Statutory damages.** In many copyright cases, both actual damages and profits are difficult to prove. For that reason, the Copyright Act provides for statutory damages—that is, damages set by law. However, only a person who has registered a work with the U.S. Copyright Office before the infringement (or within three months of publication) may receive statutory damages. Such a plaintiff in an infringement action may opt for either actual damages (and the infringer's profits, if appropriate) or statutory damages, but not both.

- For infringements that can't clearly be proven as either innocent or willful, statutory damages may be from $750 to $30,000 per infringement depending on the circumstances. The amount will depend on the seriousness of the infringing act and the financial worth of the infringer. On the other hand, an innocent infringer may have to pay as little as $200, while an intentional infringer may have to pay as much as $150,000 for a single infringement of one work.

Copyright Act: § 504. Remedies for infringement: Damages and profits

(a) In General.—Except as otherwise provided by this title, an infringer of copyright is liable for either—

  (1) the copyright owner's actual damages and any additional profits of the infringer, as provided by subsection (b); or

  (2) statutory damages, as provided by subsection (c).

(b) Actual Damages and Profits.—The copyright owner is entitled to recover the actual damages suffered by him or her as a result of the infringement, and any profits of the infringer that are attributable to the infringement and are not taken into account in computing the actual damages. In establishing the infringer's profits, the copyright owner is required to present proof only of the infringer's gross revenue, and the infringer is required to prove his or her deductible expenses and the elements of profit attributable to factors other than the copyrighted work.

(c) Statutory Damages.—

   (1) Except as provided by clause (2) of this subsection, the copyright owner may elect, at any time before final judgment is rendered, to recover, instead of actual damages and profits, an award of statutory damages for all infringements involved in the action, with respect to any one work, for which any one infringer is liable individually, or for which any two or more infringers are liable jointly and severally, in a sum of not less than $750 or more than $30,000 as the court considers just. For the purposes of this subsection, all the parts of a compilation or derivative work constitute one work.

   (2) In a case where the copyright owner sustains the burden of proving, and the court finds, that infringement was committed willfully, the court in its discretion may increase the award of statutory damages to a sum of not more than $150,000. In a case where the infringer sustains the burden of proving, and the court finds, that such infringer was not aware and had no reason to believe that his or her acts constituted an infringement of copyright, the court in its discretion may reduce the award of statutory damages to a sum of not less than $200. The court shall remit statutory damages in any case where an infringer believed and had reasonable grounds for believing that his or her use of the copyrighted work was a fair use under section 107, if the infringer was:

     (i) an employee or agent of a nonprofit educational institution, library, or archives acting within the scope of his or her employment who, or such institution, library, or archives itself, which infringed by reproducing the work in copies or phonorecords; or

     (ii) a public broadcasting entity which or a person who, as a regular part of the nonprofit activities of a public broadcasting entity (as defined in subsection (g) of section 118) infringed by performing a published nondramatic literary work or by reproducing a transmission program embodying a performance of such a work.

(d) Additional Damages in Certain Cases.—In any case in which the court finds that a defendant proprietor of an establishment who claims as a defense that its activities were exempt under section 110 (5) did not have reasonable grounds to believe that its use of a copyrighted work was exempt under such section, the plaintiff shall be entitled to, in addition to any award of damages under this section, an additional award of two times the amount of the license fee that the proprietor of the establishment concerned should have paid the plaintiff for such use during the preceding period of up to 3 years.

Related terms: criminal copyright infringement; infringement action; injunctions; innocent infringement of copyright; profits as damages.

dance

See choreography and pantomime.

databases, copyright of

See computer databases.

de minimis

This term, derived from the Latin expression, "*de minimis non curat lex*," ("the law does not concern itself with trifles") is applied in two ways under copyright law. As used by the U.S. Copyright Office, the term characterizes changes in an existing work that are too small to warrant a separate registration. U.S. Copyright Office regulations allow only one registration per version of a work. If an author makes several minor changes to a work and tries to register the new version, the U.S. Copyright Office will consider the changes "*de minimis*" and reject the attempted new registration.

The term is also used in copyright litigation. If a court determines that the infringement is insubstantial, the copying will be excused as *de minimis*. This is not a fair use defense; it is a defense based solely upon the inconsequential amount of infringing material. For example, several photographs appeared briefly in the film *Seven*. A court determined that a lay observer would have been unable to identify them. Therefore, the momentary use of the photos was so insubstantial that the copyright was not infringed. (*Sandoval v. New Line Cinema Corp.*, 147 F.3d 215 (2d Cir. 1998).)

Related terms: derivative work; single registration rule.

deep linking

See linking.

defective copyright notice

Until March 1, 1989, works published in the United States needed a copyright notice for the copyright to remain in force. A defective notice could and did permanently nullify copyright protection for many works. However, after the March 1, 1989, date, no notice is required, but only recommended (to give people notice that the work is protected by copyright).

A correct notice is either the little "©" or the words "Copyright" or "Copr." followed by the date and the author's name. In the case of a sound recording, the proper symbol is a "P" in a circle.

A defective copyright notice might be one with an error in or omission of the author's name, the copyright symbol, or the date (an error of more than one year).

Related terms: innocent infringement of copyright; international copyright protection; notice of copyright; omission of copyright notice.

defenses to copyright infringement

The common defenses to an allegation of copyright infringement are:

- The use was a "fair use," that is, the use was for a transformative purposes such as a parody, or in a critical commentary.
- The allegedly infringing work was independently created, that is, it wasn't copied.
- The statute of limitations has run (the plaintiff waited too long to file suit— filing must be within three years of discovering the infringement).
- The work (or the portion) copied was in the public domain.
- The use was authorized, that is the copyright owner gave permission.

Related terms: authorized use of copyrighted material; fair use; independent creation; innocent infringement of copyright; public domain—copyright context; statute of limitations.

deposit with U.S. Copyright Office

Part of the copyright registration process requires the deposit of actual copies, photographs, or other representations of an original work of authorship with the U.S. Copyright Office. For most categories of published works, it is necessary to deposit two copies of the work's best edition. For some types of works, however, including computer programs, motion pictures, and most unpublished works, only one copy need be deposited. The form a deposit must take differs according to the media in question but must generally be sufficient to identify the work being registered. Users of the Copyright Office's electronic filing system (eCO) should upload one digital copy of a published work (if the applicant meets the deposit requirements) or mail in two hard copies of a published work. The eCO program provides a preprinted mailing label.

Related terms: identifying material; registration.

derivative work

A derivative work is one based upon preexisting material to which enough original creative work has been added so that the new work represents an original work of authorship. The term (as defined in 17 USC § 101) encompasses any form into which a work may be recast, transformed, or adapted.

The author of a derivative work must obtain permission from the owner of the copyright in the earlier work to copy, sell, or distribute the derivative work. For example, a foreign language translation of a book is based on the book as it was originally written and is subject to the copyright in the original version; a movie that borrows the main characters, the story line, and some dialogue from a novel is based on that novel and is subject to that novel's copyright; and a song that has substantially the same melody as an earlier song is based on that song, even if the words are different, and is subject to the earlier song's copyright.

As a general rule, the more expression a subsequent work uses from an earlier work, the more likely it is to be considered a derivative work and therefore subject to the earlier work's copyright. However, assuming permission is obtained from the owner of the copyright in the earlier work, the derivative work is itself subject to copyright protection as an independent work.

Examples of derivative works are:

- an English translation of a book written in French
- a computer program rewritten in a different programming language
- a movie based on a play or book
- condensed or abridged versions of articles, such as those found in *Reader's Digest*
- annotations to literary works (for example, *CliffsNotes*), and
- a jazz version of a popular tune.

Derivative works may also be fictionalizations, recordings, or even editorial revisions. Compilations and collective works are not normally considered derivative works because they are collections of different underlying works, rather than a new work based upon an original work.

The exclusive right to make derivative works is an important part of the bundle of rights that make up every copyright. Absent an explicit transfer of this right by a written license, or by permission from the owner (voluntary or forced in the case of a compulsory license), no one else can exercise it except for personal use.

> **EXAMPLE:** Joe wants to adapt a popular novel into an interactive computer program. Because the program will be based on the novel, it will constitute a derivative work and therefore cannot legally be marketed without permission from the novel's copyright owner.

Copyright Act: § 101. Definitions

A "derivative work" is a work based upon one or more preexisting works, such as a translation, musical arrangement, dramatization, fictionalization, motion picture version, sound recording, art reproduction, abridgment, condensation, or any other form in which a work may be recast, transformed, or adapted. A work consisting of editorial revisions, annotations, elaborations, or other modifications which, as a whole, represent an original work of authorship, is a "derivative work."

Copyright Act: § 103. Subject matter of copyright: Compilations and derivative works

(a) The subject matter of copyright as specified by section 102 includes compilations and derivative works, but protection for a work employing preexisting material in which copyright subsists does not extend to any part of the work in which such material has been used unlawfully.

(b) The copyright in a compilation or derivative work extends only to the material contributed by the author of such work, as distinguished from the preexisting material employed in the work, and does not imply any exclusive right in the preexisting material. The copyright in such work is independent of, and does not affect or enlarge the scope, duration, ownership, or subsistence of, any copyright protection in the preexisting material.

Related terms: collective work; copyright; copyright infringement; independent creation.

Digital Millennium Copyright Act

This federal statute addresses a number of copyright issues created by the use of the Internet. Among other things, it outlaws attempts to get around processes, methods, or devices that limit copying of copyrighted works. For example, if a copyright owner installs a digital rights management (DRM) system that limits copying of a motion picture, and a user circumvents the system (even without copying the underlying movie), a violation of the DMCA has occurred. In short, the DMCA has made it possible for a person to violate copyright law without infringing a copyright.

The act has numerous exceptions allowing for override of DRMs, including:

- works exempted by the Copyright Office, under rules to be issued in the future
- nonprofit libraries, archives, and educational institutions that need to decide whether to add the protected work to their collections
- reverse engineering for the purpose of determining interoperability (the ability of computer programs to exchange information, and of such programs mutually to use the information which has been exchanged)
- legitimate encryption research
- legitimate security testing
- law enforcement and intelligence activities, and
- legitimate consumer privacy needs (the need to disable the protective device in order to prevent the unwanted acquisition of personal information or the tracking of activities on the Internet).

In addition to DRM rules, the DMCA has many other requirements including:

- The DMCA prohibits the production, marketing, or sales of a product or service designed to circumvent these technological protections. For example, the movie industry was able to use the DMCA to prohibit circumvention of DVD technology when it stopped a programmer from distributing a software code designed to decode DVDs and permit their copying. (*Universal City Studios Inc. v. Corley,* 273 F.3d 429 (2d Cir. 2001).)

- The DMCA puts restrictions on the import, distribution, and sales of analog video cassette recorders and camcorders that don't have a certain type of copy-proof technology.

- The DMCA prohibits the falsification of copyright management information and the distribution of works that contain such falsified information.

- The DMCA contains a number of provisions relating to transmission of copyrighted materials over Internet service providers (ISPs). The DMCA takes ISPs off the hook for infringement for transient transmissions automatically passing through their computers. Under its "safe harbor" provisions, the DMCA also allows ISPs to escape liability for infringement regarding more permanent materials if they promptly remove infringing materials upon request. The DMCA sets up a procedure in case the owner of the removed materials protests. In exchange for escaping liability for infringement, service providers must designate an agent to accept service of legal papers. The DMCA also relieves ISPs from liability for unknowingly linking to a site that does contain infringing material. Finally, the DMCA authorizes U.S. district court clerks to issue subpoenas to service providers requiring them to identify an alleged online infringer.

The DMCA is often used by angry copyright claimants seeking to have an ISP remove infringing works under its "notice and takedown" procedures, described above. To protect against the unjustified use of this provision, Congress provided section 512(f), which permits Internet publishers to bring affirmative claims against copyright owners who knowingly and materially misrepresent that infringement has occurred. In a 2004 case, two ISPs successfully used this provision to fight back against a DMCA notice and takedown procedure instigated by Diebold over the republication of an email archive. The emails from Diebold engineers allegedly sounded an alarm over flaws in Diebold's electronic voting machines. A court ruled that the republication of the emails was a fair use because there was no commercial harm and no diminishment of the value of the works. (*Online Privacy Group v. Diebold,* 72 USPQ 2d 1200 (N.D. Cal. 2004).)

In 2008, a district court ruled that prior to requesting a takedown notice, a copyright owner must consider the likelihood of a claim of fair use. In that case, Universal Music issued a takedown notice for a video of a child dancing to the song, "Let's Go Crazy," by Prince. The owner of the video claimed that because Universal didn't consider the issue of fair use, Universal could have not had a "good faith belief" they were entitled to a takedown. Faced with this novel issue, a district court agreed that the failure to consider fair use when sending a DMCA notice could give rise to a claim of failing to act in good faith. (*Lenz v. Universal Music Corp.*, 572 F. Supp. 2d 1150 (N.D. Cal. 2008).)

The DMCA allows a copy of a computer program to be made for the purpose of repairing or maintaining a computer. In addition, the DMCA contains new laws regarding the licensing of motion pictures and phonorecordings and the innovative designs of vessel hulls.

Violations of the DMCA can result in civil remedies consisting of injunctive relief, actual damages, and statutory damages. Repeat violators may be tagged with treble damages. A willful violation of the DMCA for personal or financial gain can result in stiff criminal penalties (up to ten years in prison).

The first criminal prosecution under the DMCA occurred when the U.S. government indicted Dmitri Sklyarov for creating and distributing software that could permit electronic book owners to convert the Adobe eBook format. A jury later acquitted Sklyarov of all criminal charges.

One of the more novel attempts at applying the DMCA occurred in 2003 when a printer manufacturer, Lexmark, sued a rival company, Static Control Components, which sold replacement toner cartridges. Lexmark's printers contained a software program that read information embedded on a chip in the toner cartridge. If the toner wasn't "authorized" (made by Lexmark or a licensee), the toner cartridge would not work in the printer. Static Control created Smartek chips that sent a message to the Lexmark printer authorizing the use of its toner cartridges. Lexmark argued that the Smartek chips circumvented Lexmark technology in violation of the DMCA. In March 2003, a district court in Kentucky agreed with Lexmark and enjoined Static Control from selling its Smartek chip or incorporating it in cartridges. That decision was later vacated by a federal Court of Appeals. (*Lexmark International Inc. v. Static Control Components Inc.*, 387 F.3d (6th Cir. 2004).) In a different case, the federal Circuit Court of Appeals upheld the dismissal of a case involving garage door openers in which a company unsuccessfully argued that a competitor's ability to offer universal remote control devices was prohibited under the DMCA. (*Chamberlain Group, Inc. v. Skylink Techs., Inc.*, 381 F.3d 1178 (Fed. Cir. 2004).)

Related terms: Copyleft; digital rights management (DRM); *ElcomSoft, U.S. v.;* Internet, copyright regulation of.

digital rights management (DRM)

A term that encompasses various processes or methods of restricting usage of (or access to) a copyrighted work. Initially DRM technologies were created solely to prevent copying of software, but since the late 1990s they have been used in conjunction with creative works such as music, books, databases, and movies. DRMs are implemented at the discretion of the copyright owner. Cracking, reproducing, or tampering with DRM technologies has resulted in several lawsuits, usually brought under the Digital Millennium Copyright Act (which prohibits such activities). For example, the DRM system used on DVDs known as Content Scrambling System (CSS) was the subject of considerable litigation, as was the DRM system used to limit copying of Adobe eBooks. Despite claims made by their creators, no DRM has yet proven uncrackable.

Circumventing DRM is not excused just because DRM-cracking tools are widely available. In a 2010 case, Apple sued a company that had circumvented its DRM system. The defendant company argued in defense that tools for cracking the DRM were widely available and that therefore, the DRM itself was so ineffective as to be meaningless. The court disagreed and held that if the DRM could not be circumvented without outside information or tools, it would be considered as effective DRM. (*Apple Inc. v. Psystar Corp.*, 673 F. Supp. 2d 931 (N.D. Cal. 2009).)

New rules. The Library of Congress issued rules in 2010 stating that wireless phone owners could break access controls on their phones in order to switch wireless carriers. Other rules issued: computer users could bypass security dongles if the dongle no longer works and can't be replaced; users of eBook readers could break digital locks to use read-aloud software, and educators and filmmakers could circumvent DVD protection for noncommercial purposes.

Related terms: Digital Millennium Copyright Act; *Elcomsoft, U.S. v.*

display a work

The exclusive right to display an original work of authorship is one of the bundle of rights that together form the overall copyright. (17 USC § 101.) The Copyright Act of 1976 defines "display" as: "to show a copy of it, either directly or by means of a film, slide, television image, or any other device or process or, in the case of a motion picture or other audiovisual work, to show individual images nonsequentially" (as in movie previews).

> **EXAMPLE:** Marylou photographs Juan's copyrighted print for the purpose of using it in her photography show. Because Juan has the exclusive right to display his work, Marylou must obtain Juan's permission before she displays the photo.

This particular right has become increasingly important as more creative works have been placed into digital form for display through the Internet and through the large online services which charge users for the time they spend viewing displayed materials.

Related terms: copyright.

dramatic works

In the copyright sense, a dramatic work is one that carries a story line and is intended to be performed before an audience, either directly or through use of a tangible medium such as paper, film, videotape, or videodisc. Dramatic works include movies, plays, satires, comedies, and pantomimes. Like other original works of authorship, they are fully protectable by copyright.

Related terms: original work of authorship.

duration of copyrights

How long a copyright lasts in the United States depends on when the work covered by the copyright was first created or published:

- **Works created on or after January 1, 1978.** Under the Copyright Act of 1976, copyrights on works created on or after January 1, 1978, last for a defined period of time. If the "author" is an individual, and the work appears under that person's name, the copyright lasts for the life of the author plus 70 years. If the "author" is an employer or the commissioner of a work made for hire, or uses a pseudonym or remains anonymous, the copyright lasts for 95 years from the date of publication or 120 years from the date the work was first created, whichever comes first.
- **Works created or published before January 1, 1978.** If the work was published before 1978, the copyright lasts for 95 years from the date of publication, assuming the copyright was (or is) timely renewed (by filing a renewal application with the U.S. Copyright Office). The copyright in works created before 1978 lasts at least to December 31, 2047, if published before

December 31, 2002. All unpublished works created by authors who died 70 or more years ago are now in the public domain in the United States. This is so whether the author was American or a non-American. Unpublished works made for hire created more than 120 years ago are also in the U.S. public domain.

Countries that are members of the Berne Convention and countries that have signed the GATT treaty (which requires its members to honor the Berne Convention's copyright protection standards) extend copyright protection for the life of the author plus a minimum of 50 years. The countries in the European Union also extend copyright protection for the life of the author plus 70 years.

The value of works such as books, films, art, and songs (that is, their ability to generate copyright fees) may last well beyond the term of the copyright, in which case the author's inheritors are out of luck. On the other hand, computer-related works seem likely to be more short-lived, so copyright protection will probably last for more than enough time to protect them for their entire commercial life expectancy.

Below is a chart that shows the duration of copyrights for different publishing dates.

Copyright Duration Chart	
Date and Nature of Work	**Copyright Term**
Published before 1923	The work is in the public domain
Published 1923–1963 and never renewed	The work is in the public domain
Published 1923–1963 and timely renewed	95 years from the date of first publication
Published between 1964 and 1977	95 years from the date of publication (renewal term automatic)
Created, but not published or registered, before 1978	Single term of 120 years from creation for unpublished works made for hire, and unpublished or pseudonymous works
Created before 1978 and published 1978–2002	Copyright will expire January 1, 2048
Created 1978 and later	Life of author + 70 years

Copyright Act: § 302. Duration of copyright: Works created on or after January 1, 1978

(a) In General.—Copyright in a work created on or after January 1, 1978, subsists from its creation and, except as provided by the following subsections, endures for a term consisting of the life of the author and 70 years after the author's death.

(b) Joint Works.—In the case of a joint work prepared by two or more authors who did not work for hire, the copyright endures for a term consisting of the life of the last surviving author and 70 years after such last surviving author's death.

(c) Anonymous Works, Pseudonymous Works, and Works Made for Hire.—In the case of an anonymous work, a pseudonymous work, or a work made for hire, the copyright endures for a term of 95 years from the year of its first publication, or a term of 120 years from the year of its creation, whichever expires first. If, before the end of such term, the identity of one or more of the authors of an anonymous or pseudonymous work is revealed in the records of a registration made for that work under subsections (a) or (d) of section 408, or in the records provided by this subsection, the copyright in the work endures for the term specified by subsection (a) or (b), based on the life of the author or authors whose identity has been revealed. Any person having an interest in the copyright in an anonymous or pseudonymous work may at any time record, in records to be maintained by the Copyright Office for that purpose, a statement identifying one or more authors of the work; the statement shall also identify the person filing it, the nature of that person's interest, the source of the information recorded, and the particular work affected, and shall comply in form and content with requirements that the Register of Copyrights shall prescribe by regulation.

(d) Records Relating to Death of Authors.—Any person having an interest in a copyright may at any time record in the Copyright Office a statement of the date of death of the author of the copyrighted work, or a statement that the author is still living on a particular date. The statement shall identify the person filing it, the nature of that person's interest, and the source of the information recorded, and shall comply in form and content with requirements that the Register of Copyrights shall prescribe by regulation. The Register shall maintain current records of information relating to the death of authors of copyrighted works, based on such recorded statements and, to the extent the Register considers practicable, on data contained in any of the records of the Copyright Office or in other reference sources.

(e) Presumption as to Author's Death.—After a period of 95 years from the year of first publication of a work, or a period of 120 years from the year of its creation, whichever expires first, any person who obtains from the Copyright Office a certified report that the records provided by subsection (d) disclose nothing to indicate that the author of the work is living, or died less than 70 years before, is entitled to the benefits of a presumption that the author has been dead for at least 70 years. Reliance in good faith upon this presumption shall be a complete defense to any action for infringement under this title.

Related terms: *Eldred v. Ashcroft;* GATT (General Agreement on Tariffs and Trade); international copyright protection; Sonny Bono Copyright Term Extension Act; work made for hire.

electronic filing of copyright applications

Using the eCO electronic filing system, users can file a copyright application online (currently for $35). The process is fairly straightforward (and discussed in the Forms portion of this text, following this section). You may upload a digital copy of your work (if you qualify) or you may mail in hard copies of your deposit materials.

Eldred v. Ashcroft

During the past four decades, Congress has extended copyright terms 11 times. After the Sonny Bono Copyright Term Extension Act added a 20-year term extension, Eric Eldred and other users of public domain commercial materials sued, claiming that Congress's continual extensions of the copyright term violated the Constitution. In 2003, the U.S. Supreme Court disagreed and ruled the 20-year copyright extension did not violate the U.S. Constitution. (*Eldred v. Ashcroft,* 537 U.S. 186 (2003).)

Related terms: Copyleft; duration of copyrights; Sonny Bono Copyright Term Extension Act.

end-user license (aka EULA, shrinkwrap, or clickwrap agreement)

Copyright owners, particularly software and website publishers, may want to limit how purchasers use their products and services. For example, a software maker may insist that customers use its program only for personal, not commercial, purposes. To impose these restrictions, most publishers employ a contract known as an end-user license agreement (EULA).

These EULAs were originally known as "shrinkwrap licenses" because—at least in the early days of software production—the user would consent to the EULA (visible on the back of the package) by breaking the box's shrinkwrap. A user who proceeds to use the program is deemed to accept the terms. A user who doesn't want to accept the terms can return the program to the manufacturer for a refund.

Nowadays, most EULAs are known as a "clickwrap agreements," because the user enters into the agreement online and must click to accept the conditions before accessing a website or using software.

Initially, there was doubt as to whether EULAs could be enforced in court, especially if the provisions were inconsistent with the Copyright Act. The reason for doubt is because the typical EULA isn't negotiated between seller and purchaser at the time of sale, and so the purchaser shouldn't be held to its terms, especially if the user must waive rights under the Copyright Act. For example, some licenses may prohibit the user from copying the software, even though the Copyright Act permits the purchaser to make an archival copy.

In 1996, a federal Court of Appeal ruled that shrinkwrap licenses are valid as long as a user who disagrees with the terms can return the product for a refund. The court also ruled that a license restricting rights that a purchaser would have otherwise had under the Copyright Act is legal. (*ProCD v. Zeidenberg*, 86 F.3d 1447 (7th Cir. 1996).)

The same standards apply to clickwrap agreements: "[C]lickwrap license agreements are an appropriate way to form contracts." (*i.Lan Systems Inc. v. Netscout Service Level Corp.,* 183 F. Supp. 2d 328 (D. Mass. 2002).) In a case involving America Online, a court upheld a clickwrap agreement between AOL and a Massachusetts man requiring that legal disputes with AOL be settled in Virginia. (*Hughes v. AOL,* 2002 U.S. Dist. LEXIS 9569 (D. Mass 2002).)

A EULA was ineffective in a case involving the Adobe Software company. In 2001, a federal court ruled that, despite the language of an Adobe license agreement, the purchaser of a bundle of Adobe software programs could resell the individual components (separate programs on CDs). (*Softman Products Co. LLC v. Adobe Systems Inc.,* 171 F. Supp. 2d 1075 (C.D. Cal. 2001).) The district court in that case determined that Adobe had sold, rather than licensed, its products to distributors, permitting the resale of the components under the first-sale doctrine.

In 2000, federal legislation—the Electronic Signatures in Global and International Commerce Act—was enacted, which helped remove some of the uncertainty that previously plagued e-contracts and prevented a contract from being challenged simply because it was created electronically. Some proponents of software licenses urged passage of the Uniform Computer Information Transaction Act (UCITA), a proposed law that would legitimize all software licenses. However, the UCITA was adopted in only two states, Virginia and Maryland.

Another company, as a condition of its EULA, prohibited reverse engineering of its software. To the dismay of software programmers, a federal court upheld

Copyright Law: Definitions

this provision. (*Bowers v. Baystate Technologies, Inc.*, 320 F.3d 1317 (Fed. Cir. 2003).)

Even more disconcerting for many scholars and consumers was the intro-duction of nonsoftware EULAs. For example, a book publisher used a shrinkwrap agreement to prohibit the resale of books. A museum required viewers to waive the right to claim fair use when copying material from its website. (Both of these rights—resale and fair use—are otherwise permitted under the Copyright Act.)

Related terms: computer software; licensing of copyrights; UCITA.

ephemeral recording

Under some circumstances, the Copyright Act permits making copies of works for purposes of later transmission. For example, a disc jockey is permitted to copy a song from compact disc to tape in order to prepare a radio broadcast. These ephemeral recordings are commonly used in radio, cable, and Internet broadcasting.

exclusive copyright rights

A copyright owner is exclusively entitled to a bundle of rights consisting of:

- the right to reproduce (copy) the work
- the right to prepare derivative works
- the right to distribute copies of the work
- the right to perform the work, and
- the right to display the work.

Copyright Act: § 106. Exclusive rights in copyrighted works

Subject to sections 107 through 122, the owner of copyright under this title has the exclusive rights to do and to authorize any of the following:

(1) to reproduce the copyrighted work in copies or phonorecords;

(2) to prepare derivative works based upon the copyrighted work;

(3) to distribute copies or phonorecords of the copyrighted work to the public by sale or other transfer of ownership, or by rental, lease, or lending;

(4) in the case of literary, musical, dramatic, and choreographic works, pantomimes, and motion pictures and other audiovisual works, to perform the copyrighted work publicly;

(5) in the case of literary, musical, dramatic, and choreographic works, pantomimes, and pictorial, graphic, or sculptural works, including the individual images of a motion picture or other audiovisual work, to display the copyrighted work publicly; and

(6) in the case of sound recordings, to perform the copyrighted work publicly by means of a digital audio transmission.

Related terms: copyright; exclusive license; infringement action.

exclusive license

An exclusive license, which must be in writing, is a contract in which a copyright owner authorizes another person or entity (called the licensee) to exclusively exercise one or more of the rights (or portion of such rights) that belong to the copyright owner under the copyright. The licensee is said to "own" the rights granted in the license and is often referred to as a "copyright owner."

> EXAMPLE: Jeanette, a U.S. author, publishes a successful cookbook specializing in East African recipes. Aaron believes the book will sell well in other countries and approaches Jeanette for permission to sell it on the international market. Jeanette may choose to grant Aaron an exclusive license to copy, distribute, and translate (prepare derivative works from) the book for marketing in all countries outside of the United States. She might, instead, license Aaron to market the book only in one or a few countries—for example, France, the Canadian province of Quebec, and all Caribbean and African countries where French is a primary language. In addition to foreign rights, Jeanette is interested in finding someone to help her market the book to cooking stores within the United States. To reach this market, she grants an exclusive license to a cookware wholesaler. Finally, she exclusively licenses a cookbook publisher to publish and distribute the book to the book trade (exclusive of cooking stores) in the United States.

Under an exclusive license, the licensee as a "copyright owner" has the right to file an infringement action in court to stop all infringing activities, assuming that the copyright was properly registered and the license was recorded with the U.S. Copyright Office.

Related terms: copyright owner; transfers of copyright ownership.

expedited registration

The U.S. Copyright Office has a special procedure to register a work if a copyright owner needs the registration quickly. Only three reasons are permitted for receiving special handling: pending or prospective litigation, customs matters, or contract or publishing deadlines that necessitate the expedited issuance of a certificate. Expedited registration—called "special handling" by the U.S. Copyright Office—costs an additional $760 (as of September 2011). For more on special handling, review Circular 10 at the Copyright Office.

Copyright owners must register their work prior to suing for infringement under the provisions of 17 USC § 411(a). However, the Fifth, Seventh, and Ninth Circuits have interpreted this to mean that a lawsuit can proceed if an application has been filed, provided that a registration eventually issues. The Tenth and Eleventh Circuits have held to a stricter requirement and require a Certificate of Registration.

Related terms: copyright infringement; infringement action.

expression, protection of, under copyright law

See copyright; original work of authorship.

factual works

Factual works are those that legitimately may be classified as nonfiction. Histories, instruction manuals, trade catalogs, travel guides, and biographies are all examples of factual works. Under copyright law, factual works receive less (or "narrower") protection than works of fiction because the underlying facts are legally considered to be in the public domain. Therefore, factual works do not contain as much protectable material as fictional works.

EXAMPLE: Tim writes a travel book on the Comoros Islands, a small island country off the east coast of Africa. In this book, he catalogs all the usual items, including lodging, tourist sites, and food. A year later, Alice publishes a competing book that contains much of the same information plus some additional facts about the Comorean political system. Tim writes Alice, accusing her of copyright infringement. Alice responds that she used Tim's book to visit the Comoros and that because his facts were remarkably accurate, she had no choice but to include them in her book. Because facts such as those found in Alice's and Tim's books are in the public domain, Alice has not infringed Tim's copyright.

In a 2009 case involving a play and a book—both examining the death of Pope John Paul I—a New York district court ruled that historical facts, theories interpreting those facts, and plots based on the chronology of historical events are unprotectable. (*Crane v. Poetic Products, Ltd.*, 593 F. Supp. 2d 585 (S.D. N.Y. 2009).)

Related terms: *Feist Publications Inc. v. Rural Telephone Service Co.*; merger doctrine.

failure to deposit work

To properly register a copyright with the U.S. Copyright Office, the registrant must deposit one or more copies of the underlying work. Failure to deposit within three months after a demand for the deposit is made by the Register of Copyrights will require the owner to forfeit the copyright application fee and reapply. In that case, the owner will not be entitled to the original filing date.

Related terms: copyright infringement; registration.

fair use

The fair use doctrine permits the unauthorized use of copyrighted material if it is used for certain transformative purposes such as criticism, commentary, or parody. The Copyright Act permits any person to make "fair use" of a published or unpublished copyrighted work—including the making of unauthorized copies—in these contexts:

- in connection with criticism of or comment on the work
- in the course of news reporting
- for teaching purposes, or
- as part of scholarship or research activity.

As a practical matter, fair use is primarily an affirmative defense to a claim of copyright infringement—that is, the defense is that even if infringement occurred, there is no liability, because the infringing activity was excusable as a fair use of the original work.

Whether or not a particular instance of copying without permission qualifies as a fair use is decided on a case-by-case basis and depends on four basic factors. These are:

- the purpose and character of the use, including whether such use is of a commercial nature or for nonprofit, educational purposes
- the nature of the copyrighted work
- the amount and substantiality of the portion used in relation to the copyrighted work as a whole, and
- the effect of the use upon the potential market for, or value of, the copyrighted work.

Below we examine each of these factors separately. Note that when we use the term "defendant" we are referring to the person accused of infringement.

The **first factor** is considered the most important and requires an analysis as to whether the use is transformative. That is, did the defendant change the original by adding new expression or meaning? Did the defendant add value to the original by creating new information, new aesthetics, new insights and understandings? If the use was transformative, this weighs in favor of a fair use finding. In a parody, for example, the parodist transforms the original by holding it up to ridicule. The brief use of photographs in a film was considered to be transformative because the images were used in furtherance of the creation of a distinct aesthetic and overall mood. The defendant's work doesn't have to transform the original work's expression as long as the purpose is transformative, for example, scholarship, research, education, or commentary.

Determining what is transformative—and the degree of transformation—is often challenging. For example, the creation of a Harry Potter encyclopedia was determined to be "slightly transformative" (because it made the Harry Potter terms and lexicons available in one volume), but this transformative quality was not enough to justify a fair use defense in light of the extensive verbatim use of text from the Harry Potter books. (*Warner Bros. Entertainment, Inc. v. RDR Books*, 575 F. Supp. 2d 513 (S.D. N.Y. 2008).)

When considering the **second factor**—nature of the copyrighted work—a court will generally consider whether the work being copied is informational or entertaining in nature. As the Supreme Court indicated, "copying a news broadcast may have a stronger claim to fair use than copying a motion picture." Why? Because copying from informational works such as scholarly, scientific, or news journals encourages the free spread of ideas and encourages the creation of new scientific or educational works, all of which benefits the public. In addition, a defendant has a stronger case of fair use if material is copied from a published work rather than an unpublished work. The scope of fair use is narrower with respect to unpublished works because of the author's right to control the first public appearance of his expression.

As for the **third factor**—amount and substantiality of portion used—the more that is taken from a work, the more difficult it becomes to justify it as a fair use. For example, in one case the court found that copying more than half of an unpublished manuscript was not considered a fair use. When considering the amount and substantiality of the portion taken, the court considers not just the quantity of the material taken but the quality of the material taken. Determinations regarding "quality" or "substantiality" are subjective and may be difficult to reconcile. For example, the copying of one minute and 15 seconds of a 72-minute Charlie Chaplin film, used in a news report about the comedian's death, was considered substantial and not a fair use. However, in another case, the court determined that copying 41 seconds from a boxing match film was not substantial and permitted it as a fair use in a movie biography of Muhammad Ali.

In certain rare cases, copying of a complete work may be considered a fair use. (*Universal City Studios v. Sony Corp.*, 464 U.S. 417 (1984).) For example, the Supreme Court in the Sony case permitted the off-the-air copying of complete television programs by consumers who owned video recorders (VCRs).

As for the **fourth factor**—effect of the use on the potential market—a judge must consider the effect on the actual and potential market for the copyrighted work. This consideration goes beyond the past intentions of the author or the means by which the author is currently exploiting the work. For example, in one case a photograph was adapted into a wood sculpture without the authorization of the photographer. The fact that the photographer never considered converting the photograph into a sculpture was irrelevant. What mattered was that the potential market existed, as demonstrated by the fact that the defendant earned hundreds of thousands of dollars selling such sculptures.

Some uses are not considered to undermine the potential market. Copying a magazine cover for purposes of a comparative advertisement is a fair use, because the comparative advertisement does not undermine the sales or need for the magazine. Similarly, a court found that the appearance of a poster in the background of a television series for less than 30 seconds did not harm the potential market for the poster.

Similarly, a court held that a search engine's practice of creating small reproductions ("thumbnails") of images and placing them on its own website (known as "inlining") did not undermine the potential market for the sale or licensing of those images. One of the reasons for this fair use ruling was that the thumbnails were much smaller and of much poorer quality than the original photos and served to index the images and help the public access them. (*Kelly v. Arriba Soft Corp.*, 336 F.3d 811 (9th Cir. 2003).)

A similar result was reached by the Ninth Circuit Court of Appeals in a case involving Google. The court determined that Google's use of thumbnails was permitted as a fair use in a case involving reproductions of images from an adult men's magazine website. (*Perfect 10, Inc. v. Amazon.com, Inc.*, 508 F.3d 1146 (9th Cir. 2007).)

In a case involving the reproduction of concert posters within a book, the Second Circuit Court of Appeals determined that the reduced reproduction of concert posters within the context of a timeline was a fair use. (*Bill Graham Archives v. Dorling Kindersley Ltd.*, 448 F.3d 605 (2d Cir. 2006).) In a similar case, a district court held that the reproduction of movie monster magazine covers, in a book about the cover artist, was a fair use. (*Warren Publishing Co. v. Spurlock d/b/a Vanguard Productions*, 645 F. Supp. 2d 402, (E.D. Pa., 2009).)

In addition to these four fair use factors, a court may consider other factors, if relevant. The drafters of the Copyright Act of 1976 were careful to advise that the four fair use factors were intended only as a guideline and the courts are free to adapt the doctrine to particular situations on a case-by-case basis.

In some cases, however, the facts preclude raising the defense at all. For example, a defendant in a music file sharing case could not claim a fair use defense because he had failed to provide evidence that his copying of music files involved any transformative use (an essential element in proving fair use). The court held that "In the end, fair use is not a referendum on fairness in the abstract ..." (*Capitol Records Inc. v. Alaujan*, 593 F. Supp. 2d 319 (D. Mass., July 27, 2009).)

A thorough and current source of fair use information is the Copyright and Fair Use site (http://fairuse.stanford.edu) operated by the Stanford University Libraries.

Copyright Act: § 107. Limitations on exclusive rights: Fair use

Notwithstanding the provisions of sections 106 and 106A, the fair use of a copyrighted work, including such use by reproduction in copies or phonorecords or by any other means specified by that section, for purposes such as criticism, comment, news reporting, teaching (including multiple copies for classroom use), scholarship, or research, is not an infringement of copyright. In determining whether the use made of a work in any particular case is a fair use the factors to be considered shall include—

(1) the purpose and character of the use, including whether such use is of a commercial nature or is for nonprofit educational purposes;

(2) the nature of the copyrighted work;

(3) the amount and substantiality of the portion used in relation to the copyrighted work as a whole; and

(4) the effect of the use upon the potential market for or value of the copyrighted work.

The fact that a work is unpublished shall not itself bar a finding of fair use if such finding is made upon consideration of all the above factors.

Related terms: copyright infringement; infringement action; inlining; published work.

false representation in copyright registration application

A deliberate lie on a copyright registration form, such as a false statement that no preexisting works are included in the work being registered, may invalidate the legal effect and benefits of the registration. On the other hand, an innocent mistake should not invalidate the registration if the copyright owner makes timely moves to correct it.

Related terms: supplemental registration.

Family Entertainment and Copyright Act of 2005

This Act—a collection of provisions reflecting the interests of various lobbying groups—(1) makes it a criminal violation of copyright law to videotape or transmit video signals from inside a movie theater, (2) exempts from copyright and trademark claims those who filter movies to eliminate objectionable content, (3) makes it a crime to knowingly place a copyrighted computer program, musical work, motion picture or other audiovisual work, or sound recording on a computer network accessible to the public for purposes of copying, (4) directs the Copyright Office to establish a preregistration procedure for works that have not yet been published, (5) establishes rules for the National Film Preservation Act, and (6) permits, during the last 20 years of any term of copyright of a published work, certain rights of reproduction and distribution of copyrighted works for libraries or archives engaged in the preservation, scholarship, or research of those works.

Related terms: duration of copyrights; filtering.

Feist Publications Inc. v. Rural Telephone Service Co.

In this court case, a publisher of a residential telephone directory sued a competitor who had copied the directory verbatim. The Supreme Court ruled that the original phone directory was not protected under copyright because:

- it consisted of facts in the public domain (the residence and phone number of each person listed in the directory)
- the information was not arranged in a creative manner (the listings were in alphabetical order).

Although the phone book publisher argued that it wasn't fair to allow a competitor to capitalize on the labor and expense that had gone into the original directory, the Supreme Court ruled that copyright only protects original expression, not labor and expense. (*Feist Publications Inc. v. Rural Telephone Service Co.,* 499 U.S. 340 (1991).)

Related terms: compilations; computer databases.

Copyright Law: Definitions

filtering

Filtering is the process by which an individual can skip or mute over objectionable content in audio or video content of motion pictures. The technology was created to allow parents the ability to bypass content such as graphic violence, sex, nudity, and profanity during DVD playback. In September 2002, several Hollywood movie studios and directors sued the manufacturer of the process, claiming that the process violated trademark and copyright law. However, in 2005, the lawsuit became moot when President George W. Bush signed into effect the Family Entertainment and Copyright Act of 2005, which includes a provision, The Family Movie Act of 2005, creating an exemption from copyright or trademark infringement for anyone who uses this technology for home viewing.

Related terms: Family Entertainment and Copyright Act of 2005.

filtration test for determining substantial similarity

In the case of *Computer Associates Int'l v. Altai,* 982 F.2d 693 (2d Cir. 1992), a federal appellate court first applied a now commonly used technique called "filtration" to distinguish those aspects of software or software interfaces that are protected by copyright from those that are not. Filtration works by first eliminating from a software-related work such unprotectable elements as:

- ideas
- elements dictated by efficiency (that is, there is no other sensible way to write the code or handle the task)
- elements determined by external factors (such as the nature of the mechanical specifications of the computer on which the program is intended to run, compatibility requirements, manufacturers' design standards, and the intended user base), and
- material taken from the public domain.

What's left of the work is then examined to see whether it qualifies for copyright protection.

The *Altai* case itself dealt with whether a computer program interface was entitled to copyright protection. After the court applied the filtration process to the interface in question, nothing was left to protect; thus, copyright protection was denied.

Related terms: computer software.

first-sale doctrine

The first-sale doctrine permits the purchaser of a legal copy of a copyrighted work to treat that copy in any way desired, as long as the copyright owner's exclusive copyright rights are not infringed. This means the copy can be destroyed, sold, given away, or rented. A common example is the rental of movie videos, where the store purchasing the videotapes is entitled to rent them out without paying any royalties to the owner of the copyright rights in the movie. If, however, the store made additional copies of the movie and also rented them out, the underlying copyright would be infringed. The term "first-sale doctrine" comes from the fact that the copyright owner maintains control over a specific copy only until it is first sold.

As with many areas of copyright law, there is some confusion as to the boundaries of the first-sale doctrine. Two cases involving the framing of artwork seem to have arrived at different results.

EXAMPLE 1: A company purchased a book of prints by the painter Patrick Nagel, then cut out the individual images in the book and mounted them in frames for resale. The Ninth Circuit Court of Appeals in California held that this practice was an infringement and was not permitted under the first-sale doctrine. (*Mirage Editions, Inc. v. Albuquerque A.R.T. Co.,* 856 F.2d 1341 (1988).) A similar result was reached in *Greenwich Workshop Inc. v. Timber Creations, Inc.,* 932 F. Supp. 1210 (C.D. Cal. 1996).)

EXAMPLE 2: A company purchased notecards and mounted them on tiles. A federal court in Illinois determined that this practice was not an infringement and was permitted under the first-sale doctrine. (*Lee v. Deck the Walls, Inc.,* 925 F. Supp. 576 (N.D. Ill. 1996).) The Seventh Circuit affirmed this decision and singled out the Ninth Circuit for criticism. (*Lee v. ART Co.,* 125 F.3d 580 (7th Cir. 1997).) (A similar result occurred in *C.M. Paula Co. v. Logan,* 355 F. Supp. 189 (D.C. Texas 1973).)

Under these rulings, a person in California cannot mount individual images from an art book, while a person in Illinois can mount individual notecards. Should it matter whether the object that is mounted is from an art book or from a note card? In the California case, the justices felt that mounting the Nagel images separately created a derivative work. In the Illinois case, the judge did not believe that mounting an image on a tile created a derivative work, because the image was not altered or modified.

Copyright Law: Definitions

Another first-sale decision added some confusion regarding the rights of software companies. A federal court ruled that the purchaser of a bundle of software programs could resell the individual components (separate programs on CDs). *(Softman Products Co. LLC v. Adobe Systems Inc.,* 171 F. Supp. 2d 1075 (C.D. Cal. 2001).)

There are exceptions to the first-sale doctrine. As a result of lobbying by the computer and music industries, the rental of computer programs and sound recordings is prohibited. The sound recording exception is limited to musical works; it does not extend to audiobooks. (*Brilliance Audio, Inc. v. Haights Cross Communications, Inc.,* 2007 474 F.3d 365 (6th Cir. 2007).) It is also not permissible under the first-sale doctrine to destroy a fine art or photographic work that meets the requirements of the Visual Artists Rights Act (for example, signed and numbered photographs created in limited editions of 200 or fewer copies).

The first-sale doctrine does not apply if the copyrighted work is made and sold outside the U.S. In a 2008 case, Costco bought Omega watches (with copyrighted designs) outside the U.S. and resold them in U.S. stores. When sued for infringement, the company used a first-sale defense. The Ninth Circuit Court of Appeals rejected that defense holding that the first-sale doctrine—the freedom to resell copyrighted goods—did not apply when the goods are made and first sold outside the U.S. (*Omega v. Costco,* 541 F.3d 982 (9th Cir. 2008).) A similar result was reached in another case when a New York district court ruled that an importer of less expensive foreign-published textbooks was prohibited from claiming the first-sale doctrine as a defense to copyright infringement for distributing those books in the U.S. (*John Wiley & Sons Inc. v. Kirtsaeng,* 2009 WL 3364037 (S.D. N.Y. 10/19/09).)

Copyright Act: § 109. Limitations on exclusive rights: Effect of transfer of particular copy or phonorecord

(a) Notwithstanding the provisions of section 106 (3), the owner of a particular copy or phonorecord lawfully made under this title, or any person authorized by such owner, is entitled, without the authority of the copyright owner, to sell or otherwise dispose of the possession of that copy or phonorecord ...

  (A) Notwithstanding the provisions of subsection (a), unless authorized by the owners of copyright in the sound recording or the owner of copyright in a computer program (including any tape, disk, or other medium embodying such program), and in the case of a sound recording in the musical works embodied therein, neither the owner of a particular phonorecord nor any person in possession of a particular copy of a computer program (including any tape, disk, or other medium embodying such program), may, for the purposes of direct or indirect commercial advantage, dispose of, or authorize the disposal of, the possession of that phonorecord or computer program (including any tape, disk, or other medium embodying such program) by rental, lease, or lending, or by any other act or practice in the nature of rental, lease, or lending. Nothing in the preceding sentence shall apply to the rental, lease, or lending of a phonorecord for nonprofit purposes by a nonprofit library or nonprofit educational institution. The transfer of possession of a lawfully made copy of a computer program by a nonprofit educational institution to another nonprofit educational institution or to faculty, staff, and students does not constitute rental, lease, or lending for direct or indirect commercial purposes under this subsection.

(B) This subsection does not apply to—

    (i) a computer program which is embodied in a machine or product and which cannot be copied during the ordinary operation or use of the machine or product; or

    (ii) a computer program embodied in or used in conjunction with a limited purpose computer that is designed for playing video games and may be designed for other purposes.

Related terms: end-user license (aka EULA, shrinkwrap, or clickwrap agreement); work of visual art.

fixed in a tangible medium of expression

In the United States and most other countries, an original work of authorship first qualifies for copyright protection when it is reduced to some physical form or representation—that is, when it is fixed in a tangible medium of expression. Under the Copyright Act of 1976, a work is considered fixed in a tangible medium of expression when "its embodiment in a copy or phonorecord, by or under the authority of the author, is sufficiently permanent or stable to permit it to be perceived, reproduced, or otherwise communicated for a period of more than transitory duration."

When a computer program is first reduced to paper or electronic patterns on a disk, it becomes fixed in a tangible medium of expression and is protected under the copyright laws. Similarly, when a song is recorded, a holograph photographed, a movie filmed, a video game recorded on tape, or an ornamental design molded, each is fixed in a tangible medium of expression and protected by copyright.

A work consisting of sounds, images, or both that is being transmitted live is considered "fixed" if some record of the work is being made simultaneously with its transmission. A live transmission of a baseball game is therefore subject to copyright protection at the instant of transmission, because the images being broadcast are also captured on videotape or sound recording.

Although copyright protection arises the instant a work becomes fixed, many countries, including the United States, allow the copyright owner to take additional steps to strengthen this protection, such as including a correct notice of copyright and registering the copyright with a government agency.

Copyright Act: § 101. Definitions

A work is "fixed" in a tangible medium of expression when its embodiment in a copy or phonorecord, by or under the authority of the author, is sufficiently permanent or stable to permit it to be perceived, reproduced, or otherwise communicated for a period of more than transitory duration. A work consisting of sounds, images, or both, that are being transmitted, is "fixed" for purposes of this title if a fixation of the work is being made simultaneously with its transmission.

Related terms: copyright; international copyright protection; registration.

flow charts, registration of

Flow charts that constitute original works of authorship qualify for copyright protection and may be registered with the U.S. Copyright Office. When registering flow charts, it is necessary to categorize them as a literary work (used for flow charts that communicate information primarily through text) or a visual arts work (used for charts that communicate information primarily through a graphic arrangement of symbols and boxes).

Related terms: registration.

Form CA

The U.S. Copyright Office requires Form CA for supplemental registrations, including the correction of errors.

Related terms: registration; supplemental registration; U.S. Copyright Office.

Form CO

Form CO (which debuted in 2008) is intended to speed up the registration process for applicants who use a paper application and mail it in. Form CO is an all-purpose fill-in PDF form that includes 2-D barcode scanning technology. The applicant completes it on a computer, prints out the form, and mails it in with a $50 fee and deposit materials.

Form PA

One of several forms that the U.S. Copyright Office now disfavors (and charges $65 for its use) and hopes to replace with Form CO (currently $50). Form PA is a paper form used to register all works involving the performing arts, including dramatic works, audiovisual works (such as movies, audio tapes, and training films), and CD-ROM-based multimedia products that feature a graphical user interface.

Related terms: musical works and sound recordings distinguished; registration; U.S. Copyright Office.

Form RE

The U.S. Copyright Office requires Form RE to renew copyrights on works first published prior to January 1, 1978.

Related terms: duration of copyrights; registration; U.S. Copyright Office.

Form SE (short, regular, and group)

The U.S. Copyright Office provides several versions of the SE form for the registration of works consisting of newspapers, serials, or periodicals such as magazines. Which form to use depends on a number of factors, including the number of items to be registered, the period of time for which the items are to be registered, and whether the constituent parts of the items are works made for hire.

Related terms: registration; U.S. Copyright Office.

Form SR

One of several forms that the U.S. Copyright Office now disfavors (and charges $65 for its use) and hopes to replace with Form CO (currently $50). Form SR is used to register published and unpublished sound recordings.

Related terms: musical works and sound recordings distinguished; registration; U.S. Copyright Office.

Form TX

One of several forms that the U.S. Copyright Office now disfavors (and charges $65 for its use) and hopes to replace with Form CO (currently $50). Form TX is a paper form used to register all works classified as literary and nondramatic. These include books, poems, computer programs and documentation, essays, and articles.

Related terms: registration; U.S. Copyright Office.

Copyright Law: Definitions

Form VA

One of several forms that the U.S. Copyright Office now disfavors (and charges $65 for its use) and hopes to replace with Form CO (currently $50). Form VA is a paper form used to register all sculptural or graphic works, such as paintings, photographs, and designs.

Related terms: pictorial, graphic, and sculptural works; registration; U.S. Copyright Office.

framing

Framing occurs when one website displays a Web page of another company usually within a bordered area on its own site (similar to the "picture-in-picture" feature offered on some televisions). For example, when a user enters a search engine request, the search engine might display the contents of an online store within the search engine's website, framed by the search engine's text and logos. When a website is framed within another website, the URL or domain name of the website within the frame is not displayed, and users are not able to bookmark the site.

Framing may trigger a dispute under copyright and trademark law theories because a framed site arguably alters the appearance of the content and creates the impression that its owner endorses or voluntarily chooses to associate with the framer. A court fight involving two dental websites failed to fully resolve the issues. Applied Anagramic Inc., a dental services website, framed the content of a competing site. The frames included information about Applied Anagramic as well as its trademark and links to all of its Web pages. A federal district court ruled that a website containing a link that reproduced Web pages within a frame may constitute an infringing derivative work. The court reasoned that the addition of the frame modified the appearance of the linked site and such modifications could, without authorization, amount to infringement. (*Futuredontics Inc. v. Applied Anagramic Inc.,* 46 U.S.P.Q. 2d 2005 (C.D. Cal. 1997).)

The Ninth Circuit Court of Appeals may have provided the final word on framing. According to the court, the relevant test as to whether framing amounts to infringement is the "server test"—that is, whether the alleged infringing site hosted and physically transmitted the framed content. The court rejected the "incorporation test"—that is, whether the framed content is incorporated in the alleged infringer's site. Google's framing was found not to infringe because it only provided a method for the user's computer to retrieve the framed content. (*Perfect 10, Inc. v. Amazon.com, Inc.,* 508 F.3d 1146 (9th Cir. 2007).)

Related terms: Digital Millennium Copyright Act; inlining; Internet, copyright regulation of; linking.

freedom of speech and copyright protection

The First Amendment to the U.S. Constitution prohibits the government from placing restrictions on a person's freedom of speech, except in certain situations. Copyright laws, however, prohibit speech that would infringe on somebody's copyright. For example, a court can issue an injunction to prevent the publication of material that would damage a copyright owner by infringing on a copyright. These two legal rules sometimes conflict and one of the means of resolving the issue is the fair use defense in copyright. For example, educators, news reporters, and scholars can invoke the statutory defense of fair use when they use small amounts of copyrighted material as part of teaching, criticizing, or commenting on the copyrighted material.

Related terms: fair use.

freelancer rights

See *New York Times v. Tasini*.

GATT (General Agreement on Tariffs and Trade)

Commonly known as GATT, the General Agreement on Tariffs and Trade is a comprehensive free-trade treaty signed by 117 nations, including almost every developed country. GATT created an international regulatory body known as the World Trade Organization (WTO) to enforce compliance with the agreement.

The portion of GATT that affects copyright law (and other forms of intellectual property) is contained in a special agreement known as Trade Related Aspects of Intellectual Property Rights (TRIPS for short). Probably the most important provision of the TRIPS agreement is that all members of GATT must now adhere to the Berne Convention (except for the Berne requirement that moral rights be respected), even if they haven't signed it. This means that 12 countries that were not members of the Berne Convention—including Haiti, Indonesia, Kuwait, Malaysia, and some of the countries of the former Soviet Union—now agree to offer basic copyright protection under that treaty because of their GATT membership.

Other important GATT provisions applicable to all members include:
- Live musical performances must be protected from unauthorized distribution (bootlegging) through the means of fixing the performance

in a tangible medium (tape, video, and so on) or communicating the performance to the public by wireless means.

- Computer programs are to be treated as literary works under the Berne Convention.
- Works by foreign authors that entered the public domain in the United States because of their failure to comply with U.S notice requirements in effect prior to March 1989 are to have restored copyright protection.
- Substantive penalties for copyright infringement are to be provided, including injunctive relief that prevents further infringement and adequate monetary damages for past infringement.
- Members must implement procedures that stop infringing materials from crossing the borders of other member countries.
- Software copyright owners may prevent the commercial rental of their protected works.

Related terms: Berne Convention; international copyright protection; restored copyright under GATT; Universal Copyright Convention (U.C.C.).

grant of rights

This phrase, commonly used in license agreements and other contracts pertaining to intellectual property, refers to the rights being transferred under the agreement. For example, an author makes a grant of rights when she licenses all print rights to her publisher in advance of publication.

Related terms: assignment of copyright; transfers of copyright ownership.

graphic and pictorial works

See pictorial, graphic, and sculptural works.

Grokster (Metro-Goldwyn-Mayer, Inc. v. Grokster Ltd.)

See peer-to-peer.

hot news doctrine

This refers to a legal theory that goes beyond copyright and prohibits the theft of "hot news." It's based on the 1918 case of *International News Service v. Associated Press* in which a rival news agency "stole" and "rewrote" AP news articles. Some states still uphold this approach; others consider it invalid. To qualify as the theft of hot news, the theft must be of "time-sensitive" news and must not involve material protected under copyright law. If the material is protected under copyright, the hot news doctrine is inapplicable and considered "pre-empted" under copyright law. That's what happened in a 2011 case, when Barclays's Bank complained that its research reports qualified as hot news. The Second Circuit disagreed and ruled that the claim was preempted by copyright law. *(Barclays Capital, Inc. v. TheFlyOnTheWall.com, Inc.,* ___ F.3d ___ (2d Cir. 2011).)

HTML

HTML (Hypertext Markup Language) is a collection of computer symbols and codes that are used to create documents that can be displayed on the Internet. HTML works in conjunction with a Web browser—a software program such as Google Chrome, Mozilla Firefox, or Internet Explorer that allows users to surf the Internet. Although typical HTML commands such as "bold" or "indent" are not protectable under copyright law, the visual or literary expression resulting from complex HTML code—for example, as manifested in the appearance of websites—is protected under copyright law.

ideas, not protected under copyright

Ideas as such are not protected through the copyright process. Only the actual expression of an idea is subject to copyright protection.

> **EXAMPLE:** Janice authors a new computer program that permits a homemaker to keep a running inventory of household goods. If Kim likes the idea and independently writes a competing program, no copyright infringement has occurred, because Kim copied Janice's idea, but not the expressive aspect of the program.

Other legal doctrines, such as patent law and trade secret law, are available to protect some ideas in certain contexts. For example, an idea that adds to a business's competitive position and is not generally known or used in the trade may be treated as a trade secret, and others may be prevented from disclosing or using it without permission. Similarly, an idea may qualify for protection as a utility patent if it is novel, nonobvious, and useful and has either been reduced to practice (that is, demonstrated to work) or been adequately described in a patent application. An idea for a design may also qualify for a patent if it is for a nonfunctional ornamental design of a manufactured product.

Copyright Act: § 102(b). Subject matter of copyright: In general

(b) In no case does copyright protection for an original work of authorship extend to any idea, procedure, process, system, method of operation, concept, principle, or discovery,

Copyright Law: Definitions

regardless of the form in which it is described, explained, illustrated, or embodied in such work.

Related terms: copyright and patent compared.

See also Part 4 (Trade Secret Law): idea submission; ideas as trade secrets.

identifying material

To register a copyright, it generally is necessary to deposit at least one, and often two, complete copies of the work with the U.S. Copyright Office. However, some kinds of works (for instance, holographs and virtual reality scenarios) are not easy to deposit. In other cases, the author may wish to maintain certain ideas as trade secrets and fears their disclosure if a true or complete copy of the work is to be deposited.

To accommodate the needs of registrants in these types of situations, the U.S. Copyright Office will accept a deposit of only a portion of the work or a representation of the entire work. The portion deposited is labeled as "identifying material" in order to satisfy the deposit requirement in the copyright law. Examples of identifying material include photographic prints, transparencies, photostats, drawings, or similar two-dimensional reproductions visible without the aid of a machine.

To deposit computer software, the U.S. Copyright Office will accept the first and last 25 pages of a program as identifying material, if the program runs beyond 50 pages. For databases, identifying material consists of a portion of each file in the database.

In addition to these rules, the U.S. Copyright Office is willing to provide special relief for individual deposits on a case-by-case basis. For instance, if a software developer wants to deposit source code but doesn't want to disclose certain trade secrets, the U.S. Copyright Office will allow the developer to black out certain portions of the code so that it cannot easily be understood and copied by potential infringers. Deposits accomplished under the special relief doctrine are also considered to be "identifying material."

Related terms: deposit with U.S. Copyright Office; object code; source code; special relief.

importing of infringing works

U.S. copyright and customs laws authorize the U.S. Customs and Border Protection to prevent material that infringes a U.S. copyright from entering the

United States. Under GATT, all member countries are supposed to enact a similar procedure.

In the United States, the procedure is supposed to work like this: The copyright owner records his or her work with the U.S. Customs and Border Protection Service. Any imported copies that are the same as or highly similar to the recorded works are temporarily seized. The copyright owner is informed of the seizure and provided time in which to obtain a court order barring the materials from being imported to the United States.

As a practical matter, this remedy is seldom used, due to the inability of the Customs and Border Protection Service to check imports carefully against recorded copyrights. However, Customs will act if alerted by the copyright owner.

The U.S. customs law also authorizes copyright owners to file a complaint with the International Trade Commission to have infringing works excluded from the United States on the ground their importation would constitute an unfair method of competition.

Related terms: international copyright protection; international rules on notice of copyright.

indecent or immoral works, not protected

Copyright protection is not available for works that a court or the U.S. Copyright Office deems to be indecent or immoral. The current position of U.S. Copyright Office is to accept registration for even fairly explicit material and to let the courts decide the issue if anyone objects.

independent creation

When an author independently creates a work, it is considered original, even though it may be highly similar to another work created by someone else. Accordingly, if a defendant in an infringement lawsuit can prove independent creation, the infringement action will fail, even if the plaintiffs have proved the necessary elements for infringement (substantial similarity and access).

Although some situations are relatively clear-cut, there is also a large gray area where it is difficult to tell whether subsequent works are independent creations or derivatives of earlier ones. In the latter case, permission to use the earlier work would be required.

EXAMPLE: Tim writes a book in English that is similar to one Antoine has written in French, but it is not, strictly speaking, a translation. Is this an independent creation? No, if the court finds that Tim's book was based on the

Copyright Law: Definitions

French one, and yes, if the court finds that Tim's book was created without relying on or borrowing from Antoine's book. Which of these results will occur depends on the degree of similarity between the works, whether Tim had access to Antoine's work, and the probability of Tim's independently creating a similar work.

Determining whether a work is an independent creation or a derivative work is especially difficult in the cases of:

- **Computer graphics.** Expression can easily be reduced to digital form, allowing incremental modifications (called "morphing" in the case of moving images) to be made easily, with the result that one expression can be transformed into another without a clear line of demarcation.
- **Musical sampling.** Sounds can be digitally captured and then modified and mixed to a point that the result has very little resemblance to any of the original material.

Related terms: based on an earlier work; copyright; copyright infringement; derivative work.

infringement action

A lawsuit brought against someone who uses a copyrighted expression without permission is commonly known as an infringement action. Under the Copyright Act, a copyright owner is entitled to file an infringement action in federal court against a person who, without proper authorization of the owner:

- makes copies of a copyrighted work
- prepares derivative works from a copyrighted work
- distributes copies of a copyrighted work
- displays a work protected by copyright, or
- performs any original work of authorship protected by the copyright.

To prevail in an infringement action, a plaintiff (copyright owner) must establish that copying occurred. Because direct evidence of copying is almost never available, the plaintiff usually must establish that the infringing work is substantially similar to the infringed work and that the alleged infringer had access to the infringed work in order to copy it.

If these elements are proven, the defendant (who allegedly infringed the copyright) has several defenses, including claims that:

- the work was the product of an independent conception, and is therefore an original work of authorship

- the use falls under the "fair use" exception
- the defendant had permission to use the work.

Infringement actions offer the successful plaintiff the possibility of a wide variety of judicial relief, depending on the circumstances and whether the work is registered with the U.S. Copyright Office. Most important, the court is authorized to grant immediate but temporary relief in the form of a temporary restraining order and, pending a full-scale trial, more extended relief in the form of an injunction. Either or both of these devices can halt publication or distribution of the offending work.

The preliminary injunction can be vital to a copyright owner's interests, because a regular injunction (or permanent injunction) can only be obtained as a part of a final judgment, which can take years. A preliminary injunction used to be relatively easy to obtain, once substantial evidence had been presented to the court showing a probability that an infringement is occurring. However, that standard appears to have changed. In a 2010 case, the Second Circuit held that the old test no longer applied in light of the Supreme Court's ruling in *eBay v. MercExchange, L.L.C.,* a patent case in which the Supreme Court ruled that showing a likelihood of infringement was not enough; the party seeking the preliminary injunction must apply a more traditional four-factor test. (*Salinger v. Colting,* 607 F.3d 68 (2d Cir. 2010).)

In addition to court orders prohibiting further infringing activity, plaintiffs may be awarded a money award known as damages. This can consist of actual losses suffered as a result of the infringement and the profits realized by the defendant because of the infringement. As an alternative to seeking damages and profits, copyright owners who have timely registered their copyright may pursue statutory damages, which can be awarded without any proof of harm or defendant's profits.

Copyright owners who timely register their copyright and/or record their ownership interest also qualify to have their attorney fees and court costs paid by an unsuccessful defendant. This alone can be a powerful incentive to register the copyright at the earliest possible time.

Copyright Act: § 503. Remedies for infringement: Impounding and disposition of infringing articles

(a) At any time while an action under this title is pending, the court may order the impounding, on such terms as it may deem reasonable, of all copies or phonorecords claimed to have been made or used in violation of the copyright owner's exclusive rights, and of all plates, molds, matrices, masters, tapes, film negatives, or other articles by means of which such copies or phonorecords may be reproduced.

(b) As part of a final judgment or decree, the court may order the destruction or other reasonable disposition of all copies or phonorecords found to have been made or used in violation of the copyright owner's exclusive rights, and of all plates, molds, matrices, masters, tapes, film negatives, or other articles by means of which such copies or phonorecords may be reproduced.

Copyright Act: § 505. Remedies for infringement: Costs and attorney's fees

In any civil action under this title, the court in its discretion may allow the recovery of full costs by or against any party other than the United States or an officer thereof. Except as otherwise provided by this title, the court may also award a reasonable attorney's fee to the prevailing party as part of the costs.

Related terms: access; copyright infringement; damages for copyright infringement; defenses to copyright infringement; injunctions; registration.

infringement of copyright

See copyright infringement.

injunctions

Once copyright infringement is established, courts often are willing to issue an order (termed an injunction) to prevent the infringer from making or distributing further unauthorized copies of the original work of authorship. To the extent that the infringing work heavily relies on the infringed work, an injunction can have a severely adverse economic impact on the infringer.

> EXAMPLE: When Apple Computer Inc. obtained an injunction preventing Franklin Computer from further copying the Apple Computer operating system, Franklin was effectively unable to market its computers, because they would not work without using the infringing material. (*Apple Computer, Inc. v. Franklin Computer Corporation*, 714 F.2d 1240 (3d Cir. 1983).)

Injunctions come in three forms:

- **Temporary injunctions or temporary restraining orders (TROs).** These are technically restricted to a situation when the plaintiff is on the brink of suffering irreparable injury and needs to stop some immediate action pending further consideration of the case. TROs generally last only for a week or two until the court can consider whether to grant a preliminary injunction.

- **Preliminary injunctions.** Courts will issue a preliminary injunction if the plaintiff makes a strong showing that the plaintiff is likely to prevail at the trial of the case and the plaintiff will suffer greater economic harm than the defendant if such interim relief is not granted. Preliminary injunctions can last as long as it takes to get to trial—sometimes years.
- **Permanent injunctions.** These are, as billed, permanent prohibitions against using or distributing the unauthorized work.

Prior to a Supreme Court ruling regarding patents (*eBay Inc. v. MercExchange, L.L.C.*, 547 U.S. 388 (2006)), courts generally presumed that a likelihood of copyright infringement caused irreparable injury and often issued TROs and preliminary injunctions if infringement appeared likely. A more modern approach is to require that the plaintiff prove both a likelihood of infringement, *and* irreparable harm.

If an injunction is issued, the court will usually require the plaintiff to post a bond to compensate the defendant for any harm caused by the injunction if later on the defendant ends up winning the case. Whether or not preliminary relief is granted, the court will determine after a trial whether injunctive relief is appropriate on a more permanent basis.

As a practical matter, losing a preliminary injunction often spells defeat for the defendant, regardless of the legal strength of the case. This is because few defendants can afford to keep the allegedly infringing work off the market pending trial and also meet the costs of a full-blown defense to the infringement charges. Because by definition a judge has already determined that infringement will mostly likely be found to exist when the case goes to trial, defendants normally find it economically prudent to settle early on the plaintiff's terms and get on with their business.

Copyright Act: § 502. Remedies for infringement: Injunctions

(a) Any court having jurisdiction of a civil action arising under this title may, subject to the provisions of section 1498 of title 28, grant temporary and final injunctions on such terms as it may deem reasonable to prevent or restrain infringement of a copyright.

(b) Any such injunction may be served anywhere in the United States on the person enjoined; it shall be operative throughout the United States and shall be enforceable, by proceedings in contempt or otherwise, by any United States court having jurisdiction of that person. The clerk of the court granting the injunction shall, when requested by any other court in which enforcement of the injunction is sought, transmit promptly to the other court a certified copy of all the papers in the case on file in such clerk's office.

Related terms: *Apple Computer, Inc. v. Franklin*; damages for copyright infringement; infringement action.

inlining and thumbnails

Inlining (sometimes referred to as "mirroring") is the process of incorporating a graphic file from one website onto another website. Thumbnails are small low-resolution versions of images commonly used by websites and search engines that provide links to full-size versions of the same images.

In a case involving inlining, an image search engine called ditto.com used inline links to reproduce full-sized photographic images from a photographer's website. By clicking on the link, the user was presented with a window containing a full-sized image imported from the photographer's website, surrounded by the search engine's advertising. The lower court held that this inlining constituted copyright infringement—it violated the photographer's exclusive right to display his images. A court of appeals reversed this ruling but did hold that that the search engine's practice of creating small reproductions ("thumbnails") of the images and placing them on its own website was permitted as a fair use. The thumbnails were much smaller and of much poorer quality than the original photos and served to index the images and thereby help the public access them. (*Kelly v. Arriba Soft Corp.*, 336 F.3d 811 (9th Cir. 2003).)

A similar result was reached by the Ninth Circuit Court of Appeals in a case involving Google. The court determined that Google's use of thumbnails was permitted as a fair use in a case involving reproductions of images from an adult men's magazine website. (*Perfect 10, Inc. v. Amazon.com, Inc.*, 508 F.3d 1146 (9th Cir. 2007).)

innocent infringement of copyright

Innocent infringement—when an author honestly believes, based on the circumstances, that a work is not protected under copyright—does not excuse infringement. It is, however, a mitigating factor when determining the remedies for infringement. For example, a court may halt the activity but may not be inclined to award damages. Innocent infringement should be distinguished from the fair use doctrine. Under fair use, infringement is excused because of the nature of the material and the context in which it was used, not because of the author's belief as to whether the work was copyrighted.

Related terms: fair use; international rules on notice of copyright; omission of copyright notice.

instructional text

A literary, pictorial, or graphic work that is prepared for use in day-to-day instructional activities is an instructional text. For example, a textbook would be an instructional text, but a novel used in a literature class would not be an instructional text. Instructional text is one of the enumerated categories listed for determining whether a work can qualify as a commissioned work made for hire. This distinction is important because if a work was commissioned and it did not fall within one of the enumerated categories, it would not be a work made for hire even if there was a signed agreement stating that the work was made for hire. If a work qualifies as a work made for hire, the copyright is owned by the hiring party, not the author.

Related terms: work made for hire.

Insurance, copyright

See advertising injury.

international copyright protection

Over 120 nations have signed treaties in which they agree to extend reciprocal copyright protection to works authored by nationals of the other signing countries as well as works first published in one of the other signing countries. This reciprocal approach is commonly called "national treatment."

The two main copyright treaties are the Berne Convention and the Universal Copyright Convention (U.C.C.), both of which the United States has signed. To the extent the provisions of these two treaties overlap, the author is entitled to the more liberal protection available—usually found in the Berne Convention.

Most countries of the world have ratified GATT (General Agreement on Tariffs and Trade), which binds them to comply with the provisions of the Berne Convention (except for its moral rights provision) whether or not they are already members. The GATT treaty makes the Berne Convention by far the more important international treaty; the U.C.C. will play an increasingly minor role in international copyright protection.

Besides establishing reciprocal protection rights, the Berne Convention also establishes the minimum protections that must be afforded and specifies that no formalities—such as copyright notice—are required for gaining such protection. The Berne Convention does not impose on any country a definition of what can and cannot be copyrighted, but virtually all of the signatory countries (and GATT members) will fully protect such traditional items as books, art works, movies, and plays. In addition, GATT requires that all members treat computer programs as literary works under the Berne Convention.

Authors seeking to invoke international protection under the Berne Convention (authors in the U.S. and in most large industrialized nations, including all nations that ratify the GATT treaty) need not apply any copyright notice to their works.

Authors seeking to invoke international copyright protection under the Universal Copyright Convention (the relatively few countries that have not signed the Berne Convention or the GATT treaty) must use the following notice: "© (year of publication) (author or other basic copyright owner)."

For example, the correct U.C.C. notice for this book would be: "© 2011 Richard Stim." Or, if Nolo owned the copyright, the correct notice would be: "© 2011 Nolo."

Related terms: Berne Convention; GATT (General Agreement on Tariffs and Trade); international rules on notice of copyright; Universal Copyright Convention (U.C.C.).

Internet, copyright regulation of

Congress attempted to establish some regulation and predictability for copyrights on the Internet by enacting the Digital Millennium Copyright Act (DMCA). Among other things, the DMCA prohibits circumvention of digital antipiracy devices and the removal of secret codes known as digital watermarks from digital files. The DMCA also limits liability for companies that provide access to the Internet (Internet Service Providers—ISPs) in the event that an infringing copy is offered online. In addition, the DMCA establishes licensing standards by which companies can webcast music (broadcast over the Internet).

Despite the DMCA, technology continues to outpace copyright legislation, and new, unresolved issues continue to emerge in cyberspace. In another attempt to legislate Internet uses, Congress passed the Family Entertainment and Copyright Act of 2005, which made it a criminal violation of copyright law to knowingly place a copyrighted computer program, musical work, motion picture or other audiovisual work or sound recording on a computer network accessible to the public for purposes of copying.

Related terms: Copyleft; Digital Millennium Copyright Act; digital rights management (DRM); framing; *Grokster* (*Metro-Goldwyn-Mayer, Inc. v. Grokster Ltd.*); linking; MP3.

Internet service provider (ISP)

An Internet Service Provider (ISP)—also sometimes referred to as an Online Service Provider (OSP)—is any business that provides access to the Internet. That includes big access providers like AOL, Yahoo!, and Google, or it can refer to companies that provide website hosting, commercial Wi-Fi services, or FTP services. ISPs can sometimes be held accountable for copyright violations for material posted by subscribers and users but are usually protected by the "safe harbor" provisions of the Digital Millennium Copyright Act.

Related terms: Digital Millennium Copyright Act; Internet, copyright regulation of.

inverse ratio rule

In some federal circuits, noticeably the Ninth Circuit, the higher the degree of access to a work, the less the degree of similarity required to prove infringement, a principle known as the "inverse ratio" rule.

joint copyright ownership

See joint work.

joint work

Under the Copyright Act of 1976, a joint work is defined as "a work prepared by two or more authors who intend to merge their contributions into inseparable or interdependent parts of the whole." (17 USC § 101.) The U.S. Copyright Office will accept for registration works that meet this statutory definition and will treat the authors as having equal rights to register and enforce the copyright, regardless of what the joint authors arrange among themselves.

> EXAMPLE: Tom and Mary have a partnership agreement, under which Tom owns three-fourths of the copyright and Mary one-fourth. If the copyright is registered with the U.S. Copyright Office with Tom and Mary listed as coauthors, they will be simply listed as coauthors without reference to their independent, unequal ownership arrangement. However, the partnership agreement will govern issues that may arise between Tom and Mary, such as who gets what share of the any royalties earned on the work, who is entitled to license the work to others, and who can sue to enforce the copyright.

Related terms: coauthors.

Copyright Law: Definitions

laws, judicial opinions, and model codes, copyrightable subject matter

There has long been a judicial consensus that neither the opinions of judges, nor the statutes enacted by Congress or state legislatures, can be protected by copyright. This principle is derived from a Supreme Court opinion, *Wheaton v. Peters,* 33 U.S. 591 (1834). Although anyone is free to quote or reproduce these statutes and legal opinions, various publishers and reporting systems have claimed proprietary rights to the way these statutes and opinions are annotated or organized. For example, West Publishing unsuccessfully argued that its page numbering system could not be copied onto CD-ROMs by a rival publisher. (*Matthew Bender & Co. v. West Publishing Co.,* 158 F.3d 674 (2d Cir. 1998).) These decisions and their underlying rationale—that the laws and opinions created by public officials belong in the public domain—do not necessarily apply to model codes. Model codes are regulations created by a private business that may later be adopted by a public entity.

> **EXAMPLE:** The Southern Building Code Congress International (SBCCI) is a nonprofit organization that develops modern building, fire, and mechanical codes. These codes are adopted by municipalities, and the SBCCI earns revenues by publishing and selling the codes or licensing the codes for publication. In 1997, Peter Veeck, the operator of a website, posted the building codes for two small towns in North Texas. The SBCCI sued for copyright infringement. In 2002, the Fifth Circuit Court of Appeals ruled that a company that creates a model code may not claim copyright in it once the code has been adopted into law. (*Veeck v. Southern Building Code Congress International, Inc.,* 293 F.3d 791 (5th Cir. 2002).)

Related terms: factual works; merger doctrine; public domain—copyright context.

Library of Congress

With few exceptions, under the Copyright Act of 1976, an author is required to deposit at least one copy of his or her published work with the Library of Congress. This requirement is automatically met if the work is registered with the U.S. Copyright Office, which requires a deposit of either one or two copies of the best edition of the work, depending on the type of work. However, even if an author decides not to register a work with the U.S. Copyright Office, the author generally has an obligation to make the Library of Congress deposit, except for computer programs and certain other types of works. Failure to make the deposit carries no penalty unless the Library of Congress makes a demand. In that case, failure to deposit within three months may result in a relatively nominal fine.

Copies of works deposited for copyright registration or in fulfillment of the mandatory deposit requirement are available to the Library of Congress for its collections. The Library reserves the right to select or reject any published work for its permanent collections based on the research needs of Congress, the nation's scholars, and of the nation's libraries. For more information on the Library's selection policies, contact: Library of Congress, Collections Policy Office, 101 Independence Avenue, S.E., Washington, D.C. 20540.

Related terms: best edition of a work; deposit with U.S. Copyright Office.

license fee, payable by innocent infringer

See innocent infringement of copyright.

license recordation

See recordation of copyright transfers.

licensing of copyrights

A copyright license is a method by which the owner of a copyright gives permission for another to use or copy an original work of authorship. Because the essence of a copyright is the exclusive right to make copies, in order to commercially exploit the product, a copyright owner often needs to pass this and associated rights to a publisher or distributor.

A license may be either exclusive or nonexclusive and can be restricted by territory, time, media, purpose, or by virtually any other factor desired by the parties. Exclusive licenses must almost always be in writing to be valid. In all cases, licenses should be recorded with the U.S. Copyright Office.

Related terms: exclusive license; transfers of copyright ownership.

linking

Any component of a Web page that connects the user to another Web page or another portion of the same Web page is a link (also known as "hyperlink"). Clicking on underlined text or a graphic image activates most links. Although it is not a copyright violation to create a link, it is a violation of the law to create a link that contributes to unauthorized copying of a copyrighted work if the linking party knew or had reason to know of the unauthorized copying and encouraged it.

Copyright Law: Definitions

EXAMPLE: A website posted infringing copies of a church's copyrighted handbook at its site. The website was ordered to remove the handbook but subsequently provided links to other sites that contained infringing copies of the handbook. These links were different from traditional links, because the website knew and encouraged the use of the links to obtain unauthorized copies. The linking activity constituted contributory copyright infringement. (*Intellectual Reserve, Inc. v. Utah Lighthouse Ministry, Inc.*, 75 F. Supp. 2d 1290 (D. Utah 1999).)

A link that bypasses a website's home page and instead goes to another page within the site is often called a "deep link." Many copyright experts believe that deep linking is not copyright infringement—after all, the author of a novel can't prevent readers from reading the end first if they so desire, so why should a website owner have the right to determine in what order a user can access a website? Some well-known websites such as Amazon.com welcome deep links. However, some websites—even the listener-friendly National Public Radio—have asserted rights against deep linkers under both copyright and trademark law principles. In 2002, a Danish court prevented a website from deep linking to a newspaper site. In 2003, Germany weighed in on the issue when its federal court ruled that deep linking was not a violation of German copyright law. (*Handelsblatt v. Paperboy,* Federal Superior Court of Germany (Bundesgerichtshof) 17 July 2003.)

literary works

"Literary works" is one of the broad categories of material protected under the copyright laws. The phrase has little legal significance and is used primarily to classify materials that must be registered with the U.S. Copyright Office in a copyright application.

According to the U.S. Copyright Act of 1976, literary works are "works, other than audiovisual works, expressed in words, numbers, or other verbal or numerical symbols or indicia, regardless of the nature of the material objects, such as books, periodicals, manuscripts, phonorecords, film, tapes, disks, or cards in which they are embodied." (17 USC § 101.)

Examples of literary works include computer programs, books, poems, plays, newspapers, magazines, software documentation, training films consisting primarily of dialogue, and flow charts consisting primarily of text.

Related terms: registration.

manufacturing clause

The manufacturing clause is a now-defunct U.S. statute that barred the importation of more than 2,000 copies of any nondramatic literary material written in English by an American author, unless it had been manufactured in the United States or Canada. The manufacturing clause has not been in effect since the 1980s.

mask work

See Semiconductor Chip Protection Act of 1984.

mechanical rights

The right to reproduce a song on physical media such as compact disc, vinyl recordings, cassette tape, or DVD (collectively known as phonorecords) is referred to as a mechanical right. In contrast, broadcasting a song over the radio, TV, or Internet or incorporating a song in a movie, video, or video game is not a mechanical right; it is known as a performance right.

Every time a song is "pressed" (or fixed) on a phonorecord, the songwriter is entitled to a payment for this mechanical right, known as a mechanical royalty. Mechanical royalty rates are set by law (known as the statutory rate), but artists and songwriters are free to negotiate a lower rate. The advantage of paying the statutory rate is that an artist does not have to seek permission to record the song provided that certain requirements are met (see "compulsory license").

Sometimes a songwriter accepts less than the statutory rate. Why? Often the songwriter has no choice because it is a condition of a recording agreement or because it is the only way to attract a specific artist to record the song.

Mechanical royalty rates are constantly changing. For example, it was common in the 1970s for a songwriter to receive 0.02 cents for every song pressed on a recording. The current fee for recordings is 9.1 cents per song (or 1.75 cents per minute of playing time). To verify the current rate, check the Copyright Office website (www.copyright.gov/carp) and click "Mechanical Royalty Rate." If a song is three minutes long and an artist makes 10,000 compact discs containing the song, the fee paid to the song's owner would be $910. A recording artist does not have to use the compulsory license, and many recording artists seek permission directly from the song owner and negotiate for a lower rate.

Related terms: compulsory license; music publisher.

merger doctrine

This court-made rule severely limits copyright protection—or denies it altogether—to a work that involves very little creativity if its ways of expressing

Copyright Law: Definitions

the ideas in the work are very limited. For example, there are limited ways to express the instructions for activating a fire alarm, or how to perform a yoga pose. When it is very difficult to separate the expression in a work from the underlying ideas, the two are said to merge. Under the merger doctrine, a work will only be protected against verbatim copying, assuming there is any protectable expression at all in the work.

The merger doctrine has been the basis for a series of court decisions that deny protection to computer user interfaces, for example *Computer Associates Int'l v. Altai,* 982 F.2d 693 (2d Cir. 1992). The merger doctrine also applies to factual works such as histories, biographies, and scientific treatises.

Related terms: *Computer Associates Int'l v. Altai; Feist Publications Inc. v. Rural Telephone Service Co.*

microcode and copyright

Microcode is software embedded in a computer chip for the purpose of performing the computer's basic purpose: to process information. One court has ruled that microcode is subject to copyright protection. (*NEC Corp. v. Intel Corp.,* 10 U.S.P.Q.2d 1177 (N.D. Cal. 1989).) However, this protection is likely to be limited to "virtually identical copying," as it was in the *Intel* case, because microcode is very much determined by external constraints such as heat and space, and the underlying unprotectable idea would therefore be merged with any protectable expression in the code.

Related terms: computer software; merger doctrine.

mistakes in registration, correction of

See supplemental registration.

money damages in infringement action

See damages for copyright infringement.

moral rights

Every copyright owner who lives or publishes in a country that has signed the Berne Convention is supposed to have moral rights that are personal to the author and that cannot, therefore, be taken away or abridged. Sometimes referred to by the French term "*droit moral,*" these rights include the author's right to:

- proclaim authorship of a work
- disclaim authorship of a work, and

- object to any distortion, mutilation, or other modification of the work that would be injurious to the author's reputation as an author.

Even though the United States is a signatory nation to the Berne Convention, it doesn't specifically recognize moral rights, taking the position that a number of different U.S. statutes provide equivalent and adequate protection. For instance, Section 106 of the Copyright Act, as amended, provides that the artist of a work of visual art (as defined by the statute) can control whether his or her name is on the art and object if the integrity of the work is threatened. And under a federal statutory scheme that primarily governs trademarks (known as the Lanham Act), an author may sue anyone who misrepresents authorship.

Most art law experts believe this piecemeal approach to moral rights leaves the moral rights provision in the Berne Convention largely unimplemented in the United States. Although the moral rights provision of the Berne Convention applies to all works of expression, it is seldom an issue in any area other than the visual arts.

Related terms: Berne Convention; international copyright protection; work of visual art.
See also Part 3 (Trademark Law): Lanham Act.

motion pictures, copyrights

According to Section 101 of the Copyright Act of 1976, as amended, "Motion pictures are audiovisual works consisting of a series of related images which, when shown in succession, impart an impression of motion, together with accompanying sounds, if any." Motion pictures are entitled to copyright protection under the audiovisual work category and may be registered with the U.S. Copyright.

Related terms: best edition of a work; registration of copyright.

MP3

The most common system for music downloads from the Internet is known as MPEG 1 Layer 3, or "MP3" for short. MP3 technology compresses sound files so that approximately 60 minutes of music can be stored on 32 megabytes of computer memory.

Internet sites that facilitate the copying, transfer, or sale of unauthorized MP3s have been the subject of lawsuits from the recording industry. In 2000, both MP3.com and Napster.com—a file sharing system—were the subjects of record company litigation. In both cases, judges rejected fair use arguments and found that the websites facilitated the distribution of unauthorized recordings. In other words, even though a company does not store or offer unauthorized recordings at its website, the company is still violating copyright law if it has established a system that allows others to infringe copyrights.

By 2003, several legitimate—that is, authorized—distributors of MP3s (and similar formats) began offering pay-to-use or subscription-based services. Most notable was the Apple iTunes website that became the leading site for acquiring legitimate copies of songs. Despite Apple's success—and despite lawsuits brought by the RIAA against individual users of file sharing networks—file sharing sites offering unauthorized copies have continued to maintain their popularity with a large segment of Internet music fans and it is estimated that 95% of the music that is downloaded is unauthorized. In 2005, the Supreme Court determined that individuals or companies who own or permit the use of networks that promote copyright infringement are liable for the resulting acts of infringement by third parties using the network. (*Metro-Goldwyn-Mayer, Inc. v. Grokster Ltd.*, 545 U.S. 913 (2005).)

In 2005, Congress made it a criminal violation of copyright law to knowingly place an MP3 or other computer program, musical work, motion picture or other audiovisual work, or sound recording on a computer network accessible to the public for purposes of copying.

Related terms: Audio Home Recording Act; *Grokster (Metro-Goldwyn-Mayer, Inc. v. Grokster Ltd.)*; Internet, copyright regulation of.

music publisher

Music publishers own song copyrights and collect revenue, handle business formalities, sue infringers, and look for new ways to exploit songs. Music publishers acquire ownership of song copyrights when the songwriter transfers copyright ownership in exchange for payments or an ongoing royalty. Most music publishers offer an upfront sum or "advance" to the songwriter and share the revenue with the songwriter as the song earns money. That is, the songwriter continues to earn a percentage of the revenue through the life of the copyright. For example, even though Paul McCartney does not own the copyright in the Beatles songs, he still receives revenue from the music publisher that now owns the copyright.

musical works and sound recordings distinguished

There are two types of copyrights for music: musical works copyrights, that protect songs and compositions, and sound recording copyrights, which protect the manner in which music is arranged and recorded—that is, the sounds fixed on the recording. These forms of copyright protection create two overlapping sources of income. Songwriters earn income from the exploitation of songs. Recording artists and record companies earn money from the sale of recordings. The same person or business can own both types of copyrights, but the musical works copyright is usually owned by the songwriter or a music publisher, and the sound recording copyright is usually owned by a record company.

Form CO can be used to register published or unpublished musical works and sound recordings.

national treatment

This approach to international copyright protection, taken by the Berne Convention and other major copyright treaties, requires a signatory country to extend to nationals of other signatory countries the same copyright protection as is extended to its own citizens.

Related terms: Berne Convention; international copyright protection.

new version

See derivative work; single registration rule.

New York Times v. Tasini

This 2001 Supreme Court case (*New York Times v. Tasini,* 533 U.S. 483), stands for the principle that permission is required from freelance writers if their material is published as part of an unrevised collective work in new media, not specifically covered in the original freelance agreement.

A group of freelance authors who wrote articles for the *New York Times, Time,* and several other publications sued these publications when their articles were reproduced without their consent on the LexisNexis database and when microfilm reproductions of the publications were also reproduced on two CD-ROM products.

The freelance authors argued that their contracts did not grant permission for these uses of the material. The publishers argued that the freelancers' permission was not required, because the act of placing the articles on electronic databases constituted modified versions of the collective works. In 2001, the Supreme Court rejected the publishers' argument, reasoning that electronic databases such as LexisNexis are not revisions of collective works (such as *The New York Times),* because the databases store and retrieve articles individually—articles that are part of a vast database of diverse texts. They do not store intact copies of newspapers or other collective works as originally published. In contrast, the court suggested that microfilm copies of newspapers and other collective works are revisions of the collective works, because copies of entire intact editions are stored together on the microfilm rolls.

Under *Tasini,* permission from the writers would not be required if the re-publication in the new media qualified as reproduction or modification of the collective work (magazine, newspaper, or other publication). For example, permission would not be needed if a newspaper was published both in print form and online, because the online edition would surely qualify as a revision of the original print edition.

But what about republishing articles and other materials on CD-ROMs? In *Tasini,* the Supreme Court had affirmed the right of freelance writers to prevent publishers from reprinting their works in computer databases. But in that case, the Supreme Court also stated that image-based reproductions of periodicals, such as microfilm and microfiche, are permissible under the Copyright Act because the articles appear in the exact position in which they appeared in print.

Applying that logic in a case against *National Geographic Magazine,* the Eleventh Circuit Court of Appeals ruled that *National Geographic* could reproduce archived works on CD-ROMs and DVDs (although not in computer databases, absent permissions) without seeking additional permissions from freelance photographers. (*Greenberg v. National Geographic Society,* 244 F.3d 1267 (11th Cir. 2007).) Therefore, the rule appears to be that where a magazine or newspaper is simply scanned onto media with no conversion or reconstruction, no additional permissions are required by the publishers from freelancers. But if the material is reconstructed—for example, as when preparing text articles for a database, or pulling photos out of articles for a slideshow—then the publisher must seek additional permission.

news reporting, fair use
See fair use.

nonexclusive license
A copyright owner grants a nonexclusive license when the owner (licensor) authorizes another person or institution (the licensee) to exercise one or more of the rights belonging to the owner under the copyright on a shared (nonexclusive) basis. Legally, no transfer of copyright ownership takes place under a non-exclusive license, because the licensee shares the right with the original owner and,

perhaps, with additional nonexclusive licensees. Although a nonexclusive license need not be in writing to be valid, most are.

> **EXAMPLE:** Steve builds an electronic legal dictionary featuring intellectual property terminology for the purpose of selling it to law firms. Rather than sell the dictionary outright, Steve distributes it under nonexclusive licenses that permit licensee law firms to make copies for use in personal computers belonging to the law office staff (a site license). The nonexclusive license prohibits a licensee from transferring the dictionary to another firm and requires payment of a set amount each year for renewal of the license. Under this arrangement, thousands of law firms might be nonexclusive licensees, but none of them would be considered as a copyright owner, because none has the exclusive right to use and therefore enforce the copyright.

Related terms: exclusive license; licensing of copyrights.

notice of copyright

Often referred to as a "legend" or "bug," a notice of copyright is the little "©" plus the date of publication and author's name.

For works published in the United States after March 1, 1989, no such copyright notice is required for copyright protection within the United States. Nor is a notice required in any of the other countries that have signed either the Berne Convention or GATT. However, the notice is still useful to:

- remind others that the work is protected by copyright
- preclude the use of the "innocent infringer" defense in a copyright infringement case, and
- point a would-be user of the work in the right direction if he or she wants permission to use it.

For works published in the United States prior to March 1, 1989, a copyright notice is required to preserve the copyright in the work.

To provide adequate notice where such notice is desired, the copyright notice must be placed where it will easily be seen by a person viewing the work—that is, it must provide "reasonable notice of the claim of copyright." Under guidelines published by the U.S. Copyright Office:

- For literary works, notice may appear on either the front or the back of the title page.

- For computer software, notice may appear on the disk or cassette or in the program itself, or it may be placed to appear when the program appears on the computer screen.
- For audiovisual works, notice may appear on the screen with the credits.
- For phonorecords, audiotapes, and CDs, notice may appear on the record cover or CD and tape enclosures.

There is no limit to the number of different places a copyright notice can appear.

Copyright Act: § 401. Notice of copyright: Visually perceptible copies

This statute explains the proper form for a copyright notice, as well as when, where, and why a copyright notice should be placed on a work of expression.

(a) General Provisions.—Whenever a work protected under this title is published in the United States or elsewhere by authority of the copyright owner, a notice of copyright as provided by this section may be placed on publicly distributed copies from which the work can be visually perceived, either directly or with the aid of a machine or device.

(b) Form of Notice.—If a notice appears on the copies, it shall consist of the following three elements:

  (1) the symbol © (the letter C in a circle), or the word "Copyright," or the abbreviation "Copr."; and

  (2) the year of first publication of the work; in the case of compilations, or derivative works incorporating previously published material, the year date of first publication of the compilation or derivative work is sufficient. The year date may be omitted where a pictorial, graphic, or sculptural work, with accompanying text matter, if any, is reproduced in or on greeting cards, postcards, stationery, jewelry, dolls, toys, or any useful articles; and

  (3) the name of the owner of copyright in the work, or an abbreviation by which the name can be recognized, or a generally known alternative designation of the owner.

(c) Position of Notice.—The notice shall be affixed to the copies in such manner and location as to give reasonable notice of the claim of copyright. The Register of Copyrights shall prescribe by regulation, as examples, specific methods of affixation and positions of the notice on various types of works that will satisfy this requirement, but these specifications shall not be considered exhaustive.

(d) Evidentiary Weight of Notice.—If a notice of copyright in the form and position specified by this section appears on the published copy or copies to which a defendant in a copyright infringement suit had access, then no weight shall be given to such a defendant's interposition of a defense based on innocent infringement in mitigation of actual or statutory damages, except as provided in the last sentence of section 504 (c)(2).

Copyright Act: § 402. Notice of copyright: Phonorecords of sound recordings

This statute governs how, when, where, and why to place a copyright notice on a phono-record (the media on which sounds are fixed for the purpose of distribution essentially, and reproduction).

(a) **General Provisions.**—Whenever a sound recording protected under this title is published in the United States or elsewhere by authority of the copyright owner, a notice of copyright as provided by this section may be placed on publicly distributed phonorecords of the sound recording.

(b) **Form of Notice.**—If a notice appears on the phonorecords, it shall consist of the following three elements:

(1) the symbol P (the letter P in a circle); and

(2) the year of first publication of the sound recording; and

(3) the name of the owner of copyright in the sound recording, or an abbreviation by which the name can be recognized, or a generally known alternative designation of the owner; if the producer of the sound recording is named on the phonorecord labels or containers, and if no other name appears in conjunction with the notice, the producer's name shall be considered a part of the notice.

(c) **Position of Notice.**—The notice shall be placed on the surface of the phonorecord, or on the phonorecord label or container, in such manner and location as to give reasonable notice of the claim of copyright.

(d) **Evidentiary Weight of Notice.**—If a notice of copyright in the form and position specified by this section appears on the published phonorecord or phonorecords to which a defendant in a copyright infringement suit had access, then no weight shall be given to such a defendant's interposition of a defense based on innocent infringement in mitigation of actual or statutory damages, except as provided in the last sentence of section 504 (c)(2).

Related terms: defective copyright notice; innocent infringement of copyright; international rules on notice of copyright; omission of copyright notice.

object code

Most computers work through the use of compilers, which translate programs written in a programming language (called source code) into a language that the computer can recognize (called object code). The source code typically consists of words and a formal grammatical syntax. The object code consists of ones and zeros which, in all respects, are equivalent to the source code's meaning and syntax but feed the program to the computer in a binary form (one = on and zero = off), which the computer can then process and act on. This is very much like translating a written message into short and long Morse Code signals for telegraphic transmission.

Although object code is unintelligible to most human readers, the courts have held that it qualifies for copyright protection as a form of expression and, as such, can be registered with the U.S. Copyright Office. The reason to register object code rather than source code is that because source code can be readily understood by skilled readers, registering it may give away trade secrets that have been maintained in the software.

When someone registers object code rather than source code, the U.S. Copyright Office places the registration under what's termed "the rule of doubt." This means that because the U.S. Copyright Office can't read or understand what was deposited, it expresses no opinion on whether the object code qualifies for copyright protection. In short, the U.S. Copyright Office does not consider the object code deposit the best edition of the underlying work and expressly favors the source code as a computer program deposit instead.

The U.S. Copyright Office offers a number of alternatives to the deposit of pure object code, which are designed to preserve trade secrets in a program while providing the U.S. Copyright Office with something intelligible to its employees. For example, acceptable deposits include parts of the source code with strategic sections blacked out, or a mix of source code and object code.

Related terms: computer software; deposit with U.S. Copyright Office; source code, copyrights.
See also Part 4 (Trade Secret Law): trade secret.

omission of copyright notice

Although the use of a copyright notice on copies is no longer required in the United States as of March 1, 1989, for many years previous to that, omission of the notice voided copyright protections. A work of authorship published prior to January 1, 1978, without the proper notice of copyright qualified for no copyright protection. A work published between January 1, 1978, and March 1, 1989, without the proper notice of copyright lost its copyright protection unless the work was republished after March 1, 1989. But even then, the old copies remained unprotected unless the work was registered with the U.S. Copyright Office within five years of its original publication, and an earnest attempt was made to have correct notices placed on all copies that were already distributed.

While works publicly distributed in the United States after March 1, 1989, do not need a notice to protect the copyright, it is still a good idea to include one. If a copyright infringement lawsuit becomes necessary and the work has the correct notice on it, the infringer will not be able to claim an innocent infringement—a legal status that makes it far harder for the copyright owner to recover damages.

Under GATT, works that entered into the public domain in the United States because they lacked a proper copyright notice may have their copyright restored if they were otherwise protected by the Berne Convention when created.

Copyright Act: § 405. Notice of copyright: Omission of notice on certain copies and phonorecords

(a) Effect of Omission on Copyright.—With respect to copies and phonorecords publicly distributed by authority of the copyright owner before the effective date of the Berne Convention Implementation Act of 1988, the omission of the copyright notice described in sections 401 through 403 from copies or phonorecords publicly distributed by authority of the copyright owner does not invalidate the copyright in a work if—

(1) the notice has been omitted from no more than a relatively small number of copies or phonorecords distributed to the public; or

(2) registration for the work has been made before or is made within five years after the publication without notice, and a reasonable effort is made to add notice to all copies or phonorecords that are distributed to the public in the United States after the omission has been discovered; or

(3) the notice has been omitted in violation of an express requirement in writing that, as a condition of the copyright owner's authorization of the public distribution of copies or phonorecords, they bear the prescribed notice.

(b) Effect of Omission on Innocent Infringers.—Any person who innocently infringes a copyright, in reliance upon an authorized copy or phonorecord from which the copyright notice has been omitted and which was publicly distributed by authority of the copyright owner before the effective date of the Berne Convention Implementation Act of 1988, incurs no liability for actual or statutory damages under section 504 for any infringing acts committed before receiving actual notice that registration for the work has been made under section 408, if such person proves that he or she was misled by the omission of notice. In a suit for infringement in such a case the court may allow or disallow recovery of any of the infringer's profits attributable to the infringement, and may enjoin the continuation of the infringing undertaking or may require, as a condition for permitting the continuation of the infringing undertaking, that the infringer pay the copyright owner a reasonable license fee in an amount and on terms fixed by the court.

(c) Removal of Notice.—Protection under this title is not affected by the removal, destruction, or obliteration of the notice, without the authorization of the copyright owner, from any publicly distributed copies or phonorecords.

Related terms: defective copyright notice; innocent infringement of copyright; notice of copyright.

Copyright Law: Definitions

open source

Open source loosely describes software that is created free of proprietary rights and royalty restrictions. Proponents of open source seek to collaborate and build upon code freely and to provide the software to the public without restrictions. There is an organized movement, the Open Source Initiative (OSI) (www.opensource.org), that established open source standards. Despite the restriction-free premise of open source software, its proponents often take the position that the software is subject to one of two general open source licenses: a general public license (GPL) and a lesser-used general public license (LGPL).

One of the most popular open source software codes is Linux, an operating system initially developed by Linus Torvalds that runs on various hardware platforms including PCs and Macs. Because it is distributed for free, Linux has become a popular choice for some operating systems. Several companies have also been successful selling versions of Linux licensed under GPLs. However, the freedom associated with Linux (and the open source movement) has been threatened by a rash of lawsuits by companies that own or claim to own copyrights on portions or versions of Linux. One company, SCO, has taken the position that it is the owner of the underlying UNIX code and that anyone using Linux who lacks a license from SCO is violating SCO's rights. The smoke has not cleared yet on these lawsuits, and once these cases (and their appeals) have ended, the fate of the open source movement should be clearer.

original work of authorship

Under the Copyright Act, an "original work of authorship" encompasses, with a few exceptions, any type of expression independently conceived of by its creator. Authorship embodies a certain minimum level of creativity and originality. But as long as a particular expression has been independently arrived at, it need not be original in the sense of "new." For example, if Thomas never heard of or read *One Flew Over the Cuckoo's Nest,* by Ken Kesey, but somehow managed to write a play very similar to it, Thomas's play would qualify as "original" and would thus be subject to copyright protection. Of course, when one work is very much like another, the odds favor the likelihood that copying occurred.

Among the many creations that qualify as works of authorship are sheet music, movies, recordings, video productions, video games, cartoons, artistic designs, magazines, and books. Computer software also counts as a work of authorship, in both source code and object code form.

A few categories of expression do not qualify as "original works of authorship" either because they are too short to deserve copyright protection or they involve little or no creativity or originality. Among these are titles of books, movies, and songs; short phrases and slogans; printed forms; compilations of facts; and works consisting entirely of information that is public domain property—for instance, lists and tables taken from public documents or other common sources.

Related terms: compilations; *Feist Publications Inc. v. Rural Telephone Service Co.*

orphan work

An orphan work is one that is owned by a hard-to-find copyright owner. For example, in 1975, a child sends a drawing to Elvis Presley. In 2008, a biographer wants to include the drawing in a Presley biography. The problem for publishers (as well as libraries and academics) is that the artist can't be found and the publisher doesn't want to reproduce the image without permission. A work categorized as an orphan work does not lose its copyright protection. Two bills proposed in Congress in 2007 to provide limited uses of orphan works met with opposition from artist rights organizations, and did not pass.

Related terms: computer software.

overlapping transfers of copyright

Overlapping transfers of copyright rights occur when a copyright owner:
- transfers all or part of the same exclusive right to two or more separate parties
- transfers an exclusive right when that right has already been the subject of a nonexclusive license, or
- grants a nonexclusive license involving a right that has already been transferred by an exclusive license.

The following rules determine ownership in these situations:
- In a case of conflicting exclusive rights, the first right granted is entitled to the protection if the right is recorded in the U.S. Copyright Office within one month of the underlying work's publication (within two months if the right was granted outside of the United States).
- If the exclusive right is not recorded on time, the first transfer recorded is entitled to protection (even if it was the second one granted), as long as the grantee received it in good faith (without knowledge of the earlier one).
- Whether recorded or not, a nonexclusive written license will coexist with a later transfer of an exclusive right.

- Whether recorded or not, a nonexclusive written license will coexist with an exclusive right that was transferred earlier if both the grant of the non-exclusive license occurred before the earlier transfer was recorded and the recipient of the nonexclusive license did not know of the earlier exclusive-rights transfer.

Related terms: exclusive license; nonexclusive license; recordation of copyright transfers.

ownership of copyright

See copyright owner, defined.

pantomimes and choreographic works, copyrights

See choreography and pantomime.

parody and fair use

Parody occurs when one work ridicules another work (usually a well-known one) by imitating it in an amusing or comedic way. Normally, under U.S. law and the First Amendment to the Constitution, Americans perceive public ridicule such as this as a form of free speech. However, to the extent that the parody copies material protected by copyright, a parody may also be considered as copyright infringement. Courts reconcile these two legal interests by excusing unauthorized parodies under the principle of fair use.

Not all parodies qualify. The courts first decide whether a particular work qualifies as parody. If so, the court then determines whether the work qualifies as a fair use. If it does, then the parodist is not liable for the infringement.

To determine whether a work is a parody, the courts decide whether the work actually comments on the original work or just invokes the original work as a means of calling attention to itself in the marketplace. The key question to be addressed in deciding whether a work is a parody is whether the new work "adds something new, with a further purpose or different character altering the first with new expression, meaning, or message; it asks in other words whether and to what extent the new work is transformative." (*Campbell v. Acuff-Rose,* 510 U.S. 569 (1994).)

> EXAMPLE: The Paramount motion picture company released an advertisement for the movie *Naked Gun 33⅓* that showed Leslie Nielsen's face superimposed on the famous nude photo of a pregnant Demi Moore (which originally appeared on the cover of *Vanity Fair* magazine). Annie Leibovitz,

the photographer, sued Paramount for copyright infringement. In holding the work to be a parody, the Court held that the "ad may reasonably be perceived as commenting on the seriousness and even pretentiousness of the original." The Court went on to note that the parody differed from the original "in a way that may, reasonably, be perceived as commenting, through ridicule, on what a viewer might reasonably think is the undue self-importance conveyed by the subject of the Leibovitz photograph." (*Leibovitz v. Paramount Pictures Corp.,* 137 F.3d 109 (2d Cir. 1998).)

At the same time, a work does not become a parody simply because the author models characters after those found in a famous work. For example, in a case involving the author J.D. Salinger, an author wrote a book in which a character known as Mr. C was allegedly modeled after the character of Holden Caulfield, from Salinger's *Catcher in the Rye.* After Salinger sued, the sequel's author claimed that his work was a parody, an argument rejected by the district court primarily because the work was not transformative. Aging the character and placing him in present day does not add something new, particularly because the character's personality remains intact as derived from the original work. (*Salinger v. Colting,* 641 F. Supp. 2d 250 (S.D. N.Y. 2009).) (Note, the district court's decision in *Salinger v. Colting* was vacated and remanded by the Second Circuit (*Salinger v. Colting,* 607 F.3d 68 (2d Cir. 2010).) The Second Circuit agreed with the district court regarding its fair use analysis but vacated the judgment because the district court failed to incorporate new standards regarding preliminary injunctions.)

Once a work is found to be a parody, the court then must go on to decide whether the other tests used to determine fair use apply to the case. Briefly, these tests are:

- the purpose and character of the use, including whether such use is of a commercial nature or is for nonprofit educational purposes
- the nature of the copyrighted work
- the amount and substantiality of the portion used in relation to the copyrighted work as a whole, and
- the effect of the use upon the potential market for or value of the copyrighted work.

It is often difficult to discern whether a work is a parody. Cases involving Dr. Seuss and the book *Gone With the Wind* (below) show how difficult it can be to know for sure whether a parody qualifies as a fair use.

EXAMPLE 1: Two authors wrote a book called *The Cat NOT in the Hat! A Parody* by Dr. Juice. The book told the story of the O.J. Simpson trial through poems and sketches similar to those in the famous *The Cat in the Hat* children's stories by Dr. Seuss. The work was narrated by Dr. Juice, a character based on Dr. Seuss, and contained a character called "The Cat NOT in the Hat." The owners of the copyrights in Dr. Seuss sued for copyright infringement. The authors claimed that their work was a fair use of the Dr. Seuss stories because it was a parody. They argued that by applying Dr. Seuss's style to adult subject matter, their work commented on the "naiveté of the original" Dr. Seuss stories as well as on society's fixation on the O.J. Simpson trial. The court disagreed. It said that a parody was a literary or artistic work that imitates the characteristic style of an author for comic effect or ridicule. *The Cat NOT In the Hat!* didn't qualify, because the authors' poems and illustrations merely retold the Simpson tale. Although they broadly mimicked Dr. Seuss's characteristic style, they did not hold it up to ridicule or otherwise make it an object of the parody. The court opined that the authors used the Seuss characters and style merely to get attention or avoid the drudgery of working up something fresh. It upheld an injunction that barred Penguin Books from distributing 12,000 books it had printed at an expense of $35,000. (*Dr. Seuss Enterprises v. Penguin Books USA, Inc.,* 109 F.3d 1394 (9th Cir. 1997).)

EXAMPLE 2: In a case involving the legendary Civil War novel *Gone With the Wind,* an author wrote a book, called *The Wind Done Gone,* that chronicles the diary of a woman named Cynara, the illegitimate daughter of a plantation owner, and Mammy, a slave who cares for his children. Without obtaining permission from the copyright owner of *Gone With the Wind,* the author of *The Wind Done Gone* copied the prior book's characters, famous scenes, and other elements from the plot and dialogue and descriptions. The Margaret Mitchell estate sued both the publisher and author for copyright infringement.

The court held that *The Wind Done Gone* was protected by the fair use privilege, and thus the Mitchell estate could not obtain a court order halting its publication. The court concluded that *The Wind Done Gone* was a parody because "its aim is to comment upon or criticize a prior work by appropriating elements of the original in creating a new artistic, as opposed to scholarly or journalistic, work." *The Wind Done Gone* satisfied this test because it was a specific criticism of and rejoinder to the depiction of slavery and the relationships between blacks and whites in *Gone With the Wind*. (*Suntrust Bank v. Houghton Mifflin Co.*, 268 F.2d 1257 (11th Cir. 2001).)

Related terms: copyright infringement; fair use.

patent and copyright

See copyright and patent compared.

peer-to-peer

Peer-to-peer file sharing networks, the most popular of which are currently based on the BitTorrent protocol, permit access to (and free distribution of) electronic files, usually consisting of copyrighted music, films, and software. These networks commonly permit users to either communicate directly with each other, (not using central servers) or to allow users to reassemble files, the elements of which are stored on many computers, using BitTorrent protocols.

In other words, these networks and the data they manage, often lack a central location from which material is transmitted and received; all participants are both clients and servers. In 2005, the Supreme Court determined that individuals or companies who own or permit the use of such networks, with the goal of promoting their use to infringe copyright, are liable for the resulting acts of infringement by third parties using the network. (*Metro-Goldwyn-Mayer, Inc. v. Grokster Ltd.*, 545 U.S. 913 (2005).)

Also striking a blow against peer-to-peer file sharing, Congress passed the Family Entertainment and Copyright Act of 2005 which, among its provisions, made it a criminal violation to knowingly place a copyrighted computer program, musical work, motion picture or other audiovisual work, or sound recording on a computer network accessible to the public for purposes of copying.

In 2005, a woman was sued for copyright infringement for downloading 30 songs using peer-to-peer file sharing software. She argued that her activity was a fair use because she was downloading the songs to determine if she wanted to later buy them. Because numerous sites, such as iTunes, permit listeners to sample and examine portions of songs without downloading, the court rejected this "sampling" defense. (*BMG Music v. Gonzalez*, 430 F.3d 888 (7th Cir. 2005).)

Defendants in a peer-to-peer file sharing case may also have difficulty asserting a fair use defense. One defendant was denied that right because he had failed to provide evidence that his copying of music files involved any transformative use (an essential element in proving fair use). (*Capitol Records Inc. v. Alaujan*, 593 F. Supp. 2d 319 (D. Mass. 2009).)

In 2010, a district court determined that BitTorrent protocols violated copyright law in the same manner as other peer-to-peer infringements (for example, as used in the *Grokster* case) despite the lack of a central server containing infringing copies of the material. (*Columbia Pictures Industries, Inc. v. Fung,* ___ F. Supp. 2d ___ (C.D. Cal. 2009).)

Related terms: BitTorrent, Family Entertainment and Copyright Act of 2005.

performing a work

The exclusive right to perform a work is one of the bundle of rights that make up a copyright. To perform a work publicly has a much broader meaning under copyright law than the common concept of a performance. The drafters of the Copyright Act stated that "to perform a work means to recite, render, play, dance, or act it, either directly or by means of any device or process or, in the case of a motion picture or other audiovisual work, to show its images in any sequence or to make the sounds accompanying it audible." Section 101 of the Copyright Act states that to perform a work "publicly" means that there is performance of the work where the public is gathered or the work is transmitted or otherwise communicated to the public. (17 USC § 101.)

Examples of public performance include:

- A disc jockey plays a phonorecord in a nightclub.
- A novelist reads aloud from her work at a bookstore.
- A dancer presents a performance during halftime at a football game.
- A motion picture company authorizes a showing of its latest film.
- A songwriter performs an original composition at a nightclub.
- A radio station plays a record containing a copyrighted song.
- A television station broadcasts a television show.
- A cable TV company receives a television station broadcast and rebroadcasts it via cable transmission.

The performance right does not extend to pictorial, graphic, or sculptural works, because these works cannot be performed; they can only be displayed, so these rights are covered by the display right. In 1994, the Copyright Act was amended to include digital performance rights for sound recordings and to prevent the bootlegging of live musical performances.

Related terms: copyright infringement; exclusive copyright rights; public performance of a work.

performing music at a business

Performing rights societies collect fees from establishments where music is performed, such as clothing stores, bars, or restaurants. The "performance" of a song has a broad meaning encompassing live concerts; playing of a recording at a business or club; and transmission of a song via radio, television, cable, or digital signals.

Some businesses are exempt from these pay-for-play rules. Businesses that play the radio or television do not have to pay performances fees if they meet one or more of the criteria below:

- The business is a restaurant or bar under 3,750 square feet.
- The business is a retail establishment under 2,000 square feet.
- The business, regardless of size, has no more than six external speakers, but not more than four per room, or four televisions measuring 55 inches or less, but not more than one per room.

The exemptions above apply only to establishments that play radio and television. Establishments playing prerecorded music, such as compact discs, must still pay performance fees. Permission is not required to play a song in a record store or if the song is played via licensed jukebox.

Related terms: mechanical rights; musical works and sound recordings distinguished; performing a work; performing rights societies.

performing rights societies

Performing rights societies monitor the performance of music (whether it is live concerts, playing of a recording at a business or club, or transmission of a song via radio, television, cable, or digital signals). These societies then collect royalties from those who perform the music and distribute them to copyright owners (known as "performance royalties"). For the most part (see below) the collection of payments is on behalf of song owners, not sound recording owners. That's because, except for digital audio transmissions, there is no public performance right associated with sound recordings; it is only associated with musical compositions (songs).

It would be impractical if the proprietors of radio and TV stations or nightclubs had to contact each song owner for permission each time a song was publicly performed. Performing rights societies were established in order to negotiate and collect these fees. In the United States, a song owner affiliates with one of three performing rights societies: ASCAP, BMI, or SESAC. These societies act as agents for song owners, surveying radio stations on a regular basis and using the surveys

Copyright Law: Definitions

as a basis for payments to songwriters. TV stations furnish logs of music played, and agreements are also made with club owners where phonorecords are played or with concert halls where live music is performed.

Since 1996, owners of a sound recordings have had a performance right for digital audio transmissions—specifically interactive digital services as popularized on the Internet (for example, Pandora and Spotify). These royalty payments are collected from webcasters by SoundExchange and distributed to sound recording owners.

Related terms: mechanical rights; musical works and sound recordings distinguished; performing a work; performing music at a business.

permission

Many kinds of media publications—small and large—use words, music, and imagery that are protected by copyright laws. Is permission required for all uses of someone else's work? For example, is permission needed to reproduce a photo taken by a club member, a friend, or a relative? The short answer is, "yes." Copyright protection extends to any original work regardless of who created it and permission is required for reproduction, display, or distribution of the work.

The reason for acquiring permission is to avoid a lawsuit. The copyright owner controls the use of the work, and a person who uses it without permission could be sued for financial damages. If a friend or family member has consented to the use, the concern over a lawsuit diminishes, as does the need for a written permission agreement. An oral consent is valid, although an email or written consent is preferred as it is easier to prove in the event of a dispute. Sometimes the process of acquiring consent can be simplified by using the services of a copyright clearinghouse.

It is wise to operate under the assumption that all art, music, and writings are protected by copyright law. A work is not in the public domain simply because it has been posted on the Internet (a popular fallacy) or because it lacks a copyright notice (another fallacy). As a general rule, permission is needed to reproduce copyrighted materials including photos, writing, music, and artwork.

Do not assume that clip art, shareware, freeware, or materials labeled "royalty-free" or "copyright-free" can be distributed or copied without authorization. Read the terms and conditions in the "click to accept" agreement or "readme" files ordinarily accompanying such materials to be certain that an intended use is permitted. One company failed to honor the terms of a clickwrap agreement and was found liable for illegally distributing three volumes of software clip art.

Also, don't assume that because a site permits the download of a story that this story can be posted on another website. Each type of activity—emailing, copying, printing, and posting—requires authorization.

Permission is sometimes needed to reproduce a trademark including any word, symbol, or device that identifies and distinguishes a product or service. For example, the word "McDonald's," the distinctive yellow arches, and the Ronald McDonald character are all trademarks of the McDonald's company. Permission would be needed to use these trademarks at a commercial website if consumers are likely to be confused by the use or if the commercial use damages the reputation of McDonald's.

Related terms: clearinghouses, copyright; end-user license (aka EULA, shrinkwrap, or clickwrap agreement).

phonorecords

The U.S. Copyright Act of 1976 defines phonorecords not only as the traditional "record" but also as audio tape recordings, compact discs, laser discs, and any future technology for reproducing sound. The statute covers "material objects in which sounds, other than those accompanying … [an] audiovisual work, are fixed by any method now known or later developed, and from which the sounds can be perceived, reproduced, or otherwise communicated, either directly or with the aid of a machine or device. [It] … includes the material object in which the sounds are first fixed." (17 USC § 101.)

An original work of authorship contained on a phonorecord may be registered as a sound recording with the U.S. Copyright Office on Form SR.

Copyright Act: § 101. Definitions

"Phonorecords" are material objects in which sounds, other than those accompanying a motion picture or other audiovisual work, are fixed by any method now known or later developed, and from which the sounds can be perceived, reproduced, or otherwise communicated, either directly or with the aid of a machine or device. The term "phonorecords" includes the material object in which the sounds are first fixed.

"Sound recordings" are works that result from the fixation of a series of musical, spoken, or other sounds, but not including the sounds accompanying a motion picture or other audiovisual work, regardless of the nature of the material objects, such as disks, tapes, or other phonorecords, in which they are embodied.

Related terms: compulsory license; Form SR; musical works and sound recordings distinguished; registration.

photocopies and copyright law

The photocopy machine is a familiar part of life in America, and copyrights are frequently infringed by its use. Because much photocopying occurs in private and doesn't involve commercial distribution, this type of infringement is seldom discovered. Also, unless the copyright owner has been damaged in some manner or profits were gained from the infringement, an infringement lawsuit is usually out of the question. The increased popularity of scanners, and electronic books, and the diminishing popularity of print books and copy machines, make photocopy infringement less of a priority for copyright owners.

Nevertheless, in situations where photocopying is discovered by a copyright owner and it appears that sales of the item being copied may be adversely affected, a copyright lawsuit may be the result. For instance, in the case of *Basic Books, Inc. v. Kinko's Graphics Corp.,* 758 F. Supp. 1522 (S.D. N.Y. 1991), a group of seven major publishers obtained a $510,000 judgment against a duplicating business for copying excerpts from books without permission, compiling them into "course packets," and selling them to college students. Almost 20 years later, the same issues and the same result occurred in *Blackwell Publishing, Inc. v. Excel Research Group,* 661 F. Supp. 2d 786 (E.D. Mich. 2009).

Related terms: copies; fair use; infringement action.

photography

Photographic images are protectable under copyright law whether in print or digital format. The photographer is considered the author and original owner of copyright. Absent an agreement transferring rights, a person who is photographed does not acquire copyright ownership in the photo. However, a person who is the subject of the photograph may be able to prevent its reproduction under legal theories such as the right of publicity, defamation, or invasion of privacy.

Along with the right to control reproduction, the photographer acquires the right to create derivatives of the work. These derivatives may even be three-dimensional. For example, in one case, the photographer Art Rogers created the photograph entitled "Puppies," which features a man and woman sitting on a bench and holding eight puppies. The artist Jeff Koons purchased two postcards of the image and, without obtaining Mr. Rogers's authorization, created a wood sculpture based on the image. Even though Koons had demonstrated sufficient originality in his statues, he could not sell his works because he failed to obtain permission from the photographer of the underlying copyrighted work. (*Rogers v. Koons,* 960 F.2d 301 (2d Cir. 1992).)

What's protectable about a photograph? It's not the subject matter per se. Everyone, for example, can photograph the Golden Gate Bridge or a presidential candidate. But other elements in the making of a photograph may be protectable. In one decision, a district court judge ruled that photographic elements such as rendition (the technical choices made when photographing a subject) and timing—taking a picture at the right time and right place—may be original and protectable elements in some photographs. For example, a photographer could potentially infringe the famous photo of servicemen installing the flag at Iwo Jima by recreating the photographic elements using models. (*Mannion vs. Coors Brewing Company*, 377 F. Supp. 2d 444 (S.D. N.Y. 2005).)

At the same time, a photograph that is merely a "slavish reproduction" of an existing work is unlikely to be protected under copyright. For example, a federal judge ruled against a company trying to claim copyright in a perfect reproduction of a public domain painting. (*Bridgeman Art Library Ltd. v. Corel Corp.*, 25 F. Supp. 2d 412 (S.D. N.Y. 1997).) In a similar vein, the Tenth Circuit Court of Appeals held that a detailed three-dimensional computer photo-perfect replication of an automobile—in this case, a Toyota—did not demonstrate sufficient originality such that the software company that created the imagery could claim copyright. (*Meshwerks Inc. v. Toyota Motor Sales U.S.A. Inc.*, 528 F.3d 1258 (10th Cir. 2008).)

Two cases from 2010 highlight the confusion regarding registration of collections of photographs. In one case, a photographer licensed 150 works to Corbis. Corbis included the photos in a group registration of approximately 12,000–16,000 photographs. A district court ruled that the photographer could not rely on the group registration because it identified Corbis as the author of the works, not the photographer. Because each author must be identified, the compilation registration did not register copyrights in the individual works. (*Bean v. Houghton Mifflin Publishing, Co.*, 95 USPQ 2d 1489 (D. Ariz. 2010).) A related result occurred in *Muench Photography, Inc. v. Houghton Mifflin Harcourt Publishing*, 712 F. Supp. 2d 84 (S.D. N.Y. 2010). In that case, a New York district court ruled that copyright registration in an automated database of photographs must contain the names of each of the photographers in order for an individual photographer to sue for infringement.

Related terms: inlining and thumbnails.

Copyright Law: Definitions

pictorial, graphic, and sculptural works

Works of expression using graphic and physical representations of objects and ideas, rather than text, are entitled to copyright protection. The Copyright Act covers "two-dimensional and three-dimensional works of fine, graphic, and applied art, photographs, prints and art reproductions, maps, globes, charts, technical drawings, diagrams, and models." (17 USC § 101.)

The original design of a toy, package, implement, or other product can qualify for copyright protection if it is created for expressive rather than functional purposes. For instance, a pitcher designed as a unicorn may be subject to copyright protection as long as the unicorn shape is not directly related to the pitcher's function—that is, the unicorn shape does not affect how the pitcher stores and pours liquids. Whether or not a design is functional or expressive can only be decided on a case-by-case basis. (Functional works are also known as "useful articles.")

This issue arose in two 2010 cases. In *Universal Furniture International, Inc. v. Collezione Europa USA, Inc.*, 618 F.3d 417 (4th Circuit 2010), the Fourth Circuit ruled that highly ornate furniture design can be separable and copyrightable despite its utilitarian function. In *Lanard Toys Ltd. v. Novelty Inc.*, 2010 U.S. App. LEXIS 7585 (9th Cir. 2010), the Ninth Circuit held that there was sufficient evidence to demonstrate that a launcher and flying toy were copyrightable despite their function.

Designs of an article of manufacture that are not functional may also qualify for patent protection under a design patent.

Copyright Act: § 101. Definitions

"Pictorial, graphic, and sculptural works" include two-dimensional and three-dimensional works of fine, graphic, and applied art, photographs, prints and art reproductions, maps, globes, charts, diagrams, models, and technical drawings, including architectural plans. Such works shall include works of artistic craftsmanship insofar as their form but not their mechanical or utilitarian aspects are concerned; the design of a useful article, as defined in this section, shall be considered a pictorial, graphic, or sculptural work only if, and only to the extent that, such design incorporates pictorial, graphic, or sculptural features that can be identified separately from, and are capable of existing independently of, the utilitarian aspects of the article.

A "useful article" is an article having an intrinsic utilitarian function that is not merely to portray the appearance of the article or to convey information. An article that is normally a part of a useful article is considered a "useful article."

Related terms: copyright and patent compared; Form VA; registration of copyright.

See also Part 1 (Patent Law): design patents; Part 3 (Trademark Law): trade dress.

piracy

A colloquial term without legal significance, piracy is used to describe the illegal activity of willful copyright infringers.

Related terms: copyright infringement; criminal copyright infringement.

placement of copyright notice

See notice of copyright.

plagiarism

Deliberately passing off somebody else's original expression or creative ideas as one's own is colloquially known as plagiarism. Plagiarism can be a violation under the copyright laws if original expression is copied.

Often, however, plagiarism does not violate any law but marks the plagiarist as an unethical person in the political, academic, or scientific community where the plagiarism occurs.

Related terms: copyright infringement; original work of authorship.

plot, protection of

Copyright will protect the plot of a novel or other nonfiction work, provided that the author's expression is somehow separable from the underlying premise or concept of the plot. For example, the idea of boy-meets-girl, boy-loses-girl, boy-gets-girl plot is not protectable. But the embellished plot variations of that premise or theme—such as *When Harry Met Sally*, or *An Affair to Remember*—can achieve protection. The standard was best described by Judge Learned Hand in *Nichols v. Universal Pictures*, 45 F.2d 119 (2d Cir. 1930). In that case the author of the popular play, *Abie's Irish Rose*, sued the producers of a movie, *The Cohens and the Kellys*. Both plots involved children of Irish and Jewish families who marry secretly because their parents are prejudiced. At the end of each work there is a reconciliation of the families, based upon the presence of a grandchild. Beyond that, the works had little in common except for ethnic clichés.

Judge Hand established a standard to separate the idea from the expression. He used the term "abstraction," which is a process of removing or separating something. He stated: "Upon any work, and especially upon a play, a great number of patterns of increasing generality will fit equally well, as more and more of the incident is left out." In other words, every narrative work is built around an underlying idea, in this case the basic plot summary. The idea may be similar to other plots—many people believe there are only between seven and 30 basic plots—but the author's embellishments, the series of details and incidents that separate the idea from similar plots, trigger copyright protection.

> **EXAMPLE:** A writer sued the makers of the movie *E.T.—The Extra Terrestrial*. The writer claimed that the film infringed her musical play, *Lokey From Maldemar*, a social satire designed to "illustrate the disunity of man, divided by egotism." The district court applied the abstractions test and determined that the only similarity in both works was the basic idea of the plot line—aliens with powers of levitation are stranded on earth, pursued by authoritarian characters and finally bid their earthly friends farewell. (*Litchfield v. Spielberg*, 736 F.2d 1352 (9th Cir. 1984).)

podcasting

Podcasting—a term derived from the popular audio player, the iPod—is the process of scheduling an audio file for automatic download. The process permits listeners, for example, to arrange for automatic delivery of radio shows, audio-books, music, or other audio programs. Because podcasting involves digital distribution, performance, duplication, and transfer, the process may trigger the same gamut of copyright issues raised by MP3 downloads and digital copying.

preemption

Under Section 301 of the Copyright Act, states are prohibited from creating or enforcing laws that are equivalent to any of the exclusive rights granted under copyright law. This principle—known as preemption (or "pre-emption")—is sometimes used by a defendant in a lawsuit who claims that a state lawsuit should be dismissed because it actually involves a right similar to copyright—for example, a dispute involving the right of publicity or a shrinkwrap license.

preliminary injunctions

See injunctions.

preregistration of copyright

As a result of legislation in 2005, the U.S. Copyright Office instituted a preregistration procedure for certain classes of works that have a history of pre-release infringement. According to the Copyright Office, preregistration serves as a placeholder for limited purposes, mainly where a copyright owner needs to sue for infringement while a work is still being prepared for commercial release. Preregistration is not a substitute for registration, and its use is appropriate only in certain circumstances.

A work submitted for preregistration must meet three conditions:

- The work must be unpublished.
- The work must be in the process of being prepared for commercial distribution in either physical or digital format—that is, film copies, CDs, computer programs to be sold online—and the applicant must have a reasonable expectation of this commercial distribution.
- The work must fall within the following classes of works determined by the Register of Copyrights to have had a history of infringement prior to authorized commercial distribution. The works determined to be eligible under this requirement are: motion pictures, sound recordings, musical compositions, literary works being prepared for publication in book form, computer programs (which may include video games), and advertising or marketing photographs.

Preregistration is not a form of registration but is simply an indication of an intent to register a work once the work has been completed and/or published. When the work has been completed, it may be registered as an unpublished work, and when it has been published, it may be registered as a published work.

A person who has preregistered a work must register the work within one month after the copyright owner becomes aware of infringement and no later than three months after first publication. If full registration is not made within the prescribed time period, a court must dismiss an action for copyright infringement that occurred before or within the first two months after first publication.

To preregister, a copyright owner must apply online; no paper application form is available. The effective date is the day on which the completed application and fee for an eligible work have been received in the Copyright Office.

Related term: Family Entertainment Act of 2005.

printed forms, not copyrightable

Printed forms do not usually qualify for copyright protection because they are designed for recording information and do not in themselves convey information or original expression. In other cases, the forms contain information that can only be expressed in a limited number of ways (for example, a job application form) and such works will not be protected under the merger doctrine—that is the idea and expression are merged.

Related terms: copyright; merger doctrine; original work of authorship.

profits as damages

Profits reaped by an infringer as a result of a copyright infringement (called defendant's profits) are one possible element of monetary damages a court may require the infringer to pay the copyright owner. Defendant's profits will only be awarded where these profits exceed the amount of profits lost by the copyright owner as a result of the infringement.

To establish the amount of an infringer's profits, the plaintiff copyright owner first must prove the defendant's gross profits from the sales of the infringing goods or services. The defendant then is entitled to deduct his or her demonstrable costs from the gross revenues from selling the infringing material. The resulting amount is then compared with the plaintiff's lost profits, if any. Damages that will be awarded will be the greater of defendant's profits attributable to the infringement or the plaintiff's lost profits.

EXAMPLE: Janet infringed Jeffrey's copyright by stealing his dissertation and publishing it first. Jeffrey proves that he lost $20,000 in publishers' advances and royalties based on the reasonably anticipated sale of the dissertation as a scholarly book. Because Janet's publisher did a super job selling foreign rights, she ended up with $35,000. Janet would have to pay Jeffrey $35,000, because her profits were greater. However, if instead Janet's net profits were only $15,000, she would have to pay him $20,000, his lost profits, because his lost profits were greater than her actual ones.

Related terms: damages for copyright infringement.

programs, computer, copyright of

See computer software.

pseudonym

A "pseudonymous work" is one on which the author is identified under a fictitious name. Copyright laws protect an author who publishes a work under a pseudonym almost as well as (and in some cases better than) they do an author who uses his or her real name. The main difference is that the copyright will last 95 years for a pseudonymous work, instead of the author's life plus 70 years for an author-identified work.

Related terms: anonymous; author as owner of copyright; duration of copyrights.

public domain

Any work of authorship that is not protected under copyright law is said to fall within the public domain. This means that anyone can use the work without obtaining permission from the author or the author's heirs. There are several common reasons why works may be considered to be in the public domain:

- The work was published before 1923.
- The work was published between 1923 and 1963 and never renewed.
- The work consists solely of facts or ideas. (Facts and ideas are not protected by copyright, although the means used to express them may be protected to some extent.)
- The work was published before 1978 and lacked a proper copyright notice. (But the copyright in many of these works has been restored.)
- The work was published between 1978 and 1989, the notice on the work was defective, and inadequate efforts were made to correct the defects. (Copyrights by non-U.S. authors covered by the Berne Convention that expired for this reason can be restored under GATT.)
- The copyright owner deliberately placed the work in the public domain by making a statement to that effect.
- The work was prepared by an officer or employee of the United States Government as part of that person's official duties.
- The work was created before 1978 but not published before December 31, 2003.

Related terms: factual works; *Feist Publications Inc. v. Rural Telephone Service Co.*; original work of authorship; restored copyright under GATT; work of the U.S. Government.

public performance of a work

Among the bundle of rights making up a copyright is the exclusive right to publicly perform or display an original work of authorship. The Copyright Act considers a public performance to be: (1) when a work is performed or displayed at a place open to the public or at any place where a substantial number of persons outside of a normal circle of a family and its social acquaintances is gathered; or (2) when a performance or display of the work is transmitted or otherwise communicated to the public, by means of any device or process. (17 USC § 101.)

In 2009, it was held that it is not a public performance of a song when the song is used as a ringtone. ASCAP, a society that collects money for songwriters, claimed that Verizon's sale of ringtones amounted to violation of the public performance right and required payment of licensing fees. A New York court held that the ringtones—which were stored on user's phones—were exempt from public performance licensing under 17 USC Sec. 110(4). (*In re Application of Cellco Partnership*, 663 F. Supp. 2d 363 (S.D. N.Y. 2009).)

Copyright Act: § 101. Definitions

To perform or display a work "publicly" means—

(1) to perform or display it at a place open to the public or at any place where a substantial number of persons outside of a normal circle of a family and its social acquaintances is gathered; or

(2) to transmit or otherwise communicate a performance or display of the work to a place specified by clause (1) or to the public, by means of any device or process, whether the members of the public capable of receiving the performance or display receive it in the same place or in separate places and at the same time or at different times.

Related terms: copyright; copyright infringement; exclusive license.

publication

See published work.

published work

An original work of authorship is only considered published under the Copyright Act when it is first made available to the public on an unrestricted basis. It is thus possible to display a work, or distribute it with restrictions on disclosure of its contents, without actually "publishing" it (or what is sometimes referred to as a "limited publication").

> EXAMPLE: Andres writes an essay called "Blood Bath" about the war in Iraq and distributes it to five human rights organizations under a nonexclusive license that places restrictions on their right to disclose the essay's contents. "Blood Bath" has not been "published" in the copyright sense.

Does posting material on the Internet for unrestricted access amount to publication? Although the Copyright Office does not take an official position on the issue, it is generally considered that unrestricted Internet displays amount to publication. In 2002, a federal court ruled that the posting of a website on the Internet amounted to publication. This ruling enabled the website owner to collect statutory damages from an infringer who copied the website. (*Getaped.com v. Cangemi*, 188 F. Supp. 2d 398 (S.D. N.Y. 2002).)

Published and unpublished works are both entitled to copyright protection, but there are some legal distinctions, such as:

- For works created after 1977, if the "author" is an employer or the commissioner of a work made for hire, or uses a pseudonym or remains anonymous, the copyright lasts for 95 years for published works and 120 years for unpublished works.
- The publication date sets the time running for a timely registration of the copyright with the U.S. Copyright Office.
- It is more difficult for an infringer to claim fair use when the infringed work is unpublished because the infringing publication deprives its copyright owner of the right to determine its publication date.
- A valid copyright notice on a published work can prevent the claim of innocent infringement from being raised in a copyright infringement lawsuit.

Copyright Act: § 101. Definitions

"Publication" is the distribution of copies or phonorecords of a work to the public by sale or other transfer of ownership, or by rental, lease, or lending. The offering to distribute copies or phonorecords to a group of persons for purposes of further distribution, public performance, or public display, constitutes publication. A public performance or display of a work does not of itself constitute publication.

Related terms: fair use; international copyright protection; notice of copyright; registration.

recordation of copyright transfers

Recordation refers to the filing of documents that evidence the ownership or transfer of copyright or of specific rights associated with copyright. When one or more exclusive copyright rights are transferred, it is important for the recipient of the rights to record the transfer immediately with the U.S. Copyright Office. This is because the first party to record has greater rights in the event of conflicting or overlapping transfers.

Recordation also provides all persons with "constructive notice" of the transfer of rights. This means that the law will presume infringers should have found out about it, even if they didn't actually know. Without recordation, although the owner of transferred rights can sue an infringer, it may be hard to prove that the infringement was not innocent.

Copyright Law: Definitions

To record a transfer, the new owner must file with the U.S. Copyright Office a written document describing the work involved and the transfer granted and bearing the signature of the person granting the transfer.

Related terms: overlapping transfers of copyright; transfers of copyright ownership.

recordings, sound

The U.S. Copyright Office calls all sound recordings "phonorecords," no matter what medium is actually used.

Related terms: phonorecords.

Register of Copyrights

This is the official title of the person who heads the U.S. Copyright Office.

Related terms: registration; U.S. Copyright Office.

registration

Registration occurs when the Copyright Office receives all of the required application materials associated with an author's claim, and approves the application.

Registration is not required to obtain copyright protection; that occurs automatically when a work of authorship is fixed in a tangible medium of expression. Nevertheless, registration is recommended because it provides several advantages in case of infringement:

- If a copyright is registered either before an infringing activity has begun, or within three months of first publication of the work, the copyright owner may collect statutory damages for the infringement, plus attorneys' fees, if the issue ends up in court. These benefits often make the difference between an owner being able to afford litigation and having to forgo copyright rights.
- In an infringement action, the registered copyright owner is presumed to be the actual owner, and the statements in the registration application are presumed to be true. Such presumptions make it easier to present a viable court case, because they put the burden on the other side to disprove the plaintiff's right to relief.
- Copyright owners must register their work prior to suing for infringement. (See below.)

The registration process is relatively simple. It requires three elements: a completed application form, deposit materials, and payment of a fee. An applicant can register online, or prepare a written application form and mail it in.

Using the Copyright Office's eCO system, you can file an application for $35. The process is fairly straightforward (and discussed in the Forms portion of this text, following this section). The applicant may upload a digital copy of the work (if the applicant qualifies), or in the case of most published works, the applicant mails in two physical copies to the Copyright Office.

If you have a computer with a printer, you can also use Form CO, which is intended to speed up registration for applicants who use the mail. Form CO is an all-purpose fill-in form that includes 2-D barcode scanning technology. The applicant completes it on a computer, prints out the form, and mails it in with the $50 fee and deposit materials.

The U.S. Copyright Office provides a number of preprinted forms, for different types of works. The filing fee for these forms is $65 (apparently to discourage their use).

- Form TX is used for all nondramatic literary works, including software code.
- Form PA is used for published and unpublished works of the performing arts, such as musical and dramatic works, pantomimes, motion pictures, and graphically based multimedia works on CD-ROM.
- Form VA is used for the visual arts.
- Form SR is used for sound recordings.
- Form SE (there are several variations) is used for serials like newspapers, periodicals, and journals.

All forms can be downloaded from the Copyright Office's website at www.copyright.gov. Users of print forms must send the forms to the Copyright Office with a proper deposit of the work itself, or with material that satisfactorily identifies the work (called identifying material). The Copyright Office has specific regulations governing the form of the deposit. Special rules apply in the case of computer software, phonorecordings, and mask works.

In certain cases, the Copyright Office grants "special relief" by waiving formal deposit or other registration requirements. This means, for example, that the Copyright Office will accept deposits in a different medium or form from what is normally required. There are no specific rules for when specific relief will or will not be granted.

Copyright Law: Definitions

Assuming that the registration materials are properly completed, the Copyright Office will normally register the work and send a certificate of registration. On the other hand, if information is either left out of the form or clearly erroneous on its face, the Copyright Office will send the form back and indicate how to correct it.

After registration, information provided in the initial registration can be corrected or updated by filing a supplemental registration form (Form CA).

Registration is a prerequisite to filing an infringement action (17 USC § 411(a).) However, the Fifth, Seventh, and Ninth Circuits have interpreted this to mean that a lawsuit can proceed if an application has been filed, provided that a registration eventually issues. The Tenth and Eleventh Circuits have held to a stricter requirement and require a Certificate of Registration. Registration is not required to file an infringement lawsuit for non-U.S. works that meet the definition of Berne Convention works (that is, when the author is a national of a Berne Convention country and the work was first published in a Berne Convention country). (See 17 USC § 101.) Registration is also not required to file an infringement lawsuit for works of visual art (fine art limited editions of 200 or fewer copies as defined in 17 United States Code, Sections 101 and 106A).

Copyright Act: § 411. Registration and infringement actions

This statute requires, with some exceptions, that a copyright be registered with the U.S. Copyright Office before a lawsuit for copyright infringement may be filed.

(a) Except for an action brought for a violation of the rights of the author under section 106A (a), and subject to the provisions of subsection (b), no action for infringement of the copyright in any United States work shall be instituted until registration of the copyright claim has been made in accordance with this title. In any case, however, where the deposit, application, and fee required for registration have been delivered to the Copyright Office in proper form and registration has been refused, the applicant is entitled to institute an action for infringement if notice thereof, with a copy of the complaint, is served on the Register of Copyrights. The Register may, at his or her option, become a party to the action with respect to the issue of registrability of the copyright claim by entering an appearance within sixty days after such service, but the Register's failure to become a party shall not deprive the court of jurisdiction to determine that issue.

(b) In the case of a work consisting of sounds, images, or both, the first fixation of which is made simultaneously with its transmission, the copyright owner may, either before or after such fixation takes place, institute an action for infringement under section 501, fully subject to the remedies provided by sections 502 through 506 and sections 509 and 510, if, in accordance with requirements that the Register of Copyrights shall prescribe by regulation, the copyright owner—

(1) serves notice upon the infringer, not less than 48 hours before such fixation, identifying the work and the specific time and source of its first transmission, and declaring an intention to secure copyright in the work; and

(2) makes registration for the work, if required by subsection (a), within three months after its first transmission.

Copyright Act: § 412. Registration as prerequisite to certain remedies for infringement

This statute establishes the penalty for failure to timely register a copyright with the U.S. Copyright Office and states when a registration will be considered timely.

In any action under this title, other than an action brought for a violation of the rights of the author under section 106A (a) or an action instituted under section 411 (b), no award of statutory damages or of attorney's fees, as provided by sections 504 and 505, shall be made for—

(1) any infringement of copyright in an unpublished work commenced before the effective date of its registration; or

(2) any infringement of copyright commenced after first publication of the work and before the effective date of its registration, unless such registration is made within three months after the first publication of the work.

Related terms: copyright infringement; copyright owner; deposit with U.S. Copyright Office; identifying material; infringement action; special relief; timely registration; preregistration of copyright.

registration of copyright license

See recordation of copyright transfers.

registration of copyrights in unpublished works

See unpublished work.

reliance party, when copyright restored

See restored copyright under GATT.

renewal of copyright

See duration of copyrights.

restored copyright under GATT

Until the United States became a member of the Berne Convention in March 1989, works originating in Berne Convention countries often lost their copyright in the United States because they failed to observe certain formalities required by the U.S. copyright laws, such as copyright notices. Under the General Agreement on Tariffs and Trade (GATT), copyright protection has been restored in all such works. However, parties who used these restored works without permission in reliance on the fact that they weren't protected by copyright (called reliance parties) cannot be sued for copyright infringement and may continue using the works under certain circumstances if they pay a reasonable license fee to the restored copyright owner under a type of compulsory license.

Related terms: GATT (General Agreement on Tariffs and Trade).

revocation of license

Most copyright licenses contain conditions under which the license must be exercised. If these conditions are broken, the copyright owner generally has a right to revoke the license. The license revocation should always be done in writing. Any exercise of the licensed right after revocation will constitute an infringement of the copyright.

Revocation of a license should not be confused with the right to terminate transfers under the Copyright Act. In that situation (and in addition to any provisions in the license itself), the original copyright owner (or his or her heirs) has a legal right to terminate any transfer after 35 to 40 years have passed.

Related terms: licensing of copyrights; termination of transfers.

rule of doubt

The U.S. Copyright Office allows object code (for software registrations) to be deposited in connection with a computer program registration. There is, however, an express understanding that doubt exists as to whether the code qualifies for copyright protection should litigation later ensue. In essence, the U.S. Copyright Office is saying, "We will let you deposit object code, but because we can't read or understand it, we won't commit ourselves as to its copyrightability."

If the registration is accomplished under the rule of doubt, the copyright owner may be unable to claim the presumption of ownership—an important benefit of registration—should the issue end up in court because of an alleged copyright infringement.

Related terms: computer software; special relief.

safe harbor

See Digital Millennium Copyright Act.

sampling

The digital recording process has made it possible to "sample" a portion of a sound recording. These digital samples can be manipulated to replay once or twice or repeat as a "loop" throughout a new recording. The unauthorized use of a sample almost always infringes the sound recording copyright and may infringe the musical works copyright held on the underlying sampled music.

Whether the use qualifies as an infringement depends upon the portion sampled and its qualitative or quantitative importance to the copyrighted work. Initially, the courts took a rigid approach prohibiting any use of digital samples. Then, in a 1997 case, a court determined that the rap group Run DMC's use of a drum sample from a 1973 recording was not infringing. (*Ruff 'N' Rumble Mgmt. v. Profile Records, Inc.,* 42 U.S.P.Q.2d 1398 (S.D. N.Y. 1997).)

However, the pendulum swung against sampling in a 2004 case when the Sixth Circuit Court of Appeals ruled that the use of a two-second sample was an infringement of the sound recording copyright. The court went even further, stating that when it came to sound recording there was no permissible minimum sanctioned under copyright law. (*Bridgeport Music v. Dimension Films,* 383 F.3d 390 (6th Cir. 2004).) No other courts have yet endorsed this extreme view of sound recording protection, which ignores the defense of fair use.

Although industry custom requires that two licenses be obtained to sample recorded music (from the sound recording and musical work owners), a federal court ruled in 2002 that the use of a six-second flute sample, repeated throughout a Beastie Boys song, "Pass the Mic," required permission only from the sound recording owner, not from the composer. (*Newton v. Diamond,* 2002 U.S. Dist. LEXIS 10247 (C.D. Cal. 2002).)

Sound recordings were not protected by copyright law until 1972. The use of a musical sample from a work created prior to 1972 would not be an infringement of a sound recording copyright, although it may be a violation of applicable state laws (or what is sometimes referred to as "common law copyright"). In order to avoid claims of infringement, popular artists seek sample clearance from copyright owners.

Semiconductor Chip Protection Act of 1984

This statute protects semiconductor chip manufacturers against the unauthorized copying or use of semiconductor chips and the templates that are used to manufacture them.

Semiconductor chips are a complex combination of tiny circuits that are designed to manipulate electronic data. They are mass-produced from multi-layered three-dimensional templates that are called "chip masks" in the trade and "mask works" under the Semiconductor Chip Protection Act.

Mask works (and the resulting semiconductor chips) are very difficult and expensive to design, but very easy to copy. Accordingly, semiconductor chip manufacturers have long sought protection of these devices as a form of intellectual property. Because technological advances in these chips have been incremental in nature, most improvements have been considered obvious and, therefore, not patentable. Before 1984, the chips did not qualify for copyright protection, due to the fact that their design was considered functional rather than expressive. To plug this gap, Congress passed the Semiconductor Chip Protection Act.

Under this statute, the owner of the exclusive rights in the mask work (generally the manufacturer) is given an exclusive ten-year right to:

- reproduce the mask work
- import or distribute a semiconductor chip product in which the mask work is embodied, and
- license others to exercise these rights.

These rights are forfeited, however, if the owner fails to register the mask work with the U.S. Copyright Office within two years of its commercial exploitation anywhere in the world.

A party who innocently purchases a semiconductor chip product that has been manufactured in violation of these exclusive rights is not liable for copyright infringement but must pay a reasonable royalty for each unit the innocent party imports or distributes after notice of the infringement.

Related terms: computer software; innocent infringement of copyright.

shrinkwrap and clickwrap license

See end-user license (aka EULA, shrinkwrap, or clickwrap agreement).

simultaneous publication

Previous to March 1, 1989, the United States belonged to the Universal Copyright Convention (U.C.C.) but not to the Berne Convention. If an author wished to obtain protection under both the Berne Convention and the U.C.C., he or she could do so by causing the initial publication of the work to simultaneously occur in the United States and a Berne Convention country, such as Canada. In March

1989, however, the United States joined the Berne Convention, so U.S. authors have no further reason for simultaneous publication.

Related terms: Berne Convention; international copyright protection; Universal Copyright Convention (U.C.C.).

single registration rule

The U.S. Copyright Office generally allows only one registration for each original work of authorship. There are exceptions, however. A new registration is permitted when an unpublished work is later published. A new registration is also allowed to substitute an author's name.

Changes, updates, or translations of a given work will merit a second registration only if they are substantial enough in quantity or quality to qualify the work as a new version. Practically, unless the modified work is significantly changed or contains a great deal of new material, the original registration should provide adequate protection. However, certain minor or technical changes in an existing registration sometimes warrant filing a supplemental registration.

If a new version is registered, that registration applies only to the new material contained in the work. The material taken from the original work is still covered under the original registration.

Related terms: best edition of a work; supplemental registration.

site license

Some software publishers grant a single license to a company that allows a set number of copies of the software to be installed on individual computers. For instance, if a company with 100 employees wants its employees to use a particular graphics program, it can either buy 100 copies of the program or try to get a site license that would permit use of 100 copies of the software at a reduced rate per copy.

Related terms: computer software; end-user license (aka EULA, shrinkwrap, or clickwrap agreement); licensing of copyrights.

software and copyrights

See computer software.

Sonny Bono Copyright Term Extension Act

This Act, signed by the president on October 26, 1998, extended the copyright term in the United States by 20 years for all works published after January 1,

1998. The act also extended the duration of the copyright term on works created or published prior to 1978.

In 2003, the U.S. Supreme Court ruled that the 20-year copyright extension did not violate the U.S. Constitution. (*Eldred v. Ashcroft,* 537 U.S. 186 (2003).)

Related terms: Copyleft; duration of copyrights; *Eldred v. Ashcroft.*

sound recordings

See phonorecords.

source code

Source code refers to the program code in which a programmer writes a software program. Source code can be written in various computer languages (for instance, Cobol, C++, Visual Basic) and contains not only the commands for the computer, but also the programmer's comments regarding the purpose and meaning of the different lines of code. It is relatively easy for a skilled computer programmer to examine the source code for a particular program and figure out how to produce the same result with a different program. Thus, access to source code will reveal a program's trade secrets and allow a competitor to use its ideas in a competing program.

For this reason, programmers like to keep their source code as confidential as possible. Accordingly, when registering a program with the U.S. Copyright Office, many software authors prefer to deposit only object code, which is extremely difficult to decipher because it appears in the form of ones and zeros, hexadecimal, or some other inscrutable form.

Nevertheless, the U.S. Copyright Office considers a program's source code to be the best edition of the work and, accordingly, prefers it as a deposit. In fact, the U.S. Copyright Office will accept a deposit of portions of the source code with critical parts blacked out, or a mixture of source code and object code. But the U.S. Copyright Office will also accept a deposit of the object code under what is called the rule of doubt—that is, it has no opinion as to whether the registered code qualifies for copyright protection, because it can't read it.

Related terms: computer software; object code; open source; registration; rule of doubt.

sovereign immunity

Sovereign immunity is a principle that a government is immune from civil suit or criminal prosecution. For purposes of copyright, it refers to the fact that state governments cannot be liable for copyright infringement. For example, in 2000 a suit was dismissed in which a man sued the University of Houston (a state-run institution) for copyright infringement. (*Chavez v. Arte Publico Press,* 204 F.3d 601 (5th Cir. 2000).)

Neither the federal government nor local municipal or county governments enjoy similar sovereign immunity. Moreover, civil copyright remedies can be pursued against any government (federal, state, or local) employee who commits infringement in his or her individual capacity. Finally, a state institution should not assume it has freedom to commit copyright infringement. State laws vary, and some states may waive or limit sovereign immunity in certain situations.

special relief

The U.S. Copyright Office sometimes gives a special variance to depart from its usual requirements for copyright registration or deposit. This variance is known as "special relief." Applicants for copyright registration may have one or many reasons to seek exemptions from the formal requirements for registration and deposits—for example, an unusual shape, size, or composition of the work to be deposited or the need to maintain a trade secret expressed by the work. Often the U.S. Copyright Office will grant such special relief to applicants who request it and explain in a cover letter to their registration application why they need it.

Related terms: best edition of a work; deposit with U.S. Copyright Office; registration.

states, copyright infringement suits against

See sovereign immunity.

statute of limitations

A statute of limitations sets the legal time limit by which a person bringing an infringement lawsuit must file the suit. In civil copyright cases, this limit provides that you can't file suit more than three years after the discovery of the infringement, or after it reasonably should have been discovered. (In criminal copyright cases, the government must bring an action within five years after the infringement occurred.) The theory behind the statute of limitations is that plaintiffs can't be allowed to "sit on their rights" and accumulate damages but must act reasonably promptly to prevent further damage once it is discovered.

Because it is not always easy to discover the existence of a copyright infringement, it's fairly common to file a lawsuit after the three-year deadline, claiming recent discovery. Unfortunately, the courts do not agree on what types of acts start the calendar running for purposes of the three-year statute of limitations period.

Copyright Act: § 507. Limitations on actions

(a) **Criminal Proceedings.**—Except as expressly provided otherwise in this title, no criminal proceeding shall be maintained under the provisions of this title unless it is commenced within 5 years after the cause of action arose.

(b) **Civil Actions.**—No civil action shall be maintained under the provisions of this title unless it is commenced within three years after the claim accrued.

statutory damages under copyright act

See damages for copyright infringement.

substantial similarity

See copyright infringement.

supplemental registration

Certain errors in a copyright registration may be corrected, changed, or amplified by filing a supplemental registration. Form CA, a downloadable form that you can fill out on your computer and print out, is available for this purpose.

Supplemental registration is appropriate for both trivial mistakes and more serious errors, such as:

- The author's name was misspelled.
- The author's birth date was incorrect.
- The title of the work has changed since the original registration.
- The owner's address has changed.
- An unpublished work was registered as published.
- The author or copyright claimant was misidentified, omitted, or has a changed name (not because of a transfer).
- Some aspect of the application information needs clarification.

The first three of these situations are trivial and need not be changed for the copyright to remain valid. An address change need not be noted for legal purposes, but an accurate address will obviously enable potential licensees and transferees to locate the copyright owner. The other errors, and the need to correct them, are more important, because they affect both the validity of the copyright and the owner's ability to vindicate his or her rights in court.

Related terms: single registration rule.

Tasini

See *New York Times v. Tasini.*

temporary restraining order (TRO)

See infringement action; injunctions.

termination of transfers

For works published after January 1, 1978, any exclusive copyright right that has been transferred by the author—for example, the author had assigned or licensed the rights to a publisher—may be terminated by the author, the author's surviving spouse, or the author's children or grandchildren, provided that the termination occurs after 35 years from publication of the work or 40 years after the transfer is made, whichever comes first. However, the termination must occur within five years of the date the author or heirs become eligible to do so, or the right to terminate is lost forever. This termination right does not apply to works made for hire.

> **EXAMPLE:** Bill composes a song and grants the rights to record and market the song to Ecotopia Enterprises. The transfer takes effect January 1, 1995. When first published in January 1996, the song becomes a classic, continuously recorded by a succession of artists. In 2031, Bill will have the right to terminate the "grant of rights" and recapture full ownership of the copyright. However, if Bill fails to exercise this option to terminate by 2036, he will lose it.

Although all copyright transfers after 1977 may be terminated through this process, any derivative works that have been legally prepared in the meantime will continue to belong to their authors, rather than reverting to the original copyright owner. For instance, if under a broad grant of rights from Bill (which included the right to use the song for all legal purposes) Ecotopia had prepared and marketed a television series based on the song, all rights to the television series will remain with Ecotopia or anyone to whom it transferred the series.

Related terms: exclusive license; licensing of copyrights.

thin copyright

When a work features a limited number of original features, the copyright is said to be "thin," and the owner can only stop others from copying those original features, not other unprotectable elements. For example, in one case, a California glass artist created glass-in-glass jellyfish sculptures. The works were successful—

some sold for hundreds of thousands of dollars—and another glass artist who saw them began making similar works. The California glass artist sued, but a court ruled against him, stating that he could not prevent others from depicting the natural shape of jellyfish, their naturally bright colors, or their vertical-swimming appearance. Nor could the artist prevent others from portraying jellyfish in glass. On that basis, the artist had a thin copyright and could only prevent near-exact duplications of his work. (*Satava v. Lowry,* 323 F.3d 805 (9th Cir. 2003).) A similar determination was made in a case in which a photographer of a vodka bottle claimed infringement when the vodka company used similar lighting and setting to create a similar photograph. (*Ets-Hokin v. Skyy Spirits,* 323 F.3d 763 (9th Cir. 2003).)

timely registration

To obtain all the benefits of registration, a work must be registered with the U.S. Copyright Office within certain time limits. Timely registration entitles a copyright owner to statutory damages and attorney fees in an infringement suit, which may make affordable a suit that is otherwise prohibitively expensive and risky.

For a published work, timely registration must occur within three months of first publication or before the infringement begins. For unpublished works, registration is timely as long as it occurs before the infringement begins.

Copyright owners must register their work prior to suing for infringement under the provisions of 17 USC § 411(a). However, the Fifth, Seventh, and Ninth Circuits have interpreted this to mean that a lawsuit can proceed if an application has been filed, provided that a registration eventually issues. The Tenth and Eleventh Circuits have held to a stricter requirement and require a Certificate of Registration.

Related terms: copyright; registration.

Trade Related Aspects of Intellectual Property Rights (TRIPS)

See GATT (General Agreement on Tariffs and Trade).

transfers of copyright ownership

According to the Copyright Act, a transfer of copyright ownership is any grant of an exclusive right, or an assignment, mortgage, exclusive license, or any other conveyance of a copyright or of any of the exclusive rights constituting a copyright. A transfer does not include a nonexclusive license.

Because a copyright consists of a bundle of rights that can be divided, a transfer can involve the entire copyright or only a portion of it. For example, a grant of rights may be limited by time, geography, or media. The right to make copies of an original work, the right to sell the work, the right to display the work, and the right to make derivative works of the work are also separate transferable rights.

EXAMPLE: Ruth writes a book called *Nurse Ruth*. She registers the copyright with the U.S. Copyright Office and lists herself as the owner. Although Ruth could publish and market the book herself, more likely she will let others do the job for her. For example, she might execute a written license giving Able Publishers the exclusive right to sell, display, and make copies of the book. She may also transfer some or all of the remaining rights (for instance, film, radio and TV, and magazine) to Able, or she can choose to transfer some of them to others, retaining for herself only a few or perhaps only the exclusive right to make derivative works.

In fact, an almost infinite number of transfers can occur for a copyrighted work. The only prerequisites for a transfer of ownership are that:

- The transfer must be in writing.
- The transfer must be signed by the owner.
- The right that is transferred must be an exclusive grant.

EXAMPLE 1: Ruth retains at least one of the exclusive copyright rights in the book *Nurse Ruth*, so she remains the owner of the "copyright" as far as the U.S. Copyright Office is concerned and continues to have her name on the notice of copyright. Although Able Publishers may own a number (but not all) of the rights and is considered a legal copyright owner, it owns only the exclusive rights transferred in the license and is not named as owner in the U.S. Copyright Office or on the notice of copyright.

EXAMPLE 2: Ruth decides to transfer all of her copyright rights in *Nurse Ruth* to Able Publishers (including the right to make derivative works). Able is the new "owner" in the U.S. Copyright Office and on the copyright notice. On the other hand, if Ruth transfers all rights to Able except the derivative works, which she transfers to someone else (her sister Edna, perhaps), Ruth will still be the "owner," even though she has transferred all her rights to other people. This is because the U.S. Copyright Office considers the original owner to remain the owner unless all of the copyright rights are transferred together to a single person or entity.

Copyright Law: Definitions

Although transfers can be valid without being recorded with the U.S. Copyright Office, it is better practice to record them. This record will serve as evidence in case of an argument about the scope of the rights granted. Also, the date of recordation helps determine which transfer prevails in case of overlapping transfers.

Copyright Act: § 201. Ownership of copyright
(d) Transfer of Ownership.—
   (1) The ownership of a copyright may be transferred in whole or in part by any means of conveyance or by operation of law, and may be bequeathed by will or pass as personal property by the applicable laws of intestate succession.
   (2) Any of the exclusive rights comprised in a copyright, including any subdivision of any of the rights specified by section 106, may be transferred as provided by clause (1) and owned separately. The owner of any particular exclusive right is entitled, to the extent of that right, to all of the protection and remedies accorded to the copyright owner by this title.
(e) Involuntary Transfer.—When an individual author's ownership of a copyright, or of any of the exclusive rights under a copyright, has not previously been transferred voluntarily by that individual author, no action by any governmental body or other official or organization purporting to seize, expropriate, transfer, or exercise rights of ownership with respect to the copyright, or any of the exclusive rights under a copyright, shall be given effect under this title, except as provided under title 11.

Copyright Act: § 204. Execution of transfers of copyright ownership
This statute sets out the requirements for transfers of copyright ownership (assignments).
(a) A transfer of copyright ownership, other than by operation of law, is not valid unless an instrument of conveyance, or a note or memorandum of the transfer, is in writing and signed by the owner of the rights conveyed or such owner's duly authorized agent.
(b) A certificate of acknowledgement is not required for the validity of a transfer, but is prima facie evidence of the execution of the transfer if—
   (1) in the case of a transfer executed in the United States, the certificate is issued by a person authorized to administer oaths within the United States; or
   (2) in the case of a transfer executed in a foreign country, the certificate is issued by a diplomatic or consular officer of the United States, or by a person authorized to administer oaths whose authority is proved by a certificate of such an officer.

Related terms: overlapping transfers of copyright; recordation of copyright transfers; termination of transfer.

translation rights
See compulsory license; derivative work.

UCITA

The Uniform Computer Information Transaction Act (UCITA) was drafted by an organization of law professors, judges, and attorneys in an attempt to create uniformity in the way in which courts treat software licenses. The Act legitimizes software licenses, making them fully enforceable, including those licenses that prevent reverse engineering of computer code. The UCITA has been adopted in different forms in only two states, Virginia and Maryland. The Act has been met with considerable opposition and has generated controversy in the software and Internet community. (In 2003, the American Bar Association refused to endorse it.)

Related terms: end-user license (aka EULA, shrinkwrap, or clickwrap agreement).

Universal Copyright Convention (U.C.C.)

This is an international copyright treaty that offers national treatment to any work first published in a U.C.C. member country or by a national of any U.C.C. country. In addition, it limits the formalities that a U.C.C. country may require to confer copyright protection. A member country may require only that the work carry this notice of copyright: "© (year of first publication) (name of the author)."

The U.C.C. also requires that each member country offer a minimum copyright duration of at least the life of the author plus 25 years. With one exception, each author is also given the exclusive right to translate his or her own work. If, however, the work is imported to another U.C.C. treaty country and not translated within seven years of the work's original publication, the government of that country may authorize a translation into that country's language under a compulsory licensing system (along with payment of a fair fee).

Although the U.C.C. continues to have some importance in areas not covered by the Berne Convention, the Berne Convention is normally the governing international treaty, especially because the GATT treaty provides that all of its signatories agree to be bound by the Berne Convention.

Related terms: Berne Convention; GATT (General Agreement on Tariffs and Trade); international copyright protection.

unpublished work

An original work of authorship that is fixed in a tangible medium of expression but has not yet been made available to the general public without restriction is considered to be an unpublished work and automatically qualifies for copyright protection. Displaying a work—for example, exhibiting a painting in a gallery—or distributing a work with restrictions on disclosure—for example, distributing

Copyright Law: Definitions

galleys of a book under the terms of a nondisclosure agreement—are also not considered publications.

Unpublished works may be registered with the U.S. Copyright Office, but the more common practice is to wait until a work is published before registering. If the registration occurs before an infringement of the unpublished works begins, the copyright owner may recover statutory damages and possibly attorneys' fees.

All unpublished works created by authors who died 70 or more years ago are now in the public domain in the United States. This is so whether the author was American or a non-American. Unpublished works made for hire created more than 120 years ago are also in the U.S. public domain. Unpublished works that were created after 1977 that are works made for hire are protected for 120 years.

Note: It is more difficult for an infringer to claim fair use when the infringed work is unpublished because the infringing publication deprives its copyright owner of the right to determine its publication date.

Copyright Act: § 201. Ownership of copyright

(d) Transfer of Ownership.—

   (1) The ownership of a copyright may be transferred in whole or in part by any means of conveyance or by operation of law, and may be bequeathed by will or pass as personal property by the applicable laws of intestate succession.

   (2) Any of the exclusive rights comprised in a copyright, including any subdivision of any of the rights specified by section 106, may be transferred as provided by clause (1) and owned separately. The owner of any particular exclusive right is entitled, to the extent of that right, to all of the protection and remedies accorded to the copyright owner by this title.

(e) Involuntary Transfer.—When an individual author's ownership of a copyright, or of any of the exclusive rights under a copyright, has not previously been transferred voluntarily by that individual author, no action by any governmental body or other official or organization purporting to seize, expropriate, transfer, or exercise rights of ownership with respect to the copyright, or any of the exclusive rights under a copyright, shall be given effect under this title, except as provided under title 11.2

Related terms: fair use; published work; registration of copyright.

useful article

See pictorial, graphic, and sculptural works.

U.S. Copyright Office

Established by Congress, the U.S. Copyright Office—a branch of the Library of Congress—oversees the implementation of the federal copyright laws. It issues regulations, processes applications for registration of copyrights, and accepts and (for some types of works) stores deposits made in connection with registration. The U.S. Copyright Office also issues opinions on whether certain types of items are subject to copyright protection.

The U.S. Copyright Office has a website (www.copyright.gov) where you can download forms and find a great deal of useful copyright information.

The mailing address for the U.S. Copyright Office is:

Register of Copyrights
U.S. Copyright Office
101 Independence Avenue, SE
Washington, DC 20559-6000

version

See derivative work; single registration rule.

visual artists' rights

See work of visual art.

webcasting

Webcasting is the digital audio transmission of music over the Internet. There are various types of webcasting systems: interactive sites (in which the listener requests music), passive sites (in which the station chooses the play lists), subscription sites (in which listeners pay a fee), and nonsubscription sites. Webcasters can also include terrestrial stations—commercial and noncommercial AM and FM radio stations— that simulcast musical programming over the Internet.

The Copyright Arbitration Royalty Panel ("CARP") recommends rates and terms for the statutory license for eligible nonsubscription services. Under CARP guidelines, in order for these services to play recordings (including simultaneous Internet retransmissions of over-the-air AM or FM radio broadcasts), a webcaster must pay a royalty of 7 cents per song played. Simulcasts of noncommercial radio stations (AM or FM) incur a 2-cents-per-song royalty.

In 2002, the Copyright Office announced an agreement between rival webcasting groups that set rates for small commercial webcasters. Small commercial webcasters—those that meet the eligibility requirements established in 17 United States Code, Sections 112 and 114—may operate under rates and terms set forth in the negotiated agreement, or they may operate under the rules previously established by the Copyright Office.

Unhappy with rates established by Congress in 2007, webcasters sought to modify the arrangement for payment of royalties with the digital music industry's licensing agent, SoundExchange. Two agreements were made—the Webcaster Settlement Act of 2008 and the Webcaster Settlement Act of 2009—that gave an alternative set of rates to pureplay webcasters—Internet broadcasters whose primary business is streaming audio, for example Pandora.com and Lala.com.

website

A website is a collection of pages or documents, stored on a server, and accessible and viewable over the Internet. A website is usually written in a computer language known as HTML and is accessed by typing in a domain name such as www.nolo.com. Although the website is written in computer code, it incorporates, displays, and performs many media, including text, photography, music, animation, sound, artwork, and movies. All of these media may contain copyrightable expressions. To that extent, the website's creator must obtain permission to use these media. The unauthorized use of these materials is an infringement unless permitted as a fair use.

In turn, a website or Web page is protected under copyright law and may be registered with the Copyright Office. The procedure for registration is established in Copyright Circular 66, which is available at the Copyright Office website (www.copyright.gov). Copyright protection for a website does not extend to the layout or "look and feel" or design of the site. In other words, the website's style cannot be protected under copyright law. But it is possible that the style or style features may be protected as trade dress under trademark laws.

Related terms: caching; DMCA; Internet, copyright regulation of.

work made for hire

For purposes of the Copyright Act, a work made for hire is:
- a work created by an employee within the scope of employment, or
- certain works specified in the Copyright Act (see below) created by an independent author under a written contract specifying that the project is a work made for hire.

Copyright of a work made for hire belongs either to the party who commissioned it or the party who employed the creator, not the party who created it.

Works made for hire most typically result when an employee authors an article, computer program, or other original work of authorship within the scope of employment. "Within the scope of employment" means that it is the kind of work the employee is paid to perform, it is prepared substantially within work hours at the workplace, and it is prepared, at least in part, to serve the employer.

Unless an employer and employee agree otherwise, anything an employee creates outside the scope of employment is not a work made for hire. This is so even if the work arises out of the employee's activities on the employer's behalf.

EXAMPLE: Ned uses company time to write a training manual for his employer. The employer owns the copyright in the manual as a work made for hire. By contrast, if Ned used his own time to write the manual, Ned would own the copyright, even though the manual's main purpose was to help Ned's employer.

Who is an employee for purposes of the work-made-for-hire rule? If a court determines that an employment relationship exists, even if the author is not technically employed, the work-made-for-hire rule treats the author as an employee for the purpose of determining copyright ownership. The courts examine 11 factors to decide whether an employment relationship exists. All of the factors address who has the right to control the manner and means by which the work is created. These factors are:

1. the skill required to do the work
2. the source of tools and materials used to create the work
3. the duration of the relationship
4. whether the commissioning person has the right to assign additional projects to the creative party
5. who determines when and how long the creative party works
6. the method of payment
7. who decides which assistants will be hired and who pays them
8. whether the work is in the ordinary line of business of the person who commissions it
9. whether the creative party has his/her own business
10. whether the creative party receives employee benefits from the commissioning person, and
11. the tax treatment of the creative party.

If there is no employment relationship, a work will still be considered a work made for hire if both parties sign a written work-for-hire agreement and the work fits within one of the following nine categories of works (17 USC § 101):

1. a work specially ordered or commissioned for use as a contribution to a collective work

2. a part of a motion picture or other audiovisual work, such as a screenplay

3. a translation

4. a supplementary work

5. a compilation

6. an instructional text

7. a test or answer material for a test

8. an atlas, or

9. a sound recording.

EXAMPLE: Nolo plans to publish a series of educational texts on copyright, trademark, and patent law. They hire Charles, an author who is not employed by Nolo, to write the books. For Nolo to own copyright as a work made for hire, Charles will have to sign a work-made-for-hire agreement and the resulting texts must fall within one of the enumerated work-made-for-hire categories. It's possible that the texts may qualify as "instructional texts," but only if they are intended to be used in day-to-day teaching activities. If the texts do not fall within one of the enumerated categories, the works will not be works made for hire even though a work-made-for-hire agreement has been signed. In that event, the only other method by which Nolo could acquire copyright ownership is to require Charles to assign his rights under his publishing agreement.

The duration of copyrights on works for hire is different from that on copyrights for author-owners. A copyright on a work made for hire lasts for the shorter of 75 years from the date of publication or 120 years from the date of creation in the case of unpublished works.

Copyright Act: § 101. Definitions

A "work made for hire" is—

(1) a work prepared by an employee within the scope of his or her employment; or

(2) a work specially ordered or commissioned for use as a contribution to a collective work, as a part of a motion picture or other audiovisual work, as a translation, as a supplementary work, as a compilation, as an instructional text, as a test, as answer material for a test, or as an atlas, if the parties expressly agree in a written instrument signed by them that the work shall be considered a work made for hire. For the purpose of the foregoing sentence, a "supplementary work" is a work prepared for publication as a secondary adjunct to a work by another author for the purpose of introducing, concluding, illustrating, explaining, revising, commenting upon, or assisting in the use of the other work, such as forewords, afterwords, pictorial illustrations, maps, charts,

tables, editorial notes, musical arrangements, answer material for tests, bibliographies, appendixes, and indexes, and an "instructional text" is a literary, pictorial, or graphic work prepared for publication and with the purpose of use in systematic instructional activities.

In determining whether any work is eligible to be considered a work made for hire under paragraph (2), neither the amendment contained in section 1011(d) of the Intellectual Property and Communications Omnibus Reform Act of 1999, as enacted by section 1000(a)(9) of Public Law 106–113, nor the deletion of the words added by that amendment—

(A) shall be considered or otherwise given any legal significance, or

(B) shall be interpreted to indicate congressional approval or disapproval of, or acquiescence in, any judicial determination, by the courts or the Copyright Office. Paragraph (2) shall be interpreted as if both section 2(a)(1) of the Work Made For Hire and Copyright Corrections Act of 2000 and section 1011(d) of the Intellectual Property and Communications Omnibus Reform Act of 1999, as enacted by section 1000(a)(9) of Public Law 106–113, were never enacted, and without regard to any inaction or awareness by the Congress at any time of any judicial determinations.

The terms "WTO Agreement" and "WTO member country" have the meanings given those terms in paragraphs (9) and (10), respectively, of section 2 of the Uruguay Round Agreements Act.

Related terms: copyright; duration of copyrights.

work of the U.S. government

All works prepared by an officer or employee of the U.S. government as part of that person's official duties are considered part of the public domain and are not entitled to copyright protection. This rule does not apply to state or local governmental employees.

Copyright Act: § 101. Definitions

A "work of the United States Government" is a work prepared by an officer or employee of the United States Government as part of that person's official duties.

Related terms: public domain—copyright context.

work of visual art

All art works (photos, paintings, and so on) are protected under copyright. But certain visual art that is produced in a single copy or limited edition of 200 copies or fewer signed and numbered copies receives special protection under an amendment to the Copyright Act known as the Visual Artists Rights Act (VARA). (17 USC § 106A.)

VARA amends the Copyright Act by defining a "work of visual art" as: (1) a painting, drawing, print, or sculpture, existing in a single copy, in a limited edition of 200 copies or fewer that are signed and consecutively numbered by the author, or, in the case of a sculpture, in multiple cast, carved, or fabricated sculptures of 200 or fewer that are consecutively numbered by the author and bear the signature or other identifying mark of the author; or (2) a still photographic image produced for exhibition purposes only, existing in a single copy that is signed by the author, or in a limited edition of 200 copies or fewer that are signed and consecutively numbered by the author.

VARA incorporates certain rules developed in Europe to protect the moral rights of artists. European law grants certain rights to artists based upon moral principles. For example, the creator of a work of fine art (or the artist's heirs) can share in subsequent sales of the work and can prevent the destruction or mutilation of a work. Under these principles, known as *droit de moral*, the artist's rights continue after the sale of the art. An unknown artist who sold a work inexpensively could share in revenues if the work later appreciated in value.

The United States refused to recognize moral rights for most of the 20th century. However, in order to join in an international treaty known as the Berne Convention, Congress amended the Copyright Act in 1990 to include VARA. VARA incorporates two of the features of European *droit de moral*: attribution and integrity. Attribution is the right to claim or disclaim authorship of a work. That is, the artist has a right to demand that credit be given or that credit be removed from an artwork. The right of integrity is the right to prevent distortion, mutilation, or other modification of the work. These rights are independent of the other rights granted under copyright law.

What's Protected and What's Not Protected by VARA	
Protected by VARA	**Not Protected by VARA**
A limited edition of 20 copies of a silkscreen, numbered and signed by the artist.	A silkscreen image reprinted on 1,000 posters.
A sculpture of Noah's ark.	Miniature replicas of Noah's ark sold by a mail-order company.

What happens if an oil painting is reproduced in a museum booklet or in a magazine review? Does that mass production remove the work from VARA status? No; the artist could still exert VARA rights over the oil painting. However, the artist could not prevent destruction or mutilation of the reprints in the booklet, because these would not be covered by VARA, although they would still be covered under normal copyright principles.

Under Section 106A, the creator of a work of visual arts can prevent the "intentional distortion, mutilation, or other modification of that work which would be prejudicial to his or her honor or reputation." This is the most powerful right granted under the VARA provisions. For example, if a collector buys a limited edition photograph (that is, fewer than 200 prints were made), the collector cannot destroy it without permission from the artist. If the work is destroyed, the artist can sue under VARA and recover damages.

The rule regarding destruction does not apply if: (1) the work was created prior to enactment of the VARA provisions on December 1, 1990; (2) the artist specifically waives the rights in a written statement signed by the artist and owner of the artwork; or (3) the destruction or modification results from the passage of time or because of the materials used to construct the work. For example, certain works such as ice sculptures and sand sculptures self-destruct, and the owner would have no obligation to affirmatively prevent such destruction.

Under certain circumstances, the person who employs an artist or commissions artwork acquires copyright ownership. This principle is known as work made for hire. If artwork is created as work made for hire, there are no VARA rights. That is, although normal copyright law applies to the work, neither the artist nor the person commissioning the work can claim rights of integrity or attribution under VARA.

The rights granted under VARA—attribution and integrity—are not transferable. Only the artist can exert these rights. Although copyright protection normally lasts for the life of the author plus 70 years, the rights granted under VARA last only for the life of the artist. That is, once the artist has died, the work can be destroyed under VARA without the destroyer seeking consent from the artist's estate.

Keep in mind as well that, as one court put it, "Not every artist has rights under VARA, and not everything called 'art' is protected by such rights." When an artist attempted to claim rights under VARA for a political banner commissioned by an advocacy group, a court noted that Congress has specifically excluded advertising and promotional materials, and that the banner, even though it involved political advertising, was within this exemption. (*Pollara v. Seymour,* 344 F.3d 265 (2d Cir. 2003).)

Copyright Law: Definitions

At least one court has ruled that in order for VARA to apply, the work at issue must have more than "artistic merit" or "some level of local notoriety"; it must be of "recognized stature" as an artistic work. In that case, the court permitted unauthorized dismantling of a 6,000-pound swan sculpture, (*Scott v. Dixon*, 309 F. Supp. 2d 395 (E.D. N.Y. 2004).)

Unfinished artwork is also protected by VARA. A Swiss artist, unhappy with the manner in which his art was being installed in a museum, sued under the Visual Artists Rights Act (VARA). The First Circuit determined that VARA was intended to protect the integrity of works of art, even those that are not completed. (*Massachusetts Museum of Contemporary Art Foundation, Inc. v. Buchel*, 593 F.3d 38 (1st Cir. 2010).)

Some states, such as California, have passed more comprehensive statutes regarding art preservation and resale. Under the California statute (California Civil Code Sections 986–989), for example, an artist is entitled to 5% of the resale of a work of fine art. These rights survive for 20 years after the death of the artist. New York and eight other states also have laws that grant certain rights to artists.

Copyright Act: § 101. Definitions

A "work of visual art" is—

(1) a painting, drawing, print, or sculpture, existing in a single copy, in a limited edition of 200 copies or fewer that are signed and consecutively numbered by the author, or, in the case of a sculpture, in multiple cast, carved, or fabricated sculptures of 200 or fewer that are consecutively numbered by the author and bear the signature or other identifying mark of the author; or

(2) a still photographic image produced for exhibition purposes only, existing in a single copy that is signed by the author, or in a limited edition of 200 copies or fewer that are signed and consecutively numbered by the author.

A work of visual art does not include—

(A) (i) any poster, map, globe, chart, technical drawing, diagram, model, applied art, motion picture or other audiovisual work, book, magazine, newspaper, periodical, data base, electronic information service, electronic publication, or similar publication;

(ii) any merchandising item or advertising, promotional, descriptive, covering, or packaging material or container;

(iii) any portion or part of any item described in clause (i) or (ii);

(B) any work made for hire; or

(C) any work not subject to copyright protection under this title.

Copyright Act: § 106A. Rights of certain authors to attribution and integrity

(a) **Rights of Attribution and Integrity.**—Subject to section 107 and independent of the exclusive rights provided in section 106, the author of a work of visual art—

   (1) shall have the right—

      (A) to claim authorship of that work, and

      (B) to prevent the use of his or her name as the author of any work of visual art which he or she did not create;

   (2) shall have the right to prevent the use of his or her name as the author of the work of visual art in the event of a distortion, mutilation, or other modification of the work which would be prejudicial to his or her honor or reputation; and

   (3) subject to the limitations set forth in section 113 (d), shall have the right—

      (A) to prevent any intentional distortion, mutilation, or other modification of that work which would be prejudicial to his or her honor or reputation, and any intentional distortion, mutilation, or modification of that work is a violation of that right, and

      (B) to prevent any destruction of a work of recognized stature, and any intentional or grossly negligent destruction of that work is a violation of that right.

(b) **Scope and Exercise of Rights.**—Only the author of a work of visual art has the rights conferred by subsection (a) in that work, whether or not the author is the copyright owner. The authors of a joint work of visual art are coowners of the rights conferred by subsection (a) in that work.

(c) **Exceptions.**—(1) The modification of a work of visual art which is a result of the passage of time or the inherent nature of the materials is not a distortion, mutilation, or other modification described in subsection (a)(3)(A).

   (2) The modification of a work of visual art which is the result of conservation, or of the public presentation, including lighting and placement, of the work is not a destruction, distortion, mutilation, or other modification described in subsection (a)(3) unless the modification is caused by gross negligence.

   (3) The rights described in paragraphs (1) and (2) of subsection (a) shall not apply to any reproduction, depiction, portrayal, or other use of a work in, upon, or in any connection with any item described in subparagraph (A) or (B) of the definition of "work of visual art" in section 101, and any such reproduction, depiction, portrayal, or other use of a work is not a destruction, distortion, mutilation, or other modification described in paragraph (3) of subsection (a).

Related terms: Copyright Act of 1976; work made for hire.

World Trade Organization (WTO)

See GATT (General Agreement on Tariffs and Trade).

Copyright Law: Forms

Preparing a Copyright Application

There are three ways to file a copyright application:
- file the all-purpose Form CO (unveiled in 2008), which can be used for any literary work, visual arts work, performing arts work, motion picture or other audiovisual work, sound recording, or single serial-issue type of work
- file online (using the Copyright Office's electronic eCO system), or
- file a traditional printed copyright form (Forms PA, TX, VA, SR, etc.), each of which is specific to the type of work (for example, Form TX is only for text works).

Which is right for you?

- If you want to use paper and are eager to obtain your registration, use Form CO because it will be processed faster than the traditional print application due to the incorporated 2-D bar code technology.
- If you're comfortable with electronic filing—that is, preparing and filling out forms online—the eCO system is less expensive ($35 instead of $50 for Form CO, or $65 for Forms VA, TX, PA, and SR) than using paper forms, and will likely result in faster turnaround.
- If you are used to the traditional application or feel more comfortable using a form that is specific to your type of work, use the familiar forms (Forms VA, TX, PA, SE, or SR) and pay a higher fee ($65 per application).

On the following pages, examples of the various copyright application forms are provided, along with a few screenshots from the electronic filing procedure. Regardless of which type of application is used, the information required for an application is the same. The primary differences in the three types of applications are how and in what order the information is collected.

The Copyright Office provides extensive help for the application process. There are downloadable circulars that explain registration procedures for every type of work—for example, the Copyright Office provides advice on registering comic books, software, songs, websites, and much more. The eCO electronic system is also heavily documented with online guidance. For example, the Copyright Office website offers a *PowerPoint* presentation, FAQs, and more. All of this can be found at www.copyright.gov. Click "Circulars and Brochures" for advice on filing. Click "Forms" to access copyright application forms. An explanation for each of the three primary methods of filing is provided below. Note, the fees for each application may have changed. Check with the Copyright Office for current fees.

Preparing a Form CO Copyright Application

The all-purpose Form CO can be used for any literary work, visual arts work, performing arts work, motion picture (or other audiovisual work), sound recording, or single serial-issue type of work. Form CO may be downloaded from the Copyright Office website. The download is in PDF format (the Adobe Acrobat format) and each downloadable application form is considered "fillable," meaning that you can type information directly into the form visible on your screen. Although you can print the completed form, you can't save the data. So, once you close the PDF form (or turn off your computer), you'll lose any information you typed into the form.

After you print out the form, do not alter it by hand. That's because the information used by the Copyright Office is primarily stored in the barcodes on the form. If you want to register a series of similar works, keep the form open after you print it, then make the necessary changes and print the subsequent version, as well.

Single- or double-sided printing of Form CO is acceptable. As with other forms, use a laser printer, when possible. Laser copies are preferable over ink-jet printer copies (which sometimes require enlarging). Dot-matrix printer copies are not acceptable.

Once you complete the form, you must mail the completed application, your $50 fee (payable to the Register of Copyrights), and your deposit materials (two copies if the work is published; one if it is unpublished). Send all three elements in the same envelope or package to:

> Library of Congress
> Copyright Office
> 101 Independence Avenue, SE
> Washington, DC 20559-****

To speed your claim, in place of ****, use the following:

> Literary work—6222
> Visual arts work—6211

Performing arts work—6233

Motion picture/AV work—6238

Sound recording—6237

Serial-issue—6226

Below are instructions for completing Form CO. Much of this information is taken verbatim from the instructions provided by the Copyright Office.

Section 1—Work Being Registered

Note: * indicates a required field, ** indicates required alternate fields (one of two fields required).

1a.* Type of work being registered. Check the appropriate box for the type of work—literary work, visual arts work, performing arts work, motion picture (or other audiovisual work), sound recording, or single serial-issue type of work. If your work contains more than one type of authorship, choose the type for the predominant authorship in the work.

1b.* Title of work. Enter the title. Give the complete title exactly as it appears on the copy. If there is no title on the copy, give an identifying phrase to serve as the title, or state "untitled." Use standard title capitalization without quotation marks; for example, Retire Happy. If you want to include additional title(s)—for example, titles of individual works in an unpublished collection or works owned by the same claimant—click the "additional title" button.

1c. Serial-issue. A serial is a work issued or intended to be issued in successive parts bearing numerical or chronological designations, and intended to be continued indefinitely. The classification "serial" includes periodicals, newspapers, magazines, bulletins, newsletters, annuals, journals, proceedings of societies, and other similar works. Enter the ISSN (International Standard Serial Number) without dashes. The Copyright Office does not assign these numbers. For information on obtaining an ISSN, go to www.loc.gov/issn.

1d. Previous or alternative title. If the work is known by another title, give that title here.

1e.* Year of completion. Give the year in which creation of the work was completed—the date you stood back and said, "I'm done." If the work has been published, the year of completion cannot be later than the year of first publication.

1f. Date of publication. Give the complete date, in mm/dd/yyyy format, on which the work was first published. If you're unsure, write a date as close as reasonably possible. Do not give a date that is in the future. Leave this line blank if the work is unpublished. For an explanation of "publication," see the Definitions section of the Copyright Act of 1976 in the "Definitions" section of this part.

1g. ISBN. If an International Standard Book Number (ISBN) has been assigned to this work, provide it here, without dashes. The Copyright Office does not assign these numbers. For information on obtaining an ISBN, contact R.R. Bowker at www. bowker.com.

1h. Nation of publication. Give the nation where the work was first published. If the work was first published simultaneously in the United States and another country, you can list the United States. Leave this line blank if the work is unpublished.

1i. Published as a contribution in a larger work entitled: If this work has been published as part of a larger work—for example, it's one song from a CD, or an article from a magazine—enter the title of the larger work.

Section 2—Author Information

2a.** or 2b.** Personal name/Organization name. Complete either 2a or 2b, but not both. Generally, an individual is the author except in the case of a work made for hire. If you are the author, provide your name, unless you wish to be anonymous or pseudonymous (in which case, write Anonymous or Pseudonymous). Also provide your date of birth and nationality. Repeat this for anyone who coauthored your work. For an explanation of "coauthors," see the "Copyright Definitions" section of this book. (Generally, a coauthor is someone who, at the time the work was created, made a copyrightable contribution.)

Complete section 2B only if the work is made for hire, in which case the hiring party is the author. For an explanation of "work made for hire," see the "Definitions" section of this part of the book. Give the most complete form of the corporate or organizational name of the hiring party.

2c. Doing business as. In the event the author does business under a DBA (doing business as) provide the DBA here.

2d. Year of birth & 2e. Year of death. Give the year the author was born (and deceased, if applicable). The year of birth is optional but is very useful as a form of author identification because many authors have the same name. Your birth date will be made part of the online public Copyright records and cannot be removed later.

2f. Citizenship/domicile. Check the United States box if applicable, or, if the author is a citizen of another country, enter the name of this nation. Alternatively, identify the nation where the author is domiciled (resides permanently).

2g. Author's contribution. If this line is applicable, check only one box. For an explanation of "made for hire," "anonymous," and "pseudonymous," see the "Definitions" section of this part of the book. If you wish to remain anonymous and your name is given in line 2A, it will be made part of the online public records produced by the Copyright Office and accessible on the Internet. This information cannot be removed later from those public records.

2h.* This author created. Here you check the appropriate box (or boxes) that describes this author's contribution to this work. Give a brief statement on the line after "other" only if it is necessary to give a more specific description of the authorship, or if none of the check boxes apply. Examples of other authorship statements are choreography, musical arrangement, translation, dramatization, or fictionalization. The Copyright Office recommends against giving any of the following terms: idea, process, procedure, system, method of operation, concept, principle, discovery, title, or name.

For a single serial-issue, the preferred description of the authorship is typically "collective work." Give this statement at the "other" line. This indicates that the claim is in the collective work as a whole and may include text, editing, compilation, and contribution(s) in which copyright has been transferred to the claimant.

For sound recordings and musical works: Sound recordings and musical works are separate works. To register a claim in both, the copyright claimant(s)/owner(s) must be the same. This requirement generally means the author(s) must be the same. The author of a sound recording is the performer or producer, and the authorship is "sound recording/performance." The author of a musical work—a song, for example—is the composer or songwriter, and the authorship is "music" or "music" and "lyrics." See Circular 56a, *Copyright Registration of Musical Compositions and Sound Recordings*, for more information.

Section 3—Copyright Claimant Information

3a.** and 3b.** Personal name/Organization name. Again, as with Sections 2a and 2b, complete one or the other, but not both. The person or entity who owns the copyright—either the author, or the person or organization to which the copyright has been transferred by an author or other authorized copyright owner—is listed here.

3c. Doing business as. Complete this if the claimant is using a DBA.

3d. Address, email, and phone number. The claimant postal address will be made part of the online public Copyright records and cannot be removed later. However, the email address and phone number will not appear in the public record unless it is also included in section 5, Rights and Permissions Contact.

3e. Copyright ownership acquired by. If the claimant (the person claiming copyright ownership) is the author of the work, skip this line. Transfer information is required if the claimant is not an author but has obtained ownership of the copyright from the author or another owner. In that case, check the appropriate box to indicate how ownership was acquired. When you check "written agreement," that includes a transfer by assignment or by contract. "Will or inheritance" applies only if the person from whom copyright was transferred is deceased. If necessary, check "other" and give a brief statement indicating how copyright was transferred.

Section 4—Limitation of Copyright Claim

You do not need to complete this section unless the work contains or is based on previously registered or previously published material, material in the public domain, or material not owned by this copyright claimant. The purpose of section 4 is to exclude such material from the claim and identify the new material upon which the present claim is based.

4a. Material excluded from this claim. Check the appropriate box or boxes to exclude any previously registered or previously published material, material in the public domain, or material not owned by this claimant. For example, if you were registering the text for a novel but not the illustrations, you would check the "artwork" box to indicate you were excluding the art.

4b. Previous registration(s). If the work for which you are now seeking registration, or an earlier version of it, has been registered—for example, this is the second edition of your book—give the registration number and the year of registration. If there have been multiple registrations, you may give information regarding the last two. If you are registering the first published edition of a work that is identical to a previously registered unpublished version (contains no new material not already registered), check the "other" box in line 4a and state, "First publication of work registered as unpublished." In this case, skip line 4c.

4c. New material included in this claim. Check the appropriate box or boxes to identify the new material you are claiming in this registration. Give a brief statement on the line after "other" only if it is necessary to give a more specific description of the new material included in this claim or if none of the check boxes apply.

For example, if you are providing a new arrangement of a public domain song, you would check the "text" and "music" boxes in Section 4a and state "new arrangement" on the "Other" line in 4c. If you updated the text in a new edition of a book, you would check the "text" boxes in 4a and 4c. If you translated a French novel into English, you would check "text," in 4a and write "English translation" on the other line of 4c.

A "compilation" is a work formed by the collection and assembly of preexisting materials, or of data that are selected, coordinated, or arranged in such a way that the resulting work as a whole constitutes an original work of authorship. A claim in "compilation" does not include the material that has been compiled. If that material should also be included in the claim, check the appropriate additional boxes.

Section 5—Rights and Permissions Contact

Here is where Form CO differs from previous copyright applications. Form CO asks for a listing of the person to contact for permission to use the material. If this is the same as the first copyright claimant (see above), you can simply check the box and the information will be generated to complete this section. Again, all the information given in this section, including name, postal address, email address, and phone number, will be made part of the online records produced by the Copyright Office and cannot be removed later from those public records.

Section 6—Correspondence Contact*

This is the person the Copyright Office should contact with any questions about this application. If this is the same as the first copyright claimant or the rights and permissions contact, simply check the appropriate box. (Information given only in this space will not appear in the online public record.)

Section 7—Mail Certificate To

This is the person to whom the registration certificate should be mailed. If this is the same as the first copyright claimant, the rights and permissions contact, or the correspondence contact, simply check the appropriate box. (Information given only in this space will not appear in the online public record.)

Section 8—Certification

8a.* Handwritten signature. After you print out the completed application, be sure to sign it.

8b.* Printed name. Enter the name of the person who will sign the form.

8c.* Date signed. Choose "today's date" or "write date by hand." In the latter case, be sure to date the application by hand when you sign it. If your application gives a date of publication, do not certify using a date prior to the publication date.

8d. Deposit account number. Leave this line blank unless you have a Copyright Office deposit account and are charging the filing fee to that account.

8e. Applicant's internal tracking number. If you have an internal tracking number, enter it here.

Sample Form CO (page 1)

UNITED STATES COPYRIGHT OFFICE
Form CO · Application for Copyright Registration

APPLICATION FOR COPYRIGHT REGISTRATION   VA

* Designates Required Fields

1 WORK BEING REGISTERED

1a. * Type of work being registered *(Fill in one only)*

☐ Literary work   ☐ Performing arts work
☒ Visual arts work   ☐ Motion picture/audiovisual work
☐ Sound recording   ☐ Single serial issue

1b. * Title of this work *(one title per space)*

Hayden Dolls

ApplicationForCopyrightRegistration

WorkTitles

1c. For a serial issue: Volume [   ] Number [   ] Issue [   ] ISSN [   ]

Frequency of publication: [   ]

1d. Previous or alternative title

[   ]

1e. * Year of completion [2 | 0 | 0 | 9]

Publication *(If this work has not been published, skip to section 2)*

1f. Date of publication [03/07/2010] *(mm/dd/yyyy)*   **1g.** ISBN [   ]

1h. Nation of publication   ☒ United States ☐ Other

1i. Published as a contribution in a larger work entitled

[   ]

1j. If line 1i above names a serial issue   Volume [   ] Number [   ] Issue [   ]

On pages [   ]

1k. If work was preregistered   Number PRE-[| | | | | | | | | |]

Sample Form CO (page 2)

UNITED STATES COPYRIGHT OFFICE

Form CO · Application for Copyright Registration

For Office Use Only

WorkBeingRegistered

2 AUTHOR INFORMATION

2a. Personal name   * complete either 2a or 2b

First Name	Middle	Last
Margaret		Zimet

2b. Organization name

2c. Doing business as

2d. Year of birth   1 9 8 7   **2e.** Year of death

2f. * ☒ Citizenship   ☒ United States   ☐ Other
     ☐ Domicile

2g. Author's contribution: ☐ Made for hire   ☐ Anonymous
        ☐ Pseudonymous

Continuation of Author Information

2h. * This author created (*Fill in only the authorship that applies to this author*)

☐ Text/poetry	☐ Compilation	☐ Map/technical drawing	☐ Music
☐ Editing	☐ Sculpture	☐ Architectural work	☐ Lyrics
☐ Computer program	☐ Jewelry design	☐ Photography	☐ Motion picture/audiovisual
☐ Collective work	☐ 2-dimensional artwork	☐ Script/play/screenplay	☐ Sound recording/performance

Other: 3D cloth doll

For Office Use Only

AuthorInformation

Page 2 of 7

Copyright Law: Forms

Sample Form CO (page 3)

UNITED STATES COPYRIGHT OFFICE
Form CO · Application for Copyright Registration

3 COPYRIGHT CLAIMANT INFORMATION

Claimant   *complete either 3a or 3b* - If you do not know the address for a claimant, enter "not known" in the Street address and City fields.

3a. Personal name

First Name	Middle	Last
Margaret		Zimet

3b. Organization name

3c. Doing business as

3d. Street address *

950 Parker Street

Street address (line 2)

City *	State	ZIP / Postal code	Country
Berkeley	CA	94710	United States

Email	Phone number	
tz@nolo.com	510-555-1234	*(Add "+" and country code for foreign numbers)*

3e. If claimant is **not** an author, copyright ownership acquired by: ☐ Written agreement ☐ Will or inheritance ☐ Other

For Office Use Only

CopyrightClaimantInformation

4 LIMITATION OF COPYRIGHT CLAIM

Skip section 4 if this work is all new.

4a. Material excluded from this claim *(Material previously registered, previously published, or not owned by this claimant)*

☐ Text ☐ Artwork ☐ Music ☐ Sound recording/performance ☐ Motion picture/audiovisual

Other:

Page 3 of 7

Copyright Law: Forms

Sample Form CO (page 4)

UNITED STATES COPYRIGHT OFFICE
Form CO · Application for Copyright Registration

4b. Previous registration(s)   Number _____   Year ____

Number _____   Year ____

4c. New material included in this claim (*This work contains new, additional, or revised material*)

- ☐ Text
- ☐ Poetry
- ☐ Computer program
- ☐ Editing
- ☐ Compilation
- ☐ Sculpture
- ☐ Jewelry design
- ☐ 2-dimensional artwork
- ☐ Map/technical drawing
- ☐ Architectural work
- ☐ Photography
- ☐ Script/play/screenplay
- ☐ Music
- ☐ Lyrics
- ☐ Motion picture/audiovisual
- ☐ Sound recording/performance

Other: _____

For Office Use Only

LimitationOfCopyrightClaim

5 RIGHTS AND PERMISSIONS CONTACT

☒ Check if information below should be copied from the **first** copyright claimant

First Name: Margaret   Middle: Last: Zimet

Name of organization:

Street address: 950 Parker Street

Street address (line 2):

City: Berkeley   State: CA   ZIP / Postal code: 94710   Country: United States

Email: tz@nolo.com   Phone number: 510-555-1234   (*Add "+" and country code for foreign numbers*)

Copyright Law: Forms

Sample Form CO (page 5)

UNITED STATES COPYRIGHT OFFICE
Form CO · Application for Copyright Registration

For Office Use Only

RightsAndPermissionsContact

6 CORRESPONDENCE CONTACT

☒ Copy from **first** copyright claimant ☐ Copy from rights and permissions contact

First name *	Middle	Last *
Margaret		Zimet

Name of organization

Street address *
950 Parker Street
Street address (line 2)

City *	State	ZIP / Postal code	Country
Berkeley	CA	94710	United States

Email *	Daytime phone number	
mz@nolo.com	510-555-1234	*(Add "+" and country code for foreign numbers)*

For Office Use Only

CorrespondenceContact

7 MAIL CERTIFICATE TO:

* Complete either 7a, 7b, or both

☒ Copy from **first** copyright claimant ☐ Copy from rights and permissions contact ☐ Copy from correspondence contact

7a. First Name	Middle	Last
Margaret		Zimet

Page 5 of 7

Copyright Law: Forms

Sample Form CO (page 6)

UNITED STATES COPYRIGHT OFFICE
Form CO · Application for Copyright Registration

7b. Name of organization

7c. Street address *

950 Parker Street

Street address (line 2)

City *	State	ZIP / Postal code	Country
Berkeley	CA	94710	United States

For Office Use Only

MailCertificateTo

8 CERTIFICATION

17 U.S.C. § 506(e): Any person who knowingly makes a false representation of a material fact in the application for copyright registration provided for by section 409, or in any written statement filed in connection with the application, shall be fined not more than $2,500.

I certify that I am the author, copyright claimant, or owner of exclusive rights, or the authorized agent of the author, copyright claimant, or owner of exclusive rights, of this work, and that the information given in this application is correct to the best of my knowledge.

Sign Here

8a. Handwritten signature

Margaret Zimet   9/3/2010

8b. Printed name   **8c.** Date signed

8d. Deposit account number   Account holder

8e. Applicant's internal tracking number (optional)

Page 6 of 7

Preparing an Electronic (eCO) Copyright Application

The electronic copyright (eCO) application process has three parts. The applicant:

- completes the online interview
- pays the fee (payment can be made by credit/debit card, ACH, or by setting up a deposit account), and
- uploads or mails copies of the work. Unpublished works, works published only electronically, published works for which the deposit requirement is ID material, or published works for which there are special agreements required can be uploaded. All other works must be sent by U.S. Postal Service (USPS). You will be instructed to print out a shipping slip to be attached to the work for delivery by the USPS.

In order to use eCO, the user must disable pop-up blockers and third-party toolbars. As of October 2008, the eCO system works with Microsoft Internet Explorer 6.0 (and higher) and Netscape Navigator 7.02 (and higher). Firefox 2.0 users must adjust the Tabs setting to "New pages should be opened in: a new window." (The Safari browser is not currently certified for use with the eCO system.)

Need help? The Copyright Office has done a nice job of explaining the process and making it user-friendly. There is an excellent tutorial and set of FAQs to walk you through the electronic filing process. In addition, the eCO process is peppered with helpful drop-down menus, as well as hypertext links that provide pop-up explanations for each aspect of the application process. The explanations for paper forms provided earlier in this section should aid you in answering the online interview—for example, how to respond to questions regarding the nature of work, title, date of publication, etc.

You will also need to create a user account and password. The eCO system includes a special "Save for Later" feature that will preserve your work in the event you sign off and then sign on at a later time.

Below are some screenshots with explanations to give you an idea of how eCO functions.

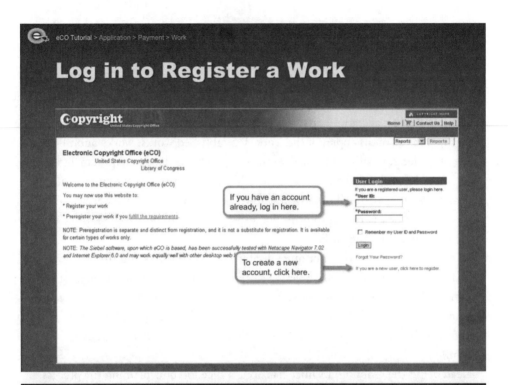

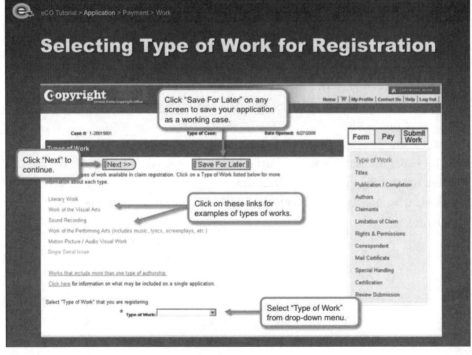

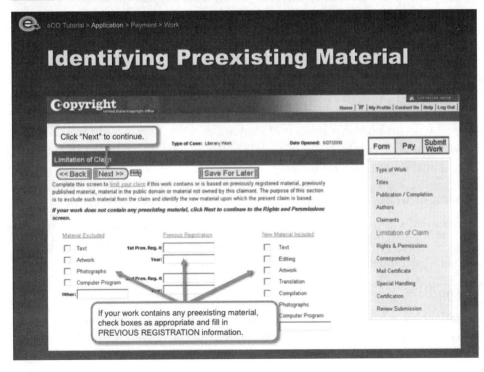

Preparing a Traditional Print Copyright Application

The traditional copyright application forms—Form TX, Form VA, Form PA, Form SE, and Form SR—can be downloaded from the Copyright Office website. The Forms are in PDF format (the Adobe Acrobat format) and each downloadable application form is considered "fillable," meaning that you can type information directly into the form visible on your screen. Although you can print the completed form, you can't save the data. So, once you turn off the computer or close the program, you'll lose any information you typed into the form. The fees for filing these print forms are currently $65 per application.

After you've completed the application, print the two pages of the form onto one sheet of paper printed head to head (top of page 2 is directly behind the top of page 1) using both sides of a single sheet. You must use either an ink-jet or laser printer (lasers are preferable). Forms printed by a dot matrix printer will not be accepted by the Copyright Office. Below are the basic requirements for completing these forms.

Title of the work

Space 1 requires that you provide the title and alternate or previous title of your work. The Copyright Office requires the title in order to index the work in its records. Nondescriptive titles such as "Work Without a Title" can be used. If you're registering a group of works, use a title that indicates it's a collection—for example, "12 Summer Stories." The alternate or previous title refers to any additional title under which someone searching for the registration might look.

Nature of Work

Space 1 of Form VA also requires information about the "nature of the work." Provide a brief description—for example, needlework, mosaic, jewelry design, fabric design, or three-dimensional sculpture.

Publication as a Contribution

If your work is textual and was first published as part of a serial publication or as part of a collective work—for example, your work first appeared in *Rosie* magazine—present the required information about the magazine.

The Author

Copyright law refers to you—the person who created the work—as "author." Provide your name in Space 2 unless you wish to be anonymous or pseudonymous.

Also provide your date of birth and nationality. Repeat this procedure in subsequent spaces for anyone who coauthored your work. A coauthor is someone who, at the time the work was created, made a copyrightable contribution.

Works Made for Hire

If you created this work by yourself, and you were neither commissioned to make it nor working for a business at the time, check "no" under the question, "Was this contribution to the work a work made for hire?" Otherwise, review the information about works made for hire in "Copyright Law: Overview" and "Copyright Law: Definitions."

Nature of Authorship

Generally, this means the extent of your authorship. For example, if you wrote a book, you would type "Entire Text" in Form TX. On Form VA, check the box that most closely describes your work, for example, 3-Dimensional Sculpture or Jewelry Design.

Creation and Publication

In Space 3, provide information about the dates of creation and first publication of the work. Your work was created on the day you completed it—the date you stood back and said, "I'm done." Give the full date (that is, month, day, and year) when the work was published. If you're unsure, it's okay to write "approximately" (for example, "approximately June 4, 2008").

The Copyright Claimant

In Space 4, provide information about the person claiming copyright—probably you or your business. Use your or your business's full legal name and address.

Transfer

If the person named as copyright claimant is not the same as the person in Space 2 (the "Author"), explain how the transfer from author to claimant occurred. For example, if you created the work but then transferred the rights in it to your corporation, you would write, "by written contract" or "by written assignment." (Don't attach the transfer documents. These should be recorded separately or at a later date with the Copyright Office.) The procedure for recording such documents is described in Circular 12, issued by the Copyright Office.

Copyright Law: Forms

Previous Registration

Here in Space 5, you must indicate any previous copyright registrations for this work or for earlier versions of the work. The Copyright Office is only concerned with whether this work or a previous version has been *registered*, not whether it's gained any other copyright protection. If it hasn't been registered, check the "No" box.

Basis for Seeking New Registration

If you checked the "Yes" box earlier in Space 5, then check the box that best describes why you're seeking a new registration—for example, if this is a changed version of the work, or if this the first application submitted by you as copyright claimant.

Previous Registration Number and Year of Registration

If this work was previously registered, indicate the registration—the number listed on the upper right-hand corner of the registration beginning with the letters VA, for example, VA-13-800.

Derivative Work or Compilation

In Space 6, you must determine whether the work you're registering is a derivative work or a compilation.

A derivative work is a modification of a previous work (regardless of whether the previous work was registered). For example, if you wrote a short story and then later used the same material and converted it to a novel, or you carved a wood block design, then created a second design adding additional flora, the second design would be a derivative.

A compilation is a collection of material—for example, a book titled *The 100 Greatest Essays on Dentistry*—in which someone assembled, selected, or organized the preexisting materials without transforming them. The author of a compilation seeks to protect the collection, not the individual works.

If you're registering a derivative work, complete 6a and 6b. If you are registering a compilation, complete 6b.

Deposit Accounts and Correspondence

If you have a deposit account—an account for applicants registering works on a regular basis—complete this section (Space 7). (It's usually not worth obtaining a deposit account unless you are registering hundreds of works.) Otherwise, skip this portion and provide your correspondence information so the examiner can contact you if any questions arise.

Certification

Check the Author box in Space 8 if you're filling out the form and if you are the person (or one of the persons) named in Space 2 of the application. In some circumstances, you may also prepare the application if you're someone other than the author. For example, the author may be deceased and you've been granted legal power to prepare the registration on behalf of the author's family.

Check Other Copyright Claimant if you're filling out the application and you're the copyright claimant in Space 4 (that is, you obtained your copyright ownership by purchasing or licensing it from the creator).

Check Owner of Exclusive Rights if you're filling out the application and you own a limited right—for example, the exclusive right to reproduce the work for a period of years—but you're not the author or the copyright claimant.

Check Authorized Agent if you're filling out the form as the authorized representative of the author, claimant, or owner of exclusive rights.

Signature

After you check the appropriate box in Space 8, type or print your name and date in Space 9 and sign it where marked. Bear in mind that by signing the application, you will be certifying to the Copyright Office that the information contained in the application is correct to the best of your knowledge. A "false representation of a material fact" in a copyright application may result in a fine of up to $2,500.

Mailing Information

After the application has been processed, it will be mailed back in a window envelope, and the space entitled "Mailing Information" will be your own address, showing through.

The Fee

A filing fee is required along with the application and deposit material. The fee is currently $35 per online application, $50 per Form CO, and $65 per paper application. But check the Copyright Office for current fee information before sending your application. You can pay by personal check, cashier's check, or money order, but don't send cash. If your checking account has insufficient funds, the

Copyright Office will not proceed with registration or will revoke the registration if it has already been issued.

Including Copies of Your Work With the Registration Application

You must include copies or images of your work with your application. As a general rule, one copy is deposited for unpublished works; two for published. If your work is three-dimensional, send two-dimensional "identifying material" such as photographs of your works. The photographs should clearly and accurately represent the work. If you've ever sent in jury photos of a work, you've already got a good idea of how to achieve this.

Sending Your Registration Application

If you are concerned about delays or that mail will be lost, you might want to send your parcel by U.S. Express Mail or some other overnight courier. This does not guarantee faster processing, but it does guarantee proof of receipt.

If you must have your application dealt with quickly after it reaches the Copyright Office, review the procedures for expediting copyright applications at the Copyright Office website.

Sample Form PA (front)

Copyright Office fees are subject to change.
For current fees, check the Copyright Office
website at www.copyright.gov, write the Copyright Office, or call (202) 707-3000.

Privacy Act Notice: Sections 408-410 of title 17 of the *United States Code* authorize the Copyright Office to collect the personally identifying information requested on this form in order to process the application for copyright registration. By providing this information you are agreeing to routine uses of the information that include publication to give legal notice of your copyright claim as required by 17 U.S.C. §705. It will appear in the Office's online catalog. If you do not provide the information requested, registration may be refused or delayed, and you may not be entitled to certain relief, remedies, and benefits under the copyright law.

Form PA
For a Work of Performing Arts
UNITED STATES COPYRIGHT OFFICE

REGISTRATION NUMBER

PA   PAU
EFFECTIVE DATE OF REGISTRATION

Month   Day   Year

DO NOT WRITE ABOVE THIS LINE. IF YOU NEED MORE SPACE, USE A SEPARATE CONTINUATION SHEET.

1 TITLE OF THIS WORK ▼
And Then You Die

PREVIOUS OR ALTERNATIVE TITLES ▼

NATURE OF THIS WORK ▼ See instructions
Screenplay

2
a NAME OF AUTHOR ▼
David Griffith

DATES OF BIRTH AND DEATH
Year Born ▼ 1935   Year Died ▼

Was this contribution to the work a "work made for hire"?
☐ Yes
☒ No

AUTHOR'S NATIONALITY OR DOMICILE
Name of Country
OR { Citizen of U.S.A
     Domiciled in

WAS THIS AUTHOR'S CONTRIBUTION TO THE WORK
Anonymous? ☐ Yes ☒ No
Pseudonymous? ☐ Yes ☒ No
If the answer to either of these questions is "Yes," see detailed instructions.

NOTE
Under the law, the "author" of a "work made for hire" is generally the employer, not the employee (see instructions). For any part of this work that was "made for hire" check "Yes" in the space provided, give the employer (or other person for whom the work was prepared) as "Author" of that part, and leave the space for dates of birth and death blank.

NATURE OF AUTHORSHIP Briefly describe nature of material created by this author in which copyright is claimed. ▼
Entire text

b NAME OF AUTHOR ▼

DATES OF BIRTH AND DEATH
Year Born ▼   Year Died ▼

Was this contribution to the work a "work made for hire"?
☐ Yes
☐ No

AUTHOR'S NATIONALITY OR DOMICILE
Name of Country
OR { Citizen of
     Domiciled in

WAS THIS AUTHOR'S CONTRIBUTION TO THE WORK
Anonymous? ☐ Yes ☐ No
Pseudonymous? ☐ Yes ☐ No
If the answer to either of these questions is "Yes," see detailed instructions.

NATURE OF AUTHORSHIP Briefly describe nature of material created by this author in which copyright is claimed. ▼

c NAME OF AUTHOR ▼

DATES OF BIRTH AND DEATH
Year Born ▼   Year Died ▼

Was this contribution to the work a "work made for hire"?
☐ Yes
☐ No

AUTHOR'S NATIONALITY OR DOMICILE
Name of Country
OR { Citizen of
     Domiciled in

WAS THIS AUTHOR'S CONTRIBUTION TO THE WORK
Anonymous? ☐ Yes ☐ No
Pseudonymous? ☐ Yes ☐ No
If the answer to either of these questions is "Yes," see detailed instructions.

NATURE OF AUTHORSHIP Briefly describe nature of material created by this author in which copyright is claimed. ▼

3
a YEAR IN WHICH CREATION OF THIS WORK WAS COMPLETED
2010   Year
This information must be given in all cases.

b DATE AND NATION OF FIRST PUBLICATION OF THIS PARTICULAR WORK
Complete this information ONLY if this work has been published.
Month _____ Day _____ Year _____
_____ Nation

4 COPYRIGHT CLAIMANT(S) Name and address must be given even if the claimant is the same as the author given in space 2. ▼
David Griffith
666 Hollywood Blvd.
Hollywood, CA 90000

See instructions before completing this space.

TRANSFER If the claimant(s) named here in space 4 is (are) different from the author(s) named in space 2, give a brief statement of how the claimant(s) obtained ownership of the copyright. ▼

DO NOT WRITE HERE
OFFICE USE ONLY

APPLICATION RECEIVED

ONE DEPOSIT RECEIVED

TWO DEPOSITS RECEIVED

FUNDS RECEIVED

MORE ON BACK ▶ • Complete all applicable spaces (numbers 5-9) on the reverse side of this page.
• See detailed instructions.   • Sign the form at line 8.

DO NOT WRITE HERE
Page 1 of _____ pages

Copyright Law: Forms

Sample Form PA (back)

		FORM PA
EXAMINED BY		
CHECKED BY		FOR COPYRIGHT OFFICE USE ONLY
☐ CORRESPONDENCE Yes		

DO NOT WRITE ABOVE THIS LINE. IF YOU NEED MORE SPACE, USE A SEPARATE CONTINUATION SHEET.

PREVIOUS REGISTRATION Has registration for this work, or for an earlier version of this work, already been made in the Copyright Office?

☒ Yes ☐ No If your answer is "Yes," why is another registration being sought? (Check appropriate box.) ▼ If your answer is No, do **not** check box A, B, or C.

a. ☐ This is the first published edition of a work previously registered in unpublished form.

b. ☐ This is the first application submitted by this author as copyright claimant.

c. ☐ This is a changed version of the work, as shown by space 6 on this application.

If your answer is "Yes," give: **Previous Registration Number** ▼   **Year of Registration** ▼

5

DERIVATIVE WORK OR COMPILATION Complete both space 6a and 6b for a derivative work; complete only 6b for a compilation.

Preexisting Material Identify any preexisting work or works that this work is based on or incorporates. ▼

a

Material Added to This Work Give a brief, general statement of the material that has been added to this work and in which copyright is claimed. ▼

b

6

See instructions before completing this space.

DEPOSIT ACCOUNT If the registration fee is to be charged to a Deposit Account established in the Copyright Office, give name and number of Account.

Name ▼   **Account Number ▼**

a

CORRESPONDENCE Give name and address to which correspondence about this application should be sent. Name/Address/Apt/City/State/Zip▼

David Griffith
666 Hollywood Blvd.
Hollywood, CA 90000

Area code and daytime telephone number 213) 666-6666   Fax number (   )

Email

b

7

CERTIFICATION* I, the undersigned, hereby certify that I am the

Check only one ▶ {
☒ author
☐ other copyright claimant
☐ owner of exclusive right(s)
☐ authorized agent of _____
        Name of author or other copyright claimant, or owner of exclusive right(s) ▲

of the work identified in this application and that the statements made by me in this application are correct to the best of my knowledge.

8

Typed or printed name and date ▼ If this application gives a date of publication in space 3, do not sign and submit it before that date.

David Griffith   Date May 1, 2010

Handwritten signature (X) ▼

☞   x _____

Certificate will be mailed in window envelope to this address:	Name ▼ David Griffith	YOU MUST: · Complete all necessary spaces · Sign your application in space 8
	Number/Street/Apt ▼ 666 Hollywood Blvd.	SEND ALL 3 ELEMENTS IN THE SAME PACKAGE: 1. Application form 2. Nonrefundable filing fee in check or money order payable to Register of Copyrights 3. Deposit material
	City/State/Zip ▼ Hollywood, CA 90000	MAIL TO: Library of Congress Copyright Office-PAD 101 Independence Avenue SE Washington, DC 20559-6230

9

*17 U.S.C. §506(e): Any person who knowingly makes a false representation of a material fact in the application for copyright registration provided for by section 409, or in any written statement filed in connection with the application, shall be fined not more than $2,500.

Form PA–Full Rev: 02/2009 Print: 06/2010—50,000 Printed on recycled paper   U.S. Government Printing Office: 2010-357-993/80,085

Sample Form TX (front)

Copyright Office fees are subject to change. For current fees, check the Copyright Office website at *www.copyright.gov*, write the Copyright Office, or call (202) 707-3000.

Form TX
For a Nondramatic Literary Work
UNITED STATES COPYRIGHT OFFICE

REGISTRATION NUMBER

TX	TXU

EFFECTIVE DATE OF REGISTRATION

Month	Day	Year

DO NOT WRITE ABOVE THIS LINE. IF YOU NEED MORE SPACE, USE A SEPARATE CONTINUATION SHEET.

1 TITLE OF THIS WORK ▼

A Fish Story

PREVIOUS OR ALTERNATIVE TITLES ▼

PUBLICATION AS A CONTRIBUTION If this work was published as a contribution to a periodical, serial, or collection, give information about the collective work in which the contribution appeared. **Title of Collective Work ▼**

If published in a periodical or serial give: Volume ▼   Number ▼   Issue Date ▼   On Pages ▼

2

a NAME OF AUTHOR ▼

Felix Founder

DATES OF BIRTH AND DEATH
Year Born ▼ 1955   Year Died ▼

Was this contribution to the work a "work made for hire"?
☐ Yes
☒ No

AUTHOR'S NATIONALITY OR DOMICILE
Name of Country
OR { Citizen of ▶ U.S.A.
{ Domiciled in▶

WAS THIS AUTHOR'S CONTRIBUTION TO THE WORK
Anonymous? ☐ Yes ☐ No
Pseudonymous? ☐ Yes ☐ No
If the answer to either of these questions is "Yes," see detailed instructions.

NOTE

Under the law, the "author" of a "work made for hire" is generally the employer, not the employee (see instructions). For any part of this work that was "made for hire" check "Yes" in the space provided, give the employer (or other person for whom the work was prepared) as "Author" of that part, and leave the space for dates of birth and death blank.

NATURE OF AUTHORSHIP Briefly describe nature of material created by this author in which copyright is claimed. ▼
Entire text of unpublished novel

b NAME OF AUTHOR ▼

DATES OF BIRTH AND DEATH
Year Born ▼   Year Died ▼

Was this contribution to the work a "work made for hire"?
☐ Yes
☐ No

AUTHOR'S NATIONALITY OR DOMICILE
Name of Country
OR { Citizen of ▶
{ Domiciled in▶

WAS THIS AUTHOR'S CONTRIBUTION TO THE WORK
Anonymous? ☐ Yes ☐ No
Pseudonymous? ☐ Yes ☐ No
If the answer to either of these questions is "Yes," see detailed instructions.

NATURE OF AUTHORSHIP Briefly describe nature of material created by this author in which copyright is claimed. ▼

c NAME OF AUTHOR ▼

DATES OF BIRTH AND DEATH
Year Born ▼   Year Died ▼

Was this contribution to the work a "work made for hire"?
☐ Yes
☐ No

AUTHOR'S NATIONALITY OR DOMICILE
Name of Country
OR { Citizen of ▶
{ Domiciled in▶

WAS THIS AUTHOR'S CONTRIBUTION TO THE WORK
Anonymous? ☐ Yes ☐ No
Pseudonymous? ☐ Yes ☐ No
If the answer to either of these questions is "Yes," see detailed instructions.

NATURE OF AUTHORSHIP Briefly describe nature of material created by this author in which copyright is claimed. ▼

3

a YEAR IN WHICH CREATION OF THIS WORK WAS COMPLETED
2010 ◀Year
This information must be given in all cases.

b DATE AND NATION OF FIRST PUBLICATION OF THIS PARTICULAR WORK
Complete this information ONLY if this work has been published.
Month ▶   Day ▶   Year ▶   ◀ Nation

4

COPYRIGHT CLAIMANT(S) Name and address must be given even if the claimant is the same as the author given in space 2. ▼

Felix Founder
1000 Bonito Way
Tampa, FL 10000

See instructions before completing this space.

TRANSFER If the claimant(s) named here in space 4 is (are) different from the author(s) named in space 2, give a brief statement of how the claimant(s) obtained ownership of the copyright. ▼

APPLICATION RECEIVED

ONE DEPOSIT RECEIVED

TWO DEPOSITS RECEIVED

FUNDS RECEIVED

DO NOT WRITE HERE OFFICE USE ONLY

MORE ON BACK ▶ · Complete all applicable spaces (numbers 5-9) on the reverse side of this page.
· See detailed instructions.   · Sign the form at line 8.

DO NOT WRITE HERE
Page 1 of _____ pages

Sample Form TX (back)

	EXAMINED BY	FORM TX
	CHECKED BY	
	☐ CORRESPONDENCE Yes	FOR COPYRIGHT OFFICE USE ONLY

DO NOT WRITE ABOVE THIS LINE. IF YOU NEED MORE SPACE, USE A SEPARATE CONTINUATION SHEET.

PREVIOUS REGISTRATION Has registration for this work, or for an earlier version of this work, already been made in the Copyright Office?

☐ Yes ☒ No If your answer is "Yes," why is another registration being sought? (Check appropriate box.) ▼

a. ☐ This is the first published edition of a work previously registered in unpublished form.

b. ☐ This is the first application submitted by this author as copyright claimant.

c. ☐ This is a changed version of the work, as shown by space 6 on this application.

If your answer is "Yes," give: **Previous Registration Number** ▶   **Year of Registration** ▶

5

DERIVATIVE WORK OR COMPILATION

Preexisting Material Identify any preexisting work or works that this work is based on or incorporates. ▼

a

Material Added to This Work Give a brief, general statement of the material that has been added to this work and in which copyright is claimed. ▼

b

6

See instructions before completing this space.

DEPOSIT ACCOUNT If the registration fee is to be charged to a Deposit Account established in the Copyright Office, give name and number of Account.

Name ▼   **Account Number** ▼

a

CORRESPONDENCE Give name and address to which correspondence about this application should be sent.   Name/Address/Apt/City/State/Zip ▼

Felix Founder
1000 Bonito Way
Tampa, FL 10000

Area code and daytime telephone number ▶ 813-123-4567   Fax number ▶

Email ▶

b

7

CERTIFICATION* I, the undersigned, hereby certify that I am the

Check only one ▶

☒ author
☐ other copyright claimant
☐ owner of exclusive right(s)
☐ authorized agent of _____

of the work identified in this application and that the statements made by me in this application are correct to the best of my knowledge.

Name of author or other copyright claimant, or owner of exclusive right(s) ▲

8

Typed or printed name and date ▼ If this application gives a date of publication in space 3, do not sign and submit it before that date.

Felix Founder   Date ▶ May 1, 2010

Handwritten signature ▼

Certificate will be mailed in window envelope to this address:	Name ▼ Felix Founder	YOU MUST: • Complete all necessary spaces • Sign your application in space 8
	Number/Street/Apt ▼ 1000 Bonito Way	SEND ALL 3 ELEMENTS IN THE SAME PACKAGE: 1. Application form 2. Nonrefundable filing fee in check or money order payable to *Register of Copyrights* 3. Deposit material
	City/State/Zip ▼ Tampa, FL 10000	MAIL TO: Library of Congress Copyright Office 101 Independence Avenue SE Washington, DC 20559-6222

9

Copyright Law: Forms

Sample Form VA (front)

Copyright Office fees are subject to change. For current fees, check the Copyright Office website at *www.copyright.gov*, write the Copyright Office, or call (202) 707-3000.

Form VA
For a Work of the Visual Arts
UNITED STATES COPYRIGHT OFFICE

REGISTRATION NUMBER

VA   VAU

EFFECTIVE DATE OF REGISTRATION

Month   Day   Year

DO NOT WRITE ABOVE THIS LINE. IF YOU NEED MORE SPACE, USE A SEPARATE CONTINUATION SHEET.

1

Title of This Work ▼

NATURE OF THIS WORK ▼ See instructions

All About Everything   Photographs

Previous or Alternative Titles ▼

Publication as a Contribution If this work was published as a contribution to a periodical, serial, or collection, give information about the collective work in which the contribution appeared. **Title of Collective Work ▼**

If published in a periodical or serial give: **Volume ▼**   **Number ▼**   **Issue Date ▼**   **On Pages ▼**

2

NOTE

Under the law, the "author" of a "work made for hire" is generally the employer, not the employee (see instructions). For any part of this work that was "made for hire" check "Yes" in the space provided, give the employer (or other person for whom the work was prepared) as "Author" of that part, and leave the space for dates of birth and death blank.

a NAME OF AUTHOR ▼

Mike Minolta

DATES OF BIRTH AND DEATH
Year Born ▼   Year Died ▼
1940

Was this contribution to the work a "work made for hire"?
☐ Yes
☒ No

Author's Nationality or Domicile
Name of Country
OR { Citizen of U.S.A.
     Domiciled in

Was This Author's Contribution to the Work
Anonymous?   ☐ Yes ☒ No
Pseudonymous? ☐ Yes ☒ No
If the answer to either of these questions is "Yes," see detailed instructions.

Nature of Authorship Check appropriate box(es). **See instructions**
☐ 3-Dimensional sculpture   ☐ Map   ☐ Technical drawing
☐ 2-Dimensional artwork   ☐ Photograph   ☐ Text
☐ Reproduction of work of art ☒ Jewelry design   ☐ Architectural work

b Name of Author ▼

Dates of Birth and Death
Year Born ▼   Year Died ▼

Was this contribution to the work a "work made for hire"?
☐ Yes
☐ No

Author's Nationality or Domicile
Name of Country
OR { Citizen of
     Domiciled in

Was This Author's Contribution to the Work
Anonymous?   ☐ Yes ☐ No
Pseudonymous? ☐ Yes ☐ No
If the answer to either of these questions is "Yes," see detailed instructions.

Nature of Authorship Check appropriate box(es). **See instructions**
☐ 3-Dimensional sculpture   ☐ Map   ☐ Technical drawing
☐ 2-Dimensional artwork   ☐ Photograph   ☐ Text
☐ Reproduction of work of art ☐ Jewelry design   ☐ Architectural work

3

a Year in Which Creation of This Work Was
Completed   This information must be given
2010   Year in all cases.

b Date and Nation of First Publication of This Particular Work
Complete this information   Month May   Day 11   Year 2010
ONLY if this work has been published.   U.S.A.   Nation

4

See instructions before completing this space.

COPYRIGHT CLAIMANT(S) Name and address must be given even if the claimant is the same as the author given in space 2. ▼

Mike Minolta
100 Grant St.
Chicago, IL 50000

Transfer If the claimant(s) named here in space 4 is (are) different from the author(s) named in space 2, give a brief statement of how the claimant(s) obtained ownership of the copyright. ▼

DO NOT WRITE HERE OFFICE USE ONLY

APPLICATION RECEIVED

ONE DEPOSIT RECEIVED

TWO DEPOSITS RECEIVED

FUNDS RECEIVED

MORE ON BACK ▶ • Complete all applicable spaces (numbers 5-9) on the reverse side of this page.
• See detailed instructions.   • Sign the form at line 8.

DO NOT WRITE HERE

Page 1 of _____ pages

Copyright Law: Forms

Sample Form VA (back)

EXAMINED BY	FORM VA
CHECKED BY	
☐ CORRESPONDENCE Yes	FOR COPYRIGHT OFFICE USE ONLY

DO NOT WRITE ABOVE THIS LINE. IF YOU NEED MORE SPACE, USE A SEPARATE CONTINUATION SHEET.

PREVIOUS REGISTRATION Has registration for this work, or for an earlier version of this work, already been made in the Copyright Office?

☐ **Yes** ☒ **No** If your answer is "Yes," why is another registration being sought? (Check appropriate box.) ▼

a. ☐ This is the first published edition of a work previously registered in unpublished form.

b. ☐ This is the first application submitted by this author as copyright claimant.

c. ☐ This is a changed version of the work, as shown by space 6 on this application.

If your answer is "Yes," give: **Previous Registration Number** ▼   **Year of Registration** ▼

5

DERIVATIVE WORK OR COMPILATION Complete both space 6a and 6b for a derivative work; complete only 6b for a compilation.

a. Preexisting Material Identify any preexisting work or works that this work is based on or incorporates. ▼

b. Material Added to This Work Give a brief, general statement of the material that has been added to this work and in which copyright is claimed. ▼

6
a
b
See instructions before completing this space.

DEPOSIT ACCOUNT If the registration fee is to be charged to a Deposit Account established in the Copyright Office, give name and number of Account.

Name ▼   **Account Number** ▼

7
a

CORRESPONDENCE Give name and address to which correspondence about this application should be sent. Name/Address/Apt/City/State/Zip ▼

Mike Minolta
100 Grant St.
Chicago, IL 50000

Area code and daytime telephone number (312) 555-5555   Fax number (   )

Email

b

CERTIFICATION* I, the undersigned, hereby certify that I am the

check only one ▶ { ☒ author
☐ other copyright claimant
☐ owner of exclusive right(s)
☐ authorized agent of _____
  Name of author or other copyright claimant, or owner of exclusive right(s) ▲

of the work identified in this application and that the statements made by me in this application are correct to the best of my knowledge.

8

Typed or printed name and date ▼ If this application gives a date of publication in space 3, do not sign and submit it before that date.

Mike Minolta   Date July 1, 2010

Handwritten signature (X) ▼

X _____

Certificate will be mailed in window envelope to this address:	Name ▼ Mike Minolta	**YOU MUST:** • Complete all necessary spaces • Sign your application in space 8
	Number/Street/Apt ▼ 100 Grant St.	**SEND ALL 3 ELEMENTS IN THE SAME PACKAGE:** 1. Application form 2. Nonrefundable filing fee in check or money order payable to *Register of Copyrights* 3. Deposit material
	City/State/ZIP ▼ Chicago, IL 50000	**MAIL TO:** Library of Congress Copyright Office 101 Independence Avenue SE Washington, DC 20559-6000

9

Form VA Rev: 07/2006 Print: 07/2006—30,000 Printed on recycled paper   U.S. Government Printing Office: 2004-320-958/60,126

Part 3: **Trademark Law**

Trademark Law: Overview..379

    What are trademarks and service marks?...379

    What is trade dress?...379

    What is trademark law?..380

    What kinds of trademarks and service marks receive protection
       under trademark law?...380

    What cannot be protected under trademark law?..381

    How is trademark ownership determined? 383

    What about federal registration of a mark? 383

    How can you tell if a mark proposed for use is already being used by
       another business?...385

    Do mark owners need to provide notice to the public?..................................386

    How is ownership of a mark enforced? 386

    Can a trademark owner stop use of a similar mark on unrelated goods? 386

    If a company has registered its trademark, does it need to register
       its "trademark.com"?...387

    What's new in trademark law since the last edition? 387

    Trademark resources..389

    Trademark resources..389

Trademark Law: Definitions...391

Trademark Law: Forms..503

    Preparing a Federal Trademark Application 503

    The Trademark Application: the TEAS System..504

       Disclaimers..506

    Example of a TEAS Plus Application 509

Trademark Law: Overview

Trademark law consists of the legal rules by which businesses protect the names, logos, and other commercial signifiers used to identify their products and services. One of the principal goals of trademark law is to prevent consumers from being confused in the marketplace. Another goal is to prevent a business from trading off another business's good will. (Good will is that mysterious factor by which consumers associate certain standards with a company.)

What are trademarks and service marks?

A trademark is a distinctive word, phrase, logo, graphic symbol, or other device that is used to identify the source of a product or service and to distinguish it from competitors. Some examples of trademarks are Toyota for cars and trucks, Frito-Lay for food products, and iTunes for music services.

A trademark can be more than just a brand name or logo. It can include other nonfunctional but distinctive aspects of a product or service that tend to promote and distinguish it in the marketplace, such as shapes, letters, numbers, sounds, smells, or colors. Titles, character names, or other distinctive features of movies, television, and radio programs can also serve as trademarks when used to promote a product or service.

For all practical purposes, a service mark is the same as a trademark— except that trademarks promote products while service marks promote services. Some familiar service marks include McDonald's (food service), FedEx (delivery service), MTV's logo (television network service), and the Olympic Games' multicolored interlocking circles (international sporting event).

What is trade dress?

Trademark law protects more than names and logos. The law also offers some protection to distinctive shapes (the Coca-Cola bottle) or packaging (the choice of colors on the Netflix envelope). Likewise, a service may be identified by its distinctive decor (the decorating motif used by the Old Navy clothing stores). Collectively, these types of identifying features are commonly termed "trade dress." Functional aspects of trade dress cannot be protected under trademark law.

What is trademark law?

Trademark law addresses the overlapping and conflicting uses of trademarks, service marks, and trade dress by different businesses. Commonly, trademark law is applied to resolve disputes when competing businesses adopt similar product names or logos. The rules for resolving these disputes usually favor whichever business was first to use the name, logo, or trade dress on a category of goods within a geographic area. These rules come from decisions by federal and state courts (the common law) and from U.S. government statutes known collectively as the Lanham Act.

The Lanham Act also establishes the trademark registration system and provides for judicial remedies in cases of trademark infringement. In addition to the Lanham Act, most states provide for some means of registering trademarks with a state agency and allow for remedies in case of infringement.

Finally, federal and state courts have applied their own set of rules to activity deemed "unfair competition," which usually occurs when one business competes unfairly with another. Trademark laws are a subset of unfair competition laws. Trademark law also addresses treaties signed by a number of countries that make it easier to obtain international trademark protection.

What kinds of trademarks and service marks receive protection under trademark law?

Trademark law confers the most protection to distinctive names, logos, and other marketing devices. Trademarks become distinctive (or strong) in two ways: They are born distinctive (inherently distinctive) or they achieve distinction through sales and advertising. Inherently distinctive trademarks don't describe the goods or services for which they are used—for example, Arrow for shirts or Yahoo! for Internet services.

Trademarks that are classified as inherently distinctive consist of:
- creatively unique logos or symbols
- words that are created specifically to be a trademark ("fanciful" marks), such as Exxon, Pepsi, or Kodak
- common words that are used in a surprising or unexpected manner ("arbitrary marks"), such as Amazon for retail services or Diesel for clothing, and

- words that cleverly connote qualities about the product or service without literally describing these qualities ("suggestive" marks), such as Slenderella diet food products or Netscape Internet browser.

If a mark describes some aspect of the goods or the services (a weak mark), it can become distinctive (or strong) from sales and advertising, often over several years. Typical examples are:

- terms that attempt to literally describe the product or its characteristics (Vision Center for an optics store, Computerland for a computer store, Park 'N Fly for airport parking services)
- surnames (Sears, Gallo, Newman's Own), and
- geographic terms (Bank of America, Washington Mutual).

Descriptive marks become distinctive if they achieve significant public recognition through exposure in the marketplace. A mark that has become distinctive in this way is said to have acquired a "secondary meaning."

What cannot be protected under trademark law?

There are five common instances in which a company cannot acquire trademark protection for a term or logo:

- **Nonuse.** Trademark rights are derived from the continued use of a mark in commerce. If there is a significant break in the chain of trademark usage, the owner may lose rights under a principal known as abandonment. Abandonment can occur in many ways, but the most common way is nonuse, that is, the mark is no longer used in commerce and there is sufficient evidence that the owner intends to discontinue use of the mark. For example, the owner of a mark for hotel services closed its hotels and failed to use the mark on similar services for a period of 30 years. This was sufficient proof that the owner abandoned the mark. Under the Lanham Act, a trademark is presumed to be abandoned after three years of nonuse. This presumption does not mean that the mark is automatically classified as abandoned after three years of nonuse. It means that the burden of proof shifts to the owner of the mark to prove it is not abandoned. The owner must prove an intention to resume commercial use.
- **Generics and genericide.** A generic term describes an entire group or class of goods or services. For example, the terms "computer," "eyeglasses," and "eBook" are all generic terms. The public associates these terms with a type of goods, not a specific brand. For example, there are many brands of computers—Gateway, Dell, and Sony—but there is no brand of computer

known simply as Computer. If protection were granted to generics, one company would have a monopoly and could stop all others from using the name of the goods. For example, if only one company could use the term "Jam," any other company would be prevented from using that term with their brand of jam. Consumers are used to seeing a generic term used in conjunction with a trademark (for example, Avery labels or Hewlett-Packard printers). From a grammatical point of view, generics are generally nouns, trademarks are generally adjectives, and the generic term almost always follows the trademark. On some occasions a company invents a new word for a product (for example, Kleenex for a tissue). That term may function so successfully as a trademark that the public eventually comes to believe that it is the name of the goods, not the trademark. This is what happened with the term "cellophane." This word, originally a registered trademark of the DuPont corporation, became so popular that consumers began to think of cellophane as the generic term for the clear plastic sheets. Other famous terms to move from trademark to generic are "aspirin," "yo-yo," "escalator," "thermos," and "kerosene." The process of moving from trademark to generic is referred to as genericide.

- **Confusingly similar marks.** A mark will not be registered or otherwise protected under trademark law if it so resembles another mark currently registered or in use in the United States as to cause confusion among consumers. This standard, known as "likelihood of confusion," is a foundation of trademark law. Many factors are weighed when considering likelihood of confusion. These factors are derived from the case of *Polaroid Corp. v. Polarad Elect. Corp.,* 287 F.2d 492 (2d Cir. 1961). However, the most important "confusion factors" are generally the similarity of the marks, similarity of the goods, degree of care exercised by the consumer when purchasing, intent of the person using the similar mark, and any actual confusion that has occurred.

- **Weak marks.** A weak (or descriptive) trademark will not be protected unless the owner can prove that consumers are aware of the mark and associate it with their product or service ("secondary meaning"). There are three types of weak marks: descriptive marks, geographic marks that describe a location, and marks that are primarily surnames (last names). When an applicant attempts to register a weak mark, the U.S. Patent and Trademark Office (USPTO) will permit the applicant to submit proof of distinctiveness or to move the application from the Principal Register to the Supplemental Register. If the applicant fails to prove distinctiveness (known as secondary meaning), the USPTO will reject the application. If the applicant disagrees with the USPTO decision, the applicant can appeal the decision to the federal district court.

- **Functional features.** Trademark law, like copyright law, will not protect functional features. Trademark disputes about this issue (sometimes referred to as functionality) arise in cases involving product shapes or product packaging (sometimes referred to as trade dress). Unfortunately, there is no simple definition for "functional," because this area of law is always evolving. Generally, a functional feature is essential to the usability of a product. That is, the feature is necessary for the item to work. When the feature is not necessary for the item to work, it will be protected under trademark law. For example, the body of an electric guitar can be made in innumerable shapes (as witnessed by oddly shaped guitars favored by musicians such as Bo Diddley, Kiss, and ZZ Top). The design of these guitars may become a trademark because the design is not dictated by the ability of the guitar to function. (The design may also be protectable as a design patent.)

How is trademark ownership determined?

As a general rule, a mark is owned by the business that is first to use it in a commercial context—that is, the first to associate the mark with a product or service. After the first use, the owner may be able to prevent others from using it, or a similar trademark, for their goods and services as long as the owner continues to use the mark in connection with its goods and services. The rights of the trademark owner, particularly for a trademark that is not registered with the federal government, may be limited by the geographic extent of the use.

First use can also be established by filing an intent-to-use (ITU) trademark registration application with the U.S. Patent and Trademark Office. The filing date of this application will be considered the date of first use if the applicant puts the mark into actual use within required time limits (between six months and three years, depending on the reasons for the delay and whether the applicant seeks and pays for extensions) and follows up to obtain an actual registration.

What about federal registration of a mark?

Registering a trademark or service mark with the USPTO makes it easier for the owner to protect it against would-be copiers and puts the rest of the country on notice that the mark is already taken. The registration process involves filling out a simple application and paying an application fee. The fee is $325 per class if filing electronically using the TEAS system ($275 per class if using TEAS Plus), and $375 if filing a paper application. TEAS Plus has stricter requirements than the regular TEAS form. However you file, you must also be prepared to work with an official of the USPTO to correct any errors in the application.

To qualify a mark for registration with the USPTO, the mark's owner first must put it into use "in commerce that Congress may regulate." This means the mark must be used on a product or service that crosses state, national, or territorial lines or that affects commerce crossing such lines—such as would be the case with a catalog business or a restaurant or motel that caters to interstate or international consumers. If an intent-to-use application is being filed (the applicant intends to use the mark in the near future but hasn't begun using it yet), another document must be filed for a fee once the actual use begins, showing that the mark is being used in commerce (as defined above).

Once the USPTO receives a trademark registration application, it determines the answers to these questions:

- Does the application have to be amended (because of errors) before it can be examined?
- Is the mark the same as or similar to an existing mark used on similar or related goods or services?
- Is the mark on a list of prohibited or reserved names?
- Is the mark generic—that is, does the mark describe the product or service itself rather than its source?
- Is the mark descriptive—that is, does it consist of words or images that are ordinary or that literally describe one or more aspects of the underlying goods or services?

When the USPTO can answer all of these questions in the negative, it will publish the mark in the *Official Gazette* (an online publication of the USPTO) as being a candidate for registration. Existing trademark and service mark owners may object to the registration by filing an opposition. If this occurs, the USPTO will schedule a hearing to resolve the dispute. Even if existing owners don't challenge the registration of the mark at this stage, they may later attack the registration in court if they believe the registered mark infringes one they already own.

If there is no opposition, and use in commerce has been established, the USPTO will place the mark on the list of trademarks known as the Principal Register if it is considered distinctive (either inherently or because the applicant has shown that the mark has acquired secondary meaning). Probably the most important benefit of placing a mark on the Principal Register is that anybody who later initiates use of the same or a confusingly similar mark will be presumed by the courts to be a "willful infringer" and therefore liable for large money damages. However, it is still possible to obtain basic protection for a mark from the federal courts under the Lanham Act without prior registration.

If a mark consists of ordinary or descriptive terms (that is, it isn't considered distinctive), it may be placed on a different list of trademarks and service marks known as the Supplemental Register. Placement of a mark on the Supplemental Register produces significantly fewer benefits than those offered by the Principal Register but still provides notice of ownership. Also, if the mark remains on the Supplemental Register for five years—that is, the registration isn't cancelled for some reason—and also remains in use during that time, it may then be placed on the Principal Register under the secondary meaning rule (secondary meaning will be presumed).

How can you tell if a mark proposed for use is already being used by another business?

A "trademark search" is an investigation to discover potential conflicts between a proposed mark and an existing one. Generally done before or at the beginning of a new mark's use, a trademark search reduces the possibility of inadvertently infringing a mark belonging to someone else.

Often, a professional search agency is used to conduct the trademark search—by first checking both federal and state trademark registers for identical or similar marks and then checking journals, telephone books, and magazines to see whether the mark is in actual use. It is also possible to conduct a preliminary online trademark search to determine if a trademark is distinguishable from other federally registered trademarks. This can be accomplished using the USPTO's free searchable TESS (Trademark Electronic Search System) database. Using TESS, a trademark owner has free access to records of federally registered marks or marks that are pending (applications undergoing examination at the USPTO). At the USPTO website (www.uspto.gov), click "Search TM database" under Trademarks.

Privately owned fee-based online trademark databases often provide more current USPTO trademark information. Three private online search companies are: Thomson Compumark (www.compumark.com), Dialog (www.dialog.com), and LexisNexis (www.lexis.com).

Do mark owners need to provide notice to the public?

Many owners like to put a "TM" (or "SM" for service mark) next to their mark to let the world know that they are claiming ownership of it. There is no legal necessity for providing this type of notice—nor are any specific legal benefits acquired by its use. The use of the mark, not the use of the symbol, is the act that confers rights.

The "R" in a circle (®) is a different matter entirely. The Lanham Act prohibits use of this notice (or any other signifier indicating federal registration such as "Reg. U.S. Pat. & TM Office") with a trademark unless the trademark has been registered with the USPTO. Once a trademark is federally registered, the owner should apply the "R" in a circle to signify its registration. Failure to use the notice with a federally registered mark may limit the damages that can be recovered in an infringement lawsuit.

How is ownership of a mark enforced?

The owner of a trademark has the burden of enforcing trademark rights. Whether or not a trademark is federally registered, the owner may sue to prevent someone else from using it or a confusingly similar mark. Courts will examine such factors as:

- whether the trademark is being used on competing goods or services (goods or services compete if the sale of one is likely to preclude the sale of the other)
- whether consumers would likely be confused by the concurrent use of the two companies' trademarks, and
- whether the products or services are offered in the same part of the country or are distributed through the same channels.

If the mark is infringing and the mark's owner can prove a financial loss or show that the competitor gained economically as a result of the improper use, the competitor may have to pay the owner damages based on the profit or loss. If the court finds the competitor intentionally copied the owner's trademark, the infringer may have to pay other damages, such as punitive damages, fines, or attorney fees. On the other hand, if the trademark's owner has not been damaged, a court has discretion to allow the competitor to also use the mark under very limited circumstances designed to avoid the possibility of consumer confusion.

Can a trademark owner stop use of a similar mark on unrelated goods?

Under a principle known as "dilution," owners of a famous trademark may prevent it from being used by others on unrelated goods if both of the following are true:

- The mark is well known.

- The later use would dilute the mark's strength—that is, impair or tarnish its reputation for quality or render it common through overuse in different contexts (even if it is unlikely that any consumers would be confused by the second use).

If a company has registered its trademark, does it need to register its "trademark.com"?

Unless a company is establishing some service unique to its Internet business—for example, downloadable audio services or assistance in filling out a mortgage application—there is usually little to be gained from registering the ".com" version of a federally registered trademark. For example, if a company sells books under the federally registered mark ReadMe, it is not necessary to federally register its domain name ReadMe.com when the company sells books at its website. Why? The owner of a federally registered trademark can stop others from using the mark for similar goods or services whether they are sold online or off. In addition, the USPTO requires that applicants disclaim ".com" in order to prevent any person from claiming a proprietary right to this generic term. However, if the website provides services or products unique to the online experience—for example, a record store that provides a musical downloading service separate from its retail outlets—then the business may want to register the .com version of the name in connection with those Internet services.

What's new in trademark law since the last edition?

Below are the major changes in trademark law since the last edition was published.

- **Functional aspects: towel design cannot be protected under trademark law.** A company that claimed trade dress on a round beach towel design lost all trade dress rights when the Seventh Circuit determined that the towel design was primarily functional (despite the fact that the trade dress had been registered and had achieved incontestable status). (*Jay Franco & Sons, Inc. v. Franek*, 615 F.3d 855 (7th Cir. 2010).)

- **One more time … keyword sales of trademarks do not amount to infringement.** A district court determined that Google's sale of the Rosetta Stone mark as a keyword in Google's *AdWords* program did not infringe the mark. Among the issues in Google's favor: the district court found that Google's use was functional and that consumer awareness of the Rosetta Stone's mark increased by 60% during the four years following the introduction of

Google's program. *(Rosetta Stone Ltd. v. Google, Inc.,* 2010 WL 3063152 (E.D. Va. 2010).)

- **Advertise.com is generic.** The Ninth Circuit reversed a lower court ruling that the registered mark "Advertise.com" was not generic. The mark which had been registered by AOL was intended for "online or Internet advertising." The Ninth Circuit noted that the addition of a top-level domain such as ".com" to an unprotectable term rarely results in distinctive composite. *(Advertise.com v. AOL Advertising, Inc.,* 166 F.3d 974 (9th Cir. 2010).)

- **Ninth Circuit provides guidelines for distinguishing between suggestive and descriptive marks.** A company registered the mark, "Would You Rather … ?" and sued a competitor over a similar mark. A district court determined that the mark was descriptive and lacked secondary meaning. The Ninth Circuit reversed and discussed three tests for distinguishing suggestive and descriptive marks. One acceptable test was the "imagination test" which asks whether a leap of imagination is required to understand the mark's relationship to the product. (The Ninth Circuit held that the district misapplied this test and that the record lacked evidence in the form of consumer surveys.) A second test was also considered—the "competitors' needs" test—that focuses on the need of competitors to use a similar mark. Another test was also examined—the "extent of use" test—that considers the extent to which other competitors have used the mark. Based on the application of these three tests, the Ninth Circuit determined that the mark was suggestive. *(Zobmomondo Entertainment, LLC v. Falls Media, LLC,* 602 F.3d 1108 (9th Cir. 2010).)

- **Substantial similarity not required to show blurring of trademark.** In a 2010 case, the Second Circuit determined that the term "Charbucks" does not tarnish the reputation of the Starbucks mark merely based on the evidence of an association and a negative connotation. Charbucks may blur the Starbucks mark but the district court's standard of substantial similarity was not appropriate—all that was required was a measurement of the degree of similarity, a different standard. *(Starbucks Corp v. Wolf's Borough Coffee, Inc.* 588 F.3d 97 (2d Cir. 2009).)

- **Web page is improper specimen for goods unless the page demonstrates a way to order the goods.** The USPTO rejected an applicant's specimen of a Web page that showed images of goods (and described applicant's services) because it failed to provide a user with direct means to order the goods. *(In re Quantum Foods Inc.,* 665 F. Supp. 2d 727 (S.D. Tex. 2009).)

- **File extension "DWG" can function as word mark.** A district court permitted the use of "DWG" (the file extension for drawings) as a trademark when used by Autodesk as part of a RealDWG software library. (*Autodesk, Inc. v. Dassault Systems SolidWorks Corp.*, 685 F. Supp. 2d 1001 (N.D. Cal. 2009).)

Trademark resources

If you're interested in protecting your trademark or service mark, you may want to consult *Trademark: Legal Care for Your Business & Product Name*, by Richard Stim and Stephen Elias (Nolo). This book shows how to choose a distinctive name, conduct a trademark search, register a mark with the USPTO, and protect the mark once it's in use.

The Internet offers convenient access to an enormous amount of trademark materials, including:

- Nolo (www.nolo.com) offers self-help information about a wide variety of legal topics, including trademark law. (See the Intellectual Property topic in the Legal Encyclopedia, which incidentally includes selected entries from this part of the book.)
- U.S. Patent and Trademark Office (www.uspto.gov) is the place to go for recent policy and statutory changes and transcripts of hearings on various trademark law issues. This site also offers four useful online programs: TESS, TEAS, TDR, and TARR. TESS is a searchable database of federally registered trademarks; TARR provides information on the status of pending registrations; TDR is an advanced electronic portal to PDF viewing, downloading, and printing of documents for hundreds of thousands of trademark applications; and TEAS is a system for electronic filing of trademark registrations.
- International Trademark Association (INTA) (www.inta.org) provides trademark services, publications, and online resources.
- Martin Schwimmer's Trademark Blog (www.schwimmerlegal.com) is the most interesting (and popular) source of daily trademark news.
- The TTABlog (http://thettablog.blogspot.com) is the most thorough analysis of Trademark Trial and Appeal Board (TTAB) rulings.
- Dear Rich: Nolo's Patent, Copyright & Trademark Blog (www.dearrichblog.com). Nolo's intellectual property blog operates as a companion to this book. Answers are provided to common IP questions.

Trademark Law: Definitions

I n this section we provide definitions of the words and phrases commonly used in trademark law. Note that we use the word "mark" to refer broadly to trademarks, service marks, certification marks, and collective marks—that is, for any identifier for a service or product that distinguishes it from competing products and services.

abandonment of mark

Abandonment—the loss of trademark rights due to nonuse—commonly occurs when there is sufficient evidence that the owner intends to discontinue use of the mark.

Under the Lanham Act, a mark registered with the U.S. Patent and Trademark Office is presumed abandoned if it is not used for a continuous period of three years or more. This means that the mark's owner cannot prevent someone else from using the mark unless the owner can convince a court that the mark really wasn't abandoned, despite the lack of use. Some reasons that may acceptable for this purpose are:

- temporary financial difficulty
- bankruptcy proceedings, or
- the need for a product revision.

A company can also prove that a mark is not abandoned by furnishing documents that indicate the company intended to resume use or by the continued existence of customer goodwill.

> EXAMPLE: The owners of the Rambler trademark (for cars) were able to demonstrate that the trademark had not been abandoned even though the company had not manufactured any new automobiles in many years. They proved nonabandonment by demonstrating that there were many Rambler autos (and related supplies) bearing the mark still in use, signs featuring the trademark were still posted, and many consumers still wanted Rambler products as evidenced by Rambler fan clubs. *(American Motors Corp. v. Action Age, Inc.*, 178 U.S.P.Q. 377 (TTAB 1973).)

Proving abandonment is often difficult and expensive. It is also affected by a procedure known as Section 8 affidavit, a document that must be filed by the owner in order to demonstrate continued use. The abandonment presumption is located in the definitions section of the Lanham Act. (15 United States Code, Section 1127.)

Abandonment of a trademark is different from abandonment of a trademark application (see below), in which the owner fails to complete the trademark application process. In that case, the rights to the trademark may not be lost. Abandonment of trademark is also distinguished from cancellation of a trademark, in which an existing mark is terminated as result of a cancellation proceeding or because the trademark owner failed to file a Section 8 declaration or a Section 15 renewal. Note that new (stricter) rules for reviving an abandoned trademark resulted from the passage of the Madrid Protocol.

The Lanham Act: § 1127. (§ 45) Construction and definitions

A mark shall be deemed to be "abandoned" if either of the following occurs:

(1) When its use has been discontinued with intent not to resume such use. Intent not to resume may be inferred from circumstances. Nonuse for 3 consecutive years shall be prima facie evidence of abandonment. "Use" of a mark means the bona fide use of such mark made in the ordinary course of trade, and not made merely to reserve a right in a mark.

(2) When any course of conduct of the owner, including acts of omission as well as commission, causes the mark to become the generic name for the goods or services on or in connection with which it is used or otherwise to lose its significance as a mark. Purchaser motivation shall not be a test for determining abandonment under this paragraph.

Related terms: abandonment of trademark application; continuous use of mark; loss of mark; naked license; opposing and canceling a trademark application.

abandonment of trademark application

The U.S. Patent and Trademark Office (USPTO) considers a trademark application abandoned if the applicant fails to respond in a timely manner to actions or requests initiated by the USPTO. An application may also be abandoned for procedural failures—for example, an intent-to-use applicant fails to file a statement of use. It's possible to monitor trademark application progress and status online at the USPTO's website (www.uspto.gov). To do so, click "trademarks" on the home page. Then click "Check Status," which will access TARR (Trademark Applications and Retrieval System). In the event an application has been abandoned, an owner who would still like to seek federal registration can either petition the USPTO to have it revived or begin the application process anew (in the hopes that previous obstacles can be overcome). Additional information about trademark applications can be found at the USPTO's TDR (Trademark Document Retrieval) database.

Note that under rules resulting from enactment of the Madrid Protocol, the USPTO has the ability to grant a "partial abandonment." This occurs if the applicant fails to respond to a refusal limited only to certain goods/services in an application or registration. Previously, this failure to respond would have caused the entire application to be abandoned.

Also, under Madrid Protocol rules, if more than two months have passed since the Notice of Abandonment was mailed, it can only be revived if the applicant claims it was not received and the applicant has been checking the status of the application or registration at least every six months after filing the application. Even if a petition to revive is successful, related international rights under the Madrid Protocol are likely to be terminated. In other words, if a U.S. application or registration becomes abandoned, related international registrations will likely be abandoned as well.

Related terms: abandonment of mark.

Acceptable Identification of Goods and Services Manual

When filing an application for federal trademark registration or deciding whether one mark infringes another, it is useful to classify the mark in question according to the kinds of goods or services it is used with. There are 45 classes of goods and services (34 for goods, 11 for services) that are used by the U.S. Patent and Trademark Office (USPTO) for this purpose. Because of the limited number of classes, it is often difficult to tell which class a particular good or service fits within. To help this process along, the International Trademark Association has published the Acceptable Description of Goods and Services Manual, an alphabetical listing of hundreds of discrete goods and services with appropriate descriptions and suggested classification numbers. The Manual is available on the USPTO's website (www.uspto.gov).

aesthetic functionality

Aesthetic functionality refers to visually appealing but unprotectable features of a trademark. For example, the wide mouth spout of a milk product may be distinctive and aesthetically pleasing, but it is primarily a functional feature and not protected under trademark law. Similarly, the bright yellow color of a tennis ball is visually appealing but it is primarily functional, allowing players to see the ball in diminished light.

affidavit of use

See Section 8 Declaration; Section 15 Declaration.

Allegation of Use for Intent-to-Use Application, with Declaration

When a trademark application is filed on an intent-to-use basis, the actual registration won't occur until you file a document with the USPTO stating that the mark is now in actual use and pay an additional fee. The form to use for this purpose is called Allegation of Use for Intent-to-Use Application. The Allegation of Use form may be filed at any time prior to the date the USPTO authorizes the publication of the proposed mark, and any time after the USPTO issues a Notice of Allowance. It may not be filed between those two dates.

Amendment to Allege Use

See Allegation of Use for Intent-to-Use Application, with Declaration.

Anticybersquatting Consumer Protection Act

The Anticybersquatting Consumer Protection Act (ACPA) was enacted in order to protect businesses against the practice of cybersquatting. (15 United States Code, Section 1125(d).) A cybersquatter registers a well-known trademark as a domain name, hoping to later profit by reselling the domain name back to the trademark owner. This law authorizes a trademark owner to sue an alleged cybersquatter in federal court and obtain a court order transferring the domain name back to the mark's owner. In some cases, the cybersquatter must pay money damages. In order to stop a cybersquatter, the mark's true owner must prove all of the following:

- The domain name registrant had a bad-faith intent to profit from the mark.
- The mark was distinctive at the time the domain name was first registered.
- The domain name is identical or confusingly similar to the mark.
- The mark qualifies for protection under federal trademark laws—that is, the mark is distinctive and its owner was the first to use the mark in commerce.

If the person or company who registered the domain name had reasonable grounds to believe that the use of the domain name was fair and lawful, they would avoid a court decision that they acted in bad faith. In other words, if the accused cybersquatter can demonstrate a reason to register the domain name other than to sell it back to the trademark owner for a profit, then a court will probably determine the domain was not acquired in bad faith. In addition to the rules provided under the ACPA, domain name owners can alternatively use the dispute resolution procedures that are overseen by ICANN, the international agency that oversees domain names. ICANN offers a Uniform Dispute Resolution Procedure (UDRP), an arbitration procedure that is usually resolved within two months.

Related terms: cybersquatting; domain names.

antidilution statutes

See dilution.

arbitrary mark

A word or phrase is classified as an arbitrary trademark if the choice is unrelated to any quality or characteristics of the goods or services. For example, Penguin (books), Arrow (shirts), and Beefeater (gin) are arbitrary terms in relation to the products they advertise and therefore stand out because they are original and surprising. Arbitrary marks are considered to be inherently distinctive, entitling them to the highest degree of trademark protection available.

Related terms: distinctive mark.

assignment of mark

An assignment is a permanent transfer of ownership rights and goodwill associated with a mark. Assignments commonly occur when a company is sold. An assignment may also occur as part of a bankruptcy or may be used as a security interest when a business seeks to obtain a loan.

Once the assignment is made, the business buying the trademark rights (the "assignee") becomes the owner, and the seller (the "assignor") has no further ownership interest. On some occasions, an assignment may be transferred back to the original owner if certain conditions are met. The Lanham Act requires the assignment of a registered mark to be in writing. Assignments should be recorded with the U.S. Patent and Trademark Office (USPTO), and the new owners can obtain new certificates of registration in their names. Using the USPTO's ETA system (Electronic Trademark Assignment), a trademark owner can file a trademark assignment electronically.

The Lanham Act: § 1057. (§ 7) Certificates of registration
(b) Certificate as prima facie evidence

… A certificate of registration of a mark may be issued to the assignee of the applicant, but the assignment must first be recorded in the Patent and Trademark Office. In case of change of ownership the Director shall, at the request of the owner and upon a proper showing and the payment of the prescribed fee, issue to such assignee a new certificate of registration of the said mark in the name of such assignee, and for the unexpired part of the original period.

The Lanham Act: § 1060. (§ 10) Assignment
This statute sets out the conditions under which a mark that has been, or is to be, registered may be sold (assigned) to another party.

(a) (1) A registered mark or a mark for which an application to register has been filed shall be assignable with the good will of the business in which the mark is used, or with that part of the good will of the business connected with the use of and symbolized by the mark. Notwithstanding the preceding sentence, no application to register a mark under section 1051 (b) of this title shall be assignable prior to the filing of an amendment under section 1051 (c) of this title to bring the application into conformity with section 1051 (a) of this title or the filing of the verified statement of use under section 1051 (d) of this title, except for an assignment to a successor to the business of the applicant, or portion thereof, to which the mark pertains, if that business is ongoing and existing.

(2) In any assignment authorized by this section, it shall not be necessary to include the good will of the business connected with the use of and symbolized by any other mark used in the business or by the name or style under which the business is conducted.

(3) Assignments shall be by instruments in writing duly executed. Acknowledgment shall be prima facie evidence of the execution of an assignment, and when the prescribed information reporting the assignment is recorded in the United States Patent and Trademark Office, the record shall be prima facie evidence of execution.

(4) An assignment shall be void against any subsequent purchaser for valuable consideration without notice, unless the prescribed information reporting the assignment is recorded in the United States Patent and Trademark Office within 3 months after the date of the assignment or prior to the subsequent purchase.

(5) The United States Patent and Trademark Office shall maintain a record of information on assignments, in such form as may be prescribed by the Director.

(b) An assignee not domiciled in the United States may designate by a document filed in the United States Patent and Trademark Office the name and address of a person resident in the United States on whom may be served notices or process in proceedings affecting the mark. Such notices or process may be served upon the person so designated by leaving with that person or mailing to that person a copy thereof at the address specified in the last designation so filed. If the person so designated cannot be found at the address given in the last designation, or if the assignee does not designate by a document filed in the United States Patent and Trademark Office the name and address of a person resident in the United States on whom may be served notices or process in proceedings affecting the mark, such notices or process may be served upon the Director.

Related terms: certificate of registration; goodwill; Lanham Act; ownership of mark in the United States.

attorney fees in trademark infringement actions

The Lanham Act authorizes a court to award attorney fees only in cases of "exceptional" infringement. To qualify as such a case, the defendant must have acted willfully, intentionally, or maliciously. This does not mean that all willful infringements result in such awards. However they are more likely when there are facts showing that the infringer was fully aware of the infringement and simply hoped to get away with it.

Attorney fees may also be awarded if infringement occurred as a result of a breach of contract or license that itself provides for attorney fees. In these cases, there is no need to show willfulness.

Related terms: infringement; innocent infringer; Lanham Act.

average reasonably prudent consumer

In deciding trademark conflicts, courts often try to imagine whether an average reasonably prudent consumer would likely be confused by the two marks. This viewpoint is particularly helpful in deciding:

- if an infringed mark is distinctive enough to warrant protection by the court, and
- whether the infringing mark would be likely to mislead or confuse the public.

If a court determines that a hypothetical consumer would be likely to know the infringed mark because of its distinctiveness and also would be confused by the use of the infringing mark, then infringement may be found.

In a trademark infringement action where consumer confusion is alleged, the parties typically conduct consumer polls to discover the actual views of the "average consumer" and introduce the results of such polls in support of their case.

Related terms: likelihood of confusion.

award, use of trademark in ratings or

A company that receives a rating or award may desire to include information about that award (or an image of the award) in its advertising—for example, a software company may want to feature a "World Class Award" from *PC World* magazine in its ads or on its packaging. Because such uses are commercial and may confuse consumers, permission should be acquired before using another company's trademark. Most companies that provide ratings or awards have guidelines for the use of their marks in advertising. Some require a written agreement from the user; some have a policy not to permit the use of their trademarks for other companies' products regardless of the rating, review, or award. For example, Consumers Union, the publisher of *Consumer Reports*, opposes use of its trademark in product advertisements.

Bureau of Customs and Border Protection

Under the U.S. Customs Act, a trademark owner whose mark is on the Principal Register may record the mark with the U.S. Bureau of Customs and Border Protection (BCBP). (19 Code of Federal Regulation Part 133, Subparts (A) and (B).) This authorizes customs inspectors to seize any products bearing infringing marks and to contact the mark's owner. If the infringing importer agrees to remove the offending mark, or the mark's owner waives the right to object, the goods will be released. Otherwise, they will be destroyed. As a practical matter, most customs enforcement occurs at the behest of trademark owners who conduct their own investigations and tip off the BCBP to the arrival of infringing goods. Currently, the recording cannot be made electronically. However the BCBP (www.cbp.gov) has prepared a Trademark Recordation Application Template that can be downloaded and mailed.

Related terms: Principal Register; protection of marks under Lanham Act.

cancellation of registration

See opposing and canceling a trademark registration.

certificate of registration

A certificate of registration is proof that a mark has been registered with the U.S. Patent and Trademark Office (USPTO) on the Principal Register. The certificate reproduces the mark and sets out the date of the mark's first use in commerce. In addition, the certificate lists:

- the type of product or service on which the mark is used

- the number and date of registration
- the term of registration
- the date on which the application for registration was received at the USPTO, and
- any conditions and limitations that the USPTO has imposed on the registration, such as restricting use to a certain marketing area to avoid conflict with another registered mark.

The certificate of registration substantially simplifies the task of obtaining relief from a court if it is necessary to file a trademark infringement lawsuit. Besides proving registration, the certificate will be accepted by a court as proof that the registration is valid and that the registrant owns the mark. The exclusive right to use the mark in commerce on the product or service is also specified in the certificate.

The Lanham Act: § 1057. (§ 7) Certificates of registration

(a) Issuance and form

Certificates of registration of marks registered upon the principal register shall be issued in the name of the United States of America, under the seal of the Patent and Trademark Office, and shall be signed by the Director or have his signature placed thereon, and a record thereof shall be kept in the Patent and Trademark Office. The registration shall reproduce the mark, and state that the mark is registered on the principal register under this chapter, the date of the first use of the mark, the date of the first use of the mark in commerce, the particular goods or services for which it is registered, the number and date of the registration, the term thereof, the date on which the application for registration was received in the Patent and Trademark Office, and any conditions and limitations that may be imposed in the registration.

Related terms: ownership of mark in the United States; presumption of ownership; protection of marks under Lanham Act.

certification mark

A certification mark certifies regional or other origin, material, mode of manufacture, quality, accuracy, or other characteristics.

EXAMPLE: The California Certified Organic Farmers have established a standard to certify that food is free of pesticides. Farmers who meet these standards may use the CCOF certification mark on their food.

Certification marks have been described as a "special creature" of trademark law because a certification mark is never used by its owner. For example, the

CCOF mark is owned by a voluntary trade association based in Santa Cruz, California. The group never uses the CCOF mark, because it doesn't sell products. Instead, California farmers who meet organic farming standards use the CCOF label in conjunction with their brand name. For example, if you purchased Molino brand tomatoes, you would see the CCOF certification mark as well as the Molino trademark on the tomatoes.

A certification mark may attest to different qualities. For example, the mark can certify:

- **Safety.** The certification mark UL indicates that electrical equipment meets safety standards of the Underwriters Laboratory.
- **Quality.** Grass seed that includes the Lawn Institute Seal of Approval is certified as being "capable of yielding a fine-textured lawn which is normally perennial in the climate where marketed."
- **Accuracy.** The certification mark SPER Certified guarantees the accuracy of weather-forecasting equipment.
- **Materials used.** Clothing with the certification mark Grown and Made in the USA guarantees the apparel was made in the United States with cotton grown in the United States.
- **Mode of manufacture.** The Log Splitter Manufacturer's Association certification mark indicates that a log-splitting device has been built according to the manufacturing standards established by the LSMA.
- **Regional origin.** The certification mark Roquefort authenticates that cheese was manufactured from sheep's milk in the caves of Roquefort, France, according to long-established methods.
- **Source of labor.** ILGWU—UNION MADE certifies that a garment was manufactured by the International Ladies Garment Workers Union.
- **Morality.** The Intelligent Sex Seal of Approval certifies that books and videotapes discuss or portray "sexual relations in a constructive and healthy manner as part of an intelligent nondegrading relationship between fully consenting adults."

Certification marks are registered under the Lanham Act. The certifier (that is, the organization granting the certification) is the only party permitted to file the certification mark application. The certifier must submit a copy of the certification standards (that is, what it takes to qualify to use the certification mark). However, the USPTO does not verify these standards. The owner of the certification mark is usually engaged solely in the certification process, but it is possible that the owner may also engage in sales or services. For example, the

Rust-Oleum Company sells a rust preventive coating. The company also has a certification mark, Protected by Rust-Oleum, that certifies those who provide the rust preventive services.

Certification marks must be retained by the persons or groups originating them. Assigning or licensing a certification mark to others destroys any meaning the mark may have had and constitutes an abandonment of the mark. Certification marks may be registered in the United States under the Lanham Act in the same manner as other marks.

Related terms: geographic terms as marks; protection of marks under Lanham Act; trademark.

characters as trademarks

Fictional characters such as Mickey Mouse or Mr. Clean may serve as trademarks. All that is required is that the character, like any trademark, be sufficiently distinctive or have acquired secondary meaning. Trademarked characters can be graphic or "drawn" characters such as the Pillsbury Doughboy or characters portrayed by actors, such as "Mr. Whipple" (Charmin bathroom tissue).

classes of goods and services

See International Schedule of Classes of Goods and Services.

coined terms

See fanciful terms.

collective mark

A collective mark is a symbol, label, word, phrase, or other mark used by members of a group or organization to identify goods members produce or services they render. A common use of collective marks is to show membership in a union, association, or other organization. Collective marks are entitled to registration and the same federal protection as other types of marks.

A collective mark differs from a trademark or a service mark in that use of the collective mark is restricted to members of the group. The mark's primary function is to inform the public that specific goods or services come from members of a group, thus distinguishing them from products or services of nonmembers. However, the organization itself, as opposed to its members, cannot use the collective mark on any goods it produces. If the organization itself wants to identify its product, it must use its own trademark or service mark.

EXAMPLE: The letters "ILGWU" on a shirt is a collective mark identifying the shirt as a product of members of the International Ladies Garment Workers Union and distinguishes it from shirts made by nonunion shops. If the ILGWU actually started marketing its own products, however, it could not use the ILGWU collective mark to identify them.

Related terms: protection of marks under Lanham Act.

color as an element of a mark

If registering a mark in which color is claimed as a component, the applicant must submit the image of the mark in color, not black and white, as well as a separate statement describing where the color(s) appear on the mark. See the *Trademark Manual of Examination Procedures* § 807.07 for further information.

Related terms: color used as mark.

color used as mark

In 1985, a federal appeals court ruled that a single color—pink—could function as a trademark for fiberglass products. (*In re Owens-Corning Fiberglass Corp.*, 774 F.2d 1116 (Fed. Cir. 1985).) This does not preclude every other business from using pink, only other makers of fiberglass and related products. In 1995, the U.S. Supreme Court ruled that a single color—green—could function as a trademark for ironing pads. (*Qualitex Company v. Jacobson Prods. Co.*, 514 U.S. 159 (1995).) The Supreme Court held that a single color is registrable if both are true:

- Over time, consumers have come to view the color as an identification or the source of the product (rather than the product itself).
- The color has no function.

EXAMPLE: In the *Qualitex* case (*Qualitex Company v. Jacobson Prods. Co.*, 514 U.S. 159 (1995)), the product in question was a green-gold pad designed for dry cleaning presses. The green-gold color was not associated with dry cleaning pads as such, had no functional purpose, and operated only to identify the pads as originating with Qualitex. Once these facts were established, the court saw no reason why the color couldn't qualify as a trademark as long as it could be shown that consumers relied on the color to identify the source of the pads.

If, on the other hand, a color has a function—for instance, the color blue used to signify nitrogen content, or bright yellow used for tennis balls so they can be seen in limited lighting—it won't qualify as a trademark.

Related terms: color as an element of a mark; distinctive mark; trade dress; trademark.

commerce that Congress may regulate

To qualify for registration and/or protection of a trademark under the Lanham Act, a mark must have first been used "in commerce that Congress may regulate." The Lanham Act defines commerce as business or trade that the federal government, through the U.S. Congress, is authorized by the U.S. Constitution to control. Technically, this means that to qualify for protection under the Lanham Act, a business must do at least one of the following:

- ship a product across state lines, as do most manufacturers, wholesalers, ecommerce sellers, or mail order businesses
- ship a product between a state and a territory or a territory and another territory (for instance, between New York and Puerto Rico or between Puerto Rico and the Virgin Islands)
- ship a product between a state or territory and another country (for instance, between California and Hong Kong or between Puerto Rico and Cuba)
- conduct a service business across state lines, as do most trucking operations and many 900 numbers
- conduct a service business in more than one state (Taco Bell, Chevron, Hilton Hotels) or across international or territorial borders, or
- operate a business that caters to domestic or international travelers, such as a hotel, restaurant, tour guide service, or ski resort.

An applicant cannot attempt to circumvent the commerce requirement with a sweetheart sale—a transaction made solely to satisfy the interstate commerce requirement, for example, selling a carton of wine to a cousin in Alabama.

The reason for the "commerce" requirement is that Congress only has power under the commerce clause of the Constitution to regulate U.S. businesses to the extent they engage in interstate, interterritorial, or international activity. Thus, the Lanham Act (the statute governing trademark registration) can only affect marks in commerce as defined here. Because Congress has no power under the commerce clause to affect marks used in only one state, the regulation of such marks is up to the individual states.

Trademark Law: Definitions

As a general rule, the U.S. Patent and Trademark Office (USPTO) doesn't question a registration applicant's assertion that a mark is being used in "commerce," which means the issue of commerce will arise only if the validity of the registration is called into question in an opposition or cancellation proceeding or in an infringement lawsuit. Also, the prevalence of commerce on the Internet, which by definition crosses state, territorial, and international boundaries, has made the determination even less of an issue.

Related terms: Lanham Act; state trademark laws; use of mark.

commercial name

See trade name.

Commissioner for Trademarks

The Commissioner for Trademarks is the title of the person who manages the trademark division of the U.S. Patent and Trademark Office. The previous title for this position was the Assistant Commissioner for Trademarks.

Related terms: Director of the U.S. Patent and Trademark Office; U.S. Patent and Trademark Office (USPTO).

Community Trademark

In 1996, the European Union began accepting applications for a community trademark, a registration that is good in 25 EU countries. To qualify for registration, the proposed mark must be acceptable in all 25 countries. Applications are to be submitted to the Office for Harmonization of the Internal Market, in Alicante, Spain. For more information on the Community Trademark, visit the Office of Harmonization website at http://oami.europa.eu.

competing and noncompeting products

When the sale of one product might preclude the sale of another product, the products are said to be competing. For instance, if one company sells a car, it obviously competes with another company's ability to sell a similar car, but it may also compete with the sales of pickup trucks or motorcycles.

Products are noncompeting when consumers could reasonably purchase both items—that is, the purchase of one is not at the expense of the other. For example, perfume does not compete with long-haul trailer trucks.

If the marks used on two competing products or services are similar enough to potentially confuse consumers, the owner of the mark found to be infringed upon may sometimes be awarded money damages measured by the amount of profits the other mark's owner earned as a result of the infringement (called defendant's profits). The owner may also be entitled to prevent future infringing use of the mark by the infringing party.

When goods are found to be not competing but are related enough to warrant a finding of potential consumer confusion (for example, they are distributed in the same channels to the same consumer base), the mark's owner can collect any actual damages and also prevent the other party from using the mark in the future. However, the defendant's profits are generally not awarded in this situation, because the infringer by definition did not earn its profits at the expense of the mark's owner.

Related terms: infringement; related products and services.

composite mark

Marks that consist of several words—for example, the slogan "Don't Leave Home Without It" owned by American Express—are sometimes referred to as composite or hybrid marks. The strength of a composite mark depends on the effect of the whole mark, not just its individual terms. That is, every term in the mark may be ordinary, and yet the whole may be a distinctive and therefore protectable mark.

When registering a composite mark with the U.S. Patent and Trademark Office, the applicant is usually required to disclaim ownership of the unregistrable parts in order to register the mark as a whole. This may mean that each individual term in the mark is disclaimed, even while ownership in the entire mark is asserted.

Related terms: disclaimer of unregistrable material.

concurrent registration

In some circumstances, two or more owners of identical or similar marks may be allowed to register their marks with the U.S. Patent and Trademark Office (USPTO). This can happen if both of the following are true:

- Both marks were in use in commerce before either owner applied for registration.
- The likelihood of consumer confusion is slight, either because the products or services to which the marks will be connected are not closely related or because they will be distributed in entirely different markets.

When allowing concurrent registrations, the USPTO may specify marketing and use limitations on each of the marks to preclude consumer confusion. For

Trademark Law: Definitions

example, the USPTO may restrict the use of one mark to ten western states and allow the use of the other mark in the rest of the states. Or the use of the respective marks may be restricted to their original products or services.

Related terms: competing and noncompeting products; interference; related products and services.

confusion of consumers

See likelihood of confusion.

Related terms: average reasonably prudent consumer; initial interest confusion; infringement.

constructive notice of mark under Lanham Act

When a mark is placed on the federal Principal Register, the law assumes that all other mark users anywhere in the United States will know that someone else owns that registered mark. This means that even if a second user has no actual knowledge of the registered mark, such knowledge will be implied, because the Principal Register is a public record, available for inspection.

This constructive (assumed) notice precludes anyone else's legal use of the mark anywhere in the United States, unless such use began before the registration. Assuming the mark's owner affixed proper notice of registration to the mark (usually an "R" in a circle: ®), the constructive notice also means the trademark owner qualifies to recover large (treble) damages and perhaps attorney fees.

The courts commonly refuse to find infringement if the marks in question are used in geographically separate markets. However, this rule has less importance as Internet commerce increases, thus extending the geographic reach of most companies. If the owner of a registered mark later chooses to expand into a market in which the infringing mark is being used, the infringer will have to give up the mark, unless its use predated the registration. As a result, it is always wise to do a trademark search before selecting a new mark to make sure the mark is available in all regions and for all products anticipated.

Related terms: geographically separate market; infringement; Principal Register.

continuous use of mark

A mark that is continuously used for five years after placement on the federal Principal Register may qualify as "incontestable." That means that the mark may no longer be challenged by another user on the ground that it is too weak (ordinary) to warrant legal protection. Any showing of a substantial interruption in the use of the mark during the five-year period may, however, prevent the mark from becoming incontestable.

Related terms: duration of federal trademark registration; incontestability status.

contributory infringer

"Contributory infringement occurs when the defendant either intentionally induces a third party to infringe the plaintiff's mark or supplies a product to a third party with actual or constructive knowledge that the product is being used to infringe the service mark." (*Lockheed Martin Corp. v. Network Solutions, Inc.,* 194 F.3d 980, 983 (9th Cir. 1999).) Like a criminal accomplice, a contributory infringer is a party who furthers or encourages the infringing activity of another. For example, a store that sells records carrying an infringing mark is considered a contributory infringer, as is the wholesale distributor of the records and any other person or business whose actions contribute to the infringement.

Contributory infringers are not liable for damages or defendant's profits as long as they were innocent (they didn't know about the infringement), but they may be enjoined (barred) from any further contributory activity. Thus, the record store owner might have to stop selling the infringing records unless the offending mark were removed. But if a contributory infringer knows of the infringement, he or she can be held liable on the same basis and in the same amount as the principal infringer. For example, eBay was not found to be liable for sale of counterfeit Tiffany jewelry because eBay did not know or had no reason to know which sellers were infringing on Tiffany's marks. A district court determined that Tiffany—not eBay—had the burden of protecting its trademark at the auction site. (*Tiffany (NJ) Inc. v. eBay, Inc.,* 576 F. Supp. 2d. 475 (S.D. N.Y. 2008).) The Second Circuit upheld the trademark ruling. (*Tiffany (NJ) Inc. v. eBay, Inc.,* 600 F. 3d 93 (2d Cir. 2010).) In a different case, however, a district court held that an Internet Service Provider (ISP) that hosted several websites selling fake Louis Vuitton merchandise could be liable for contributory infringement. The district court likened the ISPs in this case to the proprietor of the flea market found liable for contributory infringement. (*Louis Vuitton Malletier v. Akanoc Solutions,* 591 F. Supp. 2d 1098 (N.D. Cal. 2008).)

Related terms: infringement; innocent infringer; publishers of advertising matter.

counterfeit

Counterfeiting is the act of making or selling lookalike goods or services bearing fake trademarks, for example, a business deliberately duplicating the Adidas

Trademark Law: Definitions

trademark on shoes. Likelihood of confusion is self-evident in counterfeiting, because the counterfeiter's primary purpose is to confuse or dupe consumers. Even when a buyer knows that the product is a fake, the business is still liable for counterfeiting, because the product can still be used to deceive others. Counterfeiting is not limited to consumer products such as watches and handbags. A website that copied the Playboy Bunny logo for adult sex subscription services was assessed $10,000 for trademark counterfeiting. (*Playboy Enterprises Inc. v. Universal Tel-A-Talk Inc.*, 1999 U.S. Dist. LEXIS 6124 (E.D. Pa. 1999).)

Proving infringement is easier when dealing with counterfeits because there is usually no need to conduct a factor-by-factor analysis of likelihood of confusion. In a case involving two merchandising companies, the district court ruled that by their very nature, counterfeit goods cause confusion. (*Bravado International Group Merchandising Services v. Ninna, Inc.*, U.S. Dist. LEXIS 78040 (E.D. N.Y. October 6, 2008).)

The remedies for trademark counterfeiting under the Lanham Act are much harsher than for traditional trademark infringement and unless a court finds some mitigating circumstances, treble damages or profits and a reasonable attorney fee award will be awarded if the counterfeiter knew that the goods were counterfeit and intended to offer them for sale. In addition, the counterfeiter must have duplicated the trademark on the goods or services for which the trademark was federally registered. For example, it is not counterfeiting to put the Gucci mark on automobile seat covers, as these are not goods for which Gucci has a registered trademark.

An offer to sell counterfeit products can also trigger liability as a counterfeiter. For example, an individual offered to sell counterfeit jeans and provided a sample to an undercover police officer. Proof of actual production or sale of the jeans was not necessary to prove counterfeiting.

Similarly, an Internet Service Provider (ISP) that hosted several websites selling fake Louis Vuitton merchandise could be liable for contributory infringement. The district court likened the ISPs in this case to the proprietor of the flea market found liable for contributory infringement. (*Louis Vuitton Malletier v. Akanoc Solutions,* 591 F. Supp. 2d 1098 (N.D. Cal. 2008).)

Related terms: likelihood of confusion; related products and services; same or similar mark.

Customs, Bureau of

See Bureau of Customs and Border Protection.

cybergriping

See free speech and trademark law.

cybersquatting

Cybersquatting originated at a time when most businesses were not savvy about the commercial opportunities on the Internet. Some entrepreneurial souls registered the names of well-known companies as domain names with the intent of selling the names back to the companies when the companies finally realized the economic potential of the Internet. Panasonic, Fry's Electronics, Hertz, and Avon were among the early victims of cybersquatters. Opportunities for cybersquatters are rapidly diminishing, because businesses now know the importance of registering domain names and because there are two legal mechanisms of wresting the name from the cybersquatter.

A common variation on cybersquatting is typosquatting, in which misspellings of a domain name are used to mistakenly attract or mislead consumers. Typosquatting can be lucrative when tied to the use of an Internet advertising scheme such as Google Adsense. For example, in a 2006 case a typosquatter purchased domain names such as lnadsend.com and landswnd.com, and then, after sending the customer to the legitimate Lands' End website, charged Lands' End, claiming that these were referrals under the Lands' End referral program (for which the typosquatter belonged under another, legitimate domain). Lands' End filed suit, and the defendant's attempts to dismiss the suit were rejected. (*Lands' End, Inc. v. Remy*, 447 F. Supp. 2d 941 (W.D. Wis., September 1, 2006).)

The failure to sell or offer the names is not the only evidence of bad faith. For example, in one case a company registered domain names that combined elements of Bank of America and Merrill Lynch—for example bofaml.com. The defendant argued that it had never sold a domain name. The court rejected that argument since the defendant earned considerable sums by "parking" the domains—that is, by generating pay-per-click revenue. (*Webadvisor v. Bank of America Corp.*, S.D. N.Y., No. 09-cv-05769-DC, February 16, 2009).)

Related terms: Anticybersquatting Consumer Protection Act; dilution of mark; domain name; UDRP.

Trademark Law: Definitions

damages in trademark infringement cases

If the infringed mark was federally registered and the owner provided proper notice of registration when using the mark (that is, "®" or "Reg. U.S. Pat. Off."), a court is also authorized under the Lanham Act to award the owner:

- treble damages—that is, up to three times the actual money damages suffered as a result of the infringement (37 United States Code, Section 1117)
- defendant's profits—the profits made by the defendant from the infringing activity (usually only awarded if infringement was deliberate on products or services that compete in the marketplace), and
- attorney fees, in clear-cut cases of deliberate infringement.

The court may not, however, award the owner of the infringed mark defendant's profits and money damages on the same lost sales.

The Lanham Act: § 1117. (§ 35) Recovery for violation of rights

This statute sets out the types of money damages that the owner of a registered or unregistered mark is entitled to recover in a trademark infringement lawsuit and provides for attorney fees to be awarded in exceptional cases.

(a) Profits; damages and costs; attorney fees

When a violation of any right of the registrant of a mark registered in the Patent and Trademark Office, a violation under section 1125 (a) or (d) of this title, or a willful violation under section 1125 (c) of this title, shall have been established in any civil action arising under this chapter, the plaintiff shall be entitled, subject to the provisions of sections 1111 and 1114 of this title, and subject to the principles of equity, to recover

(1) defendant's profits,

(2) any damages sustained by the plaintiff, and

(3) the costs of the action. The court shall assess such profits and damages or cause the same to be assessed under its direction. In assessing profits the plaintiff shall be required to prove defendant's sales only; defendant must prove all elements of cost or deduction claimed. In assessing damages the court may enter judgment, according to the circumstances of the case, for any sum above the amount found as actual damages, not exceeding three times such amount. If the court shall find that the amount of the recovery based on profits is either inadequate or excessive the court may in its discretion enter judgment for such sum as the court shall find to be just, according to the circumstances of the case. Such sum in either of the above circumstances shall constitute compensation and not a penalty. The court in exceptional cases may award reasonable attorney fees to the prevailing party.

(b) Treble damages for use of counterfeit mark

In assessing damages under subsection (a) of this section, the court shall, unless the court finds extenuating circumstances, enter judgment for three times such profits or damages, whichever is greater, together with a reasonable attorney's fee, in the case of any violation of section 1114 (1)(a) of this title or section 220506 of title 36 that consists of intentionally using a mark or designation, knowing such mark or designation is a counterfeit mark (as defined in section 1116 (d) of this title), in connection with the sale, offering for sale, or distribution of goods or services. In such cases, the court may in its discretion award prejudgment interest on such amount at an annual interest rate established under section 6621 (a)(2) of title 26, commencing on the date of the service of the claimant's pleadings setting forth the claim for such entry and ending on the date such entry is made, or for such shorter time as the court deems appropriate.

(c) Statutory damages for use of counterfeit marks

In a case involving the use of a counterfeit mark (as defined in section 1116 (d) of this title) in connection with the sale, offering for sale, or distribution of goods or services, the plaintiff may elect, at any time before final judgment is rendered by the trial court, to recover, instead of actual damages and profits under subsection (a) of this section, an award of statutory damages for any such use in connection with the sale, offering for sale, or distribution of goods or services in the amount of—

(1) not less than $500 or more than $100,000 per counterfeit mark per type of goods or services sold, offered for sale, or distributed, as the court considers just; or

(2) if the court finds that the use of the counterfeit mark was willful, not more than $1,000,000 per counterfeit mark per type of goods or services sold, offered for sale, or distributed, as the court considers just.

(d) Statutory damages for violation of section 1125 (d)(1)

In a case involving a violation of section 1125 (d)(1) of this title, the plaintiff may elect, at any time before final judgment is rendered by the trial court, to recover, instead of actual damages and profits, an award of statutory damages in the amount of not less than $1,000 and not more than $100,000 per domain name, as the court considers just.

deceptive terms as marks

Related terms: geographic terms as marks; prohibited and reserved marks under Lanham Act.

defendant's profits

Profits earned by a defendant as a result of infringing a mark may be awarded to the owner of a mark federally registered under the Lanham Act if:

- The owner placed proper notice of registration next to the mark (that is, " ®" or "Reg. U.S. Pat. Off.").
- The infringement was deliberate rather than innocent.

- The underlying goods or services competed with each other in the marketplace.

Awarding defendant's profits to the injured party prevents an infringer from realizing any gain from infringement.

To recover defendant's profits, the owner only needs to prove the amount the defendant earned from the sales of the goods or services. Then, the defendant is given the opportunity to establish his or her costs (for instance, cost of production, sales attributable to other factors, and so on) and deduct them from the gross sales amount to arrive at the amount of profits.

Related terms: competing and noncompeting products; damages in trademark infringement cases; related products and services.

deliberate infringer (or willful infringer)

As a general rule, an infringement will be deemed deliberate if it begins after the mark in question has been federally registered, because the infringer is deemed to have notice of the existing mark.

Related terms: constructive notice of mark under Lanham Act; contributory infringer; innocent infringer.

descriptive mark

Descriptive marks are considered ordinary and therefore weak. Weak marks do not merit much judicial protection unless the owner can demonstrate sufficient sales and advertising. That's because a mark that describes the characteristics of a product or service does not effectively distinguish it from similar products or services offered by others. Protecting descriptive marks does not fulfill the primary purpose of the trademark laws, which is to protect marks that operate as indicators of origin. Also, the law doesn't want to grant a trademark owner the exclusive use of words and phrases that are in common use as descriptive adjectives, because that would limit others' legitimate need to use such a word in their advertising. A descriptive mark will only be protected under trademark law if it achieves secondary meaning—that is, it becomes distinctive because consumers associate the mark with specific goods or services.

Marks that are judged to be descriptive and which do not have secondary meaning do not qualify for placement on the Principal Register under the Lanham Act. Instead, they are placed on a list called the Supplemental Register, which offers much less protection than the Principal Register. After a descriptive mark has been in continuous use for five years, however, it can be moved to the Principal Register under the theory that it has developed secondary meaning: It has become a well-known identifier of a product or service through public exposure. At that point, a descriptive mark does act to distinguish certain products or services from others.

If a descriptive mark is mistakenly placed on the Principal Register by the USPTO, another party may challenge the mark's validity up until the time the mark becomes incontestable (five years on the Principal Register). Once incontestability occurs, the mark is immune from a challenge on the ground that it is descriptive.

Related terms: incontestability status; secondary meaning; Supplemental Register.

dilution

Dilution occurs when someone uses a famous mark in a manner that blurs or tarnishes the mark. In other words, dilution diminishes the capacity of a famous mark to identify and distinguish goods or services, regardless of the presence or absence of:

- competition between the owner of the famous mark and other parties, or
- likelihood of confusion, mistake, or deception (15 United States Code, Section 1527).

Dilution is therefore different from trademark infringement, because trademark infringement always involves a probability of customer confusion, whereas dilution can occur even if customers wouldn't be misled. For example, if a person sells sex aids named "Microsoft," no consumer is likely to associate Fred's products with the software company, Microsoft. However, because Microsoft has become such a strong and famous mark, the use of the word on sex aids would definitely trivialize the software company's mark (dilute its strength by tarnishing its reputation for quality or blurring its distinctiveness).

Until the Federal Trademark Dilution Act was enacted in 1996, (15 United States Code, Section1125(c)), there was no federal law prohibiting trademark dilution and only about half the states provided some recourse—usually an injunction against further use of the mark. As with the state statutes, the federal law applies only to famous marks and provides primarily for injunctive relief (a court order requiring the infringing party to stop using the mark). However, if the famous mark's owner can prove the infringer "willfully intended to trade on the owner's reputation or to cause dilution of the famous mark," the court has discretion to award the owner attorneys' fees and defendant's profits as well as actual damages.

Trademark Law: Definitions

In March 2003, in a case involving Victoria's Secret, the Supreme Court confirmed what many practitioners already knew: that the federal dilution law (unlike traditional trademark law) was not intended to protect consumers but rather to protect famous trademarks. The Supreme Court determined that in order to prevail on a federal dilution claim, the owner of a famous mark must demonstrate actual dilution has occurred, not the likelihood of dilution. In other words, dilution can only be proven by evidence of actual harm to the famous mark—for example, survey evidence or other direct proof that shows that consumers perceive the famous mark less favorably. (*Moseley v. V Secret Catalogue, Inc.*, 537 U.S. 418 (2003).)

Unfortunately, the Supreme Court did not provide much guidance on the type or amount of proof required to prove dilution. Since *Moseley* was decided, the owners of famous marks bringing dilution claims have had the best results when seeking to prevent dilution of an identical mark. In *Savin Corp. v. The Savin Group*, 391 F.3d 439 (2d Cir. 2004), the U.S. District Court of Appeals ruled that when the marks are identical, not merely similar, no further proof is required. Still, the issue of proof remains unresolved. In one case, for example, a district court rejected expert witness testimony based on assumptions and hypothetical consumers. (*Monster Cable Products, Inc. v. Discovery Communications Inc.*, 2004 WL 2445348 (N.D. Cal. 2004).)

The Trademark Dilution Revision Act. Much of this turmoil was resolved in 2006, when Congress enacted the Trademark Dilution Revision Act (TDRA). That revised the Lanham Act by eliminating the need to demonstrate actual or likely confusion, competition, or actual economic injury when the owner of a famous mark seeks an injunction to stop dilution by blurring or tarnishment. Still some confusion remains as to the standards required to prove blurring and tarnishment.

> EXAMPLE: In a 2010 case, the Second Circuit determined that the term "Charbucks" does not tarnish the reputation of the Starbucks mark merely based on the evidence of an association and a negative connotation. Charbucks could blur the Starbucks mark but the district court's requirement of substantial similarity was not appropriate—all that was required was a measurement of the degree of similarity. (*Starbucks Corp. v. Wolf's Borough Coffee, Inc.*, 588 F.3d 97 (2d. Cir. 2009).)

The revision defined a mark as being "famous" if it is widely recognized by the general consuming public as a designation of the source of the goods or services of the mark's owner, and it allows the court to consider all relevant factors when determining whether a mark is famous, including: (1) the duration, extent, and geographic reach of advertising and publicity of the mark; (2) the amount, volume, and geographic extent of sales of goods or services offered under the mark; (3) the extent of actual recognition of the mark; and (4) whether the mark was registered on the principal register.

The revision defined "dilution by blurring" as an association arising from the similarity between a famous mark and a similar mark or trade name that impairs the distinctiveness of the famous mark, and allows the court to consider all relevant factors when determining whether a mark or trade name is likely to cause dilution by blurring, including: (1) the degree of similarity; (2) the degree of inherent or acquired distinctiveness of the famous mark; (3) the extent to which the owner of the famous mark is engaging in substantially exclusive use of the mark; (4) the degree of recognition of the famous mark; (5) whether the user of the mark or trade name intended to create an association with the famous mark; and (6) any actual association between the mark or trade name and the famous mark. "Tarnishment" was defined as an association arising from the similarity between a mark or trade name and a famous mark that harms the reputation of the famous mark.

The TDRA also declared that certain acts are not actionable as dilution by blurring or tarnishment, including: (1) any fair use of a famous mark by another person other than as a designation of source for the person's own goods or services, including for advertising or promotion that permits consumers to compare goods or services, or identifying and parodying, criticizing, or commenting upon the famous mark owner or the owner's goods or services; (2) all forms of news reporting and news commentary; and (3) any noncommercial use of a mark.

And finally, the TDRA allows the owner of a famous mark to seek additional remedies in an action if the person against whom the injunction is sought:

- first used the mark or trade name in commerce after the date of enactment of this act;
- willfully intended to trade on the recognition of the famous mark; or
- willfully intended to harm the reputation of the famous mark.

Ownership of a valid registration is a complete bar to an action under state common law or statute that seeks to prevent dilution by blurring or tarnishment, or that asserts any claim of actual or likely damage or harm to the distinctiveness or reputation of a mark, label, or form of advertisement.

In the first appellate case heard under the TDRA, the Fourth Circuit Court of Appeals held that the Louis Vuitton trademark was not diluted by the use of the term "Chewy Vuitton" for a pet chew toy that was "evocative" of a Louis Vuitton bag. The defendant produced a line of chew toys that parodied famous designers such as "Furcedes" (parodying Mercedes) and "Chewnel No. 5 (Chanel No. 5). The court determined that Chewy Vuitton was a parody and that a successful parody would not dilute the famous brand but in fact may make it even more famous. (*Louis Vuitton v. Haute Diggity Dog*, 507 F.3d 252 (4th Cir 2007).)

While it is still possible to sue for dilution under a state statute, most actions to stop dilution are now brought under the new federal law. One exception to this is when use of the famous mark also tarnishes its reputation. For example, in the Microsoft sex aid example, the association of "Microsoft" with sex aids may fairly be said to detract from the dignity of the Microsoft mark (there is little room for humor in the commercial world). Under state statutes, an action may be brought for tarnishment as well as dilution, whereas the federal act does not speak to tarnishment at all, although many observers believe that the courts will interpret the statute to include it as a basis for relief.

The Lanham Act: § 1125. (§ 43c)

(c) Dilution by blurring; dilution by tarnishment

    (1) Injunctive relief

        Subject to the principles of equity, the owner of a famous mark that is distinctive, inherently or through acquired distinctiveness, shall be entitled to an injunction against another person who, at any time after the owner's mark has become famous, commences use of a mark or trade name in commerce that is likely to cause dilution by blurring or dilution by tarnishment of the famous mark, regardless of the presence or absence of actual or likely confusion, of competition, or of actual economic injury.

    (2) Definitions

      (A) For purposes of paragraph (1), a mark is famous if it is widely recognized by the general consuming public of the United States as a designation of source of the goods or services of the mark's owner. In determining whether a mark possesses the requisite degree of recognition, the court may consider all relevant factors, including the following:

        (i) The duration, extent, and geographic reach of advertising and publicity of the mark, whether advertised or publicized by the owner or third parties.

        (ii) The amount, volume, and geographic extent of sales of goods or services offered under the mark.

        (iii) The extent of actual recognition of the mark.

(iv) Whether the mark was registered under the Act of March 3, 1881, or the Act of February 20, 1905, or on the principal register.

(B) For purposes of paragraph (1), "dilution by blurring" is association arising from the similarity between a mark or trade name and a famous mark that impairs the distinctiveness of the famous mark. In determining whether a mark or trade name is likely to cause dilution by blurring, the court may consider all relevant factors, including the following:

(i) The degree of similarity between the mark or trade name and the famous mark.

(ii) The degree of inherent or acquired distinctiveness of the famous mark.

(iii) The extent to which the owner of the famous mark is engaging in substantially exclusive use of the mark.

(iv) The degree of recognition of the famous mark.

(v) Whether the user of the mark or trade name intended to create an association with the famous mark.

(vi) Any actual association between the mark or trade name and the famous mark.

(C) For purposes of paragraph (1), "dilution by tarnishment" is association arising from the similarity between a mark or trade name and a famous mark that harms the reputation of the famous mark.

(3) Exclusions

The following shall not be actionable as dilution by blurring or dilution by tarnishment under this subsection:

(A) Any fair use, including a nominative or descriptive fair use, or facilitation of such fair use, of a famous mark by another person other than as a designation of source for the person's own goods or services, including use in connection with—

(i) advertising or promotion that permits consumers to compare goods or services; or

(ii) identifying and parodying, criticizing, or commenting upon the famous mark owner or the goods or services of the famous mark owner.

(B) All forms of news reporting and news commentary.

(C) Any noncommercial use of a mark.

The Lanham Act: § 1127. (§ 45) Construction and definitions; intent of chapter

The term "dilution" means the lessening of the capacity of a famous mark to identify and distinguish goods or services, regardless of the presence or absence of—

(1) competition between the owner of the famous mark and other parties, or

(2) likelihood of confusion, mistake, or deception.

Trademark Law: Definitions

Related terms: famous mark; Victoria's Secret case (*Moseley v. V Secret Catalogue, Inc.*).

Director of the U.S. Patent and Trademark Office
Related terms: Commissioner for Trademarks; U.S. Patent and Trademark Office.

disclaimer of trademark use
A disclaimer is a statement that disassociates any connection created by the use of another business's trademark. A disclaimer, by itself, cannot guarantee that a trademark use is permissible. However, courts have recognized prominently placed disclaimers as a factor in reducing consumer confusion. An effective disclaimer must be:

- **Prominently placed.** It must be reasonably close to the other business's trademark so that a consumer is likely to read the statement when viewing the trademark.
- **Permanently affixed.** Detachable tags and labels will not provide adequate notice.
- **Capable of being read and understood.** The disclaimer must provide a clear statement that the companies and their goods are not associated.
- **Have the effect of minimizing confusion.** Many courts seek proof that the disclaimer actually has the desired effect. For this reason, a company may want to test its disclaimer on consumers to be certain it will have the desired effect. Statements such as "unauthorized" may be too general to avoid consumer confusion.

EXAMPLE: A publisher advertised a Godzilla filmography book. The book's front cover included the statement, "Unauthorized." A brief disclaimer was included on the back cover. The owner of the Godzilla trademark sued for copyright and trademark infringement. The court ruled in favor of the trademark owner; the publisher's disclaimer was inadequate because the word "unauthorized" conveyed limited information. An appropriate disclaimer would have been: "The publication has not been prepared, approved, or licensed by any entity that created or produced the original Toho Godzilla films," and should have been printed on the front cover and spine of the book in a distinguishing color or typestyle. (*Toho Inc. v. William Morrow and Co.*, 33 F. Supp. 2d 1206 (C.D. Cal. 1998).)

disclaimer of unregistrable material

Often a trademark will consist of a distinctive word (for instance, "Nolo") in combination with one more unprotectable terms (such as "Press" as in Nolo Press, or ".com" as in Nolo.com). Or the entire mark may consist of unprotectable terms that taken together are distinctive because of how the terms are combined.

When owners of these types of marks seek to register them with the U.S. Patent and Trademark Office (USPTO), the USPTO will normally require the applicants to "disclaim" (agree to give up any claim to) ownership of the unprotectable terms, even though the mark itself would be registered. Thus, the owner of "Snappy Salsa" would have to disclaim "Salsa." These disclaimers make it clear that other businesses are free to use the disclaimed terms, as long as they don't use them in a way that would conflict with the distinctive aspects of the registered mark.

Related terms: composite mark; geographic terms as marks; protection of marks under Lanham Act.

disparaging mark

See prohibited and reserved marks under Lanham Act.

distinctive mark

Only marks that are distinctive (or "strong")—that is, that distinguish products and services—can function as trademarks. Some marks are "born" distinctive (sometimes referred to as "inherently distinctive") because in the context of their use they are memorable—for example, the mark may consist of terms that are arbitrary (Target Stores), suggestive (Jaguar cars), or fanciful (Reebok shoes). In addition, mundane or common marks—typically people's names, geographic designators, and descriptive terms—can become distinctive if they become well known over time (such as Microsoft Windows).

Distinctive marks excel in distinguishing their products or services from competing ones, which qualifies them for maximum judicial protection under state and federal laws. Because of this protection, distinctive marks are considered to be legally stronger than are marks considered common or ordinary because they describe the product's qualities (descriptive marks), use the owner's name, or are in widespread use for the particular product or service (in common use).

For example, any mark using the term "Kodak" would be considered infringing, since "Kodak" is a very strong mark and has no meaning other than as a mark. On the other hand, a mark with a common term like "data" will probably not infringe on another use of "data," since that word is already in wide use among large numbers of high-tech businesses.

A mark must be distinctive to qualify for placement on the Principal Register under the Lanham Act. A descriptive mark will only be protected under trademark law if it achieves secondary meaning—that is, it becomes distinctive because consumers associate the mark with specific goods or services.

Related terms: arbitrary mark; coined terms; descriptive mark; dilution of mark; generic terms; Principal Register; secondary meaning; strong mark; suggestive mark.

domain names

Consider www.nolo.com. The letters www (that stand for "World Wide Web") are automatically a part of almost every domain name. The middle part—Nolo—is the unique name that you select and register for your business.

When it comes to what are referred to as the generic top level domains (TLD)—typically the last part of a domain name, for example, .com—there are currently 21 choices:

- .aero, for the air transport industry
- .asia, for people and entities in the Asia-Pacific region
- .biz, restricted to businesses
- .cat, for users of Catalan language and culture
- .com, for commercial enterprises
- .coop, restricted to business cooperatives
- .edu, for educational institutions
- .gov, restricted to government agencies
- .info, for information providers
- .int, restricted to organizations endorsed by a treaty between two or more nations
- .jobs, for employment-related sites
- .mobi, for devices using mobile Internet
- .museum, restricted to museums and related persons
- .name, restricted to individuals.
- .net, for network-related entities
- .org, for nonprofit organizations
- .pro, restricted to licensed professionals
- .tel, for internet communication services
- .travel, for the travel industry, and
- .xxx for pornography

In addition, the .mil domain is reserved exclusively for the United States military. Finally, commencing in January 2012, companies should be able to apply for TLD suffixes that mirror company names and marks—for example .nike or .apple.

Every country also has a country code that serve as a TLD. For example, the country code suffix for the United States is .us. For France it's .fr, and for Greece it's .gr. The rules for obtaining one of these vary from country to country. Your business may qualify for a country code suffix even if it's not physically present in that country.

Occasionally, a business will choose a country code because the letters have some supposed promotional value. For example, the country code for Tuvalu is .tv, making it possible to acquire www.comedy.tv as a domain name. Similarly, the country code for Moldova is .md, so a doctor can nail down www.johnsmith .md. The country code for Andorra is .ad, making it a popular choice for commercial advertising businesses.

For now, the use of country codes is considered a novelty, outside mainstream business practice. In addition, many nations place additional burdens on registrants—for example, to obtain an Andorran .ad, you must register the business name as a trademark in Andorra.

For up-to-date information about the status of TLDs, go to www.icann.org/tlds.

Keep in mind that the guidelines for many of these suffixes are not strictly enforced. For example, anyone can usually acquire a .com, .net, .org, .biz, or .info domain name regardless of the type of business they operate. But strictly enforced standards put the .edu and .gov suffixes in the hands of government and educational institutions, respectively. Similarly, the .name extension is for individuals, not businesses. The extensions .coop, .aero, .museum, and .pro are also restricted—for example, a .aero registration will be issued only to a business in the air transport industry.

Most businesses in this country have chosen a .com designation. In fact, registrations for .coms have outpaced any other by ten to one. While it's dangerous to predict the future, many observers believe that the preference for .com will continue. Rightly or wrongly, businesspeople seem to feel that the .com designation provides familiarity to consumers and confers an extra measure of prestige on the business using it.

A domain name can be registered under several suffixes—for example, nolo. com, nolo.net, and nolo.org.

Because each domain name must be unique—so that all the computers attached to the Internet can find it—it is impossible for two different businesses to have the same domain name. A simple way to check ownership of a domain is to use www.whois.net.

Beware that some registrants, especially those acting in bad faith, may supply false information about domain name ownership, and, in these cases, there's not much that can be done to track down the domain name holder. This lack of information should not stop those pursuing a cybersquatter—a speculator who is holding a domain name for ransom. There are ways to wrestle a domain name from a bad faith registrant even if the identity or location of the cybersquatter is unknown.

Keep in mind that even if a company owns a federally registered trademark, someone else may still have the right to own the domain name. For example, many different companies have federally registered the trademark Executive for different goods or services. All of these companies may want www.executive.com, but the first one to purchase it—in this case, Executive Software—is the one that acquired the domain name.

When registering a domain name, a company should be sure that nobody else is using it as a trademark for similar goods and services. If another business is selling similar goods or services with a similar name, the use of the domain name can be terminated under trademark law principles.

EXAMPLE: Jim's catalog company, Ahab, has been selling ocean-themed artwork and merchandise since 1980. Jim has registered the Ahab trademark with the U.S. Patent and Trademark Office (USPTO). Bob registers the domain name ahab.com and uses it to sell artwork depicting whales. Jim can stop Bob's use of the domain name ahab.com. If Bob were using ahab.com to sell Ahab-brand educational software, Jim could not stop Bob's use of the domain name.

Registration of a domain name can be accomplished at any of the approved domain name registrars. A complete list is provided at both InterNIC (www. internic.net) and ICANN (www.icann.org). An applicant completes the online domain name registration form indicating basic contact information (name, telephone number, and address). The fee is usually $5 to $35 per year, although some registrars offer lower rates. The whole procedure takes a matter of minutes and the domain name registrant is notified by email of the domain name owner-ship, which is effective immediately.

Payment of the annual fee for a domain name only grants ownership of an address on the Internet; it doesn't establish a website presence. In order to use it in conjunction with a website, a business must establish a Web hosting arrangement with an ISP (Internet Service Provider), usually for a fee of approximately $5 to $20 per month. The business must also construct and upload a website and coordinate the reassignment of the domain name from the domain name registrar to the ISP. Usually an ISP will assist the company through the process. Domain name registration grants exclusive title to the domain name owner, who can stop others from using it with the following exceptions:

- **Failure to pay annual domain name fees.** Domain name ownership, unlike trademark ownership, must be renewed either every year or every two years (depending on the initial arrangement with the registrar). Failure to pay fees will result in cancellation of the domain name ownership, which may eventually be sold to another buyer.

- **The domain name registrant is a cybersquatter.** If a domain name is registered in bad faith, for example, for the purpose of selling it back to a company with the same name, the domain name can be taken away under federal law or under international arbitration rules for domain name owners.

- **The domain name infringes a trademark.** If a domain name is likely to confuse consumers because it is similar to another trademark, the domain name use may be terminated. For example, if a company registered adoobie.com for the purposes of selling software, it's very likely that the Adobe company, makers of graphics software, would be able to stop the use.

- **The domain name dilutes a famous trademark.** If a domain name dilutes the power of a famous trademark, the owner of the famous mark can sue under federal laws to stop the continued use. Dilution refers to the fact that the domain name is being used for commercial purposes and blurs or tarnishes the reputation of a famous trademark. For example, if a company registered guccigoo.com for the purpose of selling baby diapers, the owners of the Gucci trademark could stop the use of the domain name under dilution principles.

Related terms: Anticybersquatting Consumer Protection Act; cybersquatting; dilution of mark.

domain names, effect of trademark law on

- Registration of a domain name does not automatically create trademark rights.

- A trademark owner can sue a domain name owner who is likely to confuse consumers or who dilutes a famous trademark.

Domain name registration, by itself, does not permit the registrant to stop another business from using the name for its business or product. For example, if Sam acquires the domain name greatgrammar.com, that does not mean Sam can stop others from using Great Grammar for services or products online or off. It only means that Sam has the right to use that specific Internet address.

A domain name will function as a trademark only if it is used in connection with the sale of goods or services and consumers associate the name with the Internet business. When that happens, the domain name owner can stop others from using a similar name.

Consider Amazon.com, a domain name that functions as a trademark because consumers associate the name with a certain company and its services. Amazon.com achieved trademark status because the company was the first to use this distinctive name for online retail sales, and the name has been promoted to consumers through advertising and sales. If another company sold books on the Internet or off under the name Amazon, the owners of Amazon.com could sue under trademark law to stop the use.

In short, to be protectable as a trademark, a domain name must be distinctive or must achieve distinction through consumer awareness, and the owner must be the first to use the name in connection with certain services or products.

A domain name owner can run into problems if the domain name legally conflicts with an existing trademark. For example, if a company launched a website with the domain name Xon.com to sell automobile accessories, that company could be stopped from using the name by the owners of the Exxon trademark. That's because Exxon has the right to stop lookalike and soundalike business names that are likely to confuse consumers of a wide range of auto products.

Whether a domain name would legally conflict with an existing trademark depends on which was first put into actual use and whether the existing mark is famous or use of the domain name would confuse customers regarding the existing mark. The legal standards used in these conflicts are no different from other trademark disputes.

Related terms: Anticybersquatting Consumer Protection Act; confusion of customers; dilution of mark; domain names; free speech and trademark law; initial interest confusion; keyword; metatags; UDRP.

domain tasting

Domain tasting occurs when someone registers a number of domain names and then waits several days before paying for them. In the interim, the "buyer" checks website analytics to see which domain names attract the most visitors and then only pays for the popular ones. There a few problems with domain tasting, most notably that it used as a springboard for typosquatting. In addition, during the period between registration and payment, the domain names are shown as being registered, which creates problems for legitimate businesses and trademark owners. Domain tasters commonly operate at high volume. For example, in one case, a domain taster registered, but did not pay for, 1,400 variations on "verizon" misspellings. In that case, a court determined that the practice was a violation of the Anticybersquatting Consumer Protection Act. (*Verizon California, Inc. v. Navigation Catalyst Systems, Inc.* 568 F. Supp. 2d 1088 (C.D. Cal. 2008).)

duration of federal trademark registration

Once a trademark or service mark is placed on the Principal Register, the owner receives a certificate of registration good for an initial term of ten years.

Although the initial registration is good for a ten-year period, the registration may lapse unless the registrant files a sworn statement within six years of the filing date (the "Sections 8 and 15 Affidavit") that the mark is either still in use in commerce or that the mark is not in use for legitimate reasons that do not constitute abandonment. (Note, if the registration occurred before November 16, 1989, the initial term of the mark is 20 years, not ten.)

The original registration may be renewed indefinitely for additional ten-year periods if the owner timely files the required renewal applications (called a Section 9 Affidavit) with the U.S. Patent and Trademark Office. Failure to renew a registration does not void all rights to the mark; however, unless it is reregistered, the mark's owner will not have the benefits of federal registration, such as the presumed nationwide notice and the presumption of validity.

EXAMPLE: Carolyn registers a service mark for her graphic design business on May 1, 2001. The registration is good for ten years, or until May 1, 2011. To keep the registration in force, Carolyn must file a Section 8 and 15 Affidavit between May 1, 2006 (five years after her registration date), and May 1, 2007, and she must renew it between May 1, 2011, and April 30, 2012, and again between May 1, 2021, and April 30, 2022. By continuing to renew the mark in this manner, Carolyn can keep it on the Principal Register indefinitely.

The Lanham Act: § 1058. (§ 8) Duration of registration

(a) In general

Each registration shall remain in force for 10 years, except that the registration of any mark shall be canceled by the Director for failure to comply with the provisions of subsection (b) of this section, upon the expiration of the following time periods, as applicable:

(1) For registrations issued pursuant to the provisions of this chapter, at the end of 6 years following the date of registration.

(2) For registrations published under the provisions of section 1062 (c) of this title, at the end of 6 years following the date of publication under such section.

(3) For all registrations, at the end of each successive 10-year period following the date of registration.

(b) Affidavit of continuing use

During the 1-year period immediately preceding the end of the applicable time period set forth in subsection (a) of this section, the owner of the registration shall pay the prescribed fee and file in the Patent and Trademark Office—

(1) an affidavit setting forth those goods or services recited in the registration on or in connection with which the mark is in use in commerce and such number of specimens or facsimiles showing current use of the mark as may be required by the Director; or

(2) an affidavit setting forth those goods or services recited in the registration on or in connection with which the mark is not in use in commerce and showing that any such nonuse is due to special circumstances which excuse such nonuse and is not due to any intention to abandon the mark.

(c) Grace period for submissions; deficiency

(1) The owner of the registration may make the submissions required under this section within a grace period of 6 months after the end of the applicable time period set forth in subsection (a) of this section. Such submission is required to be accompanied by a surcharge prescribed by the Director.

(2) If any submission filed under this section is deficient, the deficiency may be corrected after the statutory time period and within the time prescribed after notification of the deficiency. Such submission is required to be accompanied by a surcharge prescribed by the Director.

(d) Notice of affidavit requirement

Special notice of the requirement for affidavits under this section shall be attached to each certificate of registration and notice of publication under section 1062 (c) of this title.

(e) Notification of acceptance or refusal of affidavits

The Director shall notify any owner who files 1 of the affidavits required by this section of the Commissioner's acceptance or refusal thereof and, in the case of a refusal, the reasons therefor.

(f) Designation of resident for service of process and notices

If the registrant is not domiciled in the United States, the registrant may designate, by a document filed in the United States Patent and Trademark Office, the name and address of a person resident in the United States on whom may be served notices or process in proceedings affecting the mark. Such notices or process may be served upon the person so designated by leaving with that person or mailing to that person a copy thereof at the address specified in the last designation so filed. If the person so designated cannot be found at the address given in the last designation, or if the registrant does not designate by a document filed in the United States Patent and Trademark Office the name and address of a person resident in the United States on whom may be served notices or process in proceedings affecting the mark, such notices or process may be served on the Director.

The Lanham Act: § 1059. (§ 9) Renewal of registration

This statute sets out the procedure for renewing a trademark registration.

(a) Period of renewal; time for renewal

Subject to the provisions of section 1058 of this title, each registration may be renewed for periods of 10 years at the end of each successive 10-year period following the date of registration upon payment of the prescribed fee and the filing of a written application, in such form as may be prescribed by the Director. Such application may be made at any time within 1 year before the end of each successive 10-year period for which the registration was issued or renewed, or it may be made within a grace period of 6 months after the end of each successive 10-year period, upon payment of a fee and surcharge prescribed therefor. If any application filed under this section is deficient, the deficiency may be corrected within the time prescribed after notification of the deficiency, upon payment of a surcharge prescribed therefor.

(b) Notification of refusal of renewal

If the Director refuses to renew the registration, the Director shall notify the registrant of the Commissioner's refusal and the reasons therefor.

(c) Designation of resident for service of process and notices

If the registrant is not domiciled in the United States the registrant may designate, by a document filed in the United States Patent and Trademark Office, the name and address of a person resident in the United States on whom may be served notices or process in proceedings affecting the mark. Such notices or process may be served upon the person so designated by leaving with that person or mailing to that person a copy thereof at the address specified in the last designation so filed. If the person so designated cannot be found at the address given in the last designation, or if the registrant does not designate by a document filed in the United States Patent and Trademark Office the name and address of a person resident in the United States on whom may be served notices or process in proceedings affecting the mark, such notices or process may be served on the Director.

Related terms: incontestability status; Section 8 Declaration; Section 15 Declaration; Supplemental Register.

eTEAS

See TEAS.

exclusive right to use mark

See ownership of mark in the United States.

fair use of trademarks

In trademark law, fair use is a defense to a claim of infringement in which the defendant asserts that the use is to describe the goods, not to trade off the trademark owner's good will. For example, the maker of an electric dishwasher may describe the "joy" of clean dishes without infringing the trademark Joy for dishwashing liquid. A company promoting toothpaste may state that it is the "choice of dentists" without infringing the trademark Dentist's Choice. And a fragrance company may include advertising copy using the term "love potion" even though that term is a registered trademark for fragrances. The fair use defense is set forth in the Lanham Act. (15 United States Code, Section 1115(b)(4).)

In 2005, the U.S. Supreme Court ruled that a defendant may assert the fair use defense even if the trademark owner has demonstrated likelihood of confusion. In other words, a court will permit some confusion if the use is considered a fair use. (How much is a matter to be decided by the courts.) (*K.P. Permanent Make-Up, Inc. v. Lasting Impression,* 543 U.S. 111 (2004).)

The following noncommercial uses of trademarked terms—though not technically trademark fair use—are sometimes lumped in the same category:

1. comparative advertising
2. journalistic accounts of the owner of the mark or the goods or services identified by the mark, and
3. parodies involving the mark.

For example, a California district court determined that an artist's project including nude Barbie dolls and imagery entitled "Malted Barbie" and "The

Barbie Enchiladas" was a noncommercial fair use of the Mattel company's Barbie trademark. (*Mattel Inc. v. Walking Mountain Productions, Inc.*, 353 F.3d 792 (9th Cir. 2003).) Note, trademark fair use is distinguishable from the fair use defense applied in copyright law.

Related terms: free speech and trademark law; parodies of trademarks.

false advertising

False advertising occurs when advertisers materially mislead and deceive consumers. A business that makes misleading advertising statements about its products or another company's products can be sued in federal court under section 43(a) of the federal Lanham Act. (15 United States Code, Section 1125(a).) It is not necessary to have a federally registered trademark to make a claim under section 43(a). All that is required is that a business has made false or misleading statements as to its own product or another's, that there is actual deception or at least a tendency to deceive a substantial portion of the intended audience, and that the advertised goods traveled in interstate commerce. The deception must be material, that is, likely to influence purchasing decisions, and there must be likelihood of injury to another company in terms of declining sales or loss of goodwill. In other words, if the false advertising has no impact on purchasers, goodwill, or sales, then the claim will be dismissed.

For purposes of section 43(a), advertising is more than traditional print and television advertisements; it is any commercial speech intended to influence consumers and disseminated to the relevant purchasing public. "Commercial speech" refers to statements generally made for the purposes of promoting a business or trade, not editorial or informational speech protected under free speech principles. For example, it is not commercial speech to make statements about a product in a newspaper article.

Deceptive advertising is generally categorized as either statements that are simply untrue (or "false on their face") or statements that are accurate but deceptive. An example of a statement that is false on its face would be falsely claiming that a motor oil additive will increase mileage. An example of a statement that is accurate but deceptive would be that a motor oil additive protects against engine corrosion, but failing to mention that the protection is for boat engines and not automobile engines. In cases of accurate but deceptive claims, a court must examine evidence, for example, to determine if a company's test results have been distorted or exaggerated.

Trademark Law: Definitions

The Lanham Act: § 1125. (§ 43a) False designations of origin and false descriptions forbidden

(a) Civil action

(1) Any person who, on or in connection with any goods or services, or any container for goods, uses in commerce any word, term, name, symbol, or device, or any combination thereof, or any false designation of origin, false or misleading description of fact, or false or misleading representation of fact, which—

(A) is likely to cause confusion, or to cause mistake, or to deceive as to the affiliation, connection, or association of such person with another person, or as to the origin, sponsorship, or approval of his or her goods, services, or commercial activities by another person, or

(B) in commercial advertising or promotion, misrepresents the nature, characteristics, qualities, or geographic origin of his or her or another person's goods, services, or commercial activities, shall be liable in a civil action by any person who believes that he or she is or is likely to be damaged by such act.

(2) As used in this subsection, the term "any person" includes any State, instrumentality of a State or employee of a State or instrumentality of a State acting in his or her official capacity. Any State, and any such instrumentality, officer, or employee, shall be subject to the provisions of this chapter in the same manner and to the same extent as any nongovernmental entity.

(3) In a civil action for trade dress infringement under this chapter for trade dress not registered on the principal register, the person who asserts trade dress protection has the burden of proving that the matter sought to be protected is not functional.

Related terms: unfair competition; unregistered mark, protection of.

famous mark

Under federal law and most state laws, only owners of famous marks can file claims alleging dilution. Examples of famous marks include the NBA logo of a silhouetted basketball player, Saks Fifth Avenue for retail stores, Hyatt for hotel services, and Godzilla for entertainment services.

As a result of the Trademark Dilution Revision Act of 2006, a mark is "famous" if it is widely recognized by the general consuming public as a designation of the source of the goods or services of the mark's owner, and it allows the court to consider all relevant factors when determining whether a mark is famous, including: (1) the duration, extent, and geographic reach of advertising and publicity of the mark; (2) the amount, volume, and geographic extent of sales of goods or services offered under the mark; (3) the extent of actual recognition of the mark; and (4) whether the mark was registered on the Principal Register.

Related terms: dilution.

fanciful terms

Fanciful terms (sometimes referred to as "coined marks") are invented words or phrases with no other purpose than to act as a trademark. Coined terms generally are considered strong or distinctive mark and courts will tend to protect them against unauthorized use. The easiest way to assure protection for a mark is to make up, or "coin," a new word.

A coined term may consist of any combination of letters and/or numerals that are not already in use to identify or distinguish another product or service. Thus, "4711 water" is a coined phrase used as the trademark for a particular brand of cologne. Other common examples of coined terms are Sybex (publisher of computer books), Kodak (cameras), Tylenol (analgesic), Maalox (antacid medicine), and Unix (computer operating system).

Related terms: strong mark.

Federal Trademark Dilution Act of 1995

See dilution.

federal trademark registration

Federal registration of a mark entails all of the following:
- The mark must be used in commerce (used across state, national, or territorial lines or used in a way that affects interstate, interterritorial, or international commerce).
- A registration application, a Statement of Use, or an Application Alleging Use (if an intent-to-use application was previously filed) must be filed with the USPTO.
- If the mark qualifies for the Principal Register, it will be published in the *Official Gazette* by the USPTO.
- If another party claims ownership of the mark in a pending application, the USPTO may declare that an interference exists and schedule a hearing. Similarly, an interested party may file an opposition to the registration after publication in the *Official Gazette*, and the owner may have to refute or reply to the opposition.
- If there is no interference or opposition, the USPTO will issue a certificate of registration on either the Principal Register or the Supplemental Register.

Once a mark is registered, the trademark registration symbol "(®)" or "Reg. U.S. Pat. Off." should always appear next to the mark whenever it is used.

Trademark Law: Definitions

Without this designation, it may be harder to collect damages if a federal court lawsuit is filed over an infringement of the mark.

Applications for federal trademarks registration may be made electronically at the USPTO website (www.uspto.gov).

To qualify for federal registration, a mark:

- must not infringe another mark that is already registered.
- cannot include certain types of pictures, words, and symbols—the U.S. flag; other federal and local governmental insignias; names of living persons without their consent; names or likenesses of dead U.S. presidents without their widows' consent; words or symbols that disparage living or dead persons, institutions, beliefs, or national symbols; deceptive geographical names; or marks that are judged immoral, deceptive, or scandalous.

A trademark can be registered at the USPTO on one of two lists of registered trademarks and service marks:

- the Principal Register, or
- the Supplemental Register.

The Principal Register is reserved for distinctive marks and marks that have become distinctive through acquiring secondary meaning. There are many benefits to having a mark on the Principal Register rather than the Supplemental Register. Chief among these are:

- Potential competitors will be assumed to know that the marks are off limits.
- The mark can achieve incontestability status if it remains on the Principal Register for five years.

The Supplemental Register is for marks that are not yet distinctive and do not merit the same protection as Principal Register marks. However, registration on the Supplemental Register allows placement of the trademark registration symbol (®) on the mark, which is likely to scare away most potential copiers.

The Lanham Act: § 1051. (§ 1) Application for registration; verification

(a) Application for use of trademark

    (1) The owner of a trademark used in commerce may request registration of its trademark on the principal register hereby established by paying the prescribed fee and filing in the Patent and Trademark Office an application and a verified statement, in such form as may be prescribed by the Director, and such number of specimens or facsimiles of the mark as used as may be required by the Director.

    (2) The application shall include specification of the applicant's domicile and citizenship, the date of the applicant's first use of the mark, the date of the

applicant's first use of the mark in commerce, the goods in connection with which the mark is used, and a drawing of the mark.

(3) The statement shall be verified by the applicant and specify that—

   (A) the person making the verification believes that he or she, or the juristic person in whose behalf he or she makes the verification, to be the owner of the mark sought to be registered;

   (B) to the best of the verifier's knowledge and belief, the facts recited in the application are accurate;

   (C) the mark is in use in commerce; and

   (D) to the best of the verifier's knowledge and belief, no other person has the right to use such mark in commerce either in the identical form thereof or in such near resemblance thereto as to be likely, when used on or in connection with the goods of such other person, to cause confusion, or to cause mistake, or to deceive, except that, in the case of every application claiming concurrent use, the applicant shall—

      (i) state exceptions to the claim of exclusive use; and

      (ii) shall specify, to the extent of the verifier's knowledge—

         (I) any concurrent use by others;

         (II) the goods on or in connection with which and the areas in which each concurrent use exists;

         (III) the periods of each use; and

         (IV) the goods and area for which the applicant desires registration.

(4) The applicant shall comply with such rules or regulations as may be prescribed by the Director. The Director shall promulgate rules prescribing the requirements for the application and for obtaining a filing date herein.

The Lanham Act: § 1052. (§ 2) Trademarks registrable on principal register; concurrent registration

No trademark by which the goods of the applicant may be distinguished from the goods of others shall be refused registration on the principal register on account of its nature unless it—

(a) Consists of or comprises immoral, deceptive, or scandalous matter; or matter which may disparage or falsely suggest a connection with persons, living or dead, institutions, beliefs, or national symbols, or bring them into contempt, or disrepute; or a geographical indication which, when used on or in connection with wines or spirits, identifies a place other than the origin of the goods and is first used on or in connection with wines or spirits by the applicant on or after one year after the date on which the WTO Agreement (as defined in section 3501 (9) of title 19) enters into force with respect to the United States.

(b) Consists of or comprises the flag or coat of arms or other insignia of the United States, or of any State or municipality, or of any foreign nation, or any simulation thereof.

(c) Consists of or comprises a name, portrait, or signature identifying a particular living individual except by his written consent, or the name, signature, or portrait of a deceased President of the United States during the life of his widow, if any, except by the written consent of the widow.

(d) Consists of or comprises a mark which so resembles a mark registered in the Patent and Trademark Office, or a mark or trade name previously used in the United States by another and not abandoned, as to be likely, when used on or in connection with the goods of the applicant, to cause confusion, or to cause mistake, or to deceive: provided, that if the Director determines that confusion, mistake, or deception is not likely to result from the continued use by more than one person of the same or similar marks under conditions and limitations as to the mode or place of use of the marks or the goods on or in connection with which such marks are used, concurrent registrations may be issued to such persons when they have become entitled to use such marks as a result of their concurrent lawful use in commerce prior to

(1) the earliest of the filing dates of the applications pending or of any registration issued under this chapter;

(2) July 5, 1947, in the case of registrations previously issued under the Act of March 3, 1881, or February 20, 1905, and continuing in full force and effect on that date; or

(3) July 5, 1947, in the case of applications filed under the Act of February 20, 1905, and registered after July 5, 1947. Use prior to the filing date of any pending application or a registration shall not be required when the owner of such application or registration consents to the grant of a concurrent registration to the applicant. Concurrent registrations may also be issued by the Director when a court of competent jurisdiction has finally determined that more than one person is entitled to use the same or similar marks in commerce. In issuing concurrent registrations, the Director shall prescribe conditions and limitations as to the mode or place of use of the mark or the goods on or in connection with which such mark is registered to the respective persons.

(e) Consists of a mark which

(1) when used on or in connection with the goods of the applicant is merely descriptive or deceptively misdescriptive of them,

(2) when used on or in connection with the goods of the applicant is primarily geographically descriptive of them, except as indications of regional origin may be registrable under section 1054 of this title,

(3) when used on or in connection with the goods of the applicant is primarily geographically deceptively misdescriptive of them,

(4) is primarily merely a surname, or

(5) comprises any matter that, as a whole, is functional.

(f) Except as expressly excluded in subsections (a), (b), (c), (d), (e)(3), and (e)(5) of this section, nothing in this chapter shall prevent the registration of a mark used by the applicant which has become distinctive of the applicant's goods in commerce. The Director may accept as prima facie evidence that the mark has become distinctive, as used on or in connection with the applicant's goods in commerce, proof of substantially exclusive and continuous use thereof as a mark by the applicant in commerce for the five years before the date on which the claim of distinctiveness is made. Nothing in this section shall prevent the registration of a mark which, when used on or in connection with the goods of the applicant, is primarily geographically deceptively misdescriptive of them, and which became distinctive of the applicant's goods in commerce before December 8, 1993.

A mark which when used would cause dilution under section 1125 (c) of this title may be refused registration only pursuant to a proceeding brought under section 1063 of this title. A registration for a mark which when used would cause dilution under section 1125 (c) of this title may be canceled pursuant to a proceeding brought under either section 1064 of this title or section 1092 of this title.

The Lanham Act: § 1063. (§ 13) Opposition to registration

This statute sets out the procedure to be followed if a person or organization believes that a mark published for comment should not be registered.

(a) Any person who believes that he would be damaged by the registration of a mark upon the principal register, including as a result of dilution under section 1125 (c) of this title, may, upon payment of the prescribed fee, file an opposition in the Patent and Trademark Office, stating the grounds therefor, within thirty days after the publication under subsection (a) of section 1062 of this title of the mark sought to be registered. Upon written request prior to the expiration of the thirty-day period, the time for filing opposition shall be extended for an additional thirty days, and further extensions of time for filing opposition may be granted by the Director for good cause when requested prior to the expiration of an extension. The Director shall notify the applicant of each extension of the time for filing opposition. An opposition may be amended under such conditions as may be prescribed by the Director.

(b) Unless registration is successfully opposed—

(1) a mark entitled to registration on the principal register based on an application filed under section 1051 (a) of this title or pursuant to section 1126 of this title shall be registered in the Patent and Trademark Office, a certificate of registration shall be issued, and notice of the registration shall be published in the *Official Gazette* of the Patent and Trademark Office; or

(2) a notice of allowance shall be issued to the applicant if the applicant applied for registration under section 1051 (b) of this title.

Related terms: constructive notice of mark under Lanham Act; Principal Register; protection of marks under Lanham Act; Supplemental Register; trademark search.

filtering

Filtering is the process by which an individual can skip or mute over objectionable content in audio or video content of motion pictures. The technology was created to allow parents the ability to bypass content such as graphic violence, sex, nudity, and profanity during DVD playback. In September 2002, several Hollywood movie studios and directors sued the manufacturer of the process, claiming that the process violated trademark and copyright law. However, in 2005, the lawsuit was preempted when President Bush signed into effect the Family Entertainment and Copyright Act of 2005, which includes a provision, the Family Movie Act of 2005, creating an exemption from copyright or trademark infringement for anyone who uses this technology for home viewing.

See also Part 2 (Copyright): Family Entertainment and Copyright Act of 2005.

first-to-file countries

See prior registration countries.

first to register

See ownership of mark in the United States.

first to use mark in United States

See ownership of mark in the United States.

flags as marks

See prohibited and reserved marks under Lanham Act.

foreign language equivalent terms

See phonetic or foreign language equivalents for marks.

foreign nationals registering in United States

A citizen, permanent resident, or business of another country is entitled to federally register a mark in the United States if the other country affords reciprocal trademark rights to U.S. citizens and if the mark meets U.S. requirements for registration.

Registration of a mark by a foreign national in the United States may be accomplished if any of the following are true:

- The mark has been placed in use in interstate, interterritorial, or international commerce in the United States.
- The mark has been registered within the last six months in another country with which the United States has a reciprocal treaty.
- The mark has been the subject of an intent-to-use application filed in the United States.

If the basis for registration in the United States is a previous registration in another country, the date of filing in the other country establishes the filing date in the United States as well.

A foreign national who registers a mark in the United States but lives abroad must designate a U.S. representative to receive notices and official communications from the U.S. Patent and Trademark Office.

Related terms: Inter-American Convention for Trademark and Commercial Protection; international trademark rights; Paris Convention.

franchising, service marks

Over 750,000 businesses in the U.S. are franchises—privately owned businesses adhering to a corporate business model and built around principles of licensing and service marks. Examples of successful franchises are Subway, McDonald's, 7-Eleven, H&R Block, Dunkin' Donuts, and Great Clips. Among other fees, franchise owners (franchisees) pay a royalty for the use of the franchiser's marks. In return, the franchiser has an obligation to monitor the franchisee's use of the trademark (and its accompanying services) so that they adhere to standards of quality and consistency. For more on these standards, see the entry regarding "naked licenses."

Fraud at Trademark Office (Fraud on the USPTO)

Statements made as part of a trademark application are made under oath, and fraudulent statements can result in the loss of trademark rights. For example, in one year, the USPTO cancelled three trademark registrations after receiving evidence from a competitor that the trademark owner had made fraudulent statements regarding the dates of first use in commerce. (*Standard Knitting, Ltd. v. Toyota Jidosha Kabushiki Kaisha*, 77 U.S.P.Q.2d 1917 (TTAB 2006).) Note, not every false statement made on a trademark application amounts to fraud. For example, a misstatement regarding whether commerce was intrastate or interstate did not amount to a fraudulent statement. (*Maids to Order of Ohio, Inc. v. Maid-to-Order, Inc.*, 78 U.S.P.Q.2d 1899 (TTAB 2006).)

The standard for judging fraud on a USPTO trademark filing was clarified in 2009 when the Court of Appeals for the Federal Circuit (CAFC) terminated its "should have known" standard for judging fraud—that is, the applicant should have known the statement was fraudulent. Henceforth, proving fraud on the USPTO required proving intent. (*In re Bose Corp.*, 580 F.3d 1240 (Fed. Cir. 2009).) Subsequent cases have followed this precedent—for example, when an applicant incorrectly listed "transmission of oil" as one of its services, the Trademark Trial and Appeal Board (TTAB) held that absent proof of "deceptive intent," there was no fraud. (*Enbridge, Inc. v. Excelerate Energy Limited Partnership*, 92 U.S.P.Q.2d 1537 (TTAB 2009).) And in *Asian and Western Classics B.V. v. Lynne Selkow*, 92 U.S.P.Q.2d 1478 (TTAB 2009), the TTAB stated that a pleading of fraud must include "an allegation of intent."

free speech and trademark law

Free speech laws permit the use of another company's trademark for purposes of commentary or criticism. For example, the owner of a newsletter can write an article critical of Microsoft and use the Microsoft logo. Two factors may convert such commentary and criticism into a lawsuit based on trademark infringement or dilution: The newsletter is offering goods and services as part of its criticism, or the newsletter is likely to confuse readers as to whether Microsoft is a sponsor of the newsletter. In addition, if the newsletter is making false statements regarding Microsoft, this may trigger additional claims including product disparagement, false advertising, and trade libel.

However, if it is clear that the use does not confuse consumers and is not being used deceptively, courts will permit use of trademarks for purposes of commentary.

> EXAMPLE: A disgruntled former customer of the Bally Health Club created a website featuring the company's logo over which appeared the word "sucks" and included a statement that the site was "Unauthorized." A court permitted this use because the site had distinguished itself from the legitimate Bally site by prominent use of disclaimers and the site was not offering competing goods or services. (*Bally Total Fitness Holding Corp. v. Faber,* 29 F. Supp. 2d 1161 (C.D. Cal. 1998).)

The *Bally* case triggered widespread registration of "sucks" domain names (despite the fact that the defendant had not registered ballysucks.com) and opened up a world of "cybergriping" in which angry consumers maintained websites whose sole purpose is to complain about company practices or products. Disgruntled consumers of other companies registered domain names such as nikesucks.com, toysrussucks.com, walmartsucks.com, and cadillacsucks.com. In some cases, companies have successfully stopped the use of these "sucks" domain names either because they were determined to be in violation of the law or because the domain name owner refused to respond to the legal action. Keep in mind when using trademarks under free speech principles: Even though there is right of free speech, this doesn't prevent a trademark owner from filing a lawsuit. The economics of litigation often silence company critics despite their free speech rights.

In 2003, free speech rights triumphed over trademark rights when the first cybergriping case reached a federal Court of Appeals. (*The Taubman Co. v. Webfeats*, 319 F.3d 770 (6th Cir. 2003).) In *Taubman*, a Web designer created a site in support of a nearby shopping center. The site also contained a link to the designer's girlfriend's T-shirt business. The owners of the shopping center complained of the site, even though it contained a conspicuous disclaimer indicating that the site was not affiliated with the center. Alas, the previously supportive designer became angry and registered several "sucks" domain names related to the shopping center, the company owning the center, and the lawyers for the center. The owners sued for trademark infringement. The designer discontinued the link to his girlfriend's business—thereby rendering his cybergriping sites as noncommercial—and prevailed in the subsequent litigation. The court in *Taubman* pointed out that the qualifying moniker "sucks" removes any confusion as to the source of the goods or services. Keep in mind that the rule enunciated in *Taubman* is unlikely to apply in cases in which the cybergriping site has a commercial purpose—that is, offers services or products for sale or provides advertising.

In E.S.S. Entertainment 2000, Inc. v. Rock Star Videos, Inc., 547 F.3d 1095 (9th Cir. 2008), the Ninth Circuit permitted a parody under First Amendment principles noting that artistic use of a mark is permitted when (1) the use has artistic relevance to the work at issue (the video game), and (2) it doesn't explicitly mislead consumers as to the source of the mark or the work—a test adopted by the Ninth Circuit in *Mattel v. Walking Mountain*. In *E.S.S. Entertainment*, the video game "Grand Theft Auto: San Andreas" included a parody of the East Los Angeles strip club, "The Play Pen," (referred to as the "Pig Pen" in the game).

In addition to these rights, trademark law permits the use of trademarks for comparative advertising and for descriptive purposes.

Keep in mind that defending your right to free speech can be expensive, costing tens of thousands of dollars. The chances of a legal confrontation increase when using a famous trademark without permission.

Related terms: fair use of trademarks; parodies of trademarks.

generic terms

Words or symbols commonly used to describe an entire type of product or service rather than to distinguish one product or service from another are known as generic. Generic terms never receive protection because such terms cannot fulfill the function of a mark, which is to distinguish specific goods or services from competing ones. Therefore they belong in the public domain rather than to an exclusive owner.

> EXAMPLE: "Raisin bran" is a generic phrase that describes a kind of cereal; it defines the product itself rather than its source. Several different cereal manufacturers produce raisin bran, each of which is identified by its own mark—for instance, Post Raisin Bran, Kellogg's Raisin Bran, Skinner's Raisin Bran. While each of these manufacturer's marks is entitled to protection, the words "raisin bran" are not.

Combining a generic term with other terms may sometimes result in a protectable composite mark. However, often, the generic term must be disclaimed before the USPTO will grant trademark registration for the composite mark. Combining a generic term with a top level domain such as ".com" rarely results in a protectable composite mark. For example, the Ninth Circuit reversed a lower court ruling that the registered mark "Advertise.com" was not generic. The mark which had been registered by AOL was intended for "online or Internet advertising." (*Advertise.com v. AOL Advertising, Inc.*, 166 F.3d 974 (9th Cir. 2010).)

Some protectable marks may lose their protection by becoming generic. "Genericide" occurs when a mark is used widely and indiscriminately to refer to a type of product or service, rather than the service or product of one company. For example, "escalator" was originally a protected trademark used to designate the moving stairs manufactured by a specific company. Eventually, the word became synonymous with the very idea of moving stairs and thus lost its protection. Other examples of marks that have become generic are lite beer, soft soap, and cola.

How can a company keep a mark from becoming generic? To begin, most companies need not worry about this issue, since very few products or services are successful enough to produce a generic mark. But for those that are, the

Xerox campaign is instructive. The "Xerox" mark was in danger of becoming generic because it was so commonly used to describe photocopiers, the process of photocopying, and the result. To counter this threatened genericide, the Xerox Corporation spent millions of advertising dollars advising the public that Xerox is in fact a registered mark, should only be used as a proper adjective in connection with a noun (for instance, Xerox brand photocopier), and should not be used as a verb (that is, to xerox something) or as a general noun indicating the result of the photocopying process (a xerox). Google, the Internet search engine company, has embarked on a similar crusade. For example, the company has sent letters to online dictionaries making it clear that the term "Google" refers to only one company's services, not to all Internet searching. (Despite that fact, Google is commonly used as a verb as in, "I Googled that.") If anyone challenges Xerox or Google on the grounds that their trademarks have become generic, these companies may prevail if they can show that they took steps to avoid genericide and that people continue to consider the trademarks as a brand, rather than generic, name.

Related terms: loss of mark; unfair competition.

geographic terms as marks

Geographic terms (sometimes referred to as geographic designations) are naturals for trademarks because they either identify regional origin (San Francisco Sourdough bread) or conjure up a quality (the image of Prudential's Rock of Gibraltar). Geographic terms can indicate a specific location such as a street (Park Avenue), river (Rio Grande), city (Hollywood), state (Wisconsin), or mountain (Everest), or even a nickname such as Quaker State for Pennsylvania. The manner in which a geographic term is used and the type of mark—for example, trademark, certification mark, and so on—affects protection. Geographic terms are generally categorized as follows:

Descriptive. A geographic term that describes the origin, location, or source of the product or service (for example, First National Bank of Omaha for a bank located in Omaha, Nebraska) is usually considered to be weak and is not protectable unless there is a demonstration of secondary meaning. The reason for this rule is that consumers cannot differentiate the Bank of Omaha from other banks in Omaha (or New York Life from other life insurance companies in New York) without some advertising or marketing effort.

Arbitrary or suggestive. A geographic term that is used arbitrarily (for example, Atlantic for a magazine) or suggestively to conjure up a regional feeling (for example, Arizona for an iced tea drink) is considered to be strong.

Misdescriptive. When a geographic term misleads consumers into believing that the product originates from a region when it does not, it is not protectable as a trademark—for example, Danish Maid Cultured Products is geographically misdescriptive because the cultured products were not from Denmark.

Many companies use "America" or "American" as a geographic term in their trademarks (for example, American Flyer for wagons and American Express for financial services). Most uses of "America" are weak (geographically descriptive), such as Bank of America or American Diabetes Association, because the terms primarily connote American origin. Some uses, however, are strong (arbitrary or suggestive), such as American Girl for shoes, because the use of America is not primarily to connote origin. In those cases, no proof of secondary meaning is required. Some uses are geographically misdescriptive and protection is denied (that is, "barred"). For example, American Beauty for a sewing machine was barred because the sewing machine was made in Japan.

In the mid-1990s, international makers of wines and spirits successfully lobbied the United States for a special amendment to the Lanham Act that prohibited registration of geographic marks that are inaccurate as to the source of the wine. Although the amendment reiterated the existing rules regarding geographically misdescriptive marks, above, it also reassured foreign winemakers that terms such as Champagne could only refer to a bubbly wine from the Champagne region of France.

Terms that are not primarily geographical in nature (do not refer to defined locations) may be used and protected as marks if they are distinctive in the context of their use or gain a secondary meaning through extended exposure in the marketplace—for example, Southern Comfort (whiskey), Metropolitan (life insurance), and Globe (realty).

Geographical terms are also acceptable in certification marks, and the owners of such marks are entitled to full protection under the Lanham Act.

Related terms: disclaimer of unregistrable material; prohibited and reserved marks under Lanham Act; secondary meaning.

geographically separate market

When goods or services coming from different sources are sold geographically far enough away from each other to preclude consumers from getting confused, they are said to be in geographically separate markets. In general, using the same or similar marks in geographically separate markets does not constitute infringement.

Related terms: constructive notice of mark under Lanham Act; infringement; ownership of mark in the United States.

goodwill

Goodwill refers to the tendency or likelihood of a consumer to repurchase goods or services based upon the name or source. In a sense, it is name recognition, or at least a recognition of buying habits—for example, consumers who are loyal to one brand of cola. A trademark is considered to be inseparable from its goodwill. When a trademark is infringed, the infringer gets a free unauthorized ride on another company's goodwill. Any assignment of trademark rights must include a transfer of the goodwill associated with the mark.

Related terms: assignment of mark.

gray market goods

U.S. trademark owners often authorize the manufacture and sale of their goods for non-U.S. markets. For example, a cigarette maker may authorize production and sale of its brand in Germany. Usually, the arrangement prohibits the export of those cigarettes to the United States (or other territories). When these goods are imported into the United States without the consent of the trademark owner, they are referred to as gray market goods (sometimes known as parallel imports). One problem for the trademark owner who files a trademark suit over gray market goods is that these goods are not counterfeit or infringing, since they were produced under the direction of the trademark owner. U.S. trademark owners have two major remedies to prevent the importation and sale of gray market goods: Section 42 of the Lanham Act (15 United States Code, Section 1124), blocking sale and import of gray market goods; and Section 526 of the Tariff Act (19 United States Code, Section 1526), prohibiting importation of gray market goods and permitting their seizure.

hybrid mark

See composite mark.

ICANN

The Internet Corporation for Assigned Names and Numbers (ICANN) is the agency that oversees domain name registration and dispute resolution procedures (www.icann.org).

Related terms: cybersquatting; domain names; UDRP.

immoral marks

See prohibited and reserved marks under Lanham Act.

incontestability status

When a mark has been in continuous use for five years after being placed on the Principal Register, it may be classified as incontestable, or immune from legal challenge. (37 United States Code, Section 1065.) Because of the fact that incontestability can be challenged on several grounds, the term "incontestable" really means "somewhat difficult to contest" (as explained in more detail below).

A trademark owner seeking to make its mark incontestable must be able to demonstrate all of the following:

- No final legal decision has issued against the mark.
- No challenge to the mark is pending.
- A Sections 8 and 15 Declaration describing the mark's use was filed on a timely basis.
- The mark is not and has not become generic.

In essence, achieving "incontestability status" conclusively establishes ownership of the mark for the uses specified in the Sections 8 and 15 Declaration that is filed between the fifth and sixth year after the mark is placed on the Principal Register.

The issue of whether a mark is incontestable usually arises in a lawsuit for infringement where the party being sued attempts to defend by challenging the validity of the plaintiff's mark. If the plaintiff can establish that the mark is incontestable, the mark will be presumed valid unless the defendant can establish one or more of the following:

- The registration or the incontestable right to use the mark was obtained by fraud.
- The registrant has abandoned the mark.
- The mark is used to misrepresent the source of its goods or services (for instance, use of the mark involves palming off).
- The infringing mark is an individual's name used in his or her own business, or is otherwise prohibited or reserved under the Lanham Act.
- The infringing mark was used in commerce first—before the incontestable mark's registration.
- The infringing mark was registered first.
- The mark is being used to violate the antitrust laws of the United States.

Even though an incontestable mark can still be challenged on these grounds, it is safe from attack on the otherwise common ground that it lacks distinctiveness. Thus, when Park 'N Fly, Inc. sued Dollar Park and Fly, Inc. for trademark infringement, the U.S. Supreme Court ruled that because the Park 'N Fly mark had obtained incontestability status, Dollar Park and Fly, Inc., could not allege as a defense that its rival's mark is actually descriptive. (*Park 'N Fly v. Dollar Park and Fly.* 469 U.S. 189 (1985).)

The Lanham Act: § 1065. (§ 15) Incontestability of right to use mark under certain conditions

This statute defines the reasons that may be used to attack the validity of a mark that has been in continuous use for at least five years after its registration. Unless one of these reasons is present, the statute provides that the mark shall be considered incontestable. Except on a ground for which application to cancel may be filed at any time under paragraphs (3) and (5) of section 1064 of this title, and except to the extent, if any, to which the use of a mark registered on the principal register infringes a valid right acquired under the law of any State or Territory by use of a mark or trade name continuing from a date prior to the date of registration under this chapter of such registered mark, the right of the registrant to use such registered mark in commerce for the goods or services on or in connection with which such registered mark has been in continuous use for five consecutive years subsequent to the date of such registration and is still in use in commerce, shall be incontestable: provided, that—

(1) there has been no final decision adverse to registrant's claim of ownership of such mark for such goods or services, or to registrant's right to register the same or to keep the same on the register; and

(2) there is no proceeding involving said rights pending in the Patent and Trademark Office or in a court and not finally disposed of; and

(3) an affidavit is filed with the Director within one year after the expiration of any such five-year period setting forth those goods or services stated in the registration on or in connection with which such mark has been in continuous use for such five consecutive years and is still in use in commerce, and other matters specified in paragraphs (1) and (2) of this section; and

(4) no incontestable right shall be acquired in a mark which is the generic name for the goods or services or a portion thereof, for which it is registered.

Subject to the conditions above specified in this section, the incontestable right with reference to a mark registered under this chapter shall apply to a mark registered under the Act of March 3, 1881, or the Act of February 20, 1905, upon the filing of the required affidavit with the Director within one year after the expiration of any period

Trademark Law: Definitions

of five consecutive years after the date of publication of a mark under the provisions of subsection (c) of section 1062 of this title.

The Director shall notify any registrant who files the above-prescribed affidavit of the filing thereof.

Related terms: federal trademark registration; infringement; loss of mark.

infringement

Trademark infringement is the unauthorized use of a trademark or service mark (or a substantially similar mark) on competing or related goods and services. The success of a lawsuit to stop the infringement turns on whether the defendant's use causes a likelihood of confusion in the average consumer.

When infringement occurs, a trademark owner (the plaintiff) may file a lawsuit against the infringing user of the same or similar mark (the defendant) to prevent further use of the mark and collect money damages for the wrongful use. An infringement action may be brought in state court or in federal court if the mark in question is protected under the Lanham Act, which applies to both registered and unregistered marks that are used in commerce that Congress may regulate.

The success of an infringement normally turns on whether the defendant's use causes a likelihood of confusion and so weakens the value of the plaintiff's mark. A mark need not be identical to one already in use to infringe upon the owner's rights. If the proposed mark is similar enough to the earlier mark to risk confusing the average consumer, its use may constitute infringement if the services or goods on which the two marks are used are related to each other—that is, they share the same market. For more on the standards of confusion see the entry, likelihood of confusion.

The extent of damages awarded in an infringement action will usually depend on whether the infringement was willful and on the actual amount of harm that the plaintiff can prove.

Related terms: likelihood of confusion; constructive notice of mark under Lanham Act; incontestability status; injunctions against infringement and unfair competition; opposing and canceling a trademark registration; trade dress; unfair competition.

ingredient, use of a trademarked product as an

Unless it's authorized, a company should not give undue prominence to a ingredient's trademark. For example, if a candy contains Grand Marnier liquor, advertisements should not lead a consumer to believe that the candy is a product of (or endorsed by) the Grand Marnier company. A prominently placed explanatory disclaimer may also help reduce consumer confusion.

Related terms: disclaimer of trademark use.

initial interest confusion

In a 1999 case, Internet surfers were temporarily misled by the use of metatags containing the term "movie buff." When they typed the term into a search engine, they received results that favored a rival video business rather than the trademark owner. Although consumers were not prevented from locating the desired search result, a judge ruled that this momentary search engine confusion—referred to as initial interest confusion—was enough to sustain a claim for trademark infringement. (*Brookfield Communications v. West Coast Entertainment*, 174 F.3d 1036 (9th Cir. 1999).) Many commentators have criticized the standard, claiming that Internet users are sophisticated enough to sort through these momentary search engine diversions. Those arguments and the dwindling importance of metatags, has caused the initial interest confusion principle to disappear from the legal radar. The last sighting appears to be a California case in which a court prohibited www.taxes.com from using 75 references to a competitor in its metatags. (*J.K. Harris v. Steven Kassel*, 2002 U.S. Dist. LEXIS 7862 (N.D. Cal. 2002).)

Related terms: free speech and trademark law; keyword; metatags.

initials as trademark

Initials can function as a trademark and can be registered on the Principal Register, provided they meet the traditional trademark standards—the initials serve as a distinguishable indicator for the goods or services. One issue that often arises is whether the initials are signifiers for a generic term. For example, However, it is unlikely that someone selling wire fabric can register the initials WWF because within the trade, these are the commonly used initials for welded wire fabric. However, WWF can function as a registered trademark for the World Wildlife Fund.

Some other issues to consider in regard to initials:

- **Initials of government agencies.** 15 USC 1052 (b) bars the registration on either the Principal Register or the Supplemental Register of marks that consist of insignia of the United States or any simulation of such symbols. However, TMEP § 1204.02(d) states that initials, words, or letters that merely identify people and things associated with a particular agency or department of the United States government, instead of representing the authority of the government or the nation as a whole, are generally not considered to be "insignia of the United States" within the meaning of § 2(b). In other words, you can register FDA, FAA, or CIA unless specifically prohibited by a federal law. For example, 18 USC § 709 prohibits the use of F.B.I. (or any colorable imitation). Technically the application is not refused because of these statutes. Instead, if someone not authorized on the statute uses the mark, the application will be refused on the basis that the mark is not in lawful use in commerce, See Sec. 1205.01 TMEP.

- **Initials and surnames.** If initials are used with a surname, for example, P.J. Fitzpatrick, it is often easier to obtain a registration for the surname because the trademark conveys the impression of a personal name (a name associated with a specific person) versus merely being a surname (for example, "Fitzpatrick") which is considered a weak or descriptive mark. Curiously, a single initial, for example, I. Lewis Cigar Mfg., may be considered merely a surname. (1211.01(b)(iii) TMEP.)

injunctions against infringement

The winner in an infringement lawsuit can obtain an injunction: a court order that prevents further infringing activity or unfair competition. The state and federal laws of trademarks, service marks, and unfair competition authorize courts to require or prohibit any action or inaction necessary to protect the owner of a mark from economic harm.

Because lawsuits often take years to resolve, the courts have the power to issue interim injunctions. Promptly upon filing the case, the plaintiff may be able to obtain a temporary restraining order if the judge is convinced that irreparable injury is occurring. A few weeks later, the court will hold a formal hearing and, if it appears that the plaintiff is likely to prevail when the case is finally decided and irreparable harm will result if the injunction is not issued, the court will issue a preliminary injunction that will last until the case is over.

If, after a trial, a court finds that infringement or unfair competition has occurred, it will issue a permanent injunction ordering the defendant to stop using the infringing mark. In addition, the defendant may be required to destroy items or labels carrying the offending mark if necessary to prevent further use of the mark. In some cases, especially if the defendant was an innocent infringer, the court may allow some continued use of the mark in a particular locality, but bar it in other parts of the country.

The courts have broad powers ("equity" powers) to fashion their injunctions to obtain justice under varying circumstances. If necessary, an injunction that addresses the parties in a case may be enforced against other parties as well.

Related terms: infringement; preliminary injunction.

injury to business reputation

See dilution.

innocent infringer

An infringer who didn't know that he or she was infringing a mark is termed an innocent infringer. When an infringer is considered innocent, the owner of the infringed mark will usually be able to prevent future infringements but will not be able to collect money damages or defendant's profits. In some cases, the owner may not even be able to prevent the innocent infringer from continuing to use the mark, at least in a limited geographical area that doesn't create the risk of consumer confusion.

If a mark has been federally registered on the Principal Register before an infringement of the mark begins, the infringer cannot claim innocence. This is because the registration provides notice that the mark is already owned by someone else, and the infringer could have discovered this fact by doing a trademark search. However, if registration occurs after the infringing activity begins, the infringer may still be able to claim innocence until he or she actually learns of the registration.

Related terms: contributory infringer; infringement; injunctions against infringement and unfair competition; unfair competition.

intent-to-use application

The Lanham Act permits the owner of a mark that hasn't been used in commerce to reserve that mark for later registration. This is accomplished by filing an intent-to-use (ITU) application (sometimes referred to as a "1b application") with the U.S. Patent and Trademark Office (USPTO). The initial reservation is for six months from the date the USPTO approved the mark (which may be six months to a year after you file your application) and can be extended for up to five additional six-month periods for good cause. The date of the original ITU application serves as the priority date in case of conflict, regardless of when the use actually begins, as long as the applicant completes the registration process.

Actual registration will occur once the owner begins to use the mark in commerce and files an Allegation of Use for Intent-to-Use Application informing the USPTO of that fact. Without the timely filing of one of these forms, or a purchase of an extension, the ITU application will lapse. Filing an intent-to-use application requires more than a desire to use the mark; it requires actual evidence of the intent—for example, business, advertising, or marketing plans. (*Intel Corp. v. Emeny*, TTAB Opposition No. 91123312 (May 15, 2007).) An applicant that was unable to provide any documents or other evidence of an actual intent to use a mark can not claim rights as an "intent-to-use" applicant. (*L.C. Licensing, Inc. v. Berman*, 86 U.S.P.Q.2d 1883 (TTAB 2008).) A foreign registrant who "has not had activities in the U.S. and has not made or employed a business plan, strategy, arrangements or methods there," and "has not identified channels of trade that will be used in the United States," does not have a bona fide intent to use the mark. (*Honda Motor Co., Ltd. v. Friedrich Winkelmann*, 90 U.S.P.Q.2d 1660 (TTAB 2009).)

The initial intent-to-use application costs the same as an actual use application, plus an additional $150 for each additional six-month extension and $100 to file the Statement of Use—when you finally start using it in commerce.

The Lanham Act: § 1051. (§ 1(b)) Application for registration; verification

(b) Application for bona fide intention to use trademark

(1) A person who has a bona fide intention, under circumstances showing the good faith of such person, to use a trademark in commerce may request registration of its trademark on the principal register hereby established by paying the prescribed fee and filing in the Patent and Trademark Office an application and a verified statement, in such form as may be prescribed by the Director.

(2) The application shall include specification of the applicant's domicile and citizenship, the goods in connection with which the applicant has a bona fide intention to use the mark, and a drawing of the mark.

(3) The statement shall be verified by the applicant and specify—

(A) that the person making the verification believes that he or she, or the juristic person in whose behalf he or she makes the verification, to be entitled to use the mark in commerce;

(B) the applicant's bona fide intention to use the mark in commerce;

(C) that, to the best of the verifier's knowledge and belief, the facts recited in the application are accurate; and

(D) that, to the best of the verifier's knowledge and belief, no other person has the right to use such mark in commerce either in the identical form thereof or in such near resemblance thereto as to be likely, when used on or in connection with the goods of such other person, to cause confusion, or to cause mistake, or to deceive.

Except for applications filed pursuant to section 44 [15 USC § 1126], no mark shall be registered until the applicant has met the requirements of subsections (c) and (d) of this section.

(4) The applicant shall comply with such rules or regulations as may be prescribed by the Director. The Director shall promulgate rules prescribing the requirements for the application and for obtaining a filing date herein.

Related terms: Allegation of Use for Intent-to-Use Application, with Declaration; Principal Register; Statement of Use.

Inter-American Convention for Trademark and Commercial Protection

This treaty provides reciprocal trademark rights between the United States and a number of Latin American nations that are not signatories to the Paris Convention. These countries are Brazil, Colombia, Cuba, the Dominican Republic, Guatemala, Haiti, Honduras, Nicaragua, Panama, Paraguay, and Peru.

Related terms: international trademark rights; Paris Convention.

inter partes proceeding

This type of an administrative hearing is conducted by the Trademark Trial and Appeal Board to resolve:

- conflicts between pending applications (called interferences)
- the merits of opposition and cancellation petitions, and
- disputes over decisions of the Commissioner of Patents and Trademarks about applications for registration under the Lanham Act.

Related terms: interference; opposing and canceling a trademark registration.

interference

When two or more marks awaiting registration in the U.S. Patent and Trademark Office (USPTO) appear to overlap or conflict with each other, an "interference" is said to exist and the applicants are informed of this fact. Any applicant may then request that the USPTO set up an interference hearing to decide who should be the registered owner. Interference hearings tend to be expensive, lengthy, and rare. Most often, applicants facing an interference will simply withdraw their application and devise a new mark, which is then made the subject of a new application.

When an interference hearing is held, the USPTO uses a set of rules developed by the courts over the years to decide which applicant is entitled to the registration. The rules are based on such variables as:

- who was first to use the mark anywhere
- who was first to use the mark in commerce
- who was first to file the registration application, and
- if the first filer is not also the first user, whether the first filer knew or should have known of the previous use.

Related terms: inter partes proceeding; ownership of mark in the United States.

International Convention for the Protection of Industrial Property of 1883

See Paris Convention.

International Schedule of Classes of Goods and Services

All marks that are federally registered are classified by the U.S. Patent and Trademark Office according to a master list called the *International Schedule of Classes of Goods and Services* (used by virtually all countries). Classification allows marks to be efficiently stored and retrieved according to the class assigned to such product or service.

Because a mark's meaning is inseparable from the product or service to which it is attached, all registered marks must be classified by the category of goods or services they identify. Because many marks naturally fall into two or more categories, simultaneous registration in different classes is permitted, with an extra fee for each extra class.

If a mark has been registered for use on one type of product or service, and the mark's owner wants to use it on a type of product or service that falls in a different class, the mark must be registered anew.

> EXAMPLE: Sweets Inc., a candy manufacturer, attaches the trademark "TummyYummy Candies" to its line of chocolate candies. Later on, Sweets decides to enter the fresh fruit juice market. If it wants to use the trademark "TummyYummy Fruit Juice," it should obtain a new registration, since fruit juice and candy are in different classes.

See the accompanying list of "short titles" as a means to quickly identify the general content of numbered international classes. The titles are not designed to be used for classification but only as information to assist in the identification of numbered classes. To determine the classification of particular goods and services, refer to the *Alphabetical List of Goods and Services* at the UPSTO website.

Related terms: federal trademark registration; protection of marks under Lanham Act; trademark.

International Schedule of Classes of Goods and Services

Goods

1. Chemicals

2. Paints

3. Cosmetics and cleaning preparations

4. Lubricants and fuels

5. Pharmaceuticals

6. Metal goods

7. Machinery

8. Hand tools

9. Electrical and scientific apparatus

10. Medical apparatus

11. Environmental control apparatus

12. Vehicles

13. Firearms

14. Jewelry

15. Musical instruments

16. Paper goods and printed matter

17. Rubber goods

18. Leather goods

19. Nonmetallic building materials

20. Furniture and articles not otherwise classified

21. Housewares and glass

22. Cordage and fibers

23. Yarns and threads

24. Fabrics

25. Clothing

26. Fancy goods

27. Floor coverings

28. Toys and sporting goods

29. Meats and processed foods

30. Staple foods

31. Natural agricultural products

32. Light beverages

33. Wines and spirits

34. Smokers' articles

Services

35. Advertising and business

36. Insurance and financial

37. Building construction and repair

38. Telecommunications

39. Transportation and storage

40. Treatment of materials

41. Education and entertainment

42. Computer, scientific, and legal

43. Hotels and restaurants

44. Medical, beauty, and agricultural

45. Personal and legal

Trademark Law: Definitions

international trademark

There is no such thing as an international trademark. It is possible to file one application for a group of countries using a procedure known as the Madrid Protocol. The Madrid Protocol includes 77 countries. In addition, you can file one application and obtain protection in 25 European countries (known as a Community Trademark). Otherwise, you must seek protection on a country-by-country basis.

Related terms: Community Trademark; Madrid Protocol.

international trademark rights

Trademark rights in each country depend solely on the trademark laws of that country; there is no set of international laws. Mark owners must start anew to establish rights to a mark in every new country they enter for commercial purposes, a concept known as "territoriality." In other words, previous use or registration in other countries is generally irrelevant.

In the United States, first use often decides who owns a mark. Most other countries, however, award ownership to whoever is the first to register a mark (although use on the same or related goods usually must follow within a reasonable time). As a result, if the seller of wood patio furniture under the mark "Sueno" wants to expand to a first-to-register country, it will have to pick a new mark if "Sueno" is already registered in that country. This is true even if the U.S. seller was first to use the mark and even if the company that registered that mark in the other country does not currently make related goods. This "registration" system often allows people to anticipate international marketing trends and to register the rights to valuable marks before another company thinks to do so.

In an attempt to correct some of these conflicts, in 2003 the Madrid Protocol, an international treaty, went into effect, allowing U.S. trademark owners to file for registration in member countries by filing a single standardized English-language application at the U.S. Patent and Trademark Office (USPTO). The Madrid Protocol provides a truly international centralized trademark application system. Information regarding rules and membership can be found at the WIPO's website (www.wipo.int/madrid). The Madrid Arrangement on International Registration of Trademarks and the Madrid Protocol, use an international bureau, the World Intellectual Property Organization (WIPO), as a central registration office for trademarks in use in the member countries.

The territoriality rule (discussed above) has an important exception: Countries that have established treaty rights among themselves, like the United States and

Syria, may permit nationals of other treaty countries to establish their right to a mark based on prior use or registration in their own country alone. In the United States, the Lanham Act allows nationals of the Paris Convention countries to register their marks in the United States based on registration in their native country without alleging use here first (if they allege a bona fide intention to use the mark in the United States within a reasonable time).

Related terms: foreign nationals, registering in United States; Inter-American Convention for Trademark and Commercial Protection; Madrid Protocol; Paris Convention; phonetic or foreign equivalents for marks; prior registration countries.

Internet domain names

See domain names.

keyword

Keywords (or adwords or keying) are terms (words or phrases) sold by search engines to advertisers. When an Internet searcher types the keyword into a search engine, an advertisement related to the keyword appears. For example, typing the keyword "patent" might trigger specific ads by Nolo for its patent products. Trademark issues sometimes arise when keywords are trademarks—for example a competitor of Nolo buys "nolo" as a keyword.

The key issue, as with most trademark disputes, is whether consumers are confused and when consumer confusion is not found (which has been the general tendency of courts), the practice is permitted. (*Gov't Employees Ins. Co. v. Google*, 330 F. Supp. 2d 700 (E.D. V.A. 2004).), In a 2004 case, a district court held that consumers were not confused by Google's sale of the keyword "Geico." (*GEICO v. Google*, 330 F. Supp. 2d 700 (2004).) In 2010, a district court determined that Google's sale of the Rosetta Stone mark as a keyword in Google's AdWords program did not infringe the mark. Among the issues in Google's favor: the district court found that Google's use was functional and that consumer aware-ness of the Rosetta Stone's mark increased by 60% during the four years following the introduction of Google's program. (*Rosetta Stone Ltd. v. Google, Inc.,* 2010 WL 3063152 (E.D. Va. 2010).)

In Rescuecom Corp. v. Google Inc., 562 F.3d 123 (2d Cir. 2009), Rescuecom sued Google over its sale of Rescue.com trademark as a keyword to trigger competitors' ads. The Second Circuit Court of Appeals permitted the case to go forward because 15 United States Code Section 1127 defines "use in commerce" to include when "displayed in the sale or advertising of services."

When a competitor's sponsored link is triggered by its trademark and also includes the trademark within the sponsored ad—for example, a competitor of Gucci buys the Gucci keyword and includes Gucci in its ad—a court is likely to halt the sale. (See *Romeo & Juliette Laser Hair Removal, Inc. v. B. Assara I L.L.C.,* WL 750195 (S.D. N.Y. March 20, 2009).) The issue becomes even more complex when companies do business outside the United States. A French court ruled against the sale of trademarks as keywords in 2005.

Related terms: metatags, pop-up advertising.

Lanham Act

The Lanham Act is the main federal statute that governs trademarks, service marks, and unfair competition. It covers such matters as: (1) when owners of marks may be entitled to federal judicial protection against infringement of a mark by others; (2) the types of remedies for infringement that the federal courts are authorized to provide, such as injunctive relief, money damages, and defendant's profits; (3) procedures for registering marks with the U.S. Patent and Trademark Office (on the Principal Register or Supplemental Register); (4) guidelines for when trademarks become incontestable; and (5) remedies for activity that constitutes unfair competition.

The degree of protection offered to a mark under the Lanham Act (the federal statute that addresses trademark protection) depends on many variables, such as:

- whether the mark is listed on the Principal Register or the Supplemental Register
- the length of time the registration has been in effect
- whether the registrant is the senior user or the junior user, and
- whether the infringer had either actual knowledge or constructive knowledge of the registrant's mark.

Protection under the Lanham Act varies in scope and effectiveness. The owner of a registered mark can prevent others from later using a similar mark if such use would likely confuse the average reasonably prudent consumer as to the source of the product or service.

In addition, owners of such marks can prevent persons in other countries from using the same or a similar mark on their goods or services anywhere in the United States where consumer confusion is likely to result. On the other hand, the owner of a registered mark may have to accept another's use of the same or a similar mark in a specific marketing area where the mark has already been in use by the other party.

Although state and federal statutes and court decisions offer unregistered marks some local protection against mark infringement, this protection is greatly expanded if the mark is federally registered under the Lanham Act. For example, by federally registering a mark that's in use in two or three states, its owner may reserve the rest of the country for the trademark, except in places where the same or similar mark is already in use.

Some provisions of the Lanham Act are available to unregistered trademarks. For example, Section 43(a) of the Lanham Act protects against unfair competition. It makes liable anyone who causes another business to suffer damages as a result of the use of a false designation of origin; a false description; or a misleading mark, word, symbol, or name on any goods or services in commerce, in a way that is likely to cause confusion. This is the section most often used when a plaintiff claims that its trade name, unregistered mark, or trade dress has been misappropriated.

Related terms: commerce that Congress may regulate; unfair competition; unregistered mark, protection of; use of mark.

licensing of marks

The owner of a mark (licensor) grants a "license" when the owner authorizes another party (licensee) (usually in writing) to use the mark for commercial purposes. Such licenses should be very carefully drafted to provide control over the use of the mark, because the unfettered use of a mark by another party can harm the mark's value as a reliable identifier of a particular product or service. In an extreme case, allowing someone to use a mark without adequate restriction and supervision may result in the mark being considered abandoned (a "naked" license.)

Related terms: abandonment of mark; assignment of mark; naked license; ownership of mark in the United States.

likelihood of confusion

In order to stop trademark infringement, the senior user—the first business to adopt and use a particular mark in connection with its goods or services—must prove likelihood of confusion. When determining likelihood of confusion, courts use several factors derived from a 1961 case. (*Polaroid Corp. v. Polarad Elecs. Corp.*, 287 F.2d 492 (2d Cir. 1961).) These factors, sometimes known as the "*Polaroid* factors," may vary slightly as federal courts apply them throughout the country. The factors are intended as a guide, and not all factors may be particularly helpful in any given case.

- Strength of the senior user's mark. The stronger or more distinctive the senior user's mark, the more likely the confusion.
- Similarity of the marks. The more similarity between the two marks, the more likely the confusion.
- Similarity of the products or services. The more that the senior and junior user's goods or services are related, the more likely the confusion.
- Likelihood that the senior user will bridge the gap. If it is probable that the senior user will expand into the junior user's product area, the more likely there will be confusion.
- The junior user's intent in adopting the mark. If the junior user adopted the mark in bad faith, confusion is more likely.
- Evidence of actual confusion. Proof of consumer confusion is not required, but when the trademark owner can show that the average reasonably prudent consumer is confused, it is powerful evidence of infringement.
- Sophistication of the buyers. The less sophisticated the purchaser, the more likely the confusion.
- Quality of the junior user's products or services. In some cases, the lesser the quality of the junior user's goods, the more harm is likely from consumer confusion.

Related terms: initial interest confusion; infringement; average reasonably prudent consumer.

loss of mark

Ownership of an otherwise valid trademark may be lost in several situations. This occurs when a mark is deliberately abandoned (nonuse), when it becomes the generic term for the goods (genericide), when it is used improperly (in violation of antitrust laws), or when an unfavorable decision is made in a cancellation or interference proceeding (which passes the mark's ownership to another party).

Related terms: abandonment of mark; generic terms; interference; opposing and canceling a trademark registration.

Madrid Protocol

Prior to the Madrid Protocol, a U.S. trademark owner (or applicant) had to apply for registration in each country, a process that required spending thousands of dollars for fees, agents, and translators. Under the Madrid Protocol, U.S.

trademark owners can file for registration in various countries by filing a single standardized English-language application at the U.S. Patent and Trademark Office (USPTO).

Under the Madrid Protocol rules, any trademark owner with an application filed in or a registration issued by the USPTO (referred to as the "basic application" or "basic registration") and who is a national of, has a domicile in, or has a real and effective business establishment in the United States can submit an international application through the USPTO. The USPTO certifies that the same information is in the international application and the U.S. basic application and then forwards the international application to the International Bureau.

The applicant must pay the U.S. certification fees at the time of submission and identify at least one other nation (Contracting Party) in which a registration (referred to as "extension of protection") is sought. The certification fee is currently $100, per class, if the international application is based on a single U.S. application or registration.

The international registration isn't really a single registration; it triggers a process in which the application is individually examined in each country named in the registration. If a country has a basis for refusing the application, it must do so within 12 months. If an initial refusal isn't made within 12 months, the registration will automatically take effect in the designated country. If a country issues a refusal, the examination may be extended up to 18 additional months, and even more if an opposition is filed. International registrations have a duration of ten years and have one registration number. The result of all this is to speed up and simplify the international registration process.

This process doesn't preclude applicants from following the old path and filing a separate application in each country in which registration is sought. One big difference, however, is that if the owner of a U.S. mark uses the international registration, all resulting registrations around the world are dependent upon what happens in the United States for the first five years. In other words, international registrations end if the U.S. application is refused, cancelled, or abandoned. Note, all is not lost if a U.S. trademark is cancelled. The owner can still can file individual national applications within three months of the cancellation (and retain the benefit of the original filing date).

To file using the Madrid Protocol, start with the TEAS system at the USPTO website. If you later wish to add other nations to your application, you may do so by filing a "Subsequent Designation," also provided in TEAS format.

Trademark Law: Definitions

An international registration has a ten-year term, a single registration number, a single renewal date, and a single renewal fee (currently approximately U.S. $100). Likewise, any assignment or other such postregistration filing requires only one communication and one fee, payable in U.S. dollars.

Although the Madrid Protocol has primarily affected rules for international registration, it also affects U.S. trademark activity by:

- making the rules stricter for reviving abandoned applications and registrations
- providing for "partial abandonments" of trademark applications
- changing rules regarding the methods and time periods for opposing applications
- modifying rules regarding the submission of color trademarks, and
- establishing rules for the size of electronic images provided to the USPTO.

Related terms: abandonment of application.

mark

This book uses "mark" to refer broadly to:

- trademarks
- service marks
- certification marks
- collective marks, and
- trade dress (when used as a trademark or service mark).

The term "mark" generally encompasses any means that a business uses to identify or distinguish its product or service from competitors in the marketplace. Features of the mark must be nonfunctional and may include symbols, shapes, designs, logos, phrases, colors, tunes, and smells.

Related terms: trademark.

mark dilution

See dilution.

metatags

A metatag is programming code used in the creation of a website. Metatags do not affect the appearance of a website and are not visible when you look at a Web page, but they provide information regarding the content of the site. Metatags initially were used extensively by search engines that wade through the programming code and text of each page. When a search engine found a search term in a metatag, it indexed the Web page and displayed it in the search results. In other words, metatags had a direct effect on the frequency with which a search engine would find a website. This led many website owners to game the system by including rival sites' names and products in their metatags. One company went so far as to copy and use all of the metatags at a rival site. This kind of deceptive use of another company's trademark in a metatag is a form of trademark infringement when it confuses consumers. One judge described the practice as similar to a shop owner posting a sign with another company's trademark in front of its shop. (*Brookfield Communications v. West Coast Entertainment*, 174 F.3d 1036 (9th Cir. 1999).)

In some cases, using competing metatags was permissible. In one case, former Playmate Terri Welles created a website and used Playboy and Playmate in her site's metatags. This use of *Playboy*'s trademarks was permitted because Ms. Welles was using the terms to describe herself and to properly index the pages. In addition, the court was influenced by the fact that most of the free Web pages at the site included a disclaimer at the bottom: "This site is neither endorsed, nor sponsored by, nor affiliated with Playboy Enterprises, Inc. PLAYBOY, PLAYMATE OF THE YEAR, and PLAYMATE OF THE MONTH are registered trademarks of Playboy Enterprises, Inc." (*Playboy Enterprises, Inc. v. Welles*, 279 F.3d 796 (9th Cir. 2002).)

Within a decade of these decisions, most major search engines had eliminated or discounted metatags as a major factor in providing search results and legal issues regarding metatags have disappeared from the courts.

Related terms: fair use of trademarks; free speech and trademark law; keyword.

misuse of mark

See loss of mark.

money damages for mark infringement

See damages in trademark infringement cases.

naked license

A trademark owner who fails to supervise a licensee and maintain quality control over the licensed products or services has created a "naked license." A naked license may cause the owner to lose rights in the mark, a process known as "abandonment." This occurs when the mark is used on goods and services of varying quality so that it no longer identifies and distinguishes specific products and services from competing ones and does not indicate a particular level of quality attached to some product or service.

EXAMPLE: Barcamerica licensed its registered trademark, Leonardo DaVinci, to Renaissance Vineyards for the sale of wines. The licensing agreement did not contain a quality control requirement, and there was no evidence that Barcamerica controlled the quality of the licensed wine. When Barcamerica sued to stop another company, Tyfield, from using a similar mark, Tyfield argued that Barcamerica abandoned its rights as a result of its naked license. A federal court agreed and Barcamerica lost its rights to the Leonardo DaVinci mark and federal registration. (*Barcamerica International USA Trust v. Tyfield Importers, Inc.*, 289 F.3d 589 (9th Cir. 2002).)

EXAMPLE: A family owned the "Eva's Bridal" trademark. The family licensed the trademark to two people to open a Chicago store. After the license expired in 2002, the owners of the store continued to use the mark but stopped paying the trademark license fees. The store owners claimed that they didn't need to pay; the mark had been abandoned because the owners had not maintained quality control (it was a naked license). The trademark owners claimed they didn't need to supervise or maintain quality control because the bridal gowns at the store were of the same high quality (and from the same suppliers) as the other Eva's Bridal shops. In other words, quality control wasn't necessary because the store's goods were of high quality. The court responded that it wasn't "high" quality that was demanded; it was consistent quality—for example, the kind of supervision that guaranteed the dressing rooms were clean and that the customer experience was consistent across the franchise. As the judge stated, "The trademark's function is to tell shoppers what to expect—and whom to blame if a given outlet falls short. The licensor's reputation is at stake in every outlet, so it invests to the extent required to keep the consumer satisfied by ensuring a repeatable experience." (*Eva Bridal Ltd. v. Halanick Enterprises Inc.*, ___ F.3d ___ (7th Cir. 2011).)

A trademark license agreement should contain language assuring quality control and permitting the trademark owner to inspect products and services—for example, many toy licensors require pre- and post-production samples. In addition, the trademark owner of a franchise operation should perform personal inspections to guarantee consistency.

Related terms: abandonment of mark; licensing of marks.

names as marks

Names that are primarily surnames (last names) are considered weak and cannot be listed on the Principal Register unless they acquire a secondary meaning (for example, Heinz, Macy's, Miller). First names and nicknames, unless very unusual or memorable as a mark but not as a name, need to acquire secondary meaning by becoming very well known over time before others can be stopped from using them.

> EXAMPLE: "Henry's" is a mark used to advertise the Henry Weinhart's line of beers. Over time, "Henry's" has become associated in the public's mind with the underlying product and therefore has taken on a secondary meaning. If Henry Clark came along and used his first name to advertise his line of beers, the Henry Weinhart company could probably successfully sue him for infringement of its "Henry's" mark.

Related terms: prohibited and reserved marks under Lanham Act; secondary meaning; surnames as marks.

noncompeting goods

See competing and noncompeting products.

nonprofit corporations and trademarks

A nonprofit corporation is entitled to the same protection as a for-profit entity for its trademarks and service marks.

Related terms: state trademark laws; trade name.

notice of trademark registration

To denote that a mark is registered with the U.S. Patent and Trademark Office (USPTO) under the Lanham Act, a symbol must be placed next to the mark. The most commonly used symbol in the United States is an "R" in a circle (®), but "Reg. U.S. Pat. Off." is equally valid. Both symbols indicate that the mark is registered with the USPTO on either the Principal Register or the Supplemental Register (a list of marks that didn't qualify for the Principal Register because they lacked distinctiveness).

If a mark owner systematically does not use one of these symbols to identify a registered mark when using it to promote a product or service, the owner cannot collect treble damages or defendant's profits for an infringement, unless he or she can show that the infringer actually knew the mark was registered.

Trademark Law: Definitions

EXAMPLE: While searching for a name for his new computer game, Phil Hacker sees an advertisement in the newspaper for a new database manager called "Sorcerer's Apprentice." No notice of registration appears in the advertisement, so Phil concludes the mark is probably not registered and proceeds to use the name as a trademark for his program. The mark had in fact been registered. While the owners of the mark "Sorcerer's Apprentice" could sue Phil for infringement, they won't be able to collect treble damages, defendant's profits, or attorney fees unless they can show that they generally did accompany the mark with a proper notice of registration, and that the absence of a notice on the advertisement was an oversight.

Related terms: constructive notice of mark under Lanham Act; damages in trademark infringement cases.

Official Gazette

As part of the application process for placing a mark on the Principal Register, the U.S. Patent and Trademark Office (USPTO) publishes the mark in an online publication called the *Official Gazette* (OG), also available at the USPTO website (www.uspto.gov).

The OG contains lists of marks proposed for registration on the Principal Register, together with examples of their designs, to give other mark owners notice of the impending registrations. If any other mark owners believe the new mark would infringe on or dilute theirs, they can file an opposition to protest the registration.

If no one objects to the mark's registration within 30 days of the publication date, the USPTO will register the mark. If, however, any interested person files a timely opposition to the registration, the USPTO will schedule an administrative (inter partes) hearing to resolve the dispute.

Related terms: opposing and canceling a trademark registration; Principal Register; U.S. Patent and Trademark Office (USPTO).

opposing and canceling a trademark registration

Under the Lanham Act, any party who may be damaged by the actual or proposed registration of a mark is entitled to challenge the registration. If the mark has been published for proposed registration on the Principal Register, the party—usually the owner of a competing mark—can oppose the registration. The opposition must be in writing and be filed within 30 days of the proposed mark's publication in the *Official Gazette*. The U.S. Patent and Trademark Office (USPTO) may grant extensions of the 30-day period upon written request.

Under rules promulgated by the Madrid Protocol, if a party wants to oppose a trademark registration, the period for filing an opposition cannot be extended more than 180 days from the date the application was published. Those extensions must be now requested in one of two ways. A party opposing registration can, after the first 30-day period, either:

- request an extension of 30 days (granted upon request), followed by a second request for a further extension of 60 days (upon a showing of good cause), followed by a final further extension of 60 days (upon stipulation or written consent of the applicant), or
- request an extension of 90 days (upon a showing of good cause), followed by a final further extension of 60 days (upon stipulation or written consent of the applicant).

A party who intends to oppose a Section 1 or Section 44 trademark application can do so electronically or on paper. An opposition to a Section 66 application (an application under the Madrid Protocol) must be filed electronically.

If the mark has already been placed on the Principal Register, the party may petition the USPTO for cancellation of the registration. (15 United States Code, Section 1064.) A cancellation petition may be filed:

- within five years from the date the mark is published in the *Official Gazette*
- any time if the mark becomes generic or is abandoned or its use becomes fraudulent in some way, or
- any time, if the mark is a certification mark and it is being misused (for instance, the registrant no longer exercises control or the registrant begins to manufacture goods subject to the certification).

Marks proposed for placement on the Supplemental Register are not published for opposition. If a party believes that a mark's placement on the Supplemental Register may cause it harm, the party may file an application with the USPTO to have the registration cancelled. (15 United States Code, Section 1092.)

When a petition for opposition or cancellation is filed, or the USPTO declares an interference, an inter partes proceeding to resolve the dispute will be scheduled before the Trademark Trial and Appeal Board. (15 United States Code, Section 1067.) At the conclusion of this hearing, the Patent and Trademark Commissioner may:

- refuse to register the opposed mark (in an opposition case)

Trademark Law: Definitions

- cancel the registration of a mark or place restrictions on its use (in a cancellation case)
- refuse to register any mark, or some or all of several marks (in an interference case)
- register the opposed mark or marks of persons who are found to be entitled to ownership, or
- order concurrent registration of marks along with conditions or restrictions on their use designed to prevent consumer confusion in the marketplace.

The USPTO will cancel a mark on its own—without anyone asking for it—if the mark's owner fails to timely file a Section 8 Declaration showing that the mark is still in use. Because this form must be filed between the fifth and sixth year following the initial registration, and because the USPTO doesn't send a reminder, the registrations of many marks are cancelled for this reason. And because the USPTO also doesn't send notice of the cancellation, many trademark owners continue to use their marks in the belief that they are registered, when they're not.

The fact that a mark's registration is cancelled in no way affects the right of the mark's owner to challenge other users of the mark on the basis of first use. But as long as the mark remains unregistered, the owner will not be entitled to the benefits of registration should a trademark infringement suit become necessary.

Related terms: federal trademark registration; interference; ownership of mark in the United States.

ownership, presumption of

See presumption of ownership.

ownership of mark, international

See international trademark rights.

ownership of mark in the United States

In the United States, ownership of a mark generally comes from first use. Use of a distinctive mark on goods or services in the marketplace is sufficient to establish ownership in that mark unless either of the following is true:

- Someone else is already using the same or similar mark on related goods or services.
- An intent-to-use (ITU) application has been filed for the mark.

If, however, a business that is first to use a mark does not federally register it, and a second business uses the mark in a geographically separate market (which means no consumer confusion is likely), it is possible for both businesses to concurrently own the mark.

As mentioned, ownership of a mark may arise from the filing of an ITU registration application, before a mark goes into use. The ownership vests (becomes effective) when the mark is put in use and the application process is complete, but ownership will begin on the date the ITU application was filed.

Whether derived from actual use or from the ITU application, ownership of a mark confers an exclusive right to use that mark in a certain way and in a certain place.

Ownership rights may last forever, unless the mark is abandoned or becomes generic. The fact that a mark is not registered or that a registration is cancelled or not renewed does not affect the basic ownership of the mark, which is primarily based on use. However, additional remedies provided by federal registration will not be available to the owner of an unregistered mark if an infringement occurs.

Although the exclusive right to use the mark initially exists in the geographic area where the mark is being used, if someone uses the same or a similar mark in the United States, the scope of this right depends on the following factors:

- Which mark was first used anywhere in the United States?
- Which mark was first subject to a registration application under the Lanham Act on the basis of actual use or an intent to use the mark in the future?
- Was the first registrant under the Lanham Act the junior user or the senior user?
- If the first registrant under the Lanham Act was the junior user, did that party know of the mark's prior use by the senior user?
- Is there geographical proximity between areas in which two conflicting marks are used?
- Are the types of products or services to which the marks are attached related or unrelated?
- Is confusion of consumers likely to result from the use of the two marks?

EXAMPLE 1: Malou markets her marshmallow cookies, "Malou's Marvelous Mallows," in California only. Because there is no interstate use, Malou is only entitled to register her mark under her state's trademark laws. Lou, who lives in Colorado, decides to market cookies exclusively in Colorado under the name of "Lou's Marvy Mallows." Although Lou's mark is confusingly similar to that used by Malou, Malou probably would have no recourse as long as Lou's mark was confined to the Colorado market (there would be no likelihood of consumer confusion).

EXAMPLE 2: Suppose now that Malou markets cookies only on the West Coast, while Lou markets his cookies only in the East. Even if Malou federally registered her mark before Lou started using his mark, Malou will not be able to force Lou to stop using his mark unless she can show a likelihood of consumer confusion as a result of the two uses. But since Malou is the national owner of the mark, if Malou later decides to start marketing her product in the East, Lou could be forced to stop using his mark.

EXAMPLE 3: Using the same facts, with a last wrinkle. If Lou federally registers before Malou and Lou does not know of Malou's prior use of the mark, Lou will become entitled to exclusive use on a national basis except where Malou is already marketing. If Lou does know of Malou's prior use or if Malou objects to the registration, however, his registration may be deemed fraudulent and set aside.

These priorities can be somewhat complicated and obviously depend greatly on the facts of each case. Trademark law as it exists today developed at a time when geography played an important role in resolving trademark conflicts. If the same trademark was used by different businesses in different parts of the country, there was no likelihood of customer confusion and therefore no need for intervention by a court unless and until one of the users expanded into the other user's territory. As more and more businesses start to do commerce on the Internet, however, this concept of territory is becoming less and less important. Although most businesses are still local in the sense that they aren't franchises or chain stores, doing business on the World Wide Web automatically extends a business's marketing activity to all parts of the country and the world simultaneously.

Related terms: assignment of mark; infringement; licensing of marks; protection of marks under Lanham Act.

palming off

A person engages in palming off (also called "passing off") when he or she intentionally causes one product or service to be confused with another for commercial gain. Examples of palming off include:

- substituting one product for another—for instance, representing a computer as having one kind of microprocessor when it has another, or

- deliberately infringing a mark belonging to another—for instance, using "IBM" as a mark on a new computer line.

Although the phrase "palming off" is appropriate only in situations where there is an intent to confuse, it is sometimes used colloquially to designate any infringement where there is a likelihood of confusion, even where the infringer may not have intended it.

Related terms: likelihood of confusion; infringement; innocent infringer; reverse palming off.

Paris Convention

The primary treaty regulating trademark relations between the United States and other countries is called the Paris Convention. The Paris Convention provides that each signatory country will give members of other signatory countries the same protections regarding marks and unfair competition that it affords its own nationals.

Related terms: foreign nationals, registering in United States; international trademark rights.

parodies of trademarks

A trademark parody occurs when someone imitates a trademark in a manner that pokes fun at the mark, for example, distributing a newspaper called *The San Francisco Comical* in order to poke fun at the *San Francisco Chronicle*. Below are some trademark parody court cases.

- A college student sold T-shirts at Myrtle Beach depicting a red, white, and blue beer can with the phrase, "This Beach Is for You." Anheuser-Busch, the owners of the Budweiser trademark, filed a lawsuit, seized all of the T-shirts, and raided the college student's home and his mother's business. A jury determined that the T-shirts were a parody, but the judge overturned the jury verdict and ruled for Anheuser-Busch. An appeals court ruled that the use was a parody. Seven years and several lawsuits later, the parties reached a settlement in which Anheuser-Busch granted a license for sales of the T-shirt. (*Anheuser-Busch, Inc. v. L & L Wings, Inc.*, 962 F.2d 316 (4th Cir. 1992), cert. denied, 113 S.Ct. 206 (1992).)
- During a half-time show, the "San Diego Chicken" mascot initiated a fistfight with Barney, the popular purple dinosaur. A court held the use of the Barney trademark a permissible parody because the aggressive manner

in which Barney behaved was not likely to cause consumer confusion. (*Lyons Partnership L.P. v. Giannoulas*, 14 F. Supp. 2d 947 (N.D. Texas).)

• A gaudy, '60s style nightclub in Houston used the trademark "The Velvet Elvis" and, after being sued by the owner of the Elvis trademark, claimed that the club's name was an Elvis parody. A court disagreed, pointing out that the intent of the club's name and decor was to parody the Las Vegas lounge scene and the velvet painting craze, not to parody Elvis. (*Elvis Presley Enterprises v. Capece*, 141 F.3d 188 (5th Cir. 1998).)

• In *E.S.S. Entertainment 2000, Inc. v. Rock Star Videos, Inc.*, 547 F.3d 1095 (9th Cir. 2008), the Ninth Circuit Court of Appeals permitted a parody under First Amendment principles noting that artistic use of a mark is permitted when: (1) the use has artistic relevance to the work at issue (the video game), and (2) it doesn't explicitly mislead consumers as to the source of the mark or the work—a test adopted by the Ninth Circuit in *Mattel v. Walking Mountain*. In *E.S.S. Entertainment*, the video game "Grand Theft Auto: San Andreas" included a parody of the East Los Angeles strip club "The Play Pen" (referred to as the "Pig Pen" in the game).

• In the first appellate case heard under the Trademark Dilution Revision Act of 2006 (TDRA), the Fourth Circuit determined that Chewy Vuitton (for dog chews) was a parody, stating, "For trademark purposes, [a] parody is defined as a simple form of entertainment conveyed by juxtaposing the irreverent representation of the trademark with the idealized image created by the mark's owner." More importantly, the court held (1) that Chewy Vuitton was a parody that was not likely to confuse consumers as to its source, and (2) that a successful parody, such as Chewy Vuitton, would not dilute the Louis Vuitton brand but in fact might make it even more famous. The court stated, "[B]y making the famous mark an object of the parody, a successful parody might actually enhance the famous mark's distinctiveness by making it an icon. The brunt of the joke becomes yet more famous." (*Louis Vuitton Malletier S.A. v. Haute Diggity Dog, L.L.C.*, 507 F.3d 252 (4th Cir. 2007).)

Conflicting case law and the discretionary power of judges make it difficult to predict the outcome of a lawsuit based on trademark parody. It is also difficult to predict when a company will take action against a parodist. Some companies, like Anheuser-Busch, prefer to fight to the end, while others believe that chasing parodists generates negative publicity and prefer to let the parody run its course.

As a general rule, a trademark parody is less likely to run into problems if it:

- **Doesn't compete.** That is, the use of the parody product does not directly compete with the trademark product.
- **Doesn't confuse.** That is, the parody does not confuse consumers; they get the joke and do not believe the parody product comes from the same source as the trademarked goods.
- **Does parody.** Keep in mind that all humorous uses are not parodies. To avoid trouble, the use should specifically poke fun at the trademark.

Related terms: fair use of trademarks; free speech and trademark law; infringement.

partial abandonment

See abandonment of trademark application.

passing off

See palming off.

Patent and Trademark Depository Library

See trademark search.

phonetic or foreign equivalents for marks

In trademark law, a word that sounds the same as another mark, or one that means the same in another language, will normally be treated similarly. If a word or phrase is descriptive or generic (ineligible for protection), simply misspelling or translating it will not make it distinctive (that is, eligible for protection).

> EXAMPLE: If DateTime is too descriptive for a singles dating service, then Dayttyme won't work, either. Or, if GoodTimes is considered too descriptive for a party-catering service, then using the French equivalent BonTemps will not help.

Related terms: composite mark; generic terms; international trademark rights.

pictures and symbols used as marks

Pictures and symbols may be protectable as marks if they are distinctive rather than descriptive. For example, the Quaker man on Quaker Oats cereals is a strong, distinctive pictorial mark. Similarly, the apple on Apple computer products is very distinctive and nondescriptive. A generic illustration such as the no-smoking symbol—a diagonal bar through a burning cigarette within a circle—is not distinctive and would be barred from trademark use for an antismoking product or service.

Related terms: descriptive mark; secondary meaning; trademark.

pop-up advertising

Pop-up advertising occurs when a new window opens to display an advertisement while a viewer is visiting a website. In some cases, a pop-up can be generated by a competitor. In one case, a company selling contact lenses filed suit after visitors to the company's website saw pop-up ads appear for a direct competitor. In 2005, the Second Circuit Court of Appeals rejected this infringement claim, holding that the practice was not infringement because the use of the trademarked name—for the purpose of triggering a pop-up ad—did not amount to a "use" under the Lanham Act. (*1-800 Contacts, Inc. v. WhenU.com, Inc.,* 414 F.3d 400 (2d Cir. 2005).)

Related terms: keyword.

preliminary injunction

A preliminary injunction in a trademark case is a court order that requires one party to stop the use of an infringing or diluting mark, at least until the case has been resolved. Stopping an infringing use early provides a tactical advantage and usually encourages a speedy settlement. But to win a preliminary injunction, the party seeking it must demonstrate that it is likely to prevail when the case gets to trial and that it will suffer irreparable harm if the injunction is not granted. For example, in a 2011 case involving Apple and Amazon, Apple was unable to obtain a preliminary injunction stopping Amazon's use of the "App Store" because Apple failed to demonstrate that it would prevail at trial.

Related terms: injunctions against infringement

presidents' names and likenesses as marks

See prohibited and reserved marks under Lanham Act.

presumption of ownership

If a trademark infringement suit is filed, a court will assume that the trademark owner who is listed on a certificate of registration on the Principal Register is the owner of the mark. This presumption means that the owner does not have to present further evidence to support the ownership claim unless the defendant offers evidence to the contrary. In that event, the certificate holder will need to introduce evidence to back up the ownership claim.

The presumption of ownership is not available for marks on the Supplemental Register (a list of marks that didn't qualify for the Principal Register because they lacked distinctiveness).

The Lanham Act: § 1057. (§ 7) Certificates of registration

(b) Certificate as prima facie evidence

A certificate of registration of a mark upon the principal register provided by this chapter shall be prima facie evidence of the validity of the registered mark and of the registration of the mark, of the registrant's ownership of the mark, and of the registrant's exclusive right to use the registered mark in commerce on or in connection with the goods or services specified in the certificate, subject to any conditions or limitations stated in the certificate.

Related terms: certificate of registration; infringement.

Principal Register

The Principal Register is the list on which distinctive trademarks and service marks approved for federal registration are placed. Benefits of placement on the Principal Register include all of the following:

- It provides official notice to all would-be copiers that the mark is in use on particular goods or services, and that someone claims ownership of the mark for that use.
- It gives the owner the right to file an infringement action in federal court.
- It creates a presumption, in the event of litigation, that the registrant owns the mark, requiring the other party to challenge the registrant's ownership. (Placing the burden of proof on the challenger can often make the difference between winning and losing a lawsuit.)
- It gives the owner the right to seek an award of treble damages, defendant's profits, and attorney fees.
- It gives the owner the right to register in countries that afford reciprocal rights to the United States.
- It confers on the owner the right to exclusive use of the mark in all parts of the United States, except where a senior unregistered user may have already been using the mark at the time of registration.
- After the mark is on the Principal Register for five years, it gives the mark's owner the right to file for incontestability status. If granted, incontestability status prevents a challenger from challenging the registrant's ownership on

the basis that the registered mark lacks sufficient distinctiveness to warrant protection.

Related terms: incontestability status; opposing and canceling a trademark registration; prohibited and reserved marks under Lanham Act; Supplemental Register.

prior registration countries

Most countries determine ownership of a mark by who registers first, instead of who uses it first. These are called prior registration countries (or first-to-file countries) to distinguish them from countries that base trademark rights on first use, such as the United States.

Related terms: international trademark rights.

profits

See defendant's profits.

prohibited and reserved marks under Lanham Act

Under the Lanham Act, certain marks may be refused federal registration. (15 United States Code, Section 1052.) These are:

- Marks that comprise "immoral," "deceptive," or "scandalous" matter. For example, a mark resembling a sex organ would be considered immoral; a mark suggesting miracle properties in a product that are not substantiated would be deceptive; and a mark showing a mutilated corpse would be scandalous.
- Marks that disparage or falsely suggest a connection with persons (living or dead), institutions, beliefs, or national symbols.

EXAMPLE: A mark that showed Clara Barton clad only in a Red Cross-decorated bikini would constitute a disparagement of a person, of an institution (the Red Cross), and, if she were wearing the bikini while embracing Uncle Sam, of a national symbol. A baseball insignia with Babe Ruth's face would falsely suggest a connection with Babe Ruth unless authorized by his heirs.

- Marks comprising the flag or coat of arms or other insignia of the United States, or of any state or municipality, or of any foreign nation, or any simulation of these items.

- Marks that consist of or comprise a name, portrait, or signature identifying a particular living individual (except with his or her written consent), or the name, signature, or portrait of a deceased president of the United States during the life of his widow, if any, except with the written consent of the widow.
- Marks that so resemble marks previously registered with the U.S. Patent and Trademark Office that their use is likely to cause confusion or mistake or to deceive consumers.
- Marks that are merely descriptive, that is, are primarily surnames, geographical names, or terms that describe the qualities or characteristics of the product or service. This last category of marks may be placed on the Supplemental Register until they have become well-known enough to qualify as distinctive under the secondary meaning rule.

In addition to these prohibitions, certain organizations, such as the Boy Scouts and the U.S. Olympic Committee, have the exclusive right to use their marks and symbols mandated by statute. Similarly, the use of the character and name "Smokey the Bear" is reserved to the Department of the Interior.

Related terms: Principal Register; Supplemental Register.

protection of marks under state law and common law
See state trademark laws.

PTO
See U.S. Patent and Trademark Office (USPTO).

public domain
See generic terms.

publication of mark in *Official Gazette*
See Official Gazette.

publishers of advertising matter
If an infringement of a mark occurs in advertising copy carried in a magazine, newspaper, or other periodical, and the publisher has not been made aware of the infringement, the Lanham Act exempts the publisher from liability for money damages or profits. (15 United States Code, Section 1114.)

A court may bar (enjoin) the publication from any future advertising copy carrying the infringing mark unless the effect of the injunction would be to delay the normal publication, delivery, or distribution of a scheduled issue. Such a compromise is needed to prevent the injunction from harming the innocent publisher.

If a publisher engages in infringing activity after becoming aware of the infringement, it can be treated like any other deliberate infringer and money damages may be assessed.

Related terms: contributory infringer; false advertising.

puffery

When advertising claims are so broad that consumers do not take them seriously, they are referred to as "puffery," and they do not give rise to claims of false advertising. For example, grand and immeasurable statements such as "world's greatest detergent" or "the best hamburger in the world" are considered as puffery. Consumers understand that these claims are generalities intended to "puff up" a product. However, if the statement is capable of being measured or the puffery is related to specific attributes, the statement may be subject to false advertising claims.

> EXAMPLE: Pennzoil advertised that its motor oil "outperforms any leading motor oil against viscosity breakdown" and provides "longer engine life and better engine protection." A court determined that these statements were measurable, went beyond puffery, and were "literally false." (*Castrol Inc. v. Pennzoil Co.*, 987 F.2d 939 (3d Cir. 1993).)

Related terms: false advertising.

punitive damages

In trademark infringement lawsuits, the Lanham Act bars a court from awarding punitive damages: civil damages that are intended to punish a wrongdoer and serve as an example to future potential wrongdoers. The Lanham Act does, however, authorize treble (triple) damages in instances of egregious and intentional infringement. Also, unfair competition and related laws of many states provide for either punitive or treble damages. Therefore, in an effort to qualify for more generous damages, it is common to charge an alleged infringer with violations of both the Lanham Act and any applicable state laws.

Related terms: damages in trademark infringement cases; state trademark laws; unfair competition.

reasonably prudent consumer

See average reasonably prudent consumer.

reconditioned goods

A business selling reconditioned goods, for example, rebuilt Apple computers, must make it obvious to consumers—unless authorized by the trademark owner—that the goods are reconditioned or contain generic, nontrademarked parts. The words "Repaired," "Used," or "Reconditioned" must be prominently displayed with an explanation on the cartons and all printed matter. A claim for false advertising, dilution, or infringement may result if consumers are misled to believe that the company is related to, or is an authorized representative of, the trademarked goods. If a reconstruction of goods is especially extensive, the trademark should be removed from the goods and all advertising.

> EXAMPLE: A company customized Rolex watches by replacing internal and external elements and adding diamonds to enhance the appearance. The company then advertised and sold these as Rolex watches. The owner of the Rolex trademark (Rolex Watch U.S.A.) sued the company, claiming that the addition of non-Rolex parts affected the quality of the watch and its waterproofing and the insertion of diamonds affected the functioning of the watch hands. A court prohibited the promotion and sale of the watches under the Rolex trademark, since the reconditioning was so extensive that it was a misnomer to call the resulting watch a Rolex. (*Rolex Watch U.S.A. Inc. v. Michel Co.*, 50 U.S.P.Q.2d 1939 (9th Cir., 1999).)

"Reg. U.S. Pat. Off." or "®"

See notice of trademark registration.

registered mark

Although the term typically refers to federally registered trademarks, technically, any trademark, service mark, certification mark, or collective mark that is placed on a state or federal list of protected marks is considered registered. Registered marks are usually entitled to a higher degree of protection than unregistered marks. However, under Section 43(a) of the Lanham Act, unregistered marks used in commerce receive protection comparable to that provided marks placed on the federal Principal Register. As noted, the phrase "registered mark" commonly is understood as applying only to federally registered marks, specifically marks placed on the Principal Register.

registrable matter

Under the Lanham Act, certain parts of a mark may meet the standards for registration while others do not. The parts that do are called registrable matter; those that don't are disclaimed as unregistrable.

Related terms: disclaimer of unregistrable material; Principal Register; protection of marks under Lanham Act.

registrant

A registrant is any person or business who registers a mark under the Lanham Act or under state registration laws. The registrant is also usually the owner at the time of registration.

Related terms: registered mark.

registration

See federal trademark registration; state trademark laws.

related products and services

Deciding whether goods or services are related is a key determination in trademark conflicts and in deciding whether a mark qualifies for federal registration. This is because the extent to which goods or services are related will determine whether marks used on them are likely to confuse consumers if the marks are the same or very similar to one another.

How closely related goods or services are considered to be depends on many factors, the most important of which are:

- The international product/service categories (international classes) to which the goods and services belong. If they are in the same class, they will be presumed to be related, and the U.S. Patent and Trademark Office will usually not register the second mark.
- Whether the goods and services pass through related marketing channels. For example, if goods are sold in similar outlets, marketed in similar media, placed near each other in stores, and generally considered similar by the consumer, they will be considered related.

The courts have developed a number of additional criteria to determine when one product or service is related to another, which are used in infringement cases. These are:

- the likelihood that the goods or services of one business will be mistaken for those of the other

- the likelihood that one business will expand its activities so that its goods or services will compete with those of another business
- the extent to which the goods or services of businesses have common purchasers or users
- the market relationship, if any, between the goods produced, or the services provided, by the two businesses
- the degree of distinctiveness of the mark in question when compared to a competing mark
- the degree of attention usually given to trademarks or service marks in the purchase of goods or services of the type provided by the two businesses
- the length of time during which the allegedly infringing business has used the designation, and
- the intent of the allegedly infringing business in adopting and using the mark in question.

When products or services are considered to be totally unrelated, the courts will generally find that use of the same or a similar mark does not constitute infringement. On the other hand, if the products or services are found to be related, infringement may be found to exist, assuming the other requirements for infringement are also present.

Whether a product or service is considered related or unrelated depends on the exact facts of the case, how the criteria listed above are weighed in light of the facts, and the subjective perceptions of the judge, based on the evidence, as to whether the average consumer might be confused by the use of the same or similar marks on different products or services. In short, there is no firm dividing line between marks that are ruled to be related and those that are not.

EXAMPLE: Ethereal Fragrance Company produces a line of very successful perfumes with the distinctive federally registered trademark "Ekbara Scents," which it markets nationally to boutiques. If Ruben Santiago opens a small printing company specializing in business cards and calls his product "Ekbara Cards," a court is unlikely to find the two products to be related. Purchasers of business cards will not likely think they come from a fragrance company. In addition, neither business is likely to begin competing with the other. Therefore, the uses are unrelated and there is no infringement. On the other hand, if Ruben had created a line of scented greeting cards and marketed them under the Ekbara mark to boutiques as well as card shops, he might have a more difficult time proving the two products are not related.

Trademark Law: Definitions

Although the use of the same or a similar mark might not result in a finding of infringement under the "related/unrelated" analysis, this does not mean that the alleged infringer may continue to use the mark. Even though no infringement is found, the court may rule that the use of the allegedly infringing mark constitutes dilution of the original mark and restrict further use of the mark on that ground. However, the dilution rule only applies if the original mark is famous.

Related terms: competing and noncompeting products; dilution; ownership of mark in the United States.

renewal of registration

See duration of federal trademark registration.

reservation system for acquiring ownership of mark

See intent-to-use application; international trademark rights.

reverse confusion

In traditional trademark infringement cases, the second user of a trademark confuses consumers into believing that they are buying goods from the first user. However, it is possible that through massive advertising, a second user may create the impression that it is actually the first to use a trademark and that the real senior user is the infringer. This is known as reverse confusion.

> EXAMPLE: Big O Tires, a midsized regional tire distributor, began marketing a bias-belted tire under the unregistered mark BigFoot in early 1974. The tire giant Goodyear decided to market a radial tire under the BigFoot mark in late 1974. The larger company pumped millions of dollars into its advertising effort, which overlapped Big O's advertising effort to some extent. As a result, the public began coming to Big O asking for Goodyear's tire. Angry and disappointed, consumers suspected Big O of stealing the idea from Goodyear. But, in fact, Goodyear had become aware of Big O's prior use of the same mark midway into its marketing plans and had unsuccessfully negotiated to buy the mark from them. Nevertheless, they continued to use the mark. Under a theory of reverse confusion, Big O was awarded a judgment of $4.7 million. (*Big O Tire Dealers, Inc. v. Goodyear Tire & Rubber Co.*, 408 F. Supp. 1219 (D. Col. 1976) affirmed 561 F.2d 1365 (10th Cir. 1977).)

The *Big O* case introduced the theory of reverse confusion, a form of unfair competition, to trademark law. Goodyear competed unfairly because it intentionally undertook conduct with its trademark that deceived the public into thinking poorly of a competitor. The traditional likelihood of confusion factors are used in a reverse confusion dispute. The only difference is that the court focuses on the strength of the junior user's mark rather than the senior user's. That's because the essence of reverse confusion is that the senior user's mark may be less well-known than that of the powerful junior user.

Related terms: likelihood of confusion; unfair competition.

reverse palming off

Palming off occurs when goods are marketed in a way that makes people think they are really manufactured by someone else; to do this, an infringer usually uses the true trademark on substitute goods—for example putting a Levi's label on non-Levi's jeans. Reverse palming off, on the other hand, occurs when a noninfringing label is placed on someone else's goods and the goods are then sold under the noninfringing name—for example, a designer takes the Levi's label off Levi's jeans and puts the designer's label on the Levi's.

Either way, the public is being deceived and the owner of the original goods or mark may file a lawsuit under Section 43(a) of the Lanham Act to prevent this type of activity and recover damages caused by it.

Related terms: palming off.

right of publicity

The right of publicity is the right of a person to prevent the use of his or her name or persona for commercial purposes. Although the right of publicity is commonly associated with celebrities, every person, regardless of how famous, has a right to prevent unauthorized use of his or her name or image to sell products. The right extends beyond the commercial use of a person's name or image and includes the use of any personal element that implies an individual's endorsement of a product, provided that the public can identify the individual based upon the use.

For example, the right of publicity extends to a performer's identifiable voice. For this reason, courts have ruled that vocal performances that sounded like singers Tom Waits or Bette Midler could not be used to sell products. In many states, the right of publicity survives death and can be exercised by the person's estate. Because the right of publicity can trigger a claim of false endorsement or false advertising, these claims are sometimes brought under unfair competition laws, such as Section 43(a) of the Lanham Act. (15 United States Code, Section 1125(a).)

Related terms: false advertising; infringement; unfair competition.

same or similar mark

Any mark that is enough like another mark in appearance or meaning to lead the average, reasonably prudent consumer to confuse the two under the circumstances is considered "the same or similar." Whether any mark is deemed the same as or similar to another mark is necessarily decided on a case-by-case basis.

Related terms: likelihood of confusion; counterfeit; infringement.

secondary meaning

Marks that are not distinctive when they are first used can become so in the minds of the consuming public over time and through long, widespread use and/ or intensive advertising. This distinctiveness arises from the fact that the mark has acquired a secondary meaning as a mark that transcends the literal meaning of its words.

> EXAMPLE: The mark "Dollar a Day" initially just described a service: car rentals for a dollar a day. However, over time, and with the help of an advertising campaign and virtually exclusive use of the phrase by the firm, the phrase lost its descriptive literal meaning and instead stood for a specific car rental service.

If the owner of a nondistinctive mark can show (usually through consumer polls) that the mark has acquired a secondary meaning, the mark will qualify for placement on the Principal Register. Even without such a showing, a mark that is kept in continuous and exclusive use by its owner for five years will be presumed to have acquired such secondary meaning and will qualify for registration on the Principal Register as a distinctive mark.

Related terms: descriptive mark; Principal Register; Supplemental Register.

secondary register

See Supplemental Register.

Section 8 Declaration

Sometime during the fifth year after federal registration, the trademark owner must file a Declaration of Use of a mark declaring the continued use of the mark (or an explanation as to the special circumstances for any period of nonuse). The declaration must also be filed at the time of trademark renewal. The requirements for the declaration are set forth in Section 8 of the Lanham Act. (15 United States Code, Section 1058.) The fee must be enclosed along with a specimen of the mark as it is currently used for each class of goods or services. In lieu of the specimen, the trademark owner may recite facts as to the sales or advertising that demonstrates that the mark is in use.

If the owner fails to timely file the Section 8 Declaration, federal trademark rights will be canceled. There are no extensions for filing the declaration. The only way to reclaim federal trademark rights is to file a new application for registration. In the event that the mark has been assigned to a new owner since registration, the Section 8 Declaration is filed by the current owner, and the change in ownership should be reflected by the current owner filing a copy of the assignment with the U.S. Patent and Trademark Office (USPTO). When the Section 8 Declaration is filed for the first time (between the fifth and sixth years of registration), it is usually combined with a Section 15 Declaration. Forms for the Section 8, Section 15, and combined Sections 8 and 15 Declaration can be downloaded from the USPTO website (www.uspto.gov).

Related terms: Section 15 Declaration.

Section 15 Declaration

After five years of consecutive use from the date of federal registration, a mark may be declared incontestable. An incontestable mark is immune from challenge except if it has become the generic term for the goods or abandoned for nonuse, or if the registration was acquired under fraudulent conditions. In order to achieve incontestability, a Declaration of Incontestability must be filed containing the requirements as provided in Section 15 of the Lanham Act. (15 United States Code, Section 1065.)

A Section 15 Declaration is not necessary for maintaining ownership or rights under trademark law, and the failure to file the declaration does not result in the loss of any rights. However, the filing of the Section 15 Declaration is recommended because it expands trademark rights by making it more difficult to challenge the mark. A Section 15 Declaration form can be downloaded from the U.S. Patent and Trademark Office (USPTO) website (www.uspto.gov). The Section 8 Declaration and Section 15 Declaration can be combined into one declaration, and a copy of this combined declaration can be downloaded from the USPTO website.

Related terms: Section 8 Declaration.

Section 43(a)

See false advertising; unfair competition; unregistered mark, protection of.

selling goods or services with infringing marks

See contributory infringer.

senior and junior users of marks

When a dispute exists over the ownership of a mark, the person (or entity) who first used the mark is called the senior user, and the second person or entity to use the mark is termed the junior user. Although the senior user will usually be found to be the owner of the disputed mark, this is not always so. For example, if the junior user did not know about the senior user and is first to register the mark under the Lanham Act or under state laws, the junior user may still be able to use the mark in areas other than where the senior user's mark is being used.

Related terms: infringement; ownership of mark in the United States.

service mark

A service mark distinguishes a service in the same way that a trademark distinguishes a product. Examples of services and their marks are Jack-in-the-Box (food services), Blue Cross (health insurance services), Cirque de Soleil (entertainment services), and Virgin America (transportation services).

In the United States, the rules for determining when and how service marks qualify for protection are the same as the rules applicable to trademarks. This means that when you read this book or other sources of information on trade-marks, every time you read "trademark" (or "mark") in relation to a product, you can substitute the words "service mark" and "service" instead. One exception to this general rule is that some states will register trademarks but refuse to register service marks.

Note that a service mark is different from a trade name. A service mark is the name under which the service is promoted; a trade name is the name of the business that does the promoting. McDonald's Corp. (trade name) prepares and sells food under the service mark McDonald's and sells a specific product under the trademark Big Mac. Especially for small businesses, the service mark and trade name are often the same words, but used in different contexts. For instance, Universal Auto Repair is both the name of a business (it appears on the company checks, invoices, and stationery) and the name that appears on the sign designed to bring consumers into the shop (that is, a service mark).

Related terms: trade name; trademark.

similar marks, use of

See ownership of mark in the United States; same or similar mark.

slogans used as marks

Advertising slogans that function as marks may be protected as marks. To qualify as protectable marks, slogans must be either:

- inherently distinctive and creative, or
- have developed enough secondary meaning to immediately call a product or service to mind.

The more mundane a slogan is, the more secondary meaning the owner will need to show to obtain protection from imitators. For example, the owners of Excedrin had to prove that "Extra Strength Pain Reliever" had developed a strong secondary meaning.

Related terms: composite mark; secondary meaning; strong mark.

sounds used as marks

Many companies have registered sounds (or "aural trademarks") including NBC (chimes), MGM (roaring lion), and 20th Century Fox (Alfred Newman's triumphant theme). Although there is no prohibition against claiming trademark rights in a sound, the applicant seeking registration faces hurdles. For example, the sound must create an exclusive association with the company, a hurdle that the Harley Davidson motorcycle company found too difficult to overcome (the company pursued registration for the chugging sound of its well-known twin-engine sound for many years before throwing in the towel). In addition the sound must not be functional, a hurdle that an alarm clock company found equally difficult to overcome. (*In re Vertex Group LLC,* 89 U.S.P.Q.2d 1694 (TTAB 2009).) Finally, despite the fact that snippets of tones and music can be registered, a musician cannot register one of his signature songs as a trademark. When the Romantics, a pop group from the 1980s attempted to claim trademark rights in one of its hit songs, a district court rejected the trademark argument as being unsupported by case law and an "unwarranted extension intro an area already protected by copyright law." (*Romantics v. Activision Publishing Inc.,* 88 U.S.P.Q.2d 1243 (E.D. Mich. 2008).)

specimen

For purposes of filing a trademark application, the specimen is an actual example of the trademark being used on goods or in the offer of services. The specimen

Trademark Law: Definitions

must be filed with the application, or, in the case of ITU applications, the specimen must be filed later, together with a document entitled "Amendment to Allege Use." An actual specimen, rather than a facsimile, is preferred. When filing electronically, the USPTO provides a means for attaching a digital image of the specimen. For products, a label, tag, or container for the goods is considered to be an acceptable specimen of use for a trademark. A letterhead or business card is unacceptable as a trademark specimen because it doesn't follow the goods through the stream of commerce. A Web page is an acceptable specimen for services or goods provided the specimen page submitted shows a way to order the goods or services.

> **EXAMPLE:** The USPTO rejected an applicant's specimen of a Web page that showed images of goods (and described applicant's services) because the page failed to provide a user with direct means to order the goods. In other words, there was no "Click to Buy" or "Click to Order" feature on the page. (*In re Quantum Foods Inc.*, 665 F. Supp. 2d 727 (S.D. Tex. 2009).)

state trademark laws

In addition to the federal Lanham Act, all states have laws under which marks may be registered and receive judicial protection should infringement occur. State trademark protections are, like federal law, based on use. However, unlike federal law, no state offers registration on an intent-to-use basis; use of a mark must always precede its state registration. Registering with the state does not give a mark owner significantly greater rights, but it does offer notice to potential infringers who bother to search the registration list and, in a few states, may provide litigation benefits (for instance, attorney fees, presumptions of validity of the ownership claim, punitive damages).

Generally, marks used only within a state are limited to invoking state law protections, while marks used in two or more states (interstate), or across territorial or international boundaries, may use both national and state trademark laws. Simultaneously registering under both state and federal systems is a way to provide notice to both local and national competitors of claims of ownership of a mark. It also provides a choice of remedies and courts in which to sue. Also, because the laws of many states provide for punitive damages in situations where the Lanham Act does not, it is common for an infringement action to claim violations of both federal and state trademark statutes.

In addition to trademark infringement laws, most states have laws prohibiting unfair competition (business practices that confuse or deceive the consumer).

Often the facts that prove infringement of a mark will also prove unfair competition; thus, most states offer at least two theories under which a business's mark will be protected.

Although the federal Lanham Act has generally replaced state law as the most important source of protection for marks on goods and services that move between states or across territorial or national borders, the state systems are still the only source of trademark or service mark protection for those businesses, nonprofit organizations, craftspersons, dance and artist groups, theater companies, and restaurants that only operate on a local basis.

Finally, a number of states offer protection against dilution of a famous mark. This protects against the use of a famous mark in a context where consumers aren't likely to be confused but the use is likely to detract from the distinctiveness of the mark. Since the Federal Trademark Dilution Act was signed into law in January 1996, these state statutes are expected to diminish in importance.

A listing of state trademark agencies can be found on the Internet at www. ggmark.com.

Related terms: dilution; presumption of ownership; unfair competition.

Statement of Use

See Allegation of Use for Intent-to-Use Application, with Declaration.

strong mark

A mark that effectively identifies the origin of a product or service rather than its characteristics is a strong (good) mark, and a court can protect it from most or all uses by others. For example, the word "Cobalt" as a mark for a music recording label would be strong. Because it means a metal and a blue color, its use on music is original and in no way descriptive. Thus, it is distinctive and highly protectable. As a general rule, strong marks are made up of terms that are:

- arbitrary (a term that is used for a purpose other than its plain meaning such as Owl Ice Co. or Diesel clothing)
- fanciful (a made-up term such as Rackafrax Wax), or
- suggestive (a term that suggests without describing the goods or services such as ShadeTree Restaurant).

Only strong marks are entitled to be listed on the federal Principal Register; however, even unregistered strong marks are entitled to wide protections. Courts can enjoin (prevent) almost any infringing use of a strong mark. The test is whether the allegedly infringing use is likely to cause consumer confusion. The stronger the mark, the greater the likelihood that its use by another will confuse consumers. Because a strong mark stands out as the mark of a particular service or product, any imitation of it would be confusing.

Descriptive marks are weak, but they can be made strong by advertising and consumer awareness (secondary meaning). The weaker the mark, the more reluctant a court will be to find it has been infringed, and the less protection it will receive.

Related terms: strong mark; Principal Register; related products and services; secondary meaning; weak mark.

"sucks" domain names

See free speech and trademark law.

suggestive mark

A suggestive mark is a lesser cousin of the family of distinctive marks, which also includes arbitrary and fanciful marks. Suggestive marks qualify for the federal Principal Register but are not as strong as their cousins. They escape being descriptive, however, because they suggest interesting qualities or concepts about a product or service rather than directly describing it. Examples of suggestive marks are "Roach Motel" insect traps and "Accuride" tires.

Whether a mark is descriptive or suggestive is a highly subjective determination, depending on how a consumer (or a judge) perceives the word in relation to the product or service. For example, the mark "Enduring" can be descriptive on lipstick, suggestive on a photographic service, and arbitrary on ice cream.

Courts use various tests to determine whether a mark is descriptive or suggestive.

EXAMPLE: A company registered the mark, "Would You Rather … ?" and sued a competitor over a similar mark. A district court determined that the mark was descriptive and lacked secondary meaning. The Ninth Circuit reversed. One acceptable test for distinguishing between descriptive and suggestive marks was the "imagination test," which asks whether a leap of imagination is required to understand the mark's relationship to the product. The Ninth Circuit held that the district misapplied this test and that the record lacked evidence in the form of consumer surveys. A second test was also considered—the "competitors' needs" test—that focuses on the need of competitors to use a similar mark. Another test was also examined—the "extent of use" test—that considers the extent to which other competitors have used the mark. Based on the application of these three tests, the Ninth Circuit determined that the mark was suggestive. (*Zobmomondo Entertainment, LLC v. Falls Media, LLC*, 602 F.3d 1108 (9th Cir. 2010).)

As a general rule, the more brainpower it takes to see the descriptive qualities underlying a suggestive mark, the greater the protection it will receive.

Related terms: descriptive mark; strong mark.

Supplemental Register

The federal Supplemental Register is a secondary list maintained by the U.S. Patent and Trademark Office for trademarks and service marks that do not qualify for the Principal Register. Any name or symbol may be placed on the Supplemental Register as long as it is in actual use in commerce that Congress may regulate and can in some way distinguish the applicant's goods or services from others.

Descriptive, surname, and geographical term marks all qualify for the Supplemental Register. Generic terms do not qualify, since by definition a generic term calls to mind a type of product rather than a specific product. For instance, "Blue Jeans" means any pants made of blue denim, rather than a specific manufacturer's jeans. Marks that are barred from the Principal Register for reasons other than sheer descriptiveness are also barred from the Supplemental Register.

It is often difficult to prove infringement of a mark listed on the Supplemental Register, because such registration is an admission by the mark's owner that the mark is insufficiently distinctive to be placed on the Principal Register. Neither trademark nor unfair competition laws protect marks in any significant way unless consumer confusion is likely to result. Consumers are not likely to be confused by dual uses of any marks unless they are well known or memorable—in other words, distinctive. As a result, marks on the Supplemental Register do not receive all the protections given to those on the Principal Register. Specifically, placement on the Supplemental Register does not:

- provide constructive notice of ownership or a presumption of ownership in the event of infringement litigation
- support a later claim of incontestability status
- imply the right to exclusive use of the mark, or
- allow the mark's owner to request exclusion of imports by the Bureau of Customs.

Trademark Law: Definitions

On the other hand, supplemental registration does offer some benefits such as:

- the right to use the circled "®" or "Reg. U.S. Pat. Off." abbreviation to discourage would-be infringers
- the ability to register the mark in countries that offer reciprocal trademark rights, and
- the right to obtain injunctive relief, money damages, treble damages, and defendant's profits in the unlikely event that the mark owner should win an infringement action (assuming that the mark bore the proper notice of registration).

An applicant should always apply for the Principal Register first. If rejected, an applicant can then apply for the Supplemental Register.

The Lanham Act: § 1091. (§ 23) Supplemental register

This statute establishes a supplemental register for the purpose of registering marks that are insufficiently distinctive to warrant placement on the principal register. In addition, it sets out the procedures for applying to have a mark placed on the supplemental register.

(a) Marks registerable

In addition to the principal register, the Director shall keep a continuation of the register provided in paragraph (b) of section 1 of the Act of March 19, 1920, entitled "An Act to give effect to certain provisions of the convention for the protection of trademarks and commercial names, made and signed in the city of Buenos Aires, in the Argentine Republic, August 20, 1910, and for other purposes," to be called the supplemental register. All marks capable of distinguishing applicant's goods or services and not registrable on the principal register provided in this chapter, except those declared to be unregistrable under subsections (a), (b), (c), (d), and (e)(3) of section 1052 of this title, which are in lawful use in commerce by the owner thereof, on or in connection with any goods or services may be registered on the supplemental register upon the payment of the prescribed fee and compliance with the provisions of subsections (a) and (e) of section 1051 of this title so far as they are applicable. Nothing in this section shall prevent the registration on the supplemental register of a mark, capable of distinguishing the applicant's goods or services and not registrable on the principal register under this chapter, that is declared to be unregistrable under section 1052 (e)(3) of this title, if such mark has been in lawful use in commerce by the owner thereof, on or in connection with any goods or services, since before December 8, 1993.

(b) Application and proceedings for registration

Upon the filing of an application for registration on the supplemental register and payment of the prescribed fee the Director shall refer the application to the examiner in charge of the registration of marks, who shall cause an examination to be made and if on such examination it shall appear that the applicant is entitled to registration, the registration shall be granted. If the applicant is found not entitled to registration the provisions of subsection (b) of section 1062 of this title shall apply.

(c) Nature of mark

For the purposes of registration on the supplemental register, a mark may consist of any trademark, symbol, label, package, configuration of goods, name, word, slogan, phrase, surname, geographical name, numeral, device, any matter that as a whole is not functional, or any combination of any of the foregoing, but such mark must be capable of distinguishing the applicant's goods or services.

Related terms: commerce that Congress may regulate; prohibited and reserved marks under Lanham Act; unfair competition.

surnames as marks

The use of surnames (family names) is sometimes a controversial issue, because some business owners believe they have an inalienable right to use their own name as a trademark. They are surprised to find they cannot register their name or that someone else has preempted the field. For example, anyone with the family name McDonald or Denny would not be able to obtain a trademark for restaurant services.

A mark that is primarily a surname does not qualify for placement on the Principal Register under the Lanham Act unless the name has become well known as a mark through advertising or long use—that is, until it acquires a secondary meaning. Until then, surname marks can only be listed on the Supplemental Register. To register a mark that consists primarily of the surname of a living person (assuming the mark has acquired secondary meaning), the mark owner must have the namesake's written permission to register the mark.

Surnames are treated this way because, theoretically, everyone should be able to use his or her own name to promote their own business or product. In practice, however, as soon as someone establishes secondary meaning for a surname, it becomes off-limits for all uses that might cause consumer confusion. Del Monte, Disney, Spiegel, and Johnson & Johnson are just a few of the hundreds of surnames that have become effective marks over time.

A trademark is "primarily a surname" if the public would initially recognize it as a surname. A trademark application for a surname need not automatically be denied simply because it is a surname, or similar in sound or appearance to other surnames. Examination of an application for a surname should focus on how many people have that same surname and thus would be affected by registration of the surname. Extremely rare or obscure surnames—such as the surname

"Baik"—do not necessarily require proof of secondary meaning. (*In re Joint-Stock Company "Baik,"* Serial No. 78341041 (TTAB 2006).) However, a mark that is part surname and part distinctive mark may be registrable if the mark as a whole is distinctive, or if the surname is disclaimed as unregistrable material.

For example, two names may be combined (Smith and Wesson), or perhaps a name used with a design may be registrable. The reason for this is that when a surname is used with other matter, the "other matter" can affect public perception diminishing (or perhaps reinforcing) the impact of the surname. If a surname has a dictionary meaning (that is, it also functions as a word), it is treated like any other trademark. For example, King and Bird both have significance other than as family names.

Whether registered or not, if a name mark has become well known, even a person with the same name may not be able to use that name as a mark. Courts do, however, sometimes permit two conflicting uses of the same surname with modifications to try to minimize consumer confusion. For instance, if McGuffy's Bar faces a crosstown competitor by the same name, the second McGuffy may be forced to use a modifier, such as McGuffy's Cross-Town Bar.

A person who obviously tries to capitalize on his own name to take advantage of an identical famous mark (for example, Fred Ford opens Ford's Muffler Service) can be forced to give up all use of that name.

Related terms: composite mark; dilution; disclaimer of unregistrable material; names as marks; right of publicity; Supplemental Register.

symbols and pictures as marks

See pictures and symbols used as marks; prohibited and reserved marks under Lanham Act.

tacking

Often a trademark owner may wish to vary a trademark to capitalize on marketing and cultural trends. However, an issue arises as to whether this modification results in a new mark or whether it is a continuation of the first mark and can claim priority on that basis. If a trademark is properly "tacked," then the trademark owner claims the mark is a continuation of the earlier mark and is able to claim the date of first use of the earlier mark. Proper tacking requires that the two trademarks "must create the same, continuing commercial impression, and the later mark should not materially differ from or alter the character of the mark attempted to be tacked." (*Van Dyne-Crotty, Inc. v. Wear-*

Guard Corp., 926 F.2d 1156, 1159 (Fed. Cir. 1991).) For example, tacking such as changing Ego to Alter Ego or changing Polo to Marco Polo were not examples of acceptable tacking.

TARR

TARR (Trademark Application and Registration Retrieval) is a database and search system at the U.S. Patent and Trademark Office (USPTO) website enabling users to retrieve information about the status of an application or the status of registered marks.

Related terms: TDR; TEAS; TESS.

TDR

TDR (Trademark Document Retrieval) is the one of the many USPTO online services. It offers the public an electronic portal to PDF viewing, downloading, and printing of an array of information and documents for more than 460,000 trademark applications totaling more than eight million document pages. More than 300,000 application files are added annually.

Related terms: TARR; TEAS; TESS.

TEAS

TEAS (Trademark Electronic Application System) is a system for electronic filing of trademark, collective mark, certification mark, Statement of Use/Amendment to Allege Use, or other application and postregistration forms. To encourage the use of the eTEAS system (versus filing paper trademark applications), the U.S. Patent and Trademark Office (USPTO) has staggered the application fee. Currently (as of August 2011), the fee for a TEAS Plus application is $275 per class; for a regular TEAS trademark applications,$325; and for paper applications, $375. TEAS Plus has stricter requirements than the regular TEAS form.

Related terms: registration; TARR; TDR; TESS.

TESS

TESS (Trademark Electronic Search System) is a database and search system enabling users to access federal trademark registrations and prior-filed applications.

Related terms: TARR; TDR; TEAS.

Trademark Law: Definitions

TM

Although only marks that are federally registered can use the "®" symbol, any business that uses a mark can place the "TM" symbol after it to publicly claim ownership of the mark. The "TM" mark has no legal significance other than to notify the public that the mark owner views the words, design, and/or symbol as a protectable trademark. It also may serve as evidence against a claim of innocent infringement by a junior user, and thus enhance the possibility of collecting damages.

Related terms: damages in trademark infringement cases; infringement.

trade dress

Trade dress consists of all the various elements that are used to promote a product or service. For a product, trade dress may be the packaging, the attendant displays, and even the configuration of the product itself. For a service, it may be the decor or environment in which a service is provided—for example, the distinctive decor of the Hard Rock Cafe restaurant chain.

As with other types of trademarks, trade dress can be registered with the U.S. Patent and Trademark Office (USPTO) and receive protection from the federal courts.

To receive protection, both of the following must be true:

- The trade dress must be inherently distinctive, unless it has acquired secondary meaning.
- The junior use must cause a likelihood of consumer confusion.

For trade dress to be considered inherently distinctive, one court has required that it "must be unusual and memorable, conceptually separable from the product, and likely to serve primarily as a designator of origin of the product." (*Duraco Products Inc. v. Joy Plastic Enterprises Ltd.*, 40 F.3d 1431 (3d Cir. 1994).)

The U.S. Supreme Court found that a Mexican restaurant chain's decor could be considered inherently distinctive because, in addition to murals and bright colored pottery, the chain also uses a specific indoor and outdoor decor based upon neon colored border stripes (primarily pink), distinctive outdoor umbrellas, and a novel buffet style of service. (*Two Pesos, Inc. v. Taco Cabana, Inc.*, 505 U.S. 763 (1992).) However, the Supreme Court ruled that product designs such as the appearance of a line of children's clothing are not inherently distinctive and can only be protected if they acquire distinctiveness through sales or advertising. (*Wal-Mart Stores, Inc. v. Samara Brothers, Inc.*, 529 U.S. 205 (2000).) Similarly, the "Cuffs & Collar" design mark used by Chippendale's exotic male dancers was found not to be inherently distinctive. (*In re Chippendales USA, Inc.*, 90 U.S.P.Q.2d 1535 (TTAB 2009), affirmed by the Federal Circuit in 2010.)

Functional aspects of trade dress cannot be protected under trademark law. For example, a company that claimed trade dress on a round beach towel lost their rights when the Seventh Circuit determined that the towel design was primarily functional (despite the fact that the trade dress had been registered and had achieved incontestable status). (*Jay Franco & Sons, Inc. v. Franek*, 615 F.3d 855 (7th Cir. 2010).) Only designs, shapes, or other aspects of the product that were created strictly to promote the product or service are protectable trade dress.

> **EXAMPLE:** Many liqueur bottles have a unique shape designed for advertising rather than for any particular function. The tall, tapered shape of the bottle used for Galliano is not necessary to hold the product but helps to identify it and is therefore protectable as trade dress.

The trade dress aspect of packaging may be protected if a showing can be made that the average consumer would likely be confused as to product origin if another product is allowed to appear in similar dress. Legal protection is provided under the Lanham Act provisions relating to registered and unregistered marks.

It's also possible to assert a claim of dilution based on unregistered trade dress. To do so under federal law the trade dress owner must prove: (1) the claimed trade dress, taken as a whole, is not functional and is famous; and (2) if the claimed trade dress includes any mark or marks registered on the Principal Register, the unregistered matter, taken as a whole, is famous separate and apart from any fame of such registered marks.

Related terms: likelihood of confusion; Lanham Act; trademark, defined; unfair competition; *Wal-Mart Stores, Inc. v. Samara Brothers, Inc.*

trade name

Trade names are used to identify both nonprofit and for-profit business entities, whereas marks are used to identify products and services produced by such entities. Under the Lanham Act, a trade name is the name of any commercial firm, association, corporation, company, or other organization capable of suing and being sued in a court of law.

Trade names cannot be registered under the trademark and service mark provisions of the Lanham Act. However, they are entitled to protection under the unfair competition provision of the Lanham Act. (15 United States Code, Section 1125.) They are also protected under state unfair competition statutes and court decisions, if the public is likely to be confused by the use of the same or a similar name.

Companies frequently use their trade names as trademarks or service marks for their products and services—that is, as designators of origin in their advertising and on the products. For instance, Apple Computer Corporation uses the trade name "Apple" as a trademark, and the McDonald's fast food chain uses "McDonald's" as a service mark. In these situations, the trade name may be registered in its capacity as a mark and may receive additional protection under the Lanham Act's provisions applicable to infringement of marks.

Related terms: likelihood of confusion; service mark; trademark; unfair competition.

trademark

Manufacturers and merchants use trademarks for the sole purpose of distinguishing their products from those of others in the marketplace, not for any functional purpose. A trademark usually consists of a word, phrase, logo, or other graphic symbol. Examples of trademarks are Honda (automobiles), Cap'n Crunch (cereals), Apple (computer equipment), and Quicken (software). A trademark is not limited to a brand name or logo. It can also consist of a distinctive shape, letters, numbers, package design, sound, smell, color, or other aspects of a product that tend to promote it. Titles, character names, or other distinctive features of movies, television, video games, and radio programs can serve as trademarks when used to promote a product.

Many people use the term "trademark law" to refer broadly to all the laws that cover how businesses distinguish their products and services from those of others. This includes subjects like trade names, trade dress, commercial misappropriation, unfair competition, unfair business practices, and palming off. The above definition, however, focuses on the narrower meaning of "trademark" as a product identifier.

Related terms: federal trademark registration; *International Schedule of Classes of Goods and Services*; service mark; trade dress.

trademark dilution

See dilution.

Trademark Dilution Act of 2006

See dilution.

trademark infringement action

See infringement.

trademark owner

See ownership of mark in the United States.

trademark protection

See Lanham Act; state trademark laws.

trademark search

A trademark search is an investigation to discover any potential conflicts between a proposed mark and an existing one. Preferably done before a proposed new mark is used, a trademark search reduces the possibility of inadvertently infringing a mark belonging to someone else.

Trademark searches are extremely important. If a chosen mark is already owned and/or registered by someone else, the proposed mark may have to be replaced. Obviously, no one wants to discover that a new mark infringes another mark and must be changed after time and expense have been put into marketing, advertising, and implementing usage of the mark. In addition, if the earlier mark was registered under the Lanham Act prior to an infringing use, the infringing mark's owner may have to pay the mark's rightful owner any profits earned from the infringing use (defendant's profits).

Although the most thorough trademark searches are accomplished by professional search firms such as Thomson & Thomson, it is also possible to conduct a preliminary online trademark search to determine if a trademark is distinguishable from other federally registered trademarks. This can be accomplished using the U.S. Patent and Trademark Office's (USPTO's) free trademark database at www.uspto. gov, which provides free access to records of federally registered marks or marks that are pending (applications undergoing examination at the USPTO).

Privately owned fee-based online trademark databases often provide more current USPTO trademark information. Three private online search companies are: Thomson Compumark (www.compumark.com), Dialog (www.dialog.com), and LexisNexis (www.lexis.com).

It's also a good idea to check the Internet for a possible conflict with existing domain names as well as for names of firms already doing business there. The report issued by the searcher notes all uses of identical or similar marks and the products or services on which they are used.

If the search fails to disclose use of the same or similar mark by anyone in a related business, the mark owner can feel free to use it and register it federally (if used in commerce) or with the state (if used within only one state).

Trademark Law: Definitions

Related terms: damages in trademark infringement cases; domain names; federal trademark registration.

Trademark Trial and Appeal Board

An administrative arm of the U.S. Patent and Trademark Office, this body hears and decides disputes involving the registrability of, or conflicts between, marks. The Trademark Trial and Appeal Board consists of the Trademark commissioner, the deputy commissioner, assistant commissioners, and members appointed by the trademark commissioner. For a thorough reporting of decision making at the TTAB, see the TTABlog (www.ttablog.com).

Related terms: opposing and canceling a trademark registration; U.S. Patent and Trademark Office (USPTO).

typosquatting

See cybersquatting.

UDRP

The international agency that oversees domain names (ICANN) has established a dispute resolution procedure for trademark owners who believe that their domain name has been hijacked. The Uniform Dispute Resolution Procedure (UDRP) is a nonbinding arbitration procedure that is usually resolved within 60 days— much faster than any court decision would take. However, some commentators have argued that the UDRP procedure has become more cumbersome and expensive than originally intended and occasionally unpredictable in its outcome. In addition, since the UDRP results are not binding, either party can take the case to a local court if unhappy with the result. Also, based upon past ICANN arbitrations, the odds seem to be stacked heavily in favor of the person who has or claims to have trademark rights. To review the ICANN dispute resolution rules, go to www.icann.org/udrp/udrp.htm.

unfair competition

Unfair competition is the legal umbrella that governs any commercial activity that tends to confuse, mislead, or deceive the public about the sale of products or services. Such diverse activities as trademark infringement, trade name infringement, simulation of trade dress and packaging, palming off, false advertising, false designation of origin, and theft of trade secrets all constitute unfair competition. Once a court defines any given activity as "unfair competition," it generally is authorized to enjoin (judicially prevent) further activity from occurring and to award money damages.

Although most unfair competition law in the United States has been fashioned by legislatures and courts at the state level, Section 43(a) of the Lanham Act provides remedies for a broad range of activity generally described as unfair competition.

State unfair competition laws provide judicial relief in situations where a mark or trade name has been copied or simulated but where federal or state trademark infringement laws don't apply. Also, in most cases where trademark or service mark infringement is alleged, unfair competition claims are also raised as an alternative basis for judicial relief, in part because state law may offer the successful plaintiff the chance to get more money in the form of damages.

Related terms: false advertising; loss of mark; secondary meaning; unregistered mark, protection of.

unregistered mark, protection of

Unregistered distinctive marks are entitled under the Lanham Act to nearly as much protection from infringement as are registered ones. Federal registration does, however, make it easier to prove infringement and recover significant damages; thus strong marks should be registered.

The federal unfair competition statute, Section 43(a) of the Lanham Act (15 United States Code, Section 1125), is the main mechanism for protecting unregistered marks and trade names in interstate commerce. It prohibits two basic types of commercial activity (which are, in most cases, also treated as unfair competition under state laws):

- the use of a mark or label to designate falsely the origin of any product or service, and
- the description of a product or service in false terms (that is, false advertising).

If the products or services carrying the false designation or description were used in interstate commerce, anyone who engages in such activity may be sued in federal court by a person or business who can prove resulting economic injury.

This type of unfair competition suit for infringement of unregistered marks is not technically a trademark infringement action, due to the lack of registration. Such an action does, however, enable the owner of an unregistered mark to use the federal courts to stop the use of a similar mark that is likely to lead to consumer confusion. But the plaintiffs in such an action do not get some of the litigation benefits of federal registration, such as presumption of ownership, constructive notice, and incontestability. They are, however, entitled to recover triple damages and possibly attorneys' fees in case of a willful infringement.

Related terms: false advertising; Lanham Act; registered mark; unfair competition.

unregistrable material

See disclaimer of unregistrable material.

unrelated goods and services

See related products and services.

U.S. Patent and Trademark Office (USPTO)

The USPTO is the federal governmental wing of the U.S. Department of Commerce that governs trademark registration. As a practical matter, the USPTO determines the initial degree of protection that a mark is likely to receive in the courts. If registration of a mark is disputed, the Trademark Trial and Appeal Board, an arm of the USPTO, will hold hearings to resolve the dispute.

Related terms: federal trademark registration; *Official Gazette.*

use it or lose it

See abandonment of mark.

use of mark

The term "use" has a special meaning when it comes to protection and registration under the Lanham Act. As a general rule, "use" means that the mark has been, is being, or will be actually utilized in the marketplace to identify goods and services. This doesn't mean that the product or service actually has to be sold, as long as it is offered to the public under the mark in question.

A mark is being used for a service if the service is being marketed under the mark and the service can be legitimately delivered upon request by a consumer.

A mark is used for goods if the mark is placed on the goods or on labels or tags attached to them and the goods are shipped to a store for resale. However, sales made only for the purpose of getting a mark in use don't count.

Related terms: commerce that Congress may regulate; service mark; trademark.

USPTO

See U.S. Patent and Trademark Office (USPTO).

Victoria's Secret case (*Moseley v. V Secret Catalogue, Inc.*)

Victor's Secret, a New Jersey store, sold adult videos, adult novelties, hosiery, temporary tattoos, and lingerie. Victoria's Secret—a lingerie and clothing company that distributes over 400 million catalogs annually—asked the New Jersey store to change its name. The store complied, altering its name to "Victor's Little Secret." When the store refused to modify the name further, Victoria's Secret sued for dilution, arguing that Victor's Little Secret tarnished and blurred their famous mark. The district court and court of appeals agreed with Victoria's Secret, but the Supreme Court reversed. The Supreme Court acknowledged that the Victoria's Secret trademark was a valuable and famous mark and that consumers made a mental association when seeing the two trademarks—Victoria's Secret and Victor's Little Secret. But the mental association, by itself, was not enough to prove dilution. In order to prove dilution, the Court ruled that the trademark owner must demonstrate more than the likelihood of harm; the owner must actually prove—through consumer surveys or other evidence—that the mark has been damaged. The case was remanded for a new trial. However, perhaps to head off any further litigation, the defendants changed the name of their shop to "Cathy's Little Secret." Many commentators believe that the ruling will make it harder for some famous marks to claim dilution, because the trademark owner will have to demonstrate that consumers actually believe that the mark is tarnished or blurred by the second use. (*Moseley v. V Secret Catalogue, Inc.*, 537 U.S. 418 (2003).)

Related terms: dilution; trade dress.

Wal-Mart Stores, Inc. v. Samara Brothers, Inc.

In *Wal-Mart Stores, Inc. v. Samara Brothers, Inc.*, 529 U.S. 205 (2000), the Supreme Court ruled that product designs, like colors, are not inherently distinctive. Samara created a line of children's clothing that featured one-piece seersucker outfits decorated with appliques of hearts, flowers, fruits, and the like. Wal-Mart authorized another clothing company to copy Samara's designs and then sold the knock-offs at a lower price than that offered by Samara. Samara sued Wal-Mart and a district court ordered Wal-Mart to pay Samara $1.6 million. The Supreme Court eventually overruled that decision, holding that the designs were not protected under trademark law because they were not distinctive. The result is that no matter how creative and clever a product design is made, it will only be protected under trademark law if the owner can demonstrate secondary meaning—that the public associates that product design with one source.

weak mark

Trademark protection is based around a "strength" classification system. Strong trademarks are distinctive and are protectable. Weak trademarks are not distinctive. Weak marks cannot be registered or protected unless the trademark owner pumps up the mark with consumer awareness or "secondary meaning."

As a general rule, the more that the mark describes the goods or services (for example, Shake 'n Bake), the weaker or less distinguishable the mark. In some cases, if a mark is so descriptive that it is indistinguishable from the goods or service (for example, Light Beer for a beer low in calories), then it may be generic or too weak to ever obtain protection.

There are three common types of weak marks: descriptive marks that merely describe the nature, quality, characteristics, ingredients, or origin of a product or service; geographic marks that describe the origin or location of the goods or services; and family names (surnames) that are used as trademarks. All weak marks are capable of becoming strong if secondary meaning can be demonstrated.

Related terms: descriptive mark; generic terms; geographic terms as marks; surnames as marks.

willful infringer

See deliberate infringer (or willful infringer).

words in common use

See weak mark.

World Intellectual Property Organization (WIPO)

See international trademark rights.

zombie trademark

Abandoned trademarks that still have brand name recognition are referred to as zombie trademarks. Also known as "ghost brands," "orphan brands," and "graveyard brands," these revived marks pose a conundrum in trademark law. On the one hand, anyone is free to use an abandoned trademark; on the other, the new owner rarely replicates the quality formerly associated with the brand. Zombie marks are attractive to speculators who sometimes file intent-to-use applications to preclude others from using them. Some potential zombie marks include: Brim (coffee), Bonwit Teller (apparel), Coleco (toys and games), and Nuprin (analgesics).

Trademark Law: Forms

Preparing a Federal Trademark Application

In this section, we explain how to complete a federal trademark application and provide an example of a completed application. Applicants can also obtain help from the instructions provided at the U.S. Patent and Trademark Office (USPTO) website (www.uspto.gov).

The USPTO site only assists in the preparation and processing of electronic applications. The fees have changed to reflect this new electronic bias. A paper filing—should you prepare a paper application on your own—is $375 per class. An electronic TEAS filing is $325 per class, and a TEAS PLUS filing is $275 per class. (TEAS Plus has stricter filing standards and if you use the TEAS Plus version of the form, you must pay an additional fee of $50 per class if, at any time during the examination of the application, the USPTO decides you did not meet the requirements.)

Before you begin your federal application, you'll need to figure out what theory it's based on. Most federal trademark applications are based on either "use in commerce" or an applicant's intention to use the trademark (referred to as an "intent-to-use" or ITU application). The process for both "in use" and "intent-to-use" application involves three steps:

- **Preparation and filing of application.** A trademark application consists of a completed application form, a drawing of the mark, the filing fee, and a specimen of the mark. You can either mail the materials to the USPTO or file the application electronically and pay by credit card.
- **Examination by the USPTO.** Upon receipt, the trademark application is given a number and assigned to a USPTO examining attorney. If there is an error or inconsistency in the application, or if the examining attorney believes that registration is inappropriate, the attorney will contact the applicant to discuss the objection. The applicant can respond to the objections or can abandon the application. The examining attorney will either approve the mark for publication or reject it. If it is rejected, the applicant may challenge the rejection.

- **Publication in the *Official Gazette*.** Once the examining attorney approves the mark, it is published in the *Official Gazette*. The public is given 30 days to object to the registration. If no one objects, a trademark registration will be issued (or in the case of an ITU application, the mark is allowed pending use in commerce). If there is an objection from the public, the matter will be resolved through a proceeding at the USPTO.

The total time for an application to be processed may range from a year to several years, depending on the basis for filing and the legal issues that may arise in the course of examining the application. The registration expires ten years from the date of registration. You have certain obligations to maintain your trademark registration—for example, you must file a Section 8 Declaration of Continued Use between the fifth and sixth anniversary of the registration. Information about these maintenance requirements can be obtained at the USPTO website or by reviewing *Trademark: Legal Care for Your Business & Product Name,* by Richard Stim and Stephen Elias (Nolo).

The Trademark Application: the TEAS System

The preferred method of preparing the federal trademark application is to use the online Trademark Electronic Application System (TEAS) located at the USPTO's website (www.uspto.gov/teas/index.html). TEAS is an interactive system in which the user is asked a series of questions. If a question is not answered or an essential element is not completed, the applicant is asked to correct the error. The system is remarkably easy to use and there's a low probability of error in preparing the form. (In addition to the electronic system, applicants can create their own application forms by typing the necessary information onto a sheet of paper and paying the higher fee.) The information provided below is intended for use on a standard TEAS application.

Basis for Application

On the trademark application, you will be asked the basis for your application. If you have already used the mark in connection with the sale of crafts goods or services, then you would check "Yes" under "Use in Commerce." As for dates of use, you will need to provide the date (or your best guess as to the dates) you first sold goods or services using the trademark, anywhere. You will also need to provide the date when you first sold your work or services outside your state (for example, through an Internet sale or during travel to a crafts fair). If you have not yet used the mark but have a bona fide intention to use the mark, check, "Yes" under "Intent to Use."

Identification of the Class of Goods or Services

You will need to identify your class of goods. The USPTO uses the *International Schedule of Classes of Goods and Services* to group related goods. This helps them make appropriate comparisons of the mark. For example, glassware, porcelain, and earthenware are in Class 21. You can register your work in many classes, but each class registration costs $325 when filing electronically with the standard TEAS application (check current fees at the USPTO website).

To identify the class for your goods, search the USPTO's goods and services manual online. Go to the home page, click "Trademarks" (on the left side of the page), then click "Identification Manual." On the page titled "Acceptable Identification of Goods and Services Manual," click "Search" and type in the types of product or service that you sell. The class number is indicated after the letter G (for Goods) or S (for Services). Two online sources for guidance in identifying goods are the *Trademark Examiners Manual of Procedure* (*TMEP*) and the *U.S. Patent and Trademark Office Acceptable Identification of Goods and Services Manual*.

Description of the Goods or Services

Along with the class for the goods you will need to provide a description of the goods or services. This description is different from the listing of the International Class. For example, if you are selling key rings (International Class 6, "nonprecious metal goods"), the listing should state "key rings," not "nonprecious metal goods."

The description should be precise. If your description is too broad, the USPTO's trademark examining attorney will negotiate an appropriate description with you. (According to a USPTO survey, the applicant's identification of goods and services was questioned in more than 50% of trademark applications.)

Choosing the proper description is simplified because the TEAS system is electronically linked to the USPTO *Acceptable Identification of Goods and Services Manual*. An applicant can type in a word related to the goods and examine sample descriptions and lists of goods and services.

Identification of the Mark

If the mark is a word or group of words, identification of the mark is straight-forward. For example, the mark may be identified simply as "Hooky Wooky Hats." (Note: For the broadest protection for a word mark, register it free of any lettering style. This will give you the ability to use the trademark in various fonts, rather than being restricted to your original presentation of the mark.)

If the mark is a stylized presentation of the word, a graphic symbol, a logo, a design, or any of the other devices permitted under trademark law, a statement must be provided that clearly identifies the mark. If you're using the TEAS system, type in the word "mark" or, in the case of a stylized mark, attach a JPG graphic file.

Information About the Applicant

The applicant—your business—can be an individual; a partnership; a corporation; an association such as a union, social club, or cooperative; or a joint ownership by some combination of any these forms. If you are acting on behalf of a partnership, include the names and citizenship of the general partners and the domicile of the partnership. If you are representing a corporation, include the name under which the business or group is incorporated and the state or foreign nation under which it is organized.

Your own citizenship is required, as well as a mailing address. If you are doing business under a fictitious name, that information should be provided, especially if it is included on any specimen furnished with the application. If the mark is owned jointly by two entities, that should be stated as well. Type the appropriate information into the online form. Drop-down menus and online help screens are available to guide you.

Declaration

You are required to provide a declaration, a sworn statement, or other verification that the facts in the trademark application are true. You, or an officer of your corporation or association, should sign the declaration. The TEAS application provides an all-purpose declaration that can be used for both ITU applications and for trademarks that are in use.

Disclaimers

Many trademarks include words or phrases that, by themselves, cannot be protected under trademark law. For example, no manufacturer of cars can claim an exclusive right to the word "car" or "automobile." To allow one person an exclusive right to use such terms would decimate the English language. Therefore, the trademark office usually requires a disclaimer as to certain portions of trademarks. For example, if an applicant selling baked goods wanted to register the mark Lucky Bakery, the applicant would be required to disclaim "bakery." This means that apart from the use as a part of the trademark, the applicant claims no exclusive right to use the word "bakery."

Specimen

If your application is based on actual use of your mark in commerce, you'll need to enclose a specimen—that is, an actual example of the trademark being used on your goods or in your offer of services. In the case of ITU applications, the specimen must be filed later, together with a document entitled "Amendment to Allege Use." An actual specimen, rather than a facsimile, is preferred. When filing electronically, you'll see that the USPTO provides a means for attaching a digital photograph of the specimen. For products, a label, tag, or container for the goods is considered to be an acceptable specimen of use for a trademark. Your JPG file size must be under two megabytes and it should be scanned at 300 DPI or higher. A letterhead or business card is unacceptable as a trademark specimen because it doesn't follow the goods through the stream of commerce.

Completing the Process

You will complete the process by paying the fees, authorizing your electronic signature, and validating the application. After you click "Pay/Submit" and your transaction is successful, you will receive a confirmation.

Later, you will receive email acknowledging the submission of your application. Hold on to that email, because it is the only proof you'll have that the USPTO has your application. It is also proof of your filing date and contains the serial number assigned to your application.

After Filing

The USPTO filing receipt explains that you should not expect to hear anything about your application for approximately three months. If you have not heard anything in three and a half months, it is wise to call and inquire as to the status of your application. There are three ways to do this:

- Check TARR. The online Trademark Applications and Registrations Retrieval system page (http://tarr.uspto.gov) allows you to access information about pending trademarks obtained from the USPTO's internal database by entering a valid trademark serial number.
- If you want additional information or would prefer talking with a human, call the Trademark Assistance Center at 703-308-9400 and request a status check.

Trademark Law: Forms

You will likely receive some communication from the USPTO within three to six months. If there is a problem with your application, you will receive what's called an "action letter." This is a letter from your examiner explaining what the problems are. Most problems can be resolved with a phone call to the examiner.

When the examiner approves your application for publication, you will receive a Notice of Publication in the mail. Your mark will then be published online in the *Official Gazette*. For 30 days following publication, anyone may oppose your registration. Only 3% of all published marks are opposed, so it is very unlikely you will run into trouble.

Once your mark has made it through the 30-day publication period, and you are filing on an actual use basis, you will receive a Certificate of Registration. The USPTO sometimes has a difficult time moving applications through this long process. As a result, it may take a year or more to process your application.

If you filed on an intent-to-use basis, your mark will not be placed on the trademark register until you file an additional document with the USPTO when you put it into actual use. This form, available on the TEAS system, is called "Statement of Use/Amendment to Allege Use for Intent-to-Use Application." It tells the USPTO the date you started using the mark and completes the registration process. You must also provide a specimen at that time, showing how you are using the mark.

Communicating With the USPTO

The chances are good that you will be communicating with the USPTO after you have filed your application. Few applications sail through completely unscathed.

You are required to be diligent in pursuing your application. If you are expecting some action from the USPTO (the ball is in their court) and more than six months have elapsed without your hearing from them, immediately check the TARR system or call the USPTO Status Line (the TRAM Automated System, described above). If you discover a problem, bring it to the USPTO's attention. If you fail to respond in a timely manner to a request from a USPTO examining attorney, your application may be considered abandoned. If that happens, you may petition the Commissioner for Trademarks within 60 days to reactivate your application.

If the examiner wants you to change your application, such as claiming a different description of services or goods, there is usually some room for negotiation.

An examiner with a brief question might call you and then issue and mail you an examiner's amendment. This is a form on which the examiner records in handwriting a phone conversation or meeting with the applicant. Read the amendment carefully to make sure it matches your understanding of the conversation. If you disagree, or don't understand the amendment, first call the examiner, and then, if necessary, write the examiner a letter with your concerns, explaining your point of view on the communication.

Example of a TEAS Plus Application

The following data sheet reflects an application prepared using the new TEAS Plus system. The application is for the Nolo trademark as it is used in three classes: for books, software, and legal information services.

USPTO Generated Image

Trademark/Service Mark Application, Principal Register
TEAS Plus Application

*NOTE: Data fields with the * are mandatory under TEAS Plus. The wording "(if applicable)" appears where the field is only mandatory under the facts of the particular application.*

The table below presents the data as entered.

Input Field	Entered
TEAS Plus	YES
MARK INFORMATION	
*MARK	NOLO
*STANDARD CHARACTERS	YES
USPTO-GENERATED IMAGE	YES
LITERAL ELEMENT	NOLO
*MARK STATEMENT	The mark consists of standard characters, without claim to any particular font, style, size, or color.
APPLICANT INFORMATION	
*OWNER OF MARK	Nolo
*STREET	950 Parker Street
*CITY	Berkeley
*STATE (Required for U.S. applicants)	California
*COUNTRY	United States
*ZIP/POSTAL CODE (Required for U.S. applicants only)	94710
PHONE	510-704-2280
FAX	510-859-0027
EMAIL ADDRESS	rich@nolo.com
AUTHORIZED TO COMMUNICATE VIA EMAIL	Yes
LEGAL ENTITY INFORMATION	
*TYPE	CORPORATION
*STATE/COUNTRY OF INCORPORATION	California
GOODS AND/OR SERVICES AND BASIS INFORMATION	
*INTERNATIONAL CLASS	009
*DESCRIPTION	Computer software for the preparation of legal and business documents
*FILING BASIS	SECTION 1(a)
*FIRST USE ANYWHERE DATE	09/15/1987
*FIRST USE IN COMMERCE DATE	11/20/1987
*SPECIMEN FILE NAME	spec-6320712128-193107767 . Nolo_9.jpg
SPECIMEN DESCRIPTION	packaging for software product
GOODS AND/OR SERVICES AND BASIS INFORMATION	
*INTERNATIONAL CLASS	016
*DESCRIPTION	Books in the field of law and business topics
*FILING BASIS	SECTION 1(a)
*FIRST USE ANYWHERE DATE	06/01/1972
*FIRST USE IN COMMERCE DATE	06/01/1972
*SPECIMEN FILE NAME	spec-6320712128-193107767 . Nolo_16.jpg
SPECIMEN DESCRIPTION	cover of book

USPTO Specimens (Page 1)

PTO Form 1478 (Rev 7/2005)
OMB Control #0651-0009 (Exp. 09/30/2005)

Mark (USPTO-generated image for standard characters):

NOLO

Go Back

USPTO Specimens (Page 2)

PTO Form 1478 (Rev 7/2005)
OMB Control #0651-0009 (Exp. 09/30/2005)

Trademark/Service Mark Application, Principal Register

Serial Number: N/A

Class # 009

packaging for software product

Specimen:spec-6320712128-193107767_._Nolo_9.jpg

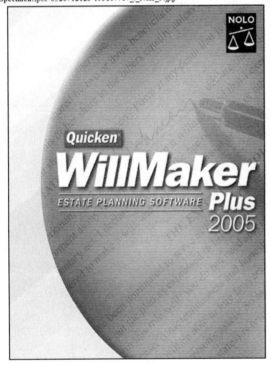

USPTO Specimens (Page 3)

Class # 016

cover of book

Specimen:spec-6320712128-193107767_._Nolo_16.jpg

 NOLO

Law for All

4th edition

Marketing Without Advertising

Inspire Customers to Rave About Your Business & Create Lasting Success

High-impact, low-cost marketing strategies that will help you:

- attract new customers
- provide great service
- "spread the word"
- plan marketing events
- use the Web ethically & effectively

 30 Years

"Anyone who wants to make the most effective use of customers for word-of-mouth marketing needs to read what Rasberry and Phillips have to say."
—Tim O'Reilly
CEO of O'Reilly & Associates

by Michael Phillips & Salli Rasberry

USPTO Specimens (Page 4)

Class # 042

screen shot of Nolo web home page

Specimen:spec-6320712128-193107767_._Nolo_42.jpg

Back

Application Prepared for Review by Applicant

PTO Form 1478 (Rev 7/2005)
OMB Control #0651-0009 (Exp. 09/30/2005)

Trademark/Service Mark Application, Principal Register

TEAS Plus Application

To the Commissioner for Trademarks:

MARK: NOLO (Standard Characters, see mark)

The mark consists of standard characters, without claim to any particular font, style, size, or color.

The literal element of the mark consists of NOLO.

The applicant, Nolo, a corporation of California, residing at 950 Parker Street, Berkeley, California, United States, 94710, requests registration of the trademark/service mark identified above in the United States Patent and Trademark Office on the Principal Register established by the Act of July 5, 1946 (15 U.S.C. Section 1051 et seq.), as amended.

    International Class 009: Computer software for the preparation of legal and business documents

For specific filing basis information for each listed item, you must view the display within the Input Table. To access, click here.

    International Class 016: Books in the field of law and business topics

For specific filing basis information for each listed item, you must view the display within the Input Table. To access, click here.

    International Class 042: Providing information relating to legal affairs

For specific filing basis information for each listed item, you must view the display within the Input Table. To access, click here.

If the applicant is filing under Section 1(b), intent to use, the applicant declares that it has a bona fide intention to use or use through the applicant's related company or licensee the mark in commerce on or in connection with the identified goods and/or services. 15 U.S.C. Section 1051(b), as amended.

If the applicant is filing under Section 1(a), actual use in commerce, the applicant declares that it is using the mark in commerce, or the applicant's related company or licensee is using the mark in commerce, or the applicant's predecessor in interest used the mark in commerce, on or in connection with the identified goods and/or services, and lists below the dates of use. 15 U.S.C. Section 1051(a), as amended.

If the applicant is filing under Section 44(d), priority based on foreign application, the applicant declares that it has a bona fide intention to use the mark in commerce on or in connection with the identified goods and/or services, and asserts a claim of priority based on a specified foreign application(s). 15 U.S.C. Section 1126(d), as amended.

If the applicant is filing under Section 44(e), foreign registration, the applicant declares that it has a bona fide intention to use the mark in commerce on or in connection with the identified goods and/or services, and submits a copy of the supporting foreign registration(s), and translation thereof, if appropriate. 15 U.S.C. Section 1126(e), as amended.

The applicant hereby appoints Richard Stim, 950 Parker Street, Berkeley, California, United States, 94710 to submit this application on behalf of the applicant.

The USPTO is authorized to communicate with the applicant or its representative at the following email address: rich@nolo.com.

A fee payment in the amount of $825 will be submitted with the application, representing payment for 3 class(es).

Declaration

The undersigned, being hereby warned that willful false statements and the like so made are punishable by fine or imprisonment, or both, under 18 U.S.C. Section 1001, and that such willful false statements, and the like, may jeopardize the validity of the application or any resulting registration, declares that he/she is properly authorized to execute this application on behalf of the applicant; he/she believes the applicant to be the owner of the trademark/service mark sought to be registered, or, if the application is being filed under 15 U.S.C. Section 1051(b), he/she believes applicant to be entitled to use such mark in commerce; to the best of his/her knowledge and belief no other person, firm, corporation, or association has the right to use the mark in commerce, either in the identical form thereof or in such near resemblance thereto as to be likely, when used on or in connection with the goods/services of such other person, to cause confusion, or to cause mistake, or to deceive; and that all statements made of his/her own knowledge are true; and that all statements made on information and belief are believed to be true.

Signature: /rwstim/ Date: 08/19/2005
Signatory's Name: Richard Stim
Signatory's Position: Legal Counsel

Back

Part 4: **Trade Secret Law**

Trade Secret Law: Overview... 519

    What kind of information qualifies as a trade secret?... 519

    How are trade secrets lost or stolen?.. 519

    Can you sell your trade secrets?... 520

    How is trade secret protection enforced?... 520

    What's new in trade secret law since the last edition?... 520

    Trade secret resources... 521

Trade Secret Law: Definitions... 523

Trade Secret Law: Forms... 569

    Preparing a Nondisclosure Agreement... 569

    Explanation for Sample Nondisclosure Agreement... 569

Trade Secret Law: Overview

A trade secret is any information that has commercial value, that has been maintained in confidence by a business, and that is not known by competitors. A business that owns trade secrets is entitled to court relief against those who have stolen the secrets or divulged them in violation of a legal duty—for example, after signing an agreement not to disclose (a nondisclosure agreement or NDA).

What kind of information qualifies as a trade secret?

Trade secrets often comprise customer lists, sensitive marketing information, unpatented inventions, software, formulas and recipes, techniques, processes, and other business information that provides a company with a business edge.

Information is more likely to be considered a trade secret if it is:

- not known outside of the particular business entity
- known only by employees and others involved in the business
- subject to reasonable measures to guard the secrecy of the information
- valuable, and
- difficult for others to properly acquire or independently duplicate.

How are trade secrets lost or stolen?

Information that qualifies as a trade secret is subject to legal protection (against theft and misappropriation) as a form of valuable property—but only if the owner has taken the necessary steps to preserve its secrecy. If the owner has not diligently tried to keep the information secret, courts will usually refuse to extend any help to the trade secret owner if others learn of the information.

Some activities that the courts will commonly treat as trade secret theft—which means the owner will be afforded some judicial relief, such as damages or an order preventing use of the stolen information—are:

- disclosures by key employees (current and former managers, scientists, and others occupying positions of trust) in violation of their duty of trust toward their employer

- disclosures by employees (current and former) in violation of a nondisclosure agreement entered into with their employer
- disclosures by suppliers, consultants, financial advisers, or others who signed nondisclosure agreements with the trade secret owner promising not to disclose the information
- industrial espionage, and
- disclosures by any person owing an implied duty to the employer not to make such disclosure, such as directors, corporate officers, and other high-level salaried employees.

When a disclosure is considered wrongful, the courts may also consider use of the information wrongful and issue an order (injunction) preventing its use for a particular period of time.

Can you sell your trade secrets?

As with other types of property—such as goods, accounts receivable, patents, and trademarks—trade secrets may be sold by one business to another. Most trade secret sales occur as part of the sale of the business owning the trade secret, but that is not mandatory.

How is trade secret protection enforced?

If the court finds that trade secret theft has occurred, it may issue an order (injunction) requiring all those wrongfully in possession of the information to refrain from using it or disclosing it to others. The court may also award the trade secret owner money damages to compensate for any monetary loss suffered as a result of the theft. In cases involving willful or deliberate theft, the court may also award punitive damages to punish the wrongdoer. Finally, in clear-cut cases, federal and state criminal antitheft laws may be invoked and the trade secret thief subjected to criminal prosecution.

What's new in trade secret law since the last edition?

There has been little change in trade secret law since the last edition. Below are some recent developments:

- **Software source code deposited with Copyright Office results in loss of trade secrecy.** A software developer registered software by submitting source code. Ten months later he submitted an email declaring that the material was a trade secret and never checked for compliance. Because the submission was available to the public, trade secrecy was forfeited. (*Kema, Inc. v. Koperwhats* 658 F. Supp. 2d 1022 (N.D. Cal. 2009).)

• **Disclosing bid without confidentiality results in loss of trade secret.** A company made a bid to another for services. An employee of the bidding company went to work for a competitor who submitted a lower bid and got the contract. Because the original bid was submitted without any requirement for confidentiality trade secret rights were terminated and the ex-employee's subsequent disclosure was not a misappropriation. (*Southwest Stainless LP v. Sappington,* 582 F.3d 1176 (10th Cir. 2009).)

• **Inevitable disclosure claim results in award of attorneys fees and costs.** An employer brought a trade secret claim against a former employee without any evidence and based solely on the claim that the employee would inevitably disclose the trade secret as part of his new employment. California (like most other states) does not permit inevitable disclosure claims and the employer was required to pay attorney fees and costs as a result of the bad faith claim. (*In Flir Systems, Inc. v. Parrish,* 95 Cal. Rptr. 3d 307 (Cal. App. 2d Dist. 2009).)

Trade secret resources

For more information on trade secret law and preparing nondisclosure agreements, see www.ndasforfree.com.

Trade Secret Law: Definitions

Below are concise definitions of the major concepts and terminology associated with explaining, protecting, and enforcing trade secrets.

accidental disclosure of trade secrets

If valuable business information is inadvertently disclosed to the public, courts commonly refuse to protect it as a trade secret. This means that accidentally disclosed information can be used by competitors without fear of a lawsuit by the information's original owner.

> EXAMPLE: Independent Robotics conducts a guided tour of its plant. One of the company's engineers accidentally leaves a top secret diagram of a new robot in full view, where it is seen by a competitor on the tour. This diagram (and the information contained in it) has lost its trade secret status due to the fact that it was discovered accidentally, without any intentional wrongdoing by the employee or the competitor.

Related terms: loss of trade secrets; reasonably precautionary measures to protect trade secrets.

advantage over competitors

See competitive advantage.

anticompetition agreements

See covenant not to compete by employee; covenant not to compete by owners of a sold business.

antitrust law and trade secrets

The primary purpose of antitrust law is to preserve a free, competitive marketplace by preventing companies from engaging in behavior that unduly dominates the marketplace or restricts free trade. Antitrust law:

- restricts businesses from engaging in practices with the intent to create a dominant or monopolistic market position, and

- prohibits businesses from making agreements with other businesses or individuals that impose significant restrictions or restraints on trade, such as price fixing, territorial restriction agreements, bid rigging, and tying arrangements.

In some circumstances, trade secret owners may violate the antitrust laws by using their trade secrets to unfairly discriminate against other companies. For example, if a clothing manufacturing company that has discovered a new method for protecting cotton from shrinkage shares this secret with one competitor for the purpose of driving a third competitor out of business, the antitrust laws may have been violated (conspiracy in restraint of trade and monopolistic practices). In general, deciding whether a particular activity violates the antitrust laws involves such variables as the intent of the actors, the degree of harm done to other companies, and the level of commerce that is affected (local, state, national, or international).

Related terms: illegal restraint of trade; licensing of trade secrets.

attorney fees

States that have adopted the Uniform Trade Secrets Act typically provide for the recovery of attorney fees if a trade secret lawsuit is brought (or resisted) in bad faith. Attorney fees may also be recovered if a nondisclosure agreement provides for recovery of fees in the event of breach of the agreement.

Uniform Trade Secrets Act: § 4. Attorney's Fees

If (i) a claim of misappropriation is made in bad faith, (ii) a motion to terminate an injunction is made or resisted in bad faith, or (iii) willful and malicious misappropriation exists, the court may award reasonable attorney's fees to the prevailing party.

beta testing and trade secrets

After new products and services are developed, they are often tested exhaustively under real-life conditions to make sure that they work properly, before being released to the public. This reality check (known as beta testing) is especially important in the case of computer software, which is usually so complex that its performance in disparate real-life situations cannot accurately be predicted on the basis of the written code. To identify any potential problems and mistakes (bugs) in the software, the software developer will commonly allow a number of people to use the software in exchange for keeping track of any problems they encounter. To preserve the software as a trade secret during the beta test phase, the developer customarily requires beta testers to sign nondisclosure agreements containing a promise to not talk about the software with anyone unless authorized by the developer.

Related terms: nondisclosure agreement; software and trade secrets.

business information as trade secret

A business's internal information can qualify as a trade secret if its disclosure would negatively affect that business's competitiveness. For example, the following types of information commonly are considered to be trade secrets because they provide a business with a competitive edge:

- information concerning the characteristics of customers
- information relevant to the cost and pricing of goods
- sources of supply, especially if disclosure would divulge the nature of a secret ingredient
- books and records of the business
- mailing lists and other sales information
- customer lists
- information regarding new business opportunities (such as the price and physical characteristics of real estate)
- information regarding the effectiveness and performance of personnel, distributors, and suppliers, and
- methods of doing business.

On the other hand, business information is not protectable as a trade secret if it can be independently developed with little difficulty. Information that might not generally qualify as a trade secret includes general employee handbooks and personnel policies that discuss the rights and responsibilities of workers based on applicable federal and state law.

Related terms: competitive advantage; compilation of information as a trade secret; customer lists; databases as trade secrets; industrial secret; know-how.

clean room

In order to demonstrate that proprietary materials were developed independently, teams are isolated and monitored in "clean rooms." These facilities provide evidence that similarities to others' works or products are due to legitimate constraints and not copying.

commercial piracy

See piracy.

Trade Secret Law: Definitions

competition by former employees

See confidential employment relationship; covenant not to compete by employee.

competitive advantage

Trade secret information, by definition, provides a business with a competitive advantage. This means that the information can potentially be exploited to enhance the income or assets of a business. If the owner of information cannot derive economic benefit from the information, there is no trade secret. Conversely, if keeping the information secret will give its owner a competitive advantage, the item may qualify as a trade secret, assuming that secrecy is, in fact, maintained.

Related terms: trade secret.

compilation of information as a trade secret

Trade secrets are often thought to involve a new approach, formula, device, or method for accomplishing a given end. However, a genuinely innovative structuring or reorganization of otherwise public information that creates a competitive advantage can also qualify as a trade secret if it is maintained as one.

Much existing information is now being reorganized so that it can be more easily stored in and retrieved from computer databases. Often referred to as "knowledge engineering," these new machine-searchable formats themselves may qualify as innovative compilations. They deserve treatment as trade secrets if maintained as such, because they enable a business to analyze old information in new ways that can lead to a competitive edge.

Related terms: business information as trade secret; customer lists; databases as trade secrets.

computer programs and trade secrets

See software and trade secrets.

confidential employment relationship

Much of trade secret law is concerned with how employees may act with respect to an employer's trade secrets during and after the period of their employment, even if these matters are not set out in a written agreement.

Each state has laws that prohibit trade secret theft. Regardless of whether an employer uses a nondisclosure agreement, an employee can be prevented, under these laws, from making unauthorized disclosures. In some cases, an employer may obtain financial damages from the employee for such disclosures. Although it is always advisable to use a nondisclosure agreement, these state laws provide a second line of defense in the event trade secrets are stolen.

In addition to state laws prohibiting disclosure, certain management and high-level employees—for example, engineers, scientists, or corporate executives—who come in contact with trade secrets during the course of their work have a special obligation (referred to as a "fiduciary duty" or "duty of trust") to treat secrets as confidential. The higher the level of expertise or responsibility possessed by the employee, the more likely this special fiduciary relationship exists. This offers an employer another method of preserving trade secrecy.

Regardless of these state laws and fiduciary duties, firms possessing trade secrets usually require all employees with access to trade secrets to sign nondisclosure agreements because these agreements provide additional rights and obligations in the event of a trade secret theft.

Related terms: duty of trust; exit interview; nondisclosure agreement.

confidentiality agreements

See nondisclosure agreement.

copyright and trade secret law compatibility

A copyright consists of the exclusive right to reproduce, display, perform, distribute, and make alterations to an original work of expression. Simply put, copyright law protects the original expressions of ideas, but not the ideas themselves.

Copyright and trade secret laws sometimes protect the same kinds of information and sometimes are mutually exclusive of each other. Here are the salient points of how trade secret and copyright legal protections can work together under the Copyright Act of 1976:

- Trade secret and copyright protection are both available for unpublished works as long as the idea (or ideas) in the work is sufficiently innovative to qualify as a trade secret (any confidential information that provides a business with a competitive advantage) and the information is kept confidential.

- Trade secret and copyright protection may both be available for works that are distributed on a limited and restricted basis under a copyright licensing arrangement requiring the licensee (user) to recognize and maintain the trade secret aspects of the work. This dual protection is especially pertinent for the computer software business.

Trade Secret Law: Definitions

- Trade secret protection is generally not available for software if the source code is made available to the public on an unrestricted basis through such means as listing it in a computer magazine or on a medium of distribution (for instance, a CD-ROM).
- Works that are widely distributed without specific licensing agreements will generally lose their trade secret status but may be entitled to copyright protection.
- The deposit of a physical copy of the work that is being registered with the U.S. Copyright Office operates to disclose any trade secrets in the work unless the deposit in some way masks the material that comprises the trade secret. For instance, it is possible to deposit samples of source code with major portions blacked out so that the parts of the code being maintained as a trade secret are not disclosed. There are several other methods for simultaneously registering a computer program and maintaining trade secrets. One common way is to withhold the source code altogether and deposit object code—which is impossible to understand when read in the U.S. Copyright Office.

Related terms: ideas as trade secrets; reasonably precautionary measures to protect trade secrets; software and trade secrets.
See also Part 2 (Copyright Law): Copyright Act of 1976.

covenant not to compete by employee

Also referred to as a "noncompetition agreement" or "noncompete," this is legalese for a written promise by an employee not to compete with his or her employer, or take employment with a competing business, for a specified length of time after the employer-employee relationship ends.

Noncompetition and nondisclosure agreements both have the same goal: to prevent a competitor from using valuable business information. The difference is that a nondisclosure prohibits disclosure to a competitor; a noncompete prohibits even working for a competitor or starting a competing business. In other words, the noncompete is broader and more heavy-handed in its approach. (So heavy-handed, in fact, that some states restrict or prohibit them.)

In some cases, noncompetes and nondisclosure agreements complement each other. For example, an Internet business might use a noncompete agreement to prohibit employees from working for competitors for a period of six months. After that, the employees may work for a competitor but will still be prohibited, under the terms of a nondisclosure agreement, from disclosing trade secrets. The six-month noncompete period guarantees that short-term business strategies won't be compromised, while the nondisclosure agreement guarantees that fundamental long-term business information and methods won't be lost in subsequent years.

By delaying former employees from going to work for competitors or starting their own competing businesses, covenants not to compete minimize the risk that trade secrets will be disclosed or used to compete with the former employer.

Agreements restricting the right of employees to compete have often proved difficult to enforce in court, as courts tend to dislike contracts that restrict a worker's right to earn a living. Employees with high levels of responsibility are more likely to be held to their promise, while those with less important responsibilities may be able to escape from the restriction on the premise that they would not be in a position to harm the employer's interest, and it would more severely affect their ability to support themselves.

Covenants not to compete are banned in some countries and banned or greatly restricted in a few states, including California. However, if an employee enters into a legal noncompete in one state and then takes a job with a competitor in California, California courts will enforce the agreement.

> **EXAMPLE:** Medtronic, a manufacturer of implantable medical devices, hired Mark Stultz to work in its Minnesota branch office. Stultz signed a noncompete agreement—legal in Minnesota—and then, after a few years, resigned and went to work for Advanced Bionics, a California medical device manufacturer. Stultz and Advanced Bionics asked a California court to invalidate the Medtronic noncompete agreement, since California does not permit noncompetes. The California Supreme Court refused; Stultz was bound by the Minnesota agreement, even in California. (*Advanced Bionics Corp. v. Medtronic, Inc.,* 29 Cal. 4th 697 (2002).)

Most state courts will, however, enforce covenants not to compete if they are seen as necessary to protect trade secrets and are drafted to minimize the restriction of the employee's right to work and/or engage in commerce.

A court is more likely to shorten the time periods for restrictive covenants when the employee works in an area of developing technology such as software or the Internet.

> **EXAMPLE:** An Internet employee's one-year restriction on working for a competitor was too long "given the dynamic nature of this [Internet] industry, its lack of geographical borders, and the employee's former cutting-edge

position." (*EarthWeb, Inc. v. Schlack,* 71 F. Supp. 2d 299, 313 (S.D. N.Y. 1999).) Another court limited an Internet employee's noncompete restriction to six months. (*DoubleClick, Inc. v. Henderson,* 1997 LEXIS 577 (Sup. Ct. N.Y. Co. 1997).)

Related terms: confidentiality agreements; reasonably precautionary measures to protect trade secrets.

covenant not to compete by owners of a sold business

As a condition of the sale of an existing business, its owners, officers, or directors are commonly required to promise in writing not to compete with the purchased business for a specific time period. These promises (or covenants) constitute recognition that part of the value of the purchased business consists of trade secrets. If former owners, officers, or directors were permitted to utilize this information in competing businesses, the purchasers of the existing business would not be getting their money's worth. For this reason, courts are usually willing to enforce these covenants.

criminal prosecution for trade secret theft

Several states and the federal government have passed laws that make the unauthorized disclosure, theft, or use of a trade secret a crime. Under these laws the government, not private businesses, arrests the perpetrators and brings criminal charges. The penalties—including imprisonment—can be much more severe than in a civil suit. For example, a person convicted of violating the federal Economic Espionage Act of 1996 can be imprisoned up to ten years.

The filing of a criminal case does not prevent the trade secret owner from filing a civil lawsuit based on the same issues. For example, in a case involving the Avery-Dennison company, a Taiwanese competitor was ordered to pay $5 million in fines to the government as a result of criminal charges and $60 million to Avery-Dennison as a result of a civil lawsuit involving claims of trade secret misappropriation, RICO (Racketeer Influenced and Corrupt Organizations Act) violations, and conversion.

Criminal prosecutions of trade secret theft are rare because many businesses prefer not to bring law enforcement officials into the fray. Also, in some cases, law enforcement officials don't wish to prosecute because there may not be sufficient evidence to obtain a conviction. Keep in mind that the standards of proof for criminal cases are higher than for civil battles.

Although state criminal laws affecting trade secrets differ from state to state, the typical law applies to anybody who intentionally:

- physically takes records or articles reflecting the trade secret
- copies or photographs such records or articles
- assists in either of these acts, or
- discloses the trade secret to another after having received knowledge of the secret in the course of a confidential employment relationship.

Related terms: federal trade secret statute; improper acquisition of trade secrets; improper disclosure of trade secrets.

customer lists

Companies are often very eager to protect their customer lists with nondisclosure agreements, particularly when a former employee might use a customer list to contact clients. If a dispute over a customer list ends up in court, a judge generally considers the following elements to decide whether or not a customer list qualifies as a trade secret:

- Is the information in the list ascertainable by other means? A list that is readily ascertainable cannot be protected.
- Does the list include more than names and addresses? For example, a customer list that includes pricing and special needs is more likely to be protected, because this information adds value.
- Did it take a lot of effort to assemble the list? A customer list that requires more effort is more likely to be protected under a nondisclosure agreement.
- Did the departing employee contribute to the list? If the departing employee helped create it or had personal contact with the customers, it is less likely to be protected under a nondisclosure agreement.
- Is the customer list personal, long-standing, or exclusive? If a business can prove that a customer list is special to its business and has been used for a long time, the list is more likely to be protected.

EXAMPLE 1: A salesman worked for an insurance company selling credit life insurance to automobile dealers. When he switched jobs to work for a competing insurance company, he took his customer list and contacted the customers at his new job. A court ruled that the customer list was not a trade secret, because the names of the automobile dealers were easily ascertainable by other means and because the salesman had contributed to the creation of the list. (*Lincoln Towers Ins. Agency v. Farrell,* 99 Ill. App. 3d 353, 425 N.E.2d 1034 (1981).)

Trade Secret Law: Definitions

EXAMPLE 2: Former employees took the client list of a temporary employee service. The former employees argued that the list could not be a trade secret since the information could be obtained through other means. A court disagreed and prevented the ex-employees from using the list, because it could not be shown, using public information, which companies were likely to use temporary employees, and because the list also included such information as the volume of the customer's business, specific customer requirements, key managerial customer contacts, and billing rates. (*Courtesy Temporary Serv., Inc. v. Camacho,* 222 Cal. App. 3d 1278 (1990).)

Wholesalers' lists of retail concerns are often hard to protect as trade secrets. Retailers are usually easy to identify through trade directories and other sources, and a list of them ordinarily does not confer a competitive advantage. But there are exceptions—for instance, a list of bookstores that order certain types of technical books and pay their bills promptly may be very valuable to a wholesale book distributor. But if the information is readily ascertainable through trade publications or other industry sources, it is not classified as a trade secret.

EXAMPLE: In a California case, a court determined that employees who left a business could use their former employer's mailing list to send out an announcement of their change of employment to former clients. The former employer's mailing list was not a trade secret because: (1) the clients became known to the ex-employees through personal contacts, and (2) the use of the customer list simply saved the ex-employees the minor inconvenience of looking up the client addresses and phone numbers. In other words, the information was easy to ascertain. (*Moss, Adams & Co. v. Shilling,* 179 Cal. App. 3d 124 (1984).)

Related terms: business information as trade secret; databases as trade secrets.

damages in trade secret misappropriation actions

If a trade secret owner has suffered monetary loss as a result of a trade secret theft, the owner may be able to get a court to award either:

- money damages measured by the profits earned by the competitor as a result of the use of the trade secret, or
- money damages measured by the loss of profits by the trade secret owner due to the improper trade secret leak.

Further, if the theft was intentional, courts in many states may impose punitive damages (damages awarded to the plaintiff for the purpose of punishing the wrongdoer and providing an example to other would-be trade secret thieves). By contrast, in other states, treble damages (three times the amount of proven actual damages) is the most that can be awarded in a trade secret case. For example, in a state that allows punitive damages, a court might award the plaintiff $1,000,000, even if the trade secret owner only proves $10,000 worth of actual damages. But in states where punitive damages are defined as treble damages, the court could only award $30,000 in the same case.

Uniform Trade Secrets Act: § 3 Damages

(a) In addition to or in lieu of injunctive relief, a complainant may recover damages for the actual loss caused by misappropriation. A complainant also may recover for the unjust enrichment caused by misappropriation that is not taken into account in computing damages for actual loss.

(b) If willful and malicious misappropriation exists, the court may award exemplary damages in an amount not exceeding twice any award made under subsection (a).

Related terms: injunctions; trade secret misappropriation action.

databases as trade secrets

A database is information of any type organized in a manner to facilitate its retrieval. An encyclopedia, for example, is a database that is organized alphabetically and contains information that can be retrieved by subject.

The term "database" currently is understood as referring to computer databases. Computer databases usually consist of information linked in a way to allow its quick retrieval, either by specific item or in combination with other items.

Databases may be protected as trade secrets. For instance, a database that allows a book publisher to identify people who purchased certain categories of books in the previous year would qualify as a trade secret if it were kept confidential.

A database often contains component materials that are protected by copyright. Sometimes this copyrighted material is owned by someone other than the database owner, as in the case of a database of archived newspaper articles where the copyright in the articles is owned by their original authors or publishers. Even so, this type of database can still be a trade secret, because the way the materials are organized is at least as valuable as the materials themselves.

Related terms: competitive advantage; compilation of information as trade secret; copyright and trade secret law compatibility; customer lists.

disclosure of confidential information

See Internet and trade secrets; nondisclosure agreement.

disclosure of confidential information during lawsuit

See litigation, disclosure of trade secrets during.

duty of trust

Over the years, the courts have recognized that certain business relationships require a higher-than-normal degree of trust between the parties. These relationships are often referred to as "fiduciary relationships," and people or businesses in these relationships are said to owe a duty of trust to each other. Those with a duty of trust have an obligation to take the interests of another person or a business into account when engaging in commercial activity potentially affecting that person or business. For instance, an employer and a high-level employee or provider of a service (expert consultant, lawyer, accountant) have a duty of trust to deal fairly with each other under all circumstances.

If a person violates (breaches) a duty of trust, the courts are usually willing to grant whatever remedy is necessary to undo the harm caused by the breach. For example, if a high-level executive breaches a duty owed to his or her employer by disclosing trade secrets to a competitor, the employer may go to court to prevent further breaches, to receive an award of damages from the employee, and to prevent the competitor from using the disclosed trade secrets.

Criminal prosecutions seldom are brought in breach of trust cases, which are almost always viewed as civil matters.

Related terms: confidential employment relationship; trade secret misappropriation action.

Economic Espionage Act of 1996

See federal trade secret statute.

email and confidentiality

How risky is it to send trade secrets by email? There's much less risk in the transmission of email than in its storage. The transmission of email usually doesn't jeopardize confidentiality, because each email message is broken into packets of information and reassembled at the delivery point, making it difficult to intercept. Also, the nature of email requires that the address be typed exactly, and, if it is not, the email almost always bounces back to the sender.

The danger from loss of confidentiality occurs when email is stored either on the sender's computer, a host computer (for example, an Internet Service Provider like America Online), or the recipient's computer. These stored files can be acquired legally by employers, lawyers, or the police, or they can be acquired illegally by hackers. Email transmissions also pose a threat to confidentiality when the information is subsequently posted on a bulletin board or in a chat group. For this reason, businesses generally institute trade secret procedures on company computers, including password protection and encryption of messages—a process that uses sophisticated software to garble the sender's words and then allows the recipient to unscramble and read them. In addition, companies prevent outsiders from penetrating the office network by the use of firewalls, protective computer hardware, or software systems.

Related terms: Internet and trade secrets.

employees, covenant not to compete

See covenant not to compete by employee.

employees, notice of trade secrets

See notice to employees of trade secrets.

employees' rights and duties toward trade secrets

See confidential employment relationship.

employment contracts and trade secrets

See covenant not to compete by employee; nondisclosure agreements.

evaluation agreement

This is a contract by which one party promises to submit an idea and the other party promises to evaluate the idea. After the evaluation, the evaluator will either enter into an agreement to exploit the idea or promise not to use or disclose the idea.

Related terms: idea submission.

exit interview

An employer may conduct an interview with a departing employee in which the employee is reminded of the trade secrets he or she has knowledge of and warned that his or her unauthorized disclosure of these trade secrets may result in being held personally liable for damages.

Related terms: duty of trust; notice to employees of trade secrets.

federal trade secret statute

The Economic Espionage Act of 1996 makes the theft of trade secrets a federal crime. The Act prohibits the theft of a trade secret by a person intending or knowing that the offense will injure a trade secret owner. The Act also makes it a federal crime to receive, buy, or possess trade secret information knowing it to have been stolen. The Act's definition of "trade secret" is similar to that of the Uniform Trade Secrets Act. The penalties for a violation of this statute include a potential prison term of 15 years and fines up to $5 million, depending on whether the defendant is an individual or a corporation.

A private party can still sue for trade secret theft even if the federal government files a criminal case under the Economic Espionage Act.

Since its adoption, the Economic Espionage Act has been enforced in several instances including:

- an attempt to steal the process for culturing Taxol from plant cells (Taxol is used in the treatment of ovarian cancer)
- the theft of a new shaving system developed by the Gillette Company
- the sale of trade secrets about a Kodak-owned device (known as the 401 machine) that inexpensively produced the clear plastic base used in consumer film
- the theft of trade secrets by a Taiwanese company from the Avery-Dennison company, and
- the theft of blueprints and bootlegged semiconductor parts from a Silicon Valley company.

Related terms: criminal prosecution of trade secrets.

fiduciary duty and trade secrets

See duty of trust.

formulas as trade secrets

Product formulas that both are kept confidential and add to a business's competitive advantage may qualify as trade secrets. A formula can consist of any combination of ingredients that results in a particular product. Examples of the many formulas that have been granted trade secret status are those for soft drinks, butter flavoring, industrial solvents, floor wax, and rat poison.

Freedom of Information Act, exemption of trade secrets

In its regulatory capacity, the federal government often requires businesses to submit information that the businesses consider to be trade secrets, such as the precise formula used in a drug for which FDA approval is being sought. The Freedom of Information Act (FOIA), located in 5 United States Code, Section 552, ordinarily provides the public with broad access to documents possessed by the executive branch of the federal government. However, to encourage businesses to file the appropriate records, trade secrets are exempt from the disclosure requirement otherwise imposed on the government by the FOIA. This means that businesses are able to comply with government regulations without necessarily giving up their secrets.

However, although the government is not required to disclose trade secrets under the FOIA, it is often difficult, if not impossible, for an agency official to tell from the information itself whether or not it is considered a trade secret by the company that submitted it. So, to protect their trade secrets, companies submitting trade secret information should clearly label the material as such. If the agency receives a request for the information, the agency is then supposed to contact the company and give it a chance to argue why the information should not be disclosed. If, however, the agency chooses to release the information in question against the company's wishes, there is little that can be done about it. The courts have prohibited affected businesses from filing lawsuits against the agencies involved (called "reverse FOIA suits").

freedom of speech and trade secrets

The First Amendment to the U.S. Constitution prohibits the government from placing restrictions on a person's freedom of speech. One exception to this "prior restraint" rule is that a court may prohibit the publication of trade secrets that have been obtained in violation of an employment agreement. Courts weigh several factors when making a prior restraint determination, including the commercial interest in the trade secrets, the individual's right to speak freely, and the illegal behavior used to acquire the trade secrets.

> EXAMPLE: A California man republished computer code from a Norwegian website. The code allowed users to bypass encryption and play DVDs on a computer—a method that was considered a trade secret by the DVD trade association. The California Supreme Court ruled that enjoining the republication of this trade secret did not violate the First Amendment. (*DVD Copy Control Association v. Bunner*, 2003 Cal. LEXIS 6295 (2003).)

Prohibiting publication is less likely if the trade secrets are obtained by legitimate means.

EXAMPLE: An attorney accidentally attaches trade secret information to a publicly filed court document. A reporter uncovers this inadvertent disclosure and arranges to publish the information in a newspaper. A court is unlikely to restrain this publication, since the information was obtained legally.

Keep in mind that some trade secret information, for example a business plan, may be protected under copyright law. In that case, the owner of the trade secret can sue, claiming copyright infringement as a result of the unauthorized publication, regardless of whether the information was obtained legally.

Journalists who republish trade secrets often seek to shield their sources under the First Amendment. In 2005, a California superior court ruled that bloggers who republished trade secrets owned by the Apple computer company could not claim this shield for their sources. The case—the first to assess the First Amendment rights of bloggers—indicates that writers for online publications may not be entitled to the same constitutional protections as traditional print and broadcast news journalists. (The unpublished decision regarding the issuance of a protective order in *Apple Computer v. Does* can be reviewed at the Electronic Frontier Foundation website (www.eff.org).)

Related terms: copyright and trade secret compatibility; injunctions; protective order; temporary restraining order.

GATT (General Agreement on Tariffs and Trade)

The General Agreement on Tariffs and Trade (GATT) is a treaty among most of the world's industrialized nations that addresses a number of factors affecting international trade, including how each signing country treats trade secrets belonging to businesses in the other signing countries. Under GATT, most industrial countries have pledged themselves to provide protection to trade secrets owned by residents of all signatory nations.

geographical licenses

See licensing of trade secrets.

head start rule

A court will often order a business that improperly possesses trade secrets to stop using the trade secrets for a period of time. The time period may depend on the length of time it would have taken the offending business to independently develop the information that constitutes the secret. In other words, the rightful trade secret owner is provided with a commercial "head start" in the information's use. This head start remedy recognizes that the essential value of a trade secret is the competitive advantage it affords its owner.

Related terms: injunctions; trade secret misappropriation action.

hiring employees from competitors to obtain trade secrets

See improper acquisition of trade secrets.

idea submission

People often come up with concepts that have not yet been exploited and may have economic value. For example, someone may conceive of an idea for a television show, but unless that person is in the business of producing television shows, the idea does not provide an advantage over competitors. In other words, it may not qualify as a trade secret. The key to protecting these idea submissions is to enter into an arrangement that respects the idea's potential value and justifies compensation.

Although the rules regarding protection of ideas vary from state to state, the best approach to protecting an idea submission is:

- maintain it with secrecy since, due to the vagaries of trade secret law, the idea may qualify as secret
- don't submit it to a company unless it has been solicited and it is clear that the arrangement is for compensation, and
- if possible, use an evaluation (or option) agreement to maintain secrecy and to demonstrate solicitation.

EXAMPLE: In 1983, two men submitted an idea to a movie studio: An African king comes to America, loses his memory, works in a restaurant, and marries an American woman and returns with her to his kingdom. The men entered into an agreement that if the studio ever produced a movie based on the idea, they would be compensated from the film's profits. The studio made *Coming to America,* a movie based on the idea, which grossed over $300 million. The studio claimed it had no obligation to pay the men because the movie was not based on their idea. The men sued and a court ruled in their favor because: (1) the movie studio had solicited the idea; (2) the parties had signed an agreement; and (3) $10,000 had been paid to the men when the idea was submitted. In the *Coming to America* case, no one factor was conclusive, but collectively these factors established that the idea submission was submitted in confidence and for economic benefit. (*Buchwald v. Paramount,* 13 U.S.P.Q.2d 1497 (1990).)

Although an evaluation or option agreement may create the presumption that an idea was solicited for compensation, a court will not always enforce it. If an idea is obvious within the industry, an agreement can be invalidated, because each party to a contract must contribute something of value. If the submitted idea has no novelty, it has no value, and therefore the contract is void. (*Nadel v. Play-by-Play Toys & Novelties, Inc.,* 208 F.3d 368 (S.D. N.Y. 1999).)

EXAMPLE: A company submitted a cross-marketing idea to the Mattel toy company and the National Basketball Association; the two entities would jointly market a Cabbage Patch Doll dressed in a basketball uniform. A court later determined that the company submitting the idea had no rights to compensation, because the idea was obvious to the NBA and Mattel. (*Khreativity Unlimited v. Mattel, Inc.,* 101 F. Supp. 2d 177 (S.D. N.Y. 2000).)

Even if a company doesn't sign an evaluation or option agreement, it's still possible to get paid for the use of an idea. An agreement can be implied from the circumstances.

EXAMPLE: The Mattel toy company invited members of an animation company to submit ideas for licensed characters. The animation company presented several ideas, including its "Flutter Faeries" characters. Mattel asked to keep copies of the presentation and soon afterwards produced dolls with characteristics similar to Flutter Faeries. A court of appeals permitted the animation company to pursue Mattel over an implied agreement. (*Gunther-Wahl Productions, Inc. v. Mattel,* 104 Cal. App. 4th 27 (2002).)

Under limited circumstances, the originator of an idea may stop someone to whom the idea is disclosed from misappropriating it if there is a "fiduciary relationship" between the parties and the idea was not generally known. In a fiduciary relationship, one person stands in a special relationship of trust, confidence, or responsibility. Fiduciary relationships are often defined by statute or case law. For example, the relationship of an attorney to a client is a fiduciary relationship, and stealing a client's idea would be a breach of that relationship.

Trade Secret Law: Definitions

Equally important is whether the parties are in a confidential relationship. If the parties have agreed not to disclose the secret without authorization, a presumption is usually created that the idea has economic value and deserves compensation.

ideas as trade secrets

Ideas alone can be protected as trade secrets only if they are generally unknown in the business community, offer a competitive advantage, and are treated confidentially. The real value of any idea will ultimately depend on its commercial success. An idea that offers the possibility of helping a business compete should be maintained as a trade secret until such time as it appears to lack feasibility or others independently think of it. Otherwise, a golden opportunity for obtaining an advantage over potential competitors may be lost.

Although the rules regarding protection of ideas vary from state to state, the maximum legal protection can be obtained by following these principles:

- Maintain an idea with secrecy and use a nondisclosure agreement.
- Don't submit it to a company unless it has been solicited and it is clear that the arrangement is for compensation.

Trade secret protection is also available for ideas that later become an invention, up to the time that a patent covering the invention issues. Once a patent issues, the underlying ideas become part of the patent. Patent information is available to the public and is no longer considered a trade secret.

Trade secret protection for ideas should be contrasted with copyright protection, which only protects the actual expression of the idea and not the idea itself. Because of this difference, trade secret law can often best protect the conception and development stages of a work before it is finally fixed in a tangible medium and published, at which point copyright protection takes over.

Related terms: copyright and trade secret law compatibility; patent application, effect on trade secrets.

illegal restraint of trade

Commercial activity by one business showing a strong tendency to restrict or curtail the free flow of commerce is considered an illegal restraint of trade. Examples of illegal restraints are tying arrangements (requiring the purchase of one product as a prerequisite to buying another), price setting agreements (two or more businesses agreeing to set prices at a particular level), and territorial restriction agreements (private agreements to restrict the use of a trade secret to certain geographical areas).

Trade Secret Law: Definitions

Related terms: antitrust law and trade secrets; licensing of trade secrets.

implied duty not to disclose trade secrets

See duty of trust.

improper acquisition of trade secrets

This phrase describes the situation where a business obtained a trade secret through means that the law considers impermissible, such as:

- deliberate theft through misrepresentation, burglary, or industrial espionage, or
- knowingly obtaining or using trade secrets that have been obtained by theft or improperly disclosed by a person who breached a nondisclosure agreement, implied duty not to disclose trade secrets, or duty of trust.

Under these circumstances, an injured trade secret owner can file a trade secret lawsuit to stop the other company from using the information, and perhaps to recover money damages and punitive damages.

> EXAMPLE: The Bayside Graphics company develops and tries to keep secret a program that greatly improves the graphics capability of a popular business-forecasting package. A competitor discovers the information by illegally stealing Bayside's trash during a five-minute period when it is left unprotected and discovers the trade secret. Improper acquisition has occurred and court relief can be obtained.

The U.S. government may also file criminal charges against the trade secret thief under the federal trade secret statute.

Uniform Trade Secrets Act: § 1 Definitions

"Improper means" includes theft, bribery, misrepresentation, breach or inducement of a breach of a duty to maintain secrecy, or espionage through electronic or other means.

Related terms: damages in trade secret misappropriation actions; federal trade secret statute; industrial espionage; trade secret misappropriation action.

improper disclosure of trade secrets

When someone communicates trade secrets to others in violation of a nondisclosure agreement, duty of trust, or confidential employment relationship, it is known as an improper disclosure of trade secrets. Those who improperly disclose trade secrets may be held liable for all resulting harm to the trade secret owner's economic interests.

Related terms: damages in trade secret misappropriation actions; improper acquisition of trade secrets; nondisclosure agreement; trade secret misappropriation action.

independent conception, defense to trade secret claim

For a trade secret owner to obtain court-ordered relief against a competitor who is using the trade secret, there must be a showing that the competitor improperly acquired it. A trade secret is not improperly acquired if it is independently conceived of or is discovered by a competitor through parallel research.

To preserve their ability to raise independent conception as a defense to a trade secret infringement action, most large companies will not:

- sign a nondisclosure agreement tendered by an outsider who wants to sell something to the company, or
- examine any work developed by an outsider unless the outsider signs a written statement giving up the right to treat the work as a trade secret.

Related terms: improper acquisition of trade secrets; parallel research; trade secret misappropriation action; unsolicited idea disclosure.

independently developed

See independent conception, defense to trade secret claim.

industrial espionage

In the trade secret context, industrial espionage consists of any activity directed toward discovering a company's trade secrets by such underhanded or illegal means as:

- electronic surveillance
- bribery of employees to disclose confidential information
- placing of a spy among the company's employees
- tapping of a company's phones, computers, or email, or
- theft of documents containing confidential information.

In the United States, an owner of trade secrets obtained by an outsider as a result of industrial espionage may recover large damages if the secrets are subsequently used by the guilty party, and the thief is subject to criminal prosecution under the federal trade secret statute. In some countries, however, trade secret theft through industrial espionage is tolerated as a normal part of doing business.

Related terms: federal trade secret statute; improper acquisition of trade secrets.

industrial innovations as trade secrets

See competitive advantage; trade secret.

industrial secret

Industrial secrets are trade secrets of a technical, technological, scientific, or mechanical nature. Secret processes, formulas, unregistered industrial designs, manufacturing techniques and methods, secret machinery, devices, and the like are all examples.

The laws of some countries, such as Japan, distinguish between industrial secrets and commercial secrets. In the United States, however, courts generally treat all trade secrets alike, regardless of their type. In other words, whether or not a trade secret is business information, industrial know-how, or an industrial secret has no legal consequence in the United States.

Related terms: know-how; trade secret.

inevitable disclosure rule (also known as the inevitability doctrine)

Even without a noncompete agreement, a few businesses have been able to prevent certain ex-employees from working for a competitor under a legal concept—appropriately titled the inevitable disclosure doctrine. This principle was popularized by a 1995 case in which Pepsico successfully argued that a former executive could not help but rely on company secrets at his new job with a rival. (*Pepsico, Inc. v. Redmond,* 54 F.3d 1262 (7th Cir. 1995).)

Some experts have been dumbfounded by this rule, since it allows a business to prevent an ex-employee from competing without the use of a noncompete agreement. From the employee's perspective, this rule is especially disturbing, since it allows a former employer to get a court order preventing employment without any proof of actual or even threatened theft or disclosure of trade secrets. In other words, the rule is used to prohibit employment, not disclosure. (*DoubleClick, Inc. v. Henderson,* 1997 N.Y. Misc. LEXIS 577 (N.Y. Sup. Ct. 1997).)

The use of the inevitable disclosure rule appears to be limited. Only a handful of courts have accepted it, and in many of the cases where it has been applied, the court has required more—for example, a showing of bad faith or underhanded dealing by the ex-employee.

Bringing a claim based solely on inevitable disclosure may backfire:

EXAMPLE: An employer brought a trade secret claim against a former employee without any evidence and based solely on an argument that the employee would inevitably disclose the trade secret as part of his new employment. California does not permit inevitable disclosure claims and the employer was required to pay attorney fees and costs as a result of the bad faith claim. (*In Flir Systems, Inc. v. Parrish*, 95 Cal. Rptr. 3d 307 (Cal. App. 2d Dist. 2009).)

injunction

A court order directed at persons or businesses who have either improperly acquired trade secrets or who threaten to improperly disclose them is known as an injunction. Typically, an injunction is sought as part of a trade secret misappropriation action, to prohibit a defendant from using a trade secret belonging to the plaintiff (the party bringing the action) or from disclosing it to others. This type of judicial relief is common in trade secret litigation, since one of the trade secret owner's primary goals is to stop any further erosion of the competitive advantage gained by keeping the information secret.

Courts are authorized to issue emergency injunctions, called temporary restraining orders (TROs), when a trade secret owner shows that a trade secret is at risk of being lost as a result of the defendant's behavior. The court must then schedule a hearing at which all sides may be heard. If, after this hearing, the court still believes that a trade secret is at stake and that the trade secret owner will probably win at trial, it can issue a provisional or "preliminary" injunction. This order will continue to prevent the defendant from using or disclosing the trade secret pending a final decision in the case. As a practical matter, once a preliminary injunction is granted, the parties will often settle rather than fight the case through to trial and beyond.

Uniform Trade Secrets Act: § 2. Injunctive Relief

(a) Actual or threatened misappropriation may be enjoined. Upon application to the court, an injunction shall be terminated when the trade secret has ceased to exist, but the injunction may be continued for an additional reasonable period of time in order to eliminate commercial advantage that otherwise would be derived from the misappropriation.

(b) If the court determines that it would be unreasonable to prohibit future use, an injunction may condition future use upon payment of a reasonable royalty for no longer than the period of time the use could have been prohibited.

(c) In appropriate circumstances, affirmative acts to protect a trade secret may be compelled by court order.

Related terms: improper acquisition of trade secrets; improper disclosure of trade secrets; trade secret misappropriation action.

Trade Secret Law: Definitions

Internet and trade secrets

The publication of confidential information on the Internet will almost always cause the loss of trade secret rights regardless of whether it was done inadvertently or maliciously. The result of such a posting is that competitors who obtain the information legally, that is, those who did not violate trade secret laws to get the information, are entitled to use it.

There are many ways a trade secret is disclosed in cyberspace. Sometimes the disclosure is the result of revenge by an angry employee or contractor, sometimes it occurs because a hacker has uncovered information without permission of the website owner, and sometimes it is the result of carelessness—often by employees of the business who may discuss secrets in online chats.

There are exceptions to the "posting equals disclosure" rule. One court ruled that posting on the Web does not automatically cause the loss of trade secret status, because the posting may not result in the secret being "generally known." The court required a review of the circumstances surrounding the posting and consideration of the interests of the trade secret owner, the policies favoring competition, and the interests—including First Amendment rights—of innocent third parties who acquire information on the Internet. (*Religious Tech. Ctr. v. Netcom On-Line Comm. Servs. Inc.,* 923 F.Supp.1231 (N.D. Cal. 1995).) In addition to violations of trade secret law, the improper disclosure of trade secrets on the Internet may lead to claims of copyright infringement.

In other cases, a defendant may argue that the posting of trade secret information is protected under free speech principles established in the First Amendment. However, this argument will not succeed if the court determines that protecting the commercial information outweighs disclosure. For example, the California Supreme Court ruled that enjoining the republication of a software code that permitted unauthorized use of a DVD did not violate the First Amendment. (*DVD Copy Control Association v. Bunner,* 2003 Cal. LEXIS 6295 (2003).)

Related terms: copyright and trade secret compatibility; email and confidentiality; freedom of speech and trade secrets; improper disclosure of trade secrets.

know-how

Know-how does not always refer to secret information. Sometimes it means a particular kind of technical knowledge that may not be confidential but that is needed to accomplish a task. For example, an employee's know-how may be necessary to train other employees in how to make or use an invention. Although know-how is a combination of secret and nonsecret information, businesses usually treat it as a protectable trade secret and require employees and contractors to whom it is disclosed to sign a nondisclosure agreement.

An organization called the International Chamber of Commerce defines "industrial know-how" to include applied technical knowledge, methods, and data that are necessary for realizing or carrying out techniques that serve industrial purposes. Industrial know-how differs from business know-how, which normally involves white collar managerial and marketing techniques.

The kind of information encompassed by the term "industrial know-how" will qualify as a trade secret if it is specialized, is not generally known in the relevant business community, provides a company with a competitive advantage, and is maintained as a trade secret.

Related terms: industrial secret; methods and techniques as trade secrets.

licensing of trade secrets

A trade secret owner may license a trade secret by permitting others to use the trade secret in exchange for an agreement to treat it as confidential. Licenses commonly are limited to specific time periods, types or fields of commerce, and purposes. There are no government agencies that oversee trade secret licenses, but trade secret licenses are subject to applicable antitrust prohibitions against monopolistic or restraint-of-trade activities.

Under a trade secret license, ownership of the trade secret remains with the original owner, while the licensee has the right to use the trade secret as long as it complies with the specific terms and time limits of the license. The license agreement should always include a clause stating that the trade secret in question is confidential information and must be maintained properly as a trade secret by the licensee.

One common type of license provides the owner with a royalty based on a percentage of the retail or wholesale price of each item sold that takes advantage of the trade secret. Many other compensation arrangements are possible. For example, the license may provide for a flat fee for each separate use of the secret, a monthly or annual fee, the reciprocal use of information belonging to the licensee, or some combination of all of these arrangements.

Related terms: antitrust law and trade secrets; trade secret owner.

Trade Secret Law: Definitions

litigation, disclosure of trade secrets during

State and federal laws establish rules regarding the use and disclosure of trade secrets during litigation. If one party requests trade secret information from another, a court will balance the interests of the litigants. If the failure to disclose would cause injustice or conceal a fraud, the owner of the trade secret will be required to disclose it. In order to preserve secrecy, the court will issue a protective order that requires that all participants in the lawsuit—the litigants, attorneys, independent contractors—maintain confidentiality. Protective orders can be made by order of the court, or the parties may agree to the protection of confidential information.

Related terms: injunction; protective order; temporary restraining order.

loss of trade secrets

Trade secrets, and the judicial protection their status confers, may be lost by any conduct that:

- releases the trade secret into the public domain, and
- does not constitute wrongful conduct such as theft, violation of a nondisclosure agreement, or breach of a duty of trust.

EXAMPLE: Sonoma Foods Inc. (SFI) conceives of a new way to lengthen the shelf life of jams and jellies. Initially, SFI takes careful steps to preserve its invention as a trade secret. However, over a few drinks at a trade show, SFI's chief executive officer tells an employee from another food company about the invention without first asking for a nondisclosure agreement. Such behavior might result in the loss of the idea as a trade secret, especially if the other company proceeds to implement the idea or tell others about it. Should SFI bring a misappropriation suit against the other company, the SFI officer's disclosure would likely constitute a successful defense. Even though the trade secret was lost, however, it might still be possible for SFI to apply for and obtain a patent on its new process.

Related terms: accidental disclosure of trade secrets; patent application, effect on trade secrets; public domain and trade secrets; public records and trade secrets; reasonably precautionary measures to protect trade secrets.

methods and techniques as trade secrets

Specialized business knowledge related to a specific process or method, commonly known as business know-how, can qualify as a trade secret in many countries if it is so treated. Examples of such know-how include specialized barbecue methods of cooking (including the use of special cuts of meat and secret sauces) and methods and techniques for running group sessions of a how-to-quit-smoking organization.

On the other hand, general business knowledge or expertise not related to a specific process or method is usually not protectable as a trade secret. The courts rarely protect information that is generally known to, or available to, the business community and thus is not secret.

Related terms: know-how; processes as trade secrets; trade secret.

misappropriation of trade secrets

Misappropriation of a trade secret occurs when secret information is acquired by improper means—for example, theft, bribery, misrepresentation, or breach of a duty to maintain secrecy. Misappropriation can also occur if a trade secret is disclosed by someone who used improper means to acquire it. Misappropriation of trade secrets is sometimes mistakenly referred to as trade secret infringement.

Uniform Trade Secrets Act: § 1 Definitions:
"Misappropriation" means:

(i) acquisition of a trade secret of another by a person who knows or has reason to know that the trade secret was acquired by improper means; or

(ii) disclosure or use of a trade secret of another without express or implied consent by a person who

    (A) used improper means to acquire knowledge of the trade secret; or

    (B) at the time of disclosure or use, knew or had reason to know that his knowledge of the trade secret was

        (I) derived from or through a person who had utilized improper means to acquire it;

        (II) acquired under circumstances giving rise to a duty to maintain its secrecy or limit its use; or

        (III) derived from or through a person who owed a duty to the person seeking relief to maintain its secrecy or limit its use; or

    (C) before a material change of his position, knew or had reason to know that it was a trade secret and that knowledge of it had been acquired by accident or mistake.

money damages

See damages in trade secret misappropriation actions.

noncompetition clauses in employment contracts

See covenant not to compete by employee.

nondisclosure agreement

The term "nondisclosure agreement" is often used interchangeably with "confidentiality agreement" or "NDA." A nondisclosure agreement is a legally binding contract in which a person or business promises to treat specific information as a trade secret and not to disclose the information to others without proper authorization. If the trade secret is disclosed in violation of the nondisclosure agreement, the trade secret owner can file a trade secret lawsuit, obtain an injunction to stop further use of the trade secret, recover money damages, and possibly recover punitive or treble damages.

Nondisclosure agreements should be used whenever it is necessary to disclose a trade secret to another person or business for such purposes as development, marketing, evaluation, or fiscal backing. Through the conscientious use of nondisclosure agreements, trade secrets can be distributed to a relatively large number of people without destroying their protected status.

Nondisclosure agreements should also be used between employees and employers, in order to require that the employee treat as confidential all trade secrets he or she learns about in the course of employment. If the employer later tries to prevent an employee from using information considered to be a trade secret, the nondisclosure agreement can establish that the employee recognized a duty to cooperate in this endeavor. Competitors who learn of trade secrets through an employee's violation of a nondisclosure agreement with a former employer may also be prevented from commercially using the information, even if they didn't know the employee had breached the agreement.

A nondisclosure agreement can also help establish that a business treated particular information as a trade secret—a necessary element to claiming legal protection.

Although nondisclosure agreements are usually in the form of written contracts, they may also be implied if the context of a business relationship suggests that such agreement was intended by the parties. For instance, a business that conducts patent searches for inventors is expected to keep the information about the invention secret, even if no written nondisclosure agreement is signed, since the nature of the business is to deal in confidential information. A sample nondisclosure agreement is provided in the Forms section of this part.

Related terms: beta testing and trade secrets; trade secret misappropriation action.

notice to employees of trade secrets

For information to qualify as a trade secret, employers must ensure that it is treated as confidential. All employees (and anyone else who may come in contact with the information) must know in no uncertain terms that the information is confidential and that they have an obligation not to disclose it.

The best way to give this notice is to require all employees coming in contact with the secret to sign nondisclosure agreements. However, an express written notice to employees regarding the status of the information and their obligation of confidentiality will also usually provide a basis for judicially protecting the information in the event of a later threatened or actual disclosure.

Companies often put employees on notice of trade secret status by using:

- signs on walk-in areas where trade secrets are being stored or used
- confidentiality labels on documents
- initial employment interviews in which the business's trade secrets are discussed and the need to keep them confidential is stressed, and
- exit interviews where departing employees are cautioned against disclosing the company's trade secrets in their new employment.

Related terms: confidential employment relationship; nondisclosure agreement; reasonably precautionary measures to protect trade secrets.

notice to former employee's new employer

When an employee with knowledge of his or her employer's trade secrets takes a new job with a competing company, the first employer will often send the new employer a letter. The first employer will emphasize that the former employee is legally bound not to disclose any trade secrets and that, if he or she does, any such disclosure may not be used by the new employer. If the new employer then makes use of the trade secrets, the first employer may obtain greater damages and other enhanced judicial relief.

Related terms: improper disclosure of trade secrets; trade secret misappropriation action.

novelty and trade secrets

For information to qualify as a trade secret, it must generally not be known or used in the relevant industry. Strictly speaking, information constituting a trade secret need not be novel in the sense of "new" or "innovative." It simply must provide its owner with a competitive advantage.

EXAMPLE: A marionette manufacturer rediscovers a principle of movement first pioneered by the 19th-century European moving doll industry. If this particular principle has been lost to the modern world, it can qualify as a trade secret, even though it is in no way novel. As long as the principle of movement provides its owner with a competitive advantage, it is legally identical to trade secrets that are independently conceived.

Related terms: competitive advantage; parallel research; trade secret.

obligation of confidentiality

See duty of trust.

ownership of trade secret rights

See trade secret owner.

parallel research

Parallel research refers to situations where similar information or ideas are developed by two or more companies through their independent efforts. Especially where cutting-edge technologies are involved, many companies are likely to be engaged in similar research and development activity, which can be expected to produce trade secrets. This means that the same basic information may be properly viewed as a trade secret by many different companies.

EXAMPLE: A new cola company inadvertently creates the exact cola formula used by an existing company. Both the new and old companies are entitled to protect their formulas as trade secrets, even though the second formula is not novel.

Related terms: head start rule; independent conception, defense to trade secret claim; unsolicited idea disclosure.

patent application, effect on trade secrets

To obtain a patent on an invention, the inventor must fully describe the invention in the patent application. The U.S. Patent and Trademark Office (USPTO) treats patent applications as confidential, making it possible to apply for a patent and still maintain the underlying information as a trade secret, at least for the first 18 months of the application period. Unless the applicant files a Nonpublication Request at the time of filing and doesn't file for a patent outside the United States, the USPTO will publish the application within 18 months of the filing date. Because a patent application is published by the USPTO, all of the secret information becomes public and the trade secret status of the application is lost.

However, if an applicant files a Nonpublication Request at the time of filing the application, the information in the patent application will become publicly available only if and when a patent is granted. If the applicant is not filing abroad and the patent is rejected, confidentiality is preserved, because the USPTO does not publish rejected applications. If the USPTO approves the patent application, it will be published in the *Official Gazette*. Inventors are willing to accept this trade-off—loss of trade secrecy for patent rights—because the patent can be used to prevent anyone else from exploiting the underlying information.

Publication after 18 months does provide one advantage for a patent applicant: If a patent later issues, the patent owner can later recover damages from infringers from the date of publication, provided that the infringer had notice of the publication.

Related terms: loss of trade secrets; reverse engineering and trade secrets.

patterns and designs as trade secrets

Patterns and designs may qualify as trade secrets if they create a competitive advantage and are kept secret. Examples of patterns and designs that have been protected as trade secrets are advanced design plans for a new minicomputer, designs for electronic circuitry, and schematic plans for an innovative metal door frame.

Related terms: industrial secret; trade secret.

physical devices, ability to maintain as trade secrets

Physical devices—for example, tools, products, and components—can qualify as trade secrets if they provide their owner with a competitive advantage and are kept secret. Such devices can easily be protected when they are used solely in the trade secret owner's manufacturing or production process. In addition, if distribution is limited and the devices are licensed rather than sold, the trade secret protection may be preserved if the license prohibits reverse engineering. However, the more the world shrinks and the faster information moves, the harder it will be to preserve trade secrecy by licensing restrictions.

Once products are widely distributed, trade secret status is usually impossible to maintain. Anyone may examine these products and figure out how they work—that is, reverse engineer them. When reverse engineering is accomplished, the trade secret enters the public domain.

Trade Secret Law: Definitions

EXAMPLE: Jason invents, manufactures, and distributes a device that allows people to use their microcomputers to preprogram their DVRs to reject certain kinds of ads. He calls it AdOut. Physically, AdOut consists of an integrated circuit board inside a black box and ports to interface it with a DVD and computer. Jason has designed the box so that it can be opened to replace the circuit board if that component fails. If Caryl were to open the box, examine the board, figure out how AdOut works, and start manufacturing her own device called AdScreen, Jason would have no grounds for relief against Caryl under trade secret laws. Why not? Because Caryl lawfully obtained the necessary information through reverse engineering. If, however, Jason owns either a patent or copyright on some aspect of the AdOut hardware or software that was copied by Caryl, Jason can obtain court relief on those grounds.

Related terms: licensing of trade secrets; reasonably precautionary measures to protect trade secrets; reverse engineering and trade secrets; trade secret.

piracy

A colloquial term, "piracy" refers to any activity directed toward the improper acquisition of a trade secret or other forms of intellectual property that belong to another. The word has no legal significance.

Related terms: criminal prosecution for trade secret theft; improper acquisition of trade secrets; industrial espionage.

predetermination of rights in technical data

Before hiring a business or consulting firm for research and development projects likely to produce patentable inventions and trade secrets, the government routinely requires a contract that contains clauses predetermining who will own the rights to the patents and secrets in question. Predetermination of rights provisions are also typically found in agreements between universities and corporations and between corporations and independent contractors. (Also, note that under the Bayh-Dole Act, enacted in 1980, universities may claim patent rights in inventions created at the university with federal funding. The university may license these discoveries to private industry—a practice some critics have likened to corporate welfare.)

Although ownership of intellectual property rights can be a subject for negotiation, the government will typically demand ownership of all rights in the main product being developed but will allow the private party to own the rights to any "side-products," including information, that can qualify as trade secrets.

Related terms: trade secret owner.

preliminary injunctions in trade secret actions
See injunction.

premature disclosure
See loss of trade secrets.

price setting
See illegal restraint of trade.

processes as trade secrets
A "process" consists of a series of steps that lead to a particular result. Any process may qualify for trade secret status if it is generally not known in the industry, adds to a business's competitive advantage, and is maintained as a trade secret. Among the processes that have been afforded protection as a trade secret in the past are those involving photographic development, silk screening, centrifugal processing for blood plasma fractionation, and the manufacture of chocolate powder and tobacco flavoring. Processes can also be protected under patent law.

Related terms: know-how; methods and techniques as trade secrets; trade secret.

professional client lists
See customer lists.

protecting a trade secret
See reasonably precautionary measures to protect trade secrets.

protective order
In the event a trade secret is disclosed as part of a lawsuit, the trade secrecy can be preserved by a protective order. This order prohibits the participants in the lawsuit from disclosing the secret, and it "seals" the court record pertaining to the trade secret, making it unavailable as a public document. Protective orders can be made by order of the court, or the parties may agree to (stipulate) the protection of confidential information. Protective orders are authorized under Section 5 of the Uniform Trade Secrets Act and under Federal Rule of Civil Procedure 26(c)(7).

Trade Secret Law: Definitions

Uniform Trade Secrets Act: § 5. Preservation of Secrecy

In an action under this Act, a court shall preserve the secrecy of an alleged trade secret by reasonable means, which may include granting protective orders in connection with discovery proceedings, holding in camera hearings, sealing the records of the action, and ordering any person involved in the litigation not to disclose an alleged trade secret without prior court approval.

Related terms: injunction; disclosure of trade secrets during litigation; temporary restraining order.

provisional relief in a trade secret action

See injunction.

public domain and trade secrets

Trade secrets are considered to be in the public domain—where their owners have no legal recourse under trade secret law against disclosure and use by others—when the owner of the trade secret:

- is negligent or impermissibly sloppy in keeping it confidential
- fails to seek relief quickly in court if the trade secret becomes known to others through wrongful behavior (for instance, in violation of a nondisclosure agreement or through industrial espionage), or
- loses the rights to court protection of the trade secret by doing something forbidden under the law (for instance, using the trade secret in violation of the antitrust laws).

EXAMPLE: Microwave Systems wants to raise some capital to fund the promotion of its new mini satellite dish system, which it plans to sell to consumers for an affordable price. To accomplish this goal, it prepares a magazine article describing its revolutionary system, without intending to disclose its trade secrets. However, Manfred reads this article and learns enough details to start his own satellite dish business. Microwave would not be able to claim misappropriation of a trade secret, since its ideas became a matter of public knowledge through its own disclosure.

Even if the secret becomes public because of someone's improper actions, such as the breaking of a nondisclosure agreement or industrial espionage, it will still be in the public domain if the information becomes well known. In short, once the trade secret is disclosed, the trade secret is gone unless the owner can somehow manage to contain the disclosure. For example, if an ex-employee discloses the secret to a rival company, it may be possible to obtain a court order preventing the other company and the ex-employee from further disclosures, and thereby maintain the trade secret status. This would not be possible, however, if the ex-employee published the trade secret for the public to see, for example, on the Internet.

It is possible for information to be in the public domain for the purpose of trade secret law but still subject to restrictions under another set of laws. For instance, certain trade secrets in a computer program might pass into the public domain under trade secret law but still be entitled to a patent. If a patent is obtained, no one can use the invention comprising the former trade secret without the patent owner's permission. Similarly, an author may treat his or her novel as a trade secret while it is being written. Once the novel is published, the trade secret aspect of the novel falls into the public domain, but the novel itself will continue to be protected by copyright.

Related terms: loss of trade secrets; trade secret misappropriation action; trade secret owner.

public records and trade secrets

Any information contained in a public record (a document, tape, disk, or other medium that is open to inspection by the public) cannot qualify as a trade secret, since by definition it is not confidential. However, because companies are often required by state and federal governments to file documents that, of necessity, contain trade secrets, there are usually laws that allow the withholding of the precise data that make up the trade secrets, even if the rest of the document is released for inspection.

Related terms: Freedom of Information Act, exemption of trade secrets; litigation, disclosure of trade secrets during; protective order.

read-only memories (ROMs) and trade secrets

Internal operating instructions and other programs that are a physical part of the computer (for instance, read-only memories or ROMs) do not usually qualify for protection as a trade secret once the computer is marketed. This is because it is usually possible to figure out the design and logic of the ROM through reverse engineering, and any trade secrets that can become known in this manner are considered to be in the public domain.

Related terms: public domain and trade secrets; reverse engineering and trade secrets; software and trade secrets.

reasonably precautionary measures to protect trade secrets

Information will only qualify as a trade secret if its owner takes appropriate measures to keep it secret. What constitutes reasonably precautionary measures depends on the type of secret and the industry involved. This issue usually arises when a trade secret action is filed and the defendant claims that the information should not be considered as a trade secret because appropriate precautionary measures were not taken. If a court determines that the business claiming misappropriation has in fact taken appropriate measures to maintain the confidentiality of the information, it will be protected. If not, judicial relief will be denied and the information will no longer be considered a trade secret. Clearly, a certain amount of judicial discretion is involved in these decisions.

Measures typically considered to be reasonable precautions include:

- requiring employees to sign nondisclosure agreements
- requiring all outside persons with whom the information is shared to sign nondisclosure agreements
- restricting physical access to areas where trade secrets are located
- consistently enforcing specific rules formulated by the company regarding confidentiality of the information and physical access to it
- using encryption or other code-like devices to make sure that trade secret information cannot easily be understood, even if read by an unauthorized person
- giving notice to all persons coming in contact with the information that it is considered a trade secret
- posting warnings on the wall of areas where trade secrets are kept or used reminding employees about company rules regarding trade secrets
- conducting exit interviews with employees, specifically warning them against improper disclosure of trade secrets
- adequately protecting against unauthorized intrusion into computer databases that contain trade secrets
- shredding sensitive documents prior to disposing of them, and
- if the scope of the operation and the value of the secrets warrants it, taking such physical security measures as posting guards, maintaining tight control over keys (including keys to the photocopy machine), and requiring visitors to wear badges.

Not all of these measures are necessary in every context, although the more of them that are employed, the better position the company will be in to claim that reasonable precautionary measures to protect the trade secrets have been taken.

Just what measures are considered to be reasonably precautionary in a given case will depend on the size of the company, the value of the trade secrets, and the nature of the technology involved.

Related terms: notice to employees of trade secrets; trade secret misappropriation action.

retail customer lists

See customer lists.

reverse engineering and trade secrets

The act of examining a product or device and figuring out the ideas and methods involved in its creation and structure is referred to as reverse engineering. Normally we think of engineering as the intellectual means by which something is built or an idea is transformed into practice. In this context, "reverse engineering" consists of taking apart and reducing a product or device into its constituent parts and concepts.

The idea of reverse engineering is of crucial importance to trade secret law. This is because of the rule that any information learned about an item through the process of legitimate reverse engineering is considered to be in the public domain for trade secret purposes and therefore no longer protectable as a trade secret. However, the fact that a particular invention or technology can be figured out through reverse engineering has no effect on whether it is entitled to protection under the patent laws.

> EXAMPLE: Ivan creates a machine capable of producing holographic games (games consisting of pictures projected onto three-dimensional space so that the images and characters appear realistic). Ivan treats the details of production as a trade secret. Once the machine is marketed, however, it will probably be possible to figure out through reverse engineering how it is constructed. If this is done, the machine can be freely manufactured and sold by the party doing the reverse engineering without Ivan being entitled to any court relief on trade secret grounds. However, Ivan would be entitled to protection under the patent laws if he has sought and obtained a patent on his invention.

There are two caveats when performing reverse engineering:
- The reverse engineering should only be performed on an authorized copy of the work—for example, it is not permissible to reverse engineer illegally copied software code.

Trade Secret Law: Definitions

- Some companies prohibit reverse engineering through the use of end-user license agreements (also known as EULAs). EULAs are created when the customer either buys the product or first uses it. As a condition of use, the agreement may prohibit reverse engineering. A customer that violates this provision may be enjoined from further use and forced to pay damages. (*Bowers v. Baystate Technologies, Inc.,* 2003 U.S. App. LEXIS 1423 (Fed. Cir. 2003).)

Related terms: physical devices, ability to maintain as trade secrets; source code as trade secret.

See also Part 2 (Copyright Law): end-user license (aka EULA, shrinkwrap, or clickwrap agreement).

sale of business, covenant not to compete

See covenant not to compete by owners of a sold business.

screening incoming information for unsolicited disclosures

See unsolicited idea disclosure.

software and trade secrets

An innovative computer program will often qualify for trade secret status at least during its development and testing stage. From a program's first conception, information and ideas about it often give an owner a competitive edge as long as they are kept secret. Once a program is fixed in a tangible medium of expression (that is, put down on tape, disk, or paper in tangible form), it may still remain a trade secret. In addition, its expression (not the ideas behind that expression) is also protected under the copyright laws.

When a program is distributed, dual copyright and trade secret protections can continue if certain precautions are taken. For instance, if all "purchasers" of the program are required to sign a license forbidding disclosure of trade secrets, both trade secret and copyright protection may be available for distributed copies (the more limited the distribution is, the more likely the trade secret protection will exist). Or, if the owner of the program only distributes object code (usually the case except for programs written in BASIC) and keeps the source code locked in a secure place, it is similarly possible to maintain both trade secret and copyright protection for the program.

If the software owner registers the program with the U.S. Copyright Office, a printout of portions of the object code—or portions of the source code with critical parts blacked out—can be deposited as part of the registration. This will permit the trade secret to be maintained along with the registered copyright.

EXAMPLE: Harry conceives of a utility that will analyze a computer user's daily use of the computer and produce a report showing which programs were used and for how long, and the overall pattern of usage. Because such a utility would have commercial value, the basic ideas behind it will qualify as a trade secret as long as Harry treats them that way. Suppose that Harry decides to press ahead with his idea. All the information produced by the development process, including the first flowcharts, the written code (the source code), and the instructions to the computer produced by the compiler (the object code), separately and together, can properly qualify as trade secrets if they are treated as such.

Once the program is up and running on the computer, Harry has others test the program to see if it actually works and whether programming bugs need to be corrected. Because Harry still considers the program to be a trade secret, he has the testers sign nondisclosure agreements in which they agree to keep the program confidential and preserve its trade secret status. In addition, because the program is now fixed in tangible form, it is protected under copyright law without losing trade secret status. When Harry registers the program with the U.S. Copyright Office, he deposits the object code.

Whether using source code or object code, the applicant at the Copyright Office should declare its trade secrecy status concurrent with the filing. Later declarations may prove fruitless.

EXAMPLE: A software developer registered software by submitting source code to the Copyright Office.. Ten months later he submitted an email declaring that the material was a trade secret and he never checked for compliance with this request. Because the submission was available to the public, trade secrecy was forfeited. (*Kema, Inc. v. Koperwhats,* 658 F. Supp. 2d 1022 (N.D. Cal. 2009).)

Related terms: beta testing and trade secrets; copyright and trade secret law compatibility; reverse engineering and trade secrets; source code as trade secret.

source code as trade secret

The specific instructions written by a programmer to tell a computer what to do are referred to as the source code. The language used to write the source code cannot usually be read directly by the computer and must be translated by a compiler into language the computer can understand, which is called object code.

When software is sold to the public, it is in object code form—that is, it is already compiled. Because object code is mostly a series of ones and zeros, it cannot readily be figured out through reverse engineering (called "decompiling" in this instance). The source code, on the other hand, can be figured out, and any trade secrets that the software owner wishes to maintain in the code can be easily obtained. For that reason, source code is usually kept secret, locked in the owner's vault.

Related terms: reverse engineering and trade secrets.

specific performance of covenant not to compete

If a former employee or owner of a business threatens to violate a contract (covenant) not to compete with the business, a court may order the owner or employee to comply with the agreement. Whether a court will issue this type of order depends on a number of "fairness" or equity factors, such as:

- the length of time competition is prohibited
- in the case of employees, the effect of the agreement on the employee's ability to make a living, and
- whether the court concludes that the original covenant not to compete agreement was unnecessarily broad.

Generally, noncompetition agreements that are limited in terms of time and scope have a better chance of being enforced than those that are open-ended. And a few states, including California, Colorado, Florida, and Oregon, severely restrict the ability of an employer to enforce a noncompetition agreement against a former employee.

Related terms: covenant not to compete by employee; covenant not to compete by owners of a sold business; injunction.

statute of limitations

States that have adopted the Uniform Trade Secrets Act typically provide that misappropriation actions be brought within three years after the theft is discovered (or should have been reasonably discovered).

Uniform Trade Secrets Act: § 6. Statute of Limitations

An action for misappropriation must be brought within 3 years after the misappropriation is discovered or by the exercise of reasonable diligence should have been discovered. For the purposes of this section, a continuing misappropriation constitutes a single claim.

The Spoliation Doctrine

Under this doctrine, a court can infer that theft of trade secrets has occurred when the defendant intentionally destroys trade secret evidence. The logic behind spoliation is that the defendant wouldn't have destroyed the information unless it indicated that trade secret theft had occurred. For example, in one case, a defendant destroyed all the files on his computer after being sued. Later, when a court-ordered image of the computer was required, the defendant deliberately left certain items out of the image, leading the judge to rule for the trade secret owner. (*Advantacare Health Partners, LP v. Access IV,* 005 U.S. Dist. LEXIS 12794 (N.D. Cal. June 14, 2005).)

temporary restraining order

A court order that can be immediately obtained by a plaintiff in an intellectual property lawsuit with little or no advance notice to the defendant is a temporary restraining order (TRO). TROs place events in a holding pattern ("maintain the status quo") until the court can more fully determine what kind of protection is required, if any. Typically, TROs only last for a few days or, at most, two to three weeks. While the TRO is still in effect, a court will hear the argument of all sides to the dispute and more thoroughly consider the underlying issues.

Related terms: injunction; trade secret misappropriation action.

tools as trade secrets

See physical devices, ability to maintain as trade secrets.

trade secret, defined

In most states, a trade secret may consist of any formula, pattern, physical device, idea, process, compilation of information, or other information that both:
- provides a business with a competitive advantage, and
- is treated in a way that can reasonably be expected to prevent the public or competitors from learning about it, absent improper acquisition or theft.

When deciding whether information qualifies as a trade secret under this definition, courts will typically consider the following factors:
- the extent to which the information is known outside of the particular business entity
- the extent to which the information is known by employees and others involved in the business
- the extent to which measures have been taken to guard the secrecy of the information

- the value of the information to the business, and
- the difficulty with which the information could be properly acquired or independently duplicated by others.

There is no crisp definition of what constitutes a trade secret. A trade secret is created and defined solely by reference to how certain information is handled, and to the value inherent in keeping it secret. Even if an item or piece of information otherwise qualifies as a trade secret, its moment-to-moment status will depend on how it is treated by its owners.

Uniform Trade Secrets Act: § 1 Definitions

(4) "Trade secret" means information, including a formula, pattern, compilation, program, device, method, technique, or process, that:

   (i) derives independent economic value, actual or potential, from not being generally known to, and not being readily ascertainable by proper means by, other persons who can obtain economic value from its disclosure or use, and

   (ii) is the subject of efforts that are reasonable under the circumstances to maintain its secrecy.

Related terms: ideas as trade secrets; reasonably precautionary measures to protect trade secrets; software and trade secrets; trade secret misappropriation action.

trade secret misappropriation action

The owner of a trade secret may bring a lawsuit, known as a trade secret misappropriation action, for the purpose of:

- preventing another person or business from using the trade secret without proper authorization, and
- collecting money damages for economic injury suffered as a result of the improper acquisition and use of the trade secret.

All persons and businesses responsible for the improper acquisition, and all those who have benefited from such acquisition, are typically named as defendants in misappropriation actions.

Among the most common situations that give rise to infringement actions are:

- Trade secrets are stolen through industrial espionage.
- An employee having knowledge of a trade secret changes jobs and discloses the secret to a new employer in violation of an express or implied nondisclosure agreement with the first employer.
- Trade secrets are improperly disclosed in violation of a nondisclosure agreement.

To prevail in a misappropriation suit, the plaintiff (person bringing the suit) must be able to show that the information alleged to be a trade secret provides the plaintiff with a competitive advantage and has been continually treated by the plaintiff as a trade secret. In addition, the plaintiff must show that the defendant either improperly acquired the information (if accused of making commercial use of the secret) or improperly disclosed it (if accused of leaking the information).

The defendants in trade secret misappropriation cases commonly attempt to defend against the plaintiff's case by proving any of the following:

- The information claimed to be a trade secret was known throughout the particular industry, and thus not a secret that should be subject to protection.
- The information was lawfully disclosed by a person having knowledge of it.
- The information was lawfully acquired through reverse engineering.
- The information was the result of an independent conception.
- The trade secret was being used by its owner in violation of the antitrust laws.

If the plaintiff can establish that a trade secret was, in fact, improperly used, disclosed, or acquired by a defendant, the court can enjoin (stop) its further commercial use. Sometimes such injunctions are permanent—that is, they are final court orders in the case. More commonly, courts will employ the head start rule. This operates to give the rightful owner of the trade secret a "head start" in commercially exploiting it, by prohibiting its use by the competitor for such period of time as the court decides it would have taken the competitor to independently develop the information.

Because lawsuits tend to drag on for years, courts are authorized to issue preliminary injunctions prohibiting the competitor from using the secret in question pending a final determination in the case. These preliminary orders are often viewed by the parties as harbingers of how the case will finally turn out and, accordingly, form the basis of a settlement (which precludes a full-scale trial).

In addition to injunctive relief (both provisional and final), a court may award damages suffered by the original trade secret owner. These can consist of lost profits resulting from sales by the trade secret thief, profits realized from the wrongfully acquired trade secret, and, occasionally, punitive or treble damages, depending on the state where the action is being tried.

Related terms: damages in trade secret misappropriation actions; independent conception, defense to trade secret claim; injunction; litigation, disclosure of trade secrets during; reasonably precautionary measures to protect trade secrets; reverse engineering and trade secrets.

Trade Secret Law: Definitions

trade secret owner

The owner of a trade secret has a right to seek relief in court in the event someone else improperly acquires or improperly discloses the trade secret. The trade secret owner is also entitled to grant others a license to utilize the secret, or even to sell it outright.

Ownership of a trade secret is usually determined by the circumstances of its creation. In general, these ownership rules apply:

- Trade secrets that arise from research and development activities conducted by manufacturing concerns belong to the company sponsoring the research and development.
- Retail customer lists belong to the business or individual who compiled the list.
- Trade secrets developed by an employee in the course of his or her employment belong to the employer.
- Trade secrets developed by an employee on his or her own time, and with personal equipment, usually belong to the employee.

EXAMPLE: A chef develops a special recipe and baking process for cheesecake during her off-work hours, and in her own kitchen. Even though she bakes the cheesecake for a restaurant, she would probably be entitled to preserve the recipe and process as her own trade secret. If, on the other hand, the recipe and process were developed at work using the restaurant facilities, the restaurant would own the trade secret.

Related terms: business information as trade secret; licensing of trade secrets.

trade secrets and antitrust laws

See antitrust law and trade secrets.

Uniform Trade Secrets Act (UTSA)

This model legislation was prepared for the ultimate purpose of creating the same trade secret laws in all 50 states. At present, 43 states and the District of Columbia have adopted it. Overall, the provisions of the Uniform Trade Secrets Act are consistent with the general principles of trade secret law adopted by the courts under the common law (law established by court case decisions). (Portions of the Uniform Trade Secrets Act are included in the relevant definitions in this section.)

unique ideas as trade secrets

See ideas as trade secrets.

unjust enrichment and trade secrets

Some courts deciding cases involving the improper acquisition of a trade secret have ordered the guilty party to pay the trade secret owner all profits earned from the trade secret in question. The legal theory underlying this type of relief is that the wrongful possessor has been unjustly enriched by profiting from these trade secrets.

The unjust enrichment approach has also been used as a theoretical basis for providing judicial protection to trade secrets. Courts have long been willing to entertain disputes where one party was being unjustly enriched at the expense of another, so the improper acquisition of a trade secret is by nature the type of unjust enrichment that deserves judicial relief.

Related terms: damages in trade secret misappropriation actions; trade secret misappropriation action.

unsolicited idea disclosure

Although many people have creative brainstorms, they usually must share their ideas with others to enlist their help in commercially developing or promoting the idea. This process frequently involves approaching a well-known company to see if it is interested in the unsolicited idea.

Although a company may benefit from ideas generated by outside parties, it often will decline to be informed about such ideas. This is because the company may already be working on a similar idea and wants to avoid later accusations of ripping off the outside party.

Companies tend to be particularly reluctant to consider ideas presented by outsiders when asked to sign a nondisclosure agreement, which treats the idea as a trade secret belonging to the outsider. In that situation, if the company rejects the idea but later markets a product or service that appears to incorporate the idea, the company may be vulnerable to charges of trade secret theft and forced into an expensive lawsuit.

Probably the best way to get past a company's mechanisms for insulating itself from outside ideas is to trust the company. Very few companies are interested in ripping off creative people; most can be counted on to play straight. On the other hand, if trust does not seem an appropriate approach for one reason or another, companies are usually willing to examine an invention if either a regular patent

Trade Secret Law: Definitions

application or a Provisional Patent Application has been filed on it (in either case, the invention is said to have "patent pending" status).

Related entries: evaluation agreement; ideas as trade secrets; idea submission; independent conception, defense to trade secret claim; trade secret misappropriation action, waiver agreement for unsolicited idea disclosure. *See also* Part 1 (Patent Law): Provisional Patent Application (PPA).

waiver agreement for unsolicited idea disclosure

Companies routinely require anyone presenting an unsolicited idea to sign a waiver agreement giving up the right to sue for trade secret infringement. If the "idea person" does not want to sign the agreement, the company will not examine the secret. Many companies go to great lengths to make sure ideas don't get past the front door absent the signing of such a waiver.

Related terms: evaluation agreement; ideas as trade secrets; idea submission; unsolicited idea disclosure.

World Intellectual Property Organization (WIPO)

This organization was formed to facilitate international agreements regulating intellectual property. WIPO is a policy-making body only, with no delegated authority to make binding decisions or impose sanctions. WIPO's membership consists of representatives from countries, and groups of countries, including:

- most European countries
- countries that are members of the United Nations body UNESCO
- Japan, and
- the United States.

Related terms: GATT (General Agreement on Tariffs and Trade).

wrongfully disclosing trade secrets

See improper disclosure of trade secrets.

wrongfully obtaining trade secrets

See improper acquisition of trade secrets.

Trade Secret Law: Forms

Preparing a Nondisclosure Agreement

In this section we provide a sample nondisclosure (NDA) agreement, followed by an explanation. A nondisclosure agreement will assure your right to sue someone who discloses secrets in violation of the agreement and demonstrates your diligence in protecting secrets. Keep in mind that you can never rely solely on a nondisclosure agreement as a basis for protection of confidential information. You must also be able to prove that you took reasonable steps to protect your secret and that the secret has not become known to the public. If you are given an NDA to sign, you can evaluate the agreement by comparing it to the model provisions.

Explanation for Sample Nondisclosure Agreement

Who Is Disclosing? Who Is Receiving?

In the sample agreement, the "Disclosing Party" is the person disclosing secrets, and "Receiving Party" is the person or company who receives the confidential information and is obligated to keep it secret. The terms are capitalized to indicate they are defined within the agreement. The sample agreement is a "one-way" (or in legalese, "unilateral") agreement—that is, only one party is disclosing secrets.

If both sides are disclosing secrets to each other you should modify the agreement to make it a mutual (or "bilateral") nondisclosure agreement. To do that, substitute the following paragraph for the first paragraph in the agreement.

> This Nondisclosure agreement (the "Agreement") is entered into by and between [*insert your name, business form, and address*] and [*insert name, business form, and address of other person or company with whom you are exchanging information*], collectively referred to as the "parties" for the purpose of preventing the unauthorized disclosure of Confidential Information as defined below. The parties agree to enter into a confidential relationship with respect to the disclosure by one or each (the "Disclosing Party") to the other (the "Receiving Party") of certain proprietary and confidential information (the "Confidential Information").

Sample Nondisclosure Agreement

Nondisclosure Agreement

This Nondisclosure Agreement (the "Agreement") is entered into by and between
_____ , with its principal offices at
_____ ("Disclosing Party"),
and _____ ,
located at _____ ("Receiving Party"),
for the purpose of preventing the unauthorized disclosure of Confidential Information as defined below. The parties agree to enter into a confidential relationship with respect to the disclosure of certain proprietary and confidential information ("Confidential Information").

1. **Definition of Confidential Information.** For purposes of this Agreement, "Confidential Information" shall include all information or material that has or could have commercial value or other utility in the business in which Disclosing Party is engaged. If Confidential Information is in written form, the Disclosing Party shall label or stamp the materials with the word "Confidential" or some similar warning. If Confidential Information is transmitted orally, the Disclosing Party shall promptly provide a writing indicating that such oral communication constituted Confidential Information.

2. **Exclusions From Confidential Information.** Receiving Party's obligations under this Agreement do not extend to information that is: (a) publicly known at the time of disclosure or subsequently becomes publicly known through no fault of the Receiving Party; (b) discovered or created by the Receiving Party before disclosure by Disclosing Party; (c) learned by the Receiving Party through legitimate means other than from the Disclosing Party or Disclosing Party's representatives; or (d) disclosed by Receiving Party with Disclosing Party's prior written approval.

3. **Obligations of Receiving Party.** Receiving Party shall hold and maintain the Confidential Information in strictest confidence for the sole and exclusive benefit of the Disclosing Party. Receiving Party shall carefully restrict access to Confidential Information to employees, contractors, and third parties as is reasonably required and shall require those persons to sign nondisclosure restrictions at least as protective as those in this Agreement. Receiving Party shall not, without prior written approval of Disclosing Party, use for Receiving Party's own benefit, publish, copy, or otherwise disclose to others, or permit the use by others for their benefit or to the detriment of Disclosing Party, any Confidential Information. Receiving Party shall return to Disclosing Party any and all records, notes, and other written, printed,

Sample Nondisclosure Agreement (continued)

or tangible materials in its possession pertaining to Confidential Information immediately if Disclosing Party requests it in writing.

4. **Time Periods.** The nondisclosure provisions of this Agreement shall survive the termination of this Agreement, and Receiving Party's duty to hold Confidential Information in confidence shall remain in effect until the Confidential Information no longer qualifies as a trade secret or until Disclosing Party sends Receiving Party written notice releasing Receiving Party from this Agreement, whichever occurs first.

5. **Relationships.** Nothing contained in this Agreement shall be deemed to constitute either party a partner, joint venturer, or employee of the other party for any purpose.

6. **Severability.** If a court finds any provision of this Agreement invalid or unenforceable, the remainder of this Agreement shall be interpreted so as best to effect the intent of the parties.

7. **Integration.** This Agreement expresses the complete understanding of the parties with respect to the subject matter and supersedes all prior proposals, agreements, representations, and understandings. This Agreement may not be amended except in a writing signed by both parties.

8. **Waiver.** The failure to exercise any right provided in this Agreement shall not be a waiver of prior or subsequent rights.

This Agreement and each party's obligations shall be binding on the representatives, assigns, and successors of such party. Each party has signed this Agreement through its authorized representative.

Signature: _____

Typed or printed name: _____

Date: _____

Signature: _____

Typed or printed name: _____

Date: _____

Trade Secret Law: Forms

Defining the Trade Secrets

Every nondisclosure agreement defines its trade secrets, often referred to as "confidential information." This definition establishes the subject matter of the disclosure. There are three common approaches to defining confidential information: (1) using a system to mark all confidential information; (2) listing trade secret categories; or (3) specifically identifying the confidential information.

What's best? That depends on your secrets and how you disclose them. If your company is built around one or two secrets—for example, a famous recipe or formula—you can specifically identify the materials. You can also use that approach if you are disclosing one or two secrets to a contractor. If your company focuses on several categories of secret information, for example, computer code, sales information, and marketing plans, a list approach will work with employees and contractors. If your company has a wide variety of secrets and is constantly developing new ones, you should specifically identify secrets. Here's an example of the list approach.

Definition of Confidential Information Example

"Confidential Information" means information or material that is commercially valuable to the Disclosing Party and not generally known or readily ascertainable in the industry. This includes, but is not limited to:

(a) technical information concerning the Disclosing Party's products and services, including product know-how, formulae, designs, devices, diagrams, software code, test results, processes, inventions, research projects and product development, technical memoranda, and correspondence

(b) information concerning the Disclosing Party's business, including cost information, profits, sales information, accounting and unpublished financial information, business plans, markets and marketing methods, customer lists and customer information, purchasing techniques, supplier lists and supplier information, and advertising strategies

(c) information concerning the Disclosing Party's employees, including salaries, strengths, weaknesses, and skills

(d) information submitted by the Disclosing Party's customers, suppliers, employees, consultants, or co-venture partners with the Disclosing Party for study, evaluation, or use, and

(e) any other information not generally known to the public that, if misused or disclosed, could reasonably be expected to adversely affect the Disclosing Party's business.

Trade Secret Law: Forms

Using a list approach is fine, provided that you can find something on the list that fits your disclosure. For example, if you are disclosing a confidential software program, your nondisclosure agreement should include a category such as "programming code" or "software code" that accurately reflects your secret material. Although the final paragraph in the example above includes "any other information," you will be better off not relying solely on this statement. Courts that interpret NDAs often prefer specificity.

If confidential information is fairly specific—for example, a unique method of preparing income tax statements—define it specifically.

Definition of Confidential Information Example

> The following constitutes Confidential Information: _business method for preparing income tax statements and related algorithms and software code_.

Another approach to identifying trade secrets is to state that the disclosing party will certify what is and what is not confidential. For example, physical disclosures such as written materials or software will be clearly marked "Confidential." In the case of oral disclosures, the disclosing party provides written confirmation that a trade secret was disclosed. Here is an appropriate provision taken from the sample NDA in the previous section.

Definition of Confidential Information Example

> (Written or Oral). For purposes of this Agreement, "Confidential Information" includes all information or material that has or could have commercial value or other utility in the business in which Disclosing Party is engaged. If Confidential Information is in written form, the Disclosing Party shall label or stamp the materials with the word "Confidential" or some similar warning. If Confidential Information is transmitted orally, the Disclosing Party shall promptly provide a writing indicating that such oral communication constituted Confidential Information.

When confirming an oral disclosure, avoid disclosing the content of the trade secret. An email or letter is acceptable, but the parties should keep copies of all such correspondence. A sample letter is shown below.

Trade Secret Law: Forms

Letter Confirming Oral Disclosure

Date:

Dear Sam,

Today at lunch, I disclosed information to you about my kaleidoscopic projection system—specifically, the manner in which I have configured and wired the bulbs in the device. That information is confidential (as described in our nondisclosure agreement) and this letter is intended to confirm the disclosure.

William

Excluding Information That Is Not Confidential

You cannot prohibit the receiving party from disclosing information that is publicly known, legitimately acquired from another source, or developed by the receiving party before meeting you. Similarly, it is not unlawful if the receiving party discloses your secret with your permission. These legal exceptions exist with or without an agreement, but they are commonly included in a contract to make it clear to everyone that such information is not considered a trade secret.

Exclusions From Confidential Information Example

Receiving Party's obligations under this Agreement do not extend to information that is: (a) publicly known at the time of disclosure under this Agreement or subsequently becomes publicly known through no fault of the Receiving Party; (b) discovered or created by the Receiving Party prior to disclosure by Disclosing Party; (c) otherwise learned by the Receiving Party through legitimate means other than from the Disclosing Party or Disclosing Party's representatives; or (d) disclosed by Receiving Party with Disclosing Party's prior written approval.

In some cases, a business presented with your nondisclosure agreement may request the right to exclude information that is independently developed *after* the disclosure. In other words, the business might want to change subsection (b) to read, "(b) discovered or independently created by Receiving Party prior to *or after* disclosure by Disclosing Party."

By making this change, the other company can create new products after exposure to your secret, provided that your secret is not used to develop them. You may wonder how it is possible for a company once exposed to your secret to develop a new product without using that trade secret. One possibility is that one division of a large company could invent something without any contact with the division that has been exposed to your secret. Some companies even establish clean room methods.

Although it is possible for a company to independently develop products or information without using your disclosed secret, we recommend avoiding this modification if possible.

Duty to Keep Information Secret

The heart of a nondisclosure agreement is a statement establishing a confidential relationship between the parties. The statement sets out the duty of the Receiving Party to maintain the information in confidence and to limit its use. Often, this duty is established by one sentence: "The Receiving Party shall hold and maintain the Confidential Information of the other party in strictest confidence for the sole and exclusive benefit of the Disclosing Party." In other cases, the provision may be more detailed and may include obligations to return information. A detailed provision is provided below.

The simpler provision is usually suitable when entering into an NDA with an individual such as an independent contractor. Use the more detailed one if your secrets may be used by more than one individual within a business. The detailed provision provides that the receiving party has to restrict access to persons within the company who are also bound by this agreement.

Provision Establishing a Duty of Nondisclosure Example

Receiving Party shall hold and maintain the Confidential Information of the Disclosing Party in strictest confidence for the sole and exclusive benefit of the Disclosing Party. Receiving Party shall carefully restrict access to Confidential Information to employees, contractors, and third parties as is reasonably required and only disclose confidential information to persons subject to nondisclosure restrictions at least as protective as those set forth in this Agreement. Receiving Party shall not, without prior written approval of Disclosing Party, use for Receiving Party's own benefit, publish, copy, or otherwise disclose to others, or permit the use by others for their benefit or to the detriment of Disclosing Party, any Confidential Information.

Trade Secret Law: Forms

In some cases, you may want to impose additional requirements. For example, a Prospective Software Licensee Nondisclosure Agreement may contain a prohibition against reverse engineering, decompiling, or disassembling the software. This prohibits the receiving party (the user of licensed software) from learning more about the trade secrets.

You may also insist on the return of all trade secret materials that you furnished under the agreement. In that case, add the following language to the receiving party's obligations.

Return of Materials Example

> Receiving Party shall return to Disclosing Party any and all records, notes, and other written, printed, or tangible materials in its possession pertaining to Confidential Information immediately if Disclosing Party requests it in writing.

Duration of the Agreement

How long does the duty of confidentiality last? The sample agreement offers three alternative approaches: an indefinite period that terminates when the information is no longer a trade secret; a fixed period of time; or a combination of the two.

Unlimited Time Period Example

> This Agreement and Receiving Party's duty to hold Disclosing Party's Confidential Information in confidence shall remain in effect until the Confidential Information no longer qualifies as a trade secret or until Disclosing Party sends Receiving Party written notice releasing Receiving Party from this Agreement, whichever occurs first.

Fixed Time Period Example

> This Agreement and Receiving Party's duty to hold Disclosing Party's Confidential Information in confidence shall remain in effect until _____ .

Fixed Time Period With Exceptions Example

This Agreement and Receiving Party's duty to hold Disclosing Party's Confidential Information in confidence shall remain in effect until _____ or until one of the following occurs:

(a) the Disclosing Party sends the Receiving Party written notice releasing it from this Agreement, or

(b) the information disclosed under this Agreement ceases to be a trade secret.

The time period is often an issue of negotiation. You, as the disclosing party, will usually want an open period with no limits; receiving parties want a short period. For employee and contractor agreements, the term is often unlimited or ends only when the trade secret becomes public knowledge. Five years is a common length in nondisclosure agreements that involve business negotiations and product submissions, although many companies insist on two or three years.

We recommend that you seek as long a time as possible, preferably unlimited. But realize that some businesses want a fixed period of time and some courts, when interpreting NDAs, require that the time period be reasonable. Determining "reasonableness" is subjective and depends on the confidential material and the nature of the industry. For example, some trade secrets within the software or Internet industries may be short-lived. Other trade secrets—for example, the Coca-Cola formula—have been preserved as a secret for over a century. If it is likely, for example, that others will stumble upon the same secret or innovation or that it will be reverse engineered within a few years, then you are unlikely to be damaged by a two- or three-year period. Keep in mind that once the time period is over, the disclosing party is free to reveal your secrets.

Miscellaneous Provisions

The sample NDA includes four miscellaneous provisions. These standard provisions (sometimes known as "boilerplate") are included at the end of most contracts. They actually have little in common with one another except for the fact that they don't fit anywhere else in the agreement. They're contract orphans. Still, these provisions are very important and can affect how disputes are resolved and how a court enforces the contract.

Relationships. Your relationship with the receiving party is usually defined by the agreement that you are signing—for example an employment, licensing, or investment agreement. To an outsider, it may appear that you have a different relationship, such as a partnership or joint venture. It's possible that an unscrupulous business will try to capitalize on this appearance and make a third-party deal. That is, the receiving party may claim to be your partner to obtain a benefit from a distributor or sublicensee. To avoid liability for such a situation, most agreements include a provision like this one, disclaiming any relationship other than that defined in the agreement. We recommend that you include such a provision and take care to tailor it to the agreement. For example, if you are using it in an employment agreement, you would delete the reference to employees. If you are using it in a partnership agreement, take out the reference to partners, and so forth.

Relationships Example

> Nothing contained in this Agreement shall be deemed to constitute either party a partner, joint venturer, or employee of the other party for any purpose.

Severability. The severability clause provides that if you wind up in a lawsuit over the agreement and a court rules that one part of the agreement is invalid, that part can be cut out and the rest of the agreement will remain valid. If you don't include a severability clause and some portion of your agreement is deemed invalid, then the whole agreement may be canceled.

Severability Example

> If a court finds any provision of this Agreement invalid or unenforceable, the remainder of this Agreement shall be interpreted so as best to effect the intent of the parties.

Integration. In the process of negotiation and contract drafting, you and the other party may make many oral or written statements. Some of these statements make it into the final agreement. Others don't. The integration provision verifies that the version you are signing is the final version, and that neither of you can rely on statements made in the past. *This is it!* Without an integration provision, it's possible that either party could claim rights based upon promises made before the deal was signed.

A second function of the integration provision is to establish that if any party makes promises after the agreement is signed, those promises will be binding only if they are made in a signed amendment (addendum) to the agreement.

Integration Example

> This Agreement expresses the complete understanding of the parties with respect to the subject matter and supersedes all prior proposals, agreements, representations, and understandings. This Agreement may not be amended except in writing when signed by both parties..

Waiver. This provision states that even if you don't promptly complain about a violation of the NDA, you still have the right to complain about it later. Without this kind of clause, if you know the other party has breached the agreement but you let it pass, you give up (waive) your right to sue over it. For example, imagine that the receiving party is supposed to use the secret information in two products but not in a third. You're aware that the receiving party is violating the agreement, but you are willing to permit it because you are being paid more money and don't have a competing product. After several years, however, you no longer want to permit the use of the secret in the third product. A waiver provision makes it possible for you to sue. The receiving party cannot defend itself by claiming it relied on your past practice of accepting its breaches. Of course, the provision swings both ways. If you breach the agreement, you cannot rely on the other party's past acceptance of *your* behavior.

Waiver Example

> The failure to exercise any right provided in this Agreement shall not be a waiver of prior or subsequent rights.

Signatures

The parties don't have to be in the same room when they sign the agreement. It's even fine if the dates are a few days apart. Each party should sign two copies and keep one. This way, both parties have an original signed agreement.

Trade Secret Law: Forms

Index

A

Abandonment of mark, 381, 391–392, 458, 460
    cancellation petition and, 465
    naked license and, 457, 461–462
    zombie trademark and, 502
Abandonment of patent application, 31
    by not replying to office action, 148
    by not rescinding NPR, 54
    as statutory bar, 163
    substitute application following, 31, 165
    trade secret and, 54
Abandonment of trademark application, 392–393
    international applications and, 459, 460
    partial, 393, 460
    See also Abandonment of mark
Abridgment, 250. *See also* Derivative work, under copyright law
Abstract in patent application, 31, 174, 186
Abstract principles, nonpatentable, 117
Accelerated Examination Program (AEP), 32, 139
Acceptable Identification of Goods and Services Manual, 393, 505
Access, in copyright law, 209–210
Accused device, 32
Actual damages for copyright infringement, 210–211, 245, 246
Actual reduction to practice, 54, 71–72, 88, 152–153. *See also* Building and testing of invention; Reduction to practice

Adaptations. *See* Derivative work, under copyright law
Admissions by inventor, 32
Advertising
    comparative, trademark in, 439
    false, 429–430, 481, 498, 499
    keyword searches and, 455–456
    pop-up, 472
    puffery in, 476
    secondary meaning gained through, 482
    trademark infringement in, 475–476
    trademark of award or ratings used in, 398
    unauthorized use of name or persona in, 481
Advertising injury, 211
Advertising slogans, used as marks, 485
Adwords, 455–456
AEP (Accelerated Examination Program), 32, 139
Aesthetic functionality, 393–394
Affidavit of use. *See* Section 8 Declaration; Section 15 Declaration
Affirmative rights, 211
Agents. *See* Patent agents
Age of inventor, and Petition to Make Special, 32, 139
AHRA (Audio Home Recording Act) of 1992, 215–216
AIPLA (American Intellectual Property Law Association), 32
Algorithms, and patentability, 33, 117
Allegation of Use for Intent-to-Use Application, 394, 449–450, 507, 508

Allowance of patent application, 33, 118

All rights reserved, 211–212, 219

Altai, Computer Associates Int'l v., 230, 268, 292

Alterations. *See* Derivative work, under copyright law

Amendment of patent application, 20, 33–34, 86

Amendments to claims. *See* Claims, amendments to

America Invents Act, 22–25
    "best mode" defense and, 23, 73
    business method patents and, 24, 45
    derivation hearings under, 25, 67–69
    filing by other than inventor in, 24, 41, 103–104
    filing date and, 84
    human organism patents banned under, 23, 90
    as imperfect reform, 34
    inter partes patent reexamination and, 97–99, 153
    major change of, 34
    new prior user defense in, 23, 63
    patent marking and, 23, 109
    Section 102 (novelty) of, 24–25, 120–121, 144–146
    Section 103 (nonobviousness) of, 24–25, 116
    timeline for changes brought about by, 34–37

American Intellectual Property Law Association (AIPLA), 32

Amino acid sequence, 156

Anonymous work, copyright for, 200, 212, 257

Anthologies, 224, 226

Anticipation of invention, 37–38
    duty to disclose, 77

    by public use, 80, 151
    specification of patent application and, 161
    See also Prior art

Anticybersquatting Consumer Protection Act, 394–395, 425

Antidilution statutes. *See* Dilution of trademark

Antishelving clause, 38–39

Antitrust law and patents, 39–40, 53, 62, 130–131
    invalidated for violation of, 168
    licensing and, 17
    patent pools and, 133
    patent thickets and, 137
    price fixing and, 142
    tying and, 39, 62, 168

Antitrust law and trademarks, 458

Antitrust law and trade secrets, 523–524, 565
    licensing and, 547

Appeals. *See* Board of Patent Appeals and Interferences (BPAI); Court of Appeals for the Federal Circuit (CAFC); Trademark Trial and Appeal Board

Apple Computer, Inc. v. Franklin, 212, 230

Apple Computer, Inc. v. Microsoft Corp., 213, 230–231

Arbitrary mark, 395
    geographic, 441
    as strong mark, 487

Arbitration of disputes, under new patent law, 69

Architectural work, 213–214

Archival copies, 214, 253

Artworks, and copyright
    copyright clearinghouses for, 223
    first-sale doctrine and, 269

magazine covers, 205–206, 266

moral rights and, 293

pictorial, graphic, and sculptural works, 314–315

registration and, 324

unfinished, 203, 242–243, 346

See also Audiovisual works; Photography; Visual Artists Rights Act (VARA)

ASCAP, 309

Ashcroft, Eldred v., 258

Assignment of copyright, 199, 214–215

claimant and, 237

ownership of copyright and, 240–241, 334–336

termination of, 215, 333

See also Copyright transfers

Assignment of mark, 395–397

after international registration, 460

Section 8 Declaration and, 483

Assignment of patent, 17, 40–41

with application filed by assignee, 24, 41, 103–104

under Bayh-Dole Act, 41–43

conflicting assignments, 26–27, 42–43

for design, 191–192

"employed to invent" doctrine and, 78–79

to employer, 78–79, 141–142

filing of, 175–176

ownership and, 131

preinvention, 141–142

recent federal court decisions on, 26–27, 28

by small entity to large entity, 40

Attorney fees

in copyright infringement action, 200, 281, 282

in trademark infringement action, 397, 408, 410, 411, 500

in trade secret lawsuit, 524

Attorneys. *See* Intellectual property lawyers; Patent attorneys

Attribution, 215

Audio Home Recording Act of 1992 (AHRA), 215–216

Audiovisual works, 216

copyright management information about, 239

copyright notice for, 298

See also Motion pictures, copyrights

Aural trademarks, 485

Authorized use, as copyright infringement defense, 217

Author of work

anonymous or pseudonymous, 200, 212, 257, 318

as copyright claimant, 237

copyright management information about, 239

death of, 257–258

defined, 216

freelance, 295–296

moral rights of, 217, 275, 285, 292–293

ownership and, 198–199

See also Work made for hire

Authorship, original work of, 302–303

Average reasonably prudent consumer, 397

same or similar mark and, 482

Award, trademark related to, used in advertising, 398

B

Bayh-Dole Act, 41–43, 554

conflicting assignments and, 26–27,
42–43

Berne Convention, 8, 202, 217, 256,
275–276, 285–286
copyright infringement and, 324
copyright notice and, 297, 301
moral rights and, 292–293
simultaneous publication and,
328–329
visual artworks and, 344

Best edition of a work, 217–218

Best mode defense, 23, 73, 96

Best mode of invention
disclosed in specification, 174,
180–181
duty to disclose, 77

Beta testing and trade secrets, 524–525,
561

Bilski, Kappos v., 104–105, 159

Biotechnology sequence, 156. *See also*
Genetic engineering and patents

BitTorrent, 218, 307–308

Blank forms, not copyrightable, 218–219,
317–318

Blocking patent, 43

Blogs
copyright and, 219
trade secret sources and, 538

Blurring. *See* Dilution of trademark

BMI, 309

Board of Patent Appeals and
Interferences (BPAI), 43, 99–100
appeal of final office action to, 86, 148,
152
appeals from decisions of, 57
patent agent representation at, 126

Bootlegging of live performance, 219,
275–276

Brand name. *See* Trade name

Breach of trust, 534

Breaking a patent, 43–44

Buenos Aires Convention, 219

Bug. *See* Copyright notice

Building and testing of invention, 44,
71–72
date of, 59
documentation of, 118
See also Reduction to practice

Business information as trade secret, 525

Business method patents, 44–45,
101–102
Kappos v. Bilski and, 104–105, 159
new patent law and, 24, 45, 102, 159
State Street Bank case and, 161–162

Busting a patent, 43–44

C

Caching of search results, and copyright,
220

Cancellation of trademark registration,
451, 458, 459, 464–466

CARP (Copyright Arbitration Royalty
Panel), 339

Cartoons, copyright clearinghouses for,
223

CCPA (Court of Customs and Patent
Appeals), 46

Cease and desist letter, in copyright
dispute, 220

Celebrity, unauthorized use of name or
image of, 481

Cell phones. *See* Wireless phones

Certificate of correction, for patent
application, 46

Certificate of registration (copyright),
220–221

Certificate of registration (trademark),
398–399, 431

assignment and, 395–396

presumption of ownership and, 472–473

receipt of, 508

Certification mark, 399–401, 460

cancellation petition and, 465

geographical terms in, 442

Certification of Validity, after patent reexamination, 154

Character names as trademarks, 496

Characters, fictional, 221–222

Characters as trademarks, 401

Chemicals. *See* Composition of matter

Choreography, 117, 222–223

CIP (continuation-in-part application), 55, 112, 148

Claims, 19, 46–49

broad, 83–84, 109–110, 111, 147, 148

broadened in reissue patent, 102–103, 149, 155

dependent, 46, 47, 67, 161, 174–175

of design patent, 194

drafting of, 174–175

fully met by prior art reference, 87

independent, 46, 47, 92, 161, 174–175

infringement and, in judge's interpretation, 109

limiting reference in, 106

means plus function clauses in, 109–110

multiple, 111, 161

narrowing, 111

nonelected, 113

product-by-process claim, 146–147

"reading on" a device or process, 74

reciting elements of, 152

rejected based on prior art, 146

rejected in final office action, 148, 152

rejected in first office action, 86, 122, 147–148, 157

of sample patent application, 184–186

scope of, 110

Section 112 of patent statutes on, 161

specification and, 110

Claims, amendments to, 86, 147–149

doctrine of equivalents and, 75, 82

after final office action, 152

after reexamination, 154

in reissue patent, 155

supplemental declaration and, 149, 165

Class Definitions, 50

Classes of goods and services, 452–453, 505

Classes of patents, 49–50

Clean room, for development of proprietary materials, 525, 575

Clearinghouses, copyright, 223

Clickwrap agreement. *See* End-user license agreement (EULA)

Clinical trial, as experimental use of unpatented invention, 81

CMI. *See* Copyright management information (CMI)

Coauthor agreement (collaboration agreement), 224

Coauthors, 223–224

duration of copyright with, 257

See also Joint work

Coined marks, 431, 487

Coinventors, 50–51

complete conception not required of, 28, 53

of design, 191

named in patent application, 175

Collaboration agreement (coauthor agreement), 224

Collective marks, 401–402, 460

Collective works, 224–225
    in conjunction with software, 225
    ownership of copyrights related to, 241

Color
    as element of a mark, 402, 460
    used as a mark, 402–403, 460, 496

Combination patent, 51

Combinations, patentability of, 51, 105, 114–115

Commerce that Congress may regulate, 403–404

Commissioned work, copyright for, 199, 200, 216
    claimant for, 237
    instructional text as, 285
    See also Work made for hire

Commissioner for Patents, 51

Commissioner for Trademarks, 404

Common law, 6
    of copyright, 225, 327
    of trademarks, 380

Community patent. *See* European Patent Convention

Community Trademark, 404, 454

Compensatory damages. *See* Actual damages for copyright infringement

Competing and noncompeting products, 404–405

Competitive advantage, 526, 551–552. *See also* Covenant not to compete

Compilation of information, as trade secret, 526

Compilations, and copyright, 205, 225–226
    collective work as type of, 224–225
    databases as, 225–226, 229

Composite mark, 405
    containing generic term, 440

    See also Disclaimer of unregistrable material

Composition of matter, 52, 164
    drawings in patent application for, 76

Compulsory licensing of copyright, 227–228, 291
    restored under GATT, 326

Compulsory licensing of patent, 52, 170

Computer Associates Int'l v. Altai, 230, 268, 292

Computer databases
    copyright protection for, 228–229
    protecting against intrusion, 558
    as trade secrets, 533
    trade secrets for reorganization of, 526
    See also Databases

Computer desktop metaphor, and copyright, 213

Computer graphics, as independent creation or derivative work, 280

Computerized patent search. *See* Patent search, computerized

Computer operating systems, copyright protection for, 212–213

Computer programs. *See* Software; Software patents

Computer read-only memories (ROMs), and trade secrets, 557

Computer security, for business secrets, 534–535

Computer security dongles, 204, 254

Computer Software Protection Act of 1980, 214

Computer user interfaces, and copyright protection, 230–231, 268, 292

Conception of invention, 52–53
    coinventor and, 28, 53
    date of invention and, 52–53, 59
    interference and, 99–101

Concerted refusal to deal, 39, 53

Concurrent ownership of mark, 466–467

Concurrent registration of marks, 405–406, 434, 466

Confidential employment relationship, 526–527, 542. *See also* Employment agreement

Confidentiality
 email and, 534–535
 idea submission and, 541
 of patent applications, 6, 53–54
 See also Nondisclosure agreement (NDA); Public use or disclosure of invention; Trade secret

Confidentiality agreement. *See* Nondisclosure agreement (NDA)

Confusion, in trademark law, 382
 initial interest confusion, 447
 reverse confusion, 480–481
 See also Likelihood of confusion, in trademark law

Constitution, U.S., 6
 copyright law and, 202
 trademark law and, 403

Constructive notice of mark, 406
 unregistered mark and, 500

Constructive reduction to practice, 54–55, 71, 72, 85, 88, 118, 149–150, 152, 153

Consumer, average reasonably prudent, 397
 same or similar mark and, 482

Consumer complaints, and trademark law, 438–439

Continuation application, 55, 86, 148, 152
 after Request for Continued Examination, 156

Continuation-in-part application (CIP), 55, 112, 148

Continuous use of mark, 406–407

Contributory infringement of copyright, 231–232
 by website linking, 290

Contributory infringement of patent, 56, 61

Contributory infringement of trademark, 407

Convention application, 56–57
 filing date in U.S. and, 84–85

Convention for the Protection of Industrial Property. *See* Paris Convention

Copies, under copyright law, 232

Copyleft, 232–233

Copyright
 for anonymous work, 200, 212, 257
 creation of work entitled to, 198, 242–243, 271–272
 of database content or design, 225–226, 228–229, 231, 278, 533
 defined, 197–198, 233–235
 design patent combined with, 236
 duration of, 200, 255–258
 exclusive rights under, 199, 233, 260–261
 freedom of speech and, 275
 international protection for, 285–286
 laws, judicial opinions, and model codes not protected by, 288
 patent combined with, 7
 patent compared to, 236
 permission for use and, 223, 224–225, 281, 310–311
 for pseudonymous work, 200, 257, 318
 thin, 333–334

trademark combined with, 6–7
trade secret and, 278, 331, 520–521,
    527–528, 538, 541, 546, 561
works protected by, 8, 10–13, 197, 234
See also Artworks, and copyright;
    Compilations, and copyright; Music
    copyright; Software copyright;
    Unpublished works, copyright
    protection for
Copyright Act of 1909, 235
Copyright Act of 1976, 202, 235
    audiovisual works under, 216
Copyright application forms, 242,
    272–274, 323, 349–376
    Form CA, 272, 332
    Form CO, 272
    Form CO, preparing, 350–356
    Form CO, sample, 357–362
    Form eCO (electronic), 363–365
    Form PA, 272–273, 371–372
    Form RE, 273
    Form SE, 273, 366
    Form SR, 273, 366
    Form TX, 273, 373–374
    Form VA, 274, 375–376
    overview of, 349–350
    preparing traditional print forms,
        366–370
    See also Copyright registration
Copyright Arbitration Royalty Panel
    (CARP), 339
Copyright claimant, 237
Copyright Cleanup, Clarification, and
    Corrections Act of 2010, 202
Copyright infringement, 198, 200–201,
    237–239
    access for, 209–210
    cease and desist letter for, 220
    contributory, 231–232, 290

criminal, 243–245, 253, 331–332
    by facilitating unauthorized music
        downloads, 294
    by file sharing networks, 218, 307–308
    by framing of Web pages, 274
    by governments, 330–331
    by imported works, 270, 278–279
    independent creation and, 279–280
    Internet service providers and,
        252–253, 287
    inverse ratio rule of, 210, 287
    by musical sampling, 327
    by photocopies, 312
    of trade secret information, 538
    willful, 247
    See also Fair use, under copyright law;
        Innocent infringement of copyright
Copyright infringement action, 200–201,
    237–239, 280–282
    defenses to, 201, 217, 249, 280–281
    by exclusive licensee, 261
    registration and, 220–221, 237, 246,
        262, 281, 322, 324–325, 334
    See also Damages for copyright
        infringement
Copyright law, 5, 6–7
    common law, 225, 327
    definitions of terms in, 209–347
    overview of, 197–208
    recent changes in, 202–207
    U.S. and international sources of, 202
    See also Digital Millennium Copyright
        Act (DMCA)
Copyright management information
    (CMI), 239–240
    credit line as part of, 243
    falsification of, 252
Copyright notice, 198, 234, 297–299
    before March 1989, 235

as copyright management information, 239

defective, 248

fraudulent, 245

fraudulent removal of, 245

GATT treaty and, 286, 297, 301

omission of, 300–301

Universal Copyright Convention and, 286

Copyright Office. *See* U.S. Copyright Office

Copyright owner, 240–241

claimant and, 237

copyright management information about, 239

licensee as, 261

publisher as, under grant of rights, 233

separate rights which may be owned by, 240

See also Copyright transfers

Copyright registration, 198, 234–235, 322–325

certificate of, 220–221

claimant for purpose of, 237

of computer databases, 229

de minimis changes and, 248

electronic filing of, 258

expedited, 261–262

false representation in application for, 245, 266–267

forms for, 242, 272–274, 323, 332, 349–376

infringement action and, 220–221, 237, 246, 262, 281, 322, 324–325, 334

preregistration, 316–317

presumption of validity not created by, 205

single registration rule, 329

special relief to applicants for, 323, 331

supplemental, 272, 324, 329, 332

timely, 334

See also Copyright application forms; Deposit with U.S. Copyright Office

Copyright transfers, 199, 334–336

overlapping, 303–304, 321

recordation of, 321–322, 336

termination of, 333

See also Assignment of copyright; Licensing of copyrights

Counterfeiting, 407–408, 411

Country code suffixes, 421

Court decisions, 6

Court decisions, recent

on copyright, 202–207

on patents, 25–28

on trademarks, 387–389

on trade secrets, 520–521

Court of Appeals for the Federal Circuit (CAFC), 24, 46, 57

Court of Customs and Patent Appeals (CCPA), 46

Court order. *See* Injunction *entries;* Temporary restraining order (TRO)

Covenant not to compete

by employee, 528–530

by owners of a sold business, 530

specific performance of, 562

Creation of work, when protected by copyright, 198, 242–243, 271–272

Creative Commons, 243

Credit Card Transmittal Form, 173

Credit line, 243

Criminal copyright infringement, 243–245

under Digital Millennium Copyright Act, 253

statute of limitations for, 331–332

Criminal prosecution for trade secret
theft, 520, 530–531, 536, 542
Critical commentary
copyright and, 249, 263, 264
trademark and, 438–440
Cross-licensing, 17, 57, 91–92
Customer lists, 531–532, 566
Customs and Border Protection, Bureau
of
copyright infringement and, 278–279
trademark infringement and, 398
Cybergriping, 438–439
Cybersquatting, 394–395, 409, 422, 423,
425

D

Damages for copyright infringement,
198, 200–201, 210–211, 245–247, 281
under Digital Millennium Copyright
Act, 253
not precluded by illegal acts, 206
profits as, 245–246, 318
by sound recordings, 204
statutory, 245, 246, 247
Damages for patent infringement, 21,
57–58, 95–96, 158
statute of limitations on, 162–163
treble, 96, 170
Damages for trademark infringement,
385, 386, 410–411
by competing or noncompeting
products, 404–405
constructive notice and, 406
court decision on, 386
punitive, 476
registration and, 386, 410, 411
Damages for trade secret
misappropriation, 520, 532–533, 565
Damages for unfair competition, 499

Dance routines
copyrightable, 222–223
nonpatentable, 117
Databases
as compilations, 225–226, 229
copyrighted material in, 533
deposit with the U.S. Copyright Office
for, 278
factual, creativity required for
copyright, 231
of photographs, 313
as trade secrets, 533
See also Computer databases; Patent
search, computerized
Date of invention, 52–53, 58–59
DDP (Disclosure Document Program),
72–73
Declaratory judgment of
noninfringement, invalidity and
unenforceability of patent, 59
Deed, patent, 126, 130, 149
Deep links, 290
Deere case, 90
Defective copyright notice, 248
Defendant's profits. *See* Profits, defendant's
Defensive disclosure of invention, 66–67
Deliberate indifference standard, 25, 93
Deliberate infringement. *See* Willful
infringement
Delphion, 134, 136
De minimis changes, 248
Dependent claims, 46, 47, 67, 161,
174–175
Deposit with Library of Congress,
288–289
Deposit with U.S. Copyright Office, 249,
288–289
best edition of work for, 217–218
failure of, 263

of identifying material, 278
of source code and object code, 300
special relief to applicants and, 331
See also Copyright registration
Derivation hearings, 25, 67–69, 99
Derivative work, under copyright law,
199, 249–251
assignment and, 214
coauthors of, 224
fictional character as, 221–222
independent creation compared to,
279–280
photographic, 312
termination of transfers and, 333
Descriptive mark, 382, 384, 385,
412–413, 475
geographic, 441
phonetic or foreign equivalents for, 471
recent case on, 388
suggestive mark distinguished from,
488–489
Supplemental Register and, 489
as weak mark, 502
Design
copyright coverage of, 314
as trade dress, 494, 495
as trade secret, 553
Designing around a patent, 69–70
doctrine of equivalents and, 75, 82
means plus function clauses and, 110
patent number marking and, 108–109
Design patent, 5, 8, 18, 70–71
application for, 191–194
on computer screen icon, 160
copyright combined with, 236
in-force period of, 21, 76
infringement of, 71, 94–95
legal requirements for, 138
term of, 191

See also Patent
Digital audio transmissions, 310,
339–340. *See also* File sharing
Digital Millennium Copyright Act
(DMCA), 251–254
copyright management information
and, 239–240
jailbreaking and, 204
willful violation of, 244
Digital rights management (DRM), 203,
251, 254
Digital sampling, 280, 327
Diligence in reducing to practice, 71–72,
88, 100–101, 144
Dilution of trademark, 386–387,
413–418, 430, 435
by domain name, 423
Trademark Dilution Revision Act,
414–416, 430
by unrelated products or services, 480
Victoria's Secret case and, 501
Dilution of unregistered trade dress, 495
Director of the U.S. Patent and
Trademark Office, 72
Directory, and copyright, 231, 267
Disclaimer of trademark use, 418
Disclaimer of unregistrable material, 405,
419, 478
generic, 440
surname as, 492
on trademark application, 506–507
Disclosure Document Program (DDP),
72–73
Disclosure Document Reference Letter,
175
Disclosure requirement for patents, 73
Disclosures of invention
limited one-year grace period for, 24,
37, 81

See also Public use or disclosure of invention

Display a work, under copyright law, 254–255

Distinctive mark, 380–381, 382–383, 384–385, 419–420
  arbitrary, 395
  product designs and, 501
  related goods or services and, 479
  secondary meaning and, 482
  unregistered, 499–500
  See also Principal Register; Secondary meaning

Distinctive trade dress, 494

Divisional application, 73–74, 148
  on nonelected claims, 113

DMCA. *See* Digital Millennium Copyright Act (DMCA)

Doctrine of equivalents, 74–75, 82, 95
  negative, 95, 112

Domain names, 420–423
  annual fees for, 423
  checking ownership of, 422
  cybersquatting and, 394–395, 409, 422, 423, 425
  generic terms in, 388, 440
  registration of, 422, 423
  "sucks" in, 438–439
  trademark law and, 422, 423–424
  trademark registration of, 387, 388
  trademark search of, 497

Domain tasting, 425

Double patenting, 74, 75

Dramatic works, 255

Drawings, copyright for. *See* Artworks, and copyright

Drawings, patent application, 75–76
  for design patent, 191, 192–193, 194
  for utility patent, 173–174, 187–190

DRM (digital rights management), 203, 251, 254

Drugs
  as compositions of matter, 52
  Food and Drug Administration and, 136

Duty of candor and good faith, toward Patent Office, 77–78

Duty of trust, and trade secrets, 527, 534, 542

DVD content filtering, 268, 436

DVD protection
  circumvented for noncommercial purposes, 204
  Digital Millennium Copyright Act and, 252, 254
  as trade secret, 537, 546

E

eBook readers, digital locks on, 204, 254

Economic Espionage Act of 1996, 530, 536. *See also* Industrial espionage

Education, fair use for purpose of, 263, 264

18-month publication system, 53–54, 116–117
  patent infringement and, 108, 132
  submarine patents and, 165
  trade secrets and, 53–54, 552–553

Eldred v. Ashcroft, 258

Electronic circuits, 106, 107

Electronic filing of copyright applications, 258. *See also* Copyright registration

Electronic Filing System (EFS-Web), 78, 128

Electronic Signatures in Global and International Commerce Act, 259

Electronic Trademark Assignment (ETA) system, 395

Email and confidentiality, 534–535

Emergency room forms, and copyright law, 203, 218–219

"Employed to invent" doctrine, 78–79

Employee

    covenant not to compete, 528–530

    exit interview for, 535, 551, 558

    of government, 207, 343

    nondisclosure agreement with, 550

    notice to, about trade secrets, 551, 558

    notice to new employer of, 551

    trade secrets developed by, 566

    See also Nondisclosure agreement (NDA); Work made for hire

Employment agreement

    design patent and, 192

    invention assignment and, 28, 40, 131–132

    as preinvention assignment, 141–142

Employment relationship

    confidential, 526–527, 542

    factors determining, 341

Enabling disclosure, 79

Encyclopedia, as collective work, 224

End-user license agreement (EULA), 258–260, 560

    nonsoftware, 260

Ephemeral recording, 260

Equivalents, doctrine of, 74–75, 82, 95

    negative, 95, 112

ETA (Electronic Trademark Assignment) system, 395

European Patent Convention, 79

European Patent Office, 56, 79, 101

European Union (EU)

    Community Trademark in, 404

    duration of copyright in, 256

    patent law relationships in, 79

Evaluation agreement, 535, 540

Examination fee, for patent, 40

Examiners, patent, 20, 130

"Examiner's Bible," 107

Examining attorney, trademark, 503–504, 505, 508–509

Exclusive copyright rights, 199, 233, 260–261

    transfer of, 334–336

Exclusive license of copyright rights, 199, 261, 289, 334–336

    conflicting, 303–304

Exclusive license of patent rights, 80

Exhaustion doctrine, 61, 64, 80

Exhibiting an unpatented invention, 80–81

Exit interview, 535, 551, 558

Expedited copyright registration, 261–262

Experimental use of unpatented invention, 38, 81, 151

Experimentation. *See* Research

Expert witness, in patent litigation, 81

Expression, protection of. *See* Copyright

Extensions of patent application prosecution, 148

F

Facts, and copyright law, 5, 197, 206–207, 234

Factual databases, and copyright, 231

Factual works (nonfiction), 262

Fair use, under copyright law, 201, 234, 249, 263–266

    attribution and, 215

    for book about magazine cover artist, 205–206, 266

    as defense in infringement action, 281

    file sharing and, 307

freedom of speech and, 275

parody and, 222, 304–307

sculpture and, in 2-D representation, 206

takedown notice under DMCA and, 205, 252–253

thumbnails as, 284

transformative nature of, 263–264, 266

waiver of, by museum website, 260

Fair use of trademarks, 428–429

False advertising, 429–430

   right of publicity and, 481

   as unfair competition, 498, 499

False designation of origin, 457, 498, 499

False representation in copyright registration application, 245, 266–267

Family Entertainment and Copyright Act of 2005, 244, 267, 268, 286, 307, 436

Family Movie Act of 2005, 268, 436

Famous mark, 430

Fanciful terms, 431, 487

Federally sponsored research

   Bayh-Dole Act and, 26–27, 41–43, 554

   predetermination of rights related to, 554–555

Federal Trade Commission proceeding, to bar imports, 82

Federal trade secret statute, 530, 536, 542, 543

Fees for patent, 20, 40

   failure to pay, 21

   increases under new law, 22, 23

   issue fee, 104

   for not filing electronically, 23

   for prioritized application, 23

Fee Transmittal Form

   for design patent application, 193

   for utility patent application, 173

Feist Publications Inc. v. Rural Telephone Service Co., 267

Festo v. Shoketsu, 82

Fictional characters, 221–222

Fiduciary duty, 527, 534

Fiduciary relationship and idea submission, 540

Field of invention, 82–83

File extension, as word mark, 389

File sharing, 218, 231, 266, 293–294, 307–308. *See also* Digital audio transmissions

File wrapper, 83, 128

File wrapper continuing application (FWC), 55

File wrapper estoppel, 61–62, 83–84

Filing date of patent application, 18, 19, 84–85

   date of invention and, 59

   foreign filing and, 129, 130

   infringement and, 23

   international, 101

   new matter and, 112

   of Provisional Patent Application, 27, 85, 124, 128, 149–150

   on receipt from USPTO, 128

Filing fee

   for design patent, 191, 193

   for utility patent, 40, 173

Filing receipt, for patent application, 84

Filtering, of motion picture content, 268, 436

Filtration test of substantial similarity, 230–231, 268

Final office action, 86, 148–149

   Request for Continued Examination and, 155–156

First office action, 86, 147–148

First-sale doctrine, in copyright law, 204, 206, 269–271
    end-user software license and, 259
First-sale doctrine, in patent law, 61, 80
First-to-file countries
    for patents, 86–87
    for trademarks, 474
First-to-file system, under America Invents Act, 22, 24, 34, 36, 37
    date of invention and, 58
    filing date and, 84
    on-sale bar and, 123
    reduction to practice and, 55
First-to-invent system, 24, 87, 153
Fixed in a tangible medium of expression, 198, 242–243, 271–272
Flow chart
    copyright registration of, 272
    in patent application, 75, 76
Food and Drug Administration (FDA), and patent term extension, 136
Foreign filing of patent, 22
    filing date in U.S. and, 84–85
    international application, 101
    Nonpublication Request and, 54, 117
    Paris Convention, 101
    See also Patent Cooperation Treaty (PCT)
Foreign national
    as inventor, 88–89
    registering a mark in United States, 436–437
Foreign ship or aircraft, with infringing technology, 167
Foreign works, and copyright infringement, 324
Forms, not copyrightable, 218–219, 317–318

Formulas
    mathematical, nonpatentable, 18, 33, 117
    as trade secrets, 536
Framing, of Web page, 274–275
Franchising
    quality control and, 462
    service marks in, 437
Franklin, Apple Computer, Inc. v., 212, 230
Fraud on the U.S. Patent and Trademark Office, 87
    duty of candor and good faith and, 77
    failure to disclose prior art as, 21, 87, 93–94, 96, 168
    patent declared invalid because of, 21, 87
    in trademark filing, 437–438
Freedom of Information Act, exemption of trade secrets, 537
Freedom of speech
    copyright protection and, 275
    trademark law and, 438–440
    trade secrets and, 537–538, 546
Freelance authors, rights of, 295–296. *See also* Independent contractors
Fully met by prior art reference, 87
Functionality, in trademark law, 383
    aesthetic, 393–394
    recent case on, 387
    trade dress and, 495
Furniture, copyrightable design of, 203
FWC (file wrapper continuing application), 55

G

GATT (General Agreement on Tariffs and Trade), 88–89, 275–276 bootlegging of live performance and, 219, 275–276

compulsory licensing disfavored under, 52

copyright and, 202, 217, 285–286

copyright duration under, 256

copyright for works of foreign authors and, 235

copyright notice and, 286, 297, 301

copyright restoration under, 325–326

importation of infringing works and, 279

trade secrets under, 8, 538

World Trade Organization and, 171

Genentech, MedImmune v., 110

Genericide, 382, 440–441, 458

Generic terms, and trademark law, 381–382, 384, 440–441

    cancellation petition and, 465

    phonetic or foreign equivalents for, 471

    recent case on, 388, 440

    as weak marks, 502

Genes, human, unpatentability of, 27, 90

Genetic engineering and patents, 52, 89–90, 112. *See also* Biotechnology sequence

Geographically separate markets, 406, 442–443, 467–468

Geographic patent license, 90

Geographic terms as marks, 382, 441–442

    Supplemental Register and, 489

    as weak marks, 502

German patent law, 169

Ghost brands, 502

Goodwill, 443

Google Patent Search, 134, 136

Government agencies

    Freedom of Information Act, exemption of trade secrets, 537

initials of, as trademark, 447–448

Governmental employees or officers, works of, 207, 343

Graham v. John Deere, 90

Grant of patent, 91

Grant of rights, 276

    by freelance programmer, 233

    See also Assignment *entries;* Licensing *entries*

Graphic, pictorial, and sculptural works, 314–315. *See also* Artworks, and copyright

Graphical user interfaces (GUIs). *See* Computer user interfaces, and copyright protection

Gray market goods

    first-sale doctrine and, 204

    trademark owners' remedies for, 443

Group art unit, 91

H

Head start rule, 538–539, 565

Health of inventor, and Petition to Make Special, 32, 139

Hot news doctrine, 276–277

HTML (Hypertext Markup Language), 277

Human organism, patents involving

    barred under new patent law, 23, 90

    court decision on gene patents, 27

Hybrid mark. *See* Composite mark

I

ICANN (Internet Corporation for Assigned Names and Numbers), 395, 443, 498

Ideas

    copyright law and, 5, 197, 234, 277–278

evaluation agreements for, 535
nonpatentable, 117
as trade secrets, 541, 567–568
Idea submission, 539–541
*Identification of Goods and Services
Manual,* 393, 505
Identifying material, deposited with U.S.
Copyright Office, 278
IDS (Information Disclosure Statement),
93–94, 146, 175
Immoral marks, 474
Immoral works, and copyright, 279
Importation of authored works,
manufactured outside U.S., 202, 291
Importation of infringing goods
patent and, 62, 82, 89
trademark and, 398
Importation of infringing works,
copyrighted, 278–279
first-sale doctrine and, 270
Improvement inventions, 91–92
Improvements to invention, continuation-
in-part application for, 148
Incontestable mark, 406–407, 413,
444–446, 483, 500
Indecent or immoral works, and
copyright, 279
Independent claims, 46, 47, 92, 161,
174–175
Independent conception, defense to trade
secret claim, 543, 565
Independent contractors, commissioned
works of, 199. *See also* Freelance authors
Independent creation, and copyright,
249, 279–280
Index of U.S. Patent Classification, 49
Inducing infringement of patent, 56,
92–93

Industrial espionage, 520, 542, 543, 564.
See also Economic Espionage Act of
1996
Industrial know-how. *See* Know-how
Industrial secrets, 544
Inevitable disclosure rule, 544–545
Information Disclosure Statement (IDS),
93–94, 146, 175
Infringement. *See* Copyright
infringement; Patent infringement;
Trademark infringement; Trade secret
misappropriation
Infringement search, 96–97, 133
Ingredient, trademarked product as,
446–447
Initial interest confusion, 447
Initials as trademark, 447–448
Injunction against dilution of trademark,
413, 416, 472
Injunction against infringer
of copyright, 200, 204–205, 253, 281,
282–284
of patent, 20–21, 95, 96
patent troll and, 137
of trademark, 448–449, 472
Injunction against publisher of infringing
advertising, 475–476
Injunction against trade secret use or
disclosure, 520, 545, 565
Injunction against unfair competition,
448–449, 499
Inlining and thumbnails, 284
Innocent infringement of copyright, 201,
247, 284
copyright notice and, 297, 301
court-ordered license for, 228
recordation of transfers and, 321
Innocent infringer of trademark, 448,
449

Instructional text, as work made for hire, 285

Insurance, general liability, advertising injury under, 211

Intellectual property (IP)
defined, 4
functional vs. aesthetic, 8
the Internet and, 7
See also Copyright; Patent; Trademark; Trade secret

Intellectual property laws
activities governed by, 5
determining which types apply, 8–9, 10–13
international, 7–8
sources of, 6
types of, 5–7

Intellectual property lawyers, 32. *See also* Patent attorneys

Intent-to-use (ITU) trademark application, 383, 384, 449–451
Allegation of Use for, 394, 449–450, 507, 508
ownership of mark and, 466–467
preparing, 503–509

Inter-American Convention for Trademark and Commercial Protection, 451

Interference, patent, 19–20, 99–101
continuation application and, 55
filing date and, 85
junior party in, 104
patent law on, 144
reduction to practice and, 44, 153
replaced by derivation hearing, 25, 67–69, 99
senior party in, 156
See also Board of Patent Appeals and Interferences (BPAI)

Interference, trademark, 431, 451–452, 458, 466

International Bureau of World Intellectual Property Organization (WIPO), 101, 129

International Convention for the Protection of Industrial Property. *See* Paris Convention

International copyright protection, 285–286. *See also* Berne Convention; GATT (General Agreement on Tariffs and Trade); Universal Copyright Convention (U.C.C.)

International intellectual property laws, 7–8

International patent application, 101. *See also* Patent Cooperation Treaty (PCT)

International patent protection, 21–22

International Schedule of Classes of Goods and Services, 452–453, 505

International Trade Commission, and importation of infringing works, 279

International trademark rights, 454–455, 458–460
for mark on Supplemental Register, 490

Internet
copyright regulation of, 286
intellectual property and, 7
publication on, 320
trademark infringement in commerce on, 406
trade secret disclosure on, 546
See also Digital audio transmissions; Digital Millennium Copyright Act (DMCA); Domain names; Family Entertainment and Copyright Act of 2005; File sharing; Webcasting; Web page; Websites

Internet Corporation for Assigned Names and Numbers (ICANN), 395, 443, 498

Internet patents, 44–45, 101–102. *See also* Business method patents

Internet searches. *See* Keywords; Patent search, computerized; Trademark search

Internet service providers (ISPs)
  contributory trademark infringement by, 407, 408
  copyright infringement and, 252–253, 287
  website hosting by, 423

Inter partes proceedings, in trademark disputes, 451, 464, 465–466

Inter partes review of patent, 22, 24, 97–99. *See also* Reexamination of patent

Intervening rights, 102–103

Invalidity of patent
  admissions by inventor and, 32
  duty of candor and good faith and, 77–78
  for fraud on USPTO, 21, 87
  for patent misuse, 130–131
  prior user defense and, 65
  reasons for declaring, 21, 168
  standard of proof for, 26, 60
  true inventors and, 51
  See also Fraud on the U.S. Patent and Trademark Office

Invalidity of patent, as infringement defense, 20, 60, 61, 87, 93–94, 96, 97
  best mode and, 23, 73
  breaking the patent and, 44

Invention
  commercialization of, 17
  defined, 18, 103
  field of, 82–83
  improvements to, 148

"not invented here" syndrome regarding, 118

"teaching" of, 166

trade secret ideas underlying, 541

working model of, 44, 71, 72, 152–153

See also Anticipation of invention; Building and testing of invention; Licensing of invention; Public use or disclosure of invention

Inventor, 103–104
  admissions by, 32
  employed, 78–79
  as patent applicant, 127
  See also Coinventors

Inventorship, 175

Inventor's notebook, 53, 73, 100, 118

Inventor's oath or declaration, 24

Inverse ratio rule, of copyright infringement, 210, 287

IP. *See* Intellectual property (IP)

ISPs. *See* Internet service providers (ISPs)

Issue fee, patent, 104, 149

ITU. *See* Intent-to-use (ITU) trademark application

J

Jailbreaking, under Digital Millennium Copyright Act, 204

Japanese patent law, 169

John Deere case, 90

Joint inventors. *See* Coinventors

Joint work, 287. *See also* Coauthors

Journalism. *See* News reporting

Junior party in interference, 104

K

Kappos v. Bilski, 104–105, 159

Keywords, 455–456

Know-how, 546–547, 548–549

Knowledge engineering, trade secrets in, 526

KSR v. Teleflex, 105, 115

L

Laches, 63, 162, 168

Lanham Act, 380, 456–457
  commerce that can be regulated under, 403–404
  false advertising and, 429–430
  gray market goods and, 443
  Paris Convention countries and, 455
  prohibited and reserved marks under, 474–475
  Section 43(a) of, 429–430, 499–500
  trademark protection without prior registration under, 385
  unfair competition and, 456–457, 499–500
  See also Trademark law, definitions relating to

Large entity, 105
  patent application fees for, 40

Latin America, trademark rights and, 451

Laws of nature, not patentable, 18, 33, 105–106, 117

Lawsuit
  for false patent number marking, 23
  by owner of intellectual property, 5
  against patent owner claiming same invention, 25, 67, 99
  See also Copyright infringement action; Patent infringement action; Trademark infringement action; Trade secret misappropriation action

Lawyers. *See* Intellectual property lawyers; Patent attorneys

Lay judge, in patent case, 106

Leahy-Smith America Invents Act. *See* America Invents Act

Legend. *See* Copyright notice

Letters patent, 126, 130

LexPat, 134

Library of Congress, 288–289. *See also* Deposit with U.S. Copyright Office

License, naked, 457, 461–462

Licensing of copyrights, 289
  compulsory, 227–228, 291, 326
  conflicting, 303–304
  exclusive, 199, 261, 289, 303–304, 334–336
  nonexclusive, 199, 289, 296–297, 303–304, 334
  ownership of copyright and, 240–241, 261
  revocation of, 326
  ringtones as exempt from, 202
  sublicensing, 202
  termination of, 326, 333
  See also End-user license agreement (EULA); Recordation of copyright transfers

Licensing of invention, 17, 106
  antishelving clause in, 38–39
  antitrust violations related to, 17
  under Bayh-Dole Act, 41, 42
  in biotechnology, 89
  challenge to patent validity by licensee, 110
  compulsory, 52, 170
  cross-licensing, 17, 57, 91–92
  declaratory judgment of noninfringement and, 59
  exclusive license, 80
  geographic, 90
  illegal practices in, 168
  nonexclusive license, 113

patent thickets and, 137
patent trolls and, 137
Licensing of marks, 457
Licensing of software. *See* Software
  licenses
Licensing of trade secrets, 547
Likelihood of confusion, in trademark
  law, 382, 457–458
    geographic territories and, 467–468
    related products and services and,
      478–479
    reverse confusion and, 481
    strength of mark and, 487–488
    trade dress and, 494, 495
    trade names and, 496
    unfair competition and, 499
Limiting reference, in patent claim, 106
Linking on websites, 289–290
Literary works, 290
Live performance, bootlegging of, 219,
  275–276
Logo, trademark including, 460, 496
Loss of mark, 458. *See also* Abandonment
  of mark
Lump-sum payment, for assignment, 40

M

Machines, as patentable subject matter,
  106, 164
Madrid Protocol, 454, 458–460
    abandoned trademark and, 392, 460
    abandoned trademark application and,
      393, 460
Maintenance fees, for patent, 107
Manual of Classification, 49
Manual of Patent Examining Procedure
  (MPEP), 107
Manufactures, as patentable subject
  matter, 107, 164

Manufacturing clause, on importation of
  literary material, 291
Manufacturing in United States, under
  Bayh-Dole Act, 42
March-in rights, to patent, 42, 108
Mark
    collective, 401–402, 460
    composite, 405, 440
    continuous use of, 406–407
    famous, 430
    phonetic or foreign equivalents for, 471
    pictures and symbols used as, 471–472
    prohibited and reserved, 474–475
    registered, 477
    same or similar, 482
    senior and junior users of, 484
    slogan used as, 485
    sound used as, 485, 496
    strong, 487–488
    suggestive, 388, 441, 487, 488–489
    trade name used as, 496
    types of, 391, 460
    unregistered, 457, 477, 487, 499–500
    use of, 500
    weak, 382–383, 488, 502
    See also Abandonment of mark;
      Certification mark; Descriptive
      mark; Distinctive mark; Names as
      marks; Ownership of mark; Service
      mark; Trademark
Marking of an invention, 108–109
    America Invents Act and, 23, 109
    false, 23, 109, 168
    infringement and, 57, 95, 108–109
    virtual, through website, 23, 109
Markman v. Westview Instruments, 109
Mask works, 328
Mathematical formulas, nonpatentable,
  18, 33, 117

Means plus function clause, 109–110, 161

Mechanical rights, 291

MedImmune v. Genentech, 110

Merger doctrine in copyright law, 207, 291–292
  printed forms and, 317

Metatags, 460–461
  initial interest confusion and, 447

Methods
  as trade secrets, 548–549
  See also Processes (or methods) as patentable subject matter

Microcode and copyright, 292

Micropatent, 134, 136

Microsoft Corp., Apple Computer, Inc. v., 213, 230–231

Misdescriptive geographic term, 442

Misuse. *See* Loss of mark; Patent misuse

Moral rights of artist, 344–346

Moral rights of author, 217, 275, 285, 292–293

Moseley v. V Secret Catalogue, Inc., 501

Motion pictures, copyrights, 255, 293
  BitTorrent and, 218
  derived work from novel, 249–250
  filtering of content, 268, 436
  licensing of, 253
  rental of videotapes, 269
  See also Family Entertainment and Copyright Act of 2005; Family Movie Act of 2005

MP3, 293–294

MPEP *(Manual of Patent Examining Procedure),* 107

Multiple claims, 111, 161

Music copyright
  for arrangements, 294–295
  Audio Home Recording Act and, 215–216
  BitTorrent and, 218, 307–308
  compulsory licensing and, 227–228
  copyright clearinghouses for, 223
  damages for infringement of, 204
  digital sampling and, 280, 327
  performing at a business and, 309
  recording of live performance and, 219
  sound recordings distinguished from musical works in, 294–295
  takedown notice for infringement of, 205, 253
  See also Digital audio transmissions; File sharing; Sound recordings

Music publisher, 294

N

NAFTA (North American Free Trade Association), 59

Naked license, 457, 461–462

Names, unauthorized use for commercial purposes, 481

Names as marks, 448, 463
  prohibited instances of, 475
  Supplemental Register and, 489
  surnames, 491–492, 502
  See also Trade name

Narrowing a claim, 111

National treatment, of copyright protection, 295, 337

Natural laws, nonpatentable, 18, 33, 105–106, 117

Naturally occurring substances, nonpatentable, 18, 89, 111–112, 117
  human organism and, 23, 27, 90

NDA. *See* Nondisclosure agreement (NDA)

Negative doctrine of equivalents, 95, 112

New matter, in patent application, 112

Newspaper, as collective work, 224

News reporting

fair use for, 263, 264

hot news doctrine and, 276–277

sources for trade secrets in, 538

New-use invention, 112–113, 164

New York Times v. Tasini, 295–296

NIH (not invented here) syndrome, 118

Noncompetition agreement

by employee, 528–530

by owners of a sold business, 530

specific performance of, 562

Nondisclosure agreement (NDA), 550

for beta tester of software, 524–525, 561

customer lists and, 531

for employees, 550, 558

ideas and, 541

implied, 550

know-how and, 547

preparing, 569–579

as reasonably precautionary measure, 558

sample of, 570–571

tendered by outsider to large company, 543, 567

trade secret disclosure in violation of, 542, 564

trade secret misappropriation in violation of, 520, 526–527, 542

Nonelected claims, 113

Nonexclusive license of copyright rights, 199, 289, 296–297

conflicting, 303–304

not a transfer of ownership, 334

Nonexclusive license of patent rights, 113

Nonobviousness, 113–116

claims and, 48–49

common sense and, 27

postgrant review based on, 24

Supreme Court guidelines for, 90

utility patent and, 18–19, 20

See also Obviousness; Section 103 of patent statutes

Nonprofit corporations and trademarks, 463

Nonpublication Request (NPR), 6, 53–54, 116–117

trade secrets and, 116–117, 552–553

See also Official Gazette, and patents

Nonstatutory subject matter, for utility patent, 117

North American Free Trade Association (NAFTA), 59

Notebook, inventor's, 53, 73, 100, 118

Notice of Allowability, 149

Notice of Allowance, 118, 149

Notice of copyright. *See* Copyright notice

Notice of references cited, 118–119

Notice of trademark registration, 463–464

Not invented here (NIH) syndrome, 118

Novelty, 119–121

anticipation and, 37, 38

claims and, 48–49

design patent infringement and, 71, 94–95

one-year rule and, 123

postgrant review based on, 24

trade secrets and, 551–552

utility patent and, 18–19, 20

See also Prior art; Section 102 of patent statutes

NPR. *See* Nonpublication Request (NPR)

Nucleotide sequence, 156

O

Object code, 299–300, 326, 528, 560, 561

Obviousness, 122. *See also* Nonobviousness

Office action, 122
    abandonment based on not responding to, 31
    final, 86, 148–149, 155–156
    first, 86, 147–148

Official Gazette, and patents, 54, 122–123
    defensive disclosure in, 66
    See also Nonpublication Request (NPR)

Official Gazette, and trademarks, 384, 431, 464, 504, 508

One-year rule, 123–124
    anticipation and, 38
    filing date and, 85
    novelty and, 119
    on-sale statutory bar and, 123, 163
    public use and, 151
    termination of, 24, 37, 60, 81, 119

On-sale statutory bar, 123, 163

Open source, 302

Operability, 124, 153

Opposing a patent (international rules), 125

Opposition to trademark registration, 410, 431, 435, 451, 464–466
    Madrid Protocol and, 460, 465
    Official Gazette and, 464, 508

Option agreement. *See* Evaluation agreement

Ordinary Observer Test, of design patent infringement, 71, 94

Original work of authorship, 302–303

Orphan brands, 502

Orphan works, 303

Overlapping transfers of copyright, 303–304, 321

Ownership of copyright. *See* Copyright owner

Ownership of mark, 383, 395–396, 466–468
    assignment and, 395–396, 483
    presumption of, 472–473
    senior and junior users and, 484

Ownership of patent, 131–132. *See also* Assignment of patent

P

Packaging
    design of, as trademark, 496
    as trade dress, 379, 494
    unfair competition and, 498

PAD. *See* Patent application declaration (PAD)

Painting. *See* Artworks, and copyright

Palming off, 468–469
    reverse, 481
    as unfair competition, 498

Pantomime, 222–223, 255

Pantros IP, 134

Parallel research, 552

Parent application, for patent, 125, 148

Paris Convention, 8, 22, 101
    trademark rights and, 455, 469
    unfair competition and, 469
    See also Convention application; European Patent Convention

Parody
    fair use and, 222, 249, 263, 264, 304–307
    involving trademark, 415, 416, 428–429, 439, 469–471

Passing off. *See* Palming off

PatBase, 134
Patent
  basic requirements for, 51
  benefits to owner of, 17
  classification of, 49–50
  copies of, 135–136
  copyright combined with, 7
  copyright compared to, 236
  creations covered by, 8, 10–13
  defined, 17, 126
  disclosure requirement for, 73
  duration of, 21, 76
  duration of, and GATT, 88
  duration of, extended due to regulatory
    process, 136
  enforcement of, 20–21
  expiration of, 21
  in force (in effect), 93
  grant of, 91
  international protection for, 21–22,
    101
  newly-issued, information on, 122–123
  offensive rights provided by, 126
  as prior art, 138, 143, 144, 145–146,
    166
  trademark combined with, 7
  trade secrets and, 6, 541, 557, 559
  types of, 17–18
  unenforceable, 168
  working a patent, 170
  See also Design patent; Fees for patent;
    Invalidity of patent; Invention; Plant
    patent; Utility patent
Patentability, 18–19, 137–138. *See
  also* Novelty; Nonobviousness;
  Unpatentability
Patentability search, 133, 138
Patent agents, 126
  to draft design patent application, 191

  for search assistance, 136
Patent and Trademark Depository
  Libraries (PTDLs), 127
Patent and Trademark Office. *See* U.S.
  Patent and Trademark Office (USPTO)
Patent applicant, 127
Patent application, 19, 127–128
  abstract in, 31, 174, 186
  allowance of, 33, 118
  approval of, 20
  certificate of correction for, 46
  confidentiality of, 6, 53–54
  conflicting applications, 19–20
  as constructive reduction to practice,
    54–55, 71, 72, 85, 88, 118, 149–150,
    152, 153
  for design patent, 191–194
  doing it yourself, 176
  duration of examination of, 139
  duty of candor and good faith
    regarding, 77–78
  electronic filing of, 78
  fees for, 40
  forms for, 173–193
  hiring a professional, 176
  initial rejection of, 33–34
  by multiple inventors for same
    invention, 19–20
  negative statements about invention
    in, 83
  opposition proceeding for
    (international), 125
  parts of, 173–175
  Petition to Make Special, 32, 139, 175
  postcard, return receipt, sent with, 175
  prosecution of, 147–149
  sample of, 177–190
  specification of, 160–161, 174–175,
    177–190

trade secrets and, 54, 552–553, 568

who files, 175–176

See also Claims; Drawings, patent application; Filing date of patent application; Foreign filing of patent; Interference, patent; Office action; Patent pending; Provisional Patent Application (PPA); Specification of patent application

Patent application declaration (PAD), 128–129, 173. *See also* Supplemental declaration

Patent assertion company, 137

Patent assignment. *See* Assignment of patent

Patent attorneys, 129

to draft design patent application, 191

for search assistance, 136

Patent Cooperation Treaty (PCT), 8, 22, 56–57, 101, 129–130

filing date in U.S. and, 85

Patent deed, 126, 130, 149

Patent examiners, 20, 130

PatentFetcher, 136

Patent infringement, 94–95

accused device in, 32

claims and, 46, 48

contributory, 56, 61

declaratory judgment of noninfringement and, 59

of design patent, 71, 94–95

by imported device, 82, 89

inducing, 56, 92–93

intervening rights and, 102

marking of invention and, 57, 95, 108–109

of plant patent, 140

reexamination and, 153–154

willful, 94, 96, 170

willful blindness standard for, 25–26

Patent infringement, defenses to claim of, 59–66

best mode defense, 23, 73, 96

exhaustion doctrine, 61, 64, 80

file wrapper estoppel, 61–62, 83–84

outside U.S. borders, 62

patent misuse, 44, 62, 130–131

prior user and, 23, 63–65

repair doctrine, 61, 155

waiting too long to file, 63, 162, 168

See also Invalidity of patent, as infringement defense

Patent infringement action, 20–21, 95–96

appeals from, 57

doctrine of equivalents in, 74–75, 82, 95

judge's interpretation of claims in, 109

jury's role in, 95, 109

new rules when joining defendants in, 23

patent trolls and, 137

presumption of validity in, 142

reexamination before filing of, 154

validity search by defendant in, 93–94, 97, 133, 170

See also Damages for patent infringement; Patent infringement, defenses to claim of

Patent law, 5

definitions of terms in, 31–171

forms related to, 173–194

overview of, 17–29

recent changes in, 34–37

sources of, 6

Title 35 of United States Code, 167

See also America Invents Act; Section 102 of patent statutes; Section 103 of patent statutes; Section 112 of patent statutes

Patent licensing. *See* Licensing of invention

Patent misuse, 62, 130–131
  breaking a patent based on, 43–44
  court decision on standard of, 28
  price fixing as, 142
  unenforceable patent due to, 168
  See also Antitrust law and patents

Patent number, 131

Patent number marking. *See* Marking of an invention

Patent owner, 131–132. *See also* Assignment of patent

Patent pending, 108, 132

Patent pending notice, 108

Patent pools, 53, 133

Patent Reform Act of 2011. *See* America Invents Act

Patent search, 133
  computerized, 134–136
  international, 129

Patent searcher, 136

Patent term extension, 136–137

Patent thickets, 39, 137

Patent Trial and Appeal Board, 24, 68

Patent troll, 26, 137

Patterns, as trade secrets, 553

PCT. *See* Patent Cooperation Treaty (PCT)

Peer-to-peer file sharing networks, 307–308. *See also* File sharing

Performance
  live, bootlegging of, 219, 275–276
  See also Public performance of a work

Performance right, 291

Performer, copyright management information about, 239

Performing music at a business, 309

Performing rights societies, 309–310

Periodical, as collective work, 224

Permission, copyright, 310–311
  clearinghouses for, 223
  for collective work, 224–225
  as defense in infringement action, 281

Permission to reproduce trademark, 311

Perpetual motion machine, 153

Person with ordinary skill in the art, 138–139, 168

Petition to Make Special, 32, 139, 175

Phonorecords of sound recordings, 311
  copyright notice for, 299

Photocopies and copyright law, 312

Photography, 312–313
  compilations and databases of photos, 203–204
  copyright clearinghouses for, 223
  copyright management information about, 239–240
  image as work of visual art, 346
  rights of person photographed, 312

Physical devices as trade secrets, 553–554

Pictorial, graphic, and sculptural works, 314–315. *See also* Artworks, and copyright

Pictures used as marks, 471–472

Piracy, 315, 554

Plagiarism, 315

Plant patent, 5, 8, 18, 89, 139–140
  genetically manipulated plants, 112
  in-force period of, 21, 76
  legal requirements for, 138
  See also Patent

Plant Variety Protection Act, 140

Plot, protection of, 315–316

Podcasting, 316

Point of Novelty Test, of design patent infringement, 71, 94–95

Polaroid factors, 457–458

Pop-up advertising, 472

Postgrant review

for business-method patents, 102

See also Inter partes review of patent

Post Office Patents, 53

PPA. *See* Provisional Patent Application (PPA)

Practicing an invention. *See* Reduction to practice

Predetermination of rights in technical data, 554–555

Preemption of copyright law, 316

Preferred embodiment. *See* Best mode

Preinvention assignments, 141–142

Preissuance submissions to Patent Office, 24

Preliminary injunction

in trademark case, 472

in trade secret case, 545, 565

Preregistration of copyright, 316–317

Presumption of ownership of mark, 472–473

Presumption of validity of patent, 142

Price fixing, 142, 541. *See also* Antitrust law and patents; Antitrust law and trade secrets

Principal Register, 384–385, 432, 473–474

benefits of placement on, 473–474

constructive notice associated with, 406

movement from Supplemental Register to, 412–413

secondary meaning and, 482

Printed forms, not copyrightable, 317–318

Printed matter, not patentable, 117

Printed publication as statutory bar, 142–143

Prior art, 19, 20, 143–146

anticipation of invention by, 37–38

cited against patent application by examiner, 34, 118

claim fully met by, 87

copyright registration and, 27

date of invention and, 59

defensive disclosure and, 66–67

defined, 143

design patent and, 71

duty to disclose, 77

exhibiting an unpatented invention as, 80

failure to disclose, 21, 87, 93–94, 96, 168

filing date and, 85

Information Disclosure Statement of, 93–94, 146, 175

infringement suit and, 60, 96

inter partes review and, 24, 97–98

new patent law and, 24

nonobviousness and, 113

novelty and, 119

patent as, 138, 143, 144, 145–146, 166

patent no longer in force as, 93

preliminary look at, 142

Provisional Patent Application as, 27, 150

reexamination based on, 153–154

swearing behind, 88, 165–166

thesis as, 167

See also Novelty; Patent search

Prior art reference, 146

Prior registration countries, 474

Prior user, sued for patent infringement, 23, 63–64

Processes (or methods) as patentable subject matter, 146, 164
    drawings in patent application for, 75
    Kappos v. Bilski and, 104–105
    See also Business method patents; Software patents
Processes as trade secrets, 555
Product-by-process claim, 146–147
Product designs
    as not inherently distinctive, 501
    as trade dress, 494, 495
Products. *See* Manufactures, as patentable subject matter
Profits, defendant's
    in copyright infringement, 245–246, 318
    in trademark infringement, 410, 411–412
    from trade secret misappropriation, 567
Programs. *See* Software; Software patents
Prohibited and reserved marks, Lanham Act, 474–475
Prosecution history estoppel, 61–62
Prosecution of patent application, 147–149. *See also* Amendment of patent application; Office action
"Protection" of intellectual property, 211
Protective order, in trade secret misappropriation action, 555–556
Provisional Patent Application (PPA), 19, 118, 124, 149–150
    as constructive reduction to practice, 54, 71, 85, 88, 152, 153
    filing date of, 27, 85, 124, 128, 149–150
    filing of, 176
    patent pending status and, 132
    as prior art, 27, 150

Pseudonymous work, copyright for, 200, 257, 318
PTDLs (Patent and Trademark Depository Libraries), 127
PTO. *See* U.S. Patent and Trademark Office (USPTO)
Public domain, authored works in, 200, 319
    attribution and, 215
    in collective work, 224, 225
    in compilation, 226
    copyright restoration under GATT, 301
    Creative Commons and, 243
    as defense to infringement suit, 249
    Eldred v. Ashcroft and, 258
    of federal employees or officers, 343
    of foreign authors before March 1989, 235, 276
    unpublished works, 256, 338
Public domain, inventions in, 21, 124, 150, 163–164
Public domain, trademark and, 215. *See also* Generic terms, and trademark law
Public domain, trade secrets and, 553, 556–557, 559
Publicity, right of, 481–482
Public performance of a work, 308, 319–320
    ringtones and, 202, 319–320
    See also Performance
Public records, and trade secrets, 557
Public use or disclosure of invention, 151–152
    anticipation and, 38
    by exhibiting an unpatented invention, 80
    one-year rule and, 85, 119, 124, 143
    as prior art, 143, 144

See also Disclosures of invention
Published work, defined, 320–321
Publishers
    of advertising matter, and trademark
        infringement, 475–476
    music, 294
Puffery, 476
Punitive damages
    trademark infringement and, 476, 486
    for trade secret theft, 520, 533
    See also Treble (triple) damages

R

®, 386, 406, 431, 463
    for mark on Supplemental Register,
        490
Race statutes, 87
Ratings, trademark related to, used in
    advertising, 398
RCE (Request for Continued
    Examination), 148, 155–156
"Read on" a device or process, 74, 152
Read-only memories (ROMs), and trade
    secrets, 557
Reasonably prudent consumer, 397
Reciting elements of a claim, 152
Reconditioned goods, and trademark,
    477
Reconsideration request, by patent
    applicant, 152
Recordation of copyright transfers,
    321–322, 336
Recordings. *See* Sound recordings
Reduction to practice, 44, 52–53,
    152–153
    constructive, 54–55, 71, 72, 85, 88,
        118, 149–150, 152, 153
    date of, 59
    diligence in, 71–72, 88, 100–101, 144

GATT and, 88–89
    interference and, 99–100
Reexamination of patent, 153–154. *See
    also Inter partes* review of patent
Re-file. *See* Substitute patent application,
    after abandonment
"Reg. U.S. Pat. Off.", 386, 431, 463
    for mark on Supplemental Register,
        490
Registered mark, 477. *See also* Trademark
    registration, federal
Register of Copyrights, 322. *See also*
    Copyright registration
Registrable matter, 478
Registrant of mark, 478
Reissue patent, 149, 155
    intervening rights and, 102–103
Related products and services, trademark
    and, 478–480
Rental of copyrighted works, 270, 276
Repair doctrine, 61, 155
Request for Continued Examination
    (RCE), 148, 155–156
Requirements contracts, 39
Research
    with biotechnology patented by
        another company, 89
    fair use for purpose of, 263, 264
    federally sponsored, 26–27, 41–43,
        554–555
    parallel, 552
    predetermination of rights in contract
        for, 554
    prior user defense and, 65
    trade secret ownership and, 566
    See also Employment agreement
Restraining order. *See* Temporary
    restraining order (TRO)
Restraint of trade, illegal, 541–542

Reverse confusion, 480–481

Reverse engineering, 156

    of software, 259, 337, 560, 576

    trade secret status and, 553–554, 557, 559–560, 565, 577

Reverse palming off, 481

Ringtones, and copyright law, 202, 319–320

ROMs (read-only memories), and trade secrets, 557

Royalties

    from assignee of patent, 40

    from franchisee for use of mark, 437

    from infringer of patent, 21, 132

    from licensee of patent, 17

    from licensee of trade secret, 547

    mechanical, 291

    for music transmission over Internet, 339–340

    for performance, 309–310

    for songwriter from music publisher, 294

Rule of doubt, of U.S. Copyright Office, 300, 326

S

Sale of business, with covenant not to compete, 530

Sale of rights. *See* Assignment of copyright; Assignment of mark; Assignment of patent

Sale of trade secret, 566

Same or similar mark, 482

Sampling, digital, 280, 327

Scientific principles. *See* Laws of nature, not patentable

Sculptural, pictorial, and graphic works, 314–315. *See also* Artworks, and copyright

Search. *See* Patent search; Trademark search

Searchers, of patents, 136

Search fee, for patent application, 40

Search results, caching of, and copyright, 220

Secondary meaning, 381, 382–383, 385, 412–413

    defined, 482

    of names, 463

    presumption of, 482

    product designs and, 501

    of trade dress, 494

    weak mark and, 502

Secrets. *See* Confidentiality; Trade secret

Section 8 Declaration, 392, 426, 482–483

    cancellation of mark for lack of, 466

Section 15 Declaration, 392, 483

Section 43(a) of Lanham Act, 429–430, 499–500

Section 102 of patent statutes, 119–121, 143–144

    claim rejections based on, 147

    new patent law and, 24–25, 120–121, 144–146

    See also Novelty

Section 103 of patent statutes, 113, 115–116

    claim rejections based on, 147

    new patent law and, 24–25, 116

    See also Nonobviousness

Section 112 of patent statutes, 147, 161

Semiconductor Chip Protection Act of 1984, 327–328

Senior and junior users of marks, 484

Senior party in interference proceedings, 156

Sequence listing, 156

Service mark, 379, 460
  defined, 484
  for franchises, 437
  on Principal Register, 473–474
  trade name used as, 496
  See also Mark; Trademark
SESAC, 309
Settlement
  by parties to derivation proceeding, 68
  in trade secret case, 565
Shapes
  as trade dress, 379, 495
  trademark including, 460, 496
Shelving of invention. *See* Antishelving
  clause
Shoketsu, Festo v., 82
Shop rights, 132, 157
Shotgun rejection of claims, 157
Shredding sensitive documents, 558
Shrinkwrap agreement. *See* End-user
  license agreement (EULA)
Similarity
  blurring of trademark and, 388
  filtration test of, for software
    copyright, 230–231, 268
Similar marks, 482
Simultaneous publication, 328–329
Single registration rule, 329
SIR (Statutory Invention Registration),
  25, 66, 163–164
Site license, 297, 329
Slogans used as marks, 485
Small entity, 157–158
  claiming status of, 173
Smart money, as damages for patent
  infringement, 158
Smells, as trademarks, 496
Software
  beta testing of, 524–525, 561

  defensive disclosure of, 66–67
  end-user license for, 258–260
  open source, 302
  trade secrets and, 520–521, 524–525,
    528, 560–562
  See also Object code; Source code
Software copyright, 229–231
  archival copies and, 214, 253
  Berne Convention and, 276
  collective work in conjunction with
    software and, 225
  copyright notice for, 298
  database of public domain information
    and, 229
  deposit with U.S. Copyright Office for,
    278, 520–521, 528, 561
  filtration approach to, 230–231, 268
  first-sale doctrine and, 259, 270
  granted by freelance programmer to
    publisher, 233
  if rewritten in different programming
    language, 250
  of microcode, 292
  of object code, 300
  software patent compared to, 236
  trade secret protection combined with,
    527
Software licenses
  site license, 297, 329
  Uniform Computer Information
    Transaction Act and, 337
  See also End-user license agreement
    (EULA)
Software Patent Institute, 135, 158
Software patents, 158–160
  for business methods, 44–45, 102
  copyright compared to, 236
  Kappos v. Bilski and, 105
  patentability and, 33

State Street Bank case and, 161–162

Sonny Bono Copyright Term Extension Act, 329–330

SoundExchange, 310, 340

Sound recordings, 322
 created before February 15, 1972, 225
 damages for copyright infringement by, 204
 musical sample and, 327
 musical works distinguished from, 294–295
 phonorecords of, 299, 311
 See also Music copyright

Sounds used as marks, 485, 496

Source code, 300, 330
 deposited with Copyright Office, 520–521, 528, 560–561
 as trade secret, 520–521, 528, 560–562

Source Translation and Optimization Patent Website, 135

Sovereign immunity, 160, 330–331

Special relief, by U.S. Copyright Office, 323, 331

Specification of patent application
 defined, 160–161
 for design patent, 192, 194
 of sample application, 177–190
 sections of, 174–175

Specific performance of covenant not to compete, 562

Specimen of trademark, 485–486, 503, 507
 with Amendment to Allege Use, 508

Spoliation Doctrine, 563

State employees, works of, 343

State laws, 6
 on art preservation and resale, 346
 copyright and, 202, 225, 235, 316

employee assignment agreements and, 131–132, 141–142, 192

musical sampling and, 327

on noncompetition agreements, 529–530

preemption of, 316

shop rights and, 157

on software licenses, 337

sovereign immunity and, 160, 331

on trade secret theft, 520, 526–527

on unfair competition, 476, 486–487, 495–496, 499

See also State trademark laws; Uniform Trade Secrets Act (UTSA)

State Street Bank and Trust v. Signature Financial Group, 161–162

State trademark laws, 380, 403, 413, 457, 467, 486–487
 dilution of trademark and, 415, 416, 430, 487
 infringement action under, 446
 registrant of mark, 478
 service marks and, 484

Statute of limitations
 for copyright infringement action, 201, 249, 331–332
 for patent infringement action, 162–163
 for trade secret misappropriation action, 562

Statutory bar to patent, 163
 on-sale bar, 123, 163
 printed publication as, 142–143, 163

Statutory Invention Registration (SIR), 25, 66, 163–164

Statutory rate, of mechanical royalty, 291

Statutory subject matter, for utility patent, 164

Strong mark, 487–488

Subclasses of patents, 49–50

Submarine patent, 164–165

Substitute patent application, after abandonment, 31, 165

Suggestive mark, 388, 488–489
geographic, 441
as strong mark, 487

Supplemental copyright registration, 329, 332
form for, 272, 324

Supplemental declaration, after amendments to claims, 149, 165

Supplemental examination, patent owner's right to, 24

Supplemental Register, 385, 412, 432, 489–491
benefits provided by, 490
cancellation of mark on, 465
protections not offered by, 489

Surnames as marks, 491–492, 502. *See also* Names as marks

Swearing behind a prior art reference, 88, 165–166

Symbols used as marks, 471–472

Synergism, 51

T

Tacking, 492–493

Takedown notice, under Digital Millennium Copyright Act, 205, 252–253

Tarnishment. *See* Dilution of trademark

TARR (Trademark Application and Registration Retrieval), 392, 493, 507, 508

Tasini, New York Times v., 295–296

Tax strategy patents, 23, 159

TDRA (Trademark Dilution Revision Act), 414–416, 430

TDR (Trademark Document Retrieval) database, 393, 493

Teach the invention, 166

TEAS (Trademark Electronic Application System), 384, 459, 493, 503, 504–509

TEAS plus, 384, 493, 503
example of application with, 509–515

Technical data, predetermination of rights in, 554–555

Teleflex, KSR v., 105, 115

Temporary presence exception, for foreign ships and aircraft, 167

Temporary restraining order (TRO), 563
against copyright infringement, 200, 281, 282, 283
against loss of trade secret, 545
against trademark infringement, 448

Territoriality of trademark rights, 454

Territorial restriction agreements, 541

TESS (Trademark Electronic Search System), 385, 493

Textbooks, foreign-published, resale of, 206

Thesis as prior art, 167

Thin copyright, 333–334

Thumbnails, 284

Timely registration of copyright, 334

Title 35 of United States Code, 167. *See also* Patent law

TM symbol, 386, 494

Tools as trade secrets, 553–554

Top level domains, 420–421
generic term combined with, 440

Toys, copyrightable designs of, 203, 207

Trade dress, 379–380, 494–495
functionality and, 383, 387
Lanham Act and, 457
simulation of, 498
unregistered, 495

used as trademark or service mark, 460
Trademark, 496
    assignment of, 395–397, 460, 483
    classification of, 393, 452–453, 478, 505
    coined, 431, 487
    constructive notice of, 406, 500
    continuous use of, 406
    copyright combined with, 6–7
    defined, 379, 496
    disclaimer of connection with, 418
    enforcement of rights, 386
    famous, 430
    goodwill associated with, 443
    incontestable, 406–407, 413, 444–446, 483, 500
    initials as, 447–448
    international, 454–455, 458–460, 490
    licensing of, 457
    loss of, 458
    online services of USPTO for, 493
    patent combined with, 7
    permission to reproduce, 311
    phonetic or foreign equivalents for, 471
    pictures and symbols used as, 471–472
    public domain materials and, 215
    specimen of, 485–486, 503, 507, 508
    tacking of, 492–493
    trade name used as, 496
    on unrelated goods, 386–387
    website resources on, 389
    zombie, 502
    See also Abandonment of mark; Mark; Ownership of mark
Trademark application. *See* Intent-to-use (ITU) trademark application; Trademark registration, federal
Trademark counterfeiting, 407–408, 411
Trademark dilution. *See* Dilution of trademark
Trademark Dilution Revision Act (TDRA), 414–416, 430
Trademark infringement, 380, 446
    by competing or noncompeting products, 404–405
    contributory, 407
    deliberate, 412
    by domain name, 423
    fair use defense to, 428–429
    geographically separate markets and, 406, 442, 467–468
    by imported goods, 398
    incontestability status and, 444–445
    innocent, 448, 449
    publishers of advertising matter and, 475–476
    recent cases on, 387–388
    registration and, 386
    related products and services and, 478–480
    on Supplemental Register, 489, 490
    as unfair competition, 498–499
    willful, 385, 397, 411–412, 500
    See also Likelihood of confusion, in trademark law
Trademark infringement action
    attorney fees in, 397
    average reasonably prudent consumer and, 397
    injunction resulting from, 448–449, 472
    presumption of ownership and, 472–473
    See also Damages for trademark infringement
Trademark law, 5–6
    broad meaning of, 496

definitions relating to, 391–502

domain names and, 422, 423–424

freedom of speech and, 438–440

goals of, 379

overview of, 379–389

property covered by, 8, 10–13

sources of, 6, 380

terms or logos not protected by, 381–383

See also Lanham Act; State trademark laws

Trademark registration, federal, 380, 383–385, 431–436

award of defendant's profits and, 411

cancellation of, 451, 458, 459, 464–466

concurrent, 405–406, 434, 466

constructive notice of, 406

damages for infringement and, 386, 410, 411

of domain names, 387, 388

duration of, 425–428

by foreign nationals, 436–437

forms for, 503–515

fraud in, 437–438

innocent infringement and, 449

maintenance requirements for, 504

notice of, 463–464

online services of USPTO for, 493

opposition to, 410, 431, 435, 451, 460, 464–466, 508

ownership of mark and, 467

proceedings on disputes about, 451–452

prohibited and reserved marks in, 474–475

related products and services and, 478–480

renewal of, 427–428

signifier of, 386, 406, 431, 463, 490

U.S. Patent and Trademark Office and, 500, 508–509

See also Certificate of registration (trademark); Disclaimer of unregistrable material; Generic terms, and trademark law; Intent-to-use (ITU) trademark application; Opposition to trademark registration; Principal Register; Supplemental Register

Trademark registration, international, 454–455, 458–460

prior registration countries, 474

Trademark registration, state, 486, 487. *See also* State trademark laws

Trademark search, 385, 493, 497–498

Trademark Trial and Appeal Board, 451, 465, 498, 500

Trade name, 457, 495–496

infringement of, 498

service mark distinguished from, 484

unfair competition and, 495–496, 499

See also Names as marks

Trade secret

accidental disclosure of, 523

beta testing and, 524–525, 561

business information as, 525

competitive advantage provided by, 526

compilation of information as, 526

copyright and, 278, 331, 520–521, 527–528, 538, 541, 546, 561

database-related, 526, 533

defined, 519, 563–564

disclosed during litigation, 548, 555–556

18-month publication system and, 53–54, 552–553

"employed to invent" doctrine and, 78
formulas as, 536
Freedom of Information Act and, 537
freedom of speech and, 537–538, 546
government contracts and, 554–555
ideas as, 541
improper disclosure of, 542–543, 546
international protection for, 8
Internet disclosure of, 546
know-how as, 546–547, 548–549
licensing of, 547
loss of, 519, 548
methods and techniques as, 548–549
Nonpublication Request and, 116–117, 552–553
notice to employees of, 551, 558
notice to former employee's new employer, 551
novelty and, 551–552
owner of, 566
patent application and, 54, 552–553, 568
patents and, 6, 541, 557, 559
patterns and designs as, 553
physical devices as, 553–554
processes as, 555
public domain and, 553, 556–557, 559
public records and, 557
read-only memories (ROMs) and, 557
reasonably precautionary measures to protect, 558–559
reverse engineering and, 553–554, 557, 559–560, 565
sale of, 520
software and, 300, 524–525, 560–561
types of information qualifying as, 8, 10–13, 519
unpublished works protected as, 527
unsolicited idea as, 543, 567–568

See also Nondisclosure agreement (NDA)
Trade secret law, 6
definitions related to, 523–568
federal statute, 530, 536, 542, 543
overview of, 519–521
sources of, 6
See also Uniform Trade Secrets Act (UTSA)
Trade secret misappropriation, 519–520, 542, 549
criminal prosecution for, 520, 530–531, 536, 542
unfair competition by, 498
See also Industrial espionage
Trade secret misappropriation action, 564–565
damages resulting from, 520, 532–533, 565
independent conception as defense in, 543
inevitable disclosure rule and, 544–545
injunction against use or disclosure in, 520, 545, 565
protective order on disclosure in, 555–556
Spoliation Doctrine and, 563
statute of limitations for, 562
unjust enrichment and, 567
waiver of right to sue, 568, 579
Transformative use, as fair use, 263–264, 266
Translation
compulsory licensing for, 228, 337
as derivative work, 249, 250
Transmittal Form
for design patent application, 193
for utility patent application, 173

Treaties and copyright protection, 285–286. *See also* Berne Convention

Treaties and patent protection. *See* Convention application; International patent protection; Patent Cooperation Treaty (PCT)

Treaties and trademark protection, 454–455. *See also* Madrid Protocol; Paris Convention

Treble (triple) damages
  for patent infringement, 96, 170
  for trademark counterfeiting, 408
  for trademark infringement, 406, 410–411, 476, 500
  for trade secret theft, 533

TRIPS (Trade Related Aspects of Intellectual Property Rights), 275

TRO. *See* Temporary restraining order (TRO)

Tying, 39, 62, 167–168, 541

Typosquatting, 409, 425

U

U.C.C. *See* Universal Copyright Convention (U.C.C.)

UCITA (Uniform Computer Information Transaction Act), 259, 337

UDRP (Uniform Dispute Resolution Procedure), 498

Unenforceable patent, 168

Unfair competition, 380, 498–499
  creations covered by, 10–13
  false designation of origin as, 457, 498, 499
  injunctions against, 448–449, 499
  Lanham Act and, 456–457, 499–500
  Paris Convention and, 469
  reverse confusion as, 480

right of publicity and, 481
  state laws on, 476, 486–487, 495–496, 499
  trade names and, 495–496, 499

Unfinished works, copyright protection of, 203, 242–243, 346

Uniform Computer Information Transaction Act (UCITA), 259, 337

Uniform Trade Secrets Act (UTSA), 524, 566
  damages under, 533
  definition of trade secret under, 564
  "improper means" under, 542
  injunctive relief under, 545
  "misappropriation" under, 549
  protective order under, 555–556
  statute of limitations under, 562

Universal Copyright Convention (U.C.C.), 285, 286, 337
  compulsory license to translate under, 228

Unjust enrichment and trade secrets, 567

Unobviousness. *See* Nonobviousness

Unpatentability
  of algorithms, 33, 117
  of human organism or gene, 23, 27, 90
  of laws of nature, 18, 33, 105–106, 117
  See also Patentability

Unpublished works, copyright protection for, 225, 234, 235, 249, 337–338
  differences from published works, 321
  duration of, 256
  fair use and, 264
  preregistration procedure for, 267

Unpublished works, trade secret protection for, 527

Unregistered mark, 457, 477, 487, 499–500

Unregistered trade dress, 495
Unregistrable material. *See* Disclaimer of unregistrable material
Unsolicited idea disclosure, 567–568
U.S. Constitution, 6
  copyright law and, 202
  trademark law and, 403
U.S. Copyright Office, 338–339
  expedited handling by, 261–262
  recording transfers of rights at, 199, 289
  registering works at, 198
  "rule of doubt" applied by, 300, 326
  special relief by, 323, 331
  See also Copyright registration; Deposit with U.S. Copyright Office
U.S. government. *See* Government agencies; Governmental employees or officers, works of
U.S. Patent and Trademark Office (USPTO), 17, 19, 169
  Commissioner for Patents of, 51
  Commissioner for Trademarks of, 404
  inadequacies of, 34
  online trademark services of, 493
  searchable patent database of, 134
  See also Patent application; Trademark registration, federal
Usefulness
  copyright law and, 203
  patent law and, 169
Use of mark, 500
Utility model, in German and Japanese law, 169
Utility patent, 5, 8, 18, 169
  inventions qualifying for, 18–19
  for plant, 140
  See also Patent

Utility patent application. *See* Patent application
UTSA. *See* Uniform Trade Secrets Act (UTSA)

V

Validity search, 93–94, 97, 133, 170
Versions, copyright protection of, 242–243, 329. *See also* Derivative work, under copyright law; Single registration rule
Victoria's Secret case, 500
Videocassette recorders (VCRs), copying of television programs with, 265
Videogames, copyright infringement of, 218
Videotaping inside movie theater, 244, 267
Virtual website patent marking, 23, 109
Visual Artists Rights Act (VARA), 203, 270, 343–347. *See also* Artworks, and copyright

W

Waiver of right to sue for trade secret infringement, 568
  nondisclosure agreement and, 579
Wal-Mart Stores, Inc. v. Samara Brothers, Inc., 501
Weak mark, 382–383, 488, 502
Webcasting, 286, 310, 339–340
Web page
  framing of, 274–275
  as specimen of trademark, 486
Website resources
  on copyright, 207–208
  on fair use, 266
  on patents, 29

on trademark, 389
on trade secrets, 521
Websites, 340
  caching of, 220
  copyrighted materials on, 340
  copyright protection of, 340
  end-user licenses for, 258–260
  framing of, 274–275
  linking on, 289–290
  metatags of, 460–461
  pop-up advertising on, 472
  thumbnail images on, 265
  visual or literary expression of, 277
  See also Domain names; Internet
Wiki, as collective work, 224
Willful blindness standard, 25–26,
  92–93
Willful infringement
  of copyright, 247
  of patent, 94, 96, 170
  of trademark, 385, 397, 411–412, 500
Wireless phones, breaking access controls
  on, 204, 254
Working a patent, 170

Working model, 44, 71, 72, 152–153
Work made for hire, 199, 340–343
  duration of copyright for, 200, 257
  ownership of, 241
  unpublished, 338
  VARA rights not applicable to, 345
  See also Commissioned work,
    copyright for
Work-made-for-hire agreement, 199, 200,
  216, 341–342
World Intellectual Property Organization
  (WIPO), 568
  international patent applications and,
    101, 129–130
  trademark rights and, 454
  See also Patent Cooperation Treaty
    (PCT)
World Trade Organization (WTO), 171
  date of invention and, 59
  See also GATT (General Agreement on
    Tariffs and Trade)

Z

Zombie trademark, 502

 **NOLO** *Keep Up to Date*

Go to Nolo.com/newsletters to sign up for free newsletters and discounts on Nolo products.

- **Nolo's Special Offer.** A monthly newsletter with the biggest Nolo discounts around.

- **Landlord's Quarterly.** Deals and free tips for landlords and property managers.

Don't forget to check for updates. Find this book at **Nolo.com** and click "Legal Updates."

Let Us Hear From You

Register your Nolo product and give us your feedback at Nolo.com/book-registration.

- Once you've registered, you qualify for technical support if you have any trouble with a download or CD (though most folks don't).

- We'll send you a coupon for 15% off your next Nolo.com order!

PCTM12

⚖ NOLO *Online Legal Forms*

Nolo offers a large library of legal solutions and forms, created by Nolo's in-house legal staff. These reliable documents can be prepared in minutes.

Create a Document

- **Incorporation.** Incorporate your business in any state.
- **LLC Formations.** Gain asset protection and pass-through tax status in any state.
- **Wills.** Nolo has helped people make over 2 million wills. Is it time to make or revise yours?
- **Living Trust (avoid probate).** Plan now to save your family the cost, delays, and hassle of probate.
- **Trademark.** Protect the name of your business or product.
- **Provisional Patent.** Preserve your rights under patent law and claim "patent pending" status.

Download a Legal Form

Nolo.com has hundreds of top quality legal forms available for download—bills of sale, promissory notes, nondisclosure agreements, LLC operating agreements, corporate minutes, commercial lease and sublease, motor vehicle bill of sale, consignment agreements and many more.

Review Your Documents

Many lawyers in Nolo's consumer-friendly lawyer directory will review Nolo documents for a very reasonable fee. Check their detailed profiles at **Nolo.com/lawyers**.

Nolo's Bestselling Books

Patent It Yourself
Your Step-by-Step Guide to Filing at the U.S. Patent Office
$49.99

The Inventor's Notebook
A *Patent It Yourself* Companion
$24.99

How to Make Patent Drawings
A *Patent It Yourself* Compantion
$39.99

Getting Permission
How to License & Clear Copyrighted Materials Online & Off
$34.99

The Public Domain
How to Find & Use Copyright-Free Writings, Music, Art & More
$39.99

Every Nolo title is available in print and for download at Nolo.com.